DISCARDED

D0148529

Competition Policy in America, 1888–1992

Competition Policy in America, 1888–1992

History, Rhetoric, Law

RUDOLPH J. R. PERITZ

New York Oxford
OXFORD UNIVERSITY PRESS
1996

Oxford University Press

Oxford New York
Athens Auckland Bangkok Bombay
Calcutta Cape Town Dar es Salaam Delhi
Florence Hong Kong Istanbul Karachi
Kuala Lumpur Madras Madrid Melbourne
Mexico City Nairobi Paris Singapore
Taipei Tokyo Toronto

and associated companies in
Berlin Ibadan

Published by Oxford University Press, Inc.,
198 Madison Avenue, New York, New York 10016

Oxford is a registered trademark of Oxford University Press

Library of Congress Cataloging-in-Publication Data
Peritz, Rudolph J. R.
Competition policy in America, 1888–1992 : history, rhetoric, law
/ Rudolph J. R. Peritz.
p. cm.
Includes Index.
ISBN 0-19-507461-0
1. Antitrust law—United States—History. 2. Competition—United
States—History. I. Title.
KF1649.P47 1996
343.73'0721—dc20
[347.303721] 95-15349

1 3 5 7 9 8 6 4 2

Printed in the United States of America
on acid-free paper

For My Parents, Martha and Hans

Acknowledgments

I would like to thank the friends and colleagues who have contributed to the completion of this book. I have profited from the comments and criticisms of David Chang, Mark Glick, Bob Lande, Arthur Leonard, Jethro Lieberman, Carlin Meyer, Nadine Strossen, and Harry Wellington. A special word of thanks goes to Jim Simon for his help and encouragement. Ed Purcell and Ted White have been especially generous with their time and their insights. At Oxford University Press, Helen McInnis has been wonderfully supportive. Nicole Gagnon and Chris Mills provided reliable and timely research assistance during the final stages of the project. The New York Law School's Mendik Law Library staff was invariably helpful; law librarian Bill Mills has been ingenious, speedy, and splendidly good-humored in tracking down the sources I needed for this project and its predecessors. My gratitude goes to New York Law School, which supported this project with a series of summer research grants and an all-too-short sabbatical. All along the way, my daughter Jessica has been a source of joyful amazement; together, we have learned a lot about creativity, logic, and love, and it has been a pleasure to share a computer with her. Finally, my biggest thanks go to Janice Peritz, whose emotional generosity, sense of humor, and sense of perspective have been as important to me as the benefit of her rigorous intellect and her professional skills as a critic and editor during my final revision of the manuscript.

Hastings-on-Hudson, N.Y. R.J.R.P.
December 1994

Contents

Introduction, 3

1. Public Debate About Competition Policy, 1888–1911: Free Competition and Freedom of Contract, 9

    The Sherman Act Debates, 1888–1890: From Concerns about Industrial Liberty and Fair Price to a Statute with Common-law Language and Uncommon Remedies, 13

    The Sherman Act in the Federal Courts, 1890–1911: Cartels and Labor Unions, Trusts and the Limits of Majoritarianism, 26

2. The Era of Cooperative Competition, 1911–1933: Trade and Labor Associations, Political Majorities, and Speech Rights, 59

    The Political Economy of Political Majorities, 63

    The Political Economy of Trade Associations, 75

    The Political Economy of Labor Associations, 89

    The Political Economy of Speech: "Free Trade in Ideas", 100

    Epilogue: The Emergence of Postclassical Economics, 106

3. The New Deal's Political Economy, 1933–1948: From Organic Body Politic to Unified Body Economic, 111

    The Early New Deal, 1933–1935: The National Industrial Recovery Act and an Organic Body Politic, 115

    The Later New Deal, 1935–1948: The Consumer and a Unified Body Economic, 142

    American Political Economy after the Close of the Second World War, 178

4. Competition, Pluralism, and the Problem of Persistent Oligarchy, 1948–1967, 181

Economic and Political Discourses of Competition, 182

Jurisprudential Currents: The Process of Pluralism as Consensus, 191

Congress and Industrial Concentration: Anti-Merger Legislation as Compromise, 195

The Supreme Court's Competition Policies: Genealogies of Agreement, Images of the Market, and a Commitment to Equality, 199

5. Rhetorics of Free Competition, 1968–1980: Efficiency, Property Rights, and Equality, 229

The Nixon-Ford Years, 1968–1976: Industrial Concentration, the Marketplace of Ideas, and the Ascendancy of Chicago-School Law and Economics, 231

The Carter Years, 1977–1980: Deregulation, Populism, and Efficiency Logics, 251

6. Rhetorics of Free Competition, 1980–1992: Free Market Imagery, Corporate Control, and the Problem of Equality, 265

The Federal Trade Commission: From "Social" to "Economic" Regulation, 271

Antitrust Law: From Regulation of Commercial Competition to Restraint of Political Power, 272

The Theory of PluPerfect Competition: Contestable Markets, 282

Corporations and Securities Law: The New Site for Commercial Competition Policy, 284

The Marketplace of Ideas: Property Rights and the Problem of Equality, 290

Concluding Thoughts: On the Limits of Competition Policy, 301

Notes, 305

Index, 365

Competition Policy in America, 1888–1992

Introduction

Competition policy has been one of twentieth-century America's most durable goods. Whether in business, politics, sports, or speech, a vision of robust rivalry—of free competition—has inspired our social theories, directed our practices, and informed our public discourse.

But from what tyranny do we want to free competition? From government power? Or from private economic power? These twin images of oppression reflect the fears animating a Hundred Years' War over particular public policy undertakings and, more generally, over the proper attitude toward political economy, over the best balance between politics and economics. If we believe that competition free from government regulation does a better job of producing and distributing capital, goods, labor, speech and other basic liberties, then not even sit-down strikes or price-fixing cartels justify government intervention. This notion of free competition has supported a commitment to individual liberty, to freedom from government power. If, however, we want to regulate private economic power because, for instance, we believe that efficiency is better served or that private power corrupts, then political oversight is justified. In this sense, free competition has involved a commitment to rough equality. Because we dread domination—both political and economic—we have called for policy that limits both kinds of power, policy that satisfies commitments to both individual liberty and rough equality.[1]

Competition policy, articulated in these twin rhetorics of free competition, has long been one way of mediating tensions between our commitments to liberty and equality. But liberty and equality are not the only concerns that have informed the making of competition policy. The other persistent concern has been private property rights. The conventional view holds that arguments for competition policy and private property rights are complementary. After all, the very idea of competition requires the capacity to buy and sell. And if anything is a basic property right, it is the freedom to buy and sell. In short, free competition seems to depend upon freedom of contract. Although this conventional understanding seems logical, the actual historical relationship between competition policies and private property rights turns out to be less logical than rhetorical.

In America, the relationship between competition policy and property rights has reflected conflict coextensive with dependency since the late nineteenth century. Consider, for example, a recurring dispute arising in antitrust policy. On the one hand, competition policy has prohibited corporate mergers that result in firms whose market power might allow them to dominate their rivals. On the other, enjoining owners from selling their business impinges upon a fundamental right to sell or exchange property.[2] A similar conflict between competition policy and property rights has erupted in the marketplace of ideas. A series of Supreme Court opinions, as well as some recent state legislation, has sought to mediate between the exercise of free speech—between competition in ideas—and the private property rights of shopping mall owners. Both examples reflect friction between competition policy and private property rights, confrontations between the twin rhetorics of free competition, between two sets of assumptions and beliefs about how to work out tensions between commitments to individual liberty and equality.

These tensions have not reached some balance, some historical equilibrium. They have been unstable, erupting or subsiding as our ideas of competition and property rights have confronted new circumstances and as our commitments to liberty and equality—themselves historically contingent—have changed. My historical investigation of competition policy approaches the subject matter as rhetorical confrontations between factions engaged in public discourse, factions informed by their own distinctive clusters of ethical commitments and logical connections. Together, rivalrous rhetorics of free competition have expressed the ethical and logical grounds, the unstable and sometimes explosive foundation, for American political economy over the last twelve decades or so.

My analytical approach depends on the notion of tension rather than on contradiction or antinomy. The notion of tension allows for a more textured understanding—for relationships of interdependence, of both complementarity and conflict, that are more in tune with the historical interplay evident in the textual materials I have studied. Certainly, this book emerges from my view of a rhetorical structure both shaping and shaped by material circumstances, a dynamic structure with room for play. Perhaps all that amounts to is a postmodernist restatement of Justice Holmes's maxim about legal formalism—that general principles do not decide concrete cases. The same can be said for general structures.

Nonetheless, we all depend on structures to help us make sense of the world. The trick is to remember that structures of thought and belief—rhetorical frameworks—survive in history as much because of their inadequacies, because of the play they allow, as because of the conditions they impose. Ideas have a complex relationship with facts, as theories do with practices. History is a way of breaking the simple cause-and-effect relationships seen by those who trumpet the objective truth of their ideas or the necessity of their practices. Theory and practice seem to be more interdependent, dialogical, and historical than objectively correct or necessary. Material circumstances and ideas about how the world works confront one another every day. They reshape one another at every turn.

What difference does it make, this new historical analysis of two rivalrous rhetorics, each with its strained allegiances to liberty and equality? To begin, a rhetorical analysis seeks to learn not only what individuals and factions wanted to do but what they could imagine doing. This view of rhetorics as ethical commitments coupled with logics—as political strategies—provides a framework for understanding the history of American competition policy as the outcome of struggles and confrontations, both among political or ideological factions and, at another level, between utopian aspirations and material conditions. Thus, this book is a history of rhetorical encounters, of debate, disagreement, and struggle, rather than an evolutionary history that would posit a progression of better economic or political ideas gaining consensus. It is not simply a history of texts or positions with later influence, such as Supreme Court majority opinions, dissenting opinions later adopted, acknowledged congressional committee reports, or economic and political theories embraced by policy makers. It is also a re-collection of the forgotten voices, rejected dissenting opinions, declined positions, and disparaged theories that were part of those debates. I want to throw open an archive of counterpolicies and counterarguments, to recall the conflicts engaged in and the alternative views so fiercely held, views whose appeal continues to inspire debate about political economy.

This book is also thematic. That is, each chapter takes the free competition rhetorics expressed during a particular period as a framework, a framework for juxtaposing major competition policy initiatives identified with the period—the decline of antitrust and the emergence of new theories of corporate and securities laws in the 1980s, airline deregulation and campaign finance reform legislation in the 1970s, the disparate treatment of labor unions and trade associations in the 1920s, and so on.

The book's historical point of departure, the opening scene in chapter 1, is the congressional debate over Senator John Sherman's antitrust bill, submitted to the Senate in 1888 and enacted in 1890. Those deliberations, as well as opinions expressed in the popular press, mark the first extended public debate in America about competition policy. Certainly, there were earlier public policy confrontations over competition—whether the *Charles River Bridge* decision (1837) or Andrew Jackson's campaign against the National Bank some five years before.[3] But the modern discourse of competition was born of the Sherman Bill's floor speeches and committee reports, whose rhetorical practices set the terms of debate over political economy in twentieth-century America—debate reflecting two sharply contrasting views of free competition. The rhetorical conflicts heard in congressional debates did not end with the passage of the Sherman Act of 1890. Rather, Supreme Court factions—familiar to antitrust scholars as "Literalists" and "Rule of Reasonists"—perpetuated the conflict, a conflict replicated in the constitutional jurisprudence associated with the well-known *Lochner* (1905) decision. The chapter explores the cross-currents running through the period's rhetorics for antitrust and constitutional jurisprudence, free markets and state regulation, commercial cartels and labor unions, and, more generally, for the confrontations between progressive legislation and a common-law judiciary.[4]

Chapter 2 looks at the ensuing two decades, which were marked by the rising tide of trade associationalism, the continuing struggles of labor unions, the World War I mobilization effort and, especially after the stock market's collapse in October 1929, an increasing level of federal regulation that would challenge the liberal formulation of individualism. These experiences would test the view that antagonism—competition—is the natural state of relations between citizens and the state, between commercial rivals, and between worker and manager. The chapter explores the political economy of associations—trade, labor, and political. In particular, it investigates the rhetorical justifications for competition policies that encouraged the trade association movement yet disapproved parallel activities by labor and political associations. Next, the period's political economy is observed through the lens of First Amendment speech jurisprudence, most clearly in the Supreme Court's rejection of Justice Holmes's economic metaphor of "free trade in ideas"—an image seemingly consistent with the Court's general approach to constitutional adjudication. The chapter concludes with a brief look at two books that signaled the close of the Hoover era's political economy: Edward Chamberlin's *The Theory of Monopolistic Competition* (1932) and Adolf Berle and Gardiner Means's *The Modern Corporation and Private Property* (1933).[5]

Chapter 3 explores the political economy of Franklin Roosevelt's presidency—in particular, the relationship between the early and later New Deals. Despite fundamental changes after 1935, the New Deal, from start to finish, revolved around a spindle of equality. Central to the New Deal was a commitment to economic enterprise free from oppressive economic power. This departure from preceding political economy was unmistakable. Nonetheless, the New Deal's own political economy would change. The early New Deal, with its National Recovery Administration, can be understood as a utopian vision of citizens—whether owners, workers, or consumers—deliberating, within an organic body politic, in order to negotiate political solutions for the hardships of ruinous competition. But after two years of dystopian experience and after the *ALA Schechter Poultry* (1935) decision's rejection of the NRA's participatory republicanist ideology, the New Deal changed course, turning away from political cooperation and toward economic competition as the strategy for economic recovery. This turn was accompanied by a rhetorical shift from citizenry to universalized consumerism, by an abandonment of the organic body politic for a unified body economic. In short, the later New Deal established "the consumer" as the unifying image for public discourse about political economy in America.

Chapter 4 takes up the two decades following the Second World War, a time of domestic economic expansion and unrivaled international influence for the United States. In the aftermath of European fascism and Japanese imperialism, American geopolitics was driven by totalitarian images—particularly the specter of a worldwide Communist conspiracy, personified by the sinister Joseph Stalin and his successors. In contrast to such totalitarianism, America saw itself as pluralistic and open, as a place where individuals were free to pursue their dreams. This vision of a pluralistic society and its horror of concentrated power provided the framework for public policy analysis in the 1950s and 1960s. Mainstream social scientists and legal scholars, as well as Congress and the Supreme Court, were inspired by the image of a free marketplace for ideas, goods and services, capital, and political decisions. Chapter 4 looks at the recurring problem in this shared vision: the undemocratic persistence of enormous disparities in power. Whether politics, economics, or jurisprudence, the dominant discourse of competition collided with the actuality of oligarchy. This chapter investigates these collisions and the array of theories and policies that they sparked—economic theories of imperfect competition, political theories of oligarchic democracy, jurisprudential theories of neutral principles and fair process, congressional attention to corporate mergers, and Supreme Court doctrine in search of a compass to navigate between the egalitarian and liberal ethics sustaining the period's visions of marketplace pluralism.

Chapter 5 traces competition policies in the Nixon-Ford administrations and the Carter presidency—a period dominated by a governmental legitimacy crisis. After Watergate, after waves of student protest not only in America but in Europe, consensus in a pluralistic marketplace of ideas seemed little more than a nostalgic delusion. In less public precincts, Chicago School policy analysts, led by law professors Richard Posner and Robert Bork, were writing voluminously, establishing their own journals, and attracting acolytes to the view that monopoly and inefficiency were almost always the result of government regulation. In 1971, Chicago School economist George Stigler wrote his influential article portraying government regulation as a commodity purchased by those seeking government protection from competition. Their message, in tune with the times, was that government was oppressive. Although such sentiments seem populist, they have an oligarchic underside. In the same year, for example, Robert Bork wrote an article whose logic leads to the unmistakable conclusion that commercial behavior merits broader protection than political speech. During that period, the Supreme Court not only abandoned antitrust concerns about economic power but, consistent with Bork's position, allowed owners of commercial shopping malls to exclude the peaceful distribution of handbills. Private property rights, in both instances, trumped public interests inspired by egalitarian commitments. Correspondingly, the Court held unconstitutional most of the campaign finance reform legislation passed by Congress in response to the Watergate scandal.

A legitimacy crisis in the political domain thus elicited two kinds of response. In academic journals and Supreme Court decisions, the view began to take hold that politics was incorrigibly corrupt, that the efficiency of private enterprise was the only available surrogate for civic virtue.[6] Public discourse surrounding the Watergate scandal, however, reflected the lingering hope for virtue in politics. In 1976, "outsider" Jimmy Carter of Georgia was elected President on a platform supported by promises of honest and efficient government. Carter, counseled by economist Alfred Kahn, initiated a surge of deregulation policies, informed by a renewed commitment to competition free of protectionist government.

Ronald Reagan's victory in the 1980 presidential campaign marked the end of an era whose political discourse was motivated by the belief that government could and should be an active, positive force. Government was now seen either as corrupt (Nixon) or ineffective (Carter). Thus, as chapter 6 describes, the shift from Carter to Reagan was not a turn to deregulation. That was already under way. What changed was the underlying political economy. Whereas Carter deregulated in order to remove the elitist mantle of government protection from corporate enterprise, Reagan deregulated to free captive corporations from the inefficient constraints of incompetent government. In contrast to Carter's populist deregulation, Reagan's was corporatist. Thus, according to the Reaganite view, the best role for government was to encourage the play of private property rights. Whether dealing with financial markets, labor relations, or corporate speech, competition policy in the Reagan-Bush years was inspired by the imagery of "free markets" and committed to an agenda of "corporate control."

In writing this rhetorical history of competition policy, I have sought to reconstruct familiar patterns of thought and familiar policies, and thereby to provoke consideration of new questions.[7] This approach encourages us to see current competition policy and current property rights, current views of liberty and equality, as the products of social and political engagement. It helps us to understand efficiency claims, First Amendment speech rights, corporate enterprise, and visions of "the free market" as contestable social and political choices, not as products of (super)natural, historical, economic, or logical necessity.

1

Public Debate about Competition Policy, 1888–1911: Free Competition and Freedom of Contract

The first extended public deliberations about enacting competition policy as positive law in America occurred around the Sherman Act debates between 1888 and 1890. In the Fiftieth Congress, differing views of free competition, freedom of contract, and their proper affiliations inspired almost two years of contentious debate, two radically different antitrust bills, and a split Senate. For two decades following passage of the Sherman Anti-Trust Act, cases calling for interpretation of the statute divided the Supreme Court into warring factions. These disputes over antitrust policy took place in a historical period rife with political and economic conflict—sometimes fought in the streets, often argued in courtrooms and legislative chambers, almost daily emblazoned across the pages of newspapers and popular magazines.[1]

During an early floor debate about his antitrust bill, Senator John Sherman expressed alarm about "the socialist, the communist, and the nihilist." Interestingly, he was not referring to the nationwide railroad strike some years earlier, or to the more recent Haymarket Affair, which provoked fears of Marxian class struggle. Nor was he expressing ideological opposition to Congress's recent enactment of the Interstate Commerce Act, which centralized supervision of the nation's railroads in the first federal regulatory commission. Rather, Sherman was dramatizing the potential for widespread social and political unrest threatened by outrage expressed toward the trusts. The era's symbol was John D. Rockefeller's Standard Oil Trust, depicted in the popular press as a menacing octopus with tentacles stretching across the country. Rockefeller's corporate charter was both granted and revoked by Sherman's home state of Ohio. For Senator Sherman and those who supported his antitrust bill, extant approaches were inadequate to the task of controlling trusts and other commercial empires.

What was needed at the federal level was competition policy as positive law. The European alternatives were seen as anarchy or communism. When viewed from a nationwide perspective, state statutes and state common laws reflected a wide range of attitudes toward cartels, trusts, and other agreements in restraint of trade. In a small number of states, trusts and cartels were the object of active regulation. For example, the attorneys general of Ohio, Michigan, and New York were actively prosecuting holding companies and trusts for exceeding the privileges granted under state incorporation statutes. An anti-monopoly persuasion led several other states—in particular Kansas and Missouri—to prosecute corporations for restraint of trade or pass new antitrust legislation. In most states, however, there was little activity. Moreover, in the years immediately preceding the Sherman Act's passage, the legislatures of New Jersey, Delaware, and New York passed new incorporation statutes allowing, and thus beckoning, trusts and holding companies. Now, these powerful new commercial enterprises could move out of states with an anti-monopoly persuasion and reincorporate in more sympathetic legal regimes. A few years later, New Jersey's invitation was accepted by John D. Rockefeller, whose attorneys were instrumental in the state legislature's passage of a particularly lenient law.[2] Were the new incorporation statutes evidence of corruption? Of commercial greed poisoning the wells of republican government? Or did they reflect a wise recognition of new economic conditions? Of commercial genius and its material benefits to the commonwealth?

Congress had entered the fray only recently. Consideration of the Sherman Act was undertaken just ten months after passage of the Interstate Commerce Act of 1887, a statute that reflected congressional confidence in its constitutional power to regulate the powerful railroad industry. Railroads were, moreover, common carriers, clothed with a "public interest" long recognized in traditional common-law doctrine and corroborated in the states' generous use of the eminent domain power, approved by Congress, to grant railroad companies ribbons of land stretching across the continent. This "public interest" was validated by the United States Supreme Court in the *Granger* cases (1877), which approved state regulation of railroads.[3]

Jurisprudential categories such as "public interest" and "liberty of contract" provided stable rhetorical forms for the Court's growing role in resolving questions of political economy. But changing circumstances, particularly the appearance of trusts and cartels, put pressure on those categories and thus threatened their stability. The Supreme Court's general principle was "liberty of contract." Legitimate grounds for state regulation, for political superintendence of private agreements, were understood as strictly limited to two categories of "public interest": to industries that fell into established common-law categories such as "common carriers" (certainly, railroads) and to industrial conditions that impinged upon "public health and public morals," therefore falling under the states' "police power." Congressional dominion over interstate commerce, particularly railroads, and the states' police power were understood as limits on one another. Despite the appearance of stability, however, the entire structure was unstable: The pull of material conditions and the push of contractarian ideology produced accordion-like categories. Still, most industries and most transactions were seen as local, as beyond federal power over interstate commerce. How, then, could Congress curb the power of trusts generally?

The interest in general antitrust regulation emerged at a time of growing tensions between rule and exception, between ideology and actuality. New economic conditions called into question the assumptions underlying classical political economy. Most troubling were the vast accumulations of wealth in the form of trusts as well as widespread industry cartelization, neither of which comported with the classical economic tenet that monopoly could persist only under government grants of "public" privilege. Given the social and economic conditions of its development, common-law regulation did not address adequately the new threat of entirely "private" monopoly—whether appearing as an individual, trust, or cartel. Liberty of contract, once conceptualized as the individual's shield against a threatening sovereign, now provided armor for powerful private interests against majoritarian government. At the same time, a beleaguered class of small businessmen, together with a growing class of wage workers, seemed to shatter the republican image of political liberty founded in widespread ownership of private property. Liberty of contract as the foundation for political economy could no longer support the weight of increasing inequality among the republic's citizenry.

Thus, material conditions called into question the standing bargain defining classical political economy. The republican ideal of civic virtue legitimating political action depended upon the belief that economic markets are self-policing and hence not menacing to the rough equality and economic independence deemed necessary for republican government. But this faith in common-law regulation, this trust in liberty of contract, was shaken by changed economic circumstances. Progressives and some conservatives understood the proliferation of large-scale commercial enterprise as a new form of commercial genius that exploded rough equality and economic independence. These new circumstances transformed the idea of "trust"—from trust as the public consensus sustaining the commonwealth to trust as a fearsome concentration of economic power that unjustly enriched a select few at the expense of the commonwealth. There raged a conflict between political and commercial figures of trust regarding the most fundamental precepts of the era's political economy.

Though under intense pressure, the classical vision of political economy was still strongly supported by the period's predominant jurisprudence. The Supreme Court's "economic due process" regime was founded on the major premise that the Fifth and Fourteenth Amendments protect individuals' natural rights by safeguarding private transactions from legislative impairment. Judges tended to write in a deductive style, beginning with the assumption that private property rights, exercised through "liberty of contract," reflect the "due process" clauses' protection of "life, liberty, and property." Although some of those judges associated liberty of contract with an idyllic domain populated by artisans, farmers, merchants, and other "small dealers and worthy men"—a domain threatened by trusts and cartels—other judges expressed concern about liberty and property rights in an era of emerging governmental activism. In both instances, however, the arguments were liberty based in principle and deductive in style. In consequence, they were relatively closed to claims of actual inequality and to other empirical argument.[4] Hence, despite new economic circumstances thick with nationwide railroads, enormous manufacturing concerns, and industry-wide cartels, there persisted the moral premise that contracting parties enjoyed equality of bargaining power.

Only in labor relations did courts act consistently on perceived inequalities. And there, they acted largely to protect the property of "individual" employers from threatening "hordes" of employees. There were, however, extraordinary conditions that did convince the Justices, from time to time, to permit state exercise of police powers to ameliorate working conditions. Nonetheless, legislative attempts to alter common-law rights of contract and property were typically seen as unjustified and destructive of individual liberty. The federal common law, supported by a contractarian interpretation of the Constitution, provided a "general jurisprudence," a categorical scheme of judging founded on an image of individualism and a standard of "reasonableness."[5]

To be sure, the disparity between ideology and actuality did have effects: demonstrations in the streets, passage of progressive legislation, and fissures in the prevailing jurisprudence. But in an era dominated by the Supreme Court's presumptive distrust of both legislative initiatives and political demonstrations, a contractarian ideology prevailed. The Court, given its normative commitments and typically deductive style, tended to produce opinions deeply suspicious of legislatures and passionately protective of private property rights.[6]

It is not surprising, then, that modern scholars, judges, and policy makers see the Sherman Act as a statute steeped in the common law.[7] That view makes good sense, not only because of the historical context but because of the Act's explicit common-law language, which proscribes "contracts . . . in restraint of trade" and "monopolization." What is surprising, however, is that modern interpreters equate the common-law language with competition policy. To do so, they must ignore the fact that Congress debated the explicit language of "full and free competition" for fifteen months, but rejected it just days before enacting a bill radically revised to reflect the language of the common law. How was "free competition" understood in the Fiftieth Congress and why was that rhetoric jettisoned? Why was common-law language substituted and how did its proponents see its relationship to "freedom of contract"? Indeed, how do we today understand those terms—free competition and freedom of contract—and the relationship between them?

By taking seriously the two competing rhetorics seen in the Sherman Act debates and in antitrust opinions written during the two decades following enactment, this chapter develops a set of principles and, with them, a framework for examining the debates and opinions, and for situating the period's political economy in a new light. Mainstream antitrust scholarship and modern Court opinions have focused on competition policy. Constitutional law scholarship of the overlapping *Lochner* era has focused on property rights. This chapter, in essence, stitches together these two fragments of the period's political economy, fastening them with threads spun from Court doctrines governing labor and race relations, free speech, and congressional regulation of the railroads. Considered in this context, the Sherman Act debates and early antitrust opinions serve as a case study of the larger ideological struggle between factions whose conflicting commitments to regulation by legislation and regulation by private property rights collided at almost every turn. Antitrust's formative period opens wide a window to the *Lochner* era's debates over political economy, debates between factions whose conflicting visions and whose common ground still inform our debates more than a century later.

The Sherman Act Debates, 1888–1890: From Concerns about Industrial Liberty and Fair Price to a Statute with Common-law Language and Uncommon Remedies

On January 21, 1888, early in the first session of the Fiftieth Congress, Congressman Henry Bacon (D.N.Y.) introduced a resolution to direct the House Committee on Manufactures to investigate trusts in several industries and to recommend suitable legislation. In the midst of the House Committee's trust investigation, President Benjamin Harrison's Republican Party and Grover Cleveland's Democrats both adopted antitrust platform planks. On July 30, the House Committee on Manufactures issued an interim report. Within two weeks, John Sherman (R.Ohio) and several other Senators introduced antitrust bills, all of which were referred to Senator Sherman's Senate Finance Committee. A month later, Committee Chairman Sherman reported to the full Senate his antitrust bill, with the following operative language: "That all arrangements, contracts, agreements, trusts, or combinations . . . made with a view, or which tend to prevent full and free competition . . . or which tend to advance the cost to the consumer . . . are hereby declared to be against public policy, unlawful, and void."[8]

Floor debate on this bill began on January 23, 1889, in the Senate's second session. During congressional debate over the bill and its House counterpart, the New Jersey legislature passed its radically liberalized incorporation statute, allowing corporations to own the stock of other corporations.[9] The Cotton Oil and the Sugar Trusts fled Louisiana and New York respectively, both incorporating in the Garden State. New York, Delaware, and several other states soon passed comparable statutes.

The Senate, after fifteen months of consideration involving sometimes heated exchange, approved by a roll-call vote of 31–28 a motion to refer Senator Sherman's bill to committee—this time to the Committee on the Judiciary. Only six days after the bill's referral, Committee Chairman George F. Edmunds (R.Vt.) returned to report a substitute bill that looked nothing like its predecessor. The Judiciary Committee's new bill replaced Senator Sherman's 1888 language of "full and free competition" and "cost to the consumer" with the common-law language of "contract . . . in restraint of trade" and "monopolize, or attempt to monopolize . . . trade." Within a week, the new bill passed by a roll-call vote of 52–1.[10]

Despite drastic differences in statutory language and despite limited debate over the substitute bill, we now take for granted that there are, or should be, no significant differences between the two versions. We assume that antitrust policy was founded on free competition and its connection to consumer prices, even though the language referring to these policies was jettisoned. Neither history nor logic compels this view.

Indeed, Senator Sherman expressed strong opposition to the substitute bill. He claimed that it would be

> totally ineffective in dealing with combinations and Trusts. All corporations can ride through it or over it without fear of punishment or detection. It is manifest that if any relief is to be had it must be as a result of popular opinion or by the action of the House, where amendments may be provided which will restore in substance the original design of the bill.[11]

Why was Sherman so adamantly opposed to the new bill? To restate the question, what significance attached to the substitution of the familiar common-law language of "restraint of trade" and "monopolization" for the discourse of "full and free competition" and "advancing the cost to the consumer"? A rhetorical analysis of the congressional debates provides an answer.

The Debates: The Competition Rhetoric of Industrial Liberty, the Property Rhetoric of Fair Price by Private Agreement

Floor debate was divided into two rhetorical camps, the same division that produced the split vote referring Sherman's bill to Edmunds's Judiciary Committee. Sherman and other supporters of the original bill's language of "full and free competition" maintained that industrial combinations, whether trusts or cartels, were antithetical to "the industrial liberty of citizens." In the opposing camp were those who believed that competition could be as dangerous as combination. They maintained that private agreements to mitigate the effects of "ruinous competition," to assure the producer a "fair price," were reasonable.[12]

Senator Sherman began the debate about his bill to secure "full and fair competition" with the familiar themes of industrial liberty and consumerism:

> This bill, as I would have it, has for its single object to invoke the aid of the courts of the United States . . . in dealing with combinations that affect injuriously the industrial liberty of the citizens. . . . It is the right of every man to work, labor, and produce in any lawful vocation. . . . This is industrial liberty and lies at the foundation of the equality of all rights and privileges. . . .
>
> The sole object of . . . [a trust] is to make competition impossible. It can control the market, raise or lower prices, as will best promote its selfish interest, reduce prices in a particular locality and break down competition and advance prices at will where competition does not exist. . . . The law of selfishness, uncontrolled by competition, compels it to disregard the interest of the consumer.[13]

Sherman's statement describes two injurious consequences of combinations. First, trusts (and cartels) harm consumers by controlling the market and advancing prices. This harm lies in high prices as well as in a lack of product alternatives. Only competition free of such market power protects consumers. Second, the closely related notion of "industrial liberty" appealed to the Sherman faction's concerns about producers. While late-twentieth-century readers typically take "industrial liberty" to mean freedom from governmental regulation, Senator Sherman and his contemporaries were concerned with another kind of freedom—freedom from corporate control of trade and commerce. Industrial liberty embodied a sense of the public as competitors and employees of new large combinations of capital, whose power rendered "the boasted liberty of the citizen . . . a myth." This strong sentiment in favor of protecting industrial liberty, of assuring a person's right to work, surpassed even the abhorrence of higher prices. Senator Henry M. Teller (R.Col.) expressed as much when he said, "I do not believe that the great object in life is to make everything cheap." In House debate, Congressman William Mason (R.Ill.) pointed out that even if "trusts have made products cheaper, . . . [they] have destroyed legitimate competition."[14] Senator Sherman and his supporters clearly saw their constituents as both workers and consumers.

The concern for consumer and producer liberty also implicated political liberty. For example, Senator John P. Jones (D.Nev.) argued that if the trusts were allowed to continue, "our Government is a farce and a fraud." Those sentiments echoed Sherman's opening statement characterizing industrial liberty as "the foundation of the equality of all rights and privileges." By that, Sherman was invoking the fundamental belief that representative government depended upon an economically independent citizenry, whose independence was secured by widespread ownership of private property. In that sense, "industrial liberty" called for entrepreneurial independence, for preservation of the "small dealers and worthy men" threatened by the new economic order of large-scale enterprise. He stated further: "They had monopolies and mortmains of old, but never before such giants as in our day. You must heed their appeal or be ready for the socialist, the communist, and the nihilist. Society is now disturbed by forces never felt before."[15] Sherman and his allies believed that rough competitive equality was important not only for economic or vocational liberty, but for political liberty in a free society as well.

The problem with this vision, of course, was the emergence of new ideas and new technologies allowing great economies of scale and thus widespread distribution of material goods. Were the great railroads and manufacturing enterprises dangerous excrescences on the natural process of competition? Or did they represent the natural and inevitable result of economic evolution? Those who believed the new economic order to be dangerous and unnatural sought, like Senator Sherman, to preserve the republicanist conception of industrial liberty. Those who believed it to be inevitable celebrated a new economic order of large-scale institutions emerging out of the very process of competition. Understandings of the clash between the old economic order and the new, as well as its consequences, were themselves in conflict.

It is not surprising, then, that some congressmen sought to preserve the freedom of contract, the natural evolutionary process they associated with trusts and cartels. Thus there were those who disagreed sharply with the Sherman faction. They argued that, under some circumstances, private agreements restraining competition should be lawful. They justified their claims in two ways. First, they claimed that both competition and combination were natural forces. Hence, both competition and private agreements in restraint of competition were inevitable. Second, they argued that combinations were good social policy because such private agreements were intended only to avoid "destructive competition." In consequence, the contracting parties should be entitled to the fair profits they sought.

First, there were those who saw competition and combination as two natural forces. These champions of private agreements restraining competition sought to draw a distinction between industrial liberty and unrestrained competition. In the heated debate just prior to the original bill's referral to the Judiciary Committee, Senator Orville Platt (D.Conn.) commented on its language of "free competition." He noted that the "bill proceeds upon the false assumption that all competition is beneficent to the country." Later, in House debate over the Conference Report on the 1890 bill as enacted, Congressman John W. Stewart (D.Ga.) stated his understanding of the new bill's common-law language: "It is just as necessary to restrict competition as it is to restrict combination."[16] In short, these congressmen expressed the belief that "unrestrained competition" is not free competition. Rather, both unrestricted competition and unrestricted combination were portrayed as undesirable extremes, as the twin evils embodied in trusts.

Congressman Stewart described competition and combination as "two great forces . . . contending for . . . mastery." They "are correctives of each other, and both ought to exist. Both ought to be under restraint." This view dovetailed with the position taken by the newly formed American Economic Association which, after initially condemning "*laissez-faire* [as] unsafe in politics and unsound in morals," in 1886 adopted a more moderate position: "Competition is not in itself bad. It is a neutral force which has already produced immense benefits, but which may, under certain conditions, bring in its train sharply defined evils."[17]

Thus, the Sherman faction's image of industrial liberty as trade rivalry among individual artisans and tradesmen was seen by some as anachronistic, indeed, as extremist. Genuine industrial liberty in an era of "great forces" and large-scale enterprise, it was argued, must be taken to mean something very different from a backward-looking Jeffersonian ethic of rough competitive equality. Time could not somehow be stopped by legislation. Industrial liberty in a dynamic, changing world was fostered by protecting liberty of contract, by respecting individual freedom to strike agreements with one's rivals to temper the harshness of ruinous competition. Prohibiting reasonable restraints in the economic sphere, it was believed, would only perpetuate the harsh excesses of ruinous competition.

The conflicting views of industrial liberty expressed in the debates can be understood in two ways. First, "liberty" was taken to mean both freedom from governmental power and freedom from market power. These two views, with their radically different concerns, implicated conflicting strategies to achieve their goals. For Stewart and those who saw in economic change the possibility of improvement, freedom from legislative intrusion was necessary. Their view of "liberty" required the courts to enforce private agreements as correctives to the great force of competition. They sought to save commercial interests from ruinous competition. In contrast, for Sherman and those who wanted to reclaim a regime of entrepreneurial rivalry among a roughly equal citizenry, "liberty" meant freedom from market power. Their view required Congress to prohibit private agreements that restrained the leveling force of competition. They sought to save the republic by distributing economic power.

These two sides of industrial liberty can also be understood in a second way—as two different impulses, one toward liberty and the other toward equality. On the one hand, industrial liberty, informed by an impulse toward liberty, can represent the belief that state regulation of private contracts in restraint of trade is bad policy when it impinges upon individual liberty of contract. This view of industrial liberty derives from both a moral precept of individual liberty and a consequentialist rationale that liberty of contract promotes economic growth and prosperity. One implication is that industrial liberty and price-fixing cartels can be perfectly compatible. On the other hand, industrial liberty, informed by a commitment to equality, can reflect the belief that state regulation of private restraints is good policy when it distributes economic power. This view derives from the moral precept of Jeffersonian entrepreneurialism and the consequentialist rationale that such competition promotes widespread economic prosperity. The implication here is that industrial liberty and price-fixing cartels are incompatible.

In spite of these fundamental disagreements, all participants in the congressional debates shared two cardinal tenets. First, no one denied the importance of government intervention. The dispute hinged on its time and form. Sherman and his allies sought government enforcement of competitive conditions as a first resort: competition as positive law. The opposing coalition preferred private agreements to administer markets and saw the governmental role as a last resort, as courts curbing the excesses of competition and combination, both reflected in unfair prices. Second, for entirely different reasons, all views held that one benefit of commercial endeavor ought to be "fair price." Those who argued for protection of competitive conditions, for equalization of market power, sought government action to dissolve private agreements such as trusts or price-fixing cartels in order to reinstate the "full and free competition" necessary to produce fair prices.[18] Those who proclaimed the liberty to enter into private agreements in restraint of trade saw combinations as contracts to protect fair prices in the face of ruinous competition. Thus, each side of the antitrust debates over the proper political economy for Progressive Era America claimed "fair price" as its own product.

The public discourse of the times included many supporters of both views of industrial liberty—freedom from undue market power and freedom to contract.[19] Yet, congressional speeches deploying an explicit rhetoric of industrial liberty championed only the freedom-from-market-power view. These speeches explicitly called for government intervention to dissolve trusts and other "unnatural" agreements in restraint of "full and free competition." Those committed to industrial freedom from government power, however, made no explicit references to liberty of contract or limited government. Rather, they invoked the rhetoric of "fair price."

For those who opposed the Sherman faction by invoking the property rhetoric of "fair price," the logic was entirely consequentialist: Genuine industrial liberty meant enforcing private agreements (when "reasonable" at common law) *because* they restrained competition or countervailed the power of trusts, *because* their purpose was to impose "fair prices" on markets otherwise overrun by the extreme force of ruinous competition. Indeed, they attacked the "industrial liberty" associated with "full and free competition" because they saw freedom of contract as the proper form of regulating trade and commerce. In short, freedom of contract protected "fair profit" or "fair return," an important social value threatened by the ravages of competition. For example, Senator Orville Platt (D.Conn.) stated:

> The true theory of this matter is that prices should be just and reasonable and fair, that prices . . . should be such as will render a fair return to all persons engaged in its production, a fair profit on capital, on labor, and on everything else that enters into its production. . . . [E]very man in business . . . has a right, a legal and a moral right, to obtain a fair profit upon his business and his work; and if he is driven by fierce competition to a spot where his business is unremunerative, I believe it is his right to combine for the purpose of raising prices until they shall be fair and remunerative.[20]

Congressman Stewart, addressing an asserted policy conflict between the antitrust bill and the Interstate Commerce Act of 1887 (Commerce Act) in the regulation of railroads, sought to emphasize a fundamental commonality based on the right to a fair return on investment: "[T]he doctrine of fair play requires . . . that the railroads should have a just compensation for their services. . . . That is only reasonable and fair."[21]

Stewart's references to "just compensation" and "fair return" echoed rationales recently expressed not only in the Commerce Act debates but also in Supreme Court decisions defining the constitutional scope of economic regulation by the states. In *Munn v. Illinois* (1877), the Court had addressed the Fourteenth Amendment due-process question of "taking" private property in the public interest. The legislation under scrutiny was one of the numerous "Granger laws" passed in the agricultural states of the Midwest and West to regulate the warehousing and transportation of grain. The statute in *Munn* defined grain elevators as public warehouses and established maximum rates for storing grain. The crucial issue involved the power of state government to regulate the owners' return on their business, thereby trumping private agreements to fix prices and limiting the investment return on private property. Writing for the Court, Chief Justice Waite drew no limits on state power to regulate, once a private business was clothed with the "public interest." In a commonwealth, there was no need for the Court to be concerned with the exercise of legislative power: "[I]t is a power which may be abused; but that is no argument against its existence. For protection against abuses by legislatures the people must resort to the polls, not to the courts."[22]

Justice Stephen J. Field dissented, insisting that the Court had a constitutional duty to define the limits of state power over private interests. This constitutional duty derived from a conviction that there was no commonwealth. There were only majoritarian and individual interests, only public and private spheres, which diverged. Hence, a common-law determination of "reasonableness" was the constitutional standard needed to adjudicate conflicting interests so that "on the one hand, the property interest of the stockholder would be protected from practical confiscation, and on the other hand, the people would be protected from arbitrary and extortionate charges." Just two years before the Sherman Act debates began, the Court adopted Field's view that the "due process" clause protected railroad property rights to a "fair return."[23]

It is important to remember precisely what the Supreme Court's rate cases and the Commerce Act debates concluded—that both congressional policy and constitutional protection of property must assure only that private investors receive a *minimum* fair profit, not the *maximum* profit possible through monopolization or private agreement. The rationale for Congressman Stewart's comments during the Sherman Act debates, and for his faction's solicitude for "fair prices," parallels the reasoning in both the Commerce Act debates and the rate cases: Just compensation requires some *minimum* rate of return. In all these cases, some minimum protection of property rights "is only reasonable and fair." Stewart's statements emphasize the value of combinations as securing for the producer a fair profit or fair return on property, whether that return derives from capital or labor. Moreover, it is clear that a fair return entails a fair price to the consumer—no more and no less.

In sum, the speeches representing the freedom-from-government view illustrate the workings of a discourse very different from the competition rhetoric of industrial liberty. They describe the contours of a property rhetoric whose foundation is the notion of a "fair profit" or "fair return." Briefly, the argument is as follows: It is an independent social good that those who work, those who put their labor or capital into the market, get a fair return on their input. This social good benefits both producers and consumers. "Fair profit" or "fair return" is a social good that the government should enforce, whether the evil be competition or combination and whether the harm be low profits or high prices. It is a social good to be enforced in much the same way that one's possession of property is protected from theft or extortion.

These notions of fair return and private administration of markets appeared alien in statements about "full and free competition." In contrast, they comfortably inhabited statements about protecting the value of one's property—whether labor, railroad rolling stock, manufacturer's goods, or retailer's goodwill. These conflicts between "full and free competition" and private property rights produced fifteen months of debate on Senator Sherman's original bill.

The Sherman Act: Common-law Language and Legislative Remedies

Only six days after the original bill's referral to the Judiciary Committee, Senator Edmunds introduced its successor. The 1890 bill replaced the old language of "full and free competition" and "cost to the consumer" with the common-law language of "restraint of trade" and "monopolization." In sharp contrast to the common-law language of liability, however, the new bill, without so much as a word of floor debate, included civil and criminal remedies lying far outside the common law's contractarian framework. One week after the new bill's introduction, after only a few hours of floor debate, both chambers quickly passed the new Sherman Act. What significance can be attributed to the radical change in language? And what are we to make of the contrast between common-law language of liability and legislative imposition of radically new remedies?

The turn to familiar common-law language was a reaction against the original bill's explicit and unmediated imposition of "full and free competition" as the only natural and legitimate form of commerce. Senator Edmunds's rendition of the Sherman bill used customary language suffused with stable images from a long common-law tradition grounded in liberty of contract principles and private property rights, including the right to a fair profit.

Senator George F. Hoar (R.Mass.), who first asked that the new bill be taken up by the full Senate, immediately expressed hope for an early vote, stating that the bill was already "well understood." Hoar declared that "[w]e have affirmed the old doctrine of the common law . . . and have clothed the United States courts with authority to enforce that doctrine." Edmunds later added that the Committee took the new bill's language "out of terms that were well known to the law already." In response to a hypothetical question about an ingenious rancher's monopoly of short-horn cattle trade with Mexico, Edmunds replied, "Anybody who knows the meaning of the word 'monopoly', as the courts apply it, would not apply it to such a person at all." A "man who merely by superior skill and intelligence . . . got the whole business," he declared, "was not a monopolist."[24]

This common-law "meaning" upon which Congress seemed to rely derived from decisions issued by state courts and British tribunals. Although the common law differed among the several states, some jurisdictions did prohibit monopolies and restraints of trade. For example, the Illinois Supreme Court held that cartel agreements between rivals to fix prices or to allocate territories were restraints of trade and thus unenforceable. Moreover, a number of states used the old common law writ of *quo warranto* to attack some of the more visible trusts. Consistent with such views, the Michigan Supreme Court, upon finding matches a public "necessity," characterized the Diamond Match Company as a monopoly at common law. Chief Justice Thomas R. Sherwood expressed the following concern: "Monopoly in trade or in any kind of business in this country is odious to our form of government. . . . Its tendency is . . . destructive of free institutions, and repugnant to the instincts of a free people, and contrary to the whole scope and spirit of the federal Constitution."[25]

Still, the doctrines of monopoly and trade restraints were an anomalous part of the common law and its classical matrix. The classical matrix included natural law as its moral foundation, freedom of contract as its primary commitment, and classical economics as its "scientific" rudiment. The common law's general rule was liberty of contract, which was understood as the condition required for competition. Thus, regulating liberty of contract was seen as government interference with a natural regime of competition. In consequence, only exceptional circumstances could justify interventionist doctrines to regulate monopolies and restraints of trade. In 1889, for example, the United States Supreme Court acknowledged as legitimate a state's common-law prohibition against a price-fixing cartel because it involved a commodity or service of "public necessity"—that is, only because the circumstances were exceptional.[26] British courts were less inclined to condemn monopolies and restraints of trade. Again in 1889, for example, Lord Bowen wrote that a maritime shipping cartel was not a common-law restraint of trade, even when financing a "fighting ship" to drive rivals out of business by carrying cargo at prices that "would not repay a shipowner for his adventure." The cartel did "nothing more," Bowen concluded in his influential decision, "than pursue to the bitter end a war of competition."[27] In short, competition was the logical consequence of liberty of contract, even when a contract restrained trade among the parties and sought to eliminate rivals.

The Sherman Act's common-law language, it seems, was well known but unsettled. Recent developments in common-law doctrines of monopoly and restraints of trade were the uneven consequences of intense pressure on the classical matrix of common-law and economics doctrines, pressure exerted by the widespread appearance and persistence of trusts and cartels. The doctrines of monopoly and trade restraints were anomalous because they explicitly called upon public policy to trump private agreements. Classical law and economics produced this exceptional category of "public interest" to take account of the sudden appearance of monopolies and cartels in an otherwise lawfully and naturally competitive marketplace driven by private enterprise.

It is easy to see why monopolies and combinations were so troubling. Their very existence called into question one of the basic tenets of classical economics and legal doctrine: the fairness of market price derived from free exchanges between roughly equal individuals. Because actual market prices could mean monopoly price, predatory price, or competitive price, actual market transactions no longer seemed constrained by the classical ideal of competitive markets. Trade could no longer be characterized as free exchanges between roughly equal individuals.

The Fifty-first Congress's familiarity with the language of the new antitrust bill, it seems, was rooted in their general understandings of classical contract and property law doctrines, as well as classical economics. This classical matrix was imbedded in their naturalistic sense of lawfulness and rationality, whether scientific, legal, economic, or religious. Hence, when Congressman Stewart spoke of "two great forces working in human society," his rhetoric reflected the imaginative structure framing the views of his colleagues. His claim of *two* natural tendencies—one to compete and the other to combine—rather than an unrivaled tendency to compete, was prompted by the changing face of American industry and labor. That is, the late nineteenth-century belief in natural law and its rationality animated a desire to characterize the economic tendency to combine as natural and rational, because the alternative—asserting the unnaturalness of the widespread practice of combination—would call into question the very belief in natural law and its rationality.[28]

Nonetheless, there remained a profound ambivalence toward business combinations, toward trusts and cartels, because their success was at odds with the familiar tenets of classical economics, which proclaimed the inevitability of competition (in the absence of government grant).[29] Under the classical view, a natural tendency to compete would not only overcome the current wave of combinations but bring with it greater prosperity and individual freedom. Government intervention was seen as unnecessary and unwise. In contrast, if Stewart was right—if there had evolved two natural tendencies and forces, competition and combination—then the prospects for competitive markets were indeterminable and government action could make a difference.

Stewart's view was also tough to swallow because it challenged the classical view that a fair price derived from free exchanges between roughly equal individuals. Under this Ricardoan labor theory of value, since commodities embody a worker's labor, it is labor that imparts market value. Free exchanges among numerous independent trading partners produce "natural" or "market" prices. Moreover, since each party was imagined as getting something in return that was proportional to his contribution, the prices and the process were seen as not only natural and free, but also fair and just.[30] Insofar as combinations charged prices higher or lower than the natural market price, classical economics considered them unnatural and unjust interlopers in competitive markets.

In hypothetical questions such as the one about a short-horn cattle monopoly discussed earlier, the classical view was faced with two further problems, one legal and the other empirical. First, can the state legitimately interfere with the rancher's accumulation of wealth and property, resulting from his hard work and ingenuity? Certainly, *Munn* and other Supreme Court opinions had already recognized a state's right to regulate profit when there was a "public interest" involved. But what about all those industries that were not clothed in something called the public interest? What about regulating the price of short-horn cattle?[31]

In House debate, Congressman George W. Fithian (D.Ill.) asserted that the state can interfere only when the rancher acted improperly by creating unnatural or "fictitious prices." Fithian's statement raises the classical problem of "fictitious prices": Even if the ingenious rancher had done nothing improper, a monopoly price would be charged. That is, a gap would appear between a classical market's "fair price" and the actual market price. Should the law characterize the actual price as an earned property right or as a fictitious price? Rather than confront the hard case of monopoly earned in the meritocracy of the competitive process, Senator Edmunds, in Senate colloquy about the same hypothetical rancher, also hedged his response: "He has not bought off his adversaries. He has not got the possession of all the horned cattle." Like his colleague in the House, Senator Edmunds avoided the tough issue: What if this gentleman rancher *had* gotten hold of all the horned cattle, using only his ingenuity, thus "prevent[ing] other men from engaging in fair competition with him"?[32]

The classical view of monopoly as transitory faced a second difficulty: the material reality of a national economy filled with combinations, with trusts and cartels. This reality called into question classical economics' foundational premise: the inevitability of competition. The experience of epidemic combination suggested that after the hypothetical rancher dominated the market, his rivals might decide to cooperate rather than compete. They might choose, even agree, to charge the price set by the dominant rancher, who might elect simply to charge his monopoly price, comfortable in the knowledge that his rivals would rather follow his lead than compete with his superior intelligence and ingenuity. For those who believed that the natural tendency to compete supported classical economic theory, price leadership was irrational conduct.[33] The economic facts all around them, however, did not fit the classical theory.

This dissonance between experience and expectations did not go entirely unnoticed. David Ames Wells, a prominent classical economist, wrote in 1889 that the new technology of steam power created such efficiencies that "overproduction" provoked "excessive competition" and thus an incentive to combine, either by cartel or by merger. In his critique of the classical view, influential economist Henry Carter Adams wrote that combinations, particularly those taking the corporate form, were destroying the "strategic equality" of classically conceived competitors. Making the imbalance even more pronounced, he wrote, was that corporations assert "rights conferred on individuals by the law of private property, and apply to themselves a social philosophy true only of a society composed of individuals." Motivated by similar concerns, other scholars, writers of the popular "literature of protest," and farmer and labor groups, as well as both Democratic and Republican party platforms, called for some antitrust action.[34]

Nonetheless, the courts held firmly to doctrines founded in the classical economics of what Harvard Law School Dean Roscoe Pound would call "abstract individual self-assertion," and thus embraced images taken from an earlier time of "pioneer, rural, agricultural America." These images served to repress impulses toward equalizing market power and to obscure the effects of gross economic inequalities on individual liberty. Together with claims by U.S. Steel founder Andrew Carnegie and by a new wave of economists that greater size always entails greater efficiency, the surge of trust-building, which began in earnest in 1889, along with the persistence of cartels, raised deeply troubling questions about the classical view that the natural process of competition would dissolve combinations.[35] Supporters of combination were calling upon the powerful idea of liberty. Individual liberty legitimized private agreements, whether or not they restrained competition, by summoning a counterfactual image of typical market transactions as free exchanges between roughly equal parties. In this way, the impulse toward liberty constituted the foundation for a freedom-of-contract regime that relied on an ideal of equal competition and viewed social and economic reality as momentary aberrations from the ideal. Thus, the impulse toward liberty provided a powerful basis not only for the classical view of competition as free trade, but also for the freedom to enter into private agreements without regard for their effects on competition. This idealized notion of liberty and its formal assumption of equality justified both competition and its restraint, both industrial liberty and fair price. It provided common ground for explaining and defending contradictory market conduct and conflicting social values.

These tensions carried profound economic, legal, and political implications. They supported both the economic tenet that individual achievement lay behind monopolization and the jural tenet that liberty of contract justified combinations in restraint of trade. In sharp contrast, social and economic realities unconstrained by such classical images exploded popular and scholarly beliefs in naturally competitive markets and in natural connections between liberty and equality. As the legislative debates demonstrate, the loss of political liberty itself became an issue. James Bryce, British historian and ambassador to the United States, observed:

> The power of groups of men organized by incorporation as joint-stock companies, or of small knots of rich men acting in combination, has developed with unexpected strength in unexpected ways, overshadowing individuals and even communities, and showing that the very freedom of association which men sought to secure by law when they were threatened by the violence of the potentates may, under the shelter of law, ripen into a new form of tyranny.[36]

The Sherman Act passed through a Congress struggling with tensions between belief and experience; tensions between, on the one side, the economic mythology of artisans and local markets together with the political ideology of a yeoman citizenry and, on the other side, the actuality of a new economic order of large-scale enterprise and national markets. Liberty—both industrial and political—seemed to need government intervention to reestablish competitive markets overrun by powerful trusts and cartels. But a return to the rigors of full and free competition was not seen as an unalloyed good. A contrasting rhetoric of fair price (as a per-version of equality), a contrasting sense of human nature as embodying a desire to associate with others, and a fundamental belief in the evolutionary nature of economic enterprise sustained arguments that some combination was a social good.

Congress's eleventh-hour turn to the common-law language of monopolization and restraints of trade sounded a retreat from the 1888 antitrust bill's explicit and unmediated imposition of competition as the only natural and legitimate form of commerce. The 1890 bill's common-law language carried familiar and stable images drawn from classical economic and legal thought—powerful though counterfactual images of mythic proportion. Economic and political impulses toward both liberty and equality were seen as best served by permitting this natural state to flourish, shorn of its excesses. Criticizing Sherman's 1888 bill, the editor of the *American Law Review* wrote that "The common law is good enough, if it were only administered."[37] Finally, the idealized portrayal of commercial markets as free exchanges between roughly equal individuals satisfied the commitment to a fair return on one's property or labor. The problem was seen as unnatural and unfair methods of competition: not the ingenious cattle rancher but rather the "monster" trusts and "extortionate" cartels.

Following the Sherman Act provisions prohibiting "all contracts . . . in restraint of trade" and "monopolization," however, appeared remedies entirely alien to the common law. At common law, the consequence of finding a restraint of trade unreasonable and thus illegal was, at worst, a judicial declaration that the agreement could not be enforced against the parties. If trusts or holding companies were found to have exceeded their authority under state incorporation statutes, their charters could be revoked. Presumably, the principals would simply reincorporate in another jurisdiction.

The Sherman Act introduced uncommon-law remedies that not only recognized new harms but threatened businessmen with the most coercive of sovereign powers—imprisonment and confiscation of property. First of all, "persons injured in their business or property" by restraints of trade or acts of monopolization could seek injunctions and "three fold the damages by him sustained, and the costs of suit, including a reasonable attorney's fee." Venturing far beyond the common-law remedy of actual damages to the contracting party injured by a breach, the Sherman Act authorized damages to third parties injured by perfect performance of a contract. In allowing injured strangers to sue, Congress created a remedial mechanism for public harms, for societal effects of contracts in restraint of trade. Now, entirely private contracts would involve something more than an individualist notion of liberty of contract—something reflecting a "public interest" in *all* commercial endeavor: a concern about "*every* contract . . . in restraint of trade," not just those falling into traditional categories (common carriers, for example) recognized at common law, whether federal or state, and authorized by the Supreme Court's "economic due process" jurisprudence. Entirely alien to the common law, multiple damages and liability to strangers were part of Sherman's original antitrust bill, along with its "competition" rhetoric of liability.[38]

Second, certain agreements were now plainly illegal. The Attorney General was instructed to prosecute, either in civil or criminal suits, those who transgressed the statute's prohibitions. Upon conviction, persons "shall be punished by fine . . . or by imprisonment . . . or by both." Even more remarkable than criminalizing contracts that were simply ignored at common law was the Sherman Act provision that empowered the Government, in prosecutions of cartels and other combinations, to exercise the most extreme of sovereign prerogatives outside of imprisonment—confiscation of private property, here for commercial conduct now likened to smuggling:

> Any property owned under any contract or by any combination or pursuant to any conspiracy (and being the subject thereof) . . . shall be forfeited to the United States, and may be seized and condemned by like proceedings as those provided by law for the forfeiture, seizure, and condemnation of property imported into the United States contrary to law.[39]

The 1890 bill's combination of civil and criminal penalties passed both chambers without debate, despite its seeming trespass of property rights traditionally safeguarded in common-law doctrine and constitutional jurisprudence. Apparently, the statute presented a synthesis of sorts: common-law categories of liability joined to radically new remedies. The Sherman Act created a mechanism for socializing common-law liability beyond the contractarian limits of "actual" injury seen in contract cases and of judicial refusals to enforce agreements in restraint of trade. In short, the statute authorized both public and private exercise of something akin to a "police power" to enforce common-law standards of commercial conduct.

In the social and political turmoil of the new economic order, the common-law Sherman Act, with its supplement of uncommon-law remedies, seemed to be reaching for a middle ground between the rhetorics of industrial liberty and fair price, between their logics of competition policy and private property rights, and between their statist and libertarian approaches. But the middle ground sometimes crumbles and supplements often prove dangerous. The statute, in the hands of federal judges and trial attorneys, would only shift the battleground for these rivalrous visions of political economy.

The Sherman Act in the Federal Courts, 1890–1911: Cartels and Labor Unions, Trusts and the Limits of Majoritarianism

Although federal antitrust law originated in a statute, judges and scholars have regarded it as a general congressional mandate to develop a federal common law of competition. Within this common-law framework, there rests an orthodox view of the two decades following the Sherman Act's passage. In it, the Supreme Court is portrayed as struggling with the statute until enough Justices got it right to adopt the "Rule of Reason" in *Standard Oil* (1911). Before "Reason" prevailed, however, Court majority opinions, characterized as "Literalist," "reveal some early confusion about the relationship of § 1's prohibition to common-law notions of 'restraint of trade.'" Indeed, the so-called Literalists are portrayed as naifs who took the Sherman Act at its word, prohibiting literally *every* contract in restraint of trade. A Literalist reading of the Sherman Act would outlaw not only price-fixing cartels but also partnership agreements and even simple contracts for the sale of goods. Certainly, Congress did not intend such folly. Accordingly, the familiar story concludes, we must apply a "Rule of Reason" as the framework for analyzing the effects of conduct "in restraint of trade." In short, only *unreasonable* restraints of trade should raise antitrust concern.[40] And so the Court wisely adopted the "Rule of Reason." The moral of this parable is clear enough—the force of Reason restrained the zeal of Literalism.

A strikingly different history emerges from a rhetorical analysis of court opinions between 1890 and 1911. We will see, first of all, that the Court's antitrust opinions chronicle a deep conflict between two factions—a series of battles over questions of political economy, battles over the relationship between competition policy and common-law property rights, encounters whose maneuvers were choreographed years earlier in congressional debates about Senator John Sherman's original Anti-Trust Bill. The lines between Literalist and Rule of Reasonist factions were clearly drawn. The Literalists, the early majority, took as their first principle an individualist image of competition, of marketplace rivalry among "small dealers and worthy men," a political economic vision embraced by Senator Sherman and his allies. The Rule of Reasonist minority, together with antitrust defendants and most federal judges, asserted the inviolable nature of property protection, particularly liberty of contract, in terms sometimes more severe than those expressed by the congressmen who called for reasonable restraints to assure a "fair return" in the marketplace. This juristic form of property rhetoric was sometimes more abstract, lending form to a discourse of natural and constitutional rights.

Justice Edward Douglass White's minority faction, who would later dominate a new Rule of Reasonist majority, saw the shift to a standard of "reasonableness" as imperative because "competition"—in the rhetoric rejected by Congress for the Sherman Act—reflected an approach to regulation at odds with the extant common-law scheme. Justice Oliver Wendell Holmes agreed, writing pointedly in his *Northern Securities* (1904) dissent that the "act says nothing about competition."[41] Holmes was not only teaching his Literalist brethren a lesson in the art of literalism; he was also advancing property logics championed by his fellow dissenting Justice White. In the early era's war over the foundations of antitrust law, Holmes joined the Rule of Reasonist faction, an imminent majority whose explicit goal was to restore the primacy of freedom of contract.

Second of all, we will see that these battles were fought on seemingly placid waters—during a historical period, that is, when a divided Court was extraordinary. It is perhaps difficult to imagine and thus easy to forget that the Court, at least in its formal record, rarely reflected the turbulence, in both city streets and state legislatures, provoked by economic and social reorganization—by conflicts between those favoring and those resisting such changes.

With relatively few exceptions, Court opinions concerning, for example, industrial or race relations, free speech, or review of economic legislation, produced strong majorities, sometimes with one or two Justices in dissent. Indeed, even antitrust opinions were largely issued by a united Court. The *Northern Securities* decision and its splintered Court, with four separate opinions, was the last of only three antitrust cases (out of about two dozen) that divided the Court in antitrust's "formative era" between 1890 and 1911. How was it that the two antitrust factions resolved their disputes? And how did they resolve other issues of political economy, particularly the role of labor unions and the power of political majorities?

The remainder of this chapter investigates these questions. The era's antitrust jurisprudence can be understood as two overlapping cycles of fission and fusion; as two sudden outbreaks of conflict provoked by factional commitments to competition policy and common-law property rights, followed by surprisingly swift resolutions. I explore each cycle of collapse and consolidation in a separate section. The first looks at the Court's struggle in the 1890s to regulate a new economy under an old common-law regime at odds with legislative efforts by both Congress and several states. Under the Sherman Act, the cases that emerged involved the conduct of associations—either commercial cartels or labor unions. Right around 1900, it became clear that common-law discourse would prevail. This discourse of "conspiracy" was wrapped around Literalist outcomes: Associations, whether commercial cartels or labor unions, were unlawful conspiracies. They were simply illegal per se. The second jurisprudential cycle dealt with large corporate size—with trusts—which were usually the result of both mergers and sharp competitive practices. Here, the collapse occurred in 1904 with the *Northern Securities* case, and the consolidation emerged seven years later in the *Standard Oil* opinion's "Rule of Reason." In harmony with the *Lochner* era's "economic due process" jurisprudence, freedom of contract and other general principles of federal common law underwrote the antitrust "Rule of Reason," which would provoke widespread legislative response even though the Oil and Tobacco Trusts were disassembled. In 1914, Congress would enact two new statutes, both written in the explicit language of "competition," to reinvigorate antitrust policy.

Gone, however, was concern about industrial liberty and the rhetoric of "small dealers and worthy men." Gone was the explicit commitment to a political economy founded on tenets associated with a commonwealth of communities populated by an independent, roughly equal citizenry. In its place stood growing admiration for the genius of large-scale enterprise, apprehension about the power of majoritarian government, and commitment to a federalist vision of free markets supervised by federal courts and agencies. The Supreme Court's solicitude for individual liberty shifted from fear of powerful commercial interests to alarm over legislative impairment of property and contract rights, despite increasing disparities of power in the economic sphere.[42] That shift was reflected in new relationships forged between free competition and freedom of contract.

First Cycle: Cartels and Labor Unions, 1890–1899

Justice Peckham's old majority first formulated its Literalist interpretation of the Sherman Act in the *Trans-Missouri Freight Association* decision (1897), which reversed the federal district and circuit courts, both in their holdings and in their reasoning. These lower court judges were simply following the uniform practice of their peers, treating the statute as a congressional grant of jurisdiction to develop a federal common law. The doctrines of monopolization and restraint of trade, familiar terms in the common laws of England and the several states, were understood as requiring judges to determine the "reasonableness" of trusts, cartels, and other restraints of trade.[43]

Federal judges were already imbedded in a federal common-law regime that had expanded into traditional state precincts in the years after *Swift v. Tyson* (1842). Indeed, the Supreme Court went so far as to distinguish federal common law from legislative regulation of commercial matters. In 1890, Justice Samuel Blatchford wrote that state legislation was regulation subject to judicial review for the constitutional purpose of ensuring that a state did not fix rates so low as to constitute a "taking" of property. Eleven years later, Justice David J. Brewer treated the Court's common law as entirely distinct from legislation, which constituted "regulation." The common law was simply the accumulated sedimentation over the centuries of well-settled principles and the customary law merchant. Together, an expansive federal common law, a restrictive view of state common law, and constitutional supervision of state legislation founded in common-law freedom of contract produced a common-law federal judiciary. Thus, federal judges saw the Sherman Act as part of a pervasive common-law regime.[44]

In the same year that district court Judge John A. Riner dismissed the Attorney General's Sherman Act suit against the Trans-Missouri Freight Association, finding their price-fixing agreement reasonable, Supreme Court Justice-to-be Howell E. Jackson wrote his influential trial court opinion in one of the Whiskey Trust cases, *In re Greene* (1892).[45] Finding for the trust, Judge Jackson reached beyond the common-law doctrine of reasonable restraints, asserting that, as a constitutional matter, the Sherman Act could not regulate the property of corporations created by a state. The opinion's "takings" rhetoric was clearly consistent with the federal courts' "economic due process" approach to evaluating state regulatory statutes. Jackson's argument was categorical: "Property" must be protected from congressional assault. Unlike the instrumentalist rhetoric of "fair price" heard in the congressional debates, Jackson was not concerned with the *effects* of a statute imposing competition. Instead, he saw the statute as threatening the destruction of an essential right of private property, as an unconstitutional taking, regardless of the effects on trade. The categorical quality of Jackson's jurisprudence contrasted sharply with the congressional concerns expressed during the Sherman Act debates about the economic ebb and flow of marketplace activity, about the need to restrain the extremes of both competition and combination to ensure a fair price.

For the most part, however, lower court judges in the seven years before the Supreme Court's *Trans-Missouri Freight Association* opinion treated Sherman Act cases as disputes governed by common-law doctrine, not by constitutional conceptions of "property" or categorical notions of "competition." Thus, the Supreme Court's rejection (by a 5–4 decision) of the lower courts' common-law reasoning was unanticipated. Justice Peckham wrote that Congress intended to drop the common-law scheme of reasonable and unreasonable restraints because it did not use that language. Instead, the statute said *every* restraint: "By the simple use of the term 'restraint of trade,' all contracts of that nature, whether valid or otherwise [at common law], would be included, and not alone that kind of contract which was invalid and unenforceable as being in unreasonable restraint of trade."[46]

The eighteen railroads constituting the Trans-Missouri Freight Association were accused of fixing uniform rates and terms in violation of the Sherman Act. Counsel for defendants had convinced the trial and appellate courts that their agreement "regulated" rather than "suppressed" competition. The trial court concluded that the Association had fixed "reasonable prices" to prevent "unhealthy competition" and "to avert personal ruin." Whether under the Interstate Commerce Act or the Sherman Act, wrote trial Judge Riner, "the public is not entitled to free and unrestricted competition, but what it is entitled to is fair and healthy competition."[47] The Eighth Circuit Court of Appeals affirmed both the holding and the reasoning.

In oral argument before the Supreme Court four years later, Freight Association attorneys repeated their claims that "competition leads in the railroad business to financial ruin and insolvency . . . [and] to the destruction of innocent stockholders." In short, the lower court opinions as well as the argument of counsel, all couched in the common-law language of reasonable restraint, framed in the Interstate Commerce Act's regulation of railroads, paralleled those congressional speeches extolling the virtue of combination, the need to restrain ruinous competition, and the property right to a fair return on capital committed to the marketplace. The economic facts seemed to corroborate their view: Between 1891 and 1897, almost 350 railroads went into federal receivership.[48]

Nonetheless, the Supreme Court reversed. Justice Peckham left no doubt that all price-fixing agreements were illegal, regardless of the reasonableness of the prices fixed: "Competition . . . is a necessity . . . for securing in the end just and proper rates." Indeed, it was impossible to determine whether any *agreed* price was reasonable. Only prices fixed by competition were reasonable. It was a matter of fundamental conviction, unshakable belief, that private agreements simply could not "regulate" competition. They could only "restrain" it. Echoing Senator Sherman's faction in the Fifty-first Congress, the five Justices signing the majority opinion agreed that "[c]ompetition, free and unrestricted, is the general rule."[49]

In response, Justice White's dissenting opinion expressed agreement with the lower court judges, the defendants, and those congressmen who wanted to restrict the extremes of both competition and combination in order to assure a fair price to all market participants. Unshakable in their belief that private regulation of commerce was not only possible but necessary, they wanted to protect competitors from ruinous competition. White's faction insisted that the "plain intention of the law was to protect the liberty of contract and the freedom of trade." White went even further, declaring, in abstract language of constitutional and natural rights reminiscent of Judge Jackson's formal "property" rights rhetoric in the *Greene* opinion, that the Court majority's "unreasonable" interpretation amounted to a subjection of liberty of contract and freedom of trade "to the mere caprice of judicial authority."[50]

Both Supreme Court factions, inspired by their commitments to either "free competition" or "freedom of contract," carried the juridical impasse over congressional intentions beyond a concern for fair prices. Mirroring the congressional debates about competition and combination, each opinion claimed that not only the economic effects but also the social and political aftermath of the other's prescription would shatter the peace and prosperity of American society.[51]

Peckham, writing for the Literalist majority, saw the problem as "motives of individual or corporate aggrandizement as against the public interest." That is, private agreements in restraint of trade would drive "out of business the small dealers and worthy men whose lives have been spent therein. . . . Mere reduction in the price of the commodity dealt in might be dearly paid for by the ruin of such a class . . . of small but independent dealers." Much like Senator Sherman's view of entrepreneurial independence as the bedrock of individual liberty, Peckham called for rivalry among roughly equal firms of relatively small size

> because it is not for the real prosperity of any country that such changes should occur which result in transferring an independent business man, the head of his establishment, small though it might be, into a mere servant or agent of a corporation for selling the commodities which he once manufactured or dealt in, having no voice in shaping the business policy of the company and bound to obey orders issued by others.

According to this industrialized mutation of the Jeffersonian ideal of independent farmers, this entrepreneurial republicanism, the problem was "combinations of capital [that] drive out of business all the small dealers in the commodity, and . . . render the public subject to the decision of the combination." The solution to maintaining this vital class of independent entrepreneurs was "competition, free and unrestricted."[52]

The problem, of course, lay in the republican or commonwealth view that political and economic spheres were not airtight compartments. In this political ideology of republicanism, an independent entrepreneur could be an independent citizen, while a "servant or an agent of a corporation" could not. At the same time, economic power and vast accumulations of wealth brought the threat of political corruption. The Literalist solution was economic competition to temper economic power. Agreements to fix prices, contracts to evade the discipline of competition, were most obviously illegal: Not only did they raise prices but they threatened the very possibility of interjecting the republican norm of rough equality into the economic sphere and thus averting the political corruption associated with economic power and great wealth.[53]

In sharp contrast to this vision of industrial liberty practiced by numerous independent entrepreneurs, Justice White saw a different problem and, not surprisingly, a different solution. The problem for White was the threat of industrial warfare, a Hobbesian vision of individualism as hostile anarchy. White's solution, however, was not imperial but liberal: "utmost liberty of contracting," as prescribed by the common law. Furthermore, according to White, the Court's commitment to free competition, its refusal to allow contracts to temper unreasonable excesses of competition, "strikes down the interest of the many to the advantage and benefit of the few."[54]

Muffled by this abstract rhetoric was the issue before the Court: the claim of a few large and powerful railroads that their price-fixing cartel should not be disturbed. To justify the railroad cartel's right to fix prices, White referred to the Court's affirmation two years earlier of a contempt order against union leader Eugene V. Debs, growing out of the infamous Pullman Company strike. The Literalist interpretation of the Sherman Act in *Debs* (1895), White claimed, made the Sherman Act "embrace every peaceable organization or combination of the laborer to benefit his condition either by obtaining an increase of wages or diminution of hours of labor." White argued that the consequence—a threat of industrial warfare—attached with the same urgency to competition between capitalists as it did to competition between capital and labor.[55] In sum, White was asserting the necessity of combination for both railroad capitalists and union wage laborers—combination not only to equalize bargaining power in labor's struggle to win a fair wage from capital, but also to eliminate competition between railroads to allow them a "fair profit" on their invested capital. In the case at hand, combination was the only civilized alternative to industrial warfare between capitalists, and well worth the price of entrepreneurial independence.

White's policy argument, like Peckham's, derived from classical political economy. Not only was competition understood as both horizontal and vertical, but questions of competition raised concerns in two dimensions: economic and political. Indeed, the disagreement between Peckham and White was expressed most vividly in political terms, with Peckham fearing the loss of virtue in the ruin of an independent entrepreneurial citizenry and White fearing the loss of liberty in the Hobbesian chaos threatened by congressional prohibition of economic cooperation.

Yet White's attack on the Literalist approach is open to serious question. Two years earlier, White and every other member of the Court had signed on to the *Debs* opinion, written by Justice David Brewer, a member of the Literalist faction. The Court had upheld a contempt citation issued against Debs, who continued to exhort the rank and file after the district court's injunction against the widespread shutdown of railways using Pullman cars. White was condemning an opinion that he had joined, an approach that he accepted in the context of a labor combination. Although *Debs* was a contempt-of-court case, not itself decided under the Sherman Act, White was nonetheless criticizing the decision for what he saw as Literalist underpinnings. Moreover, in direct conflict with his criticism, White would subsequently join a unanimous Court in the *Danbury Hatters* case (1908), which applied a Literalist approach in holding labor boycotts illegal per se under the Sherman Act.[56] Nevertheless, he was willing in the breach to argue for the huge railroad companies' right to form a cartel by analogizing their position to the condition of individual workers.

Certainly, Peckham and his Literalist faction seemed to take consistent positions. Both combinations of capitalists and unions of laborers violated the Sherman Act's ethic of individualism. Price-fixing cartels hurt individual entrepreneurs and customers; labor unions hurt individual employers. But behind this ideological consistency stood an unarticulated assumption about the nature of the combining parties. Whereas laborers actually were individuals, many capitalists were already vast combinations, not individual entrepreneurs. Indeed, Peckham's majority used the rhetoric of "small dealers and worthy men" to engage in a political economic analysis of eighteen large railroads. The Court would face this disparity between individualist ideology and cooperative actuality in the second cycle of fission and fusion—in the controversial trust cases that concluded the formative period.[57]

How could White and the others in his Rule of Reason faction square their positions in the cartel and labor cases? Was it simply a class-based political judgment about the rights of owners and employees, a judgment that owners deserve fair profits, whether through owner cartels or protection from unions? Or was it a sense that cartels, in charging only "fair prices," had no victims, whereas labor unions provoked violence and boycotts, more threatening injuries not only economically but also socially and politically? What of the view among elite lawyers and economists that combinations of capital created productive efficiencies, while combinations of labor simply raised costs? Whatever the explanation, the classical view of competition proceeded from assumptions that would make elitist rationales at once troubling and acceptable.

Competition, as understood by classical economists, was produced by freedom of contract; value and thus price derived from the labor invested in a good. It was not until 1890 that economist Alfred Marshall synthesized the work of Jevons, Ricardo, and others in his treatise *Principles of Economics*, which turned economics away from concerns about individual liberty and toward an idea of market equilibrium (between supply and demand), toward a concept of marginalism and, with it, the technical focus on markets that ultimately led, some thirty years later, to a general acceptance of the neoclassical models of perfect competition and perfect monopoly.[58] Around 1900, however, the political economic vision of competition still held sway. Two elements of that vision are relevant here. The first provides a perspective on the unanimity in the labor cases, the second a perspective on the division in the cartel cases.

First, classical political economy made no distinction between horizontal and vertical dimensions. Competition was understood as both vertical and horizontal, as involving rivalry not only among sellers but also between buyers and sellers. In the years surrounding the Sherman Act legislative debates, economist Francis Walker's *Political Economy*, well known and widely disseminated, defined competition as "the operation of individual self-interest, among buyers and sellers." This view, still respectable for the next three decades, was explicitly adopted in several influential dissenting opinions written by a well-informed Justice Holmes. In the 1890s, classical political economy's two-dimensional view of competition supported the Court's unanimity in the labor cases: Both Literalists and Rule of Reasonists felt justified in enjoining employees from combining to restrain trade with employers.[59]

Second, classical political economy was founded in liberty of contract as the primary expression of common-law property rights. Into the late nineteenth century, the "labor and skill of the workman" and the "plant of the manufacturer" were both seen as "property" and, in consequence, were understood as calling for the same legal rules regarding combination. As early as the 1870s, however, the Supreme Court was grappling with the view that "property" meant "profits," and by 1890 six Justices had adopted the position that protecting the constitutional right to property meant protecting its exchange value.[60] The Sherman Act debates also reflected the view that "fair profits" called for reasonable combinations.

The same fears of rate regulation and ruinous competition did not seem to apply to workmen who could, it was claimed, simply take their labor and skill elsewhere. "Free labor," it was argued, allowed the individual worker to bargain across industrial and geographic borders to find the employer willing to pay what the worker was worth in the free market. There was no attention paid, for example, to the firm-specific investments made by many employees—that is, to the particular skills and know-how that were often lost across industrial and geographic boundaries.[61]

It is clear that the disagreement between Literalist and Rule of Reasonist factions involved much more than a lawyerly argument over proper techniques of statutory interpretation. There was an underlying conflict, a fundamental disagreement about the political economy of competition. It involved a clash between factions holding opposing visions of society. On one side, the Literalists believed that the policy directing the antitrust laws should rest upon free and unrestricted competition among roughly equal market participants, among independent entrepreneurs or free workmen, whether or not the consequence in any particular transaction was fair or reasonable. On the other, the advocates of a Rule of Reason urged that antitrust policy should tolerate large consolidations of capital and allow private agreements that restrain trade when the agreements protect a fair return on property or some other traditional exercise of freedom of contract.[62]

At the same time, there was substantial agreement between these factions—not only in their treatment of labor unions but also, for example, in their common-law view of First Amendment speech as a concern outside the category of individual liberty. The first accommodation between antitrust factions began to take shape in the next railroad cartel case, *Joint-Traffic Association* (1898). Although another 5–4 decision (with the same factional alignment of Justices), this case reflected rhetorical shifts. First of all, Justice White's faction dissented without opinion. Calls for a Rule of Reason to forestall ruinous competition appeared only in the argument by counsel for the railroads. Next, only in the Solicitor General's argument for the Government was there mention of the prior term's republicanist concern for independent entrepreneurs. Finally, Justice Peckham's opinion was surprising because it was written in direct dialogue with the arguments of "learned counsel" for the railroads. The opinion reflects great candor. Peckham took seriously arguments posed "for the third time . . . because the eminence of counsel . . . called upon the court to again give to those arguments strict and respectful attention." Noting "so close a division of opinion in this court," Peckham proceeded to analyze the railroad industry and competition more generally, and concluded that the outcome of competition is always "uncertain." The cartel lawyers' arguments for allowing reasonable restraints, founded in the claim that ruinous competition was inevitable, were thus rejected.[63]

However, instead of carrying forward *Trans-Missouri*'s dominant theme of republicanist concern for a disappearing class of independent entrepreneurs, Peckham picked up another thread: the traditional common-law distinction between direct and ancillary restraints. Unless ancillary to the sale of a business or some other property, agreements not to compete were unenforceable at common law. Just like the earlier Trans-Missouri cartel's "direct, immediate, and necessary effect was to put a restraint upon trade or commerce," the Joint Traffic Association, a cartel of thirty-one railroads, had a "natural, direct, immediate effect . . . to prevent any competition whatsoever." Peckham concluded that competition was good for commerce because "the direct and immediate effect of free competition between carriers is to lower rates."[64] Lower rates were now presented as the primary benefit of competition policy.

Although the Literalist rhetoric changed, the result was the same. The cartel, because it was categorized as a direct restraint of commerce, was illegal under the Sherman Act, notwithstanding alternative common-law arguments to the contrary. Thus, the Court remained divided. The close division on the Court maintained its force because the two factions could not reach the kind of *normative* accommodation achieved in, for example, the labor injunction cases. In those cases, Peckham, White, and everyone else on the Court agreed that labor had no right to combine—that is, to restrain trade—because they injured the property of "individual" business owners. In the railroad cartel cases, however, we see a Court divided by fundamental disagreement over the political economy of competition in trade, a Court separated by incompatible visions of commercial society. In one camp, the Literalists held firm to their substantive view that congressional competition policy superseded the common law. In the other, the Rule of Reasonist faction endorsed combinations and cartels, insisting on the entrepreneur's liberty to contract away his independence in order to restrain destructive competition and to safeguard a fair profit.

The following term, however, brought substantive agreement, with Justice White's faction joining Peckham's unanimous opinion in the *Addyston Pipe* case (1899), the federal prosecution of the six major producers of iron pipe. Charging them with a secret agreement to fix prices and allocate contracts, Attorney General Richard Olney sought not only an injunction but also confiscation of all pipe sold and transported in interstate commerce under the conspiracy.[65]

The common ground for this rapprochement between factions seemed to be Judge William H. Taft's opinion for the Sixth Circuit, which seemed to bridge the gap between Supreme Court factions. In finding the defendants' bid-rigging scheme illegal, Taft forged an admirable synthesis in concluding that, at common law, all "reasonable and ancillary" restraints were considered valid because they promoted "the free purchase and sale of property."[66] Taft's opinion presented the relationship between the statute and common law in a new and acceptable way that promoted property interests. At the same time, in holding that the bid-rigging agreement was direct and thus illegal, Taft also conformed the common law to the Literalist rhetoric of competition.

The common ground for the Court's unanimous opinion was not, however, Taft's much-celebrated synthesis. Only in the rhetoric was synthesis possible. Ultimately, Taft himself recognized the need to choose between the two approaches: To allow some price-fixing agreements, he wrote, would entail the judicial "power to say . . . how much restraint of competition is in the public interest" and thus would require courts to "set sail on a sea of doubt."[67] In short, Taft chose to assert that competition, unrestrained by private agreement, must remain the final arbiter of reasonable price.

The Court factions found common ground elsewhere. First, there was doctrinal agreement that the secret bid-rigging agreement was fraudulent, thus violating everyone's version of the Sherman Act. White's faction could see *this sort of* price-fixing agreement, this fraud on the public, as unreasonable and thus prohibited. Second, Peckham wrote that "if it were important," the prices themselves were unreasonable. Third, there was an entirely new element in Peckham's continuing rhetorical shift away from a republicanist solicitude for "small dealers and worthy men": a new argument that appealed to the liberal sensibilities of Justice White and the Rule of Reasonist faction, an argument founded upon Justice Brewer's unanimous opinion in *Debs*: "If a State, with its recognized power of sovereignty, is impotent to obstruct interstate commerce, can it be that any mere voluntary association of individuals within the limits of that State has a power which the State itself does not possess?" Evoking the Court's ideology of "laissez-faire constitutionalism," Peckham asked, "What sound reason can be given why Congress should have the power to interfere in the case of the State, and yet have none in the case of the individual?" Given the Court's institutional self-image as the guardian of interstate commerce, everyone could agree that when "private contracts . . . result in the regulation of interstate commerce," Congress has the power to regulate because the "liberty of the citizen . . . was limited by the commerce clause."[68] In short, Peckham turned the liberal logic of the federal common law inside out, deploying it to serve republicanist concerns about commercial size: Market transactions, though presumptively private and thus protected by a constitutional liberty of contract, become public and subject to federal oversight when they "regulat[e] . . . interstate commerce."

Thus, Peckham's opinion attracted the Rule of Reasonists for three reasons. First, they agreed with the premise that the Supreme Court had the power and responsibility to keep the states out of regulating interstate commerce—that is, out of regulating private agreements. This proposition was consistent with their disdain for legislative impairment of contracts between private parties. Second, they concluded that the iron pipe cartel's effect was just as illegitimate as state regulation of interstate commerce—an exclusively federal domain. Finally, they believed that common-law tribunals, including the Supreme Court, could legitimately pass judgment on private agreements in restraint of trade. The cartel agreement in *Addyston Pipe* was fraudulent and called for unreasonable prices. Hence, it met both the Literalist (direct) and Rule of Reasonists (unreasonable) tests, both common-law standards, for illegality.

The *Addyston Pipe* opinion announced that the first impasse between Literalist and Rule of Reasonist factions was resolved. Indeed, cartel cases would almost always muster unanimous opinions during the next two decades. For example, Justice Holmes wrote for a unanimous Court in *Swift & Co.* (1905) that a combination of meat processors, in agreeing not to bid against one another in setting prices for sales to stockyards, violated the Sherman Act. Adopting a much broader notion of interstate commerce than *E. C. Knight*'s manufacture/commerce distinction only ten years earlier, Holmes's opinion seemed to signal that the Court was ready to expand its common-law regulation of interstate commerce.[69] Lost in the resolution and expansion, however, was the republicanist solicitude for "small dealers and worthy men." In its place emerged a regulatory regime of federal common law, including a libertarian rhetoric for antitrust, situated comfortably within *Lochner*'s constitutional framework, founded in liberty of contract.

The rhetorical shift seemed to have no practical consequences for cartel cases: Both antitrust visions, both free competition and freedom of contract rhetorics, portrayed cartels as always direct, always unreasonable, and thus always illegal restraints of trade. An overarching image of competition as rivalry between individuals strengthened the consensus that combinations, whether capital or labor, violated the Sherman Act. And so the first outbreak of tensions between Court factions was resolved, at least as early as *Addyston Pipe* (1899).

Yet, as I have already mentioned, something in the logic of individualism was amiss. A hint of trouble was seen in the long line of labor injunction cases. The *Danbury Hatters* decision (1908), for example, seemed on the surface to be consistent with the cartel cases. That is, the labor union strike, just like the meat processor cartel in *Swift & Co.*, was simply illegal. Whether combinations of employees or combinations of commercial competitors, the Sherman Act would strike them down. There was, however, the fundamental difference mentioned earlier: Not only manufacturing and commercial concerns in general but also employers in labor relations cases were uniformly treated as individuals, although they were typically aggregations—often incorporated groups.

It was the well-known *Northern Securities* litigation (1904) that finally presented the difficult case of distinguishing between individuals and groups in commercial associations. Certainly liberty of contract protected individual rights of property. But what constitutes an individual entity? That question appeared as an antitrust issue: Should the Sherman Act, construed under *Addyston Pipe* to prohibit price-fixing agreements among separate entities, also prohibit an agreement between separate entities to combine into a new entity—a trust or holding company? The antitrust issue was doubly difficult. On the one hand, the Sherman Act was, after all, antitrust legislation. On the other, the old common-law doctrine of ancillary restraints, adopted in the unanimous *Addyston Pipe* decision, seemed to permit mergers: At common law, the paradigm case of a permissible restraint of trade was an agreement not to compete, ancillary to the sale of a business or other property. Indeed, that is the very argument (among others) made by railroad counsel before the Supreme Court. It is not surprising, then, that the *Northern Securities* suit unraveled the accommodation reached five years earlier in the cartel cases.[70]

Second Cycle: Commercial Trusts and the Limits of Majoritarianism, 1895–1911

Northern Securities was litigated not only in the light of cartel doctrine but also in the long shadow of *E. C. Knight* (1895), the Sugar Trust merger case, which stood as the Court's authoritative statement on the Sherman Act's jurisdictional limits: Mergers, at least those between manufacturing enterprises, involved purely local concerns and hence arose outside the interstate commerce power of Congress. The Sherman Act, the Court had decided, did not reach the Sugar Trust. Certainly, the railroad cartel cases and the Court's approval of Interstate Commerce Commission power over railroads suggested that a railroad merger was different, that it would fall within the commerce power.[71]

But the relationship between railroads and interstate commerce was not without its vagaries. Thus, for example, the Court, in *Plessy v. Ferguson* (1896), could carve out of interstate railway lines an intrastate segment properly within Louisiana's police power. Despite the Fourteenth Amendment's clear racial purport, Justice Henry Billings Brown, a Michigan Republican, wrote that Louisiana could "in a technical sense interfere with freedom of contract" in a statute that "enforced separation of the races" in railroad passenger cars. Applying a rule of reason, the Court, over Justice Harlan's lone dissent, held that the Louisiana legislature "is at liberty to act with reference to the established usages, customs and traditions of the people." The Court treated railroads as raising intrastate concerns and hence as falling outside federal regulation, as best served by state majoritarian politics when the cultural values at stake were strong enough. Yet, four years earlier, the Court had voided a legislative grant of public lands to a railroad, thereby countermanding a state-level majoritarian action, although such grants had been a well-established custom for almost half a century: In the *Illinois Central Railway* decision (1892), Justice Field wrote that the equitable notion of a "trust" limited legislative powers. That is, the Illinois legislature could not grant irrevocable control of the city of Chicago's harbor to the railroad company because "such abdication is not consistent with the exercise of that trust which requires the government of the state to preserve such waters for the use of the public."[72]

Would the Court treat the Northern Securities merger as an intrastate transaction, as the sale of a business outside the reach of interstate commerce? Would it interpret the Sherman Act as a majoritarian action transgressing the common-law property rights protected by the Fifth Amendment?

In addition to long-standing questions raised about mergers and railroads, the Court had changed since the turn of the century. Two new Justices had joined the Court that heard the *Northern Securities* case: Oliver Wendell Holmes, Jr. and William Rufus Day. But it was within the staunch Literalist majority that unanticipated change erupted. Justice Peckham's majority crumbled under the pressure of this "great case," brought by Teddy Roosevelt's Attorney General to bust the great railroad trust. The Northern Securities Trust was the armistice engineered by financier J. P. Morgan between warring railroad barons James J. Hill and Edward Henry Harriman. Not only did Justice David J. Brewer announce in a concurring opinion his pending defection to the Rule of Reasonist faction, but Peckham himself abandoned the Literalist majority, leaving a plurality of four led by Justice Harlan. Among the dissenters, White and Holmes wrote separate opinions. Peckham, the leading voice of Literalism, joined the choruses of dissent.

The ideological, doctrinal, and economic circumstances made *Northern Securities* a very hard case. The economic circumstances surrounding the formation of the railroad trust added unbearable strain to the doctrinal implications of "ancillary restraints," to the surface tensions between competition and private property rhetorics, to the subterranean fault lines running through the ideology of individualism, and, finally, to the relationship between railroads and interstate commerce. Not only the well-known trend toward federal receivership seen in the railroad industry nationwide but the particular financial difficulties preceding the merger under scrutiny pressed on the Literalist doctrine developed in the cartel cases. It was Justice Harlan who chronicled the difficult economic circumstances of the case.

In his plurality opinion for the Court, Harlan began by describing the huge expanse of competing railway roads, now merged, from the Great Lakes to the Pacific Ocean: "The Great Northern Railway company and the Northern Pacific Railway Company owned . . . two lines, main and branches, about 9000 miles in length, [which] are parallel and competing lines across the continent" and "were engaged in active competition for freight and passenger traffic." The two companies also purchased more than $200 million in capital stock of the Chicago, Burlington, and Quincy Railway company, whose lines aggregated about 8,000 miles. Following that, the principals filed articles of incorporation in New Jersey for the Northern Securities Company and authorized capital stock of $400 million. Stock in this new corporation was exchanged for railroad company stocks, which were held and voted by the Northern Securities Company board of directors. The result was a holding company or trust that controlled more than 17,000 miles of track as well as rights of way, rolling stock, and other assets covering the Western United States, and that consolidated three large railroads, two of which had parallel and competing lines. No wonder Harlan had little difficulty portraying this series of transactions as contracts in restraint of trade, or as a monopolization of the railroad transportation business in a substantial part of the country.[73]

There was, however, another side to these economic circumstances: the railroads' financial distress, mentioned only in passing and only by Justice Harlan. After the Northern Pacific Railroad had entered receivership on account of insolvency, its bondholders arranged "a virtual consolidation of the two systems." In his discussion of the court decree ordering dissolution of the trust, Harlan alluded to this agreement made in advance of foreclosure, an agreement designed to save the value of Northern Pacific shareholders' property from the effects of ruinous competition. He concluded, however, that the dissolution would "destroy, not the property interests of the original stockholders of the constituent companies, but the power of the holding corporation. . . ."[74]

Perhaps Harlan felt that another willing buyer could have been found. It was unlikely, however, that anyone other than the insolvent railroad's parallel and overlapping rival would have found 9,000 miles of parallel and overlapping track attractive, especially given the recent history of fierce competition and claims of overcapitalization. More likely, Harlan believed that the overcapitalization claims were well founded and that the insolvent railroad company shareholders' alternative—selling assets for salvage value at a foreclosure sale—represented the necessary and proper workings of competition. After all, Harlan did write that there were those "who believe that [the rule of competition] is more necessary in these days of enormous wealth than it ever was in any former period of our history."[75] This statement can be understood as the last residue of republicanism, the ideological commitment to "small dealers and worthy men," the belief that the new economic order was destructive of both commerce and politics.

Peering into this crucible of volatile economic circumstances, Justice Harlan concluded that the Literalist interpretation must be applied to settle this explosive mixture of huge wealth and insolvency. Harlan posed the question directly: Does the Sherman Act forbid "every combination or conspiracy in restraint of trade" or "only such restraints as are unreasonable?" Does it require "that the operation of the natural laws of competition . . . not be restricted or interfered with by any contract, combination, or conspiracy?" In addressing those questions, no explicit reference was made to the republicanist rhetoric seen in the first railroad cartel case, *Trans-Missouri* (1897). Rather, Harlan pointed to "certain propositions . . . plainly deducible" from Court precedent: "The act is not limited to restraints . . . that are unreasonable in their nature, but embraces *all* direct *restraints*." Thus, he chose the doctrine of *stare decisis* to reject a Rule of Reason analysis. He chose to cite Court precedent holding that "Congress has, in effect, recognized the rule of free competition by declaring illegal every combination or conspiracy in restraint of interstate and international commerce." Finally, he insisted upon unfettered competition, because "as Congress has embodied that rule in a statute, that must be, for all, the end of the matter, if this is to remain a government of laws, and not of men."[76] The implication seemed to be that the Court could not legitimately impose its own political economic preferences upon the state's majoritarian institution.

Harlan also addressed the constitutional challenge raised by railroad counsel and asserted in Justice White's dissent. He began with a proposition adopted by the unanimous Court in *Addyston Pipe* and affirmed earlier that term in *Montague & Co.*: "The constitutional guarantee of liberty of contract does not prevent Congress from prescribing the rule of free competition . . ." The problem for Harlan, however, was that the merger at hand raised questions unanswered by the cartel cases. Most significant was the question of stock ownership and transfer. In citing *Addyston Pipe* as precedent, he called both the Northern Securities merger and the Addyston Pipe cartel "combinations."[77] With references to the abstract category of "combination" and with reasoning produced by a commitment to competition, Harlan avoided questions about the fundamental right to sell one's property. He could only repeat that the rule of competition was paramount—an incommensurable response to arguments that fundamental liberty and property rights were at stake.

While Harlan's opinion grappled with both the constitutional and doctrinal issues raised by the railroads' financial circumstances, dissenters White and Holmes divided the workload. White took up the Fifth Amendment question of congressional power to regulate or control ownership of state-chartered railroads; Holmes focused on the common-law doctrine of "combination" and its relationship to "competition." In sharp contrast to the Harlan opinion, the dissenting opinions exhibited an inattention to the economic circumstances, an abstract rhetoric of political economy, a concern about the reach of government power, and a vision of social chaos and warfare. In short, they exhibited high anxiety about dangerous and violent consequences attributed to a congressional policy of competition. Harlan saw the Sherman Act as imposing necessary limits on increasing economic inequality, as legitimate regulation of private economic power. White and Holmes saw the Sherman Act's Literalist interpretation as an illegitimate and dangerous exercise of government power, as an assault on the foundations of the American polity.

White rehearsed his apocalyptic vision of industrial warfare unleashed by a Literalist Court's "disregard [of] the great guaranty of life, liberty and property and every other safeguard upon which organized civil society depends." Unlike his dissent in *Trans-Missouri* (1897), however, this opinion called for Fifth Amendment protection without reference to fair profits. Like Judge Jackson's essentialist "property" rhetoric in *Greene* (1892) and the Court's categorical distinction between "manufacturing" and "commerce" in *E. C. Knight* (1895), White asserted that government prohibition of mergers was an unconstitutional confiscation of property ownership and that ownership of property is the foundation of civilized society. The "power of Congress to regulate commerce," he argued, does not entail the power "to regulate the ownership of stock in railroads, which is not commerce at all." In separating the status of property ownership from the conduct of commerce, White's argument can also be understood as a Fifth Amendment analogue to the familiar common-law doctrine that restraints ancillary to the sale of a business were reasonable. It was counsel for the railroads who explicitly made the common-law argument, citing *Addyston Pipe* as authority for the claim that the formation of the trust was simply the sale of a business to a competitor, and therefore that associated restraints were ancillary and legal.[78]

Although Justice Holmes's dissent gives a scenic tour of the common law, its itinerary leads to the same Hobbesian vision of society augured in White's companion dissent. The Literalists' refusal to recognize the Sherman Act's common-law foundations "would make eternal the *bellum omnium contra omnes*." Holmes believed that Congress did not mean to enact but instead intended to counteract this Spencerian vision of Social Darwinism. "It was the ferocious extreme of competition with others, not the cessation of competition among the partners, that was the evil feared," he asserted. The evil was maintenance of market conditions destructive of the right to a fair price: Congress feared "the sinister power exercised . . . by the combination in keeping rivals out of the business and ruining those who already were in."[79] In short, Holmes was taking up the "combination" and "fair price" side of the congressional debates—the side associated with the rhetoric of property rights.

According to Holmes, the Sherman Act does not "require all existing competitions to be kept on foot." Nor does it "invalidate the continuance of old contracts by which former competitors united in the past." Such intentions to dissolve common enterprises introduced dangers even more threatening than government sanction of ruinous competition. For Holmes, it entailed "the universal disintegration of society into single men, each at war with all the rest." Both Holmes and White envisioned chaos resulting from a congressional transgression of the boundary between economic and political domains. Despite his expansive view of legitimate majoritarian activity, his capacious view of the political domain, Holmes concluded, about a congressional purpose to prohibit commercial mergers, that "If that were its intent I should regard calling such a law a regulation of commerce as a mere pretense. It would be an attempt to reconstruct society."[80]

Justice Holmes's rush into the rhetoric of politics suggests that he too saw something important at stake in the heated conflict between factional commitments to property and competition arguments. For example, Holmes portrayed the majority's commitment as entailing a "universal disintegration of society" or a literal ban on combination, even though their jurisprudence had always turned on the common-law doctrine of indirect or ancillary restraints. But Justice Holmes and the new Rule of Reason majority would require more—the protection of private property rights from competition, the commitment to freedom of contract. Perhaps most telling is Holmes's statement that "the Act says nothing about competition." The caustic implication was that the Literalists should take seriously the *literal* language of the statute. In analyzing the common-law doctrine of "restraints of trade," rather than the meaning of "competition," Holmes quipped, "I stick to the exact words used." But his distaste for the Literalists' political economy of competition drove Holmes too far when he characterized the railroad combination as an ordinary business transaction whose effects on competition were remote.[81] Certainly the novelty, size, and complexity of this series of transactions made them anything but ordinary, and the effects of the three-way merger were immediate. Yet, for Holmes, it was the denial of a property right, the prohibition against a contract of sale, that seemed proximate.

As for Justices Brewer and Peckham, what persuaded them to abandon their Literalist colleagues for the Rule of Reasonist camp? The question as it relates to Justice Brewer allows for a quick and easy answer. His concurring opinion in this merger case announced the rationale for his impending shift to a Rule of Reason analysis in explicit property rights terms: "the inalienable right[ ] of every citizen . . . to manage his own property and determine the place and manner of its investment."[82] If nothing else, property rights must protect an individual's liberty to sell his property free from government control. In the earlier cartel cases, government policy could be understood as maintaining a natural state of competition, as prohibiting agreements that restrain individual liberty to set a price. But in this merger case, it looked as though the Literalists wanted to prohibit citizens from buying and selling property.

Justice Peckham, prolific scrivener for the Literalists, abstained from writing a separate opinion and chose instead to sign on to both dissents. Nonetheless, we can discern a link between his competition-based Literalism in the earlier cartel cases and his desertion to the Rule of Reasonist faction in this merger case. In the cartel cases, Peckham applied a notion of industrial liberty founded in his well-known reading of "liberty" as used in the Fourteenth Amendment: Writing for the Court in *Allgeyer* (1897), Peckham characterized this constitutional right as the "liberty of a citizen to pursue any livelihood or vocation, and for that purpose to enter into all contracts which might be proper, necessary and essential to carrying out those objects to a successful conclusion."[83] In *Northern Securities,* Peckham's turn from the competition rhetoric of industrial liberty to the property rhetoric of liberty of contract reflected a continuing commitment to individual liberty. In the price-fixing cases, the liberty to conduct one's business must be protected. In the merger case, the liberty to sell one's business merits the same security. Though these two facets of liberty reflect conflicting competition and property rhetorics, they do accord with Peckham's commitment to individual liberty. Thus, Peckham could sign on to both dissenting opinions and concur in both rationales—White's liberty of contract and Holmes's freedom to associate.

Peckham's shift suggests that a commitment to liberty can be understood as a meeting point between republican and liberal visions of political economy: Sometimes commitments to liberty can be at odds—as they were in the cartel cases, when a republican concern about economic inequality clashed with the liberal mandate to protect property rights from legislative distribution. At other times, commitments to liberty can coalesce—as they did in the *Northern Securities* dissents, when a republican investment in associational rights is detected in liberty of contract. Thus, for the quartet of dissenters and for Brewer as well, the Northern Securities Company merger evoked some facet of liberty—freedom of association, liberty of contract, or the property right to conduct one's own affairs. If property rights and liberty of contract protect anything at all, they must protect the right to sell one's property, to manage one's business, to choose one's associates. The conflict between property and competition rhetorics, between protecting individual liberty and leavening inequality among rivals, could not be ignored in *Northern Securities*.

Counsel for the railroads recognized that theirs was the paradigm case of an ancillary and thus permissible restraint of trade under the traditional common law. They alone argued explicitly that "[i]t has been held repeatedly that such restraints as result from the sale or the purchase of property are not within the provisions of [the] anti-trust statutes." They reminded the Court that the common law "does not require competition. The business of a rival may be purchased for the purpose of being rid of his competition." Characterizing this right in the Fifth Amendment terms we saw rejected in earlier cases, they concluded: "This constitutional provision protects the right to acquire property—equally with the right—to hold the same after it has been acquired."[84]

Little more could have been said to resolve this impasse between conflicting commitments to individual liberty. For Justice Harlan, whose thinking was inscribed with the logic of competition, as well as for his colleagues and the circuit court judge, it was enough to write, "if such combination be not destroyed, all the advantages that would naturally come to the public under the operation of the general laws of competition . . . will be lost." Competition rhetoric expressed their concerns about individuals, their fear of private economic power, and their anxieties about the future of majoritarian government. The dissenting Justices and defendants, however, saw things differently. In large part because their commitments to individualism were founded in liberty of contract, they saw Harlan's Literalism as "depriv[ing] the individual of his freedom to acquire, own and enjoy property by descent, contract or otherwise, because railroads or other property might become the subject of interstate commerce."[85] In consequence, government power exercised by unpropertied majorities, if unchecked, would overwhelm individuals and destroy the very fabric of society—individual rights of private property and private association.

One year later, the Court divided again, this time in the notorious *Lochner* case (1905),[86] which raised similar questions about liberty of contract, economic inequality, and the legitimate scope of governmental regulation. Writing for a bare majority, Justice Peckham expressed the kinds of concern about government power seen in the *Northern Securities* dissents to which he had subscribed. Once again, there was the sense, now shared by five Justices, that government regulation had gone too far; that an apparent expression of majoritarian choice had transgressed the most basic of principles—individual liberty of contract. Once again, Justice Harlan disagreed, but now in dissent, and treated the conflict as a question of judicial deference to legitimate legislative action. The Harlan and Peckham opinions, however, did agree that the question before them called for a rule of reason—a balancing of New York's police power and Joseph Lochner's freedom of contract, a libertarian vision of individual rights and government power in opposition. The factional disagreement was lodged in the determination of a proper balance. Holmes's celebrated dissent agreed with Harlan in substance but formulated an alternative analysis of legitimate majoritarianism around a critique of Peckham's liberty-based reasoning.

Although Peckham's opinion begins with a categorical statement about the unassailable importance of individual liberty of contract, there is no deductive analysis proceeding from that premise. Instead, Peckham recognizes that the state "has power to prevent the individual from making certain kinds of contracts. . . ." The "right of the individual" and the "right of the state" are then opposed in libertarian equipoise. How does Peckham resolve the confrontation? Where does he locate the line between public and private spheres? That Peckham saw the issue as one of line-drawing was absolutely clear: "It must be conceded that there is a limit to the valid exercise of the police power by the State. There is no dispute concerning this general proposition." Indeed, Harlan agreed, as did Holmes. Peckham chronicled recent Court opinions upholding "proper exercise of the police power"—eight-hour work day legislation for underground miners, compulsory vaccination, even Sunday blue laws—even though each was an interference with freedom of contract.[87] Many others, including *Plessy*, could have been added to the list. Why, then, did Peckham's majority feel compelled to draw a line prohibiting New York's regulation of bakers' hours?

According to Peckham, each of the earlier opinions upholding state police power involved some question of "safety, health, morals and general welfare of the public." Here, there was no such concern, because "to the common understanding the trade of a baker has never been regarded as an unhealthy one." If baking were harmful to their health, then bakers could "assert their rights and care for themselves." For the Court majority, the danger lurking in the legislation's justification as a health measure was that "it might be safely affirmed that almost all occupations more or less affect the health."

Thus, "no trade, no occupation, no mode of earning one's living could escape this all-pervading power." The fear of individual liberty overwhelmed by majoritarian government was palpable: "[T]here would seem to be no length to which legislation of this nature might not go." Thus, a line had to be drawn: "We think the limit of the police power has been reached and passed in this case."[88]

In short, the limits of majoritarianism were seen as the "freedom of master and employé to contract"—"all being men, *sui juris*" (that is, not under any legal disability) and "equal in intelligence and capacity." The legislature's "real object and purpose were simply to regulate the hours of labor between a master and his employés." Peckham's majority was insinuating that the New York legislature and its Court of Appeals had acted in bad faith. The statute was even "found in what is called a labor law of the State." The hours legislation would lead to similar attempts to discriminate in favor of virtually all employees: "[A] printer, a tinsmith, a locksmith, a carpenter, a cabinetmaker, a dry goods clerk, a bank's, a lawyer's or a physician's clerk, or a clerk in almost any kind of business would all come under the power of the legislature."[89]

Peckham's justification for locating the limits of majoritarian government at the moment of industrial relations had two elements. First, there was the uncontroversial proposition that majoritarianism had its limits. This statement was not controversial at least in part because "government rights" and "individual rights" were seen as separate and opposed rather than, for example, mutually constituted and interdependent. Justice Harlan's trio of dissenters agreed that judicial intervention was legitimate "when that which the legislature has done comes within the rule that if a statute purporting to have been enacted to protect the public health, the public morals or the public safety, has no real or substantial relation to those objects, or is, beyond all question, a plain, palpable invasion of rights secured by the fundamental law."[90]

The second element in Peckham's justification for limiting majoritarian control over industrial relations was the controversial assumption of formal equality. In other words, Peckham's majority was unwilling even to consider the possibility that bakers and bakery owners, or employees and masters more generally, met across fictional bargaining tables as anything but equals—*sui juris*—despite widespread recognition of inequality between owners and workers. The inequality stemmed from two sources. First, individual employees often dealt with corporate or otherwise aggregated employers. Second, employees, unpropertied and relatively numerous, needed work for wages in order to subsist. Employers as a class, propertied and relatively scarce, thus had an advantage. Given the historical circumstances, there was little doubt that the employer's common-law designation as "master" comported with material reality. Nonetheless, Peckham would allow no "room for debate and for an honest difference of opinion."[91] In short, Peckham refused to allow the New York legislature, despite widespread concerns and an exhaustive industry study, to transgress his assumption of formal equality.

It was here that disagreement lay. Joined by Justices White and Day, Harlan refused to adopt the majority's assumption of formal equality between bakers and bakery owners. In allowing that the New York legislature could plausibly have believed "that employers and employés in such establishments were not on equal footing," Harlan could treat the statute as a health measure. It was a health measure necessitated by legislative recognition that bakers did not have the economic power to bargain over unhealthy employment conditions. All of this was corroborated by studies showing that working conditions were in fact harmful to bakers' health. For Harlan's faction, the New York legislation fell well within the state's police power, and well within the legitimate scope of majoritarian politics.[92] As in his *Northern Securities* opinion one year earlier, Harlan was concerned more with the consequences of unequal bargaining power than with the threat of overreaching government power.

Finally, there was Holmes's opinion—two paragraphs following an introductory sentence announcing his regret over dissenting. The first paragraph deals with the substantive issue of state police power. Except for his pithy style, Holmes could have joined Harlan's opinion insofar as he agreed that the New York statute fell easily into the existing category of legitimate state police power. Moreover, he concurred that to the extent the legislation raised a question of economic theory, the issue was political and thus properly a legislative decision: "The Fourteenth Amendment," he concluded, "is made for people of fundamentally differing views." It is in the opinion's second paragraph that Holmes parts company with Harlan, both in its jurisprudential conception and in its majoritarian vision. The paragraph begins with the famous general proposition that "[g]eneral propositions do not decide concrete cases." According to Holmes, another maxim better describes judicial method: "The decision will depend on a judgment or intuition more subtle than any articulate major premise." Although these statements have been interpreted as an attack on Peckham's majority opinion, on the value of "liberty of contract" as a general proposition and thus on "legal formalism" more generally, they can also be seen as having another import, in particular because Holmes recognized his own complicity in the deductive style: "But I think that the proposition just stated, if it is accepted, will carry us far toward the end."[93]

As we have seen, Holmes did not oppose all general propositions. He recognized the judicial undesirability of speaking only in the particular. Although he seemed to find unsatisfactory the libertarian calculus of individual rights in opposition to government power, he did not resist all limits on majoritarianism. Indeed, "dominant opinion," in his view, must be limited when "the statute proposed would infringe fundamental principles as they have been understood by the traditions of our people and our law." What, if not liberty of contract, would count for Holmes as a principle fundamental enough to overturn a legislative pronouncement of public policy? Holmes's opinion in *Northern Securities* provides both an example of limited majoritarianism and a fundamental principle. Recall Holmes's statement that if Congress intended to prohibit merger agreements, "I should regard calling such a law a regulation of commerce a mere pretense." Its consequence would be "the universal disintegration of society into single men, each at war with all the rest, or even the prevention of all further combinations for a common end."[94] Thus, it seems, a political principle of liberty to associate—to integrate society through groups—was for Holmes a general proposition important enough to limit a majoritarian edict of economic "competition." Moreover, Holmes's explicit concerns about social strife evoke his admonition in *Lochner* that the Fourteenth Amendment did not enact Spencer's Social Darwinism.

Side by side, the fractious *Northern Securities* and *Lochner* decisions displayed conflicting visions of political economy across the United States Reports. In each case, Harlan's faction saw legislation to distribute economic power as a legitimate political act. In each case, the opposing faction sought to protect individual freedom of contract from what it saw as government impairment. For all concerned, the question was one of line-drawing. Their disagreement was over the line's location, and was derived from sharply different commitments to equality. While the Harlan faction paid attention to the economic circumstances in each case, both Peckham and White proceeded on an assumption of formal equality.[95]

For Holmes, the fundamental principle of liberty gave life not to freedom of contract but rather to a politics of association, to a political economy of combination. Thus, in the merger case, Holmes envisioned a society threatened with anarchy and violence, a dystopian horror of de-civilized society founded in civil war. Holmes did not distinguish between economic and political spheres, between commercial combinations and other sorts of social groups, in part because he subscribed to a classical theory of political economy and perhaps also because he found the Hobbesian specter of unrestrained individualism so alarming. Under such circumstances, not even dominant opinion could legitimately prohibit commercial association and thereby tear the very fabric of society.

It is in these two cases, *Northern Securities* and *Lochner*, that we can see most clearly the jurisprudential conflicts sparked by social and economic conditions in the decade following the turn of the century. Intertwined visions of political economy, as well as conflicting renditions of both "liberty" and "equality," were played out in rhetorical confrontations between Supreme Court factions espousing free competition (or, to their opposition, social conflict) and freedom of contract (or, to their opposition, anti-majoritarianism). Although the Court would again split from time to time, the next ten years would produce another accommodation, in both substantive due-process and in antitrust cases.

In 1908, for example, the Court issued four decisions corroborating the established political economy of class, gender, and race. These opinions paint a clear picture of accommodation between factions in the Court's supervision of legislative action, except regarding the *Northern Securities* problem of corporate size, which would not be resolved until *Standard Oil* (1911).[96]

The Court in *Adair* (1908) struck down a federal labor statute prohibiting anti-union contracts by interstate carriers, the opinion stating that employment relations were local "man toward man" contracts outside congressional authority to regulate interstate commerce. Yet one month earlier, the Court had applied the Sherman Act to enjoin the Danbury Hatters strike, pointing to the "vast combination" of unionists who sought to "paralyze and break down every railroad." Although seemingly inconsistent in their views of congressional power to regulate labor relations, both cases did maintain *Lochner*'s labor regime of free contracting between employers and employees, both seen as individuals. In *Adair*, Justice Harlan declared that Congress could not disturb such "equality of right." Writing for a unanimous Court in the *Danbury Hatters* case (1908), Chief Justice Fuller characterized the illegality of labor strikes in extreme language borrowed from an English common-law conspiracy case: "The very plot is an act in itself."[97] Workers' rights were individual. Neither a congressional majority nor a labor association could change that.

Later that October term, however, a unanimous Court upheld Oregon's police power to regulate the working hours of women. Unlike the fully capacitated men in *Lochner* and *Adair*, protecting women was in the public interest because of "the fact that woman's physical structure and the performance of maternal functions place her at a disadvantage." Citizen Louis Brandeis's 100-page brief in *Muller* (1908) contained almost no legal argument. Rather, it chronicled social science claims, medical reports, and expert opinions about the harmful effects of long working hours on women, opinions that urged the Court to find that women were indeed weaker than men, whose children they must raise. In the cultural framework of an expanding and unsettling women's movement led by the National American Woman Suffrage Association (1890), the National Consumers League (1899), and the Women's Trade Union League (1903), the Court could corroborate an important traditional image—that what was still "essential" about working women was their status as "healthy mothers." In sharp contrast, a voluminous study akin to the famous Brandeis brief failed to convince the *Lochner* Court to allow legislation limiting the hours of male bakers.[98]

Finally, the Court continued to carve a special place out of "laissez-faire constitutionalism" to permit state regulation of race relations. Justice Brewer wrote that the Commonwealth of Kentucky could prohibit Berea College from maintaining a school "for both white persons and negroes." Only Justice Harlan dissented. With Kentucky arguing that its public policy was to "preserve race identity . . . [and] the purity of blood," the Court held that the individual liberty celebrated in *Allgeyer* (1897) and *Lochner* (1905) did not apply to the incorporated college, which had "no natural right to teach at all." The Court upheld racist legislation denying private individuals the liberty of contract to agree among themselves, and with a private college, to enter into voluntary associations. Holmes concurred without opinion. By ignoring the constitutional premise underlying *Santa Clara v. Southern Pacific Railroad* (1886)—that constitutional rights flow through the corporate form to the natural persons who are their principals—the Court preserved the values articulated in *Plessy* (1896). In short, due process scrutiny of state regulation turned on the legislation's substantive values. When it came to unions, women, and race relations, the Court defended traditional social patterns against change, whether by enforcing freedom of contract or by defining exceptions.[99]

Against this background of accommodation, the *Standard Oil* case (1911) again raised the issue that produced four separate opinions in *Northern Securities*—the legality of trusts, indeed, the cultural symbol for all trusts, under the Sherman Anti-Trust Act. How could the Court avoid finding John D. Rockefeller's creation a Frankenstein monster? Indeed, there was reason for doubt: Brewer had already announced his defection to the Rule of Reasonists. Holmes was a fellow traveler. Moreover, *Lochner* and its progeny ordained the sanctity of individual freedom of contract. The Court would resolve the difficult question, with only Harlan dissenting in part, by treating the Standard Oil Trust as a person whose conduct was at issue. Thus, John D. Rockefeller as master with servants at his command was found to have monopolized trade under the Sherman Act by engaging in unreasonable and abnormal conduct. Corporate size was discussed. But it was a view of the trust as an extension of John D. Rockefeller, a belief in individual responsibility, that provided the ethical framework for judging the reasonableness of the Standard Oil Trust. By imagining the trust problem as a question of individual conduct rather than an instance of combination, the Court could reconcile competition policy as articulated in the cartel cases with common-law private property rights and with the constitutionalized liberty of contract propounded in Justice White's *Northern Securities* dissent.

Standard Oil and its companion case, *American Tobacco,* were argued early in 1910. Both cases presented difficulties that prompted the Court to order reargument for January 1911. A few months later, White's lengthy companion opinions for a new Rule of Reasonist majority took up right where he left off in his *Northern Securities* dissent: "The principle that the ownership of property is embraced within the power of Congress to regulate commerce, whenever that body deems that a particular character of ownership . . . may restrain commerce" is "in conflict with the most elementary conceptions of rights of property."[100] White was determined to safeguard an essentialized right of private property.

In his *American Tobacco* opinion, White remained committed to a Rule of Reason whose purpose was "to prevent [the Sherman Act] from destroying all liberty of contract and all substantial right to trade, and thus causing the act to be at war with itself by annihilating the fundamental right of freedom to trade. . . ."[101] White believed that his approach was necessary to forestall the Literalist attack on individual liberty—a citizen's right to buy and sell property. Whether constitutional (Fifth Amendment-taking), natural law (liberty and property), or common law (freedom of contract) in form, White's Rule of Reason stood for the proposition that competition could be destructive and that combinations—private agreements to protect business owners from competition—could be reasonable. In particular, "good" trusts could be lawful monopolies under the Sherman Act.

The Rule of Reason shifted the ongoing conflict between free competition and property rights advocates away from the terms heard in the legislative debates. In place of the earlier property right to a "fair price," White's formulation rested upon an essentialized liberty of contract. This rhetorical shift brought into play an implicit tension in the notion of industrial liberty. In the congressional debates, Senator Sherman's references to industrial liberty were taken to mean markets characterized by rough competitive equality. This republican image of freedom from private market power reappeared in the Literalist jurisprudence of full and free competition. The debates, however, included no reference to the other side of industrial liberty—freedom from governmental intrusion into private agreements. This unspoken libertarian ideology found juristic voice in Justice Field's jurisprudence, White's *Trans-Missouri* dissent, Peckham's opinion for the Court in *Lochner*, and now in Justice White's consensus opinions in the twin trust cases.

White's formulation of "liberty" lifted the language of industrial liberty from the rhetorical moorings established during congressional debates. Under the triumphant banner of Reason, the *Standard Oil* opinion pushed aside the old competition logic of "liberty to pursue any livelihood or vocation" with the new property logic of "freedom to acquire, own, and enjoy property." For the Literalists, the problem in cases such as *Standard Oil, American Tobacco,* and *Northern Securities* was the accumulation of property to consolidate economic power, to short-circuit industrial liberty, and, ultimately, to threaten the economic independence supporting the citizenry's civic virtue. Their Sherman Act solution entailed the regulation, the limitation, of property rights when a transaction restrained "full and free competition." For the Rule of Reasonist faction, the problem was a Literalist Sherman Act authorizing government to intrude upon individual rights of liberty and property. Their solution called for private regulation of competition to protect those individual rights. White's concerns about Literalism were clear: "If Congress deemed the acquisition by one or more individuals engaged in interstate commerce of more than a certain amount of property would be prejudicial to interstate commerce, the amount of property held or the amount which could be employed in interstate commerce could be regulated."[102] If Congress could regulate an individual's right to exchange or use property, not only would liberty of contract be destroyed but the entire institution of private property ownership would fall under the dominion of public policy. Then, Congress could limit the accumulation of property—that is, economic power—in the name of free competition.

To protect the institution of private property, Chief Justice White returned to the common law: Monopolies were not illegal because of their size and power; they "were unlawful because of their restriction upon individual freedom of contract." White stressed that the common-law standard was individual conduct: "Freedom of contract was the essence of freedom from undue restraint on the right to contract."[103] Hammering the last nail of liberal ideology into the coffin of republicanist concerns about economic power and corporate size, White insisted that government was the problem, that government could not exert the very restraints that monopolies were enjoined from imposing on individual liberty.

This common-law rhetoric of liberty effected two important changes in antitrust jurisprudence. First, the new majority was willing to allow some trusts, even though they were private agreements that restrained competition. Moreover, such "good" trusts reflected the positive social and economic benefits of individual liberty. Second, it was a particular impulse toward liberty that animated that willingness, a negative liberty turned to stopping government regulation of private market transactions among traders. The Rule of Reason represented a diminished investment in equalizing private market power, a discounted interest in promoting the positive liberty to pursue any vocation or livelihood, as well as a heightened concern for curbing governmental power. Of course, limiting government intrusion can expand the reach of everyone's liberty. Yet inattention to economic power, to gross inequalities of wealth, also conserves the status quo to the benefit of those already in possession of economic power or wealth.

Despite the Rule of Reasonist faction's inattention to equalizing economic power or curbing market domination, the common-law notion of liberty did suggest limits: An individual's exercise of the fundamental right to freedom of trade could sometimes amount to an unreasonable restraint of trade. In finding both the Standard Oil and American Tobacco trusts to be unreasonable restraints of trade and thus illegal under the common-law Sherman Act, Chief Justice White pointed out that individual liberty of contract could be exercised in some "unnatural" way, beyond the making of "normal and usual" contracts. Thus, "unusual and wrongful" *acts*, such as predatory pricing followed by the purchase of faltering rivals, or forming cartels (as in *Addyston Pipe*), properly called for sovereign intervention.[104] In the companion trust cases, evidence of predatory pricing and other kinds of "fierce competition" provided *behavioral* ground for the new majority's finding of unreasonable restraints of trade. John D. Rockefeller and James B. Duke had *acted* in ways that overstepped the bounds of common-law reason. The lower court decrees breaking up the Standard Oil and American Tobacco trusts would stand.

Thus, an ethical judgment about conduct provided the standard for determining whether a restraint of trade was reasonable, as it had under the common law. The common-law jurisprudence subtending the Rule of Reason allowed the Court to distinguish between cartels and trusts: A cartel always involved unreasonable conduct because it was viewed as a combination in restraint of trade. A trust was seen as unreasonable when it engaged in conduct seen as unfair competition. The logic driving the distinction between cartels and trusts becomes even more evident from a third perspective. That perspective is provided by a decision involving resale price maintenance—the common practice of a manufacturer's requiring retailers to charge a predetermined price for its goods. The Court's opinion in *Dr. Miles* (1910) sheds light on the distinction drawn between cartels and trusts because it deals with the antitrust significance of agency law. Somewhere between the corporate entity and the cartelian aggregate stood Dr. Miles and his independent retailers, his agents.

On the very day that lawyers for the American Tobacco Trust concluded their reargument, the Court heard attorneys for the Dr. Miles Medical Company and opposing counsel for John D. Park & Sons Company, a discounting retailer, complete their arguments in a private dispute over the power to set retail prices for Dr. Miles patent medicines. The *Dr. Miles* opinion for the Court, written by recently appointed Justice Charles Evans Hughes, is an overstuffed cookbook of common-law recipes to mediate tensions between competition and property rhetorics.[105] The published argument of counsel, Justice Hughes's opinion for the Court, and Justice Holmes's lone dissent all address at great length a series of issues concerning the extent of Dr. Miles Medical Company's property rights in the patent medicine and thus its power over those who distributed and sold its wares. Only after Hughes determined that Dr. Miles retained no common-law property rights in the product, and that John D. Park & Sons held such rights, did competition rhetoric enter the majority opinion. Holmes dissented because he believed that Dr. Miles held both property and liberty rights that empowered it to fix the resale prices of its patent medicine.

It is not surprising that the Court found Dr. Miles's attempt to set Park & Sons' resale price a violation of the Sherman Act. The same Court would shortly find the oil and tobacco trusts to be unreasonable restraints of trade. What is surprising is that the Court's property logic led it to hold that *every* agreement between manufacturers and retailers to fix a price is illegal. Why did the new Rule of Reasonist majority adopt a "Literalist" ban on resale price-fixing agreements?

Hughes's approach turned on the common-law property logics of ownership and free alienation. Counsel for Dr. Miles contended that the agreements were consignment and agency contracts, and thus that the goods were held "for sale for the account of [Dr. Miles], the title thereto and property therein to be and remain in" Dr. Miles. In short, they argued that a manufacturer has the right to fix the prices at which *its agents* sell *its property*. No one disputed that claim. Indeed, attorneys for discounter John D. Park & Sons responded that it had acquired the goods in simple sale transactions and that, accordingly, Dr. Miles retained no property interest. Hence, Dr. Miles was seeking to set the price of someone else's property. And the cartel cases had already established that practice as a violation of the Sherman Act.[106]

After considering a series of property arguments advanced by Dr. Miles, the Court found a loophole in the agency/consignment agreement that allowed distributors to sell the patent medicine free and clear. Thus, John D. Park & Sons could have acquired the goods by simple purchase from a distributor and thereby the unfettered right to set the price. Only then did competition policy come into play: Justice Hughes wrote that Dr. Miles "seeks to control not merely the prices at which its agents may sell its products, but the prices for all sales by all dealers . . . and thus to fix the amount which the consumer shall pay, eliminating all competition." In sum, eliminating competition meant fixing the price of *someone else's* property. The tension between competition and property rights rhetorics was mediated by the ancient common-law doctrine of title: A property owner always has the right to restrain competition by fixing a price for its goods. No one else does.[107]

The Court expressed no interest in the liberty of "small dealers and worthy men" who sold the patent medicine on consignment. Nor was there discussion of free competition among retailers. As it had been in the cartel cases, the Court was unwilling to consider the pure liberty of contract claim by Dr. Miles that an agreement to fix prices should be enforced against all retailers and distributors simply because it was a bargain contract between two willing parties. Justice Hughes concluded that "to sustain the restraint, it must be found to be reasonable" and that, at common law, bargain contracts to fix prices were always unreasonable.[108]

Following his practice in cartel and union strike cases since *Addyston Pipe*, Chief Justice White and the other Rule of Reasonists signed on to the Court's Literalist holding that price-fixing is illegal per se. Why? There was the precedent of cartel cases. In more recent times, we have tended to think of competition only as a horizontal phenomenon and hence we separate commercial conduct into horizontal and vertical dimensions. Classical economics, however, made no such distinction. Competition was understood as entailing rivalry not only between two patent medicine makers (horizontal) but also between a manufacturer and its retailers (vertical). In consequence, no one on the Court blinked at citing the cartel cases as precedent. Holmes, the lone dissenter who agreed on little else, concurred that competition was two dimensional.

The cartel cases influenced the Rule of Reasonist majority's willingness to adopt Literalist doctrine in a second respect, at a level not entirely reflected in the legal doctrine. There was the extended notion of individualism or personhood that, for example, allowed the Court to imbue the Standard Oil Trust with the personhood of John D. Rockefeller yet treat Addyston Pipe Company as a cartelian aggregate. If Dr. Miles had retained title to the goods—if all of its wholesalers and retailers had sold on consignment—then the case would have come out differently. In short, Dr. Miles would have been treated as principal to his agents, master to his servants. That unquestioned proposition has something to say about the political economy producing the legal distinction between cartels and trusts, between "loose" and "tight" combinations—a distinction that persists today. At the very least, everyone on the Court shared a commitment to individual liberty, to the constitutional protection of a "person's" life, liberty, and property. The difficulty came in deciding the scope of protection—that is, the measure of a "person." Certainly, individual human beings were persons. But what of groups? When could they stand independent of their members, as entities in their own right?

The intellectual enterprise of investing groups with personhood was already under way, both in the United States and in Europe. For example, some writers were conceiving of corporations and other social combinations as "organic groups" and thus as natural entities in their own right. The Supreme Court, too, was treating corporations as "persons," at least in some respects. In 1886, the Court's one-paragraph *per curiam* opinion in *Santa Clara* simply stated that corporations are persons for purposes of the Fourteenth Amendment. That is, constitutional rights flowed through corporations to their owners. Moreover, a decision issued in 1905, in the same session as *Lochner*, granted Fourth Amendment protection to corporations, again suggesting that corporations were seen as constitutional "persons," at least for certain purposes. Yet the Court made an explicit distinction between individuals and corporations in both *Northern Securities* (1904) and *Berea College* (1908), reserving individual liberty of contract to natural persons. In 1910, a series of opinions limiting state regulation of foreign corporations suggests that the Court began to think of corporations more broadly as "persons."[109] Finally, there was the ancient law merchant's well-settled category of consignment, taken up in *Dr. Miles* (1910). The Court had no difficulty treating independent retailers who took products on consignment as Dr. Miles Medical Company agents—that is, as part of the manufacturer's corporate body.

Corporate personality was well established in the cultural context of the times. Trusts and other large business enterprises were not the faceless conglomerates we perceive them to be today. Rather, they were associated with names, faces, and industries. There was no USX Corporation. Nor was there simply a U.S. Steel Corporation. There was Andrew Carnegie's steel company, Lawrence Laughlen's steel company, John D. Rockefeller's Standard Oil Company, Edward H. Harriman's Southern Pacific Railroad. It was the era that canonized captains of industry, or, as Thorstein Veblen called them, captains of business. "Tight" combinations resulted in huge enterprises—with human faces and notorious names. They were the "robber barons"—the industrial era's form of medieval lords, engaging in industrial warfare among themselves and together, against armies of unskilled laborers. It was easy to think of large corporate organizations as "persons"[110]

The social image of corporations as individuals took hold in the popular culture of the times. One of the best known symbols was the cartoon depiction of Standard Oil as a menacing octopus with John D. Rockefeller's caricatured face. Even the general category of "trust" or "monopoly" was often pictured as an oversized, obese man, in top hat and tails, overseeing the Senate or transported pasha style by gaunt servants. And the personified corporation was not limited to popular culture. Among elites as well, bureaucratic institutions were imagined in human terms. For example, in an article criticizing the *Northern Securities* decision, a member of the Columbia Law School faculty wrote in his institution's law journal that a corporation can "be regarded as a combination of the persons composing it [just as] a man, although usually regarded as a unit, may be considered as a combination of his limbs and other parts of his anatomy." Harvard economist Jeremiah W. Jenks called

Rockefeller, Duke, Henry Ford, and their peers "Napoleons," and one of J. P. Morgan's rivals considered him the financier-"king."[111]

Cartels, in contrast, were too fragmented, unstable, and untrustworthy to personify. Members retained their identities, their names, their individual interests. To serve their individual interests, they would cheat by secretly lowering prices. They would simply go off on their own. Cartels were seen as temporary associations, not persons. The distinction between (temporary) cartels and (permanent) mergers made good sense, particularly because corporate breakups, the modern aftermath of mergers, were unknown in the Progressive Era. Like divorce, corporate breakups fell outside the Victorian sensibility of propriety and stability. Moreover, just as individuals wielded power over their property, principals directed their agents and masters controlled their servants. Corporations were simply extensions of individual sovereignty, of private property. In short, the ideology of individualism cleared a cultural space for the juristic personification of the corporation, brought to life in the visages of ruthless railroad barons, pirating industrialists, calculating financiers, and even patent medicine makers.

Although the distinction that arose between corporations and associations, between mergers and cartels, was not somehow required by the ideology of individualism, these distinctions were easily produced in those terms. For those who believed in the inevitability of large-scale production or saw the financial possibilities of the corporate form, the ideology of individualism seemed natural, inspiring, or, at the very least, convenient.

Thus, antitrust's formative era would close with a truce in the factional conflict, a settlement negotiated between the public imperative of competition policy and the private demands of property rights: Reasonable restraints of trade—"good" trusts—did not violate the Sherman Act, no matter how large or how powerful they were. But Standard Oil and American Tobacco, as evidenced by the "unusual and wrongful" corporate behavior of John D. Rockefeller and James B. Duke, were bad actors, and hence they unreasonably restrained trade. Like any person, Rockefeller's Standard Oil was constrained to act reasonably in the exercise of his property rights, his freedom of contract.

In sharp contrast to the Rule of Reason standard applied to individual conduct, the Court would have no truck with combinations or conspiracies to constrain individual liberty. Dr. Miles sought to restrain the property rights of an independent commercial actor—John D. Park & Sons. Like the railroad cartel agreements and the labor union conspiracies to strike, Dr. Miles's attempt to fix prices was seen as unjustifiable, as unreasonable per se: The individual freedom to sell one's own property demanded, at the very least, the power to set the price. That power could not be bought and sold.

In two overlapping cycles, the Supreme Court's Literalist faction, with its commitment to a commercial egalitarianism expressed in the rhetorics of industrial liberty and free competition, reached accommodations with the Rule of Reasonist faction, with its rhetoric of freedom of contract, its commitment to limited government in the form of expansive judicial oversight of legislative action. These accommodations, in an era symbolized by great private accumulations of wealth and power, were achieved in part by an underlying agreement about the social and economic issue of equality. The Court factions agreed to a formal conception of equality—that is, an assumption of equality as a matter of law. Whether John D. Rockefeller or an immigrant baker working for Joseph Lochner, contracting parties were treated as equals. Not only were they equally threatened and thus equally deserving of protection from oppressive majorities, but they were equally positioned across a bargaining table from one another. Hence, the bargains struck were given the utmost respect. This abstract idea of equality was seldom unlocked to open discussion. Justice Mahlon Pitney's opinion for the majority sextet in *Coppage v. Kansas* (1915) would provide a rare moment of candor:

> No doubt, wherever the right of private property exists, there must and will be inequalities of fortune; and thus it naturally happens that parties negotiating about a contract are not equally unhampered by circumstances. This applies to all contracts. . . . And, since it is self-evident that, unless all things are held in common, some persons must have more property than others, it is from the nature of things impossible to uphold freedom of contract and the right of private property without at the same time recognizing as legitimate those inequalities of fortune that are the necessary results of the exercise of those rights.[112]

In short, the Court assumed equality because, according to Pitney, to do otherwise would undermine the regime of property and contract rights. What made this seem inevitable to the Court was its view that these inequalities were the products of fortune, the natural consequences of a property/contract regime. The choice, moreover, seemed to be categorical: Either uphold private property/contract or replace it with public/socialized ownership. No middle ground or third alternative appeared possible. In this context, it is easy to understand Peckham's concern in *Lochner* about a slippery slope to legislative regulation of all employment contracts, or the Hobbesian images of civil war painted by White and Holmes.

Thus did the Court's attention fix on majoritarian curtailment of individual liberty, understood as the public abrogation of private property rights. Lawyer, scholar, cabinet officer, United States Senator, and Nobel Peace Prize recipient Elihu Root saw the judiciary as a body in government but not of it. Expressing the view of many elite lawyers, scholars, and policy makers, he applauded judicial supervision of "government" action—of legislatures. Judicial remedies, he believed, are "the sole protection of the individual citizen against the arbitrary exercise of the tremendous powers with which the agents of government are invested." Of those "tremendous powers," perhaps the most threatening was distribution of wealth. Justice David Brewer expressed his concerns without hesitation. In an article discussing the police power of the state, he warned of the "mere force of numbers," the majoritarian impulse, whose effect was the "spoliation and destruction of private property." Not only in his *Northern Securities* (1904) concurrence but also in his early *Budd* (1892) dissent, Brewer argued against government regulation as an affront to the right of property, a right with which "men are endowed by their Creator."[113]

The *Standard Oil* (1911) opinion's Rule of Reason can be understood as closing *Lochner*'s circle of individual liberty, its vision of a private sphere defined in opposition to a public, majoritarian domain. The ideology of individualism working in Supreme Court jurisprudence and in the writings of the era's elite class no longer projected an image of Jeffersonian yeomanry, of "small dealers and worthy men" threatened by the new economic order. In place of a largely republicanist conception founded in the importance of rough economic equality, a recast ideology took normative content from a liberal conception of individuals as threatened by oppressive and corrupt political majorities. Accordingly, it was not private property rights but rather the "public interest" that required restraint.

In the two decades following the Court's adoption of an antitrust Rule of Reason, the rising tide of trade associationalism, the continuing activity of labor unions, and increasing government regulation (both state and federal), as well as the national experience of mobilizing production for World War I, would challenge the liberal formulation of individualism. These circumstances would call into question the supposition that antagonism naturally defines relationships between individual and democratic majority, between commercial rivals, and between worker and owner.[114] And, once again, competition and property rhetorics, inspired by commitments to liberty and equality, would shape the policy arguments posed to resolve such questions.

2

The Era of Cooperative Competition, 1911–1933: Trade and Labor Associations, Political Majorities, and Speech Rights

The two decades between 1911 and 1933 were a time of accelerating, sometimes cataclysmic, change in the economic, political, and cultural currents of everyday life in America. The First World War produced the most evident upheaval, not only in the physical and economic ravages of war but also in its political aftermath. In the United States, the Great War stands as the great divide between an earlier era of progressive politics and a decade of conservative Republican administrations. If the 1930s are recalled as the decade of the Great Depression, the twenty years preceding it should be remembered, much as we view the 1960s, as an era of turmoil—of tyrannies, resistances, and excesses. Not only World War I and its international aftermath, but also the first women's movement in America, urban race riots and a revival of the Ku Klux Klan, labor uprisings, repression of dissident speech, the burlesque of Prohibition, and an anti-immigrant nativism betray any effort to portray those years in harmonious terms.

In this context, the Supreme Court's "Rule of Reason," whether applied to antitrust, labor, or constitutional law, seems to have been at best hortatory, calling for a rational resolution of conflict, and at worst reactionary, wielding the iron hand of reason to maintain the status quo. Much the same can be said of the era's "cooperative competition," particularly Herbert Hoover's nationwide trade association movement. In its most favorable light, it too emerges as a hopeful vision, a peaceful and productive oasis amid a desert storm of threatening and sometimes violent struggle. In its harshest light, it appears as just another kind of factional alliance, a cartelization movement to exploit customers, suppliers, and employees.

The two decades between 1911 and 1933 can be understood as a series of efforts to make a place for cooperative associations, for the collective actions of economic and political groups, in a classical political economy and ideology founded in individualism. Classical theory and ideology were called upon to accommodate new social and economic practices. The Supreme Court in *Standard Oil* (1911) announced the antitrust Rule of Reason, which resolved the lingering question of how to treat commercial collectives organized as formal entities, as corporations or trusts: Economic power was to be tolerated unless abused. This doctrine's constitutional analogue was well settled. Fifteen years before *Lochner* (1905), the Court had already declared that political majorities could not, as a general matter, impose their will on "individuals." The political economic theory supporting the Court's limitation of majoritarian imperatives, its "economic due process" jurisprudence, was founded on the fundamental postulate that conflict defined the relationship between public interests and private rights. Inscribed in this liberal ideology, Justice Peckham's opinion for the Court in *Lochner* applied a Rule of Reason to locate the constitutional limits of state police power and, with it, a Maginot Line between public interests and individual rights.[1]

Although this conception of strictly separate public and private spheres was not identified exclusively with political and economic domains, the Court's governing jurisprudence was liberty of contract and, in consequence, the predominant images of public and private that emerged were political and economic ones. It was only a matter of time before the Court would apply the Rule of Reason not only to political but also to private associations, and use it not only to judge the constitutionality of state legislation impinging upon individual liberty but also to determine the antitrust implications of private contracts in restraint of trade. Thus did *Standard Oil* follow the path marked by *Lochner*. A difficulty, however, lay in the normative ground beneath this libertarian framework of reasonableness—the private property rights argument underlying freedom of contract. Applying property rights arguments to political majorities would naturally tend to limit their power. The same logic applied to private agreements, however, would tend toward toleration and, even more, toward solicitude.

Published in the midst of William Howard Taft's single-term presidency, the *Standard Oil* decision (1911), along with its companion case, *American Tobacco*, known as the Rule of Reason opinions, mobilized progressive legislative action in both Congress and the states. The decisions were taken as reflective of Taft's seeming turn away from the progressive politics of his predecessor and mentor, Teddy Roosevelt. In fact, the Court's political economic vision was close to Roosevelt's corporatist approach, embodied since 1903 in the Bureau of Corporations. The Bureau implemented Roosevelt's regulatory attitude toward large-scale enterprise. That is, "bad" trusts were hectored into limiting their conduct to fair methods of competition. Size did not condemn economic enterprise but was seen instead as an opportunity for informal regulation in the public interest.[2]

Roosevelt nonetheless expressed his deep disappointment in the Taft administration's perceived turn to conservatism by challenging Taft for the Republican nomination and, upon failing, by quickly organizing the Bull Moose Party. In the presidential election of 1912, Democrat Woodrow Wilson would win, with Taft finishing behind Roosevelt. Together, Wilson and Roosevelt would poll three votes to every one for Taft. Socialist Party candidate Eugene V. Debs would receive almost a million votes—about 7 percent of the total cast in the election. Both Wilson and Roosevelt campaigned on progressive platforms: Wilson's "New Freedom" called for a strong antimonopoly policy and a return to small-scale business. Roosevelt's "New Nationalism" outlined a forceful regulatory approach to the new economic order of large-scale enterprise—in essence, a revival of his progressive corporatism.

In this political context, the Rule of Reason decisions were seen as a continuation of the Court's conservative regime, driven by an "economic theory" that Justice Holmes earlier recognized in *Lochner* as out of step with majoritarian sentiments. The antitrust Rule of Reason galvanized public opinion of the Supreme Court as pro–big business despite the fact that the twin 1911 decisions had in fact affirmed the breakup of the Rockefeller and Duke trusts. Why the public outrage seen in the passage by twenty states of new antitrust provisions? Why the immediate turn by Congress to what would be the Federal Trade Commission and Clayton Acts of 1914?

Although most Supreme Court opinions do not attain cultural significance, a few become public currency. Like *Brown v. Board* (1954) and *Roe v. Wade* (1972), *Standard Oil* decided a conflict not only wrapped in ideological controversy but also rife with material consequences. Just as the two more recent opinions confronted questions of the government's role in race and gender relations, *Standard Oil* can be understood as deciding fundamental questions of political economy, if not economic class relations. The *public*'s identification with Justice Peckham's earlier antitrust image of "small dealers and worthy men" at the mercy of the powerful trusts and the symbolic power of "the Standard" to provoke fears of individual helplessness and political corruption provide a context for understanding how the Rule of Reason quickly became the pro-trust idiom that stirred public sentiment and legislative reaction, the apparently severe consequence of corporate dissolution notwithstanding.[3]

Although it is unlikely that the lawyerly niceties of the jurisprudential shift were widely appreciated, it was easy for the public to understand the difference between prohibiting every trust—every large and powerful organization of private wealth—and prohibiting only "unreasonable" ones: Most trusts would pass antitrust scrutiny because size and economic power were not in themselves deemed offensive to the Sherman Act. Consumers, grangers, small businessmen, union members, muckrakers, politicians, financiers, and industrialists could all figure out, in their own terms, who would benefit and who would lose under a regime of reasonable trusts and other powerful economic organizations. Any lingering doubts on that account were dissolved in two subsequent opinions finding the immense shoe machinery and steel trusts "reasonable restraints of trade." Although both the United Shoe Company (1918) and the United States Steel Corporation (1920) controlled at least 80 percent of their industries, although they dealt sharply with competitors, customers, and employees, the Court found that neither one "at any time abuse[d] the power or ascendancy it possessed." Antitrust, the Court maintained, would not concern itself with economic power per se, with dominant firms, even in the face of evidence of sharp dealings.[4]

The Rule of Reason decisions (1911) advanced a larger ideological commitment to political liberalism more commonly associated with *Lochner*'s constitutional doctrine of economic due process: a shift away from concerns about economic inequality among the republic's citizenry and toward a view that individuals were defined by their freedom from majoritarian sentiments. Still, this notion of individual liberty did hold the silent echo of republicanism, the concern about private collectives of economic power. Since the 1890s, the Court had enjoined both cartels and unions from imposing their collective wills on individuals, from oppressing their customers and employers. But so long as a group was characterized as agents of a private principal, as extensions of a John D. Rockefeller or James B. Duke, the group was treated as a person rather than a cartel or union. Even into the 1930s, this juridical concept of individualism, personified by the anachronistic cultural image of corporations steered by captains of industry, shaped the logic for separating trusts and cartels into discrete categories, although both were collectives.[5]

But the cultural image was dissolving. The reality of large-scale organization was showing through the ideology. Most persistently in the several states, progressive legislation had long sought to impose limits on economic associations—whether cartels, unions, or trusts. Seen in this setting, the Court's harsh treatment of cartels and unions appeared to call for recognition of the associational character of all large economic organizations and hence equally stern treatment of not only cartels and unions, but also of corporations and trusts. Or perhaps all large economic organizations should be equally treated as entities. In either event, there seemed to be pressure for equal treatment of all large economic organizations. As well, the ascendancy of neoclassical economics reflected a shift in perceptual framework among a growing number of economists and policy makers, a shift from the classical model of competition as derived from individual freedom of contract to a depersonalized, systemic paradigm of markets understood in abstract, functional terms, a shift from imagining Standard Oil as an extension of John D. Rockefeller and toward seeing it as a large economic organization.

Within this cultural context, a new form of economic organization began to take shape. It was the trade association. After the national experience of mobilization for World War I, the trade association movement swelled into a tidal wave that swept the country. While elite lawyers, commercial promoters, and influential federal officials extolled the virtues of "cooperative competition," most policy makers could not imagine the conjunction of cooperation and competition. By the mid-1920s, however, even the Supreme Court would approve of cooperative competition (also called "open competition" and the "new competition") by judging trade association activities, including conduct amounting to price-fixing, under a Rule of Reason previously reserved for unitary corporate entities. All large commercial organizations would be judged, as a general matter, under the same legal standard. The years between the World War I armistice and the stock market crash of 1929 would come to be seen as the heyday of Herbert Hoover's trade associationalism. The new solicitude for collective action, however, was reserved for trade associations. Labor associations were not judged according to the tenets of cooperative competition. Rather, labor union activities still provoked strict judicial scrutiny, as did legislative efforts to legitimize them. The *Lochner* logic limiting collective power continued to embrace both political and labor associations.

This chapter investigates the political economy of associations—trade, labor, and majoritarian—that took hold between 1911 and 1933. How did the trade association movement win freedoms denied to labor unions and power denied political majorities? Why were only trade associations permitted to pursue higher prices and dominate economic markets? Although there is no simple answer to these questions, there is a clear rhetorical framework that emerged in the writings of policy makers and in Supreme Court jurisprudence. To investigate this rhetorical framework, we need to consider the four quadrants of the era's political economy: the indulgent attitude toward trade associations, the harsh treatment of labor associations, the Court's consolidation of laissez-faire constitutionalism, and, finally, the Court's First Amendment speech jurisprudence, which developed a distinctive character during this period. The Court's quick adoption of Holmes's political rhetoric of "clear and present danger," along with its refusal to adopt his economic metaphor of "free trade in ideas," illuminates the libertarian framework for competition policy and, more broadly, for political economy in the years between 1911 and 1933.

The Political Economy of Political Majorities

This section opens with an account of the public reactions and legislative initiatives provoked by the 1911 Rule of Reason opinions, initiatives including Congress's 1914 antitrust statutes: the Federal Trade Commission and Clayton Acts. Thereafter, I investigate the Supreme Court's explicit reassertion of judicial dominance over majoritarian politics, first over federal antitrust policy and then over state price regulation. Between these inquiries into the Court's consolidation of laissez-faire constitutionalism, I pause at the *International News Service* (1918) decision. The decision's significance lies in its redefinition of property as any "pecuniary right" and, in consequence, the implicit expansion of the private or economic domain. In sum, the *Lochner* regime was wielding liberty of contract as a jurisprudential scythe to cut down both federal and state impositions of political will upon commercial transactions.

Public Reactions and Legislative Initiatives Provoked by the Rule of Reason

In the 1911 Rule of Reason cases, the Court upheld the antitrust equivalent of capital punishment. Given such harsh consequences, the Rule of Reason should have had an immediate deterrent effect on trust building. Yet, no one took these cases to represent a threat to corporate mergers, particularly not those in the business community who were intent on combining with competitors. Indeed, in Senate debate preceding passage of the Clayton Act, Senator William Thompson (D.Kan.) would read into the *Congressional Record* a list of 445 active trusts. Moreover, despite the fact that the 1911 opinions used the Rule of Reason to break up the great oil and tobacco trusts, the Court was widely perceived as pro–big business because it established a category of "good" trusts. Many believed that such a category was a contradiction in terms.

The practical effects of the *Standard Oil* decision were distressing. Senator Reed (D.Mo.) reported during the Clayton Act debates that the so-called rivals created in the oil industry produced even more wealth for their shareholders in fragmented form than they did as the Standard Oil Company of New Jersey. Indeed, Standard's offspring enjoyed unregulated regional dominance in most sections of the country. Moreover, both the oil and tobacco trusts' offspring were still engaging in predatory pricing and other forms of unfair competition against independents. Thus, in material terms, the dissolution was actually consistent with Justice White's dissenting opinion in *Northern Securities* (1904), which argued against federal regulation of an individual's purchases of property, regardless of the effects on competition. Here, property ownership—in the form of holding shares of "the Standard"—was not disturbed. The shareholders of the old Standard now held all shares of the new Standard miniatures, all of them still managed by the old Standard's executives.[6] Thus, despite the dissolutions, there was no effective change in market power or economic substance. The decrees imposed changes in form but did not distribute wealth or market power from miniatures to their trading partners or rivals. Given the continued predatory practices of the miniatures, the Rule of Reason had fostered absolutely no practical improvements in the quantity or quality of competition. In practical effect, the *status quo ante* survived intact.

However, reactions were not uniform. In the Taft Administration, for example, policy makers directing the influential Bureau of Corporations simply celebrated a doctrinal change they had advocated so fervently for years, even before the agency's creation during the preceding Roosevelt Administration. It was well known that the Roosevelt administration, through the Bureau of Corporations, had initiated the practice of granting antitrust immunity to "good" trusts and other large corporations. Nonetheless, outside the Bureau and its corporate constituency, the *Standard Oil* opinion evoked outrage, not only in the muckraking press but also in the federal and state legislatures. Within a few weeks of the opinion's publication, progressives in Congress, together with citizen Louis Brandeis and others fearful of "reasonable" trusts, held first private meetings and then public hearings.[7]

Opposition to both Court doctrine and a corporatist executive provoked legislative action at both the state and federal levels. Between 1911 and 1913, twenty states quickly passed new antitrust provisions—some of them statutes and others constitutional amendments. Then, early in Woodrow Wilson's first term, Congress passed the Clayton and Federal Trade Commission Acts.

No one doubts that the 1914 antitrust legislation was passed in reaction to the judicial Rule of Reason. As Senator Reed (D.Mo.) recounted in the congressional debates, "All will remember when the Supreme Court wrote the word "reasonable" into the Sherman Act. When that decision was announced it was recognized as being of a revolutionary character. It struck the country as being a deadly blow to trust litigation." Citizen Louis Brandeis testified before the House Committee on the Judiciary that, within days of the *Standard Oil* decision, Senator Robert La Follette (R.Wis.) had called a meeting of a dozen or so people to discuss the need for new trust legislation. In testimony before the Senate Committee on Interstate Commerce, Brandeis warned of the "extraordinary perils to our institutions which attend the trusts." His concerns went beyond the economic issues associated with competition and combination: Whether a powerful corporation "has exceeded the point of greatest economic efficiency or not, it may be too large to be tolerated among people who desire to be free." Within ninety days, La Follette introduced a bill to toughen the Sherman Act. Similar legislation was introduced in the House chamber. In describing his understanding of the House bill, Representative Carlin (D.Va.) declared that "We are engaged in an effort to bring about competition; that is the economics of this bill."[8]

It is evident that the Rule of Reason provoked a political response founded in the tenets of competition. What has not been clear before, however, is the significance of the two statutes' explicit language of "competition." Whether prohibiting conduct producing "substantial lessening of competition" under the Clayton Act or "unfair methods of competition" under the Federal Trade Commission Act,[9] this explicit competition rhetoric signaled congressional movement away from the Court's common-law jurisprudence founded in the values of "property" and "freedom of contract." The Clayton Act regulated a set of well-known practices, while the FTC Act created a new agency to identify and enjoin unfair commercial conduct. Both statutes sought to expand the enforcement powers of federal agencies and, in the process, bridle the Court's headlong rush into laissez-faire.

In institutional terms, the legislation seemed designed to rein in not only the judiciary but also the executive branch: The Clayton Act would control judicial discretion by defining a list of specific antitrust violations, including price discrimination and anti-competitive mergers. The second statute would replace the corporatist Bureau of Corporations with an independent Federal Trade Commission, envisioned as a true interstate commerce commission, empowered to define and regulate unfair competition—that is, the abuse of economic power.

But it would be wrong to conclude that the 1914 statutes simply reintroduced Senator Sherman's and the Literalists' commitments to "full and free competition." Rather, the visage of competition was changing. The Rule of Reason regime and its constellation of assumptions and beliefs about the proper legal standards for commerce were illuminating a new vision of competition, different not only from the Literalist image of independent entrepreneurs but also from the buccaneering, cutthroat practices of John D.

Rockefeller, Edward Henry Harriman, and their contemporaries. The 1914 statutes would take meaning from the new notions of "enlightened competition" or "open competition," which embodied a belief that some cooperation among rivals would produce a better kind of competition.

Further, the Rule of Reason Court of the years between 1910 and 1930, under Chief Justices Edward D. White and William H. Taft, did not hesitate for a moment to distinguish between public and private restraints of trade. That distinction rested upon a libertarian conception of segregated private and public spheres, as well as an expanding notion of private property that defined the margin between them. The result was a bifurcated treatment of commercial regulation, treatment founded in the view that free competition meant freedom from government administration, but not freedom from concerted private administration of markets.

Judicial Consolidation of Laissez-faire Constitutionalism: Federal Antitrust Policy

Both Congress and the states passed economic legislation in response to the Rule of Reason. The Supreme Court judged legislative initiatives, whether the Federal Trade Commission Act or the Pennsylvania Public Service Commission Act, by their effects on the common-law freedom of contract underwriting both *Standard Oil* (1911) and its constitutional forebear, Justice Peckham's *Lochner* opinion (1905). Assuming the mantle of common-law liberty, the Supreme Court under Chief Justices White and Taft was unrelenting in its protection of commercial activity from legislative "intervention."

Two antitrust decisions published in 1920 exemplify the Supreme Court majority's antipathy toward congressional oversight of commercial markets. The common thread was the Court's institutional self-image, its role as the final arbiter of political economy. The Court's antipathy, it should be recalled, hinged on the belief that the legislative and executive branches were political institutions, but that, in contrast, the judiciary was the nonpartisan protector of preexisting and self-evident rights, especially the constitutional right of liberty of contract. That view was contested in powerful dissenting opinions by Brandeis and Holmes. Holmes's less-than-progressive values, however, sometimes led him to join the conservative majority despite his professed distaste for a laissez-faire constitutionalism evocative of Herbert Spencer's Social Darwinism.[10]

In his confidently Progressive first term, President Woodrow Wilson set in motion the Democrats' "New Freedom" platform by filing suit against the huge United States Steel Corporation. The Department of Justice charged that the corporation's very size, achieved through a long series of mergers, allowed it to terrorize and often eliminate its competitors. The Attorney General asserted that U.S. Steel's economic mass and financial connections fueled fears of price wars, allowing it to coerce rivals to standardize prices and costs, including labor wages. Moreover, the government pointed to the trust's history of episodic industry control. In the background was U.S. Steel's recent battle with labor, its brutal suppression of employees' demands for unionization and, in particular, for improved working conditions, wages, and hours.

Writing for a divided Court in the last year of Wilson's difficult second term, Justice Joseph McKenna declared in *U.S. Steel* (1920) that the corporation violated neither section of the Sherman Act. The four-judge majority included Justice Holmes. Despite his proclaimed commitment to the Rule of Reason, McKenna read § 2 literally, as requiring complete monopolization. This sort of literalism, it should be pointed out, was consistent with the ascendant paradigm of neoclassical economics. That is, markets were understood categorically as either competitive or monopolistic. Given the model's excluded middle, anything short of complete market control was treated as competitive. Because U.S. Steel controlled only 80 to 90 percent of its major product markets, it had not achieved, in McKenna's estimation, monopoly power. Moreover, McKenna saw U.S. Steel's vertical integration, from coal mining to steel fabrication, as a natural process driven by the advantages of new production and management technologies rather than by any intent to monopolize. Finally, he refused to characterize any of U.S. Steel's tactics as unfair, even its sharp underpricing, purchase, and shutdown of competing mills.[11]

In similar fashion, McKenna found no violation of Sherman Act § 1 because, he believed, the requirement of a "contract, combination, or conspiracy" could not be met by the government's showing informal cooperation with rivals, a process that he viewed instead as helping to stabilize an industry fraught with great financial risks.[12] This attitude toward cooperation echoed the claims of those advocating the "new competition," the view that some collective action, usually in the form of trade associations, made for better competition.

The *U.S. Steel* decision stood for three important propositions. First, McKenna corroborated *Standard Oil* doctrine: Big was not bad. Massive economic size and industry domination did not violate the antitrust laws. The dissenting faction, led by Justice Day, agreed that sheer size, accomplished by merger, was not itself a violation of the Sherman Act. What concerned Day was the massive record of persistent price-fixing conspiracies that the Court portrayed as industry stabilization. Second, the opinion clearly characterized cooperation among industry rivals as good, based on the neoclassical economic tenet that cooperation tended to stabilize competitive markets, flattening their "natural" cycles of over- and under-production. That is, the underlying economics here is market-based, rather than freedom-of-contract based. Third, the Court affirmed its institutional dominance over the executive branch's Department of Justice, its sovereignty in matters of political economy.

Indeed, Justice McReynolds reaffirmed the Court's sovereignty over federal competition policy later that term in *FTC v. Gratz*. Despite dissenting Justice Brandeis's powerful call to recognize a broad congressional mandate for the new Federal Trade Commission, McReynolds, with Holmes again joining the majority, denied the Commission power to identify and enjoin unfair methods of competition outside the limited category of conduct already prohibited under the existing common law. This case is a particularly good example of the Court's institutional self-image as final authority in matters of political economy. It sheds such strong light on the Court's self-defined role because the FTC was seeking under the FTC Act to enjoin conduct—the practice of tie-ins—that was explicitly condemned under the recent Clayton Act, although condoned at common law. The FTC had issued an order forbidding Gratz from selling metal ties for baling cotton on the condition that customers also buy jute bagging. There was little doubt that Congress considered tie-ins an unfair method of competition.[13]

McReynolds based the Court's seizure of policy-making sovereignty on the claim that since Congress did not define "unfair methods of competition," it was a question of law for the courts, not a question of industrial policy for the FTC. Despite the strong dissent by Brandeis finding clear congressional intent expressed in committee reports, as well as earlier Court deference to the Interstate Commerce Commission, McReynolds refused to acknowledge any congressional mandate of agency discretion. He concluded that FTCA § 5 "does not apply to practices never heretofore regarded as opposed to good morals, because characterized by deception, bad faith, fraud, or as against public policy because of their dangerous tendency to unduly hinder competition or create monopoly."[14] Oddly, neither McReynolds nor Brandeis pointed out that the Clayton Act's tie-in provision (§ 3) offered convincing evidence that Congress viewed such conduct as unfair competition. Rather, the case was argued on the issue of sovereignty in the policy domain of political economy. In short, the Court read the statute as granting the FTC the narrow authority to enforce the common law as defined by the judiciary rather than the broad jurisdiction to regulate unfair commercial practices.

In these two cases decided during the 1920 term, the last for Chief Justice White, the Court perpetuated its preeminence in matters of political economy, despite congressional pronouncements to the contrary. Whether the competition policy-making had been delegated to the Federal Trade Commission or to the Department of Justice, the Court would have the last word. Chief Justice Taft's tenure, from 1921 to 1930, was a decade of jurisprudential continuity. Historian Paul L. Murphy has characterized the Taft Court regime as "judicial activism . . . for the recreation of laissez-faire policies." The business community seemed to appreciate the Taft Court's sentiments. The National Association of Manufacturers, for example, praised the Taft Court as the "indispensable interpreter" of the Constitution, as the sacred text's defender against the "babel voices of the mob." Herbert Hoover, both as Commerce Secretary and as President, agreed; he believed devoutly that the "public interest" was best served by commercial activity free from political control. A private, commercial domain free from majoritarian oppression was seen as the necessary ground for all constitutional rights. According to Murphy, such sentiments were carried forward most emphatically in Taft's labor and free speech cases, which demonstrate that Taft wanted to "stem the tide of social democracy" and place "property above personal rights." Again, the Taft Court was following the course set by its predecessor. Indeed, in the term immediately preceding Chief Justice White's retirement, Justice Brandeis wrote an impassioned dissent in a free speech case, *Gilbert v. Minnesota* (1920), admonishing the Court that "liberty" includes more than "liberty to acquire and to enjoy property."[15]

Interlude: International News Service *and Property as Any "Pecuniary Right"*

An understanding of the Court's conception of "private property" is necessary to comprehend the Court's central role in guarding the private sphere from public despotism and, with it, the logic of "economic due process." In a shift that began at least as early as Justice Stephen Field's dissent in the *Granger* cases (1877), the Court was confronted with the view that constitutional protection of property rights should include more than title and possession. By 1886, the Court would adopt a broader notion of property rights, which would protect a property owner's use and enjoyment from government "taking," rights that included a "fair return" on property devoted to the public interest.[16] The culminating decision was *International News Service* (1918), a common-law unfair competition case in which Justice Mahlon Pitney defined property so broadly as to include any "pecuniary" interest.

Whether the "public interest" called for competition policy or direct government regulation of price, the private interest at issue was always property rights. In classical terms, property rights connoted physical possession and control of some "thing": The owners of a small steel company, for example, should be allowed to sell their blast furnace or steel fabrication machinery—their property—to the United States Steel Trust. By the turn of the century, courts did not require property to be a blast furnace or some other "thing." It could also be an "intangible" representation of ownership such as a stock certificate. Indeed, as the *Dr. Miles Medical Company* (1910) opinions remind us, possession of the "thing" itself had not been a necessary element of property ownership for more than three centuries. Retention of "title" (a piece of paper signifying the "thing") was property enough for the entire Court, as it had been for the seventeenth century's ancient law merchant.

As the nineteenth century drew to a close, property became more and more closely tied to freedom of contract. Freedom of alienation—the right to set a price—was perceived as the fundamental liberty interest underlying property rights. In constitutionalizing freedom of contract, the *Lochner* (1905) decision propelled this transformation of property rights and, with it, confined political liberty to a market-based philosophy of liberty of contract. In all these ways, "property" was dephysicalized.[17]

Although such shifts reflected numerous and complex changes in cultural institutions of the early twentieth century, the legal and economic implications of private property were abstracted in a very specific way: Property was no longer imagined primarily in terms of possession and use value, but in terms of exchange and market value. The difficulties associated with transforming property rights from largely tangible attributes of possession and use into an abstract concept including anything with a market value, "any civil right of a pecuniary nature," materialized in the *International News Service* (1918) case.[18] While Justice Pitney labored for the Court majority to extend the traditional idea of private property beyond its common-law limitations, dissenting Justice Brandeis contended that the difficulty with Pitney's treatment lay in the very common-law view of INS's conduct as lawful.

Associated Press had sued International News Service for misappropriating AP news stories, most often stories about the war in Europe. The particular question on appeal involved AP stories that had already been published, either in AP member newspapers or on public bulletin boards. Did INS do anything wrong when it "lawfully acquired, then used" the AP stories? Justice Pitney began by stating that the issue was not "property"—not common-law rights or copyrights. The issue was "unfair competition." But what is unfair competition? Pitney asserted that it is not a property right against the public because everyone is permitted to read and use published news. Rather, it is competitors' equitable "rights as between themselves." And "news matter, however little susceptible of ownership and dominion in the absolute sense, is stock in trade." Pitney then seems to ignore his own teaching, stating that there *is* a "remaining property interest in [already published news] as between the competitors." Because "both parties are seeking to make profits at the same time and in the same field," the opinion continues, "we can hardly fail to recognize that for this purpose, and as between them, it must be regarded as quasi-property."[19]

In short, Pitney understood the common-law tort of unfair competition to require protection of gathered news as private property, even after publication, because it retained "an exchange value to the gatherer" as well as "to one who can misappropriate it." Even though INS lawfully acquired the news, without transgressing any common-law property right, "fair competition" called for protection of this exchange value "from piracy." A "court of equity concerns itself . . . [with] the right to acquire property by honest labor." The Court would not permit INS to "reap where it has not sown." In sum, a Lockean view of property appropriation by labor was yoked to a market view of property value by exchange, leading Justice Pitney to create an equitable "quasi-property" interest: "Any civil right of a pecuniary nature [is] a property right."[20] In the process, "quasi-property" rights were shifted from INS to AP. By extending property to include anything with exchange value, anything with market value, the Court not only created a new "civil right" for AP but also took a traditional property right from INS.

More broadly, Pitney's analysis brings to light the complex and sometimes contradictory relationship between property rights and competition rhetorics. Here, AP's "quasi-property right" is both a product of competition rhetoric and its limit. That is, fair competition implies AP's property right, which protects AP from competition by INS, competition stemming from the use of public information.

In separate opinions, Justices Holmes and Brandeis disputed the creation of a private "quasi-property" right. While Brandeis dissented, Holmes concurred that the injunction against INS should stand. Nonetheless, Holmes took issue with Pitney's natural, labor-based view of property, declaring that all "property is the creation of law." For Holmes, the clear implication was that all property is a public product of the state, not a preexisting natural right that called for the Court's protection. The result, however, was the same, because common-law courts could and, since time immemorial, did create property rights. Holmes was simply calling upon the Court to take responsibility for its power.[21]

Brandeis began his dissent cautiously. By its conclusion, however, his balancing of public and private interests in news was pathbreaking. Brandeis first applied common-law property rights analysis to AP's published news, finding that copyright and trade secret law would favor INS. Furthermore, no special statute granted property status to AP's news stories. Turning to the common law of unfair competition, Brandeis wrote that Pitney's use of private law cases by analogy was a dangerous exercise in judicial policymaking because important public interests rest in the news. That is, Brandeis took issue with Pitney's analogy of publicly available news to privately held inventory stock.[22] Though sympathetic to INS's doctrinal arguments, Brandeis ultimately rested his dissent on the broad political principle that the balancing of private and public interests is better left to the legislature. Brandeis was convinced that the complexity of "modern society" called for legislative balancing of public and private interests rather than judicial extension by analogy of traditional common-law rights. His preference for the legislature was based both on institutional competency and political principle.

The wider implications of Brandeis's balancing view of property in *International News Service* become clear once we appreciate both its normative and analytic aspects. Normatively, Brandeis sought to expand the realm of cognizable interests beyond the common law's private property rights, the individual's rights of contract. In his view, property rights should be defined by weighing in the balance both public and private interests, both competition and contractual restraint, both majoritarian preferences and individual property rights. Analytically, Brandeis was not daunted by the perception of persistent conflict between those interests, because he believed that a balance could always be struck. This balancing jurisprudence called for an evaluation of the social and economic consequences of the legal rule under scrutiny.

The opinions by Pitney and Brandeis thus present two radically different views of property rights. The differences are both normative and jurisprudential. To understand the normative difference, we can ask: Why protect property rights? Pitney's response would be a moral argument: because they are constitutional or natural rights protecting the fruits of individual labor. Brandeis's response would be utilitarian: when they produce societal benefits. These responses also reflect different jurisprudential approaches. Pitney treated property rights as the starting point, the general principle, for deciding concrete cases. His arguments were loosely deductive and presented as moving from general premises to particular conclusions, from the common-law doctrine of "fair competition" to the implication of AP's "quasi-property right." In contrast, Brandeis viewed property as the product of a legislative process that balanced public and private interests. This legislative balancing—a loosely inductive enterprise—moved from the specifics of societal consequences to the decision of whether to grant property status to the private interests asserted. Property was a judicial creation only in the limited sense of deferential judicial reenactment of the legislative balancing. Although no one concurred in Brandeis's opinion, it would gain influence some twenty years later.[23]

The Economic Limits of Majoritarianism: Public Price-fixing as Illegal Per Se

The constitutional necessity of Supreme Court review in state regulation cases derived from the concept of property crystallized in Justice Pitney's *International News Service* opinion: When the established rates were too low—when the shareholders' pecuniary interest was not satisfied with a "fair" return on investment—the fixed rates amounted to a government "taking" of property prohibited by the Fourteenth Amendment. Such regulation cases invited normative and institutional conflict by calling upon the common-law, conservative Court to rule on progressive-minded legislation passed in the name of the "public interest."

Two types of regulation case reached the Court. One class raised questions about the constitutional adequacy of rates issued by regulatory commissions. These cases involved economic activities indisputably within the traditional common-law category of industries "affected with a public interest"—primarily utility companies and railroads. But the vast majority of commercial pursuits were seen as private enterprise outside the narrow scope of legitimate state power to set rates, just as the Court in *Lochner* (1905) had seen the vast majority of wage laborers as working in industries outside the state police power to regulate public health and morals. In this second category, the Court consistently denied state power to regulate rates. That is, public price-fixing was illegal per se.[24]

The *Lochner* era would be thirty years old before Brandeis's and Holmes's capacious view of "public interest" would take hold in *Nebbia v. New York* (1934), which heralded an end to the era of laissez-faire constitutionalism and the start of a time of greater judicial deference to legislative judgment. But in the decade before the Court first showed a greater willingness to allow legislative regulation of economic relations, a fierce battle raged over the reach of legitimate political power. Between 1927 and 1929, for example, Justice George Sutherland, writing for the Court, concluded that the Fourteenth Amendment protected individual liberty of contract by prohibiting New York from setting prices for theater ticket agents, New Jersey from fixing employment agency fees, and Tennessee from regulating gasoline prices. None of those industries was "affected with a public interest."[25] Most striking in the decisions are the sharply conflicting formulations of public interest and private property rights expressed in majority and dissenting opinions.

The *Tyson Bros.* decision (1927) reflects two radically different views of the "public interest." Sutherland wrote for a deeply divided Court that theater ticket agents were not subject to state regulation of price, and that the New York statute took "rights of property" from the agents, apparently because there is something "sacrosanct" about one's right to set a price. Even where state licensing was justified, he would later insist, state price-fixing remained "a more serious invasion of property rights."[26] Sutherland's majority saw price-setting as the purest exercise of liberty of contract, the distilled essence of private property rights. Justices Holmes, Stone, and Sanford disagreed, each in his own dissenting opinion.

After limiting the category of "industries affected with a public interest" to those recognized under the traditional common law, Sutherland went on to define his terms: It was the "character" of the business that defined the narrow category of "public interest." Only the common-law category, fixed in time and expanse, provided an exception to the common law protection of private property rights. Sutherland concluded that neither the size of a firm nor any "public concern" about it, although "warranted," should expand the common-law category beyond its historical boundaries.[27]

Dissenting Justice Holmes maintained that "public interest" was not properly defined by reference to tradition or to natural law, but rather by legislative action reflecting popular sentiment—that is, by the very "public concern" Sutherland rejected. Holmes's opinion, in which he was joined by Brandeis, reflected both men's positions in *International News Service* (1918). Both refused to define property rights entirely in terms of common-law categories or natural rights. Both saw the legislature as the legitimate arbiter of property rights, as the political fulcrum for balancing the private and public interests that should ultimately define rights in property.[28]

But for Justice Sutherland and his colleagues in the Court majority, this view projected a dangerous image of majoritarianism unrestrained. Whether regulating mergers or reviewing utility rates, the Court would not take private economic power into account in determining the proper limits of state action. That would privilege politics over a preexisting, natural right of private property. Hence, the Court would not tolerate an expression of a political majority to govern the terms of a "private" market transaction. Judicial review of state action to restrain political excesses in the "public interest" served the goal of protecting individuals from oppressive political power.[29]

The Court's unanimous decision in *Trenton Potteries* (1927), which found private price-fixing illegal regardless of intent and competitive effect, is published just ahead of the *Tyson Bros.* opinions in volume 273 of the United States Reports. They stand side by side, as if to announce that both private and public price-fixing are just the same: Both are simply illegal. But beside the unanimity in outlawing private price-fixing stood a Court divided in evaluating state price-fixing. Justice Harlan Fiske Stone, who wrote for the united Court in

Trenton Potteries, was one of four dissenting Justices in *Tyson Bros*. For Stone, joined by Holmes and Brandeis, the difference between public and private price-fixing was clear: Price regulation was a legitimate exercise of sovereign power "when circumstances seriously curtail the regulative force of competition." In short, public rate-setting was different from private rate-setting and functionally equivalent to competitive markets: Both competitive markets and government agencies regulated private economic power to benefit the public. The Court majority's calcified *Lochner*ian commitment to a fixed common law should give way to a balancing, to an assessment of effects in construing the phrase "industries affecting a public interest." For the dissenting faction, the important point was that both competition and state rate-setting produced comparable effects—the regulation of private economic power and the lowering of prices. Furthermore, the intent must be the same—to ensure "fair prices," fair both to the regulated firms and to those trading with them.[30]

Sutherland and the majority faction took notice of an entirely different set of effects—the impact on private property rights of regulated businessmen. Whereas competition promoted their exercise of property rights and liberty of contract, state rate regulation undermined those rights for the purpose of distributing private wealth. Moreover, *all* naked price-fixing, whether public or private, was unacceptable, because such associations coerced individuals. Neither political majorities nor dominant cartels were permitted to trample individual liberty of contract, whose purest practice was the right to set sales prices.

Indeed, the vision of price-setting as the crown jewel of individual liberty was powerful enough to expand Sutherland's majority in the *Williams v. Standard Oil* decision (1929). With only Holmes dissenting, Sutherland would write that gasoline retailing involved merely the sale of a common commodity, and thus the industry was not affected with a public interest. Despite the size of the Standard Oil Company, despite the public concern over corporate domination of a commodity important to the day-to-day life of many citizens, the State of Tennessee could not regulate prices. The attempt deprived a "person," John D. Rockefeller qua Standard Oil Trust, of "his" property without due process.[31]

As I have described elsewhere, this property argument legitimized the treatment of large firms, enormous institutions, as "individuals."[32] Given this view, the Sutherland majority saw public and private price-fixing as identical because they looked at the impact on "individual" sellers. In both cases, (corporate) "persons" were restrained from exercising "individual" discretion to set prices. But the majority view ignored a fundamental difference between public and private price-fixing: the impact on private economic power. Private cartels typically created and exercised economic power to raise prices above the "fair price" of competition, while public rate-setting agencies were politically authorized to apply countervailing public power to lower prices from an uncompetitive monopoly price to a regulated "fair price." Indeed, the regulatory process typically looked to markets as benchmarks for rates, and sought to emulate market processes in setting a "fair price."

In Justice Stone's terms, "fair price" can be understood as the connective tissue between the processes of competition and regulation. Only when competition proved unworkable, when the market process failed to produce a "fair price," did regulation become necessary to fill the void. This inductive or instrumentalist approach to the "public interest" derived from a sense that private economic power was a legitimate public concern, a concern reflected in the constitutional provisions governing the relationship between majoritarianism and private property rights.

For the Sutherland majority, the exercise of private economic power did not justify state regulation of prices. Outside the narrow common-law category of public utilities and common carriers, the public interest was understood in traditional terms of safeguarding individual liberty and property. Underlying that formulation was a view of the Constitution as a liberal document designed solely to protect private property from political taking, a document with nothing to say about the consequences of private economic power. This brand of political liberalism, together with an extruded ideology of individualism, produced both the antitrust Rule of Reason and the *Lochner*ian stand against general rate regulation by government. That was why the Court *allowed* Elbert Gary's U.S. Steel Corporation, a virtual monopoly, to overwhelm "his" rivals and to purchase their assets. That was also why the Court *did not allow* the State of Tennessee to set resale prices on John D. Rockefeller's gasoline, held under the name of the Standard Oil Company. Though both firms exercised monopoly power, the Court was concerned primarily with protecting their "individual" property rights from the hands of political majorities, majorities represented by the federal and the Tennessee legislatures.

The Political Economy of Trade Associations

In the decade preceding the *Standard Oil* and *American Tobacco* decisions (1911), a new logic of "cooperative competition" began to take hold, first among industrial managers, then elite lawyers, and later economists and policy makers. The success of Woodrow Wilson's War Industries Board in organizing production and distribution, followed by postwar promotion of industry trade associations in Herbert Hoover's Commerce Department, fueled a nationwide movement to organize industries, manage them more efficiently, and foster fair competition. Although strict judicial scrutiny of economic regulation by political majorities continued to enforce a *Lochner*ian logic of individual freedom, there emerged a new and more lenient view of private administration of markets. By the mid-1920s, the Supreme Court no longer judged trade associations according to the cartel doctrine of per se illegality announced in *Addyston Pipe* (1899). The trade association came to be seen as an economic organization that was neither cartel nor trust, but a third category with unique economic virtues. As we shall see, the Court's indulgent attitude toward trade associations corresponded with its broader toleration of commercial price-fixing.

Cooperative Competition and the Rise of Trade Associations

By the 1920s, the era of cooperative competition was in full bloom.[33] The story of cooperative competition began, however, some twenty years earlier, not in the halls of government or the directives of experts but in the corridors of commerce. Although the benefits of cooperation among competitors to limit output and thus raise prices seems obvious to us today, rivals at the turn of the century were more interested in maximizing output. Maximizing output was seen as the economically logical course of conduct because experience had shown that cartels were difficult to maintain and now were illegal under the Sherman Act. Mergers, for the most part, were capitulations to more powerful rivals. The best strategy, then, was to produce as much as possible, defeat one's rivals, and then dominate the market. Although the enticing strategy of lowering output to increase price was well known, there was a missing piece to the puzzle: how to eliminate competition without resort to merger (capitulation) or to cartelization (difficult to enforce and illegal). That missing piece ultimately took the form of the trade association.

Organizing exchange of information and developing industrywide group identification, trade associations educated their members to the virtues of cooperative competition. In practice, cooperative competition displaced the buccaneering attitude associated with the late nineteenth-century personae of Rockefeller, Harriman, Duke, and their contemporaries. Encouraged by all presidential administrations between the two Roosevelts except that of Woodrow Wilson in his first term, industrial self-governance came to replace the "full and free competition" valued by Justice Peckham's Literalists and Senator Sherman's faction in Congress and carried forward in the Court's strict scrutiny of private cartels. Still, the trade association movement did have ideological roots in the Sherman Act debates, in the faction opposing Senator Sherman, those who saw "full and free competition" as destructive.

On the eve of World War I, consulting firms of industrial engineers were already organizing and managing numerous trade associations. Perhaps the most influential firm was Stevenson, Jordan & Harrison. In a widely distributed and well-known pamphlet published by his group, Charles R. Stevenson wrote: "[T]he business leader of today achieves success by managing his individual volume to his industry's volume, so as to maximize his revenue and not his physical output. . . . [B]usinessmen must manage volume so as to share the market, not to monopolize it, and, thus, to safeguard the conditions which maximize revenue." The Stevenson consulting firm began its work in 1915 and, despite criminal indictments, consent decrees, and injunctions in the late 1930s, managed thirty major trade associations in 1940. According to one government study published in 1940, the Stevenson firm implemented price stabilization programs in three stages. First, they installed a uniform method of accounting and gave rivals the information to compete with restraint. Second, if knowledge of costs was not enough to stabilize markets (because some firms chose to reduce costs by selling more at lower prices), they would compile, analyze, and disseminate statistics regarding inventory, shipments, orders, and so forth. Third, if knowledge of costs and market activity was not enough, the firm promoted "the principle of an Equitable Sharing of the available volume of business."[34]

Advocates of industrial trade associationalism called for markets administered by contract or combination—by trade associations—to replace "destructive competition" among individual rivals. But an ideological difficulty lay in the inescapable role of government: What sort of political action to rationalize markets was consistent with freedom of contract? What governmental participation would contain the "Red Scare" fears about Bolshevik Communism while producing the benefits of centralization? And what of the commitment to individualism portrayed in the image of "small dealers and worthy men"? It was a mixture of informal government participation and commercial cooperation that presented an approach to organizing production consistent with the liberal distrust of political majorities roaming freely in the private economic sphere. That mixture was "cooperative competition."

There was a broad range of public support for cooperative competition, an approach that reflected not only an ideological commitment to freedom of contract but also a practical desire to mediate between fair profits for sellers and fair prices for buyers, a desire to find a "reasonable" middle ground between the extremes of ruinous competition and unbridled monopoly. Fresh from his success at helping America's European allies begin their recovery efforts after World War I, Herbert Hoover was convinced that "the laws of Scientific Management" could provide the structure for efficient and "socially responsible economic institutions and processes." Economist John M. Clark, who would gain notoriety for his influential theory of "workable competition" in the 1940s, wrote in 1923 that trade associations enhanced competition when they promoted information exchange among members, thereby avoiding ruinous competition. Justice Holmes and his progressive brethren concurred, particularly supporting the information exchanges organized by trade associations. Holmes wrote that "the Sherman Act did not set itself against knowledge—did not aim at a transitory cheapness unprofitable to the community as a whole." Justice Brandeis agreed that the private property right to a fair profit reflected a public interest, maintaining that "the pursuit of business for private profit" served society's best interests insofar as "Congress assumed that the desire to acquire and to enjoy property is the safest and most promising basis for society."[35] In short, ruinous competition was bad for everyone. Private profits were a public good.

Stronger advocates of "cooperative competition" favored a radical departure from "full and free competition." Muckrakers such as Ida Tarbell urged a "golden rule," a "live-and-let-live" attitude among rivals. John Dewey, the preeminent philosopher of pragmatism, viewed associationalism as a practical exercise in economic democracy. In 1918 he called for "a federation of self-governing industries with the government acting as adjuster and arbiter." Not unlike John Stuart Mill's political vision of small local groups fostering civic virtue, Dewey's economic conception placed a high value on intermediating groups, because they offered a middle ground between the large institutions of government and the classical individualism often understood as its only alternative. He applied a Millsian, perhaps even a republicanist, view of groups to economic organization, seeing in group experience the best opportunity for the development of human qualities. The title page of an immensely popular book, *The New Competition* (1914), by Arthur Jerome Eddy, a prominent member of Chicago's corporate bar, displays the following phrase, italicized, underlined, within quotation marks, and in 18-point type: "*Competition Is War, and 'War is Hell.'*" Directly under the book title, Eddy described the work as "AN EXAMINATION OF THE CONDITIONS UNDERLYING THE RADICAL CHANGE THAT IS TAKING PLACE IN THE COMMERCIAL AND INDUSTRIAL WORLD—THE CHANGE FROM A *COMPETITIVE TO A COOPERATIVE BASIS*."[36]

When America finally entered World War I, the War Industries Board of 1917–1918 under President Woodrow Wilson encouraged the formation of trade associations to exchange information and stabilize markets. The Department of Commerce published a report estimating that approximately a thousand national trade associations were active in 1920. By 1933, there were more than ten thousand trade associations. Franklin Roosevelt's New Deal legislation would take those trade associations as its institutional framework for the National Recovery Administration. As historian Ellis Hawley has rightly observed, the decade of the 1920s was not a period of "inactive federal administration or . . . a return to laissez-faire." Rather, it was a shift in "policy-making power from parliamentary institutions and governmental regulators to associational networks and corporative bodies[,] part private and part public."[37]

Embraced by business managers across the country, promoted by Herbert Hoover in the 1920s, the ethic of cooperative competition, put into practice through trade associations, was transforming cutthroat rivalry into a cooperative notion of competition. Yet the trade association movement reflected an uneasy union of recent experience and old ideology. The recent experience of national mobilization during World War I under President Woodrow Wilson's War Industries Board of 1917–1918 demonstrated the awesome power of industrial cooperation under government regulation. The old ideology was a commitment to individual liberty and a distrust of expansive government, expressed in both *Lochner*'s constitutional freedom of contract and *Standard Oil*'s Rule of Reason.

Interlude: Chicago Board of Trade *and Two "Rules of Reason"*

The political economy of competition and its relationships to private property, individual liberty, and economic inequality were changing. And change was coming from two directions—one practical, the other theoretical. On one flank, actual commercial practices were challenging theoretical and jurisprudential models of proper commercial conduct. As I have already described, the experiences of cooperative competition and war mobilization did not comport with the classical matrix of economics and the common law. The lessons of experience raised a twin challenge to the classical liberal view of individualism. Not only was the oppositional relationship between individual and government being called into question—first by a minority faction on the Court and majorities reflected in legislatures, and a decade later by a New Deal majority. But the distrust of economic cooperation, the figure of rugged individualism, was also dissolving in a tidal wave of associationalism.[38]

On the other flank, there was a theoretical impetus for change in the political economy of competition. Like its practical counterpart, the theoretical challenge was double. An early challenge was carried in the neoclassical model of economics, synthesized in Alfred Marshall's 1890 treatise *Principles of Economics* and developed in the work of his American acolytes. Seen in Supreme Court jurisprudence at least as early as Justice McKenna's opinion in *U.S. Steel* (1920), the neoclassical model defined competition in functional terms, by reference to markets. Whereas the older classical model defined competition as a consequence of individual liberty of contract, the newer view, especially in its American form, presented a picture of commercial markets that was not always consistent with the classical view and its jurisprudential cognate, liberty of contract. The newer view in America was influenced, for example, by the work of Henry Carter Adams, who distinguished among industries according to their cost characteristics. This distinction suggested that some industries were naturally competitive while others were naturally monopolistic. A theory of natural monopolies raised the specter of government regulation as economically logical. This economic logic of political supervision ran headlong into the classical and jurisprudential logic of individual liberty.

There was a second, more recent theoretical challenge to the classical political economy of competition and its particular brand of individualism. That challenge to the political economy of *Lochner* and *Standard Oil* appeared almost unnoticed in Justice Brandeis's opinion for the Court in *Chicago Board of Trade* (1918). Although modern antitrust scholars still view Brandeis's opinion as a restatement of Chief Justice White's Rule of Reason expounded in his lengthy *Standard Oil* and *American Tobacco* opinions, Brandeis followed the earlier version only in name. In both jurisprudential form and normative substance, the two versions are better understood as separate and distinct Rules of Reason.

The restraint at issue in *Chicago Board* was the Board's "Call Rule," a regulation setting the daily closing price as the overnight price on all grain to arrive before morning. Government counsel characterized the rule as simple price-fixing and hence illegal per se under the cartel doctrine of *Addyston Pipe* (1899). Board attorneys argued that the call rule's purpose was "not to prevent competition or to control prices, but to promote the convenience of members by restricting their hours of business and to break up a monopoly in that branch of the grain trade acquired by four or five warehousemen in Chicago." The defendant's lawyers were asking the Court to look at purpose and consequences, rather than the implications of liberty of contract.

Seeming to adopt the classical libertarian jurisprudence expressed in *Standard Oil*, Justice Brandeis wrote that "the legality of an agreement or regulation cannot be determined by so simple a test, as whether it restrains competition. Every agreement concerning trade, every regulation of trade, restrains. To bind, to restrain, is of their very essence." Under *Standard Oil* doctrine, Brandeis would then have penned an ode to liberty of contract, a classically styled exercise in loose deduction, likely concluding that the restraint was reasonable at common law and thus pro-competitive. But Brandeis did no such thing. Rather, he inverted the Rule of Reason to construct a loosely inductive analysis consistent with his dissenting opinion in *International News Service* (1918), his pathbreaking brief in *Muller* (1908), and his constitutional standard for reviewing state regulation cases. It is Brandeis's rendition that is remembered today as the Rule of Reason's most eloquent statement:

> The true test of legality is whether the restraint imposed is such as merely regulates and perhaps thereby promotes competition or whether it is such as may suppress or even destroy competition. To determine that question the court must ordinarily consider the facts peculiar to the business to which the restraint is applied; its condition before and after the restraint was imposed; the nature of the restraint and its effect, actual or probable. The history of the restraint, the evil believed to exist, the reason for adopting the particular remedy, the purpose or end sought to be attained, are all relevant facts.

Brandeis then looked at the particular circumstances of the case and concluded that the call rule, on balance, "helped improve market conditions."[39]

In the *Standard Oil* and *American Tobacco* (1911) decisions, we saw Chief Justice White reformulate antitrust doctrine under a classical Rule of Reason, using common-law language to redefine the public policy of competition in terms of private rights secured by liberty of contract: The public policy of competition was best served by protecting private rights of contract. But Justice Brandeis's restatement of the rule in *Chicago Board* turned this deductive analysis on its head, determining inductively the reasonableness of a contract, a private restraint, by looking at its public effects: Does the private agreement "regulate[ ] and perhaps thereby promote[ ] competition or [does it] suppress or even destroy competition"?[40]

By 1925, the Court would adopt Brandeis's formulation in antitrust cases. That formulation would allow the Court to recognize the kinds of arguments made in favor of cooperative competition. In short, the shift from classical cartel doctrine to the jurisprudence we recognize as the Rule of Reason occurred between 1911 and 1925. It is most noticeable in the trade association cases.

The Trade Association Cases, 1913–1925

Although popular in the business community, trade associations as the vehicle for transmuting cutthroat into cooperative competition met pockets of strenuous resistance. Some of the resistance was expressed in the Justice Department's enforcement and interpretation of the Sherman Act, which, after all, did contain language forbidding contracts, combinations, and conspiracies in restraint of trade. The issue was met head-on in a long series of trade association cases decided by the Supreme Court.

Each side in the extended confrontation had its own framework for viewing the question of cooperative trade associations. To those opposing the movement to cooperation, the old freight association cases loomed large. It was in the *Trans-Missouri Freight Association* (1897) and *Joint Traffic* (1898) decisions that the Court first declared price fixing illegal per se. Later decisions, including *Addyston Pipe* (1899), *Montague & Co.* (1904), *Swift & Co.* (1905), and *Dr. Miles* (1910) consistently reaffirmed that price-fixing was always unreasonable. Even more recently, in *American Publisher's Association* (1913),[41] the Court had found illegal per se an agreement among booksellers and a publisher's association to fix prices for copyrighted books. Cooperation that set or stabilized prices was illegal, regardless of the particular means and regardless of the intent to safeguard a property right—a legal monopoly in copyrighted materials.

On the other side of the docket, the jurisprudential theme inspiring the larger commercial crusade for cooperation was elaborated in Justice Brandeis's opinion in *Chicago Board* (1918). Brandeis, writing for the Court, announced that "regulating" commerce was not a violation of the antitrust laws, even if the regulation affected price. Certainly, improving the informational basis for market decisions enhanced rather than restrained competition. Although "naked" price-fixing was illegal, Brandeis insisted, the publication of market information was different. In a dissenting opinion published during the Court's 1921 term, Justice Holmes agreed, lauding the exchange of price and production information, forecasts, and opinions by members of a large trade association, with the following observation: "I see nothing that binds the members . . . to anything that would not be practiced, if we could imagine it, by an allwise socialistic government acting for the benefit of the community as a whole."[42]

In trade association cases after 1925, Brandeis, Holmes, and Stone would find agreement in the Court's conservative faction, though concurrence straddled two distinct Rules of Reason. Although Sutherland, McReynolds, and their cohort were Locked into a constitutional and moral defense of property as the ground for contracts in reasonable restraint of trade, the more progressive faction rested their approval on the social value of "enlightened competition."[43] The progressives' dangerous turn to a utilitarian and legal positivist defense of property entailed a Rule of Reason different from Chief Justice White's formulation in *Standard Oil*. Indeed, writing in the Court's 1918 term, Brandeis saw both competition policy (in *Chicago Board*) and private property rights (in *International News Service*) as the outcomes of balancing public and private interests.

Most of the trade association cases involved the kind of information exchange practices developed by the Stevenson consulting firm and those who mimicked it. The information cases introduced especially difficult, vigorously contested questions of antitrust policy. The questions were especially difficult because the arguments made by association counsel and, in the later cases, taken up by the Court, concerned the purpose and effect of information sharing. And market information itself presents a dilemma: It is necessary for both competition and combination. The cases were vigorously contested because the issues of purpose and effect, and the Court's eventual shift to a Brandeisian Rule of Reason, turned on the particular facts of each case: Were the purpose and effect to restrain competition, to fix a price, as in *Trans-Missouri Freight Association*, or were they to regulate competition, to rationalize market behavior, as found in *Chicago Board*?

Although cases in which trade associations enforced open, express agreements to charge a particular price seemed easy, those that did not involve proration proved more difficult. *American Column & Lumber Company* (1921) was an early case involving no proration that reflected the Court's early distrust of all trade associations. Government attorneys began their oral argument as follows:

> This case for the first time presents directly for the consideration of this court the practices of those organizations which are known as "open price associations." The conditions of the industrial world are such, and the literature on the subject so abundant, that the court will take judicial knowledge that these associations are so numerous and so extensively organized as to threaten an economic revolution. The basic principle of these associations is cooperation.

Trade association counsel agreed, asserting that the public meetings and open dissemination of information improved market conditions, especially for the smaller firms who could not afford to produce such information. Moreover, they argued, the fact of widely varying production levels across the industry was inconsistent with the charge of an agreement limiting production. Even a report by the Department of Agriculture to Congress attributed the rise in prices to "natural causes" associated with demand pent up during World War I.[44]

In response, government attorneys observed that the extensive and immediate publication of industry data made unobserved price cutting impossible. This price stabilization increased profits. Coupled with rising demand, lack of downward movements in price had the effect of accelerating the pace of price increases. Finally, persistent group pressure to cooperate produced a series of "understandings," eliminating the need for an explicit agreement. In short, an industrywide course of conduct had the purpose and effect of increasing price by curtailing output, regardless of the underlying "natural causes."[45]

Despite the sharply opposing claims made by counsel, there was a covering rhetoric common to both views, a rhetoric different from the classical arguments about individual liberty underlying common-law cartel doctrine. Here, counsel for both parties implicitly agreed on a new form of argument about competitive effects taken from neoclassical economics and reflected, however perversely, in Brandeis's inductive Rule of Reason.

Writing for the Court, Justice John H. Clarke paid close attention to the association's written Open Competition Plan and to the report of the Association Committee who drafted it. Well over half the opinion simply quotes parts of the plan, the report, periodic publications, and written responses of association members to the plan. Clarke used the association's own verbiage to demonstrate that the industry had been "organized into one group" and had developed a "cooperative spirit." This group identity had two aspects. First, within the industry, a "cooperative spirit" was developed through a program of reeducation, overseen by F. R. Gadd, the association's "Manager of Statistics." In addition to gathering and publishing data, Gadd proselytized the canon of cooperation: "Overproduction will spell disaster." "Co-operation will only replace *undesirable competition* as you develop a co-operative spirit." "More members mean more power to do more good for the industry . . . *and you know what that means.*" Apparently, the association members did know. As one member wrote, "There seems to be a friendly rivalry among members to see who can get the best prices, whereas, under the old plan it was cutthroat competition." Second, cooperation within the group was set apart from "threats" originating outside the group—threats from buyers. It was buyers who sought to "break the hardwood market by a withdrawal of demand" and other "vigorous efforts . . . *to hammer down prices.*"[46] In short, horizontal cooperation and common stakes were contrasted to vertical competition and conflicting interests.

Given this conception of a group identity, Justice Clarke was obviously struck by the statement that "*Knowledge regarding prices actually made is all that is necessary to keep prices at reasonably stable and normal levels.*" Although there was no explicit agreement to fix prices, agreement was inferred from "the disposition of men `to follow their most intelligent competitors,' especially when powerful[,] . . . joined with the steady cultivation of the value of `harmony' of action." With this esprit de corps—this newfound commitment to wage common warfare against the real rival, the buyer—all that was necessary was someone to issue marching orders. Where was the "most intelligent competitor"? Who would lead the others into battle? Justice Clarke found his leader among the defendants in the case: F. R. Gadd, the "Manager of Statistics" for the association. Gadd was a guide rather than a commander, someone who brokered a "tacit understanding that all were to act together under the subtle direction of a single skilled interpreter of their common purposes." Gadd's handiwork identified him as that skilled interpreter. The gathering, analysis, and publication of market information was anticompetitive, Justice Clarke implied, because it was not left open to the interpretation of individual market participants. Instead, association members learned to trust a single interpretation and to follow the interpreter's lead in acting on it. Who could doubt that the common purpose and effect were to restrain competition among association members?[47]

Both Holmes and Brandeis, the latter joined by Joseph McKenna, expressed their doubts in dissenting opinions. In a brief opinion, Holmes stressed the value of "full knowledge of the facts" in attempting "to conform to . . . normal market conditions," especially the value to smaller "mills in the backwoods." But what of the evidence of a common purpose and effect—restraining competition? Certainly, Holmes had already made clear his antipathy toward a political economy of atomistic competition some seventeen years earlier in his *Northern Securities* dissent. For more on the issues at hand, Holmes directed his readers to the "elaborate discussion of the case by my brother Brandeis."[48]

Brandeis began by asking whether advice can amount to a restraint. He concluded that "words of advice seemingly innocent and perhaps benevolent, may restrain, when uttered under circumstances that make advice equivalent to command." For Brandeis, the key issue was "coercion." In this case, Brandeis saw none: "There is no claim that by agreement, force, or fraud, any producer, dealer or consumer was to be or has in fact been controlled or coerced." "The Plan is a voluntary system [whose] purpose was to make rational competition possible by supplying data not otherwise available." Brandeis disagreed not only with Clarke's view of the association's purpose, but also with his focus for determining effects: "The illegality of a combination . . . lies not in its effect on the price level, but in the coercion thereby effected. It is the limitation of freedom which constitutes the unlawful restraint." Brandeis's position was surprising in light of his *Chicago Board* (1918) opinion, which recognized that the very essence of agreement is restraint on individual freedom. The proper question, given the essentially coercive nature of agreement, would then concern its consequences rather than its (omni)presence. Brandeis's "coercion" rationale, even more surprisingly, tracked Justice White's classical Rule of Reason in that it was less concerned with anticompetitive effects than with liberty of contract—freedom to act in one's economic interests.[49]

Moreover, because Brandeis refused to acknowledge the power of group suasion under the hand of a "single skilled interpreter," he could dismiss the coercive effects on hardwood buyers in their trade with association members. Heedless to any "disposition to follow one's most intelligent competitor," he saw only voluntary transactions, with participants acting in their best interests and, hence, in society's. Their best interests were "the pursuit of business for private profit." Again evocative of White's derivation of social benefit from protecting private interests, Brandeis concluded that society's best interests were served by promoting private property rights: "Congress assumed that the desire to acquire and to enjoy property is the safest and most promising basis for society." In ignoring the inclination to follow a leader and in discounting the power of 400 mills, which produced "one-third of the total production of the United States," Brandeis could disagree with Clarke's majority opinion, its finding of a common purpose and effect to restrain competition. Instead, Brandeis, Holmes, and McKenna saw the plan as tending "to promote all in competition which is desirable." It improved competition "by substituting knowledge for ignorance . . . research and reasoning for gambling and piracy."[50]

Two years later, Justice James C. McReynolds, for a unanimous Court in *American Linseed Co.* (1923), used even stronger language to condemn twelve corporations, linseed "crushers" who subscribed to the notorious Armstrong

Bureau of Related Industries. Their subscription agreements called not only for information exchange but also for standardized price quotations and freight rates within eight geographic zones. Although the case looked like one of straightforward "naked" price-fixing, McReynolds seemed as concerned about the information exchange as he was about the price-fixing. Taking up Brandeis's rhetoric of "coercion," McReynolds wrote that "all subjected themselves to an autocratic bureau." He condemned the associated subscribers as an illegal combination, maintaining that it "took away freedom of action . . . by requiring each to reveal to all the intimate details of its affairs."[51]

But didn't each linseed crusher agree to the arrangement? Weren't they all exercising their freedom to contract? There are no indications that any party to the agreement was unhappy with it. Presumably, the Armstrong Bureau was administering a program of information exchange and price-fixing eagerly embraced by the linseed crushers. McReynolds took no notice of the contradiction in his analysis, a contradiction earlier finessed by Brandeis: Where is the coercion? In his *American Column & Lumber* dissent, Brandeis had sidestepped the question by refusing to acknowledge an implied agreement among the hardwood mills. That refusal enabled him to disregard his own admonition in *Chicago Board* (1918) that all contracts restrain.[52] But McReynolds had to face the music, because the agreement among linseed crushers was explicit. If the Bureau coerced anyone, it did so pursuant to an agreement freely joined by the twelve rivals.

The problem with the "coercion" analysis is that all parties to contracts give up some freedom as soon as they exchange promises. That is what they bind themselves to do because they believe that they are getting something at least as valuable as they are giving up. The linseed crushers did not want to be "bona fide competitors." Each one wanted to constrain its rivals' "freedom of action" because each anticipated higher profits. If anything, it was the economic logic of cooperation that convinced (coerced) them.

The difficulty lay in the very relationship between coercion and freedom of contract. That was the point made so forcefully in the writings of political economist Robert Hale: In a fundamental sense, we only enter into contracts when we cannot freely take what we want. We cannot take what we want when it belongs to someone else. That is, we do not take it under threat of coercion, of government sanction to defend private property. This understanding of contract as fundamentally coercive also raised serious questions about the very logic of laissez-faire constitutionalism underlying the *Lochner* era: How can freedom of contract be understood as a purely private institution to be protected from government "intrusion" when government action (or the threat of it) lies at the very heart of property rights and contractual relations?[53]

The narrower issue of coercion was lurking behind all of the information exchange cases because they all involved contracts, and contracts by their nature restrain the covenanting parties. In publishing market information, moreover, the manifest intent was to restrain not only the parties but everyone else by creating a common understanding, a single interpretation, a market. In short, trade association organizers perceived the value of information as providing the minor premises for an economic logic whose major premise was cooperation. In *American Column & Lumber*, F. R. Gadd's educational program for the hardwood millers had two goals: not only publishing market information but also teaching the economic logic of cooperation. For the Supreme Court, the difficulty lay in the fact that the same information could serve as minor premises for another economic logic, one whose major premise was competition. And under that logic, information exchange improved competitive conditions. Hence, a Rule of Reason would settle nothing. The reasonableness of trade association activities would turn on the Court majority faction's political economy, their choice of major premise—competition or cooperation.

In these early information exchange cases, a Court majority saw the "concerted action" as unreasonable because it produced more than simply data for "intelligent competition." It aided and abetted "the inevitable tendency to destroy real competition." It amounted to price fixing. In rejecting the premises of cooperative competition, these early decisions were out of step with the industrial self-governance encouraged by Commerce Secretary Herbert Hoover, President Calvin Coolidge, and his predecessors. The Court read the Sherman Act as demanding the "real competition" of individualized rivalry among sellers and among buyers, not coordinated battles between groups of sellers and (groups of) buyers.

Warren G. Harding appointed Herbert Hoover Secretary of Commerce in 1921, the same year the Court outlawed information exchange and the other sorts of trade association activities described in *American Column & Lumber*. Hoover had already earned a reputation for his part in the Wilson administration's war mobilization and postwar efforts to help Europe recover. Now he would turn his boundless energies and ambitions toward, as historian Ellis Hawley put it, a "type of private government, one that would meet the need for national reform, greater stability, and steady expansion, yet avoid the evils long associated with 'capital consolidations,' politicized cartels, and governmental bureaucracies." Hoover believed that temporary, *ad hoc* government commissions were needed to get industrial self-governance underway, to help build "internal machinery" at the local and regional levels. As deeply as he distrusted "big government," so did he have faith in a nascent "industrial statesmanship" just waiting in the business community. He fully expected that a modern commitment to managerial science and industrial engineering would provide the rational ground for a new commercial ethic of cooperative competition.[54]

Hoover's approach represented the only kind of government support—informal and lacking legislative foundation—that could meet the Court's libertarian standard for constitutional correctness and for its antitrust cartel doctrine, most recently expressed in the unanimous adoption of a "coercion" analysis in *American Linseed Co.* Yet it was a commercial commitment to scientific management that inspired Hoover's crusade to encourage and develop industrial trade associations. Hoover and his company of followers saw themselves as grassroots organizers and troubleshooters. They were particularly interested in reviving "problem industries," such as the lumber trade. Invited to attend the first lumber conference in 1922 were manufacturers, wholesalers, retailers, architects, railroad managers, and wood users. Everyone but labor representatives was in attendance. The conference produced the Central Committee for Lumber Standards. The next few years saw the adoption of recommended guidelines for sizing, grading, and terms of sale. As well, Hoover formed the Wood Waste Committee and the National Committee on Wood Utilization. He felt confident that the lumber industry was on its way to scientific management. Thus the *American Column & Lumber* decision infuriated Hoover, who immediately launched two counterattacks. First, he began lobbying the Attorney General to accept his view of the economic benefits of trade associations. Second, he instructed the Commerce Department to perform the data gathering and statistical work for trade associations.

Before long, Hoover's hectoring began to pay off. While finishing Harding's term, new President Calvin Coolidge appointed his own Attorney General—Harlan Fiske Stone, Dean of Columbia University Law School. Stone shared Hoover's view of corporate associationalism and began looking for a good test case involving trade association activity. They hoped to convince the Supreme Court that trade association statistical activities were not unreasonable restraints of trade.[55] The case they chose involved the Maple Flooring Manufacturers Association. By the time the case reached the Supreme Court, Stone would be sitting as an Associate Justice. Indeed, he would write the opinion for the Court, one reflecting a sharp change in attitude toward information exchange within trade associations. The change in attitude was consonant not only with Hooverian associationalism but also with Justices Holmes's and Brandeis's views of information exchange as a rational economic activity. Now less concerned with sellers' dispositions to follow intelligent rivals, with their tacit understandings, and with the impact on buyers, the Court would approve of trade association activities short of "naked" price-fixing.

In *Maple Flooring Manufacturers Association* (1925), newly appointed Justice Stone praised the association's extensive information publication activities as fostering "the intelligent conduct of business operations." Stone asserted that "the consensus of opinion [sic] of economists and many of the most important government agencies" held that the "public interest" was best served by information exchanges, which "stabilize prices, produce fairer price levels, and avoid the waste of unintelligent conduct of economic enterprise." The Maple Flooring Association published data describing average flooring costs; freight rates from Cadillac, Michigan; and sales and inventory information. Mill owners had all they needed to know to determine their rivals' prices. Moreover, there were regular meetings at which members apparently discussed a wide range of topics, although the Court was willing to accept the evidence that they never actually agreed on prices. In short, "members have been left free to sell their product at any price they choose." For Justice Stone, the failure to prove an explicit agreement was fatal. Echoing Brandeis's earlier approval of such activities, the Court majority was convinced that coercion was both the essence of restraint and the antithesis of information exchange.[56]

As Justice Clarke had recognized in *American Column & Lumber* (1921) and as the Stevenson consulting firm had formalized into a three-step plan, however, agreement was often unnecessary. With the right information and the proper group identity shared among association members, the logic of cooperation would take hold. Indeed, "it was conceded by [Maple Flooring] that the dissemination of information as to cost of the product and as to production and prices would tend to bring about uniformity of prices through the operation of economic law." But counsel for the association convinced the Court that the economic law operating was competition, not cooperation. The result was a rationalized "law of supply and demand."[57]

Judged according to this Court's Brandeisian Rule of Reason, the case would turn on its particular facts. The government was required to prove each element of the case: the association's power and purpose, and the practices' competitive effects. Consistent with the view expressed in *U.S. Steel* (1920), Stone's opinion made it clear that market power—here, the association's 70 percent market share—was presumptively benign. Purpose was assumed honorable in the absence of "unfair or arbitrary practices"—that is, explicit price-fixing agreements. And the immediate effect of association activity proved to be "fair and reasonable prices."[58] In sum, the association agreement amounted to a reasonable restraint of trade.

Under this rubric, there emerged no conflict between competition rhetoric and the property rhetoric of fair price, between rivalry and agreements among rivals, between independent action and an educated inclination to follow an intelligent competitor. An unreasonable restraint of trade required coercion rather than simply a disposition to fall in line. Trade association activity was now imagined as rational competition rather than cooperation among competitors. Agreements that stabilized prices and produced fair profits, conduct traditionally supported by the property logics of fair price and freedom of contract, now challenged the classical vision of competition. In fact, the spread of trade associations, supported by the logic of the "new competition," was boring into what was left of the classical vision of competition: the cartel logic of coercion, together with the ideology of individualism, that produced the distinction between corporations and associations. Now, there would be unified antitrust treatment of loose and tight combinations: Unless a trade association or a corporate person engaged in flagrantly anti-competitive conduct—open and obvious price control of some sort—the restraint was judged as reasonable. The new Rule of Reason, a juridical reformulation of neoclassical economics and its focus on markets rather than individual freedom of contract, embraced the logic of cooperative competition.

So powerful was this logic of cooperative competition that it influenced price-fixing doctrine as well. There emerged a sharp distinction between public and private price-fixing, a distinction that produced a dichotomous jurisprudence, cumulatively called the Rule of Reason. The classical Rule was most evident in "political conflicts"—in state price-setting and in labor disputes. The Brandeisian Rule appeared in "economic" disputes, in private price-fixing cases. The previous section examined public price-setting. The next takes up the politicized rhetoric applied to labor disputes.[59]

The Political Economy of Labor Associations

Under the classical Rule of Reason's common-law approach, the Court applied cartel doctrine to trade associations and labor associations alike. Indeed, Court consensus that cartels were illegal per se emerged from *Addyston Pipe* (1899) and its adoption of a liberal logic earlier applied to labor unions in *Debs* (1896). The classical distinction was between associations and personified corporations, between *Addyston Pipe*'s strict cartel doctrine and *Standard Oil*'s reasonable trusts.

In 1896, Justice Holmes, then sitting on the Supreme Judicial Court of Massachusetts, wrote in dissent:

> If it be true that workingmen may combine with a view, among other things, to getting as much as they can for their labor, just as capital may combine with a view to getting the greatest possible return, it must be true that when they combined they have the same liberty that combined capital has to support their interests by argument, persuasion, and the bestowal or refusal of those advantages which they otherwise lawfully control.[60]

That is, Holmes saw labor unions and corporations as juridical equivalents. His future colleagues on the Court did not. Throughout the formative era, both Literalist and Rule of Reasonist factions agreed that labor associations were always unreasonable restraints of trade under the Sherman Act. By 1895, they would reach an accommodation that commercial cartels were also illegal per se. By 1911, they would announce (with Holmes concurring) that corporations—in particular, trusts—would be judged more leniently, under a Rule of Reason.

Seven years later, Justice Brandeis articulated a post-classical Rule of Reason in *Chicago Board* (1918). It was a loosely inductive approach that allowed the Court to consider arguments not recognized under the classical Rule. Hence, Brandeis's new Rule of Reason made possible the approval of trade associations despite their cartel-ness under the classical Rule. After 1925, the Court concerned itself neither with individual freedom of contract nor with "coercion" by cartels, but rather with particular trade association practices, with factual circumstances. The classical Rule of Reason would remain alive, but in the political domain, in the Court's supervision of majoritarian associations—that is, in laissez-faire constitutionalism.

How would labor associations be treated? It seems logical to have anticipated that, like trade associations, labor associations would be judged more leniently under the new Rule of Reason, because they would be viewed as economic activities in the private domain. That did not in fact occur. Instead, labor associations were still judged according to the classical cartel doctrine otherwise reserved for illegitimate political action. Like public price-fixing, labor union activities were illegal per se.

How was it that elite lawyers and economists, federal judges and Republican administrations justified the radically different treatment accorded trade and labor associations after 1925? Although that is a complex question that does not yield an easy answer, close attention to the rhetoric of Court opinions, the practices of the Harding, Coolidge, and Hoover administrations, and writings by elite lawyers and economists recovers a common imaginative framework that justified the disparate treatment. In short, labor associations were imagined as political factions, not economic entities; as always threatening violence to person and property, rather than competing with employers. This prevailing image of labor associations as political factions, an image held in common by critics and proponents of labor unions until the early years of the twentieth century, retained influence long after union leaders decided that political aspirations were futile and long after their experience with "government by injunction" turned them to more circumscribed goals.[61]

Although both trade and labor associations were viewed with suspicion before World War I, the ensuing era of cooperative competition brought about a sharp division. Trade associations found legitimacy in the new economics practiced by Herbert Hoover and theorized in the writing of economists such as James M. Clark and corporate lawyers such as Arthur J. Eddy. For those favoring economic association, perhaps the most eloquent statement of all was the success of the Woodrow Wilson administration's mobilization efforts during World War I. In part fashioned by congressional legislation and in part the result of Wilson's broad interpretation of the President's implied war powers, national mobilization during 1917–1918 produced a corporatist structure of industry associations under government supervision. The centralization of economic decision making was not just a resounding success; it also provided a sharp contrast to the "ruinous competition" that preceded it, as well as the postwar inflation, unemployment, and underproduction that followed.

But the success of the Wilson administration's war mobilization effort provoked a deep ambivalence. On the one hand, his corporatist regime did yield the fruits of efficiency. On the other hand, its very success, along with the wartime suppression of individual liberties, especially freedoms of contract and speech, intensified a traditional distrust of "big government," a fear fanned not only by Germany's massive military buildup under Kaiser Wilhelm but also by the Bolshevik "worker" takeover of Russia in 1918. Edward A. Purcell, Jr. has written that the Bolsheviks were initially seen as anarchists. The attendant concern was instability, "mobocracy." Later, the Bolsheviks were seen as a tyrannical regime closer to the fascist dictatorships developing in Italy and Germany.[62] In either setting, the machinery of war mobilization sparked peacetime fears of political danger and revolutionary change.

Indeed, the year 1919 was momentous for more than the treaty of Versailles. Postwar dislocation and inflation produced the massive strikes of

1919, which involved more than four million workers. As well, the Supreme Court published in that year its first group of "modern" First Amendment Speech cases, adopting a narrow view of protected speech under Holmes's rubric of "a clear and present danger." European politics, labor unions, and dissident speech were all part of a threatening mix. William Howard Taft had captured the anxiety some years earlier, and exhorted those who valued law and order to "make their views and voices heard above the resounding din of anarchy, socialism, populism and the general demagogy." He continued, "The sovereign today is the people, or the majority of the people. The poor are the majority. The appeal of the rich to the constitution and courts for protection is still an appeal by the weak against the unjust aggressions of the strong."[63] What can explain the 1920 election of a torpid Warren G. Harding better than his slogan of a return to "normalcy"? In those circumstances, it was no accident that Herbert Hoover, although building a large government bureaucracy in the 1920s, first as Secretary of Commerce and then as President, characterized his efforts in apolitical, nongovernmental terms. Hoover described his program as driven by economics—by management science—not imposed by government or by politics. Although there were some both within government and without who saw trade associations as dangerous mechanisms for subverting competition, for controlling output and raising prices, Hoover's success and the Court's turnabout in *Maple Flooring* (1925) virtually silenced those critics.

The benefits of association were understood as economic. The dangers of collectivity were portrayed as political. The problem, it seems, was the separation of benefits and dangers, the differentiation of economic from political brands of association. In the era of cooperative competition, a complex cultural process effectively characterized industrial trade associations in economically beneficial terms. At the same time, the danger in association—the political content—was ascribed to labor associations.[64] In conjunction with Herbert Hoover's decade-long program to demonstrate what trade associations could do, this cultural process assured everyone of what trade associations would not do. As we will see, the cultural apparatus that differentiated beneficial trade associations from dangerous labor associations, economic efficiency from political threat, worked in three overlapping stages.

A Revised Jurisprudence of Economic Association

The first stage positioned trade associations, labor unions, and trusts in shifting triangular formations. Early on, labor and trade associations, or combinations, were differentiated from trusts and corporations, or persons. The differentiation was both cultural and juridical. The clearest example is the Supreme Court's characterization of labor disputes. In antitrust's formative era, the most notorious confrontations between workers and owners involved large associations on both sides of the picket lines. Yet, in each instance, the owners' association was represented as an entrepreneurial entity, as "the employer." Huge industrial concerns were personified as John D. Rockefeller's oil company, Henry Ford's car company. The workers' association, in contrast, was seen as a "union" or a "combination" of workers. For example, in the *Danbury Hatters* case (1908), Chief Justice Fuller wrote for the Court that the striking workers were "members of a vast combination called The United Hatters of North America, comprising about 9,000 members and including a large number of subordinate unions . . . combined with some 1,400,000 others in another association known as The American Federation of Labor, of which they are members."[65]

The consequence of this representation was devastating to labor associations: As critics of this line of representation recognized, although labor unions were seen as dangerous combinations, they were judged according to an ideology founded in individual action. As Roscoe Pound wrote in 1908,

> Why do so many [courts] force upon legislation an academic theory of equality in the face of practical conditions of inequality? Why do we find a great and learned court in 1908 taking the long step into the past of dealing with the relation between employer and employee in railway transportation, as if the parties were individuals—as if they were farmers haggling over the sale of a horse?[66]

Individual workers were required to contract with "individual" employers. Proselytizers and promoters of cooperative competition were hard at work reorienting attitudes toward trade associations. By the early 1920s, there remained few opponents to the movement. But among the opposition numbered the Department of Justice and the Supreme Court. In the year that Justice Clarke wrote his anti-trade association opinion in *American Column & Lumber* (1921), the *Harvard Law Review* published an article that repeated Pound's question about the ideology of individualism:

> [In] these days of huge and powerful corporations, which form in the eyes of the law single persons . . . why should the law be such that if two steel workers plan a certain act which the law regards as tortious, they should be subject to fine and imprisonment; but if, let us say, the United States Steel Corporation plans and executes the self-same act, the criminal law should be unable to touch it? . . . Why should a combination of individuals . . . constitute a crime if the individuals are not incorporated but be free from crime if they are incorporated?[67]

The question made good sense insofar as neither a labor combination nor a corporation was a natural person. This view of "personhood," along with classical cartel doctrine, was still influencing the Court to find both labor and trade associations illegal per se because both were still imagined as aggregates rather than personified entities.

The earliest indication that the Court's attitude toward associations, as well as its antitrust jurisprudence, was changing appeared two years before the landmark *Maple Flooring* decision. In *National Association of Window Glass Manufacturers* (1923), the Department of Justice sued to enjoin an agreement between the manufacturers' trade association and the glassblowers' trade union. The agreement set a wage scale and "prescribed the time during which the defendant manufactures should operate their factories." Under classical cartel doctrine, the agreement would have been illegal per se. But Justice Holmes, writing for a unanimous Court, found the agreement a reasonable restraint of trade. Citing *Chicago Board* (1918), Holmes wrote that the agreement's "legality requires a consideration of the particular facts."[68]

The classical analysis of restraints, derived from liberty of contract, appeared nowhere in the opinion. Instead, Holmes turned to the "dominant fact in this case"—the decline of handblown glassmaking, which was faced with competition from new, efficient machines. Thus, the economic facts pointed to the contracting parties' powerlessness: Their agreement was a last-ditch effort to save their property—in capital and in specialized skills—from immediate destruction by new technology. In short, Holmes's inductive style of analysis, under the new Rule of Reason, led a unanimous Court to find the restraint reasonable because of "the dominant fact" in the case—no economic power and, hence, no effects on competition.[69]

The 1923 case suggested that identical treatment of trade and labor associations would continue under the new Rule of Reason. In this rare crossover case, involving not only trade and labor associations but also an agreement between them, the Court unanimously applied the kind of analysis that would soon enable it (in *Maple Flooring* (1925)) to approve of trade associationalism and its policy of "new competition," its logic of "cooperative competition."

However, two years after *Maple Flooring*, after the Court explicitly applied the new Rule of Reason and the logic of cooperative competition to trade associations, a labor injunction case made it clear that labor associations would be viewed under the classical Rule of Reason, its liberty of contract logic, and its common-law cartel doctrine otherwise reserved for state price-fixing. Tracing the libertarian logic of his *Tyson Bros.* (1927) opinion, Justice Sutherland upheld an anti-strike injunction in *Bedford Cut Stone Company* (1927), an injunction that actually required striking stonecutters to go back to work. Citing classical cartel cases, both trade and labor, Sutherland wrote that the strike was "necessarily illegal if thereby the interstate trade of another is restrained." As in the *Danbury Hatters* (1908) case, the stonecutters were "guilty of a conspiracy against interstate commerce." This common-law rhetoric and its classical libertarian logic contrasts sharply with trade association cases after 1925, resembling instead the rhetoric and logic of public price-fixing cases.[70]

Justice Brandeis, joined by Holmes, was outraged, characterizing the mandatory injunction as "involuntary servitude." Moreover, he repeated the question raised by numerous progressive critics since Holmes's dissenting opinion in the Massachusetts case, *Vegelahn* (1896), some thirty years earlier:

> The Sherman Law was held in United States v. United States Steel Corporation to permit capitalists to combine in a single corporation 50 per cent. of the steel industry of the United States dominating the trade through its vast resources. The Sherman Law was held in United States v. United Shoe Machinery Co. to permit capitalists to combine in another corporation practically the whole shoe machinery industry of the country. . . . It would, indeed, be strange if Congress had by the same act willed to deny to members

> of a small craft of workingmen the right to cooperate in simply refraining from work, when that course was the only means of self-protection against a combination of militant and powerful employers. I cannot believe that Congress did so.

Such protests notwithstanding, "government by injunction" persisted throughout the 1920s. Indeed, federal judges issued more than 2,100 antilabor injunctions during the decade.[71]

Despite the resistance of Brandeis, Holmes, and many others, the triangulation of trade associations, labor associations, and trusts had shifted into a new formation. The first phase of reformulating the political economy of associations showed the following results: While both corporations and trade associations were now seen as economically beneficial market participants, labor associations were treated as inefficient political combinations of individual workers. Whereas the new Rule of Reason was applied to identify "good" trusts and "good" trade associations, the classical Rule of Reason constrained labor associations and political associations alike as illegitimate combinations in restraint of individual commercial conduct. Given the Court's prominence in the domain of political economy, this realignment reformulated competition policy in the period. This realignment reflected the Court's effort to legitimate the "new competition" without disturbing the old laissez-faire constitutionalism.

Economic Theories of Labor Associations

There were two more phases, two more stages, in the cultural apparatus that differentiated labor from trade associations in those years. Each of the three phases cast influence over the others. The second stage of differentiation unfolded in the theoretical precincts of political economy. At the very moment the Supreme Court was constitutionalizing freedom of contract, just as it was restraining competition and other regulatory policies in the straightjacket of common-law private property rights, Alfred Marshall and his disciples were transforming political economy into economics. As early as Marshall's publication of *Principles of Economics* (1890), the discipline's focus began to shift from liberty of contract to marginal revenue and elasticity of demand, from protecting *individual* industrial liberty to evaluating *market* performance in terms of price and output.

As we have seen, the classical matrix of economics, freedom of contract, and a homologous political ideology of liberalism had influenced not only the Supreme Court, but also treatise writers and lower court judges to declare that all combinations, all associations, deserved equal treatment. Treatise writer Frederick Cooke, for example, wrote that "it is not apparent why the legality of combinations among employees . . . should be subjected to any different test from that applied to combinations among employers . . . or tradesmen." "New competition" advocate Arthur J. Eddy wrote that the "capital of the laborer is his labor, together with his skill." Federal Circuit Court

Judge Caldwell maintained that the same legal rules should apply to all "property," whether the "plant of the manufacturer" or the "labor and skill of the workman."[72]

Although the change prompted by Alfred Marshall's treatise was revolutionary in some respects (it is commonly denominated the "marginalist revolution"), it did not call into question, but rather corroborated, the Court's disparate treatment of trade and labor associations after 1925. Indeed, the marginalists' work contributed directly to the cultural process of vilifying labor unions.

The second stage of distinguishing labor associations from their commercial twins flowed directly from the new economics, both its practice and its theory. Practitioners of the new management science, most notably Herbert Hoover, were convinced that industry organization would make firms more efficient and improve competition. Labor organizers, in sharp contrast, were viewed as seeking to restrain competition. For example, calls for shorter working hours were rejected as output-restricting. Further, although theorists justified trusts by reference to economies of scale, they rejected claims of increased labor efficiency resulting from organization. Instead, theorists associated labor organization with higher costs. For example, John B. Clark wrote: "Like other vendors, the laborer can get the true value of his product and he can get no more." Under conditions of perfect competition, he deduced, the earnings of laborers and capitalists will converge. Thus, "free markets" for both labor and capital were necessary.[73] Clark's analysis suffered from two counterfactual assumptions. First, his "free markets" were already inhabited by combinations of capital, called "corporations." Second, there were no free markets, given the enormous inequality of bargaining power between natural persons who labored and corporate "persons" who hired and fired them. Nevertheless, in Clark's neoclassical framework, labor associations were seen as offering no economic benefit.

Certainly, the claims about efficiency were not self-evidently true or false. Large corporations, for example, often exceeded the minimum size for economies of large-scale production. At the same time, labor organizations might have increased productivity by shortening the work day, improving working conditions, decreasing mutual hostility and worker alienation, or taking better advantage of workers' firm-specific knowledge. Moreover, both commercial associations and labor unions sought to raise prices and manage output. Nonetheless, the new economics singled out labor unions as anticompetitive and market-restricting.

The new economics, in focusing on "the market," transformed the study of commercial transactions in numerous ways. One pivotal change was the horizontalization of competition. In short, rivalry was no longer understood as a two-dimensional process. Although horizontal rivalry among buyers or among sellers became the object of close "economic" scrutiny, vertical rivalry between buyers and sellers became a "political" question of bargaining power, of wealth distribution. Political economy was effectively partitioned into vertical and horizontal planes, into economic and political domains.

Although familiar with the theoretical currents of the day, Justice Holmes did not distinguish between the vertical and horizontal dimensions of competition. His dissenting opinions in *Vegelahn* (1896) and *Dr. Miles Medical Co.* (1910), for example, were both founded on the view that buyers and sellers compete with one another. In the earlier opinion, Holmes insisted that competition "applies to all conflicts of temporal interests," not simply "to struggles between persons of the same class competing for the same end."[74]

Two-dimensional competition appears wrong, even bizarre, to modern sensibilities. We have been taught to view the contest over wages as a question of redistributing wealth between classes rather than a question of efficiency, as a question of politics rather than a question of economics. But the separation of vertical and horizontal dimensions, of distribution and efficiency questions, is not self-evidently correct. Nor is it the product of some "objective" process of science. Indeed, the division of political economy into politics and economics was itself a political, or value-driven, transformation.[75]

Moreover, the division has not enabled economics to elude its political counterpart: The basic economic concept of allocative efficiency (producing and getting goods and services to those who most value them) cannot be defined, calculated, or even understood without direct reference to distribution of wealth. For it is the distribution of wealth that conditions taste or marginal utility. When the distribution of wealth changes, as it often does, taste or marginal utility changes, and demand also changes, signaling for a new mix of goods and services. What was an efficient allocation before is no longer relevant. But the "new economics" excludes as a political question the distribution of wealth, which is the fundamental condition for determining economic efficiency. In consequence, a black hole marks the center of the depoliticized, rigorous "new economics."[76]

Notwithstanding these limitations, marginalist or neoclassical economics verified the classical view of labor unions as harmful political associations. Only the logic changed, from classical liberty of contract to neoclassical efficiency. The first and second stages of this cultural apparatus overlapped, each one corroborating the other's sharply contrasting images of labor associations and trade associations: Whereas labor unions were seen as cost-raising, output-restricting combinations of collaborators, combinations of capital were viewed either as personified, individualized employers or as cost-lowering, output-expanding associations of competing entrepreneurs. Combinations of capital could be reasonable, as corporations under the old system of individual liberty and also as trade associations under the new economics of marginalism. Combinations of workers, however, were ideologically incorrect under both regimes.

The Cultural Rhetoric of Labor Associations

The division of classical political economy into an economics of horizontal competition and a politics of vertical wealth transfers provided a powerful framework for the third phase of differentiating trade and labor associations.

The third phase, equally influenced by the aggregate view of labor unions, was a rhetorical phenomenon. Labor unions were not only seen as vast combinations of individuals, not only as inefficient and wealth redistributing factions, but also were described as physically threatening to private property and bodily integrity. Thus, trade associations were understood as a horizontal problem, an economic issue, whose resolution called for an economic analysis of their effects on competition. Labor associations, in sharp contrast, were classed as a vertical problem, an issue of politics.

Employers and employees did not "compete"; they engaged in "struggle" or "conflict." While a trade association's activities were evaluated as (un)reasonable restraints of competition, labor union activities were summarily enjoined as causing "irreparable harm" to employers' "property." The issuance of injunctions became a commonplace in large part because an expansive notion of "property," threatened by labor violence, included the very right to do business.

Of course, both trade association and labor association activities injured someone's property rights and both involved rivalry or competition. The difference in treatment was nonetheless justified in terms that denied their fundamentally similar consequences. It was justified by the imaginative distinctions drawn between economic competition and political conflict. When, for example, did National Guardsmen or United States Army soldiers aid an independent firm in breaking up a railroad boycott ordered by John D. Rockefeller? When has a boycotted firm been permitted to hire Pinkertons to engage in violence against the boycotting firms? No instances have been recorded. Why, in sharp contrast, were such responses to "property" injury seen as legitimate in labor disputes? In short, because labor unions were positioned as oppressive political associations interfering in an otherwise economic domain of freely contracting individuals. As such, their politics were seen as dangerous—redistributive, antiindividualist, anticompetitive, violent, and alien.

In the 1890s, William H. Taft, then a federal circuit court judge, described union activities as a "danger to our whole social fabric." An ardent supporter of labor injunctions throughout his long political career, Taft characterized unionized workers generally as having "contempt for the security of private property," as "avowed socialists," most often found in "large cities where foreign labor is congested." While presiding over aspects of the brutal Pullman strike, Taft wrote to his wife that the federal marshalls "have killed only six of the mob as yet. This is hardly enough to make an impression." Taft's candid description of antilabor violence, written in a private letter, was subsequently corroborated by President Cleveland's United States Strike Commission, whose investigation and public report produced overwhelming evidence that workers were victims rather than perpetrators of violence in the Pullman strike.[77]

Nonetheless, violence was attributed to union activities. Federal judges agreed that there was "no such thing as peaceful picketing, any more than there can be chaste vulgarity, or peaceful mobbing, or lawful lynching." "It was impossible," they believed, "that a strike . . . should succeed without violence." "It is idle to talk of a peaceable strike. None such ever occurred." In the face of uncontradicted testimony that union leaders "openly discouraged conflict," Taft conjured "secret terrorism," without a shred of evidence, as the foundation for finding a threat of violent coercion.[78]

The Supreme Court majority shared this view of labor activities. In *Truax v. Corrigan* (1921), for example, Chief Justice Taft wrote that "peaceful picketing was a contradiction in terms." But *Duplex Printing v. Deering* (1921) provides the most arresting example of the violence attributed to labor association activities. Justice Pitney, writing for the Court, produced an opinion filled with the rhetoric of "class war" and "conflict," even though the strike at issue was an entirely peaceful effort by trade unionists. Referring to "threats" five times and to the need to maintain "peaceable" conditions nine times, Pitney wrote that "the sinister name of picketing" itself implied intimidation—whether threatening by force or simply by persuasion. Even nonviolent demonstrations were coercive, he concluded, because they injure the employer's property by reducing output.[79]

Justice Brandeis's dissenting opinion in *Truax* (1921) warned that labor picketing involved an entirely different sort of coercion: Employers sought injunctions not so much "to prevent property from being injured [or] to protect the owner in its use, but to endow property with an active, militant power, which would make it dominant over men. In other words, that under the guise of protecting property rights, the employer was seeking sovereign power."[80] Brandeis also understood the Court's labor relations jurisprudence as a political process. In his view, however, the Court was enforcing, rather than holding off, an oppressive regime of serfdom, a political economy of involuntary servitude.

Counterfactual images of worker hordes massed against individual employers stand behind the views expressed in the Supreme Court's labor opinions, even after the 1914 Clayton Act's purported exemption of labor unions from the antitrust laws.[81] Whether or not progressives like Justice Brandeis and Senator Robert LaFollette better expressed majority sentiments, conservatives like Warren G. Harding won the presidency and appointed like-minded judges and administrators. The conservatives' vision of worker hordes erased that of the individual employee's economic plight, and portrayed her instead as a foot soldier in a massed army of workers.

Two incidents reflect the tenor of the times. First, there was the notorious Bisbee deportation, an example of the period's widespread antilabor vigilantism, sometimes assisted by the United States Department of Justice. Employers and their agents, allegedly armed with government-issued weapons, forced more than a thousand striking copper miners and their sympathizers into freight cars, releasing them in the New Mexico desert and threatening them with bodily harm should they return to Arizona. In a lawsuit ultimately argued by Charles Evans Hughes before the Supreme Court in 1920, Chief Justice White concluded that no federally protected rights were injured. The second incident was the railroad shopman's strike in 1922. Federal courts were directly implicated, granting the railroads almost three hundred antistrike injunctions, for the most part in *ex parte* hearings, based solely on uncorroborated statements by railroad representatives.[82]

This morality play of good against evil, this bourgeois drama of individual entrepreneurs fighting the alien union masses, like Custer's "last stand" or Davey Crockett at the Alamo, dramatized and legitimated the violence, attributing it to the labor unions—the aliens swarming America's last lines of defense. The violence of employers and government agents was seen as purely and devoutly defensive. Moreover, labor unions could not turn to federal courts, either for impartial hearings or protection from the virtuous violence of employers. In the view of federal judges and policy makers, as well as those who supported Warren G. Harding and his Republican successors, labor unions embodied the worst dangers of politics. Even more threatening than unregulated majoritarianism, more dangerous than legislative "takings" of private property, labor unions incarnated the menace of mobocracy, the destruction of individual liberty and property rights. Clearly, trade associations were of a different order. They were cooperative economic enterprises, motivated by "industrial statesmanship" to improve competitive conditions and, in the process, to serve the public interest.[83]

While Herbert Hoover's trade association movement was the hallmark of the cooperative competition era, labor associations served as its lightning rod. Even within the precincts of labor there was conflict—conflict between native-born, English-speaking members of trade unions and unskilled workers, largely immigrants and blacks, who produced, for example, ten million Model "T" Fords between 1915 and 1927. Indeed, in the decade preceding 1915, almost eleven million immigrants entered the United States from eastern and southern Europe. They were seen as bringing with them more than their willingness to work for low wages, more than their foreign tongues and tastes. These unruly masses also carried with them the violent tendencies that ignited Europe's World War I in 1914 and the dangerous ideas that inspired Russia's October Revolution three years later. When the United States entered World War I in 1917, German ancestry provoked particular fears, as did Bolshevik affiliations. Oregon, Nebraska, and other states, for example, passed legislation prohibiting the teaching of all modern languages except English in their schools. Congress passed the Espionage Act of 1918, which criminalized interference with army recruitment or mobilization, and which gave the Postmaster General censorship powers. The Sedition Act amended the 1918 legislation by criminalizing any "word or act" opposing the war effort. Even five years after the Versailles Treaty, Congress passed the Johnson-Reed Act (1924) setting low quotas for entry from eastern and southern Europe.[84]

Overlapping affiliations among labor associations, radical political groups, anti-war protest groups, and organizations working for black civil rights were well known (and, perhaps, exaggerated). Eugene V. Debs, after all, was not only a labor leader jailed for contempt of court, not only an anti-war dissident jailed for violation of the Espionage Act, but the five-time Socialist Party candidate for President of the United States—the last time while a prisoner in the Atlanta federal penitentiary. But Debs was just one of numerous war protestors prosecuted under the Espionage Act, though his particular case was a *cause célèbre* in progressive circles.[85] In 1919, four cases reached the Supreme Court, each of them raising arguments that the Statute violated the defendants' First Amendment right of free speech. The opinions in these cases reflect more than the overlapping affiliations feared among labor unions and political radicals. They reflect as well a political economy of speech rights unreceptive to "free trade in ideas" during an era defined by a commitment to unfettered commercial enterprise.

The Political Economy of Speech: "Free Trade in Ideas"

Like similar arguments made in several earlier labor picketing cases, free speech claims in the 1919 Espionage Act cases ultimately failed. Nonetheless, they represent the Supreme Court's first attempts to grapple with First Amendment freedoms as rights not entirely contained by the English common law. In consequence, these cases have been identified as the origin of modern free speech jurisprudence.[86]

The Court adopted Justice Holmes's formulation—his now-familiar view that speech is protected unless it presents a "clear and present danger" of something Congress can legitimately prohibit. The curiosity in the cluster of cases is Holmes's precipitous shift—from the *Schenck* majority's craftsman of the "clear and present danger" test to, later that very session in *Abrams*, the dissenter, who called instead for "free trade in ideas" and "competition in the market."[87] Why were Holmes's free-contractarian colleagues on the Court so quick to adopt his "clear and present danger" test and yet so resolute in rejecting "free trade in ideas" and "competition in the market"—metaphors clearly evocative of the laissez-faire constitutionalism expressed in *Lochner* (1905) as well as the classical Rule of Reason adopted in *Standard Oil* (1911)?

This section opens with an investigation of this question, and approaches it as a matter of political economy. I begin by reconstructing the rhetorical structure of speech jurisprudence before the 1919 cases and the transformation that followed—a change implacably liberal in its commitment to separate public and private, political and economic domains. In simple terms, the Court majorities in those cases treated speech as a political activity and thus as subject to state police power, power from which economic activities were relatively free. But the picture was not so simple, because the Court did not treat all speech as a political activity subject to government ordinance. Some speech was protected as a valuable economic activity. Not only in the informational activities of trade associations, but also in the emerging social institution of advertising, new forms of speech put pressure on the reigning orthodoxy of separate economic and political domains. By the mid-1920s, antitrust policy treated economic speech, practiced by trade associations, as procompetitive conduct. In sum, "free trade in ideas" became a commercial canon long before it would become the metaphorical key to constitutional protection of political speech.

In the years following World War I, although political speech was constrained by an expansive interpretation of Holmes's "clear and present danger" test, mass advertising was transforming the economic domain. The "advertising man" became the self-appointed spokesman for the "industrial statesmanship" attributed to trade associations and, more generally, to commercial enterprise. Moreover, the advertising industry became the arbiter of popular taste, extolling a new "democracy of goods" and, in the process, commodifying the political rhetoric of participatory government. Finally, the impact of mass advertising drained neoclassical economics of its explanatory power. That is, mass advertising called into question the power of price theory to describe consumer and producer behavior. Advertising, after all, accomplished nothing if not brand or class identification.[88] The social institution of advertising would come to dominate the marketplace of ideas.

Speech Jurisprudence as Political Economy

In the pre-1919 speech cases, the Court's deaf ear to complaints against majoritarian regulation of individual speech was, perhaps, surprising, because common-law theory generally did not differentiate between conduct and speech at a time when *Lochner*ian ideology attributed great value to individual freedom of conduct. When they were differentiated, speech received special treatment only insofar as it was protected from prior restraint. Prior restraint was permissible, however, when the speech embodied some "bad tendency," when it threatened to evoke some harmful conduct subject to the state's legitimate police power. In *Gompers v. Buck's Stove & Range Co.* (1911), for example, a unanimous Court upheld an injunction ordering the American Federation of Labor not to publicize that the employer was on the union's "We don't patronize" and "Unfair" lists. Calling such speech "verbal acts [with] a force not inhering in the words themselves," Justice Lucius Quintus Cincinnatus Lamar treated speech as conduct, as a common-law attempt or conspiracy to commit an unlawful act. Hence, the "verbal act [is] as much subject to injunction as the use of any other force whereby property is unlawfully damaged."[89]

Thus were "verbal acts" enjoined, whether the threatened damage resulted from words written in union lists or words enacted in state legislation. Neither unions nor state legislatures, I have already shown, were seen as economic actors. The images portraying them and the Supreme Court doctrine regulating their activities placed them both into a separate political sphere. Unions were political associations whose "verbal acts" in the economic sphere destroyed private property and threatened majoritarian tyranny. The very term "union," not widely adopted by labor associations until the Civil War era, resonated with the "free labor" ideology of the antislavery Union. By the late nineteenth century in America, however, such positive political valences had turned negative. Unions—whether political or labor—were no longer seen, particularly in the imagery of Supreme Court jurisprudence and of other elite policy makers, as liberating but rather as menacing. "Free labor" became a maxim expressing anti-collectivist sentiments. Unions were envisioned as specters of oppressive collectivity threatening a private, largely economic sphere of free individuals.[90]

In sharp contrast, "verbal acts" associated with economic activities were seen as less and less threatening, as increasingly valuable activities in the "new competition" theory promoting the trade association movement. Recall Arthur J. Eddy's influential *The New Competition* (1914), which extolled the virtues of cooperation and explicitly characterized traditional competition as war. Cooperative competition, founded in notions of industrial statesmanship and managerial expertise, required the production, sharing, and dissemination of information about the industry.

Indeed, the Court's approval of trade associations stemmed from changed attitudes about information and ideas in economic markets. Before that approval, the Court in *American Column & Lumber* (1921) found the hardwood trade association's informational activities illegal precisely because the association's manager of statistics was the "single skilled interpreter" of market information. That is, he persuaded association members to accept his ideas about the proper course of conduct. If analyzed under the rubric of free speech, his "verbal acts" would have presented a "clear and present danger" of something Congress could legitimately prohibit—price-fixing. The post-"free market in ideas" Holmes dissented, arguing that the association activities not only made good economic sense but merited First Amendment protection. Four years later, in *Maple Flooring* (1925), the economic danger of price-fixing would no longer persuade a Court majority that such trade association activities should be prohibited under the Sherman Act. Dangerous ideas—"verbal acts"—were now to be tolerated, indeed, encouraged, in the marketplace for goods and services. In contrast, that term's *Gitlow* (1925) decision recognized political speech as a liberty interest only in the abstract, finding that the particular speech in question—general statements about "class struggle" and "political strikes"—was too dangerous to merit constitutional protection.[91]

At the turn of the century, amid the common-law framework for free speech doctrine, long before the trade association cases, there had already been indications of solicitude toward commercial speech. In *American School of Magnetic Healing* (1902), the Court held that the Postmaster General could not refuse to deliver payments sent for Christian Science "treatments." General McAnnulty stopped mail delivery because he determined that the American School of Magnetic Healing was "engaged in conducting a scheme or device for obtaining money through the mails by some means of false and fraudulent pretenses, representations, and promises." Such conduct, the government argued, violated recent congressional legislation aimed at stopping mail fraud. Sidestepping discussion of First Amendment freedoms, Justice Peckham wrote that the government's enforcement of the statute was improper because

Magnetic Healing's activities involved not fraud but rather "mere matters of opinion upon subjects which are not capable of proof as to their falsity." There was absolutely no analysis of the utterances' "bad tendency," as there would have been had the "verbal acts" been seen as political.[92]

In sum, the common-law doctrines applied to arguments raising free speech claims treated words as deeds when they exhibited some "bad tendency" or, in Holmes's words, when they created "a clear and present danger" of something perceived as summoning the state's police power. Whatever the relationship between these two doctrines as understood by Holmes or his colleagues, both were framed in political rhetoric. Whether motivated by concern about the destruction of property or some other threat associated with state police power, the Court granted political majorities broad powers to regulate political speech. When the speech involved commercial enterprise, however, the Court was less likely to look for some "bad tendency" or "clear and present danger." In short, commercial speech was seen as less dangerous and thus more worthy of protection.

The dominant political rhetoric of speech jurisprudence, along with a recessive economic alternative, formed the discursive context for the Court's cluster of speech opinions in 1919. Thus, the Court's political economy of free speech, expressed in the "clear and present danger" doctrine, carried forward theory found in the English common law that provided the ground for its earlier approach to speech rights. The Court's treatment of free speech arguments, even after the 1919 cluster of Espionage Act opinions, however, lacked the ideological urgency that inspired the Court's laissez-faire constitutionalism, its common-law regime founded in liberty of contract. That is, the early speech cases did not proceed from the kind of commitment to individual liberty seen in *Lochner* and *Standard Oil*. Missing from the speech opinions was *Lochner*'s logic of antagonism between the vulnerable individual and the powerful state, and concern about oppressive majoritarianism at a time when the logic of individual liberty provided the rhetorical touchstone for the Supreme Court's distrust of legislative regulation of commercial conduct. In *Meyer v. Nebraska* (1923), a decision that found unconstitutional a xenophobic statute prohibiting the teaching of modern foreign languages, Justice McReynolds' majority would define liberty more broadly than freedom of contract:

> not merely freedom from bodily restraint but also the right of the individual to contract, to engage in any of the common occupations of life, to acquire useful knowledge, to marry, establish a home and bring up children, to worship God according to the dictates of his own conscience, and generally to enjoy those privileges long recognized at common law as essential to the orderly pursuit of happiness by free men.

Still, the list did not include speech rights. Two years later, just as the Court was approving the cooperative competition practiced by trade associations, Justice Edward T. Sanford finally declared that individual liberty under the Fourteenth Amendment does incorporate speech rights. Nonetheless,

Sanford's declaration in *Gitlow v. New York* (1925) was not enough to protect from criminal prosecution the defendants who made the First Amendment claim, defendants whose *Left Wing Manifesto*, calling for "class struggle" and "political strikes," was somehow found to pose a "clear and present danger" of violent government overthrow.[93]

The War to End All Wars: Political and Economic Speech Practices

These threads of speech jurisprudence were part, perhaps a relatively small part, of a larger cultural transformation in attitudes toward speech—both political and commercial. In the decades preceding America's entry into World War I, a new outlook toward words and ideas accompanied the emergence of mass advertising as a social institution. President Woodrow Wilson's administration of World War I marked a crucial juncture in the growth of advertising as a social institution with power and responsibility.

Although modern advertising had emerged in the late nineteenth century, the Wilson administration's unprecedented deployment of mass advertising in the war effort helped transform cultural attitudes toward advertising in much the same way that the War Industry Board hastened the organization of industries by trade associations and legitimized cooperative competition. The Wilson administration's advertising activities included both traditional politics and innovative finance, both wartime propaganda and mass marketing of war bonds. One year before Congress passed the Sedition Act of 1918, President Wilson issued an executive order forming the Committee on Public Information, which managed the government's wartime propaganda. Its *Official Bulletin* was the authoritative compendium of regulations, executive orders, agency publications, and court decisions affecting the conduct of the war.[94] Together with a series of executive orders, Wilson's Committee on Public Information and congressional legislation effectively controlled the flow of information and the dissemination of opinion about the war.

Under the powerful Committee on Public Information, the government entered into a joint venture with the advertising industry, organized as the Division of Advertising. From the advertising industry came an army of volunteers—artists, writers, lithographers, and others—who applied their talents in a widespread advertising program to enlist military recruits and, for the first time, to sell war bonds. Wilson had been advised that it would be impossible to sell the $3 billion in government bonds necessary to begin financing the war because there were not enough investors—fewer than 300,000. Looking to the recent success of the British government in advertising National War Bonds, Wilson emulated their program. The American advertising effort attracted six million subscribers. Indeed, the last series of war loans advertised after the Armistice, the "Victory Loan," attracted more than twenty million subscribers—one-fifth of the country's population. The mass advertising approach to floating war bonds was a shocking success.[95]

The war gave advertising men (and they were men) the "opportunity not only to render a valuable patriotic service," according to one influential ad agency, "but also to reveal to a wide circle of influential men . . . the real character of advertising and the important function which it performs." Their war effort had shown that "[i]t is possible to sway the minds of whole populations, change their habits of life, create belief, practically universal, in any policy or idea." Advertising industry spokesmen and proselytizers trumpeted the power of advertising to shape taste and opinion, and thus, to overcome the dreaded business cycle of oscillating demand. Cultural attitudes toward advertising were changing at a deeper level as well.[96]

That change, in some part associated with the "patriotic emotion" summoned by "war advertising," is captured in the *Encyclopedia Britannica*'s entries for "Advertisement"—the first version in its prewar eleventh edition (1910), the second in its postwar supplement to the eleventh edition of 1922. The pre-war entry describes "the process of . . . purchasing publicity" as a business "of relatively recent origin if it be regarded as a serious adjunct to other phases of commercial activity." The author begins his historical treatment of advertising with the following statement: "As the primeval man's wolfish antipathy to the stranger of another pack gradually diminished, and as intercourse spread the infection of larger desires, the trapper could no longer satisfy his more complicated wants by mere exchange of his pelts for his lowland neighbor's corn and oil." The obvious allusion to venereal disease betrays an ambivalent attitude toward advertising and commerce—both corporeal desire and fear of dangerous consequences—couched in a rather ascetic notion of virtue. The fear, it seems, was the spread of "larger desires."[97]

Twelve years and one world war later, *Britannica*'s new and revised entry for "Advertisement" lauded the advertising industry's "public service" during the First World War. In this light, advertising reflected not only "better quality" in writing and artistry but better "character." With "Truth in Advertising" as its credo, "advertising had become a business of high principles and well-defined ethics." Advertising offered "information," "public education." "To be effective it must be a sincere expression of the character of the advertiser." The new virtue attributed to advertising was truth. Thus, there could be confidence that "advertising is no weapon for dark causes and no advocate for unworthy goods."[98]

As attitudes changed, so did industry self-image and rhetorical practices. Advertising spokesmen saw their industry as engaged in a "cultural mission . . . to counsel and uplift" consumers, to educate them in a common culture of consumerism, producing "one people in ideals." In contrast to the persistent ethnic flavor of labor unions and urban neighborhoods, national advertising, especially in the foreign language press, was hailed as "the great Americanizer." The director of the American Association of Foreign Language Newspapers went so far as to declare that advertising in immigrant communities was "the answer to Bolshevism." Although advertising agents and their clients were surely interested, first and foremost, in successful campaigns and increased sales, the discourse of advertising reflected a self-image of industrial statesmanship, suffused with "high principles."[99]

In the mid-1920s, Edward Bernays, an advertising executive and author, described advertising and public relations as "the competition of ideas," as "an essential democratic process, for then the public can make its own choice." "It is within the structure of business," maintained Edward Filene, the Boston haberdasher and "mouthpiece for industrial America," that "the wisest and best leadership is actually being chosen by people"—that is, by consumers. Hence, mass consumption was promoted as the solution to "class thinking." A well-known advertisement of the 1920s presented, as written testimony to the Parker Pen's quality, signatures by labor leader Samuel Gompers, British author and socialist H. G. Wells, and the presidents of U.S. Steel and the B.&O. Railroad. There could be no better evidence of consumerism's noble power to produce consensus.[100] There was no better place than the marketplace of ideas.

The advertising industry's mission, informed by the economic logic of marginal utility, was to shape consumer preferences for corporate clients. Its rhetoric, however, was often political, insinuating and sometimes explicitly promising that a secular gospel of consensus, consumer democracy, and progress would defuse the dangers of class antagonism, ethnic insularity, and political dissent. Thus did the new social institution of mass advertising, with its commodification of conflict, its consumerization of factional politics, re-present the pressures of new social and economic patterns. Intensified after the stock market crash of 1929, such pressures would pulse through the arteries of party politics, speech jurisprudence, and economic theory. Herbert Hoover would abandon his Republican Party platform and pursue ideas to combat the Depression, ideas more often associated with the New Deal, such as the Reconstruction Finance Corporation, massive public works projects, direct relief to the unemployed, and assistance to agriculture. In 1931, the Supreme Court, led by recently appointed Chief Justice Charles Evans Hughes, would strike down state legislation on explicit grounds of First Amendment speech. Still, the rhetoric would remain political: The statutes were unconstitutional because they sought to prohibit speech innocent of "a clear and present danger." "Free trade in ideas" would remain the image for commercial advertising, replete with comforting political overtones.[101]

Epilogue: The Emergence of Postclassical Economics

Given its view of markets as driven by price competition, neoclassical economics could not account for the commercial practices of mass advertisers and trade associations. First of all, advertisers, even during the ensuing Great Depression, derived their marketing strategies from the assumption that consumers did not make purchasing decisions based solely on price. Second, trade associations institutionalized information exchange and other sorts of cooperation that seemed to conflict with the theory's exclusive logic of competition. Finally, persistent industry concentration did not comport with the neoclassical dichotomy of pure competition and pure monopoly. Most industries were neither. Moreover, the traditional property rights underlying neoclassical economics did not offer a useful framework for understanding relations between owners (shareholders) and their agents (managers) within the large bureaucratic corporations that had become so common.

These shortcomings did not go entirely unnoticed. Indeed, two paradigm-shattering books appeared at the margin between Hoover's cooperative competition and Roosevelt's New Deal. Edward H. Chamberlin's *The Theory of Monopolistic Competition* (1933) would soon revise economic discourse by showing how a seeming contradiction—monopolistic competition—was not only possible but likely. Chamberlin's work was so influential because it provided a pair of new economic concepts to explain what neoclassical theory could not—the practices of cooperative competition and mass advertising. Chamberlin's new economic concepts were oligopoly and monopolistic competition. The second book was Adolf Berle and Gardiner Means's *The Modern Corporation and Private Property* (1932), which documented both the concentration of American industry and the discretion of corporate managers to pursue goals other than maximizing return to shareholders, who, after all, own the corporations and employ the managers. Finding that traditional private property rights were an inadequate mechanism for owners to control the discretion of corporate managers, Berle and Means called for public regulation of the sort associated with Franklin Roosevelt's New Deal. Together, these two books reshaped economic discourse, competition policies, and the relations between them.[102]

Most markets, Chamberlin observed, were neither purely competitive nor purely monopolistic. Instead, all markets reflected some of each element. Chamberlin distinguished two kinds of "synthesis" of the "fundamental forces of competition and monopoly." The first is oligopoly, meaning a market with few sellers and an identical product, such as newsprint, steel ingot, or granulated sugar. The second synthesis is monopolistic competition, signifying a market with many sellers and differentiated products, such as stereo equipment, cosmetics, or designer jeans.[103] Competition between Coke and Pepsi, or between Post and Kellogg breakfast cereals, reflects a combination of oligopoly and monopolistic competition.

In a sense, Chamberlin's oligopoly theory only formalized the know-how behind the trade association movement, taught twenty years earlier by management consultants such as Charles R. Stevenson. Yet, by making plain the economic logics driving modern entrepreneurs, Chamberlin's rigorous analysis exploded the neoclassical assumption about unmonopolized markets as well-oiled price mechanisms. He demonstrated the rationality of cooperation for firms in oligopolies—that is, in markets with few rivals. In a perfect oligopoly, Chamberlin maintained, it is economically rational to anticipate a rival's quick reaction. For example, if one seller is considering a price decrease, it is foolish to ignore the likelihood of immediate, responsive price decreases by one's rivals. Should that occur, everyone will be worse off because an industry-wide price decrease would leave everyone with the same market share but at a lower price. If rivals act logically and regard "their total influence on price, indirect as well as direct," he concluded, the "result is the same as though there were a monopolistic agreement between them." Without a monopoly and without a cartel, it is the logic of oligopoly, the recognition of mutual interest, that produces a monopoly price.[104]

Chamberlin's oligopoly theory introduced an economic logic of cooperation to explain the lack of price competition in industries with few firms as well as those with trade associations—that is, industries organized to act as though they were oligopolies. His theory of monopolistic competition introduced a new economic logic of rivalry to explain mass advertising and, more generally, the alternatives to price competition in industries with many firms. "[I]f any significant basis exists for distinguishing the goods (or services) of one seller from those of another," then those sellers engage in monopolistic competition. A basis of distinction may be a "patent or trademark, quality, packaging, design, color, style, or even conditions of sale, including location, way of doing business, reputation, or personal links." "[I]t is evident," Chamberlin observed, "that virtually all products are differentiated."[105]

How, then, is monopolistic competition different from the competition of neoclassical theory, which posits that markets with standardized products and large numbers of sellers will produce price competition? And how is it different from oligopoly? What did Chamberlin have to say about the price mechanism as supreme allocator of goods and services in competitive markets with differentiated products?

In a perfectly competitive market, sellers have only two choices—sell all that they can produce at the market price or withdraw from the market. Powerless to affect the market price, all sellers who remain maximize profits by selling at the market price. In a perfectly oligopolistic market, all sellers recognize the profit-maximizing logic of decreasing production. Each withholds supply as part of a coordinated effort to lower industry supply in order to raise the industry price. Sellers in both competitive and oligopolistic markets, however, take industry demand as a fact. In sharp contrast, sellers in markets characterized by monopolistic competition seek to alter demand. Each seller seeks to persuade buyers (or, perhaps, help them recognize) that his product is better and thus more valuable than its substitutes, and, ultimately, that it is worth a higher price (or worth more at the same price).

Each seller engaged in monopolistic competition, according to Chamberlin, deploys some combination of three strategic alternatives to distinguish his product from those of his rivals. First, the seller can meet demand simply by competing on price. Second, he can meet demand by changing the "nature of his product"—that is, he can offer something better for the same price. Or, third, he can seek to alter demand by changing the buyer's impression of his product through "advertising outlays." The more successful a seller is in impressing buyers that there is no good substitute for his product (that is, the less elastic demand becomes), the more customer loyalty he accrues. Product differentiation succeeds and monopoly profits flow when loyal customers would rather pay higher prices than switch to a substitute.[106]

Chamberlin drew a normative distinction between changing a product and changing a buyer's impression of a product, between research and development, and advertising and promotion. That is, although he associated product change with innovation, with progress, he saw much product advertising as "useless differentiation," as manipulating surface features—signs, marks, symbols, words. Monopolistic competition, it appeared, was transforming markets for goods and services into a commercial marketplace of ideas and images.[107]

Chamberlin's concern was the proliferation of difference without innovation, form without substance. Joseph A. Schumpeter, who was Chamberlin's mentor at Harvard, took the theory of monopolistic competition one step further and, in so doing, radically shifted its tone. For Schumpeter, the proliferation of products was not the problem but the solution. He declared in *Capitalism, Socialism and Democracy* (1942), "The fundamental impulse that keeps the capitalist engine in motion comes from the *new* consumers' goods, the *new* methods of production or transportation, the *new* markets, the *new* forms of industrial organization that capitalist enterprise creates." In glorifying the "new," he dismissed with a stroke of his pen the importance neoclassical economists attributed to the price mechanism. Moreover, he did not concern himself with Chamberlin's fine distinctions between innovation and differentiation, between meeting and altering demand. Indeed, Schumpeter insisted that it was the "new," regardless of its substance, that drives capitalism relentlessly to increase output and raise standards of living. Thus, Schumpeter contended that price competition was far less important than the actual and potential competition of new products and processes. "A perennial gale of creative destruction," he maintained, was the economic force that brought progress while destroying monopoly power at its foundation. Good economic policy, Schumpeter concluded, results from understanding the dynamics of change, not the statics of existing economic arrangements.[108] The mere threat of the "new" served as the unseen seer, the invisible hand of potential competition, the radar-eluding Stealth bomber of economic warfare. One moment tranquility and the next, utter devastation. Today, monopoly; tomorrow, bankruptcy.

In short, Schumpeter rejected the value of both neoclassical price theory and Chamberlin's re-visions. Yet, in two significant respects, he propped his own theory of dyanamic competition on neoclassical assumptions about how firms and markets work. First of all, in arguing for his familiar claim that innovation requires the stability, high profits, and technical expertise found in monopolies, Schumpeter considered only the neoclassical extremes of monopoly and "a perfectly competitive industry." Avoiding even a reference to the postclassical alternatives of oligopoly and monopolistic competition cited earlier in the book, Schumpeter could easily portray monopoly as the condition precedent for innovation. Second, Schumpeter's preference for monopoly was based on the assumption that monopolies produce monopoly profits. That assumption had already been called into question by Berle and Means.[109]

In *The Modern Corporation and Private Property*, Adolf Berle and Gardiner Means presented a blend of business history, legal history, and empirical economics to support their claim that managers of large bureaucratic corporations were not driven by the neoclassical logic of maximizing returns to owners. They demonstrated that the traditional unity of property ownership and control no longer obtained in large corporations: Large, widely dispersed, unorganized groups of shareholders had given up control to small, organized groups of corporate managers. Owners in name only, shareholders retained merely a right to residual profits. Thus, traditional private property rights of ownership were an inadequate mechanism for intracorporate control, for ensuring that managers did not divert corporate profits to their own salaries and to other personal advantages as well. Moreover, industry concentration, with its oligopoly logic of cooperation, eliminated competition as the extracorporate mechanism for disciplining management. By these lights, Berle and Means called for a dangerous third category of entitlement—not protecting shareholders or rewarding corporate managers, but serving the public interest. The modern corporation, they insisted, should be recognized for what it is: "a system of community obligations," a relational web of diverse interests, including widespread ownership and networks of workers, consumers, and suppliers. Taking Thorstein Veblen's vision of engineer/managers one step further, Berle and Means called for a "neutral technocracy"—corporate management by industrial and social engineers—to balance this diverse community of interests. Much as Justices Holmes and Brandeis had envisioned property rights in their dissenting opinions in *International News Service* (1918), Berle and Means redefined the modern corporation as a combination of public interests and private rights.[110]

The implications were unmistakable: We could no longer count on competition as a self-sustaining economic policy. The logic of neoclassical price theory and its promise of economic efficiency no longer comported with the workings of actual markets. How radical was this departure from neoclassical economic theory? It was so far out of the orthodoxy that Ronald Coase, in his "Theory of the Firm" (1937) (treated like a religious relic by the Chicago School's 1970s generation of neoclassicists), made no reference to Berle and Means. It was so dangerous that some sixty years later, Berle and Means are misread as calling for the return of control to shareholders.[111] But they did nothing of the sort. Their book documented the need and thus provided legitimacy for early New Deal legislation, including not only the securities legislation of 1933 and 1934 but also the National Industrial Recovery Act and the Agricultural Adjustment Act. Indeed, the legislative history of the National Industrial Recovery Act is replete with references to the kind of "community obligations" and "neutral technocracy" recommended by Berle and Means. The discourse of postclassical economics, with eye-opening concepts such as oligopoly, monopolistic competition, innovation, and corporate control, not only unlocked a rhetorical gateway to the New Deal but also expanded the boundaries of modern competition policy for the remainder of the century.

3

The New Deal's Political Economy, 1933–1948: From Organic Body Politic to Unified Body Economic

The New Deal is understood by historians, political scientists, economists, legal scholars, and other students of political economy as two New Deals. The early New Deal, identified most of all with the National Industrial Recovery Act, is seen as a dangerous episode, as the collectivist impulse that failed. This brief period of central planning, as it is viewed, was already a national fiasco when the Supreme Court handed down the unanimous *ALA Schechter Poultry* (1935) decision, which held the NIRA unconstitutional. Within minutes of the decision, Justice Brandeis was heard to say to Tommy Corcoran, one of Franklin Roosevelt's close advisors, "This is the end of this business of centralization, and I want you to go back and tell the President that we're not going to let this government centralize everything. It's come to an end."[1] Roosevelt, and Congress, would take heed of Brandeis's warning. Indeed, the later New Deal's turn toward decentralized planning, toward competitive markets as economic regulator, was symbolized by an Antitrust Division in the Department of Justice. Yale law professor Thurman Arnold would lead the division's assault on the economy's collectivist *mentalité*, cultivated at least as early as Herbert Hoover's regime of trade associationalism.

In the twenty years preceding Franklin Roosevelt's presidency, the political economy of associationalism inspired by Herbert Hoover, first as Secretary of Commerce and later as President, produced a series of problems and resolutions. Those problems and resolutions not only reflected material conditions but also illuminated the period's freedom-of-contract ideology, with all its brilliant contradictions. As I discuss in chapter 2, it was a time governed by the dilemma of individual liberty. This dilemma produced a volatile compound of competition policies and constitutional jurisprudence, in the process throwing off unstable formulations of property rights that provoked radically different public policy responses to the trade association and labor movements—policies favoring the former and maligning the latter. Moreover, as all dilemmas do, this one issued divergent legal doctrines, including the

Supreme Court's discrepant treatment of trade and labor associations, and public and private price-fixing. Such discordant strains not only reverberated through Supreme Court doctrines and federal policy initiatives but were repeated in the intellectual themes and public discourse of political economy in the first third of the twentieth century.

The Hoover administration, confronted by the unrelenting economic depression that followed the stock market's collapse in 1929, transgressed its libertarian ideology in seeking passage of public welfare legislation. Nonetheless, throughout Hoover's single-term presidency, the dominant ideology remained laissez-faire; the welfare legislation was seen as a stopgap measure rather than part of some fundamental change in political economy.

Franklin Roosevelt's presidency inaugurated a new era whose policies and doctrines would revolve around the spindle of equality. This commitment to equality sprang from its predecessor, the freedom-of-contract ideology that formally assumed equality between transacting parties and questioned that assumption only in narrowly defined, extraordinary circumstances. But the New Deal introduced a *primary* commitment to *substantive* equality that would turn freedom of contract on its head. Henceforth, the promotion of relational equality—substantive equality between parties to a transaction—would revise the very ideas of property rights and competition, first in New Deal legislation and later in Supreme Court doctrine. In the process, this primary commitment to substantive equality would produce its own conundrum and its own array of incompatible resolutions.

The New Dealers grasped economic inequality as a fundamental social problem and viewed political action—whether inspired by the statist impulse attributed to the National Industrial Recovery Act of 1933 or the new liberal sentiment seen in the antitrust revival that followed, whether expressed in the early rhetoric of "fair competition" or the later turn to "free competition"—as the best prospect for its resolution. Although historians have paid close attention to Roosevelt's demand-side fiscal policy, to the distributive aspects (what I term the equality and property side) of the New Deal, relatively little has been said about the images of fair and free competition underlying New Deal initiatives (what I call the equality and competition side).[2] This chapter takes up the questions of fair and free competition, and, through that inquiry, the conundrum of economic (in)equality.

Without disputing the mainstream historical understanding of two New Deals,[3] I nonetheless take issue with the dominant view in several respects. First and foremost, I find that the New Deal *throughout* reflected efforts to establish free competition in the important sense of competition free from private economic power. Both the initial turn to state-supervised enterprise and the return to antitrust, both the rhetorics of "fair" and "free" competition, revolved around this spindle of equality. New Deal policy makers, from Gardiner Means to Thurman Arnold to Justice William O. Douglas, struggled to accommodate a guiding principle, an ethic, of equality.

Second, the ethic of equality was not limited to the microeconomic notion of market power, the horizontal relations between rivals. Rather, it was informed by a sensitivity to verticality, a heightened concern for the relative bargaining power of buyers and sellers—whether the transaction involved labor, corporate stock, or canned beans, whether intracorporate relations or an open-market exchange. Liberty of contract, after all, had always reflected, first and foremost, an image of transactions between individual buyers and sellers, not competition among rivals. New Dealers sought to take into account the relational inequalities assumed away in the liberty-of-contract ideology inspiring their predecessors.

Third, the early New Deal brought labor unions into the associational process because policy makers envisioned competition as organic, in terms both different from and more capacious than their Hooverian predecessors. In my estimation, this policy of inclusion had significance beyond recognizing certain fundamental rights of labor: Competition in the early New Deal took on a politicized, interest-group hue more commonly associated with the 1960s. But in contrast to the political rivalry—the zero-sum game of winners and losers associated with the 1960s—the early New Deal embodied an organic vision of a body politic, a positive-sum game of winners and winners. The ethical center of that vision was the political norm of equal representation. The process was understood as deliberation, not adversarial combat. In this ethical light, the early New Deal, particularly the NIRA, can be understood as a failed experiment in participatory republicanism rather than centralized planning.

The later New Deal both fragmented and reunified this specter of an organic body politic. The fragmentation isolated labor, consumer, shareholder, small business, and large corporate interests, statute by statute, into their own administrative arenas, their own agencies. At the same time, however, those statutes, the agencies they empowered, and the Supreme Court doctrine that followed, were all drawn into a new organic body, a new image of a unified public interest: the consumer. The rhetoric of consumerism, familiar since the 1880s, now offered a new vision, a new language to fuse fragmented interests, to negotiate conflicting producer claims, to balance competition policy and private property rights.

In sum, classical liberty-of-contract ideology was extended and thereby radically revised. Beginning with early New Deal legislation, liberty was reimagined as not only depending upon substantive equality but also demanding government mediation of economic relations to produce and protect equality. It was this progressive rendition of participatory republicanism that inspired the shift from Hoover's brand of corporatism, framed in an informal, shadow bureaucracy within the Commerce Department, to Roosevelt's formal, legislatively mandated body politic under the National Recovery Administration. New Dealers believed that liberty entailed something other than protection from majoritarian oppression. Their reformulation of classical liberalism led them to conclude that citizens should be able to call upon political processes to referee fairness in economic relations, to free them from the oppressive effects of private collectives with great economic power.

Code-drafting and enforcement provisions under the Recovery Act would embody this egalitarian impulse in the idea of "fair competition." But the "free competition" policy of the later New Deal would also embody an egalitarian ethic, and perhaps in a more radical way: Despite Thurman Arnold's antitrust metaphor of a traffic cop merely teaching the rules of the road to those in the stream of commerce, strong antitrust enforcement would require insistent cops and committed prosecutors. In consequence, Arnold's young Antitrust Division, representing "the public interest," would put business interests and government into an adversarial relationship. This distrustful relationship, reminiscent of Woodrow Wilson's New Freedom platform as well as the old Literalists' antitrust crusade against restraints of trade, contrasted sharply with the cooperative regimes overseen by Roosevelt's NRA and Hoover's Commerce Department. It was a return to liberalism's adversarial ethic, its vision of individuals threatened by collectives—but with an egalitarian twist. The threatening collectives were no longer oppressive sovereigns or political majorities. They were powerful, private economic organizations. And individuals were no longer seen as virtuous citizens but as powerless consumers.

By 1937, the Supreme Court would acknowledge that broader political oversight of economic life was legitimate at both state and federal levels. The sharp jurisprudential line separating economic and political spheres, as well as its ideological stylus—freedom of contract—would yield to a conception of two domains with permeable, if not open, frontiers. Moreover, the Court would adopt the egalitarian ethic propelling the New Dealers' revisionist liberalism. Court opinions written by Roosevelt's majority would also reflect a change in jurisprudential style—the balancing of public and private interests advocated in Justice Brandeis's *International News Service* (1918) dissent and his *Chicago Board of Trade* (1918) opinion for the Court. Together, the ethic of equality and the jurisprudence of balancing interests posed a threat of unrestrained majoritarianism: A primary commitment to substantive equality could tip the balance toward a wholesale politicization of private property and individual liberty, allowing and perhaps demanding distributive action by the state to leaven economic inequalities. But the emerging symbol for this "public interest," for this new organic body, would not be the citizen. The brooding image was no longer threateningly political. The new symbol was an economic "small fellow"—not, however, the class-identified shopkeeper or laborer, but rather the universalized consumer. The later New Deal's rhetorical image of the consumer projected the political ideology of marketplace liberalism onto the machinery of the state.

This chapter's investigation of competition policies during the New Deal is divided into two sections. The first deals with the early New Deal's major piece of legislation, the National Industrial Recovery Act of 1933—its legislative, administrative, and judicial aspects. The account begins with the utopian vision expressed in legislative hearings and ends with the *ALA Schechter Poultry* (1935) decision,[4] in which the Court held the statute unconstitutional. The second section takes up the later New Deal's antitrust legislation and jurisprudence, its influential economic studies, and its labor and constitutional law doctrines. The later New Deal arose out of the ashes of an organic body politic, still inspired by an ideology of relational equality but reshaped to accord with a new image—the consumer, representing a unified body economic.

The Early New Deal, 1933–1935: The National Industrial Recovery Act and an Organic Body Politic

The National Industrial Recovery Act of 1933 is remembered as the statist experiment that failed. Its failure was not, however, abject. Nor was its utopian vision normatively bankrupt. The social policy aspirations animating the early New Deal take on a new fullness when the Recovery Act is viewed from three perspectives: first, the utopian vision of an organic body politic, expressed in the legislative history; second, the dystopian experience of code drafting and enforcement, driven by inequalities of economic power; and third, the Supreme Court's unanimous rejection of the utopian vision, pronounced in the well-known *ALA Schechter Poultry* decision striking down the statute as an unconstitutional delegation of congressional power.

Congressional Hearings and Codes of Fair Competition: Imagining an Organic Body Politic

The National Industrial Recovery Act of 1933 authorized industrial codes of ethics to organize American business and labor. The statute established both procedural requirements for the drafting process and substantive principles for government approval—the procedural requirements founded in an ethic of equal representation, and the substantive principles embodied in a notion of fair competition. Perhaps because Franklin Roosevelt was elected so many times with such overwhelming majorities, it is often forgotten that the broad consensus expressed during legislative hearings in 1932 was followed by a divided Senate's passage of the Recovery Act and then by widespread resistance to code enforcement. This section analyzes the rhetorics and logics of both consensus and opposition as expressed in legislative hearings, with somewhat disproportionate attention paid to the opposition in an effort to understand the stresses that would so quickly produce dystopian experience from utopian vision.

In the half century between Raymond Moley's *After Seven Years* (1939) and Donald R. Brand's *Corporatism and the Rule of Law* (1988), numerous historical studies have illuminated the making and remaking of the New Deal, particularly the saga of the Recovery Act. My interest is not to repeat or revise extant studies on their own terms but, instead, to pay more attention to the legislative hearings than others have, and to do so in a new way that takes seriously the rhetoric—the discourse—of admittedly staged public hearings. It is their very staging—what language and, accordingly, what images were chosen to portray the problems, solutions, and means associated with the Recovery Act—that seems so promising to me. How did its supporters formulate public claims that it would succeed where other approaches failed? Was there opposition, express or implied, and, if so, what rhetoric did it use? For historians interested in exploring such questions, transcripts of congressional hearings become historical archives of the commitments and conflicts that animated both the problem-solvers and apologists of the day.

Sponsored by Senator Robert F. Wagner (D.N.Y.), the original bill expressed the predominant view that the country was in a state of "national emergency productive of widespread unemployment and disorganization of industry." The language of emergency evoked memories of Woodrow Wilson's War Industries Board—a symbol for the highly successful national mobilization effort for the First World War. The Recovery Act would mobilize the nation to confront another common enemy—the Great Depression. In testimony before the House Committee on Ways and Means, Henry I. Harriman, powerful industrialist and president of the Chamber of Commerce of the United States, admitted the extraordinary nature of the Chamber's support for such a bill, and explained its support in terms of the economic emergency at hand: In 1932, annual income had fallen to less than half the 1929 figure; prices of general commodities had dropped 40 to 50 percent; thirteen million workers were unemployed.[5] Harriman called for an enhanced trade associationalism to raise income, consumption, output, and price levels. Harriman's discourse echoed the "ruinous competition" and "fair price" rhetorics heard in the Progressive Era's legislative debates and railroad cartel cases, as well as in the cooperative competition era's justification for allowing contracts in restraint of trade, including the setting of reasonable prices. Moreover, it drew upon the well-known writing of Arthur J. Eddy, who began his *New Competition* (1914) with an exhortation to cooperate because "Competition is War and 'War is Hell.'"

Senator Wagner's bill promised to promote national industrial recovery by combining two strategies. First, it would "foster fair competition." Second, it would "provide for the construction of certain useful public works." This section examines the imaginative structure of "fair competition" reflected in the congressional hearings. Although Wagner characterized the bill as a plan to put people back to work, he expressed its goal in the language of fair competition: "The purpose of the present bill is not to abolish competition but to lift its standards and to raise its plane so as to eliminate destructive practices, unfair practices." Destructive and unfair practices would fall under statutory "codes of fair competition." These codes would be drafted by industry trade groups and approved by the National Recovery Administration. Code violations were to be treated as "unfair methods of competition" under the Federal Trade Commission Act and could invoke civil penalties, industry licensing procedures, and even revocation of licenses. The FTC would provide investigatory resources for the NRA.[6]

With Harriman praising the plan as a strengthened form of Hoover's associationalism, other industry leaders, as well as labor leaders, expressed approval. Accordingly, antitrust should mean only anti-monopoly, not anti-associationalism. Why? Because together, Harriman asserted, trade association codes and an anti-monopoly campaign would take the brutality out of competition. They would allow the fair prices, wages, and dividends necessary for businesses to survive.[7] The call for fair prices and wages carried with it echoes of the Sherman and Interstate Commerce Act debates, particularly the concerns expressed about ruinous competition. Now, however, the notion of ruinous competition would be applied to labor relations as well as commercial ones.

The antitrust exemption. But what of Section 5, which provided an antitrust exemption for action taken under the Recovery Act? How could that be reconciled with competition policies underlying the antitrust laws? Representative Joseph L. Hill (D.Ala.), a member of the House committee, stated that the statute "effectuate[s] the very purpose which was in the minds of the legislators at the time they enacted the antitrust law, namely, the prevention of unfair competition." Senator Wagner agreed, arguing that the Recovery Act was "supplemental to the antitrust laws." "We are going to retain competition," he insisted. "We are simply going to put competition on a high standard of efficiency rather than on a low standard of exploitation of labor."[8] In sum, antitrust policy meant fair competition free from cutthroat practices, whether by monopolists or recalcitrant rivals. And it meant fair prices, fair wages, and fair profits: neither too high nor too low. Antitrust enforcement and trade association codes of ethics were presented as complementary forms of managed competition, of fair competition.

Small enterprise. Still, this rhetoric of fair competition espoused more than regulation of competitive extremes. It expressed a commitment to protect the threatened class of individual entrepreneurs that an older generation of patrons—Justice Peckham's Literalists—called "small dealers and worthy men." Senator Wagner stated that the legislation was intended to stop "rebates, discrimination, and selling below the cost of production in order to destroy some little business man."[9]

Of course, there were other New Dealers who were more interested in the benefits of large-scale enterprise than in preserving small businesses. Donald Richberg, a labor lawyer and chief draftsman of the bill, believed that technological innovation made industrial giantism inevitable and thus that "constitutional guarantees of liberty can only be made good by laws imposing restraints upon the anarchy of unregulated individual action." He called for "a government of business—that is, an intentional orderly control of industrial processes." Much like Teddy Roosevelt's New Nationalism platform some twenty years earlier, Richberg's view was framed by a preference for the "vigorous assertion of a centralized executive authority."[10]

Nonetheless, an explicit solicitude toward small businesses was written into the Recovery Act: Section 3(a) elaborated criteria for judging codes of fair competition. First of all, the NRA would not approve codes "designed . . . to eliminate or oppress small enterprises" or codes "operat[ing] to discriminate against them." In short, the drafters seemed intent upon a codification process that would not devolve into another site for the exercise of economic power. Second, trade associations must be "truly representative" of the trade or industry. Small businesses would be empowered to protect themselves: They would have equal voice in establishing the rules of fair competition.

Those who drafted the statute draped the process and normative content of codification in the rhetoric of equality, the language of nondiscrimination. Although the language was taken to mean the assurance of equal voice to small businesses, the mandates for equal treatment and "truly representative" bodies did contain a common ambiguity, a tension: Did equal treatment mean identical treatment? Or treatment according to economically rational standards? For example, must codes provide that a supplier sell an item at the same price to all? Or should account be taken of cost differences in selling to large firms (A&P through its distribution center for central Pennsylvania) and small businesses (Kay's Korner Kupboard, State College, Pa.)? Each alternative, although inconsistent with the other, seemed to satisfy the requirement of "equal" treatment.

The same ambiguity beset the call for "truly representative" bodies. Must each market participant have equal representation, equal voice? Should each firm receive one seat or vote? Or must market share be reflected? For example, if A&P has 50 percent of some geographic market, should that be taken into account? Should seats or votes be distributed according to market share? What of two membership classes—one comprising A&P and the other everyone else—with each class having one vote?

Both sets of questions, the first substantive and the second procedural, reveal the same tension: Does equality call for identical treatment of each firm, just as one person, one citizen, is given one vote? Or does equality demand recognition of economic differences and equitable treatment according to such differences? In sum, should judgments about equality reflect political norms or economic realities? This double standard for equality, at once political and economic, mirrored a doubled rhetoric of fair competition. On the one side, fair competition was seen as contestation between roughly equal firms, as rivalry not subject to monopoly power. On the other, fair competition was understood as the product of uniformly enforced ethical codes and universally shared information, as the flowering of an egalitarian trade associationalism. Fair competition meant both contest and cooperation, both rivalry and agreement. Cooperation and agreement were political aspirations. Contest and rivalry were economic virtues.

Despite its duplicity, the language of fair competition seemed to carry one consistent message. It summoned not just an activist state, but something more striking; not just governmental supervision of commercial conduct, but something different in kind. The language of fair competition decreed a politicization of economic rivalry, a fundamental change from the perception of separate economic and political spheres, a departure from the image of a private economic domain—self-sustaining, productive, and guarded by the principle of freedom of contract—a shift toward an organic vision of an integrated process with interleaved elements, both economic and political. Tempered by the economic hardships suffered since 1929, the new rhetoric of fair competition represented, too, the belief that the old image of individualism, the classical ideology of freedom of contract, even if attractive in the abstract, projected a failed approach to solving real problems.

Labor relations. The statutory language broadcast a clear message about the legitimacy of government action in matters of economy. Yet, while the call for "truly representative" boards was importing political norms into administration of economic markets, a subsequent section of the statute explicitly concerned with labor relations was doing precisely the converse: Recovery Act Section 7 was redefining political conflict in terms of economic rivalry. In sum, the rhetoric of fair competition was interweaving political and economic ethics and images. In particular, Recovery Act Section 7(a) defined fair labor standards as a necessary part of industry codes:

> Every code of fair competition . . . shall contain the following conditions: (1) That employees shall have the right to organize and bargain collectively through representatives of their own choosing . . . and (3) that employers shall comply with the maximum hours of labor, minimum rates of pay, and other conditions . . . prescribed by the President.

These standards were characterized in the rhetoric of fair competition and invoked norms of trade associationalism. Senator Wagner sought "to get rid of the whole idea of war to the limit and to substitute for it the idea of agreements through mediation." He wanted labor and management relations to exchange the political imagery of conflict for the associationalist rhetoric of cooperative competition.[11]

This rhetorical reformulation of labor relations constituted an effort to overthrow the anti-labor attitudes of the Hoover era, whose Supreme Court opinions and federal enforcement officials portrayed union efforts to organize labor as "struggle" or "conflict" rather than competition—in short, as dangerous political uprisings rather than economically motivated behavior. In contrast, the Recovery Act sought to redress labor relations with the economic virtues of "cooperative competition" ascribed to trade associations. Implicitly rejecting the claims of John M. Clark and other economists who had equated labor organization with inefficiency and higher costs, Wagner asserted that fair labor standards would

> not abolish competition but . . . lift its standards and raise its plane so as to eliminate destructive practices, unfair practices, competition in the reduction of wages and the lengthening of hours. In other words, efficiency, rather than the ability to sweat labor and undermine living standards, will be the determining factor in business success.

Donald Richberg, the longtime counsel for railway labor organizations who drafted much of the bill, echoed Senator Wagner's statement: "The most unfair competition that existed in industry was the competition through depressed and disorganized and deflated labor." During Richberg's appearance before the House committee, Representative Harold Knutson (R.Minn.) asked: "You are setting up here a sort of cooperative machine, with the Government as the mediator?" Richberg responded: "Very largely, so far as it is possible for industry to organize and govern itself."[12]

Labor leader John L. Lewis drew a more vivid picture of American labor's position as caught between "the rapacity of the robber barons of industry in America, and the lustful rage of the Communists, who would lay waste to our traditions and our institutions with fire and sword." Lewis's rhetorical moorings are clear enough: Cooperative labor relations presented the only reasonable path between the extremes of ruinous competition and riotous politics. Both extremes threatened property rights, the first on an individual basis and the second at an institutional level. Lewis cautioned his listeners that "[l]abor in America, organized labor, is trying to maintain an equilibrium of relations in industry."[13] He wanted nothing more than a labor-management associationalism judged under an economic Rule of Reason.

The rhetorical structure of fair competition. These statute excerpts and statements from the congressional hearings reflected the mainstream discourse of American political economy in those years. This discourse, in all its complexity, rested on a triangular footing: first, competition—whether ruinous, fair, or free—and its double, monopoly; second, politics—whether legislative action or populist upheaval—and its economic double, liberty of contract; and, finally, associationalism—whether cartels, mergers, trade groups, labor unions, or political factions—and its double, individualism. For the Recovery Act, the shifting term in this triangular array was associationalism, which sometimes displayed an economic valence and other times a political spin. The rhetoric of associationalism and its double, individualism, tended to intermix political and economic strains, as it had in the treatment of trade associations and labor unions before the New Deal.

The Recovery Act and legislative hearings reflected a realignment of the rhetorical triangle. This realignment was seen in an observable shift in the language of competition: "Fair" competition displaced "free," "cooperative," "open," or "new" competition, and in so doing interwove political and economic strains, one through the other. The result was a mixed rhetoric of political economy: "fair competition." At the highest level of abstraction, politics and competition were no longer represented as mutually exclusive alternatives. In practical terms, "fair competition" allowed political supervision of trade associations without forfeiting their ideological correctness, forged so carefully in the language of competition. The Recovery Act promised to do no more than jump-start "a sort of cooperative machine." Moreover, with the simple acknowledgment that buyers and sellers compete, the domain of competition was expanded vertically. Recognizing a vertical dimension in competition not only allowed labor unions to be recognized in the language of "fair competition" but also raised concerns about the vertical effects of trade associations.

This attention to the vertical dimension of competition, this concern about transactions between trading partners, appeared prominently in Section 9 of the statute as a separate provision regulating only the oil industry. Perhaps surprisingly, Senate committee hearings generated as much verbiage about Section 9—almost 250 pages of statements and colloquy—as about all other statute sections combined. Two issues were on the table: illegally produced, or "hot," oil, and major oil company ownership of interstate pipelines. The statutory treatment of interstate pipeline ownership and control illuminates the concerns expressed about the vertical dimension of "fair competition."[14]

The major oil companies, legacies of the Standard Oil Trust, were vertically integrated. That is, they owned the oil-drilling equipment, the gasoline pumps at the corner station, and everything in between, including the few interstate oil pipelines. As a consequence, independent producers typically found themselves facing regional monopolists. With pipelines by far the cheapest form of transport, independents had two bad choices: sell in local spot markets at depressed prices or transport through pipelines at monopoly prices. Given the massive overproduction of oil in those years, the independents, dependent upon the kindness of the regional pipeline monopolies, sought legislative remedies for the unequal bargaining power working in the industry. Because the bargaining power was so asymmetric, the vertical competition so unfair, something, they implored, had to be done.

Recovery Act Section 9 offered a double-barreled solution. First, the Interstate Commerce Commission was authorized to "prescribe regulations to control the operations of oil pipe lines" and to "fix reasonable, compensatory rates" for their use. No one quarreled with this regulatory approach. But there was a second barrel pointed at the major oil companies, whose subsidiaries owned the pipelines. An antitrust-inspired provision authorized the President to "institute proceedings to divorce from any holding company any pipeline company," should it "by unfair practices or by exorbitant rates in the transportation of petroleum or its products tend[ ] to create a monopoly." The regulatory and the antitrust alternatives represented two available discourses for understanding and thus for producing solutions to the problem of verticality. The regulatory approach raised few questions, given the acknowledged power of Congress to regulate interstate commerce. But the divestiture provision threatened the dominance of major oil companies in the most fundamental sense: There could be a forced sale of property, a "divorcement" of pipeline subsidiaries from their parent holding companies.

Given the regulatory regime, the two criteria for invoking corporate "divorcement" are puzzling. The first, monopolization by "exorbitant rates," seems superfluous, because the ICC regulated rates. Did the provision simply threaten divestiture as the penalty for charging rates not authorized by the ICC? Or could the Federal Trade Commission also proceed on a theory that rates approved by the ICC were exorbitant? The second criterion for divestiture, monopolization by "unfair practices," presents a shocking array of possibilities for defining an "unfair practice": Should content be given to the phrase by reference to common-law doctrines of unfair competition? To

Federal Trade Commission policy under FTC Act Section 5? Or perhaps to the Recovery Act guidelines for industry codes of fair competition, which included fair labor standards? Could, for example, a refusal by Texaco's pipeline subsidiary to allow labor union representation provide the ground for "divorcement" of the pipeline subsidiary? How far did the concern about the vertical dimension of competition extend? These questions could not be asked of the antitrust laws. It was the Recovery Act's audacious rhetoric of "fair competition" that provided the language even to formulate such scandalous thoughts.

An organic body politic. Rhetorical connections between labor practices and corporate dissolution present only the most vivid example of the statutory framework for this political economy of "fair competition." The larger vision was organic: Associations of rivals negotiated the terms of horizontal competition. Industrial statesmanship monitored by public servants would mediate the tensions between competition and association. At the same time, buyer and seller groups would negotiate the terms of vertical competition. The most critical case of such deliberation was the "united action of labor and management" proclaimed in the Recovery Act Section 1. This organic vision portrayed the Great Depression as a national problem whose solution lay in organization of the body politic. It lay in the political will to cooperate instead of compete, or, at least, to compete in a spirit of cooperation.

The Recovery Act's rhetoric linked the image of an organic body politic to the idea of the nation-state. James A. Emery, representing the National Association of Manufacturers, summoned a nationalist effort modeled on Woodrow Wilson's World War I mobilization, complete with an embargo on imports. In an exchange with Henry I. Harriman, the powerful industrialist representing the national Chamber of Commerce, Representative Allen T. Treadway (R.Mass.) suggested, "If competitive articles are manufactured in foreign countries under different conditions . . . there should be a compensating offset to that in our law." Harriman replied, "Otherwise the act would become noneffective." Representative Frank Crowther (R.N.Y.) called for an outright two-year embargo on all competing imports.[15]

Thus, this vision of an organic body politic had an inside and an outside, a national and an international face. Turning out toward international trade, the vision of an organic body politic, "truly representative" of its constituencies, resembled an integrated trading company unwilling to "divorce" itself from any subsidiaries lest the removal destroy the internal body politic. The ideological corollary was protection against imports, against outside attack, as part of the program described in Section 1 to "reduce and relieve unemployment," to "increase consumption . . . by increasing purchasing power" and to "promote the fullest possible utilization of present productive capacity of industries."

As enacted, the Recovery Act Section 3(e) would authorize the Tariff Commission to investigate complaints that articles were being imported "on such terms or under such conditions as to render ineffective or seriously to endanger the maintenance of any code" of fair competition. When such complaints were substantiated, the President would be required to prescribe "the payment of such fees" and "limitations in the total quantity which may be imported" in order to safeguard the codes of fair competition, many of which included price-fixing provisions. The organic body politic would protect itself from external attack, whether economic or political.

Voices of opposition. Although the congressional deliberations reflected a broad consensus in favor of the Recovery Act, Franklin Roosevelt and his New Dealers certainly faced opposition. both progressive and conservative. The Recovery Act hearings produced two types of opposition. First, there were a few speakers who doubted that such an associational scheme could work. Second, there were those who expressed ideological opposition to the entire approach.

Those who suspected that the plan would fail expressed strong concerns about the anticipated treatment of small businesses and labor unions. Representative Treadway, for example, was apprehensive about "small enterprises which were not, typically, members of trade associations. How will their interests be voiced?" Senator William E. Borah (R.Idaho) demanded that an anti-price-fixing provision be added to the statute, declaring, "When the time comes that the large interests in an industry, gathered together for the purpose of making a code, do not dominate the situation, but permit the small independent to write the code for the large industry, the millennium will have been here for many years."[16]

In contrast to such progressive sentiments, speakers challenging the very call for "unity" between labor and management expressed a wider range of views. The most subdued comment came from Representative Thomas A. Jenkins (R.Ohio): "[D]on't you think it would be a long step to permit the President to take two agencies, one labor and one industry, and compel them to agree, and then have the power to punish them?" Was Jenkins questioning the likelihood of success or the legitimacy of compelling agreement? R. P. Lamont, representing the powerful American Iron and Steel Institute, left no doubts about his intentions. Perfectly clear about wanting to maintain the status quo, Lamont favored open shops and individual bargaining between employer and employee. He opposed requiring management to bargain with "representatives of employees." Charles R. Hook, president of the American Rolling Mill Company, responded to Senator Wagner's hope for getting "rid of the whole idea of war to the limit" with a rhetoric of denial symptomatic of either bare-faced mendacity or an acute form of social dyslexia: He read the recent record of labor strikes and violence as a "happy relationship between employer and employee during the past ten years."[17]

Following steel industrialists Hook and Lamont was John L. Lewis, perhaps America's most prominent labor leader, representing the United Mine Workers of America and the American Federation of Labor. Lewis pointedly began his statement with the observation that there were "no union men in any United States Steel plant." Keenly aware of the disparity chronicled in years of federal policies sanctioning trade associations while condemning their labor counterparts, Lewis asserted that "if an employer can join a trade association, an employee should have the right to join a union."[18] Lewis supported the Recovery Act in the belief that union leaders would be significant participants in the process of code-writing and enforcement.

Echoing the sentiments expressed by Hook and Lamont, Senator Thomas P. Gore (D.Okla.) voiced his opposition to the Recovery Act in language reflecting the Supreme Court's economic due-process jurisprudence seen in the *Lochner* decision (1904) and its progeny. On the morning of the first day of Senate committee hearings, Gore asked a leading question: "Doesn't the power to license and revoke the license of private enterprise deprive the owner of property, of his property, without due process of law?" Gore then answered by comparing the power to revoke licenses with the power of a "Mussolini [or] Stalin." At another juncture, Gore interrupted colloquy regarding the oil regulation provision to ask, "Do you want to be put under a dictator?" Louis Titus, representing the Independent Petroleum Association of America, later responded, "The major oil companies already fix the prices. Why not prefer the federal government?"[19]

Arguments for fair price and freedom of contract guided twin property logics criss-crossing the new rhetoric of "fair competition." While fair price called for allocation of property according to the new liberal ideology of equality, freedom of contract called for protection of property according to classical libertarian tenets. Whereas a commitment to fair price legitimized state distribution of property rights, a commitment to liberty of contract justified the current allocation of economic power—the results of bargain transactions—regardless of relative bargaining power. In this sense, the conflict between the Recovery Act supporters and the Gore faction turned on attitudes toward the current distribution of economic power. The Recovery Act was designed to equalize it, and the Gore faction opposed its new distribution.

Such statements of opposition would provoke widespread protest and resistance within months of the bill's passage. Even before the opposition took shape, those intimately involved in the work of the National Recovery Administration would see sharp divergences between vision and reality, between theory and practice. Moreover, the political ideology animating Senator Gore's spirited opposition would find voice in the Supreme Court that would issue the *ALA Schechter Poultry* decision in 1935.

Drafting and Enforcing Industrial Codes of Fair Competition: The Dystopian Experience

After less than three weeks of deliberation, Congress approved the massive Recovery Act just before noon on June 16, 1933. Although little opposition appeared in the hearings and debates, the Senate vote was very close—forty-six in favor to thirty-nine opposed. Despite his overwhelming election mandate for change, Franklin Roosevelt signed a bill that only a plurality of senators was willing to support. Yet, later that afternoon, as Roosevelt signed the legislation, more than 4,000 trade associations stood ready to join the codification crusade. In the next two years, more than 1,000 codes of fair competition would be drafted and approved.

Considerable opposition arose almost immediately after General Hugh Johnson took charge of the NRA. A career army officer, Johnson had a reputation for administrative competence: During Woodrow Wilson's national mobilization program in World War I, he had organized the Selective Service Administration and then represented the army on the crucial War Industries Board. Johnson expressed great enthusiasm about the new NRA: "The very heart of the New Deal is the principle of concerted action in industry and agriculture under government supervision looking to a balanced economy as opposed to the murderous doctrine of savage and wolfish individualism, looking to dog-eat-dog and devil take the hindmost."[20] However, Johnson's views seemed nearer Herbert Hoover's informal associationalism than the formal government supervision outlined in the Recovery Act. He favored "the concept of industrial self-government" and opposed "general rules of what should and what should not be in codes" and "resolutions requiring the Administrator to include or not to include this or that thing." Granting such broad discretion seemed at odds with the Recovery Act Section 3, which itemized general rules and imposed requirements on the administrator. Johnson's corporatism, his belief in the "industrial statesmanship" of business executives, led, according to historian Ellis Hawley, to a "bargain between business leaders on the one hand and businessmen in the guise of government officials on the other."[21]

At the very least, this belief in industrial statesmanship, shared by Johnson and his general counsel Donald Richberg, along with the reality of an unstaffed agency inundated with hundreds of code applications, produced a regime of severe under-supervision. What little government supervision there was was undertaken by young, inexperienced lawyers who approved scores of codes drafted by experienced and knowledgeable corporate attorneys. General Johnson (and, on occasion, Franklin Roosevelt himself) did, however, take an active role in negotiating codes in industries considered particularly important—automobile, coal, steel, lumber, petroleum, and cotton textiles.

Whether a failure of social consensus or an absence of industrial statesmanship, industry codes seemed to engender more conflict than agreement. By the end of 1933, only six months after the bill's passage, the NRA had a backlog of more than 10,000 code violations. In some areas, the agency stiffened code provisions; in others, agency enforcement languished. No one was satisfied. Every constituency, from small business to big, from labor unions to unorganized consumers, now seemed to oppose the Recovery Act. Labor leaders called the NRA the vanguard of corporatist fascism. Industrialists, led by early supporter Gerard Swope, head of General Electric, inveighed against the agency's increasing activism, seeing it as the beginning of bureaucratic socialism. The contentious practices of code-drafting and code enforcement showed little in common with the associationalist vision expressed in committee hearings. The Recovery Act was in a tailspin long before the Supreme

Court shot it down in the *ALA Schechter Poultry* opinion (1935).[22] By that time, tensions, both ideological and factional, had already shattered the ecumenical rhetoric of fair competition and its organic vision of political economy.

Codes and the "little fellow." From its inception, the Recovery Act reflected conflicting views of corporate size. The New Deal's patrons of small business had their adversaries: Not only Donald Richberg, Hugh Johnson, and their allies but also the recent commercial proponents of trade associationalism harbored the belief that, under the right conditions, the material benefits of large-scale enterprise and the moral fiber of industrial statesmanship would lead the nation out of its Great Depression. The ideological conflict was alive in the utopian vision of a body politic. But conflict had been anticipated, and the process for resolution was provided in the statute: Trade associations had to pass a litmus test of representativeness just to get in the door, just to begin code-writing.

But the litmus test never materialized. Representatives of large-scale enterprise dominated the agency and its constituent associations from top to bottom. Men such as Alfred Sloan of General Motors, Gerard Swope of General Electric, and Walter Teagle of Standard Oil held the top positions at the NRA. In consequence, their views dominated the codes written for industries with large firms. Moreover, large-firm influence permeated not only the NRA but the great majority of trade associations engaged in codification. It was usually by productive capacity of member firms, not by counting heads, that association majorities were determined. In short, Section 3(a)'s representational equality proviso failed to produce a process that protected the interests of the "little fellow." Political norms of representation did not leaven differences in economic power. It is not surprising that among the NRA backlog of 10,000 code complaints, "violations were more prevalent among . . . smaller and hard-pressed competitors." Of nineteen cases decided by federal district court judges, for example, fourteen dealt with "gas stations, auto dealerships, laundries and dry cleaners, and lumber yards."[23]

In response to protests by small businesses (Senate debate on January 18, 1934, included Senator Borah's claim that his office had received more than 9,000 complaints from small businesses), Franklin Roosevelt established by executive order the National Recovery Review Board and appointed Clarence Darrow to head it. The "Darrow Board" was charged with investigating the effects of codes on small businesses and recommending changes. The Darrow Board reported to Roosevelt that small businesses were "cruelly oppressed" under the NRA codes. These codes of fair competition continued to facilitate industry cartelization, price increases far greater than wage increases, and disproportionate enforcement against small businesses. As one deputy administrator wrote, "Without odds this is the damnedest mess it has ever been my misfortune to be connected with. The entire NRA is in a suspended state—crying for simplification of policy and routine—for broad simple policy determinations—and getting nothing. The . . . conflicts would be laughable were they not so serious."[24] The grand idea about an organic body politic, about a political norm of equal representation to leaven economic power, had begun its downward spiral.

Codes and labor unions. The Recovery Act was also celebrated as "Labor's Bill of Rights"—especially the rights to organize and bargain collectively enumerated in Section 7(a). All codes of fair competition would include them. Labor would finally participate in deliberations to formulate economic policy. Especially in the "Big Six" industries—automobiles, coal, cotton textile, iron and steel, lumber, and petroleum—labor would provide the countervailing power necessary to fabricate codes of fair competition.

But, from its inception, Section 7(a) embodied an uneasy compromise. On one side, labor leaders were supporting an earlier labor bill sponsored by Senator Hugo Black (D.Ala.), a radical proposal to distribute employment by imposing a thirty-hour work week. On the other side, Franklin Roosevelt had shown no inclination to protect labor's rights and, moreover, vehemently opposed the Black bill. Roosevelt and labor leaders compromised, agreeing on Congress's Section 7(a). Yet according to Donald Richberg, Roosevelt's confidant and appointee as NRA General Counsel, the compromise did not, however, provide direct labor representation on trade association boards: "There will be no labor representatives in trade associations but they have the rights of organization and collective bargaining, which equals the right to bargain with management over terms and conditions affecting labor."[25]

After Congress passed the Recovery Act, Roosevelt further isolated labor from the code-drafting mechanism by establishing a National Labor Board within the NRA. The NLB and its three lawyers would handle Section 7(a) compliance by processing complaints. The consequences of labor's separation from the micropolitics of code formulation were severe. Most of all, labor representatives could not bargain for the *industrywide* labor practices deemed crucial in the legislative debates. How could labor costs be leveled? With the NLB's authority limited to complaint processing, no one, it seems, was in a position to negotiate the labor-cost uniformity that was intended to support intra-industry fair competition. There was no associational structure for including labor in the organic body politic.

Hugh Johnson, the NRA Administrator, early declared that the agency would not "compel the organization either of industry or labor." Johnson shocked labor leaders when he added that he would not require collective bargaining as a condition precedent to ratifying the labor relations provisions of industrial codes of fair competition. Finally, Johnson announced that the NRA did not prohibit "open shop" provisions in codes: "[A]n open shop is a place where any man who is competent and whose services are desired will be employed regardless of whether or not he belongs to a union. That is exactly what the law says."[26] Given such announcements of NRA policy, code negotiations met immediate and persistent resistance, especially in the form of "Big Six" industry association refusals to include the labor rights mandated by Section 7(a).

During that summer of codification, the following events occurred: Henry Ford refused to sign the auto industry code. Roosevelt intervened in the coal code negotiations to stop violent confrontations between striking miners and employers who refused to recognize their union. To broker an agreement, Roosevelt felt compelled to approve a price-fixing provision. In the cotton textile industry, employers agreed to abolish child labor practices and little more in exchange for their own price-fixing agreement.

Still, the NLB continued to receive hundreds of complaints about labor practices. Through the winter of 1934, industry refusals to recognize unions in labor negotiations brought on bitter strikes in the steel and auto industries. That spring, a wave of labor strikes rolled across the country, approaching in both breadth and intensity the class war feared by many. Beginning in a Toledo auto-parts plant among workers bitterly dissatisfied with the auto industry settlement, the strike spread to teamsters in Minneapolis, south to textile workers, and west to longshoremen in San Francisco. Workers' anger at recent labor pacts was heightened by the sense that Roosevelt had abandoned them. Left to their own devices, union members took to the barricades, suffering injury and sometimes death at the hands of police, vigilantes, and National Guardsmen.[27]

The Recovery Act rhetoric of "fair competition," of economic rivalry, fell silent in the uproar and upheaval of industrial warfare. The utopian vision of associationalism, of cooperative competition between labor and management, succumbed to industrialists' militant refusals to recognize labor associations. Employers would rather fight than allow the equality of bargaining power needed to nourish an organic body politic. The assistance of National Guardsmen and the fainthearted opposition of NRA officials not only encouraged employers to resist but also overwhelmed the rhetoric of fair competition. Labor relations were not economic transactions but political conflict. Strikes were war and, as such, the continuation of politics by other means.

In consequence, the Recovery Act's aspiration—its political economy of expanded associationalism—expired, strangled by the unrelenting discord between employers and their employees. The Wagner Act, passed on May 16, 1935, would establish the National Labor Relations Board and, with it, a more substantial labor bill of rights was born. But its passage would also institutionalize the boundary between commerce and labor, the ideological barrier between economic competition and political battle. Chief among the Wagner Act's goals, and expressed in the political rhetoric of conflict and struggle, was the channeling of "strikes and other forms of industrial strife or unrest" into "orderly and peaceful" processes for the "friendly adjustment of industrial disputes."[28] The soothing economic rhetoric of associationalism would adhere only to commercial relations. The political discourse of conflict would again portray labor relations as dangerous. The Recovery Act, Franklin Roosevelt's all-embracing Leviathan, would give way to separate agencies with separate rhetorics and practices in separate spheres.

Codes and price-fixing. The same industrialists who endorsed armed resistance to industrywide or even firmwide wage negotiations with labor unions eagerly negotiated among themselves industrywide codes of fair competition, especially provisions regulating pricing practices. The rhetoric of "fair competition" and the ideology of associationalism, withdrawn from labor relations, would continue to subsidize agreements among rivals to restrain price competition.

A Brookings Institution study (1935) of the NRA found that almost all of the 1,000 industry codes in force included some provision restraining price competition. Historian Ellis Hawley has written that only a few codes permitted direct price-fixing, whether agreements between competitors or resale price maintenance between manufacturers and their downstream distributors and retailers. But the practices of Hooverian associationalism found their way into more than 900 codes. More than 100 codes included provisions imposing restrictions on output—the direct route to supporting price levels. Almost 450 codes created open-price systems of information exchange, many including cost data, sales information not only aggregated but also itemized by transaction, and price lists. Some also required waiting periods before the new price lists would take effect. Perhaps most telling is the fact that some 400 codes prohibited sales below cost. In terms of the Recovery Act policy, these provisions seemed to make the best sense. After all, wasn't the idea to stop ruinous competition? And weren't higher prices needed to pay higher wages? While everyone seemed to agree on the need to raise price levels, within limits, there was no consensus about the working standards for defining costs and allowing exceptions. How should cost be measured: by marginal or average variable, average total, or some other cost? Should cost mean individual firm cost, industry average, industry lowest, industry highest? What of widely divergent labor costs? Even if some agreement could be reached on costs and even if the expenses involved in information production could be met, what of an exception for meeting a competitor's lower price? Must a firm seek approval from a code authority before meeting the lower price? These examples only scratch the surface of the administrative strains and theoretical impasses that burdened the NRA.[29]

Although the NRA can be understood as trying to promote competition, to allow price competition within constraints, both its theory and its practice allowed the kinds of corporate cooperation that could lead too easily to the restraint of all meaningful competition. It seems that three elements conspired to bring about the NRA's failure. First, there was no ethical revolution, no rise of industrial statesmanship. Business planning never converged with industrial planning. Second, even more broadly, there was no political consensus beyond a vague desire for change. Finally, the NRA suffered from poor administration, whether attributed to Hugh Johnson's failure to formulate agency policies or to the utter impossibility of building a functional bureaucracy overnight.

Like Adolf Berle and Gardiner Means, who called for a regime of "quasi-public corporations" to balance the "diversity of interests" impounded by large bureaucratic corporations, the New Dealers who drafted the National Industrial Recovery Act wanted to organize economic markets under a political norm of equal representation of diverse interests, under ethical rules negotiated according to the tenets of "fair competition." But the utopian vision of an organic body politic imposing its will upon the hard times of economic depression never materialized in the frenzied practices of code drafting and enforcement.

The Supreme Court's ALA Schechter Poultry *Decision: Political Power and the Discourse of Fair Competition*

Although thousands of complaints were filed and numerous disputes adjudicated under the Recovery Act's codes of fair competition, only a few reached the Supreme Court. The best known was *ALA Schechter Poultry Corp. v. United States* (1935). With Justices Benjamin N. Cardozo and Harlan F. Stone concurring in a separate opinion, Chief Justice Charles Evans Hughes, speaking for a united Court, held the Recovery Act unconstitutional. According to Chief Justice Hughes, the problem in *ALA Schechter Poultry* was the Recovery Act's "vague standard" of "fair competition" and, with it, the unbridled discretion granted to those drafting, approving, and enforcing industry codes of ethics. The Constitution, agreed all nine Justices, does not permit Congress simply to delegate its legislative discretion, either to the President or to private associations. As Justice Cardozo put it, the Recovery Act was "delegation run riot." Nonetheless, even though historians and other scholars have paid close attention to delegation doctrine,[30] its political economy of "fair competition" remains largely uncharted.

The very ground for Chief Justice Hughes's opinion—that "fair competition" is vague—seems shaky, given the Court's prior approval of other statutes built upon equally general principles. First of all, the language of "fair competition" seemed to parallel the Federal Trade Commission Act's indefinite standard of "unfair competition." Indeed, any violation of the Recovery Act was explicitly deemed a violation of the FTC Act. Moreover, "fair competition" appears no less vague than the Interstate Commerce Act's broad prohibition of "unjust and unreasonable charges" for railroad carriage. Hughes's opinion did consider the discretion delegated to the Federal Trade and Interstate Commerce Commissions but found their limits constitutionally clear enough.

What makes the Court's finding of vagueness especially puzzling was its own institutional commitment to a federal common law of "fair competition"—seen in economic due process doctrine, trade association cases, and the "quasi-property" right created in *International News Service* (1918). By the time the Court rejected the Recovery Act's formulation of "fair competition" in *ALA Schechter Poultry*, there was a large inventory of statutory and common law templates sitting on its jurisprudential shelves. The Court opinion, nevertheless, referred only to *International News Service*. Why no references to the constitutional and antitrust lines of "fair competition" doctrine?

Finally, the shocking unanimity: What led progressives and conservatives—Brandeis and Sutherland, Stone and McReynolds, Cardozo and Butler—and everyone in between to agree on this matter of political economy? Why was *ALA Schechter Poultry* such an easy case? The Recovery Act seems merely to have integrated the state price-fixing recently authorized in *Nebbia v. New York* (1934) with the upcoming *Sugar Institute* (1936) decision's affirmation of longstanding policy favoring trade association codes of fair competition. What was wrong with the NRA and its nationwide grid of trade associations? To understand what a unanimous Court rejected in *ALA Schechter Poultry,* I examine the Court's approval of "fair competition" in two lines of cases. I begin with the economic due-process jurisprudence clustering around the *Nebbia* decision and then turn to antitrust trade association cases, culminating in *Sugar Institute* (1936).[31] In both of these areas, the Court's standard was "fair competition"—the very standard it rejected as too vague in *ALA Schechter Poultry.* We will see that the congressional vision was found unconstitutionally void for vagueness because, unlike the earlier formulations of "fair competition," this one transgressed the categorical separation of property and competition rhetorics; it trespassed boundaries between private and public spheres, between economic and political domains, between cooperation and coercion. In consequence, the statute was seen as raising administrative scaffolding for an organic body politic without deontological bounds. A body both economic and political, both cooperative and coercive, was categorically vague.

State regulation and the political rhetoric of fair competition. When Herbert Hoover appointed Hughes and Roberts to the Supreme Court in 1930, a jurisprudential impasse separated two Court factions. Hughes and Roberts joined a Court divided in two important respects. First, the two factions held radically opposed visions of society—conflicting ideas about property rights and freedom of contract. Second, the two factions practiced different forms of opinion writing. Both economic due process jurisprudence and antitrust doctrine reflected these differences in two Rules of Reason. Before Hughes and Roberts joined the Court, the conservative majority's deductive style, shaped by a powerful faith in freedom of contract, consistently dominated the inductive, balancing approach set out most prominently in Justice Brandeis's opinions in *Chicago Board of Trade* and *International News Service.* Now, Hoover's two appointees would straddle the abyss separating two factions, neither one a majority. Only one vote was needed to extend the conservative bloc's dominance, two to swing the balance.

For several years, Hughes and Roberts wavered, sometimes voting on one side, sometimes on the other. In the *O'Gorman* (1931) decision, for example, both joined Brandeis's opinion to form a bare majority, which held that the New Jersey legislature could regulate insurance agents' commissions so long as the rates were reasonable. They rejected the conservative quartet's argument, written in dissent, that the public "right to regulate a business does not necessarily imply power . . . to trespass on the duties of private management." The two recent appointees seemed unconcerned about maintaining fixed boundaries between public and private spheres.[32]

One year later, however, Hughes and Roberts joined Sutherland's opinion in *New State Ice Co.* (1932), which held an Oklahoma licensing statute unconstitutional because the legislature sought to regulate "an ordinary business"—that is, a private enterprise outside the fixed common-law category of businesses "affected with the public interest." By requiring a license to open an ice house, the Oklahoma legislature fostered "monopoly, not competition." In safeguarding liberty of contract, Sutherland was promoting the conservative bloc's conception of fair competition—that is, competition free of oppressive government supervision. Brandeis's dissent retraced the steps of his *O'Gorman* opinion, embellished only by references to the recent literature on economic regulation. Brandeis argued that it was reasonable for the Oklahoma legislature to conclude that unregulated rivalry was not fair competition.[33]

During the 1934 session, their paths ran parallel: Roberts's heralded opinion in *Nebbia,* joined by Hughes, and Hughes's opinion in *Home Building & Loan Ass'n v. Blaisdell,* joined by Roberts, were both written for progressive majorities. Thereafter, Hughes would stay the progressive course in economic due process decisions. Roberts, however, would join the conservative faction on numerous occasions.[34] In *Morehead v. New York ex rel Tipaldo* (1936), for example, Roberts joined the Four Horsemen in an opinion that drove Hughes to the uncharacteristic extreme of dissenting. Roberts's majority opinion in *Nebbia* and Hughes's dissent in *Tipaldo* provide constitutional logics of "fair competition" available to Hughes in *ALA Schechter Poultry,* while opinions by McReynolds and Butler reflect the conservative logic that opposed them. Ultimately, of course, everyone agreed, although for different reasons, that the Recovery Act's formulation of "fair competition" failed constitutional muster.

In 1933, the Milk Control Board of New York, under the state Agriculture and Marketing Law, set the price of milk at 9 cents per quart. "Nebbia, the proprietor of a grocery store in Rochester, sold two quarts and a five cent loaf of bread for eighteen cents." He was "convicted for violating the Board's order." "The question for decision is whether the Federal Constitution prohibits a state from so fixing the selling price of milk."[35] Justice Roberts, writing for a divided Court, held that the Constitution did not prohibit New York from fixing the price of milk. Nebbia's conviction stood.

After reviewing the New York legislature's 473–page study of the milk industry's difficulties, Roberts observed that New York had been regulating the industry since 1862. Moreover, he listed at length other examples of state regulation to protect "public welfare." Finally, Roberts wrote that legislatures could legitimately decide on a policy of "free competition" or determine instead that prevailing conditions of "unfair competition" called for regulation of prices. The New York study found "price-cutting and other forms of destructive competition" that kept large dairy distributors from charging prices high enough to permit them to fulfill their public responsibility of carrying the surplus milk needed to satisfy unanticipated spikes in demand. For Roberts's majority, "fair competition" resulted from regulated market conduct, including price-setting, initiated because the legislature determined that "the conditions and practices in an industry make unrestricted competition an inadequate safeguard."[36]

A large chunk of Roberts's opinion deals with the state's power to impose "fair competition"—that is, the constitutional question of the proper relationship between "private property rights and the state right to regulate."[37] Roberts's treatment reveals some of the latent ambiguities in the liberal judicial view of private property rights. In the brief course of a few paragraphs, three conflicting renditions appear.

First, we are told that property and contract rights "are normally matters of private and not public concern. . . . The general rule is that both shall be free of government interference." While neither is "absolute," clearly public concern is abnormal. The implication is that an argument for public concern about property or contracts must overcome a presumption of abnormality. This formulation resembles the conservative bloc's presumptive distrust of majoritarian action. A *close* resemblance would require a *conclusive* presumption against regulation, except for fixed categories of legitimate regulation.

However, in the very next paragraph, Roberts's opinion shifts ground. Invoking Chief Justice John Marshall as oracular authority, Roberts writes: "Equally fundamental with the private right is that of the public to regulate in the common interest." Private rights and public interests now appear as equally weighted rights. "These correlative rights, that of the citizen to exercise exclusive dominion over property and freely to contract about his affairs, and that of the state to regulate the use of property and the conduct of business, are always in collision."[38] That is, they are equally, correlatively, fractiously, constitutional rights. Given this formulation, the new normal situation seems to be equipoise—a presumption-free balancing.

This second formulation, this idiom of equality, does not, however, survive the paragraph. For Roberts concludes: "But subject only to constitutional restraint the private right must yield to the public need." This statement seems to assert a new presumption, now favoring public need. Yet, there remains the ambiguous proviso of "constitutional restraint" on the public need. How does Roberts understand the constitutional limitation on legislative power? Is it Sutherland's categorical logic of property rights? Or the unweighted balancing of correlative rights? The opinion chooses neither alternative. Instead, the constitutional constraint is presented in Brandeisian terms: "Times without number we have said that the legislature is primarily the judge of the necessity" of legislation, "that every possible presumption is in favor of its validity." In the end, the early presumption favoring private property rights is turned on its head, flipped into a strong presumption favoring the constitutionality of "fair competition" by legislative fiat.[39]

There is, nevertheless, a consistent thread running through Roberts's alternative versions of liberal judicial respect for property rights. All three renditions of due process jurisprudence proceed from an image of colliding public and private "rights," separate political and economic spheres. What is absent from *Nebbia* is a vision unbounded by spheres—whether a Holmesian, legal realist notion of all rights as ultimately political or its mirror image, the Recovery Act's sense of fair competition as the political economic lifeblood of an organic body politic.

Two years later, in *Morehead v. New York ex rel Tipaldo* (1936), public and private rights again collided in open court. *Tipaldo* was another public price-fixing case, another employee compensation case in the line of *Adkins* (1923) and *O'Gorman* (1931). On its facts, *Tipaldo* was *Adkins* all over again—a statute requiring that "minimum fair wage rates," a "living wage," be paid to women.[40] Although Justice Sutherland's opinion in *Adkins* had found a similar congressional statute for the District of Columbia unconstitutional, the *O'Gorman* decision, written by Brandeis and joined by both Roberts and Hughes, had seemingly intervened, approving a New Jersey statute regulating minimum commissions for insurance agents. Which faction would Roberts and Hughes join? Despite the fact that each had written an opinion for progressive majorities in *Nebbia* (1934) and *Blaisdell* (1934), their earlier alliance with Justice Sutherland in *New State Ice Co.* (1932) evidenced a lingering attraction to the property rights rhetoric, the freedom of contract ideology, underlying *Adkins*.

They would separate, with Roberts joining the Four Horsemen to produce a conservative majority in *Tipaldo*. Justice Pierce Butler's opinion echoed Sutherland's in *Adkins*, insisting that equal treatment was required, because women were emancipated; because, that is, they had won the vote. There were "no exceptional circumstances" meriting special treatment. Thus, the New York minimum wage statute went beyond the state's police power and violated the constitutional freedom of contract. Indeed, Butler wrote that fair competition between men and women required competition free from government restraint; otherwise, women could not compete successfully with men.[41] A formal assumption of equality was the proper ground for liberty of contract.

As much as Hughes disliked dissenting, he could not join Pierce's majority. Hughes's opinion begins with his own view of freedom of contract, developed in *Blaisdell* (1934). At issue in *Blaisdell* was the very heart of the conservative bloc's jurisprudence: Article I, Section 10 of the Constitution—the Contract Clause. Liberty of contract was the issue, pure and simple: Could the Minnesota legislature authorize judges to change the terms of contracts between mortgage lenders and farmers? As in that term's *Nebbia* (1934) decision, Hughes and Roberts joined the progressives to ratify the legislature's regulatory power. Sutherland composed his most impassioned dissent of the period, writing that "[f]ew questions of greater moment than that just decided have been submitted for judicial inquiry during this generation." The decision would lead, by Sutherland's lights, "directly to anarchy or despotism." The very "principles of constitutional liberty would be in peril, unless established by irrepealable law." Sutherland's "irrepealable law" was, of course, the Four Horsemen's commitment to liberty of contract as constitutional first principle—a legal artifact of the late nineteenth century.[42]

In rejecting Sutherland's view that the statute impaired the obligation of contracts, Hughes's opinion in *Blaisdell* seemed to deploy a legal realist rhetoric worthy of Holmes himself: "The obligation of contract is the *law* which binds parties to perform their agreement." That is, contract law, not the intent of the parties, ultimately determines the content of their obligations to one another. Although sounding like the proposed *Restatement Second of Contracts* then in circulation, Hughes's opinion sought the mantle of precedent, not controversial overtones of legal realism. The authority for Hughes's view of contractual obligations, and for the assertion that the Contract Clause not be taken "with literal exactness like a mathematical formula," was not Holmes but Justice William Johnson, appointed in 1804 by Thomas Jefferson. Hughes reached back to the Marshall Court, to a jurisprudence preceding the *Lochner* era and its constitutionalization of liberty of contract, and borrowed Johnson's words: "Societies exercise a positive control as well over the inception, construction and fulfillment of contracts, as over the form and measure of the remedy to enforce them."[43] Hughes deftly placed Sutherland's call for "irrepealable law" into a longer historical context and, in consequence, raised it on its own petard: After all, wasn't it the Four Horsemen who had "repealed" law? Hughes was merely restoring it.

With this "restoration" of liberty of contract to its "proper" historical understanding as the framework, Hughes's dissenting opinion in *Tipaldo* (1936) boldly picked up the legal realist line with which Holmes ended his *Adkins* (1923) dissent. Distinguishing between what we today would call formal and substantive equality, Holmes, in his typical aphoristic style, had quipped that suffrage did not engender equality for women: "It will take more than the Nineteenth Amendment to convince me that there are no differences between men and women." Hughes was not one to quip. But his continuing reformation of liberty of contract was spurred by the same distinction between the formal assumption of equality and a substantive inquiry into actual economic circumstances. His authority for such an inquiry was Justice David J. Brewer's opinion for a unanimous Court in *Muller v. Oregon* (1908), the presuffrage decision upholding an Oregon law limiting the hours women could work. It was the pathbreaking brief filed by counsel Louis D. Brandeis, arguing "the facts," that had convinced the Court to uphold state legislation to "secure a real equality of right" for the "weaker sex" (women). Following the example of Brewer *cum* Brandeis, Hughes looked to the factual background developed in a study by the New York legislature. Hughes observed that the study found women were "not as a class upon a level of equality in bargaining with their employers in regard to minimum fair wage standards," and concluded that "'freedom of contract' as applied to their relations with employers is illusory." Moreover, sounding very much like the concurrent Recovery Act committee hearings in Washington, the New York legislative study concluded, according to Hughes, that the "constant lowering of wages by unscrupulous employers, constitutes a serious form of unfair competition against other employers."[44]

Hughes's revival of a pre-*Lochner*ian liberty of contract, applied to an industrialized society more than a century after the Marshall Court, presented substantive "equality of bargaining" as an indispensable element of "fair competition." Beware, wrote Hughes, of "a fictitious equality." It is "important to limit freedom of contract to prevent its abuse, thereby destroying freedom of opportunity." In short, the opportunity to compete was illusory without substantive equality as a limit on freedom of contract.[45]

For the Roberts majority in *Nebbia* and for the Hughes minority in *Tipaldo*, "fair competition" was seen as government regulation that required judicial scrutiny to survive its collision with private property rights. If "free competition" was not working, then government regulation, including enforcement of fixed prices, was constitutionally permissible. Moreover, judicial scrutiny should begin with deference to legislative determinations of need for regulation to produce "fair competition." The Four Horsemen, dissenting in *Nebbia* and, with Roberts, speaking for the Court in *Tipaldo*, sharply disagreed. They insisted that "fair competition" meant "free competition." That is, only competition free of political oversight, free of coercion, was fair (except in fixed common-law categories determined by the Court).

Private price-fixing and the competition rhetoric of "fair competition." There was a second line of "fair competition" logic, also ignored by the Court in *ALA Schechter Poultry* (1935). Unlike the property-rights rhetoric of constitutional concerns about public price-setting in cases such as *Nebbia* and *Tipaldo*, antitrust concerns about trade association cases were ultimately expressed in competition rhetoric. Nonetheless, both property rights and competition rhetorics always insinuated the other—whether the regulatory takings claims against "fair competition" in *Nebbia* and *Tipaldo*, or long-standing arguments favoring agreements to stop "destructive competition," despite their effects on prices, in antitrust discourse.

Ten years had passed since Justice Stone's opinion in *Maple Flooring* (1925) set the tone of tolerance Herbert Hoover was seeking for his program of scientific management and open competition. By the mid-1930s, trade associations were organizing everything from steel production to crèpe paper manufacture. The Court's approval of trade association activities had raised the difficult ideological problem of allowing cooperation within a regime of competition. The problem was solved by mediation, by a balancing of the sort seen in Justice Brandeis's opinion in *Chicago Board of Trade* (1918). Convinced that some competition was destructive, the Court allowed cooperation to cure "evil conditions." Chief Justice Hughes, in his *Appalachian Coals* (1933) opinion for a majority with only Justice McReynolds dissenting, wrote that a collective of small, independent coal producers was a reasonable restraint of trade, even if "the correction of abuses may tend . . . to raise prices to a higher level than would prevail under the conditions of free competition." With precisely the same language he would use in *Tipaldo* (1934), Hughes warned that "free competition" was sometimes "a mere delusive liberty." In the balance, Hughes concluded, allowing small producers to cooperate and, perhaps, to survive was more important than requiring their independence and thereby hastening their demise. Indeed, such cooperation would yield "fair competition."[46]

Thus, the *Appalachian Coals* decision conformed to the distinction between free and fair competition posed in the economic due process cases. Fair competition was competition restrained—here, by a *private* agreement adjudged reasonable. Three years later, however, trade association rhetoric took a curious turn. In the last of a twenty-year string of trade association decisions, Hughes's opinion in *Sugar Institute* (1936) dissolved the dichotomy between free and fair competition as well as the ideological tension between cooperation and competition. Like *Appalachian Coals, Sugar Institute* involved trade association agreements responding to difficult economic circumstances, to competitive "evils" in industries with enormous overcapacity facing dwindling demand: "Secret price concessions" and "double dealing," as well as "economic waste" in distribution, only increased already substantial losses for both sets of association members. The associations themselves, however, held vastly different positions in the troubled industries. Whereas the Appalachian Coals Association brought together one hundred thirty-seven small coal producers from one region, the Sugar Institute was a national association of eighteen large sugar refiners who produced 70 to 80 percent of the sugar consumed in the United States. Moreover, the Sugar Institute dominated the industry by enforcing adherence to published prices, blacklisting certain classes of distributors, setting commission and transportation rates, strongly discouraging long-term contracts, and prohibiting quantity discounts. After trial, the district court judge issued a decree enjoining the Sugar Institute from forty-seven specific "unfair methods of competition."[47]

What is shocking about the case is not the intricate specificity of the decree but rather the court's decision not to dissolve the Sugar Institute. Despite a history of anticompetitive practices, the Department of Justice, the district court judge, and the Supreme Court expressed no doubt that the trade association was worth saving. The regulatory decree was premised on the belief that it was feasible and worthwhile to distinguish competitive from restraining elements of the Institute agreement. Despite his earlier view that "free competition" can be "mere delusive liberty," Hughes now portrayed "free competition" as "free and open markets." The Sugar Institute, under the proper decree, would promote such free competition.[48]

For Hughes, "free and open markets" meant freedom from coercion and open sharing of information. His opinion reverberates with the corporatist ideology of Arthur Jerome Eddy's *New Competition*, the "open competition" vision of Herbert Hoover's associationalism: Cutthroat competition is bad, while fair competition is good. Fair competition requires standards, like the Institute's code of ethics, as well as "scientific knowledge" of the industry. The grant of secret concessions headed Hughes's list of unethical conduct. "Scientific knowledge" should include both cost and price data, both past and future transactions, and advance announcement of changes in terms. Ethical standards and widely available market information were thought to produce the kind of "intelligent competition" praised by Holmes and Brandeis in their

American Column & Lumber (1921) dissents.[49] Yet the industrywide agreements that produced such "open competition" had raised troubling questions about competition policy ever since Justice Brandeis observed in *Chicago Board of Trade* (1918) that all agreements restrain and that the issue under the Rule of Reason, therefore, was whether a given restraint is reasonable under the circumstances. For Brandeis's dissent in *American Column & Lumber* (1921), the cardinal issue was coercion. If an agreement was voluntary—if there was no coercion—then the restraint was reasonable. Trade association agreements must be voluntary.

Hughes's opinion in *Sugar Institute* adopted Brandeis's distinction between coercion and freedom and, in the process, bridged the classical opposition between individual and collectivity. The classical ideology of liberty called for individual action, unrestrained by agreements and other forms of cooperation. The early entity-view of corporations, for example, satisfied this ideological mandate by treating large corporate bureaucracies as "persons." Hughes wrote instead of "the freedom of concerted action," the value of "co-operative endeavor," and the need for "voluntary action . . . to preserve . . . fair competitive opportunities." He praised the Sherman Act as a "charter of freedom," as intended to encourage cooperative enterprise to protect individual freedom from destructive competition.[50]

Given this "freedom of concerted action," what was left of the traditional view, founded in individual liberty and group restraint, of cartels? For Hughes, there remained a clear, two-part distinction. First, the Sugar Institute was prohibited from "reaching or attempting to reach an agreement or concerted action with respect to prices or production." Second, the Institute was enjoined from taking "the steps . . . to secure adherence, without deviation, to prices and terms." Hughes understood competition policy as allowing "co-operative" and "voluntary" efforts, short of transgressing the market mechanism of setting price, to soften the effects of overcapacity and declining demand. Moreover, Hughes produced a litmus test for distinguishing between compulsion and agreement, between coercion and cooperation: It was enforcement mechanisms that threw agreements outside the rhetoric of "free and open competition."[51]

In consequence, a sharp distinction between public and private logics of "fair competition" emerged. Although private agreements could seek to transform "unfair" into "fair competition," and "destructive competition" into "free and open competition," they could not deploy means reserved to legitimate political action. They could not set prices, because market pricing is the essence of "free competition." Nor could they coerce compliance with private agreements, because coercion is a political prerogative. Thus, private agreements were reasonable restraints of trade under the antitrust laws when they were voluntary, when the result was "fair competition" and the means "free and open competition." For the progressive Justices, public regulation to produce "fair competition," coercive legislation to set prices, was reasonable under the Constitution when "free competition" failed, when it devolved into "destructive" or "unfair competition." For the conservative bloc, "free competition" failed only when government policy interfered with individual freedom of contract. Thus, "fair competition" meant competition free of government regulation (except in the fixed common-law categories determined by the Court).

The ALA Schechter Poultry *decision: "Fair competition" and discourses of political economy.* It was the very phrase "fair competition" that led a unanimous Court to conclude that the Recovery Act was unconstitutional. Chief Justice Hughes wrote that the "act does not define 'fair competition.'" "Congress," he insisted, "cannot delegate legislative power to the President to exercise an unfettered discretion to make whatever laws he thinks may be needed or advisable for the rehabilitation and expansion of trade or industry."[52] Not only the Recovery Act and its legislative hearings but two well-developed lines of Supreme Court doctrine—one antitrust and the other economic due process—presented available discourses of "fair competition." What led the Court to view "fair competition" as an undefined term, even though its jurisprudence was suffused with fair competition policy?

The *statutory* formulation of "fair competition" was alien to the Court's jurisprudential framework. First of all, the congressional hearings reflected a vision that transgressed the boundary between political and economic logics of fair competition established in economic due process and antitrust doctrines to differentiate between coercion and cooperation. The National Recovery Act intended its organic body politic to blend the two logics. Such political economy was simply unacceptable. Moreover, the Recovery Act fully satisfied neither the political nor the economic logic of fair competition. In consequence, the statute was declared unconstitutional.

Early in the opinion, Hughes quickly turned back the government's argument that the Recovery Act fostered a "co-operative effort by those engaged in trade and industry." Hughes did recognize a reasonable direction, a telos of "fair competition," in the statute's "single goal—the rehabilitation of industry and the industrial recovery which unquestionably was the major policy of Congress." But for Hughes, that was inadequate because the plan "involves the coercive exercise of the lawmaking power. The codes of fair competition . . . place all persons within their reach under the obligation of positive law."[53] In short, the Recovery Act could not intermix the practices of cooperation and coercion; it could not entangle the political power of regulation with the economic freedom to cooperate. Any coercion threw it into the category of politics.

Integrated political economy was simply not recognized as an alternative vision of fair competition. That is, the Court's bifurcated discourse of "fair competition" did not comprehend the vision of an organic body politic, both driven by deliberation about *economic* relations and safeguarded by a *political* norm of equal representation. The Recovery Act was forced to satisfy either the political or economic logic of "fair competition." Justice Hughes found that the statute satisfied neither.

First of all, the ideology of economics, the rhetoric of competition, denied a proper place for coercion. As we saw in the trade association cases, cooperation was encouraged in economic matters. The Court's recognition not only in Justice Brandeis's *Chicago Board of Trade* (1918) opinion but in the early trade association cases that all cooperation, all agreement, coerces, was lost in the more recent doctrine of open competition, culminating in Hughes's assertion of a "freedom of concerted action" in *Sugar Institute*. In the process, coercion and cooperation were realigned as mutually exclusive alternatives. Even though "voluntary" economic conduct always insinuated coercion, the doctrinal element of coercion came to mean only formal enforcement mechanisms. Thus, the Court could encourage cooperation free of coercion in the economic sphere by enjoining formal enforcement mechanisms.

The very presence of enforcement mechanisms consigned the Recovery Act to the political domain. The last question, then, was whether the statute satisfied the political logic of "fair competition." Politics was seen as necessarily coercive, as embodying legal processes of enforcement. In the shadow of the statute's enforcement provisions, the Recovery Act's theory of code drafting was not seen as deliberation and consensus. Rather, the entire statute was perceived as an adversarial legal process. The image that comes to mind is Justice Jackson's collision of public and private rights described in *Nebbia* (1934): no balancing or deliberation, but only head-to-head confrontations between competing private rights of property and public rights of regulating in the public interest. Thus, Hughes gave no weight to the political norm of equal representation, central to democratic politics and required in code negotiations, but of no value in an adversarial process. Hughes wrote the remainder of the opinion based on the assumption that the creation and enforcement of codes of fair competition were to be judged as purely politico-legal matters.

At this juncture, Hughes had already rejected the Recovery Act as integrated political economy since such integration was unimaginable. He had also found it inadequate under the pure economic model of fair competition since code enforcement involved coercion. Conceiving his third framework—the political model—in purely adversarial terms, Hughes now proceeded to determine whether the statute met the standards for coercive legal processes. The question was formulated in terms of proper delegation: Did Congress provide the positive control necessary to limit the discretion of those with the power to coerce? Hughes held that delegation was improper for two entwined reasons—one substantive and the second procedural. Delegation was improper because "fair competition" neither comported with common-law jurisprudences of fair competition nor allowed for the kind of judicial review necessary to make it comport with them.

Hughes concluded his analysis by holding the Recovery Act up to three juridical models of "fair competition." First, he turned to the "limited concept" of common-law "unfair competition." Was "fair competition" under the Recovery Act simply the obverse of "unfair competition," and thus limited by reference to common-law doctrine? Hughes read the statutory language as broader than the common-law protection from "misappropriation of what equitably belongs to a competitor," as developed in *International News Ser-*

vice (1918). With no further discussion, Hughes determined that the statutory language of "fair competition" did not permit the judiciary to turn to the common law to protect property rights from misappropriation under the Recovery Act code enforcement procedures.[54]

Second, the Federal Trade Commission Act language of "unfair methods of competition" was compared to the Recovery Act's "fair competition." There were two issues here—one the preliminary question of discretion in the FTCA phrase and the other the relationship between the two statutory phrases. What of the FTCA language, which, like the Recovery Act, expressed "a broader meaning" than the common law? Hughes wrote that neither provision "admit[s] of precise definition." But Congress compensated for the FTCA's open-textured language, he observed, by setting up "a special procedure," "a commission, a quasi-judicial body." "Provision was made for formal complaint, for notice and hearing," and, most of all, "for judicial review." In contrast, the Recovery Act "dispenses with this administrative procedure."[55] The requirement of close judicial review was unquestionable, at least since Justice McReynolds's opinion in *Gratz v. FTC* (1920), which severely limited FTC discretion. Although Hughes allowed that the scope of "unfair methods of competition" was broader than the common law, the phrase would always remain a question of law for the courts, not a question of competition policy for the FTC.

With the preliminary difficulty of FTCA discretion resolved by reference to formal legal process culminating in judicial review, Hughes proceeded to the question of the relationship between the FTCA's "unfair methods of competition" and the Recovery Act's "fair competition." Again, Hughes observed that the policy described in the Recovery Act, Section 1 "embraces a broad range of objectives" including but not limited to the "elimination of 'unfair competitive practices.'" He concluded that the judiciary could not limit the discretion of those with power to coerce compliance to the Recovery Act codes by reference to the FTCA. Neither did the Recovery Act itself make "provision . . . for judicial review."[56]

Third and finally, Hughes considered the government's argument that the Recovery Act scheme was like the Interstate Commerce Commission's supervision of railroad rate and route agreements. That claim also failed, again because the ICC provided for hearings, notice, and the findings of fact needed for judicial review.[57]

In sum, Hughes found the Recovery Act language of "fair competition" unconstitutionally vague, in terms not unlike the void-for-vagueness doctrine applied to criminal statutes under the due process clauses of the Fifth and Fourteenth Amendments. Here, a unanimous Court was convinced that the NRA code enforcement commissions were in a position to take someone's liberty or property without the judicial protection arising out of limiting precepts and extended legal process.[58]

The *ALA Schechter Poultry* decision held that the Recovery Act unconstitutionally delegated legislative power to the president or to private trade associations[59] because the statute lacked the safeguards to limit discretion. Lost in the opinion's rhetorical structure was Congress's new discourse of "fair competition," the Recovery Act vision of an organic body politic with a very different sort of safeguard—the political ethic of representational equality. Lost as well was the sense of political economy as a deliberative process, an experiment, guided by a goal or telos of "fair competition," rather than a stable deontology. The Court simply could not understand or would not allow such an institution because it did not provide a stable preceptual and procedural structure for judicial oversight.

Whether or not the Court's delegation doctrine is good political philosophy for judging the Recovery Act in theory, the Recovery Act's political norm of representational equality failed as a practice. Not only were code commissions dominated by large firms but labor and consumer representation had little impact. In both theory and practice, the Recovery Act dream of an organic body politic, safeguarded by the political norm of equal representation, driven by deliberation and motivated by industrial statesmanship, devolved into a nightmare. In the end, Chief Justice Hughes's announcement of the *ALA Schechter Poultry* decision was nothing more than a wake-up call interrupting a dream whose hopeful images only prolonged the everyday hardships and cynicism of economic struggle.

The Later New Deal, 1935–1948: The Consumer and a Unified Body Economic

In January 1935, the Seventy-fourth Congress began its first session amid an unsettling downturn in the economy. The National Recovery Administration was near collapse. Federal judges were issuing injunctions right and left, preventing federal officials from carrying out New Deal legislation—more than 1,600 injunctions during that congressional term.[60] Spreading labor strife reflected not only hard times but also the pessimism accompanying deep disappointment at Franklin Roosevelt's seeming indifference to the interests of workers, especially those in the auto, steel, and energy sectors. Manufacturers and retailers, big and small, looked with disdain upon the NRA's Blue Eagle.

The second shoe dropped later that year when the Supreme Court announced its *ALA Schechter Poultry* decision, which held the Recovery Act unconstitutional. Two things were now clear about the statute and the New Deal more generally. First, actual experience with code drafting and enforcement had betrayed the legislation's underlying vision of an organic body politic: Utopian aspirations failed to leaven economic inequalities. Political norms of equal voice and policy by consensus did not evolve in NRA industry councils. Second, the Supreme Court rejected political process in the economic sphere, even in theory. The *ALA Schechter Poultry* decision's demand for a priori legislative standards and post hoc judicial review envisioned severely constrained administrative agencies, agencies functioning as the middle tier in a three-level process of constitutional government. The Court simply repudiated the concept of administrative agency as a site for political activity—that is, for ongoing deliberation and formulation of policy without the kind of legislative limits that would permit judicial oversight.

On Capitol Hill, the year 1935 also marked the passage of two statutes that, at least in retrospect, indicated a new direction for the New Deal: No longer would the Recovery Act's holistic vision of an organic body politic inspire equitable economic relations among all classes. Instead, a second-generation New Deal would produce the Wagner Act, the Public Utilities Holding Company Act, and other statutes, each of which today we associate with a particular class or interest group.

The Wagner Act of 1935 entitled workers to organize. Yet, despite the New Deal's broad strategy of elevating wages to increase demand—of turning workers back into consumers—the statute segregated labor relations not only from industrial relations but also from consumer interests. It would create the National Labor Relations Board, a separate (and sympathetic) agency to enforce a duty to bargain in good faith and to adjudicate "unfair labor practices." Like shareholders under the 1933 and 1934 securities statutes, like small business owners under the antitrust amendments of 1936–1937, and like consumers under the 1938 amendment to the FTC Act, workers would now pursue their class interests in economic and administrative isolation.[61]

The Public Utilities Holding Company Act of 1935 empowered the Securities and Exchange Commission to investigate, regulate, and dissolve utility holding companies. By stacking holding company upon holding company, a few minority stockholders with small investments had captured control of massive accumulations of assets across wide geographic areas. Although the PUHC Act is seen as securities regulation aimed at stopping utility holding companies' abusive conduct in financial markets, the legislative history is replete with references to the impact on consumers. Unlike the Wagner Act, the PUHC Act's legislative history explicitly links individual shareholders and consumers by the harms they suffered at the hands of those few minority stockholders who controlled the holding companies. Nevertheless, both statutes reflect the later New Deal's shift away from the Recovery Act's vision of an organic body politic.[62]

The PUHC Act's legislative history is representative of later New Deal rhetoric. The consumerist rhetoric suffusing its legislative history exemplifies a new vision of constituents whose problems and solutions, and whose interests, were largely economic. Thus, a new body economic emerged from first disaggregating the earlier vision of an organic body politic into separate interest groups and then reaggregating them under the universalizing image of the consumer. That is, the particular interest group protected by a later New Deal statute and agency was seen as legitimate to the extent that the special interest coincided with the neutral, all-encompassing interest of the consumer. In short, all citizens, no matter their differences, shared interests as consumers.

Unlike the early New Deal's image of a holistic body politic working through difficult economic circumstances, later New Deal legislation envisioned, for the most part, a series of attempts to work out economic tensions between the interests of buyers and sellers: Should one be given priority over the other or could their interests be balanced? Moreover, given the growth of mass production, distribution, advertising, and retailing, these interests splintered into large and small business factions. Advocates for each faction sought the legitimacy of consumer well-being. Were consumer interests and small business interests facing a common enemy in big business? What of the consumer benefits flowing from large-scale production, distribution, advertising, and retailing? The later New Deal, both in its legislation and its administrative activity, acted upon a body economic disaggregated into markets, classes, and interests, all of which appealed to a unified public interest of "consumer welfare."[63]

In those years, the Supreme Court's competition policy was in transition, marked by a complex series of movements between the classical logic of liberty of contract and the neoclassical logic of market pricing as the proper rationale for regulating markets. Reflecting the hesitant shift from a rhetoric of individual liberty to a discourse of social institutions, the Court's treatment of both public and private restraints of competition showed signs of change, the first culminating in the "constitutional revolution" of 1937 and the second in approval of the new adversarial attitude assumed by Thurman Arnold's Antitrust Division. Private interests expressed in the rhetorics of property rights and freedom of contract were giving way to public interests understood in terms of federal competition policy and state regulation, now seen as legitimate commitments to leveling economic power and to serving the individual as consumer.

This section begins with a look at the influential report by Gardiner C. Means, submitted to Congress in 1935, describing the relationship between economic concentration and inflexible prices. The report provided policymakers with a new framework—postclassical economics—for overcoming the Great Depression through commercial egalitarianism and consumerism. The next three sections take up the economic discourses of commercial egalitarianism and consumerism as they emerged in the three branches of Roosevelt's New Deal government: first, in a sequence of four statutes passed by Congress between 1935 and 1938; then in administrative initiatives, particularly the ideological shift from corporatism to anti-trust seen most clearly in Thurman Arnold's tenure as Chief of the Justice Department's Antitrust Division; and finally in Supreme Court decisions about competition policy—the "constitutional revolution" of 1937, the emergence of Holmes's "marketplace of ideas" metaphor for speech, and the approval of activist antitrust enforcement by federal agencies, especially in the 1940s. The chapter concludes with a sketch of the later New Deal's new economic discourse of commercial egalitarianism and new image of the consumer for a unified body economic in the years immediately following World War II.

The Means Report: Economic Concentration and Inflexible Prices

In mid-January, 1935, "pursuant to Senate Resolution 17," Franklin Roosevelt's Secretary of Agriculture Henry Wallace submitted to the Senate "a report prepared and just now presented to me in final form by Gardiner C. Means, [my] economic adviser on finance." The report was entitled "Industrial Prices and their Relative Inflexibility."[64] It not only presented eye-opening data describing stable industrial prices through the depths of the Great Depression but also attributed that price inflexibility to large "quasi-public" corporations and a lack of price competition in the markets that defined their economic fields of play. Fourteen weeks later, in the early spring, the Supreme Court would announce its decision in *ALA Schechter Poultry*. Means's report would prove, in retrospect, both futile and influential. As the first closely reasoned economic argument for the National Industrial Recovery Act, it would have no impact on the statute's destiny, which was ultimately determined on other grounds in another forum. Nonetheless, the report and, more generally, its approach to understanding commercial markets presented federal policy-makers with the new orthodoxy of economics.

Within a few years, most economists would no longer treat commercial markets, in the absence of pure monopoly, as if they were purely competitive. In consequence, the problem of economic power would become both more complex and more widespread. The Means report brought into the political arena this new approach for thinking about and making competition policy. The new approach interwove two separate strands of recent research: the new political economy of "quasi-public corporations" developed in *The Modern Corporation and Private Property* (1932) by Means and Adolf Berle, and the postclassical economics of "oligopoly" explicated in Edward Chamberlin's *The Theory of Monopolistic Competition* (1933). American competition policy would display these dominant strands for the next sixty years.

The Means report begins with the declaration that "inflexible administered prices" were "largely responsible for failure of the policy of laissez-faire." In short, the foundation for laissez-faire was price competition. Still, the absence of price competition did not mean the absence of all competition: A great many "vigorously competitive industries in which the number of competitors is small" had "administered prices." This non-price competition in oligopolistic markets called for new industrial policy not dependent upon the pricing mechanism of traditionally competitive markets—a new industrial policy adapted to "administered markets" with few sellers, markets identified by changes in volume of production rather than changes in price.[65]

The report does not deal with the problem of monopoly, perhaps because monopoly was rare. Moreover, it makes no mention of monopolistic competition, no mention of Chamberlin's model of competition by brand differentiation. Means defined the problem as a dichotomy: not the traditional one of competition-monopoly, but a split within competition. The traditional, unitary view of competition depicted a multitude of sellers whose only profit-maximizing strategy was to meet the market price. The Means report describes a second form of competition. This new form of competition displays both the structural and behavioral characteristics of Chamberlin's oligopoly theory. As evidence, Means presented the results of his study of price and output levels in the years 1926–1933: In markets with few sellers, he found constant price levels and changing supply levels. In markets with many sellers, he found changing prices and constant supply.[66]

"Administered prices," the report cautions, "does not indicate monopoly" and, by implication, does not call for antitrust remedies. "Modern industrial organization and modern technology" have "brought a new type of competition and inflexible administered prices which disrupt the workings of the market." For example, General Motors set the prices for its automobiles and set production levels according to its estimate of demand at those prices. But GM would compete to sell as many Chevrolets as possible at its list price, and was willing to produce as many as its dealers could sell. With GM's rivals employing the same strategy, the automobile industry can be seen as an example of the kind of rivalry produced by modern "concentration of economic activity." In this way, large-scale production "destroyed the free market and disrupted the workings of the law of supply and demand." But it also "increased productivity." The report calls for a social policy with the twin goals of attacking administered pricing and preserving the benefits of large-scale production. Thus, the antitrust solution of atomizing large firms to create traditionally competitive markets was unacceptable because small firms could not produce the benefits of large-scale production. The report urges "new techniques of control" to "supplement" the market mechanism.[67]

The objective was "to accomplish what the market is supposed to accomplish"—that is, to mimic the function of traditional competition, to emulate the price mechanism's allocation of goods and services. The problem was to "set up a framework to allow individuals and groups to act in their own interests." This process of interest-group representation, with the "Government in charge," in conjunction with "key decisions" made by experts trained in the "highly technical matter of applied economics," would create industrial policy "to produce the most effective use of human and material resources." "As the interest groups became more nearly equal in power, their decisions would tend increasingly to be in the public interest." "The public . . . includes both producers and sellers, and the public interest requires the balance of these conflicting interests."[68]

The report concludes that traditional forms of intervention failed: Antitrust was ineffective because its policies "confused the absence of monopoly with the existence of a free market." Public utility regulation "focused on the interests of property" rather than on "balancing the interests of investors, workers, and consumers." Government ownership eliminated the market mechanism entirely.[69] But the interest-group balancing approach, too, was failing, even as Gardiner Means was writing the report. Perhaps he hoped that the NRA could be saved, could be reinvigorated with a balanced deliberation process that would not fall to the interests of those with economic power.

Means's hopes aside, the NRA experiment did fail to produce the interest-group balancing process called for in the report or the deliberation hoped for in congressional hearings two years earlier. Nevertheless, New Deal policy was given new life with the theory of oligopoly markets—the view of the public as both producers and consumers—and the language of "administered prices" and "concentration of economic activity." Moreover, the two models of administrative agencies reflected in the report—as bodies of experts and as arenas for political deliberation—would underwrite modern regulatory theory and administrative practice.[70] Certainly the Means report was not the only source for these ideas. But it was a highly influential public document, widely circulated throughout Washington—a document that played an important role in introducing the new economics to those engaged in the production of public policy and legal doctrine.

Congressional Legislation: Equality, Sellers and Buyers, Consumers

In the years 1935–1938, Congress passed a series of four statutes aimed at abuses of economic power, particularly at abuses of superior bargaining power. Traditional historians and legal scholars have not understood these four statutes in series. Rather, they have seen them in isolation—as one securities law and one consumer-protection measure, sandwiched around a "Depression era" pair of special-interest amendments shielding small, inefficient businesses from the competition of large, efficient firms. When viewed as efforts to equalize bargaining power and thus to promote robust competition, however, the four statutes represent a sequence of efforts to resolve conflicts between large-scale enterprises and small businesses, conflicts arbitrated by invoking the interest of a "neutral" third party—the consumer.

Shareholders and consumers: The Public Utility Holding Company Act of 1935. In August 1935, Congress assigned to the Securities and Exchange Commission the task of regulating and disassembling the "Power Trust," thereby fulfilling one of Franklin Roosevelt's major campaign promises. This anti-Trust legislation struck at a concentrated industry whose financial abuses had been the subject of government studies since 1925, when the FTC reported that twenty holding companies controlled more than 60 percent of the operating capacity of commercial electric power plants in the United States. In the twelve months before Congress enacted the PUHC Act, the National Power Policy Committee submitted its report to Congress, the House Commerce Committee produced a six-volume study, and the FTC published a new seven-year study in eighty-four volumes.[71]

The industry's high profile is easily understood. The reports and studies detailed widespread financial abuses in an industry whose protected monopoly status was premised on the need for financial stability. Both shareholders and consumers thus suffered injury. Commercial and residential consumers paid higher electric bills because public utility commissions set rates, then as they do today, based on operating expenses and a reasonable return on assets. The regulated utility's operating expenses were inflated by paying too much for management contracts and other services provided by the upstream holding companies. Asset values were inflated as well. Moreover, inflated revenues from rate payers, even when they covered the utility's abusive practices, were not passed on to utility company shareholders. In perhaps the most outrageous example of Berle and Means's "quasi-public corporation" and the dangers of separating ownership and control, minority shareholders who controlled the holding companies directed funds to their own accounts and manipulated markets in utility stocks to their own benefit.[72]

In *Electric Bond & Share Co. v. SEC* (1938), the Supreme Court would uphold the PUHC Act and the SEC's power to prevent nonregistering holding companies from using the mails and other "instrumentalities of interstate commerce"—that is, to prevent them from doing business.[73] Only then did utility holding companies begin to comply with the statute's registration requirements and only then did the SEC start to fulfill its statutory mandate.

Nonetheless, the utility industry's trust structure and thus its economic power remained largely undisturbed until 1946, when the Supreme Court held constitutional the SEC's power under the statute to dissolve utility holding companies. The defendants in *American Power & Light Co.* were two of the five intermediate holding companies controlled by Electric Bond & Share Co. "[F]rom its headquarters in New York City," wrote Justice Francis W. Murphy, "the Bond & Share system . . . embraces utility properties in no fewer than 32 states from New Jersey to Oregon and from Minnesota to Florida, as well as in 12 foreign countries." More than 25 percent of the electric energy transmitted across state lines was handled by Bond & Share companies. Justice Murphy concluded that the remedy of corporate dissolution was a reasonable result of, on the one hand, the congressional balancing of private property rights and, on the other, "the political and general economic desirability of breaking up concentrations of financial power in the utility field too big to be effectively regulated in the interest of either the consumer or the investor."[74] Such concerns about corporate bigness reflected the view that individual shareholders and consumers were in the same boat—that their common enemy was the financial privateer who pyramided holding companies not to create the efficiencies of large-scale production, but instead to defraud the public.

Independent retailers and consumers: The Robinson-Patman Act of 1936.[75] In July 1935, House hearings were convened to consider Representative Wright Patman's (D.Tex.) bill to amend the price discrimination provision of the Clayton Act of 1914. Largely the work of H. B. Teegarden, counsel to the U.S. Wholesale Grocers Association, the Patman bill and its Senate counterpart (sponsored by Joseph T. Robinson, (D.Ark.)), sought to strengthen the provision whose judicial interpretation, according to the amendment's sponsors, left too much room for large corporations to abuse their economic power.

In the twenty years since Standard Oil and other dominant industrial firms provoked passage of the Clayton Act (and the FTC Act), the logic of mass distribution had revolutionized the wholesale and retail trades. Chain stores such as A&P, Sears & Roebuck, and Woolworth were now perceived as the threats to competition. Their competitive advantages over small, localized rivals came from economies of scale, from the lower costs of purchasing, distributing, and marketing huge volumes of consumer goods. Their sheer size, complained small rivals, also created economic power, unequal bargaining power allowing them to coerce suppliers into giving secret rebates and quantity discounts far in excess of the lower costs of selling to these chain stores. As a result of such price discrimination, small rivals (and their patrons) had to pay even more to make up for the quantity discounts extorted by chain stores.

These complaints raised a serious policy conflict: On the one hand, chain stores were charging lower prices in a time of economic hardship. An assault on A&P or Woolworth could be, as well, a charge on consumers. On the other hand, chain stores were not only demanding lower prices from suppliers already in deep economic distress but also driving small dealers out of business. The Robinson-Patman Act can be understood as an attempt to regulate competitive practices in the spirit of Gardiner Means's compromise: to balance the interests of sellers and buyers by mimicking the price mechanism. The neoclassical assumption about competitive markets underlying both the Clayton Act and its 1936 amendment was that individual sellers set their prices according to costs, and that markets balance interests by pushing prices down to cost. The Robinson-Patman Act sought to improve the balancing process by policing this cost-price logic.

The Clayton Act, as enacted in 1914, prohibited anyone engaged in commerce from "discriminat[ing] in price between different purchasers of commodities . . . where the effect of such discrimination may be to substantially lessen competition." The prohibition expressed several antitrust virtues. First, it covered much more ground than the Sherman Act, which required proof of market dominance. Second, its competition rhetoric announced a clear rejection of the Court's property rhetoric—the classical freedom-of-contract ideology underlying its Rule of Reason jurisprudence. And, finally, although it aimed to prohibit conduct identified by progressive reformers as unfair competition, it did seek to preserve the benefits of large-scale enterprise and price competition by permitting price discrimination (1) "on account of differences in grade, quality, or quantity," (2) for "difference in the cost of selling or transportation," or (3) "made in good faith to meet competition."[76] The Clayton Act's price discrimination provision was reinforced by the Robinson-Patman Act in three ways.

First, the Robinson-Patman Act included an entirely new provision for buyer liability, a provision that reflected the Seventy-fourth Congress's concern about chain stores, whose buying habits fired the wrath of those affected most directly—wholesalers and independent grocers. Just as Standard Oil had mobilized congressional sentiments in earlier years, so did A&P provide the animus for the Robinson-Patman Act. In documents submitted to accompany his lengthy testimony before the House Committee on the Judiciary, H. B.

Teegarden, the Patman bill's acknowledged draftsman, excerpted the 1934 Federal Trade Commission Report on chain stores, as well as the transcript of a recent House Special Committee on Investigation of the American Retail Federation. These excerpts, along with other documents submitted, describe abusive buying practices of A&P, Kroger, and Safeway stores. A&P was presented as the worst offender; for example, it captured fully one-half of its 1934 profits from "secret and confidential rebates" obtained through "threats and coercion."[77]

There was very little debate or disagreement over this new provision, perhaps because it was understood as benefiting both consumers and small businesses without endangering the efficiencies associated with large-scale enterprise. In sharp contrast, intense debate surrounded the second major change to the original Clayton Act provision: the prohibition of price discrimination whose effect was to injure a competitor. The Clayton Act of 1914 had prohibited price discrimination whose effect "may be to substantially lessen competition or tend to create a monopoly in any line of commerce." This language of competitive effects reflected a Senate amendment, a significant change from the original House bill, which would have prohibited price discrimination, regardless of the competitive effects, "with the purpose or intent thereby to destroy or wrongfully injure the business of a competitor." While the Clayton Act required a substantial effect on competition, the rejected House version was concerned with something different—protecting the livelihood, the property of small businesses from the predatory practices of Standard Oil and other powerful enterprises. The Robinson-Patman Act of 1936 reinstated the House version rejected in 1914: Henceforth, price discrimination would be prohibited where the effect might be either "to substantially lessen competition" or "to injure, destroy, or prevent competition with any person who either grants or knowingly receives the benefit of such discrimination."[78] The Robinson-Patman Act revived concern for the individual competitor; its proponents insisted that injury to any individual competitor by price discrimination amounts to a lessening of competition and, ultimately, harm to consumers.

Even more controversial was the third change introduced by the Robinson-Patman Act—its elimination of the original Clayton Act's provision permitting price discrimination on account of quantity discounts. Left intact, however, was the cost-justification defense. In consequence, quantity discounts would be permitted only to the extent that, penny for penny, they could be cost-justified. Even though the original Clayton Act language seemed to require that the amount of a price discount given for quantity purchases be proportional to the quantity purchased, Representative Patman and his allies wanted to clarify the provision, because the commercial practice of quantity discounting without regard to associated cost savings was widespread. Indeed, the Federal Trade Commission had just determined in *Goodyear Tire & Rubber Co.* (1936) that Goodyear's contract price to Sears was discriminatory under the original Clayton Act, because the quantity discount to Sears was not proportional to the approximate savings directly attributable to selling in such quantity. Proponents of the Patman bill wanted to codify the FTC's explicit connection between quantity discounts and cost savings. Almost two years after the Robinson-Patman Act's passage, a federal court of appeals would substantiate Patman's concern: Sitting in Cleveland, the Sixth Circuit Court of Appeals set aside the Federal Trade Commission's order in *Goodyear Tire & Rubber Co.* under the preamendment provision for quantity discounts.[79]

There was intense congressional debate over abolishing the quantity discount provision. The debate moved along two parallel tracks. At one level, opposing factions clashed over a seemingly pedestrian issue of cost accounting—an issue, it turns out, with surprisingly strong normative implications. At a second level, congressional combatants waged polemical warfare, with proponents wielding the ideological weaponry of "fair opportunity" and "equality" against their opponents' rhetorical arsenal of "competition" and "efficiency."

First, there was the accounting issue of allocating costs. Representative Hubert Utterback (D.Iowa) submitted the Committee on the Judiciary's report. The report states that the Patman bill's abolition of the quantity discount provision "limits the use of quantity price differentials to the sphere of actual cost differences . . . whether they arise in operating or overhead cost." "This," the report concludes, "permits differences in overhead where they can actually be shown . . . but precludes differentials based on the imputation of overhead to particular customers, or the exemption of others from it, where such overhead represents facilities or activities inseparable from the seller's business as a whole." Representative Emmanuel Celler (D.N.Y.), the committee member whose relentless opposition fills the *Congressional Record*, argued that the new provision limiting quantity discounts would require a buyer to "pay for all the services the seller elects to have in his business," regardless of whether the buyer's order "happens to occasion" the services. That is, the "overhead costs" associated with the seller's sales, distribution, or research and development departments, for example, would be apportioned among all buyers—not only small buyers who counted on the seller to perform those functions but large buyers who had their own departments.[80]

The underlying conflict between these two views of the proper cost accounting methodology is normative. To begin, the Patman bill not only presumes but mandates cost-based pricing. This particular view of product pricing, although consistent with the neoclassical economics of price theory, does not reflect the way business is often done.[81] The proponents' assumption of cost-based pricing would lead to the inference that a change in cost always translates into a change in price—for example, that imposing a tariff always increases the price of an imported product, or that a weaker dollar and a stronger yen or deutschemark has the same effect. But experience has shown that higher cost does not always lead to higher prices. Sometimes a strategy of maintaining market share leads to the practice of pricing to the market and absorbing some costs or lowering others, rather than raising price. Except in the most abstract, simplified, neoclassical model of perfectly competitive markets, cost is only one factor in determining price.

Celler did not question the neoclassical presumption of cost-based pricing. Instead, he argued that the decision of how to allocate costs should be left to the entrepreneur. The intrusion of government into this decision-making process, for Celler, was the important normative question. FTC oversight would, according to Celler, raise prices to consumers and put employees out of work. FTC oversight of quantity discounts was a "dam placed across the stream of competition." The new provision "would lay an ax at the tree of efficiency in the movement of essentials of life from producers to consumers." The Patman bill "strikes directly at the primary interest of the public by denying consumers the assurance of obtaining the benefits of the lowest prices the most efficient methods and equipment can bring about under free, but fair competition."[82]

For Patman's majority, FTC oversight would lower prices for many small dealers, raise prices for a few large ones, and have little if any impact on consumer prices. In contrast to Celler's invocation of "efficiency" and "free competition," the committee report emphasized that the bill was seeking "to restore, so far as possible, equality of opportunity in business by strengthening the antitrust laws." In subsequent debate, Representative John E. Miller (D.Ark.) remarked that the "bill is based upon the simple American ideals of equal opportunity and fair play." Miller concluded that, insofar as "human values are greater than property values," it was of paramount importance to safeguard the "local merchants and manufacturers" who make up the "backbone of our Nation." Representative George G. Sadowski (D.Mich.) agreed, inveighing against the "old cry of laissez-faire." Congress has the "right to impose governmental restraints upon the conduct of private business." The Patman bill is based on "equal opportunity and fair play." Sadowski concluded:

> The monopolies insist on concessions, allowances, and rebates that enable them to compete with independent merchants. This, I say, is unfair competition. Why are they afraid or unable to compete with the independent merchant on equal terms? Why are they afraid to start with goods at equal costs? The monopolies claim to have superior efficiency. Let us have an honest test.[83]

For Celler and his allies, consumer and worker interests, as well as the viability of manufacturers, depended upon the manufacturer's entrepreneurial liberty to give quantity discounts, to determine or to ignore cost allocation, and, more broadly, to take advantage of large-scale production and distribution efficiencies—both his own and that of large retailers. For Utterback, Miller, Sadowski, and the others who spoke in support of abolishing the quantity discount provision of the original Clayton Act, consumer and worker interests coincided with the survival of small-scale, independent retailers and manufacturers who, given a real opportunity to compete on equal terms with large firms, would succeed: Their lower costs and thus their lower prices would benefit everyone except their large rivals.

Evoking Justice Rufus Peckham's classical image of "small dealers and worthy men," the bill's proponents insisted that fair competition required a commitment to equality, to equal opportunity. That commitment, however, produced a contradiction—it required both the preservation and the destruction of rivalry. Competition on the merits should allow no one to have a head start. If Mom & Pop's Corner Grocery must pay more for identical items than the local A&P pays, how can we ensure fair competition? How can the race go to the swiftest, if some runners begin at a 5-yard or 5-cent advantage? Yet the metaphor of a foot race is perhaps too simple. A&P, after all, was a complex organization structured to create efficiencies in distribution, to run more swiftly. Such efforts should be encouraged, not penalized.

The Robinson-Patman Act's strategy for equalizing competition embodies a compromise between equality and efficiency, between strict government control of wholesale prices, on the one hand, and unrestrained economic power on the other. It seeks to forge a fair start by stratifying competition along levels of distribution. Thus, for example, if all rival grocers pay the same wholesale prices, then the competitive success of any given grocer will turn on the process of competition. The same holds true at the levels of manufacture and distribution. The statutory exceptions to equal treatment—the "meeting competition" and "cost-justification" defenses—are appropriately competitive and meritocratic.

This design of a fair start founded in equality at each level of distribution produces a contradiction: An equal start at any given level requires administered pricing at the preceding level. Thus, the commitment to equality both fosters and transgresses competition policy. The idea, nonetheless, is to regulate vertical relations (competition between buyers and sellers) in order to foster rivalry among competing sellers (horizontal competition). However, the consumer, as ultimate beneficiary, falls outside the statutory scheme: Retailers are permitted—indeed, encouraged—to charge different prices to different consumers. But as final beneficiary, the consumer must be free to extract the lowest prices from the most efficient competitors. In this way, fair competition determines who is the consumer's true patron—A&P or Mom & Pop.

Independent retailers, small manufacturers, consumers: The Miller-Tydings Resale Price Maintenance Act of 1937.[84] Ever since the *Dr. Miles* decision (1910), the Supreme Court had prohibited manufacturers from setting resale prices. Still, the retailer's entrepreneurial freedom to set the price was subject to the manufacturer's property rights. As the Court declared in *Dr. Miles* and again in *General Electric* (1926), the manufacturer who consigned goods or who otherwise retained legal title had the property right to set prices for "its own" goods. The result of this confrontation between competition policy and private property rights was a two-track system for large and small manufacturers: Financially powerful manufacturers, who could afford to bankroll their retailers' inventories, were free to set retail prices and thereby to restrain competition among their dealers. Hence, dominant firms such as General Electric could control distribution, set monopoly prices, and be assured that they, not their retailers, would reap the benefits. Other financially strong firms such as Dr. Miles Medicine Company who faced competition could also assure retailers that their efforts to sell the product (and the higher costs of those efforts) would be rewarded with higher profits—that discounters would not undercut their prices. But small manufacturers sat on a second track. Typically without the financial resources needed to consign their products to retailers—unable to wait for payment until retailers sold their goods—small manufacturers were subject to antitrust prosecution for setting resale prices of goods sold outright, even though distributional restraints such as pegging prices might be crucial to convincing retailers to carry new products and to bring them to the attention of consumers.

Within this context, the Miller-Tydings Act can be understood as putting small manufacturers on an equal footing with their large rivals. By permitting *all* manufacturers to set minimum retail prices for goods identified with the manufacturer (in states that permitted it), the statute would allow small manufacturers to protect the retailers whose marketing efforts were so important to their success. In the congressional debates, little was said about small manufacturers. Still, Senator Millard E. Tydings (D.Md.) did characterize the statute "as an effort to strengthen the antitrust law, to make it apply so that the small businessman shall enjoy the same privileges which larger businessmen have enjoyed under the Sherman antitrust law through all the years." For the most part, *The Congressional Record* chronicles debate over the predatory tactics of large retailing chains and their effects on local retailers. Both supporters and critics of the Miller-Tydings bill wanted to eliminate loss-leader pricing by large stores—precisely the practice that had led Dr. Miles Medical Company some twenty-five years earlier to seek an injunction against a "cut rate and department store." Both supporters and critics in the Seventy-fifth Congress saw loss-leader tactics as "predatory pricing," as a way that large retailers exerted their financial power to destroy smaller rivals.[85]

Congressional factions did not agree, however, that the Miller-Tydings bill was the best way to solve the problem of loss-leader pricing. Much of the hasty deliberations reflected differences of opinion, though overwhelming majorities in the House and Senate ultimately voted for the bill. Despite voting in its favor, Representative Celler was the bill's most vociferous critic. Celler was concerned that the bill would "nail the consumer" because it would eliminate not only loss-leader pricing but all intrabrand price competition—among, for example, Ford dealers or among Dr. Miles patent medicine retailers. The "efficient distributor" and the "efficient merchant" will suffer, warned Celler, and, in consequence, the statutory "'cure' become[s] a poison by . . . exploiting the consumer." A California study that found higher prices under the state fair-trade statute was submitted to corroborate Celler's claim.[86]

In support of the bill, Representative John E. Miller (D.Ark.) expressed his belief that the small businessman was the backbone of America:

> The grocer, the hardware dealer, the jeweler, the pharmacist were to be found shoulder to shoulder with the doctor, the lawyer, the clergyman in their efforts to upbuild and uplift. These men constituted the woof and fabric of our national life. . . . These were the men who met in legislative halls, who sat on the bench, and who were entrusted with executive authority to give force and life to the principles of opportunity for all and special privileges to none.

Miller's concern was clear: "to equalize, to some extent at least, the difference between large and small business, and to strike down the unfair advantages the big operator enjoys." The bill was intended to thwart the "break-down in social status of those once engaged in conducting their own independent businesses. [Small-business owners] see the footsteps of a new feudal system with a few in complete control of the destiny of millions."[87]

Miller's remarks resonate with Jeffersonian sentiments. They evoke the property logic, the commitments to individual liberty animating the Literalist and Rule of Reason factions in antitrust's formative era, as well as their *Lochner*ian constitutional framework. They summon the classical political economics of "small dealers and worthy men" rather than the more recent economics of efficiency and cost-price relationships framing Celler's views. Celler was concerned with allowing the efficiencies of large-scale enterprise "to pass through to the consumer."[88] For him, the public interest was economic and the public was the consumer. The proper policy, according to this view, called for market correction to allow the price mechanism to function properly.

Celler and other critics were not alone, however, in summoning the consumer as the legitimizing public interest to be served. Alongside the Jeffersonian rhetoric of Congressman Miller, other proponents were claiming that consumers would be better off with the bill as law. They insisted that the interests of independent entrepreneurs were aligned with consumer wellbeing. Miller himself was careful to point out that his bill was explicitly limited to "a commodity which bears . . . the brand or name of the producer . . . and which is in free and open competition." That is, there must be lots of interbrand competition—between Coke and Pepsi, or between Ford and Chevrolet, for example—before manufacturers could fix retail prices in those items. The bill would ensure that consumers would no longer be "sandbagged and gypped" by the "predatory cut-rater" who "lured" them into the store with the loss leader, with the "crooked" promise of low prices. "Just as the gambler knows that the sucker can be induced to remain in the game by permitting him to win occasionally," so "the wily retailer proceeds to fleece" the consumer. Such tactics have long-term effects as well, warned proponents of the bill. Consumers would not only pay more, right away, for most items sold by large retailers and for all items sold by small independent retailers, but in time retailing would be monopolized by "large operators" and, in consequence, consumers would be paying monopoly prices for everything.[89] In sum, proponents were arguing that consumer interests were better served by promoting commercial equality among both independent retailers and small manufacturers.

Consumer welfare: The Wheeler-Lea Act of 1938. This amendment to the FTC Act of 1914 did not provoke the kind of robust debate heard in congressional consideration of the Robinson-Patman and Miller-Tydings Acts. Like the hearings on the Public Utility Holding Company Act, there was little conflict over whose interests embodied the "public interest." The Wheeler-Lea Act's clear focus on deceptive advertising and other fraudulent practices pointed the congressional process toward a unified figure for the public interest—the consumer. Whatever else one was, everyone was a consumer endangered by fraud and deception. Thus, everyone—the public—would benefit from adding language to FTC Act § 5(a) to "stop unfair and deceptive" practices. Indeed, the public interest was described as "consumer welfare."[90]

The original language of § 5(a) authorized the FTC to investigate and enjoin "unfair methods of competition." The Supreme Court had interpreted this provision as requiring evidence of some injury to competitors. Thus, the FTC lacked authority to stop false advertising, for example, that harmed consumers unless it could prove that competitors suffered injury as well. Although the FTC seldom had difficulty in finding evidence of such injury, the agency recommended amendment because "there are times when such a practice is so universal in an industry that the public is primarily injured rather than individual competitors."[91]

Along with several new sections relating to false advertising of food, drugs, therapeutic devices, and cosmetics, the Wheeler-Lea Act amended FTC Act § 5(a) to prohibit "unfair or deceptive acts or practices." The new provision would now "protect the consumer as well as the honest competitor." In a world of monopolistic competition, in which advertising provided the informational grounds for exchange, false or misleading claims would, if not eliminated, poison the stream of commerce. The FTC commissioners wanted to stop such deceptive acts in interstate commerce—whether found in the national advertising campaigns of large corporations or in the flyers of potion peddlers.[92]

There is something odd, however, about the amendment to FTC Act § 5(a). It seems almost superfluous. The two concerns motivating the amendment, hardly discussed and not debated, were admittedly thin: First, false and misleading advertising had been subsumed under the old language of "unfair competition" since the 1920s. Second, the Supreme Court's requirement of showing injury to competitors had not proven to be an obstacle to the FTC.[93] Why, then, bother to amend the section? The only explanation given was the possibility that an entire industry might engage in a deceptive practice, in consequence injuring no competitors. But neither the FTC Annual Report nor the congressional debates offered any evidence of such patterns of industrywide deception. Still, such concerns were more than theoretical: Both the FTC and the Justice Department were in the midst of prosecutorial sweeps through the nation's trade associations. Perhaps the FTC commissioners were more concerned with the economic consequences of mass advertising, more attuned to Edward Chamberlin's theory of monopolistic competition—particularly to what he called "manipulative advertising."

Whatever the expressed motivations of individual commissioners or members of Congress, however, the amendment's political economy was clear: The later New Deal identified with a unified body economic, a public interest subsumed under the universal image of the consumer. This universal image was, at least within the context of the FTC, profoundly abstract: Actual living, breathing consumers had no private cause of action under the FTC Act. Rather, it would be federal policy-makers—the FTC and the federal courts—who would determine the profile of "consumer welfare."

Statutory annuals, 1935–1938, and a unified body economic. With each of the four statutes I have discussed, Congress sought to equalize bargaining power—whether between shareholders and management, suppliers and retailers, or retailers and consumers. In the hearings convened to consider these four mandates to regulate vertical relations in commerce, those congressmen supporting passage argued that, in addition to benefiting an individual producer interest (shareholders, small businesses, and so forth), consumers would benefit. In debates over the Robinson-Patman and Miller-Tydings Acts, those opposing passage argued that both large-scale producers' and consumers' interests would be harmed by the statutes. The rhetorical battle over "the public interest" and the producer-consumer relations within it produced three-way struggles among advocates for large corporate organizations, small businesses, and consumers—battles between those who wanted more direct government supervision of commercial enterprise and those who did not.

In these debates, an abstract economic body called the "consumer" emerged as the unifying image of "the public interest" that would replace the National Industrial Recovery Act's failed vision of an organic body politic, a vision founded on the political norm of equal representation. The "consumer," personifying an economic form of equality, became the rhetorical term for mediating conflicts between competition policy and private property rights, between maintaining competition and protecting competitors, between the efficiencies associated with large-scale enterprise and the multiple virtues of small businesses. The Wheeler-Lea Act's amendment to FTC Act § 5(a), although it did little else, celebrated the "consumer" as the economic image of a unified public interest.

Roosevelt Administration Initiatives: Competition Policy and Consumers

The later New Deal involved much more than proposing and supporting congressional legislation. The Roosevelt administration's turn toward a political economy committed to commercial egalitarianism and consumer well-being inspired two administrative initiatives, both begun in 1938: first, Thurman Arnold's tenure at the helm of the Justice Department's new Antitrust Division; second, the work of the Temporary National Economic Committee. These two undertakings offer clear examples of a new political economy, a political economy that propelled the Roosevelt Administration away from the NRA's corporatism and toward an adversarial relationship with business not seen since Woodrow Wilson's prewar "New Freedom" platform.

Thurman Arnold: From "Folklore" to "Bottlenecks." In 1938, Franklin Roosevelt appointed Yale law professor Thurman Arnold as Chief of the Antitrust Division. In *The Folklore of Capitalism* (1937), Arnold had written that antitrust policy was a useless exercise in manipulating cultural symbols, an exercise whose ironic result was the legitimation of large corporate organization. How could Roosevelt hand the reins of antitrust enforcement to someone who had written that antitrust had in fact aided the concentration of economic power? Although some antitrusters in Congress professed misgivings, Arnold, the antitrust chief, would approach the Division as a social organization that assembled cultural symbols in a pragmatic process of producing material economic consequences. Not at all a Brandeisian progressive, Arnold adopted a prosecutorial philosophy that emphasized benefits to consumers rather than the virtues of small business. He analogized his approach to that of a traffic cop intent upon facilitating the flow of trade and upon teaching the commercial rules of the road. As a policy maker, he was more interested in clearing the "bottlenecks of business" than in punishing corporate size. Whether of a large corporate organization or an association of small businesses, Arnold wrote in *The Bottlenecks of Business* (1940), the measure would be economic performance.[94]

Sharing the concern expressed in the FTC Annual Report for 1938 about industrywide unfair practices, Arnold's Antitrust Division tended to investigate industries rather than particular firms. Moreover, many investigations resulted in consent decrees rather than in lengthy trials and extended appeals, with defendants agreeing to end objectionable practices. When Arnold did pursue criminal sanctions, his focus remained pragmatic: Asked about two highly publicized indictments following an investigation of the milk industry, he responded that the price of milk had already fallen 4 cents, to 9 cents per quart.[95] Thus, it was the cultural symbol of the "consumer" that inspired the shift from the early New Deal's corporatism, with its cooperative vision of government and business, to the later New Deal's adversarial view, and its turn to antitrust. And notwithstanding Arnold's self-portrayal as the helpful traffic cop, when violations, whether traffic or antitrust, result in consent decrees and criminal indictments, the relationship turns adversarial. As we shall see, the Supreme Court would approve the adversarial view of government-business relations—the image of a consumer as the body economic—as the unified public interest.

TNEC Efficiency Study: corporate size and economic performance. Shortly after Arnold's confirmation as antitrust chief, the Roosevelt administration and Congress assembled the Temporary National Economic Committee, one of whose members was the new antitrust chief. Charged to investigate the causes of price rigidity and concentration of economic power, the committee produced a number of studies, including the influential TNEC No. 13, entitled "Relative Efficiency of Large, Medium-Sized, and Small Business" (1941). The TNEC Efficiency Study applied two series of tests to compare the efficiency of three classes of producers—small, medium, and large scale. The first series investigated the relationship between size and average costs. The second analyzed the association between size and return on invested capital.[96]

The first series of tests developed four separate sets of average cost data: one set each for individual plants, groups of plants, individual companies, and groups of companies. For example, in thirty-seven of the fifty-nine tests of individual companies, small companies had the lowest costs. In twenty-one of the fifty-nine tests, medium-sized companies had the lowest costs. In only one test did a large company have the lowest cost. The other three sets of cost-tests (for individual plants, groups of plants, and groups of companies) produced similar results.[97]

In the second series, eighty-four tests were run for rates of return on invested capital earned by individual companies (in eighteen different industries). Large companies showed the highest rate of return fourteen times. In fifty-seven of the eighty-four tests, medium-sized companies showed the highest rate of return, while in the thirteen remaining tests small companies showed the highest.[98]

The study also combined the two series of tests to give cumulative results. For the 233 tests considered together, the study characterized the results (either cost or rate-of-return data) as a measure of "efficiency." The study concludes, "Thus, large size was most efficient, as efficiency is here measured, in approximately 11% of the total tests, medium size was most efficient in approximately 55% of the tests, and small size was most efficient in approximately 34% of the tests."[99] Here was powerful evidence that large-scale production was less efficient than smaller-scale alternatives. What could explain the divergence between these findings and economic theory about the benefits of large-scale production? Were Brandeisians right after all—that small and medium-sized businesses produced goods not only with civic virtue but also at efficient scale? Or was something blocking the "natural" advantages of scale? Was it the lack of competition, the smug dominance of large firms, or the cozy cooperation of industry associations that sapped these potential benefits? Were economies of scale at work in the real world, but at scales far below large-firm capacities in most industries? That is, were entrepreneurs, acting in Coase's model of the firm, incompetent cost accountants? Or, instead, were Berle and Means's observations about undisciplined management the key to regaining the benefits of large-scale production? Each of these potential theories for interpreting the TNEC Efficiency Study pointed to different competition policy initiatives. All of them, however, pointed to the consumer as the rightful beneficiary of public policy in the later New Deal.

From corporatism to adversarial antitrust. The TNEC Efficiency Study influenced Thurman Arnold and other New Deal policy makers to question the view that corporate size and industrial trade organization produced efficiency. Whether pursuing dominant firms or trade associations, Arnold sought the restoration of price competition to release the economic benefits of large-scale production. He saw his job as turning federal antitrust policy into a force for revitalizing competitive conditions in order to produce better products at lower prices—that is, to benefit the consumer. The Federal Trade Commission monitored advertising practices, as it had been doing since the late 1920s, but now with the broader powers of the Wheeler-Lea Act.[100]

Although Arnold's tenure at the Antitrust Division and congressional legislation during the later New Deal have both been criticized—Arnold for a failure to bring about structural change and Congress for protectionist legislation—both can be understood as seeking to reconcile an underlying tension in economic policy-making: the often conflicting interests of buyers and sellers, consumers and producers. These conflicting desires were themselves complicated: The ideology of neoclassical economics, understood in terms of efficiency, seemed to pit consumers and large-scale enterprise against small business. The ideology of individualism, understood in Jeffersonian terms of civic virtue, seemed to pit consumer/citizens and small businesses against large corporate interests. The TNEC Efficiency Study seemed to interject a neo-Jeffersonian view that small and medium-sized businesses produced not only civic virtue but economic efficiency.

Although congressional legislation purported to serve consumers and anyone else whose interests aligned with this universalized image of the public interest, the Antitrust Division under Arnold simply sought to carry the logic of efficiency and the ideology of consumerism to their neoclassical conclusions. The FTC was turning to postclassical economic concerns about mass advertising, although the consumer protection was limited to extreme cases—outright fraud or deception. This new ideology of consumerism was emerging as a powerful force in Congress, the FTC, and the Antitrust Division for unifying the "public interest" and thus for leavening inequalities of bargaining power. The later New Deal's political economy rested on the fundamental premise that the most productive relationship between government and business was adversarial.[101]

The Supreme Court: Liberty, Property, Equality

The final arbiter of congressional legislation and other New Deal initiatives remained the Supreme Court and its twin messages. In the *Nebbia* and *Blaisdell* decisions (1934), the Court deferred to political decisions to regulate private property rights in the public interest. In *ALA Schechter Poultry* (1935), however, a unanimous Court held unconstitutional the centerpiece of the New Deal experiment—the National Industrial Recovery Act—despite numerous earlier instances of similar delegation of legislative power.[102]

The legislation that followed *ALA Schechter Poultry* reflected a shift in New Deal political economy from building an organic body politic to fragmenting interest groups, distributing them among federal agencies, and reaggregating them in the public image of the consumer. At the same time, state legislatures continued to enact minimum wage, maximum hour, and other progressive labor legislation. How would the Court treat these statutes? With Justice Roberts's epiphany—such as it was—and Justice Van Devanter's retirement, the Court would expand the public domains of state police power and congressional interstate commerce authority, thereby shrinking the private realm of contract and property rights.[103]

A new jurisprudence would emerge out of Supreme Court doctrine in labor and antitrust cases. Whether regulating the commercial marketplace for goods and services or a political "marketplace of ideas" and free speech, the new jurisprudence revealed a reformulated notion of individualism. This remodeled individualism and its rhetoric of liberty invoked twin public images that guided the Court's new concern for leveling inequality. The first image, the consumer as embodying the public interest, authorized the regulation of bargaining power in private commercial transactions; the second image, the citizen as holding a bundle of constitutional freedoms, authorized the regulation of political majorities seeking to silence individuals in the political marketplace of ideas. Both consumers and citizens were now imagined as participants in marketplaces. Hence, Court doctrine, like congressional legislation and administrative initiatives, unfolded within an economic discourse of free competition.

Labor regulation: commercial egalitarianism and consumers. Historians have described the "constitutional revolution" of 1937 as the Supreme Court's new attitude of deference to democratic institutions, as a politically correct demeanor of judicial self-restraint in matters of social and economic policy. After all, it is the elected legislature, be it federal or state, that reflects the will of the citizenry, not an appointed federal judiciary. Justice William O. Douglas soon made plain the extent of this deference, writing that the presumption of constitutionality accorded legislation was so strong that states had no burden of showing how actual economic or social conditions justified the regulation at issue.[104]

This "revolution" was accompanied by a rhetorical rift, a break in the traditional bond between liberty and property rights. Individual liberty would now encompass a commitment to equality and thus a limitation on property rights, as Justice Hughes adumbrated in his *Tipaldo* dissent (1936). Differentiating between liberty and property rights divided the constitutional integrity of liberty of contract. In consequence, liberty of contract could no longer provide the fixed molecular infrastructure for a constitutional theory of legitimate state action. Instead, a new figure emerged out of dynamic images of the citizenry as consumers, of politics as competition in ideas, and of public discourse as a marketplace of ideas—a figure that inspired the Court's reconception of majoritarianism.

How, then, did the Court reconfigure the states' police power and the federal interstate commerce power—the legitimate spheres of political action in the public interest? It was Justice Brandeis's opinions in *International News Service* and *Chicago Board of Trade* (1918) that first offered dynamic visions of property rights and competition policy, each one framed in a jurisprudence of balancing private rights and public needs. Three years later, Brandeis, dissenting in a labor injunction case, made clear his view of the relationship between property and politics, competition, and liberty. Writing for a divided Court in *Truax v. Corrigan* (1921), Chief Justice Taft had struck down a Wisconsin statute shielding labor unions from anti-strike injunctions. Brandeis, however, maintained that Taft's boilerplate logic of injunctions that purported to make the world safe for property rights made no sense insofar as "every change in the law governing the relation of employer and employee must abridge, in some respect, the liberty or property of one of the parties." Moreover, Brandeis continued, both legislative exercise of the police power and commercial competition—whether by rivals or "suppliers of merchandise or of labor"—are legitimate causes for interfering or even destroying the property or liberty right to "carry on business." Most importantly, Brandeis observed, property and liberty rights were themselves in conflict—in labor picketing cases, for example—whenever "an alleged danger to property" abridged the "constitutional rights of individuals to free speech, to a free press, and to peaceful assembly."[105] The implication was that more weight should be given to civil and political rights. After 1936, Supreme Court jurisprudence would reflect Brandeis's views. However, the jurisprudence would track the later New Deal's rhetorical shift from political to economic imagery.

The "constitutional revolution" of 1937 began, of course, with twin decisions published three years earlier. In his *Nebbia* (1934) opinion, Justice Roberts struggled to reconcile what he imagined as the colliding forces of private property rights and public need, ultimately reposing in a presumption that the New York statute and, more generally, state regulation of economic matters were presumptively constitutional interferences with private property rights. In *Blaisdell* (1934), Chief Justice Hughes faced squarely the thirty-year regime of *Lochner*'s contractarian jurisprudence, writing that freedom of contract did not exhaust the constitutional meaning of liberty. He looked back to Marshall Court Justice William Johnson for the "legal realist" view that contractual obligations are ultimately determined by contract law, not by the will of the parties. In short, public policy ultimately defines private rights. Accordingly, political action can redefine or reshape marketplace economics. And so, Hughes concluded, the Minnesota legislature could legitimately impose a moratorium on lenders' contractual rights to foreclose on farm mortgages.

Hughes's new-old view of public policy and private contract led him in *Tipaldo* (1936) to dissent from the Court's position that a state minimum wage statute for women was unconstitutional. Hughes accepted the New York legislature's findings that women were "not as a class upon a level of equality with their employers," concluding that this inequality rendered "'freedom of contract' as applied to their relations with employers illusory." Legislative concern about inequality of bargaining power was, for Hughes, a legitimate public policy basis for political action to override private agreements. With Justice Brandeis's balancing jurisprudence as the framework, Chief Justice Hughes's opinions in *Blaisdell* and *Tipaldo*, particularly their reconstruction of liberty of contract, provided the building blocks for his majority opinion in *West Coast Hotel v. Parrish*[106]—one of the "revolutionary" decisions written in 1937.

Deserting the Four Horsemen, Justice Roberts joined Hughes's majority opinion in *West Coast Hotel*, which upheld a State of Washington statute setting minimum wages for women. Writing one of the last opinions for his conservative quartet, Justice Sutherland dissented from a majority opinion that explicitly rejected his *Tipaldo* opinion for the Court, written just one year earlier. "[T]he employer and employee have equality of rights," he still insisted, "and any legislation that disturbs that equality is an arbitrary interference with liberty of contract."[107] For Sutherland's faction, a formal assumption of equality remained the proper foundation for liberty of contract.

"What is this freedom?" asked Hughes. "The Constitution does not speak of freedom of contract. It speaks of liberty." Moreover, Hughes wrote, "the Constitution does not recognize an absolute and uncontrollable liberty." Taking up language from an opinion he wrote some twenty years earlier during his tenure as an Associate Justice, Hughes maintained, "The guarantee of liberty does not withdraw from legislative supervision that wide department of activity which consists of the making of contracts, or deny to government the power to provide restrictive safeguards." Thus, he concluded,

> [L]iberty safeguarded is liberty in a social organization which requires the protection of law against the evils which menace the health, safety, morals, and welfare of the people. Liberty under the Constitution is thus necessarily subject to the restraints of due process, and regulation which is reasonable in relation to its subject and is adopted in the interests of the community is due process.

And a community—here, the State of Washington—could reasonably decide that low wages paid to women employees constituted "exploitation of a class of workers who are in an unequal position with respect to bargaining power." A minimum-wage statute is a legitimate regulation of contract "where the parties do not stand upon an equality." For Hughes's bare majority, formal equality was not enough: "[T]he Fourteenth Amendment did not interfere with state power by creating a 'fictitious equality.'"[108] Hughes and the new majority opened wide a new constitutional doorway for public policy to enter the private domain of individual liberty. Whether a minimum-wage statute or a legislative moratorium, a state could legitimately distribute property rights to equalize bargaining power in difficult economic circumstances.

Still, the new jurisprudence was not "revolutionary." Although it appealed to progressive sensibilities, it did not threaten the social institutions of private property and contract rights. Indeed, their legitimacy was perhaps strengthened by opening them to supervening public interests under exceptional circumstances—either economic emergency or gross inequality of bargaining power. Under "normal" circumstances, private property and contract remained perfectly adequate institutions for ordering society. Yet, there was the threat that the exceptions—the rhetoric of "emergency" and the logic of "equality"—might swallow the rule. Justice Sutherland and his fellow dissenters, and a wavering Justice Roberts, were troubled by the introduction of a public policy virus into the body of private property and contract rights.

The *NLRB v. Jones & Laughlin Steel* decision, also handed down in 1937, was a breakthrough for New Deal policy makers. Finding the Wagner Act of 1935 to be a constitutionally permitted exercise of congressional power to regulate interstate commerce, the Court approved the National Labor Relations Board and, in the process, ratified the federalization of labor relations. While this was undoubtedly a significant change worth all of the attention it has attracted, a pair of labor decisions published three years later offers clear sight lines into a widening rift between the imperatives of liberty and property, and the expanding reach of the new competition rhetoric of consumerism. *Thornhill v. Alabama* sought to reconcile a conflict between First Amendment liberties and property rights in the marketplace of ideas; *Apex Hosiery v. Leader* endeavored to mediate a conflict between competition policy and property rights in the marketplace for goods.[109]

Competition as a metaphor for envisioning free speech rights was not unknown to the Court, although confined to several renowned dissents by Justice Holmes. In *Thornhill* (1940), Justice Frank Murphy, with only McReynolds dissenting, relied on the competition metaphor to resolve a labor picketing dispute that threw free speech and property rights into direct conflict. The opinion adopts Justice Holmes's legitimating image for free speech—the free "marketplace of ideas" drawn in his dissenting opinions some twenty years earlier.[110]

Thornhill involved an Alabama statute that prohibited loitering and picketing. Just as federal judges issued injunctions under the antitrust laws to protect employers' property from irreparable harm, so did the Alabama legislature enact an anti-picketing statute to shield employers from the effects—whether destruction of physical property or interference with the property right to conduct business—of labor protests. When Byron Thornhill and a few fellow workers, all of whom lived in the company town owned by their employer, engaged in peaceful picketing, they were arrested and tried under the statute. The Inferior and Circuit Courts of Tuscaloosa County convicted Thornhill and sentenced him to imprisonment for seventy-three days. Before the United States Supreme Court, Thornhill's lawyers asserted that the statute violated his constitutional freedoms of speech and assembly.

The Court found the statute unconstitutional, Justice Murphy writing that in "the circumstances of our times the dissemination of information concerning the facts of a labor dispute must be regarded as within that area of free discussion that is guaranteed by the Constitution." The practice of picketing, according to Murphy, involves even more than publication of facts. It affords "an opportunity to test the merits of ideas by competition for acceptance in the market of public opinion."[111] In short, the Court understood labor relations as more than private contractual disputes between employer and employee; as, remarkably, a matter of public interest deserving of open debate in what was later christened the "marketplace of ideas." The Court's introduction of free speech rights and competition rhetoric into the labor relations discourse of property rights and struggle changed the balance of power between employer and employee. With this new admixture of politics and economics, of competition policy and property rights, labor relations were recast.

Nevertheless, the image of labor relations retained its familiar profile: First and foremost, the view of labor relations as politics not economics, as struggle not competition, held firm. Murphy described state power to modify "the rights of employers and employees" as the authority "to set the limits of permissible contest open to industrial combatants."[112] It was unquestionably legitimate for the State of Alabama to exercise its police power to protect employers and others from the anticipated dangers of industrial warfare—physical violence and injury to property. However, the Court's vision of labor relations as politics embraced a larger view of labor relations as something more than *physical* struggle. In contrast to an earlier era's view of all labor picketing as inherently threatening, Murphy's opinion recognized peaceful picketing by a few workers as political but nonphysical, nonthreatening conflict—that is, as political speech. Whether because a realist jurisprudence opened the Court to the empirical possibility of nonviolent picketing by a few workers in a company town or because a new solicitude toward labor informed the Court's deliberations, a nonthreatening rhetoric of free speech took hold. Now, so long as the picketing was peaceful, so long as it did not threaten a clear and present danger to person or property, it was political speech whose exercise was protected.

The practical significance to employers was a loss of property rights. That is, picketing was protected speech even when it interfered with the conduct of their business. Justice Murphy wrote that "picketing and loitering"

> may enlighten the public on the nature and causes of a labor dispute. The safeguarding of these means is essential to the securing of an informed and educated public opinion with respect to a matter which is of public concern. It may be that effective exercise of the means of advancing public knowledge may persuade some of those reached to refrain from entering advantageous relations with the business establishment which is the scene of the dispute. Every expression of opinion on matters that are important has the potentiality of inducing action in the interests of one rather than another group in society. But the group in power at any moment may not impose penal sanctions on peaceful and truthful discussion of matters of public interest merely on a showing that others may thereby be persuaded to take action inconsistent with its interests.[113]

In short, employers could not use their economic and political power to prevent employees from seeking to persuade others to help them by boycotting the employer's products. Employees could exert economic pressure by disseminating information to potential consumers, who might decide to do business elsewhere; consumers, who have a right to vote with their dollars. Thus, employees engaged in rhetorical struggle were not only exercising a political right. They were competing in "the market of public opinion."[114] This calming vision of politics as rhetorical rivalry, as free competition in the marketplace of ideas, displaced the older view of labor as a menacing underclass of foreigners, radicals, and other dangerous types.

This ideology of marketplace pluralism projected a new image of labor as simply one "group in society" seeking to further its interests through legitimate political means. In this light, the invocation of speech rights ruptured the idea of liberty, exposing a tension between civil liberties and private property rights. In the Anglo-American political tradition, individual liberty was understood as depending upon property rights. Indeed, Thomas Jefferson, like John Locke and James Harrington before him, thought of "freemen" as property owners.[115] Writers before the industrial revolution saw the economic independence of property ownership as a condition precedent to political freedom. But this controversy over labor picketing in a company town, in an industrialized society accompanied by enormous inequalities of property ownership, pitted individual liberty against property rights: How should the propertyless employee's freedom of speech and the employer's private property rights be adjudicated when the exercise of one inescapably trespassed upon the other? The Court turned for its answer not only to the political rights of free speech and assembly but to a new image for free speech, to a rhetoric of competition.

The Alabama statute did include a proviso limiting its application: "Nothing herein shall prevent any person from soliciting trade or business for a competitive business."[116] Justice Murphy and his strong majority determined that Byron Thornhill and his fellow picketers had a constitutional right to engage in comparable competition. Measured by Murphy's opinion, it was a very short distance from the marketplace of ideas, of public opinion, to the market for the products of Brown Wood Preserving Company. The State of Alabama could not restrain competition in ideas in order to protect the company from the threat of losing the business of those who disapproved of its labor policies. The benefits of competition, to striking employees and educated consumers alike, merited constitutional protection, despite injury to property rights suffered by the employer. Competition, as Brandeis pointed out in *Truax* (1921), always injured someone's property rights.

This political vision of economic competition came at a time when decisions such as *Nebbia* (1934) and *Parrish* (1937) were giving states broad discretion to regulate competition in goods and services. What states could not regulate so easily now was open access to the marketplace of ideas, participation in the political process of competition that legitimated their decisions.[117] In short, this Court would make substantive judgments about majoritarian decisions to limit individuals' civil rights, much as the *Lochner* Court had made such judgments about majoritarian decisions to limit individuals' property and contract rights. The more recent idea of opening access to the political process certainly served the democratic value of majoritarianism—even when it turned aside majoritarian legislation such as the Alabama statute. The process, it seems, was given more respect than its outcomes. The outcomes were, however, seen as legitimate, as serving the public interest, when everyone benefited—that is, when an image of the consumer conjured a conception of a unified body economic.

But what of labor disputes characterized as restraints of trade in commercial markets, as conduct outside the constitutionalized marketplace of ideas? Since 1895, competition policy had led the Court to issue an unbroken line of decisions approving the issuance of antistrike injunctions under the antitrust laws. *Apex Hosiery v. Leader* (1940),[118] a labor case decided during the session that produced *Thornhill,* broke that line of antitrust decisions.

In the mid-1930s, labor unions began to organize sit-down strikes, in large part because this strategy shut down employers entirely, denying them the possibility of hiring nonunion replacement labor. On May 6, 1937, a small group of labor organizers staged a violent takeover of the Apex Hosiery Company, shutting down its Philadelphia manufacturing plant, which employed more than 2,500 workers. Reinforced by union workers from other factories in the area, the American Federation of Full Fashioned Hosiery Workers picketed, obstructed shipments, and demanded a union shop. After a full trial, a jury found that the Federation's sit-down strike constituted an illegal restraint of trade under the Sherman Act. The Third Circuit Court of Appeals overturned the District Court, finding that the boycott had an insubstantial effect on competition and that the strikers did not intend to restrain interstate commerce. The Supreme Court affirmed the Court of Appeals, finding that the Sherman Act simply did not apply to the strike.[119]

Conceding that the statute applies to some labor organization activities, Justice Stone asked the following question: Is this "the kind of restraint of trade or commerce at which the Act is aimed?" Looking into the legislative history, Stone found that

> [t]he end sought was the prevention of restraints to free competition in *business and commercial* transactions which tended to restrict production, raise prices or otherwise control the market to the detriment of *purchasers or consumers* of goods and services, all of which had come to be regarded as a special form of public injury.

Stone then cited the "consumer" language of the 1888 Sherman bill—language rejected in favor of the statute's common-law rubric of restraints of trade. Stone disregarded as well the common-law rubric of the *Addyston Pipe* (1898) and *Standard Oil* (1911) opinions, including them as further examples of a primary concern about the "threat of enhancement of prices." Notwithstanding Stone's readings, both opinions were primarily concerned not about prices but rather about restraints on freedom of contract—whether imposed by political majorities or by private cartels. Indeed, *Addyston Pipe* was particularly questionable authority, given Justice Peckham's reliance on *In re Debs* (1895)—a labor case. Justice Stone concluded his rationale for the view that the Sherman Act was intended primarily to regulate "commercial competition" by paraphrasing Justice Brandeis's new Rule of Reason in *Chicago Board of Trade* (1918): "Restraints on competition . . . is [*sic*] not enough, unless the restraint is shown to have or is intended to have an effect upon prices in the market or otherwise deprive *purchasers or consumers* the advantages which they derive from free competition." Accepting the Circuit Court's finding that the strikers neither intended nor had an effect on hosiery prices, Stone concluded that this violent, destructive strike did not offend the "consumer" policy underlying the Sherman Act. Chief Justice Hughes, joined by Justices Roberts and McReynolds, disagreed on both counts and dissented.[120]

In finding the Sherman Act inapplicable, Stone evoked the same image for the public interest seen in administrative initiatives and congressional legislation of the period: the unquestionable authority of the consumer as a unified body economic. The Sherman Act, like the Wheeler-Lea Act of 1938, was intended to serve "consumer welfare." Thus, the antitrust laws could no longer provide the ground for a labor injunction—for equitable relief founded in the claim that strikes must be stopped because they do irreparable harm to the employer's property. It was not that property interests were no longer relevant. Rather, the reorientation of competition policy toward consumer welfare shifted the protected property interest to consumers. Serving the "public interest" meant protecting the interests of consumers in the low prices produced by competitive markets.

The *Apex Hosiery* and *Thornhill* decisions equalized bargaining power between employers and employees by turning to a marketplace imagery of economic competition. In the discourse of antitrust, the public interest was identified with the image of the consumer. In the discourse of constitutional law, the public interest was identified with the visage of the citizen—a citizen whose rights depended upon free competition in a marketplace of ideas. In both rhetorical formulations, competition policies were advanced to trump established private property rights. In both, the class interests of workers were reformulated by reference to neutral, unified visions of a "public interest" linked to marketplace competition—whether the consumer or the citizen-as-market-participant. At the same time, the marketplace metaphor promised that there would be no radical change but rather an adjustment in bargaining power between workers and owners/managers. Business owners could still sue under the common law to remove workers from the premises and to collect damages. They could still hire nonunion labor to break strikes. Union workers still faced prosecution for violations of criminal laws. Yet, when coupled with the Wagner Act's imperative that owners/managers bargain in good faith, the consumerist rhetoric of competition did introduce public interests to limit the reach of traditional contract and property rights in labor relations.

Antitrust regulation: the goals of competition policy and discourses of economics. Even before Thurman Arnold took the helm of the Antitrust Division in 1938, the Roosevelt administration had begun to enforce the antitrust laws more aggressively. With Arnold's arrival and with the Federal Trade Commission's investigations of industrywide practices, strengthened by the Wheeler-Lea Act's more expansive language, adversarial antitrust displaced the corporatist sensibilities of Roosevelt's National Industrial Recovery Act and Hoover's trade associationalism. In virtually all cases, the Supreme Court approved the later New Deal's aggressive antitrust enforcement. Although there were some opinions written by Justice Hugo Black that reinscribed a Jeffersonian rhetoric of "small dealers and worthy men"—a rhetoric not anchored to economics discourse—the Court acquiesced in this antitrust reformation, often invoking the same twin images that inspired the "constitutional revolution" of 1937: marketplaces of goods and ideas whose legitimate constituencies were consumers and citizens-as-market-participants.

Yet Court opinions, both majority and dissenting, often mixed conflicting ideas about competition because they frequently adopted elements from three different paradigms of economics. The goals of competition policy shifted as well, reflecting the era's congressional solicitude toward both consumer welfare and small producer interests while seeking the economic benefits of large-scale production. The opinions were so heterodoxical because there was no consistent relationship between the three economics paradigms and the three goals for competition policy. That is, antitrust jurisprudence skipped across an uneven terrain of economic discourses and, in the process, touched upon an array of goals for competition policy.

Nonetheless, antitrust doctrine did follow a rough trajectory. First, arguments framed in property rights rhetoric were increasingly unsuccessful; second, Court opinions evinced a consistent commitment to equality, around persistent concerns regarding (horizontal) market power and (vertical) bargaining power; third, the opinions often displayed metaphorical crossings of the marketplace of ideas and markets for commerce. However, the era ended in disappointment among New Deal liberal policy makers, because a surprising Court opinion imposed unanticipated limitations on economics as a discourse for serving a commitment to equality.

Competition policy had, and still has, multiple meanings. Unlike new paradigms in the physical sciences, new approaches or models in economics have never eclipsed their predecessors as sources for competition policy in America. Ever since scientists agreed, for example, in the eighteenth century that most of the invisible stuff around us should be called oxygen, with all that entails, no one who thinks in terms of phlogiston is taken seriously. But in economics, both phlogiston and oxygen continue to guide policy analysis and research programs, even today. The three economic models that continue to inform antitrust may be called classical, neoclassical, and postclassical.

The classical model of competition was founded in the view that competition is a logical deduction from freedom of contract. In the Progressive Era, both the Literalists and the Rule of Reasonists agreed that freedom of contract produced free competition, although they disagreed on the crucial question of the relationship between freedom of contract and commercial combinations. Thus, the classical model, while deductive in epistemological style, was not a formal system in the sense that the same premise would always lead to the same conclusion. Disputes over intermediate premises and definition of terms produced slack or play in the model. The classical model of competition, it seems, is better understood as the classical rhetoric or discourse of competition, as a set of terms and images for thinking and arguing about competition. Accordingly, the classical rhetoric inspired Literalist Rufus Peckham to write the *Lochner* opinion and Rule of Reasonist Edward White the *Standard Oil* opinion, both reasoning from the same major premise—freedom of contract. Yet, White could dissent in *Lochner* from within the classical rhetoric of competition. Moreover, the Literalists and Rule of Reasonists disagreed fiercely, for a short while, about the implications for cartels. The Literalists expressed deep concern about the sociopolitical effects of cartels, about the demise of independent entrepreneurship. The Rule of Reasonists argued that economic combinations of all sorts were not only historically inevitable but also consistent with commitments to social and political compacts. Both renditions of the classical rhetoric of competition, with their differing sets of intermediate premises, reappeared in opinions during the later New Deal years.

The neoclassical model of competition has taken market performance as its point of departure. As a result, the neoclassical discourse of economics displaces the language and images of individual liberty of contract with the image of a "price mechanism" and the language of supply, demand, marginal cost and revenue, output, and related quantifications of market performance. Until recent years, the neoclassical discourse of competition was imbedded in a dichotomous view of economic markets as either competitive or monopolistic. That is, neoclassicists imagined intermediate market conditions—markets short of monopolization—as competitive. Further, they questioned neither profit maximization as the universal goal driving individuals nor rivalry as the natural demeanor for achieving economic success. Although the neoclassical model's recent turn to mathematical language lends the appearance of an even more formal, more deductive, discourse than its classical predecessor, it too leaves ample room for disagreement about intermediate premises and definition of terms. The neoclassical discourse of economics, particularly its devotion to the "price mechanism," also appeared in numerous opinions during the later New Deal years.

Particularly among economists, the postclassical discourse of competition began to shape research and analysis of concentrated markets and, later, of dominant firms, concerns influenced by Edward Chamberlin's oligopoly theory. In the later New Deal years, the Supreme Court paid scant attention either to Chamberlin's theory of monopolistic competition—his theory of competition for brand loyalty—or to Joseph Schumpeter's dynamic view of competition as innovation—his "perennial gale of creative destruction." Finally, congressional debates regarding, for example, the Robinson-Patman and Miller-Tydings Acts did evidence a neo-Jeffersonian rhetoric of consumerism aligned with small producers, a rhetoric given sustenance by TNEC findings that small and medium-sized producers tended to be more "efficient" than large ones. Although this neo-Jeffersonian rhetoric does not fit neatly into any one of the three discourses of economics, its claim to refuting neoclassical tenets makes it, if only in a limited sense, postclassical.

It was not unusual for Supreme Court opinions written during the later New Deal to display flashes of friction between contending visions of competition. For example, Chief Justice Hughes, writing for a unified Court in the *Sugar Institute* decision (1936), approved much of a complex decree issued by Circuit Court Judge Mack, sitting in the Southern District of New York. The Supreme Court did not find fault with the idea of a trade association or with the Institute's organizational activities, but only with "the steps taken to secure adherence, without deviation, to prices and terms."[121] While Hughes's opinion displayed a Hooverian attraction to trade associationalism, with its rhetoric of "co-operative" and "voluntary" efforts to soften the effects of overcapacity and declining demand, there was a limit, and the limit was expressed in the neoclassical language of market pricing. The Court would not permit enforcement of explicit agreements to short-circuit the neoclassical market's "price mechanism."

The decree by Circuit Court Judge Mack, however, went beyond the discursive boundaries of neoclassical theory. Mack enjoined the practice of announcing in advance changes in prices and terms. For Hughes, the decree went too far. He believed that advance announcements were reasonable because, in his view of competition, the evil lay not in the knowledge of future prices and terms but only in their enforcement. Mack understood the anticompetitive intent—the element of enforcement—and thus the entire question of competition differently. In his view, anti-competitive restraints included not only explicit agreements to adhere to list prices and to withhold information from outsiders but also a "cooperative spirit," an intent to avoid competition. Thus, the very cooperation that Hughes celebrated as producing free competition Mack condemned as anti-competitive.[122]

The advance announcements that Hughes understood in neoclassical terms as important information for intelligent competition Mack saw as signals passed among rivals seeking tacit consensus about prices and terms. Mack's view was old hat. It had appeared in the early trade association cases now disregarded, especially Justice Clarke's opinion in *American Column & Lumber* (1921), and in the trade association literature of consulting firms such as Stevenson, Jordan & Harrison. But Mack's view was also potentially new. Postclassical economics, particularly Edward Chamberlin's theory of monopolistic competition, would soon revolutionize the understanding of markets just like those in *Sugar Institute*, markets with standardized products and few sellers: The postclassical economics discourse of tacit understandings, price inflexibility, and non–price competition would soon call into question the economic assumptions underlying Hughes's neoclassical synthesis of competition and cooperation.

A second example of economics discourses in conflict was Justice Hugo Black's surprising opinion in *Fashion Organizers Guild of American v. FTC* (1941)

(*FOGA*). Black rejected out of hand an argument by the Guild founded in the neoclassical tenet that competition is a process dedicated to consumer wellbeing, particularly as reflected by the market "price mechanism." Guild attorneys argued that the system of blacklisting buyers who purchased dresses from manufacturers who pirated their designs from Guild members, fining Guild members who dealt with offending retailers, and enforcing the system did not violate the antitrust laws "since the Federal Trade Commission did not find that the combination fixed or regulated prices, parcelled out or limited production, or brought about a deterioration in quality."[123] Their argument was consistent with Justice Stone's recent opinion in *Apex Hosiery* (1940), which presented this consumerist vision as the basis for finding that the antitrust laws were not intended to regulate even the most violent labor/management disputes. Black, writing for the unanimous Court in *FOGA*, refused even to take up neoclassical arguments about low prices and consumerism.

The problem was understood, instead, in classical common-law terms. Black turned to turn-of-the-century cartel doctrine as expressed in *Addyston Pipe* (1899), and his language reverberated with undertones of the recent *ALA Schechter Poultry* opinion (1935): "[T]he combination is in reality an extra-governmental agency, which prescribes rules for the regulation and restraint of interstate commerce, and provides extra-judicial tribunals for the determination and punishment of violations and 'thus trenches upon the power of the national legislature.'"[124] This turn away from the consumer as an image of a unified body economic reflects a mirror image of *Thornhill*'s (1940) evocation of a marketplace of ideas. Whereas Justice Murphy envisioned employees and consumers in a neoclassical marketplace of ideas, Black located citizens in a classical marketplace for goods and services. In the classical marketplace, the concern was not prices and consumers, but individual liberty. Hence, the Guild's organized attempt to protect private property rights, to enforce fair competition by stopping illegal style piracy, was prohibited under the classical model as a restraint of individual liberty, even if there was no impact on prices or consumers.

Other opinions were explicit, if not self-conscious, in their *mixture* of economic discourses. Some mixed common-law conspiracy doctrine with neoclassical concerns about market price. In others, the classical rhetoric of common-law conspiracy and the postclassical model of oligopoly, with their heightened sensitivities to tacit agreements and parallel conduct, appeared side by side, throwing together two logics and two sets of concerns for competition policy. By 1948, the Court would explicitly recognize competing models (here, neo- and postclassical), Justice Black observing in *FTC v. Cement Institute* that dueling economists gave sharply different expert opinions regarding the competitive implications of prices, identical to the one-millionth of a penny, submitted in sealed bids. Trade association experts testified that the identical bids were consistent with neoclassical expectations of intense price competition, while FTC economists testified that the identical bids reflected the kind of tacit collusion associated with postclassical assumptions about oligopoly market structure. Apparently finding neither interpretation compelling, Black acknowledged the conflict and simply deferred to the FTC administrative judge's expertise.[125]

In all three discourses of competition, Court opinions revolved around a spindle of equality—whether protecting producers or consumers, whether expressing concerns about market power (horizontal) or bargaining power (vertical). Some opinions, however, failed to keep the later New Deal's vision of a unified body economic, its neo-Jeffersonian mixture of small business and consumer welfare. Two opinions—one by Justice Hugo Black and the other by Justice William O. Douglas—present extreme examples of a rhetorical divide between small producers and consumers.

Perhaps the best known and most ruthless evocation of the consumer is Justice William O. Douglas's starkly neoclassical opinion in *U.S. v. Socony-Vacuum Oil Co.* (1940). The defendants, major oil companies, argued that their program of buying "distress oil" from small producers (who had no storage facilities and could not cap their wells) was consistent with the purposes expressed in *Appalachian Coals* (1933) to eliminate destructive competition. Given economic hard times and the added pressure of new oil discoveries, the stabilization program would help small producers avoid bankruptcy. But Douglas insisted that even price stabilization violates the antitrust laws because it is "an artificial stimulus applied to . . . market forces." "Fixing, pegging, stabilizing" or otherwise influencing price interferes with the workings of the natural body economic. Price fixing threatens the "central nervous system of the economy"—that is, the price mechanism for directing the allocation of goods and services. The "age-old cry of ruinous competition" fell on deaf ears. For Douglas and a unified Court, producers, both large and small, had no choice but submit to the market as the final arbiter of price. The Sherman Act is "a prohibition against the infliction of a particular type of public injury"—that is, injury to the consumer.[126]

At the other discursive extreme was Hugo Black's equally striking opinion in *FOGA* (1941)—not only his leap back into turn-of-the-century cartel doctrine, already described, but his revival of the Jeffersonian imagery inspiring Justice Peckham's *Trans-Missouri* (1897) opinion and abandoned in *Addyston Pipe* (1899): "Trade or commerce under those circumstances may nevertheless be badly and unfortunately restrained by driving out of business the small dealers and worthy men whose lives have been spent therein."[127] No "reduction in price" could mitigate the harm suffered by "small dealers and worthy men." In short, consumer interests in lower prices must sometimes yield to other public interests.

The Court's double vision of a body economic, together with its movement among three economic approaches, produced opinions whose doctrinal surface appears uneven and whose substructure seems incoherent. The opinions do, however, revolve around a common commitment to equality. In consequence, there was a persistent return, a looping back to questions of economic power—both horizontal (market power) and vertical (bargaining power), both multifirm and dominant-firm control of industries. While numerous Supreme Court opinions project this two-dimensional view of inequality, it is Second Circuit Judge Learned Hand's landmark opinion in the *ALCOA* (1945) monopolization case that provides the most vivid portrayal of two-dimensional effects of economic power.[128] ALCOA was essentially the only source for new aluminum ingot. Much of the ingot was sold to independent aluminum fabricators, who made storm windows, screen doors, electrical wire, and other items. But ALCOA retained a substantial amount of ingot for its own fabrication business. Thus, ALCOA both supplied and competed with independent fabricators. The trial court found that ALCOA injured independent fabricators with a "price squeeze." That is, ALCOA sold ingot to independent fabricators at a price high enough to allow it to undersell them, whenever it desired, in the market for fabricated aluminum. It squeezed them into the margin between the cost of aluminum ingot and the price for fabricated aluminum. ALCOA's economic power allowed it to control both the cost of ingot (vertical bargaining power over its customers) and the price for fabricated aluminum (horizontal market power over its rivals).

The flip side of this amplified concern about economic power was the Court's more frequent rejection of claims that restraints of trade were reasonable because they protected property rights. Property rights rhetoric is, after all, founded in the belief that a restraint is reasonable, that an exercise of economic power is justified, although it is anticompetitive, because it reflects an important property right. Whether claims of destructive competition, consignment rights, common-law unfair competition, trademark, patent, or copyright, the Supreme Court had always recognized property rights as a limitation on competition policy. But in the later New Deal years, the Court began to look with more skepticism at such claims. For example, in *Socony-Vacuum* (1940), the Court rejected the "destructive competition" argument—that agreements in restraint of trade were reasonable because they were intended only to save their businesses from the ravages of competition—earlier accepted in *Appalachian Coals* (1933). In *FOGA* (1941), defendants insisted that they were protecting themselves (and everyone else) from the "evils of piracy." They claimed that this "style piracy" constituted unfair competition at common law, and gave rise to the equitable property right recognized in *International News Service* (1918). Rejecting their claim, Justice Black wrote that their restraint of competition was unreasonable per se—that is, nothing could justify it.[129]

The Court's denial of such property rights defenses expanded the reach of competition policy by diminishing the economic power of those who were asserting their property rights. A stunning example of a property-rights defense, once again rejected by the Court, appears in *Associated Press v. U.S.* (1945), a case litigated at the celebrated intersection of First Amendment freedom of the press and Sherman Act free competition in the commercial marketplace. Writing for the renowned Second Circuit panel of Hand, Hand, and Swan, Augustus Hand's opinion turned two thumbs down to the Associated Press bylaws, which allowed its members to exclude competitors from its news-gathering service. Hand insisted that, in judging the reasonableness of AP's restraint of trade, the court consider the public interest reflected in the First Amendment presupposition "that right conclusions are more likely to be gathered out of a multitude of tongues, than through any kind of authoritative selection. To many this is, and always will be, folly," Hand observed, "but we have staked upon it our all."[130]

In argument before the Supreme Court, AP attorneys argued that "to apply the Sherman Act to this association of publishers constitutes an abridgement of the freedom of the press guaranteed by the First Amendment." At the same time, following *International News Service* (1918), they argued that news-gathering produced private property that need not be shared with competitors. News was both public goods protected by the First Amendment and private property protected by the common-law tort of unfair competition. Their twin claims of public interest and private property defenses to the Sherman Act highlighted the anomalous position of information, free in the marketplace of ideas and for sale in the marketplace of commodified news. Rejecting the private-property defense, Justice Black repudiated as well the claim that the Sherman Act was inconsistent with the First Amendment. "Surely a command that the government itself shall not impede the free flow of ideas," he declared, "does not afford non-governmental combinations a refuge if they impose restraints upon that constitutionally guaranteed freedom."[131]

The Court recognized no dilemma in the demands imposed upon information, no tension between the free flow associated with the marketplace of ideas and the private ownership protected in commercial markets. This tension, of course, is not limited to First Amendment issues. Nor is it avoided in entirely commercial markets. The same pair of conflicting demands upon information appears in commercial markets: the commodified value of information protected as private property, and the competitive market's very dependence upon fully available information kept free from private advantage. Neither dilemma has been resolved. Indeed, both attach with a vengeance to modern commercial markets whose monopolistic competition always produces commercial rivalry through the medium of images and ideas—in a commercial marketplace of ideas.

In 1946, the Court published *American Tobacco v. U.S.*—an opinion soon seen by observers of competition policy as clarifying the economics discourse of antitrust policy and settling the most troublesome inconsistencies in antitrust doctrine. A unanimous Court affirmed criminal convictions against the three major tobacco products makers—American, Liggett & Myers, and R.J.Reynolds Tobacco companies—and certain company officials for violating the Sherman Act. The Court seemed to use the common-law doctrine of conspiracy as the vehicle for expressing concerns about oligopoly structure, about concentrated industry. Conspiracy doctrine, like oligopoly theory, required neither commercial success nor an overt attempt to break the law. The major question on appeal in *American Tobacco* was the trial judge's charge to the jury under Sherman Act § 2—in particular, the explanation of "conspiracy to acquire and maintain the power to exclude competitors to a substantial extent." In short, the antitrust policy concern was industrial concentration; the charge was a conspiracy to monopolize. The government simply had to prove that "the conspirators had a unity of purpose or a common design and understanding, or a meeting of the minds in an unlawful arrangement." The Court found ample evidence, including identical price lists and terms of sale, coordinated price changes in cigarette sales, as well as collaborative control of leaf tobacco purchases. Justice Harold H. Burton described the evidence as indicating "action taken in concert," "a course of dealing."[132]

The Court's common-law discourse of conspiracy, applied to a concentrated industry, evoked oligopoly theory—by then well known. First was the very belief that a small group of powerful firms would act upon a shared sense of common benefit to produce monopoly effects, rather than compete to win a monopoly. Next was the realization that no formal agreement was necessary, that reliance on a common course of conduct was enough. A "meeting of the minds," it appeared, could describe not only the traditional view of a bargain contract and the common-law crime of conspiracy but also the esprit de corps supporting the cooperative enterprise of oligopolists. Their common interest was to control output, allowing them to charge monopoly prices. The *American Tobacco* opinion seemed to fold into a smooth mixture the discourses of classical, neoclassical, and postclassical economics. This eclectic treatment allowed the Court to oblige concerns about both the horizontal and vertical consequences of economic power—both injury to competing tobacco companies and pecuniary harm to retailers and consumers. Finally, these reconciliations were the result of an understanding of common-law conspiracy doctrine and oligopoly theory as parallel, or at the very least coincidental, in design. Antitrust, it seemed, had constructed its own unified body economic, not unlike the rhetorical images inspiring those in other precincts of the later New Deal.

In perhaps the most influential piece of antitrust scholarship in the immediate post-war years, Yale law professor Eugene V. Rostow proclaimed that the *ALCOA* (1945) and *American Tobacco* (1946) decisions heralded a new era in which antitrust would play a vital role in adjusting the "organization of industry and commerce." Rostow declared that "with revolutionary speed . . . the doctrine of the Sherman Act has lately been transformed" by a shift in concern from "freedom of contract" to "freedom of competition." His reading of recent opinions led him to conclude that "market control is now a far more important theme in Sherman Act cases than handicaps upon an individual's power to do business." Rostow proclaimed that the "Supreme Court is on the threshold of recognizing what the economists call monopolistic competition." (Rostow seemed to mean, more strictly, oligopoly theory.) Everything was in place to make the Sherman Act an instrument for "a wider dispersion of power and opportunity": the economic theory, the Court's new attitude, and the Truman administration's willingness to prosecute.[133]

One year later, in the *Columbia Steel* decision (1948), a divided Court shocked the Justice Department by holding that U.S. Steel's purchase of Consolidated Steel Corporation, the strongest independent steel fabricator on the West Coast, did not violate the Sherman Act. Like the *ALCOA* case, this one involved both vertical and horizontal considerations, because U.S. Steel not only sold rolled steel to Consolidated but also sold fabricated steel in competition with Consolidated. Judge Learned Hand had written in *ALCOA* that the antitrust laws were intended "to perpetuate and preserve, for its own sake and in spite of possible cost, an organization of industry in small units which can effectively compete with each other."[134] Although the most substantial West Coast steel fabricator, Consolidated Steel was just such a small, independent unit.

But Justice Stanley F. Reed, writing for a bare majority, turned the question of size on its head. Following the economic analysis of markets praised by Eugene Rostow, Reed determined that Consolidated's market share was so small that its elimination as a competitor would have little effect. Thus, the acquisition, whether viewed as vertical integration of a customer or purchase of a competitor, was not an unreasonable restraint of trade. Unlike the *American Tobacco* opinion, Justice Reed's analysis was relentlessly neoclassical—that is, it focused on horizontal variables, particularly market definitions and market shares. And, unlike Judge Hand in the *ALCOA* decision, Reed was unable or unwilling to find the high market share needed to satisfy a neoclassically formulated monopolization case. Convinced that there was an utter lack of competition between U.S. Steel and its acquisition, a bare majority held that the merger did not violate the Sherman Act.

Justice Douglas wrote an impassioned dissent that dwelled on the merger's economic effects. The economic effects that Douglas was referring to were not, however, derived from the neoclassical logic of market share. Douglas had something else in mind, something both classical and postclassical in ancestry: "We have here the problem of bigness." Bigness, for Douglas, was a problem regardless of market shares, because it produced two undesirable consequences. First, there was "the power of a handful of men over our economy," power over the price of a basic commodity that "determines the price of hundreds of other articles." That power was not the monopoly power of a single-firm industry understood in dichotomous neoclassical terms but rather the market dominance, the industrial concentration, described in the postclassical work of Chamberlin and of Berle and Means. In addition to the impact on prices, there was the social and political fallout, expressed in classical Jeffersonian terms:

> This is the most important antitrust case which has been before the Court in years. . . . Here we have the pattern of the evolution of the great trusts. Little, independent units are gobbled up by bigger ones. . . . Its lesson should by now have been burned into our memory by Brandeis. *The Curse of Bigness* shows how size can become a menace—both industrial and social.[135]

Rostow and others who envisioned antitrust as a tool for shaping industrial organization, as a political instrument for leveling gross disparities in economic power, had misread the purport of recent antitrust opinions. Although conspiracy rhetoric and oligopoly theory overlapped, the critical difference was that conspiracy theory did, after all, require some sort of evidence of evil intent. Buying a rival's factory was not evil. It was normal business conduct to buy and sell property. Oligopoly theory, understood as an economic theory concerned only with industrial concentration, heralded as a postclassical expression of Jeffersonian sentiments, was not the theory that impelled a Supreme Court majority. And, in an ironic turn, competition policy derived from economics discourse—here, neoclassical analysis of markets—provided the rhetorical framework for approving the huge U.S. Steel Corporation's purchase of its largest rival in the western United States.

The next twenty years of Supreme Court doctrines concerning competition policy would struggle with the implications of oligopoly theory, monopolistic competition, and their relationships to common-law conspiracy doctrine, Jeffersonian commitments, and neoclassical price theory. Congress, too, would weigh into the struggle with new legislation.

American Political Economy after the Close of the Second World War

The end of World War II saw new fears of a Communist conspiracy replace wartime fears of international cartels conspiring with the Third Reich. The Taft-Hartley Act of 1947 not only required labor leaders to make public any association with the Communist Party but, in a larger sense, began to treat labor unions as political conspiracies in restraint of trade that required close monitoring. In this context, it is not surprising to find the language of combination and conspiracy sprinkled liberally throughout Supreme Court opinions, including antitrust cases prosecuted against organized industries. The epidemic spread of conspiracy rhetoric does, however, raise questions about the closeness of any relationship imputed between common-law conspiracy doctrine and the oligopoly theory it seemed to parallel.

In 1944, Franklin Roosevelt, anticipating an Allied victory, convened a conference at Bretton Woods, New Hampshire.[136] Roosevelt invited Allied leaders to plan for postwar economic recovery, including economic reconstruction of not only the Allies but also Germany and Japan, under Allied supervision, in order to ease the sort of economic hardship and political turmoil that followed the Versailles Treaty. The conferees agreed upon economist John Maynard Keynes's plan for international organizations to support economic growth and full employment. But after the war ended, this theory never produced the independent supervisory organizations called for. In large part because the United States was the only industrialized nation left standing, the matériel—in particular, the capital—needed to lift the other industrialized nations out of their economic devastation was in the hands of American banks. American economic hegemony meant American control of the International Monetary Fund and the World Bank. It meant American dollars as the currency for international trade. Most of all, it meant that international laissez-faire was advantageous to the United States: Open borders and free trade would allow American manufacturers to enter new markets while there was no real international competition. Domestic competition policy, including antitrust, would treat the rest of the world as if it did not exist.

Before the war, Congress had passed a series of antitrust statutes whose language and intent projected an image of a unified body economic—a pluralistic array of interests situated as constituencies of federal agencies, yet reaggregated in terms of a singular "public interest" personified in the consumer. The Supreme Court had acceded to the Roosevelt Administration—both its later New Deal initiatives and its new adversarial attitude in antitrust cases, an attitude that survived Thurman Arnold's appointment to the bench and Franklin Roosevelt's death. Court opinions, throughout the war years and after, oscillated between the rhetorics of conspiracy and market analysis, between consumerist and producerist images of the public interest. When they appeared, marketplace metaphors seemed to produce a convergence of political, labor, and commercial doctrines. Expressed in an economic discourse of competitive marketplaces, these doctrines converged around a common axis of equality.

This commitment to equality, and the discursive boundaries giving it form, can be seen most clearly in the astonishing decision handed down in *Shelley v. Kraemer* (1948).[137] The result itself was surprising: The Court refused to allow enforcement of restrictive covenants whose purpose was to restrain residential property owners from selling to "Negroes and Asians." It was surprising because earlier opinions seemed to view such covenants as private matters outside the public domain regulated by the Fourteenth Amendment. Thus, it was anticipated that these covenants running with the land, ancillary and thus reasonable restraints under the common law, were beyond the reach of the Civil War amendments and their egalitarian purposes. What made the decision astonishing was Chief Justice Fred M. Vinson's opinion. Conceding that restrictive covenants are private agreements, Vinson pointed to state court enforcement as the public element, the state action, necessary to trigger the Fourteenth Amendment's protection. Shelley's liberty—here, his right to buy residential property—was unconstitutionally taken without due process when the Missouri courts sought to enforce the restrictive covenant. In short, judicial enforcement seemed to transform *all* private agreements into public policy, into state action constrained by the egalitarian impulse of the Fourteenth Amendment. The commitment to equality was threatening to turn the entire sphere of private agreement into a public domain open to federal judicial scrutiny.

Was there anything left of the private sphere? Anything shielded from judicial scrutiny under the microscope of New Deal liberalism, with its egalitarian focus? First of all, the Court would never take up *Shelley*'s full implications. Moreover, the *Shelley* opinion recognized limits. Most of all, court enforcement was required. Thus, the liberty to agree on common courses of conduct—whether industry practices or the racial composition of neighborhoods—was not disturbed. Such private agreements among property owners were voluntary and thus outside the range of public scrutiny. Of course, the Court had recognized the judiciary as a public, policy-making institution long before *Shelley*. In *Erie Railroad v. Tompkins* (1938), Justice Brandeis wrote that there is no body of "federal general common law"—in Holmes's words, "no transcendental body of law"—and thus that federal courts were impermissibly making law when they ignored state law. In short, the Court's rejection of the pre-New Deal faith in an all-encompassing liberty of contract exploded the foundation for belief in a federal common law and, with it, belief in the Supreme Court itself as above politics. Citing dissenting opinions by Justice Holmes for the proposition that courts make law, Brandeis held that federal courts must follow state court decisions as well as state legislation. Failure to follow state law, Brandeis concluded, denied citizens equal protection of the law under the Constitution, insofar as federal judges resorting to federal common law meant that federal and state courts could apply different laws to the same controversy.[138]

Thus, the New Deal Court's commitment to equality opened a wide path through the private domain of individual liberty in the decade before *Shelley*—ever since the "constitutional revolution" of 1937. This broad egalitarian impulse was seen most clearly in Chief Justice Hughes's opinion in *West Coast Hotel* and in the marketplace rhetorics of labor and antitrust cases thereafter. But the image was, after all, one of a marketplace, an image with its own limits. Those limits, glimpsed in *Shelley*, emerged more prominently in the *Columbia Steel* opinion that surprised and disappointed New Deal liberals. In that antitrust decision, the Court did not disturb a private transaction between two corporate entities. Why? Because the Court was convinced that there was more than adequate competition in the marketplace to discipline U.S. Steel. Faith in competition emerged from belief in the neoclassical vision of markets as meritocratic enclaves, fueled by individual effort, directed toward serving a unified body economic imagined as the consumer. No public regulation was necessary because the commitment to equality was served as a matter of course by the competitive conditions surrounding the acquisition.

Even in its most extreme view of private actions and their public consequences, the Court maintained the formal distinction between public and private spheres, between state and individual action. The consequences were, however, more than abstract. As *Shelley* and *Columbia Steel*—both decided in 1948—demonstrate, the rhetoric of marketplace liberalism, with its faith in competition and its preservation of a private sphere, imposed limits on the New Deal's commitment to equality. Neoclassical economics and, more generally, the marketplace metaphor of free competition provided the Court with language and images for satisfying that commitment to equality. But, as we shall see, the disparity between marketplace rhetoric and marketplace realities would soon provoke reconsideration of competition policy by Congress, the Courts, and the social science scholars who influenced their deliberations.

4

Competition, Pluralism, and the Problem of Persistent Oligarchy, 1948–1967

Although the end of World War II opened a period of domestic economic expansion and unrivaled international influence for the United States, it was also a time of intense domestic conflict and national self-doubt. The New Deal's egalitarian ethic and Harry Truman's Fair Deal platform, as well as economic growth fueled by government investment such as the GI Bill and a national highway construction program, increased pressures for more equal distribution of economic benefits and better protection of civil rights. Amid much legislation, Congress enacted the highly contested Civil Rights Act of 1948 and, two years later, the less controversial Celler-Kefauver amendment to the Clayton Act's provision regulating corporate mergers. It was the early 1960s before the Supreme Court had occasion to corroborate the egalitarian concerns driving both pieces of legislation: "one person, one vote" in the political marketplace, and "Congress' fear not only of concentration of economic power on economic grounds, but also of the threat to other values a trend toward concentration was thought to pose."[1] Today, almost fifty years later, neither the Civil Rights Act nor the Celler-Kefauver amendment has settled very much in its respective domain. Race relations too often incite physical confrontation, while proposals to regulate economic power seldom produce more than policy debate. Within its own precinct, each egalitarian impulse still provokes tensions, which have grown sharper during the last decade as more and more Americans have fallen out of the middle-class circle of prosperity created by the ethic of equality, prosperity sustained, to some extent, by those very inegalitarian institutions targeted by the legislation.

But in the postwar years, America saw itself as pluralistic and open, as a place where people were free to pursue their desires, both political and economic—so long as those desires were not "Communist."[2] Senator Joe McCarthy's (R.Wis.) vicious crusade and its counterpart, the House Un-American Activities Committee, indiscriminately painted hundreds of government officials and private citizens with the red star of Communist Party membership and, more broadly, set a tone of fear and intolerance. American geopolitics was driven by the threat of worldwide communism, symbolized by a monolithic and frightening Stalinist Soviet Union, and later by a fear of communist expansion as close as Cuba and as far away as Southeast Asia. President Dwight Eisenhower would eventually engineer the congressional censure of Joe McCarthy and order National Guard troops to Little Rock to enforce the desegregation order following *Brown v. Board of Education* (1955). The Supreme Court would eventually throw out McCarthyite laws and approve the desegregation decrees ordering school busing. America's self-image as a pluralistic society would manage to survive, at least into the late 1960s, when more insistent demands for racial equality, the spectacle of urban riots, an increasingly alienated generation of "baby boomers," and, finally, the televised horror of the Vietnam War splintered the liberal coalition held together by the later New Deal's vision of an organic body economic.

This organic vision of a pluralistic society provided the imaginative context for public policy analysis in the 1950s and 1960s. Mainstream political scientists, economists, and legal scholars, as well as Congress and the Supreme Court, shared the vision of a pluralistic society, the image of a free "marketplace"—for ideas, goods and services, capital, and political decisions. The recurring problem in this shared vision, particularly in light of the New Deal liberal consensus inspired by the ethic of equality, was the undemocratic persistence of enormous disparities in power. This chapter investigates the reactions of mainstream theorists and policy makers to threats to the legitimacy of the "marketplace" image, threats posed by perceptions of oligopoly in economic institutions and oligarchy in political ones. It traces the New Deal legacy of competition rhetoric, its crossing of economic and political domains and its pluralist impulses, through the tensions provoked between the rhetoric of competition and the presence of political and economic elites. Whether political science or economics, whether jurisprudence, congressional legislation, or Supreme Court doctrine, the dominant discourse of competition collided with the actuality of oligarchic power. This chapter examines the array of theories and doctrines thrown off by these collisions in the decades of the 1950s and 1960s—both those taken up and those left where they lay.

Economic and Political Discourses of Competition

Not only for economists but for political scientists as well, the dominant image of society during this period was the competitive marketplace. The central question was what to do about economic and political elites, elites whose power was often seen as economic in origin. Although most economists condemned oligopoly as inconsistent with competition, the most influential political theorists claimed to find that oligarchies were in fact compatible with liberal pluralism. Thus, responses ranged from affirmative embrace to condemnation, all earnestly offered as consistent with competition policy.[3]

Economic Theory: Competition's Imperfections

After the war, Edward Chamberlin's theories of oligopoly and monopolistic competition dominated microeconomics and competition policy analysis. In their well-respected and influential book, *Monopoly and Free Enterprise* (1951), economists George W. Stocking and Myron W. Watkins observed that by 1943 Chamberlin's theories were being "expounded to undergraduates across the land." As early as 1940, monopolistic competition theories were already "conquer[ing] their audience" at an "unprecedented pace."[4] That is not to say, however, that such theories constituted a coherent paradigm that brought consensus to price theory economics. Rather, intra-paradigmatic debate was intense. Chamberlin's reformulation of price theory, coupled with Berle and Means's analysis of industrial organization, provoked empirical research and scholarly exchange over three issues: the consequences of sheer corporate size, the implications of market structure, and the criteria for determining economic performance.

As empirical research showed, greater corporate size did not mean either greater efficiency or more innovation. Following the lead of the earlier TNEC Efficiency Study (1941), Harvard economist Joe Bain gathered his influential industry studies in *Barriers to New Competition* (1956). His findings seemed to corroborate the TNEC report:

> The largest several plants in an industry . . . are typically somewhat larger than the estimated optimal size of plant; on the average such plants may be from less than double to five times the estimated optimal size. . . . But generally, plant concentration plays a minor role, and multiplant development of firms a major role, in the over-all picture of concentration by firms. . . . Thus in 11 of 20 industries the existing degree of concentration by firms as measured by the average size of the 4 largest firms is significantly greater than required for these firms to have only one optimal plant per submarket.

Moreover, one of the first research teams to investigate Schumpeter's hypothesis—that innovation flourishes in large, dominant firms—found instead that "innovation is sponsored by firms in inverse order of size. . . . [Decades of inactivity] reveal the steel oligopoly as failing to compete in strategic innovations." In *Big Business and the Policy of Competition* (1956), economist Corwin Edwards concluded that the combination of political and economic power, which separately might countervail each other, leads to an antidemocratic corporatism.[5]

For others, it was market structure that was most important. In his enormously influential article analyzing restraints of trade under the Sherman Act, Harvard Law School Professor Donald Turner, antitrust chief under John Kennedy and Lyndon Johnson, introduced an extreme structuralist view of oligopoly into legal discourse—that is, the view that oligopoly structure *determined* commercial behavior. Before his conversion on the road to Chicago, economist George Stigler wrote that "an industry which does not have a competitive structure will not have competitive behavior." Scholars and those on the Supreme Court who took up Turner's view followed Chamberlin only in the sense that they seemed to overgeneralize from what Chamberlin hypothesized as *perfect* oligopoly—an unlikely environment outside armchair theorizing. Nonetheless, oligopoly theory, in both its structural and behavioral aspects, focused on markets. Thus, what fell out of economics discourse was discussion about the consequences of sheer corporate size. Yet, issues outside the framework of markets, issues of economic rather than market power, would soon reappear in the public policy domain of antitrust—most acutely in the problem of conglomerate mergers, debated in the late 1960s and then forgotten.[6]

There were those, however, who did not take oligopoly structure to entail a single ironclad logic of cooperation. In line with Joe Bain's view that economic analysis of markets should take into account not only structure but also firm behavior and industry performance, Karl Kaysen and Donald Turner argued that both market structure and individual intent, both market power and firm behavior, ought to be taken into account. Economist Edward S. Mason, convener of the Harvard discussion group that developed the approach taken up by Kaysen and Turner, wrote the foreword to their book, *Antitrust Policy: An Economic and Legal Analysis* (1959), the most influential work on antitrust in the 1960s and 1970s. Mason maintained that Kaysen and Turner's approach, whose greatest concern was with strategies for excluding potential competitors, was valuable because it stressed the importance of "the combined study of market structure and business behavior."[7] Yet, for those who believed that competition policy ought to focus on more than a structural analysis of markets, there remained not only the difficulties in delineating markets but also the contentious question of defining criteria for determining performance: Regarding the latter, should researchers look at price levels and flexibility, industry and individual output levels, innovation, profits, conduct? How should each criterion be defined, measured, and interpreted?

Understanding oligopoly discourse in the 1950s and 1960s as an admixture of concerns about structure, performance, behavior, and their interrelationships permits us to see the scope of debate and the array of contending approaches in broader and more useful terms. The influential Harvard discussion group occupied the discursive center of the debate, at least insofar as concern about both structure and performance was most acceptable to mainstream economists, who could still design research agendas, now framed by claims about the importance of market structure, that were still consistent with traditional price theory. At the same time, antitrust policy makers found the Harvard position attractive because it called upon their prior experience in identifying business behaviors and informed their recent turn to market-structure analysis.

With the Harvard group's rendition of oligopoly theory as center, three alternative theories appeared in microeconomics discourse. Two of the theories were slightly but significantly different from the center, while the third—derived from Schumpeter's work—was more distant. But as Kaysen and Turner's book demonstrated, mainstream economists sought to blend

Schumpeter's call for a longer-term dynamic analysis into the traditional static efficiency model.[8] The two mainstream alternatives can be imagined as closely flanking the Harvard group's formulation of oligopoly theory. On one side was Chamberlin's own monopolistic competition theory; on the other, John M. Clark's alternative of "workable competition."

Chamberlin launched his theory of monopolistic competition alongside his oligopoly theory. They were complementary in several respects. The oligopoly model hypothesized an economic logic of cooperation driving rivals in markets with *few* firms and an identical product. Its complement described a new economic logic driving rivals in markets with *numerous* firms. Later researchers, some of them members of the Harvard discussion group, saw the product differentiation associated with monopolistic competition as having anticompetitive effects. Joe Bain, for example, concluded that "product differentiation is of at least the same general order of importance as an impediment to entry as are economies of large-scale production and distribution." Stocking and Watkins described it as "rivalry aimed at insulating the demand for a particular product through advertising in such a way that its market cannot be captured by a rival even at lower prices." Donald Turner agreed, arguing that claims of economies in promotional costs should not be considered a factor in favor of proposed mergers.[9]

Chamberlin did not view oligopoly and monopolistic competition as somehow mutually exclusive. Indeed, he discussed the most obvious overlap between them—the combination of few firms and differentiated products. By the 1950s, there was widespread debate about both the economic and social costs and benefits of advertising by dominant firms. But both proponents and critics overlooked a deeper difficulty lurking at the theoretical boundary between the two theories. That difficulty stemmed from the very root logic of monopolistic competition: The successful proliferation of differentiated products exploded the fundamental ground for both oligopoly theory and its neoclassical predecessors—the economic fiction of discernible "markets." In short, increasing product differentiation made more obvious the limits of any useful economic analysis of product markets. Did twenty-five brands of designer jeans constitute one market, along with Levis and Wranglers? Two markets? Twenty-six? Or did they fall into a category of designer slacks? Did list prices organize them into markets? Or discounted list prices?

What sense did a market analysis make? Given a Schumpeterian gloss of perennial gales of "new" products, market share would lose all value in formulating competition policy. Should competition policy turn on distinctions between product differentiation and innovation, between manipulative advertising and announcing progress? The deeply disruptive potential of the monopolistic competition model has surfaced from time to time, most clearly in Federal Trade Commission initiatives from the mid-1960s through the late 1970, and occasionally in Supreme Court opinions, one as recently as the 1991 term.[10]

Flanking oligopoly theory on the other side was John M. Clark's notion of "workable competition." First published in 1940, Clark's formulation was most influential in the Eisenhower years, providing the framework for the widely cited *Report of the Attorney General's National Committee to Study Antitrust Laws* (1955). The *AG Report* introduced itself as a neutral document produced by rigorous debate among experts, a study "completely untrammeled by direction from any public or private source." "Workable competition" was presented as the product of economics experts, as the best of modern economics. The *AG Report* was carefully written to distance itself from the structuralist oligopoly theorists. Market structure should not, the *AG Report* insisted, be the determinative factor in antitrust policy; firm behavior and individual culpability should remain the watchwords. The *AG Report* re-presented the *Standard Oil* (1911) opinion's "rule of reason" in terms of "workable competition," as a "rule of thumb" for making antitrust judgments about particular markets. According to Clark, competition was to be judged as workable (a) if it is preferable to the best practically attained alternative and (b) if market power is not excessive, and if, in the particular industry, it does more good than ill. Clark felt confident of his view because he believed that most entrepreneurs in positions of power would give up short-term profits for increased sales in the longer term. As contemporary critics pointed out, however, whether an industry is "workably competitive will depend to a very substantial extent on the 'ideology' of the judges." Because "workable competition" essentially included all markets between perfect monopoly and perfect competition, critics saw the theory itself as unworkable.[11]

There were numerous difficulties with Clark's "workable competition," of which I will mention three. First, experience during both Herbert Hoover's associationalism and Franklin Roosevelt's NRA had already contradicted Clark's view that business managers will choose to expand output over the longer term rather than increase short-term profits—a view that led Clark to promote trade associationalism in the Hoover years. Second, giving credence to Schumpeter's view of innovation as a perennial gale of creative destruction immediately calls into question the business logic of choosing the longer-term alternative. Third, and perhaps most striking for the *AG Report*, which was intended as a position paper for future antitrust policy, "workable competition" seemed much more restrained, more likely to acquiesce in intermediate levels of market power than either oligopoly or monopolistic competition theories. Particularly in light of Clark's view that oligopoly is beneficial in that it minimizes the danger of "ruinous competition," "workable competition" theorists seemed more comfortable with the status quo. As economists Stocking and Watkins observed, "though doubtless without premeditation or design, elaboration of the workable competition concept leads to complacency."[12]

The Attorney General's committee, composed of pragmatic lawyers and economists, did not, however, produce a dogmatic *AG Report* that followed the implications of Clark's view in all respects. Rather, it offered workable competition as a better alternative than either ignoring economic learning altogether or embracing the more activist oligopoly theory (and its subversive complement, monopolistic competition). Yet the *AG Report* reshaped antitrust jurisprudence around a Rule of Reason informed by a rough-and-ready economics drawn from neoclassical price theory, rather than the postclassical work of Chamberlin, Berle and Means, and their cohorts. In this context, it is not surprising that the *AG Report* sought to limit (if not repeal) the later New Deal's statutes, such as the Robinson-Patman and the Miller-Tydings Acts, which were characterized as protectionist rather than competitive, discriminatory rather than egalitarian—a view consistent with the neoclassical indifference to corporate size and economic power. In sum, the *AG Report* writers believed they could depoliticize antitrust law by interjecting the "modern economics" of "workable competition" into their "rule of reason." Lost in the translation were the normative overtones of alternative competition policies available for "modernizing" antitrust. Most of all, there was the belief, or at least the hope, that antitrust policy could be pushed toward the economic sphere and thus away from the political domain, toward market analysis and away from economic power considerations. A policy of workable competition offered the best reason for hope.

Political Theory: Democracy as Oligarchic Competition

In the 1950s and 1960s, two themes emerged in political science discourse. The first, composed by Joseph Schumpeter, Yale political scientist Robert A. Dahl, and their acolytes, asserted a competitive process, entitled "marketplace pluralism," as the essence of democratic decision-making. The second theme, developed by Marver Bernstein and Mancur Olsen, expressed concerns about the implications of oligarchy for democracy in a bureaucratic state. Their concerns would reappear in George Stigler's work and in the more recent Public Choice school of economistic political science.

The first theme, taken from Schumpeter's early writings and carried forward by Robert A. Dahl, presented competition as the essence of democratic decision-making. For Schumpeter, democracy is a process devoid of substance, an "institutional arrangement for arriving at political—legislative and administrative—decisions." It entails no substantive values—particularly no commitment to equality. Political parties, like economic firms, are not defined by principles. Rather, "a party is a group whose members propose to act in concert in the competitive struggle for political power." Schumpeter's democracy is an extreme form of legal positivism in which citizens have no legitimate control over leaders except at election time. This democracy is not government by the people but "government approved by the people."[13]

Like consumers in economic markets, citizens are passive choosers in a political market whose range of choice is not open to question. Because citizens are capable only of "infantile discussion of public affairs," because human nature in politics is "irrational," good government calls for "leaders" (political entrepreneurs) who can organize elite governing groups. "Liberty" means no more than the proposition that "everyone is free to compete for political leadership." Democracy means only that there are no barriers to seeking entry to the governing oligarchy. In sum, the process of election is majoritarian, the process of governance elitist. Like his economic theory of dynamic competition through innovation, Schumpeter's democratic theory is founded in the antiegalitarian principle that political leadership, like its kindred entrepreneurial spirit, produces the kind of governing elites necessary to make institutions function effectively. It is not surprising to find that democratic states, like bureaucratic capitalism, depend upon a Schumpeterian entrepreneurial spirit.[14]

In *A Preface to Democratic Theory* (1956), Robert A. Dahl reshaped Schumpeter's governing elites as neither majority nor minority rule, but rather as "minorities rule"—that is, as governance by shifting and open coalitions. Historian Morton Horwitz observes that Dahl (like Schumpeter) sought to discredit "populist democracy," pointing out that "popular sovereignty and political equality . . . failed to ensure the protection of minorities." Though Dahl recognized barriers to entry ignored by Schumpeter—"Negroes were relatively defenseless in the past, just as the Communists are now"—he stubbornly insisted that there was, somewhere below the surface, an underlying consensus. But what that consensus entailed, beyond some implied agreement on the process of marketplace pluralism, remained a mystery. It was Dahl who would introduce the term "marketplace pluralism" into political discourse.[15] As a political model for group dynamics, the idea of marketplace pluralism, situated somewhere between the economic sphere of commercial competition and the constitutional image of a "marketplace of ideas," promised to secure the traditional economic tenets of individualism to the constitutional rhetoric of rights. These twin visages of competitor and citizen were sharply different from the unified body economic that emerged in the congressional legislation and administrative initiatives of the later New Deal. Dahl's double—the twin rhetorics of competition and consensus—were bound, it seemed, to create tensions. Still, the marketplace metaphor, spanning economic and political domains, was taken up as the mediating vision, as the comforting image of competition rather than conflict, of party rivalry rather than factional struggle.

Given the empiricism, the inductive logic driving social science in those years, Dahl's task was to produce empirical grounds for his claim that "interest group pluralism" described democracy in America. His study of local government in New Haven, Connecticut, provided that ground. Indeed, he found the best of all possible interest group pluralisms. Not only were the governing elites composed of shifting alliances and competing groups, but the whole system was characterized as "easily penetrated by anyone whose interests and concerns attract him to the distinctive political culture of the stratum." Dahl's interest group pluralism, which closely resembled Schumpeter's political model of oligarchic competition, was even more attractive insofar as it countered the antidemocratic implications of oligarchic rule. Dahl found that minorities, for the most part, were not insular (in the sense of Justice Stone's famous *Carolene Products* footnote). Instead, they were the shapeless amoebic foundation for democratic ruling elites.[16]

Dahl's empirical study, however, was confined to a small and perhaps unrepresentative political unit. What of Boston or New York City? What of New York State or the federal government? Just as neoclassical economic theory had little to say about large corporate bureaucracies in oligopolistic industries, Schumpeter's theory and Dahl's empirical findings, influential though they were, seem to have had little to say about the modern administrative state. Policy makers and other writers had already expressed concerns about the post-New Deal regulatory state. Congress, for example, had passed the Administrative Procedure Act of 1946, which represented a shift away from faith in agency expertise and toward the procedural legalism reflected in the *ALA Schechter Poultry* (1935) opinion. Like interest group pluralism and economic competition, procedural due process and judicial review could not assure fair outcomes. Nothing could. What was important was the fairness of the process. "Procedure," Justice Abe Fortas would write in the mid-1960s, "is to law what scientific method is to science." Although this turn to democracy as process attracted many adherents, there were longstanding doubts about process theories. Both legal realist scholars and Supreme Court jurisprudence had long ago called into question the possibility of separating process from substance, thus recognizing to some extent the immanent normativity of process.[17]

Within the context of the modern administrative state, a second theme emerged: a set of concerns about agency discretion, and then agency capture by the interests whose economic power prompted regulation. Following A. V. Dicey, political scientist Marver Bernstein argued that administrative agencies made many important policy decisions, decisions hidden from public attention but closely observed by private interests that had the most to gain or lose from those decisions. In *Regulating Business by Independent Commission* (1955), Bernstein maintained that the regulatory process tended to protect regulated firms both from competition and from public scrutiny, thus hurting rather than serving intended public interests. Ten years later, economist Mancur Olsen wrote *The Logic of Collective Action* (1965), precursor to George Stigler's "The Theory of Regulation" (1971) and the more recent work of Public Choice theorists. Olsen observed that there was long-term political advantage in those interested parties with the greatest economic stake in the outcome of particular government decisions. Those with the most to gain or lose, whether a wealthy individual, a large corporation, or, most commonly, industry trade associations such as the AMA, ABA, or National Association of Manufacturers, are most motivated to pay the costs of lobbying for their interests. An individual consumer or citizen has less to lose, faces more difficulty in organizing others to join her common cause, and thus is less likely to participate in the market for government regulation. To the extent that government officials are motivated by economic self-interests, they tend to serve private rather than public interests. The concern was regulatory capture—the power of business elites, the oligarchic results of process theories, and, paralleling Berle and Means's anxiety about the break between corporate ownership and control, the gap between old theories about democratic majoritarianism and more recent findings of oligarchic rule in the halls of bureaucratic government.[18] Thus, political theory in the 1950s and 1960s reflected a tension between faith in a competitive process, albeit a new faith made more "realistic" by an admission of competition among elites, and the impact of economic power on the formation of elites and on the rivalry that followed.

There was concern as well about the impact on democratic values of private bureaucracy—the modern corporation. A significant number of political scientists, economists, and legal scholars saw the corporation as a bureaucratic institution spanning the economic and political spheres. Although competition policy was, as we have seen, the dominant discourse in both spheres, a rhetorical backdraft of sorts drew traditional political discourse about democratic values into the debate about corporations and what to do about them.

In a widely read volume underwritten by the Rockefellers' Fund for the Republic and published by Harvard University Press, with a foreword by Adolf Berle and introduction by Edward S. Mason, fourteen essayists debated the complex issue of the book's title—*The Corporation in Modern Society* (1959). Mason observed that there was little consensus about corporate theory and policy, although opinion seemed to be polarized between two extremes: those who decried bureaucratic capitalism as the "new feudalism" or "self-perpetuating oligarchies," and those who praised its "professionalization of management" and "corporate conscience." Although the criticism in Mason's volume was subdued in tone, a discursive gap did separate enthusiasts and critics: For the most part, support sounded in the competition rhetoric of market economics, while concerns about modern corporate bureaucracy were expressed in terms echoing the early New Deal rhetoric of a body politic. Dean Eugene V. Rostow of Yale Law School, whose article just after the close of World War II had heralded the coming of an antitrust policy informed by monopolistic competition theory, insisted that corporate management's sole responsibility was and ought to be to owners, because the difficulty in giving "any palpable meaning" to "the public interest in some alternative sense" would effectively give unbridled discretion to management. In response to this markets-as-disciplining-management view, economist Karl Kaysen began by noting that market forces produced only loose constraints on large corporations. He observed, moreover, that the result of such market power was substantial managerial discretion whose influence was not only economic but also political and social. Thus, Kaysen concluded, the market rhetoric of neoclassical economics drew too narrow a profile of the modern corporation.

Two essays epitomize the discursive gap between the economic rhetoric of support and the political rhetoric of concern about corporate bureaucracy. In "The Corporation Man," W. Lloyd Warner wrote that management discretion was not the problem but, instead, the solution. Warner detected patterns of upward and downward mobility in the life-cycle of corporate executives, patterns he interpreted as evidence of competitive markets for corporate management. When combined with the view that professionalization at Harvard and other elite business schools was improving both business judgments and business ethics, Warner's description of a shifting layer of meritocratic elites, evocative of Robert Dahl's findings in his New Haven study of political elites, portrayed corporate bureaucracy as driven by competition to better performance and more progressive outlook. In "The Body Politic of the Corporation," Earl Latham analyzed the corporation in markedly different terms. Latham applied to the large modern corporation the classic Aristotelian formulation of the state as "a rationalized system for the accumulation, control, and administration of power," following as well Thomas Hobbes's view of corporations as "lesser commonwealths." He found that power was being distributed and used within American corporations in ways that transgressed prevailing democratic values. Corporate hierarchy, Latham concluded, should be restructured to allow for decision-making to be spread more democratically among corporate constituencies.[19]

Together, these four essays are representative of the debate over corporate theory, both in its rhetoric and in its policy implications, which reflected a conflict between those who believed that the presence of competitive forces would produce good results and those who believed that competition was either inadequate or simply absent. The principal discussions in both microeconomics and political theory, however, were dominated by the rhetoric of competition. Whether economists, political scientists, or cross-disciplinary groupings (including legal scholars and historians), these social scientists continued to debate questions of sheer organizational size, interorganizational structure, and organizational performance in terms of a tension between elites and the competitive process.[20]

Jurisprudential Currents: The Process of Pluralism as Consensus

The debate over corporate theory took place not only within the discourse of the social sciences but also within the realm of law and legal theory. Lawyers and legal theorists were struggling with their own form of tension between elites and democratic theory. Certainly the work of political scientists and economists made up an important part of the cultural and intellectual framework for legal thought, as did the New Deal's outburst of bureaucratic government. Moreover, the production of postwar theory was motivated by a compulsive desire for consensus—for democratic legitimacy—coupled with, it seems, a phobic rejection of authoritarian tendencies symbolized by World War II Germany and the Cold War Soviet Union, authoritarian tendencies understood as excesses of majorities and persecution of minorities.

There were two dominant themes, with later variations, that legal scholars composed within the canon of consensus. These well-known themes, closely associated with their composers, were Henry Hart and Albert Sachs's "legal process" and Herbert Wechsler's "neutral principles." Both conceptions presented the legitimacy of law-related social institutions—especially administrative agencies and courts—as dependent upon a commitment to eliminating the discretion, the political judgments, of those in positions of power.

Herbert Wechsler's well-known call for "neutral principles" as the basis for judicial decision appeared amid widespread scholarly criticism of the Warren Court's judicial activism, particularly its opinion in *Brown v. Board of Education* (1954).[21] The five years between the *Brown* decision and Wechsler's call, which was first heard in the 1959 Oliver Wendell Holmes Lecture at Harvard Law School, were marked by increasingly insistent demands for desegregation, more frequent civil disobedience, and President Dwight Eisenhower's delayed dispatch of federal marshals to enforce the desegregation order in Little Rock, Arkansas. Judicial activism—the Warren Court's insistence on choosing between conflicting normative principles to decide the case—not only provoked social strife, Wechsler seemed to suggest, but also contradicted democratic theory, that is, legitimacy through consensus.

What, asked its critics, was the Supreme Court, an elite institution, doing imposing its will on state legislatures who reflected majoritarian sentiments? Wechsler scrutinized the juridical landscape for a neutral principle to legitimate the *Brown* decision. He found none. In this melancholy process, he rejected both the "denial of equality" and "freedom to associate"—both equality and liberty—as neutral principles. To the extent that consensus was wanting, to the extent that society reflected something between Dahl's liberal pluralism and Olsen's oligarchy, there could be no neutral principles. There would be either disagreement over the principles, or, it seemed, biased impact in their application.[22]

What was clear in Wechsler's argument was that following it to its logical conclusion rendered traditional commitments to liberty and equality entirely incompatible with the call for neutral principles. Wechsler did not offer any candidate of his own to wear his crown of nonpartisanship. In consequence, neutral principles as the standard for judicial legitimacy would lead to legislative power unfettered by a judicially interpreted Bill of Rights.

Wechsler's call for consensus also invoked an extreme form of positivism, an implicit claim that legislative majorities (or some other quantitative measure of consensus) provide the only legitimate ground for decision in a democratic society. The trouble with this repose in majoritarianism was the threat of authoritarianism. Indeed, the very context Wechsler chose for his lecture at the Harvard Law School was not only the school desegregation cases but also the Supreme Court's decisions prohibiting racially restrictive covenants and the "white primary"—all three examples in black and white of majoritarian excess.

In this context, it is striking that Congress, in passing the Civil Rights Act of 1964, and particularly Title II's desegregation of "public accommodations," would rely not on the Fourteenth Amendment—neither the Equal Protection nor the Due Process clauses—but on its power under the Commerce Clause. Perhaps sensitive to an ascendant "neutral principles" approach and certainly aware that the Supreme Court in *The Civil Rights Cases* (1883) had struck down Reconstruction era legislation passed under the new Equal Protection Clause of the Fourteenth Amendment, Congress explicitly grounded the 1964 statute in its power to regulate interstate commerce. Although the Supreme Court would uphold the legislation on Commerce Clause grounds, Justices William O. Douglas and Arthur Goldberg would lament the jurisprudence, Goldberg writing that the purpose was, after all, "the vindication of human dignities and not mere economics."[23] Nonetheless, the economic imagery of free markets would provide the rhetorical ground—a sanitized if not a neutral principle—for outlawing racial discrimination. Consumer protection (along with a constitutional right to travel) would become the judicial logic of civil rights, evoking again the image of a unified body economic first seen during the later New Deal.

The second dominant jurisprudential theme—"legal process"—can be understood as a reluctant accommodation to the view that American society did not reflect consensus. If Wechsler was right—if there were no neutral principles, no underlying social compact reflected even in such basic constitutional values as liberty or equality—what was there to bind together the mix of interest groups? What could serve as a legitimate basis for adjudicating differences? Hart and Sachs's answer, their alternative vision disseminated most widely in *The Legal Process* (1958), a textbook used in most first-year law school curricula throughout the 1960s, was to reformulate the question of consensus. Accepting the liberal pluralist description of American society propounded by Schumpeter, Dahl, and others, Harvard law professors Hart and Sachs made a persuasive argument that consensus lay in the very process of adjudicating differences among factions, in the tenets of procedural due process developed by the Supreme Court to bridle the bureaucratic Leviathan of the modern welfare state. Indeed, they described the institutional arrangements and guarantees of fair hearing and appeal as the democratic bedrock, the fundamental agreement, underlying the very possibility for something like Dahl's (and Schumpeter's) liberal pluralism to flourish in the modern regulatory state. Consensus lay in the shared view that the playing field must be level and the rules consistently applied for fair competition in the political arena.[24]

Both the congressional turn to the Commerce clause and the legal process school's means/ends synthesis of procedural consensus with substantive pluralism were ingenious deflections of the threat to legal institutions generated by the tension between democratic theory and elitist practices—whether those were unelected judges dictating to citizens or local majorities discriminating against insular minorities. The major premise for both ventures was a consensus about competition as a fair process. Both Schumpeter's view of the citizen as consumer and the congressional rhetoric of public accommodations were founded in the principles of free competition. Dahl's vision of shifting elites was not possible without the congressional opening of interstate communication with government and Hart and Sachs's consecration of procedural due process administered by professional and dispassionate lawyers. The universal danger in a world of minorities was seen as factional control of adjudicatory processes. Whether oligarchy or oligopoly, Hart and Sachs's diluted formula for consensus depended upon the perception that there was rivalry robust enough to curb long-term domination by any particular faction. But the criticisms of Marver Bernstein and Mancur Olsen were already raising serious questions about long-term factional dominance as well as about the assumption that individuals could always express their interests through intermediary groups.

In the same year that Olsen published his book, a related yet different criticism of interest group pluralism appeared—a devastating criticism of modern bureaucratic society, both governmental and corporate. There was no meaningful opportunity, no real chance for "the common man," wrote Yale Law School's Charles A. Reich in "The New Property" (1964). Historically, it had been protection of private property that safeguarded individual liberty from the tyranny of the majority. In the "constitutional revolution" of 1937, however, the Supreme Court had separated property and liberty interests, giving more weight to the "public interest" and its reformulated corollary of individual liberty and less to private property rights. But, Reich observed in his seminal article, individual liberty was left out in the cold—neither protected by private property rights nor entirely consonant with the "public interest." "Civil liberties must," he insisted, "have a basis in property."[25]

Echoing those who portrayed bureaucratic capitalism as the "new feudalism," Reich argued that pervasive government largess, whether in the form of social security benefits, television broadcast licensing, or government contracts, placed individuals in positions that compromised their independence. A combination of the classical liberal's fear of political tyranny and the Brandeisian progressive's fear of economic tyranny, Reich's horror was "the combined power of government and the corporations that presses against the individual." The terrible mistake, according to Reich, was the failure to distinguish between corporations and "natural persons." The problem was not "individual property" but rather "industrial property" and the "arbitrary private power" it produced. The mistake was the result of blindness to the question of equality. Although Reich did not express it in terms of equality, the failure of "reformers" to distinguish between individuals and "large aggregations of property," between the "common man" and "private governments," cannot be taken for anything short of a full-throated call to save "small dealers and worthy men," for attention to disparities in economic power.

This blindness to questions of inequality, in Reich's view, also infected government institutional analysis based on "the public interest." When "reformers" simply opposed "the public interest" to "private property," they fell victim to a "fundamental fallacy" because the public interest with regard to any given policy issue may actually conflict with individual interests. In policy analysis, moreover, individual interests are often viewed narrowly—as the interest of only the particular individual involved in the adjudication rather than the interest of many (and perhaps most) individuals similarly situated. Yet the narrowing of individual property rights left the individual with only the public interest to protect her. Neither individual liberty nor pluralism is possible, Reich concluded, without new "institutions to carry on the work that property once did but can no longer do."[26]

In short, institutional visions founded in rivalry—whether economic competition or political pluralism—have an entangled relationship with both the old property rhetoric founded in freedom of contract and a new property rhetoric of entitlements. Vigorous rivalry requires both the independence that property ownership promises and protection from great inequalities of property ownership, from gross disparities in economic power. It was the "individual," the "common man," and thus the questions of individual liberty and equality, that Reich reinserted into the collectivist discourse subtending both political and economic brands of rivalry in the modern bureaucratic welfare state.

In the 1950s and 1960s, the social sciences were in their ascendancy and informed public policy—civil rights, antitrust, and most things in between. There was a unifying image for the social sciences, at least for political science and economics. That unifying image was the competitive marketplace. Whether political interest groups or commercial corporations, whether citizens, consumers, or producers, the relational model was rivalry. Certainly there were sharp differences among political scientists and among economists. But the dominant framework for both disciplines was rivalry. Economists argued about the adequacy of oligopoly, monopolistic competition, and workable competition models. Political scientists debated the accessibility of oligarchic elites to interested citizens. But metaphors of competition provided the common ground for debating economic power, political power, and individual rights. This ascendancy of the social sciences has been characterized as the "realization of the pluralist impulse."[27] This pluralist impulse rested not only in an epistemology of relativism but also, it turns out, a rhetoric of competition and a commitment to equality.

Notwithstanding the ascendancy of competition rhetoric in the years between Presidents Harry Truman and Richard Nixon, the discursive field was not quiescent: Mancur Olsen raised concerns about economic elites, Charles Reich called for a "new property," and others quarreled more directly with the implications of competition policy. Moreover, social, political, and economic life was, as it always is, more unruly than theoretical explanations permit. Thus, for example, mainstream competition theorists simply could not account for behavior motivated by desires other than profit maximization, desires such as market-share expansion, loyalty to local communities, or racial discrimination. Still, competition rhetoric would provide an acceptable proxy for consensus. And it would offer a flexible narrative line from which to hang congressional legislation and Supreme Court jurisprudence.

Congress and Industrial Concentration: Anti-Merger Legislation as Compromise

In economic legislation since the late nineteenth century, Congress has expressed persistent concerns about the economic and political effects of corporate consolidation. The Celler-Kefauver Act of 1950, which amended the

Clayton Act provision regulating corporate mergers, was perhaps the most aggressive expression of such concerns. It carried forward the later New Deal's adversarial attitude toward antitrust, an attitude that persisted into the mid-1970s. Spurred by the Supreme Court's approval, in *Columbia Steel* (1948), of U.S. Steel's acquisition of the largest steel fabricator on the West Coast, the statute's conception was found in Franklin Roosevelt's 1938 message to Congress urging stronger legislation to halt the increasing concentration of industrial assets in fewer corporate hands. In the TNEC Final Report (1941) and two FTC studies (1947, 1948) of mergers and increasing concentration, through a dozen bills that cleared committees and one chamber or the other, there lingered concern about corporate power and what to do about it.

Concern about corporate power was both economic and political. Representative Emmanuel Celler (D.N.Y.) began House debate on his 1949 bill by reminding colleagues of "Jefferson's admonition against monopolies." In Senate debate, Estes Kefauver (D.Tenn.) captured the moment in a query:

> I think that we are approaching a point where a fundamental decision must be made in regard to this problem of economic concentration. Shall we permit the economy of the country to gravitate into the hands of a few corporations . . . with central-office managers remote from the places where their products are made, and the destiny of the people determined by the decisions of persons whom they never see, or even know of? Or on the other hand are we going to preserve small business, local operations, and free enterprise?

It is significant that congressional debate, as well as the TNEC and FTC reports upon which Congress relied, emphasized economic concentration and economic power, not market power. In assessing mergers, the TNEC Committee recommended a six-step burden of proof for a merger's proponents, including a showing that "the size of the acquiring company after the acquisition will not be incompatible with the existence and maintenance of vigorous and effective competition." The Federal Trade Commission later agreed, adding that "the cumulative concentration of economic power" by merger caused "damage to small business." The House Committee report on Celler's bill deplored the increased concentration resulting from mergers in "traditionally 'small business' industries," as well as the "'small business' fields . . . taken over by very large corporations."[28]

Not only higher costs and higher prices but also social and political domination by "large scale collective enterprise" motivated supporters of the bill. "Like government organization, business organization has no right or function to control the activities and the lives of men," began the TNEC Final Report (1941). "The theory of competition," observed the FTC in its 1948 report, "has been the heart of the American philosophical and political system." Both concluded that "monopoly constitutes the death of capitalism and the genesis of authoritarian government." In House debate, Emmanuel Celler (D.N.Y.) read from a report filed with the Secretary of War: "Germany under the Nazi set-up built up a great series of industrial monopolies in steel, rubber, coal and other materials. The monopolies soon got control of Germany, brought Hitler to power and forced virtually the whole world into war." Whether or not the report accurately reflects historical events, it did express widespread concerns about the dangers to democratic government posed by concentrated industrial power.[29]

The Celler-Kefauver Act brought two significant changes to Clayton Act § 7. First, it closed the "assets" loophole that had immunized asset acquisitions from antitrust scrutiny. The 1914 Clayton Act referred only to stock acquisitions. Supporters of the 1950 amendment gave two explanations for the omission: first, that asset acquisitions were rare before the 1914 statute was passed, and, second, that stock acquisitions were of greater concern because they were often accomplished in secret. Although both explanations make sense, there was, I believe, something more to the omission. Very simply, Congress in 1914, like its *Lochner*ian contemporaries on the Supreme Court, saw asset acquisitions as sacrosanct contracts for the sale of physical property. Indeed, sale of physical assets was (and still is) understood as the most basic of private property rights: Certainly an individual has the right to sell his property.

Two pieces of evidence led me to look beyond the supporters' explanation for the omission. First, Supreme Court doctrine under the original Clayton Act was ferociously compulsive in its protection of the distinction between stock and asset acquisitions. In three companion cases, the Court allowed corporations to acquire stock in violation of the original § 7, vote the stock to approve acquisition of the assets, and then retain the assets. The Court required only that the acquiring corporations divest the stock of the shell corporations. The second bit of evidence is found in the Celler-Kefauver bill debates. Representative Harris Ellsworth (R.Oreg.) asked the simple question: "Would such a law preventing one individual or corporation from selling his property, assets, or stock to another be protected by the Constitution or not?" Emmanuel Celler responded that the citizen's right would be protected "so long as such sale does not tend toward monopoly or curtail competition." Later, Representative John E. Jennings, Jr. (R.Tenn.), expressed outrage that the bill "denies to all corporations the freedom of contract which has always been the very breath and life of corporate enterprise in this country."[30]

Indeed, everyone who spoke expressed concern about individual rights and about the viability of corporate enterprise. Those who opposed the bill used the rhetoric of property rights to express their desire to protect individual rights. And those who supported the bill used the rhetoric of competition to express their desire to protect individual rights. Representative John A. Carroll (D.Colo.) responded to Jennings's outrage: "Actually, competition protects and aids every element of our population. It keeps prices low and quality high. It allows a man with a new idea to build up a stable and prosperous business. It prevents any individual or firm from assuming excessive power of the economic life of the Nation. Our problem is to maintain competition."[31] Although substantive understandings of competition policy and private property rights had changed in the sixty years since the Sherman Act's passage, the Celler-Kefauver debates reflected a rhetorical repetition, the well-rehearsed confrontation between two sets of assumptions and beliefs about the rules to govern commercial markets and about the larger consequences of those rules. It was the familiar conflict between the values of competition and private property rights.

In addition to closing the "assets" loophole, there was a second significant change borne in the Celler-Kefauver Act: the explicit extension of § 7 to all corporate mergers, not just those between direct competitors. The expanded scope of merger regulation, which would now include not only horizontal mergers (between direct competitors) but also vertical integration (mergers of suppliers and customers) and conglomerate mergers (everything else), was entirely consistent with the concerns expressed about economic concentration, about corporate size. In the context of congressional debates, as well as the TNEC and FTC reports, the statute seems to be an unyielding policy imperative calling for corporate deconcentration. And perhaps it was.

But, in another context, in the shadow of the large corporate bureaucracies already in place, the statute can be understood as a compromise on the question of bigness. A radical commitment to deconcentration might have included a statutory mandate to break up existing corporate giants. A less compromising resolution might have set limits on corporate size or, at the very least, have taken up the TNEC report's recommendation to "forbid the acquisition of the assets and property of competing corporations of over a certain size."[32]

Instead, the 1950 statute embodied a compromise on corporate size, founded in a distinction between "internal" and "external" growth. As defined in the 1948 FTC report, internal growth, "referred to as natural growth, occurs through the building of new facilities or the expansion of existing properties financed out of retained earnings, loans, [or] the sale of securities." The natural process of internal growth was, moreover, directly linked to another natural process—competition. Indeed, internal growth was seen as an emblem of success. Representative Sidney R. Yates (D.Ill.) spoke lucidly of the links perceived between internal growth and competition:

> A corporation may grow big in several ways. One is to make money and use the profits to expand its operations. When this happens the expansion is an evidence of the concern's success, a result of a kind of vote of confidence which consumers have given the enterprise. Another way is to float new security issues in the market and expand with the proceeds. A concern which does this has exposed its prospects to the judgment of investment bankers and investors in competition with other companies which wish to expand.
>
> A third method of expanding, however, is inherently dangerous to competition. It consists in buying out going concerns. A desire to get rid of inconvenient competitors is one of the most probable motives for this type of expansion.[33]

In sum, concerns about economic concentration, expressed in the rhetoric of competition, produced a statute with both radical potential and conservative affinities. The debates and reports spoke of sheer corporate size, its anticompetitive impact, and its oligarchic dangers. But the debates also revealed the view, seen as early as the Sherman Act debates and as recently as Learned Hand's opinion in *ALCOA* (1945), that corporate size could be the just reward of entrepreneurial success.

Agency activities would reflect the twin tendencies seen in the legislative history. By the late 1960s, while the Department of Justice was following a moderate approach set out in the writings of Antitrust Division Chief Donald Turner, the Federal Trade Commission was pressing postclassical theories of oligopoly and monopolistic competition in an anticoncentration program seeking to stop large corporate mergers in their tracks. Within ten years, however, the pendulum would swing the other way. In the 1980s, the Reagan administration would develop the statute's conservative tendency—its high esteem for corporate size—celebrating both internal and external growth.[34]

The Supreme Court's Competition Policies: Genealogies of Agreement, Images of the Market, and a Commitment to Equality

During this period, the Supreme Court produced dozens of doctrines and hundreds of opinions in an endless process of formulating competition policies. These opinions were part of a larger discursive reservoir, a cultural context flooded with the social science discourses of competition, the yearning for consensus, the case for neutral principles, and the turn toward a second-best foundation for democracy in fair process—whether the process of competition, adjudication, or election. The most influential opinion written in those years—*Brown v. Board of Education* (1954)—is a good example of the era's jurisprudential cross-currents: Unwilling to rest solely on either normative grounds or sociological research, the unanimous opinion stood with one juridical foot on "inherent rights" derived from the Civil War amendments and the other on empirical findings of harm to segregated students. There appeared to be two neutral principles here—not only the egalitarian import of the Fourteenth Amendment but also the positivistic claims that segregated schools caused actual, measurable harms. Congressional power to ameliorate related harms had already been characterized in the Civil Rights Act of 1948 as constitutionally granted jurisdiction over interstate commerce, as legitimate protection of consumers and citizens-as-market-participants. Floating atop this jurisprudential brine were two pieces of debris, two nonbiodegradable problems—the old riddle of "agreement" and the new question of "market power."

The chronic problem of what constitutes a prohibited "agreement" floated like a clump of doctrinal flotsam atop a triangular confluence of currents—pushed on one side by postclassical oligopoly theory; pulled on the second by the political ideology of consensus (that is, political agreement); and drawn on the third side by the common-law notion of conspiracy. Thus, one persistent difficulty was separating economic from political agreements. Was a railroad freight association's effort to lobby for legislation against expanded truck licensing political and protected or economic and prohibited? What of a newspaper's running a paid advertisement libeling a Southern sheriff or some entertainer? How did the Court make sense of these crossings of politics and economics, these overlaid marketplaces of ideas and commerce?

The other piece of debris, the newer problem, was market power—that is, the postclassical economic concern about power short of monopoly. Conflicting views of competition policy were evident in the range of attitudes toward market power analysis, especially in the Court's treatment of large bureaucratic corporations. This market imagery, seen in the social science discourses of political science and economics, seeped into the Court's constitutional jurisprudence as well. Whether through the swings in obscenity doctrine between community and national standards for the appropriate marketplace of ideas, or reapportionment cases seeking to draw lines consistent with a political process founded in "one person, one vote," or jury selection questions about representativeness, there emerged a broad concern about fair process understood in structural, market-like terms. Fair process would capture and give shape to the egalitarian ethic. The concern about corporate size, taking a structuralist focus from the work of Chamberlin and of Berle and Means, would find expression in merger policy under the Celler-Kefauver amendment. In 1967, the Court would issue a series of antitrust opinions resembling a morality play, a spiritual struggle resolved in an epiphany of postclassicism exalted by policy makers and mainstream scholars but already under assault, most notably by Yale law professors Ward Bowman and Robert Bork, forerunners of a secular crusade to reform law in the name of neoclassical economics.

Competition Policy, Liberalism, and the Twin Genealogies of Agreement

In significant part, the history of competition policy has been a fable of agreement, a series of figures given life to embody distinctions between agreements allowed and those prohibited. We have already seen that corporations were distinguished from associations, and later, trade associations from labor unions. The imagery of agreement is, of course, much more complex and paradoxical than narrowly gauged economic history allows. In the realm of economics, the idea of agreement bears the shadowy ancestry of cartels, combinations, and other profane trusts. Yet in the commonwealth of politics, agreement celebrates a heritage of consensus, social compact, and other sacred trusts. Moreover, in each domain there is a substantial anomaly. Amid profane agreements threatening the realm of competition stands the hallowed corporation. Camouflaged among sacred agreements constituting democratic theory, somewhere between John Locke's social compact and *Lochner*'s freedom of contract, slouches the common law doctrine of conspiracy (known in seventeenth-century England as "tumultuous petition"). The "constitutional revolution" in 1937 opened classical liberalism's ideological border between economic and political spheres, the later New Deal returned to a political economy of competition, and the social sciences after World War II embraced competition rhetoric. These events conspired to bring the twin genealogies of agreement—sacred and profane—face to face, anomalies and all.

In the realm of antitrust policy, observers, most notably Dean Eugene Rostow, proclaimed that the Supreme Court had modernized antitrust by adopting the economic learning of monopolistic competition in place of the common-law jurisprudence of contract and conspiracy. But subsequent events, particularly the *Columbia Steel* (1948) decision and the *1955 Attorney General's Report*, raised doubts about the implication that a convergence of antitrust law and economics would oblige the Court to adopt postclassical theory and, with it, a "progressive" distrust of oligopoly.

Three sorts of questions are raised by the competition policies that were applied to commercial markets. First, what was the rhetorical relationship in Court doctrine between oligopoly theory and common-law conspiracy doctrine? Second, what were the concerns driving conspiracy doctrine? In particular, why were issues of deception, coercion, and individual freedom important? Finally, did the constitutional revolution in 1937, particularly the egalitarian commitment injected into liberty of contract by opinions such as *West Coast Hotel* (1937), tint common-law doctrine with a Jeffersonian hue? That is, were the rhetorics of common-law conspiracy and postclassical economics both inspired by an image of "small dealers and worthy men" reminiscent of the old Literalists? The short answer to these questions is that the overlap produced both common concerns and tensions. Ultimately, choices had to be made.

What was the relationship between policy makers' concerns about industry structure and the Court's common-law rhetoric of conspiracy? Between *Columbia Steel* (1948) and *The 1955 Attorney General's Report*, the Supreme Court raised doubts about the very claim of a convergence between antitrust law and economics. Writing for a majority one short of unanimity, Justice Tom Clark, in *Theatre Enterprises v. Paramount Film Distributors Corp.* (1954), pointedly chose the common-law language of conspiracy to resolve a claim that members of the oligopolistic film industry—Paramount, Warner Brothers, et al.—had jointly refused to license their films to the only suburban theater in the Baltimore area. Rejecting the strong statement of postclassical theory that oligopoly market structure imposes an economic logic of cooperation, Clark wrote that the Court "has never held that proof of parallel business behavior conclusively establishes agreement, or phrased differently, that such behavior itself constitutes a Sherman Act offense." There was an implicit tension between the new theory's deterministic logic of cooperation and the old common-law doctrine of individuals freely agreeing, conspiring to restrain competition. The tension was resolved in favor of the latter: "The crucial question," Clark declared, was whether the film distributors' refusal to license "stemmed from independent decision or from an agreement, tacit or express." The Court determined that proof of identical practices by oligopolists was not conclusive evidence of an agreement, announcing that "'conscious parallelism' has not yet read conspiracy out of the Sherman Act entirely."[35]

This caricature of oligopoly theory as a purely deterministic model of commercial conduct was made explicit by Donald Turner in an influential *Harvard Law Review* article (1962). Indeed, Turner went much further. He insisted that even when tacit agreement could be proved, even when each oligopolist's decision was shown to depend for its success upon identical decisions by everyone else, such "interdependent conscious parallelism" should not violate the antitrust laws. Turner's rationale was a reflection of common-law conspiracy doctrine's requirement of a bargain contract: How can we punish someone who is not exercising free will, someone imprisoned by the economic logic of oligopoly structure? Moreover, in practical terms, Turner charged, what sense does it make to compel an economic actor to act irrationally?[36]

The only solutions—either public utility–like rate regulation, or corporate dissolution to create a competitive market structure—were not authorized by the antitrust laws, Turner concluded. He expressed two concerns about these solutions, even if Congress were to amend the antitrust laws. First, he did not want to see an industrial organizationalist logic of market structure replace the common-law logic of conduct and the traditional antitrust notion of individual fault. Second, Turner seemed troubled by the idea that rate regulation or "radical structural reformation"—something between capital punishment and a taking of property—could result despite an absence of fault in the traditional sense.[37] This view was consistent with, although different in normative content from, Justice Clark's common-law rhetoric of conspiracy in *Theatre Enterprises*.

The rhetoric of common-law conspiracy doctrine also invoked doctrines of deception and individual freedom, neither one associated with market structure or performance. As early as the *Addyston Pipe* case (1898), common-law conspiracy had been associated not only with individualist notions of illegal conduct and predatory intent but also with the ideas of secrecy, fraud, or deception. A half century later, confronted with the seemingly illogical question of whether a corporation can conspire with itself to fix prices, the Court turned for an answer to the ideas of secrecy, fraud, and deception. Writing for a unanimous Court in the *Kieffer-Stewart* case (1951), Justice Black concluded that, indeed, a corporation could conspire with itself: "The fact that corporations are under common ownership and control does not relieve them from liability under the antitrust laws, especially where they hold themselves out as competitors."[38]

The Court's hesitancy to adopt oligopoly theory as an economic logic for "agreements" in restraint of trade, its adherence to a common-law logic of conspiracy, had material consequences. In *Klor's v. Broadway-Hale Stores* (1959), for example, a small San Francisco retailer claimed that ten national appliance suppliers had conspired, at the urging of a Bay Area department store chain, to sell to the local retailer at a higher price or not at all. The defendants argued that the matter was a "purely private quarrel." The presence of "hundreds of other retailers" was overwhelming evidence that the conspiracy had no competitive effect and thus, they insisted, there was "no public wrong."

Justice Black rejected this economic argument out of hand: A group boycott "is not to be tolerated merely because the victim is just one merchant whose business is so small that his destruction makes little difference to the economy." The illegality stemmed not from any economic effect, concluded Black, but from depriving Klor's of the "freedom to buy appliances in an open competitive market," from the collusive effort to restrain liberty of contract.[39]

Although the view that competition derives from freedom of contract seems to repeat the classical economics that informed both the *Lochner* (1904) and *Standard Oil* (1911) opinions, Justice Black's special solicitude for small business, evinced in the *Klor's* opinion's egalitarian ethic, produced a radically different kind of freedom of contract. Indeed, this new liberty of contract doctrine had a more recent genealogy: The egalitarian commitment can be traced to several of Chief Justice Hughes's constitutional law opinions—particularly, the *Tipaldo* dissent (1936) and the *West Coast Hotel* opinion (1937) for the Court during its "revolutionary" term.[40] Numerous antitrust opinions into the late 1960s adopted this new rhetoric of contract, informed by an egalitarian ethic, in two ways: Some decisions prohibited agreements when they were seen as tinged with coercion (that is, sharply unequal bargaining power), while others assessed agreements in explicitly Jeffersonian terms of their impact on independent entrepreneurs.

The relationship between coercion and agreement was a troubling one, at least since Justice Brandeis's observation in *Chicago Board of Trade* (1918) that all agreements restrain and since legal realist Robert Hale's deconstructive analysis a few years later of "freedom of contract" as fundamentally coercive. In the years that followed, the Court's Rule of Reason was presented as a jurisprudence for discriminating between reasonable and unreasonable restraints. One recurring basis for adjudging a restraint unreasonable was a finding of coercion—that is, an exercise of grossly unequal bargaining power.[41] The second rhetorical reflection of an egalitarian ethic was a direct call to Jeffersonian values, an explicit commitment to perpetuating a vibrant class of independent entrepreneurs.

Simpson v. Union Oil (1964) offers an example of both rhetorical approaches to the Court's modern freedom of contract jurisprudence, each rhetoric informed by an egalitarian ethic. The Court released Simpson, an independent gas station owner, from a "coercive type of consignment agreement" by applying a common-law contract doctrine—that of coercion—to overthrow an ancient common-law property right—retention of title in property by consignment: Even though Union Oil Company retained title to their products, they could not use coercion to set the retail price. In the process, the Court transfered a fundamental property right—the right to set the sale price—from the oil company to the station owner. Justice Douglas's rationale included a Jeffersonian spin on freedom of contract. "Dealers, like Simpson, are independent businessmen," Douglas began. "The risk of loss is on them." Yet, "[p]ractically the only power they have to be wholly independent," he concluded, "is taken from them by the proviso that they must sell their gasoline at prices fixed by Union Oil." But where the Justice Black who wrote the *Klor's*

(1959) opinion would have reposed in the common-law logic of coercion or an explicit call to Jeffersonian values, Douglas moved on. Indeed, he moved on to another jurisprudential plain. After taking explicit account of the parties' unequal bargaining power, Douglas, citing his *Socony-Vacuum* (1940) opinion, vaulted out of the rhetorical domain of common-law property rights and into the economic discourse of competition. The Union Oil Company consignment was not unreasonable simply because it was "coercive." Rather, *any* "consignment, no matter how lawful it might be as a matter of private contract law," Douglas declared, "must give way before the federal antitrust policy"—that is, competition policy. The opinion shifted ground, moving from property to competition rhetoric. The movement was more than semantic. It shook loose a cornerstone of common-law property rights secure for three hundred years: Competition policy would now trump the common-law property right of consignment.[42]

The rhetorical divergence between Justices Black and Douglas, as well as the underlying policy conflict, was neither easily nor quickly settled. Indeed, it would resurface in the Court's treatment of market power in merger cases under the Celler-Kefauver amendment discussed later in this chapter. But the problem of "agreements" in restraint of trade was resolved, at least insofar as the rhetoric for its conceptualization would henceforth come from competition policy. There remained only one question: To what model of competition would Douglas and the *Simpson* majority subscribe? "The evil of this resale price maintenance program," asserted Douglas, "is its inexorable potentiality for and even certainty in destroying competition in retail sales of gasoline." Under what theory of competition could the loss of competition between Union Oil stations be portrayed in such extreme terms? Douglas left no doubt about his view of competition, excerpting a recent article by Adolf Berle that declared: "Economists call it 'imperfect competition'—a tacitly accepted price. . . . Only big concerns can swing this sort of competition." Douglas introduced the excerpt with the following language: "A. A. Berle recently described the critical importance of price control to money making by the large oligarchies of business, or the 'behemoths' as he called them."[43]

The concern for Simpson's freedom to set a price, together with the recognition that Union Oil Company was not only a huge corporate enterprise but also part of an oligopoly, led the Court to conclude that without competition at the retail level, there would be no competition at all. The analytical apparatus used to reach this conclusion was oligopoly theory: Allowing Union Oil and other industry members to retain the right to set retail prices would simply extend to the retail level, despite the large number of gas stations, the kind of tacit agreement associated with oligopoly market structure at the manufacturing level.

The Court's, and especially Justice Douglas's, turn to an oligopoly logic of competition informed by a Jeffersonian commitment to independent entrepreneurs typically focused on the competitive freedom of retailers. In *White Motor Co. v. U.S.* (1963), however, the Court was confronted with a new problem: a dispute between two independent entrepreneurs—one a truck dealer and the other a truck manufacturer. The difficulty lay in both parties' strong claims to the mantle of Jeffersonian solicitude. On one side stood the familiar figure of the retail dealer who wanted to compete free of restraints imposed by his supplier. But on the other side of this dispute was a small manufacturer struggling to compete in an industry dominated by the "Big Three" oligopoly of General Motors, Ford, and Chrysler. White Motor argued that their territorial and customer limitations on dealers, their restraint of competition among their own dealers, was a crucial incentive for active and costly dealer efforts to market and service their product. Dealers would be less likely to exert the kind of effort necessary to compete against the Big Three if they also risked losing customers to lower-cost discounters—to White Motor dealers who could "free ride" on their costly efforts and then steal their customers.[44]

What distinguished White Motor from Union Oil Company in the *Simpson* decision was White's smaller size and weak market position. White's "free rider" argument was as old as the hills—at least as old as *Dr. Miles* (1911), the Court's early decision resolving a dispute about restraints on distribution. But Justice Douglas's opinion in *White Motor Co.* recognized an argument now understood in terms of oligopoly theory, an egalitarian ethic, and, moreover, the theory of monopolistic competition. The theory of monopolistic competition entered competition policy in the form of a distinction between interbrand and intrabrand competition. White Motor's argument was based on that distinction. Without the concepts of brand identification and customer loyalty, the claim that restraining its dealers (intrabrand competition) would enhance competition against the Big Three (interbrand competition) made no sense. That is, White Motor asserted that its fortune must depend not on price competition but rather on marketing and service—on successful product differentiation, not on lower price.

The Court majority, with Justice Brennan concurring, concluded that the effects on competition were not clear enough to treat the restraints as illegal per se. In short, the Court took seriously White Motor's argument, founded in monopolistic competition theory, that a Jeffersonian ethic should apply to independent producers. Justice Clark dissented, characterizing White Motor's argument as nothing more than an attempt "to make a virtue of business necessity, which has long been rejected as a defense."[45]

By the mid-1960s, the Court's notion of "agreement" under Sherman Act § 1 had come full circle, or perhaps full spiral: from *Sugar Institute*'s (1936) neoclassically informed view of cooperative competition to *Theatre Enterprise*'s (1954) common-law doctrine of conspiracy to *White Motor*'s recognition of a "free rider" argument derived from the theory of monopolistic competition. Lodged within this uncoiling notion of agreement there remained, however, a stable center: Express agreements between competitors, whether to fix prices or to boycott rivals, were always seen as unreasonable.[46]

But what of an open agreement between competitors to lobby Congress for rate regulation—that is, for public price-fixing? Or to lobby a state legislature for market entry restrictions whose practical effect would be market foreclosure to all new competition? Do agreements seeking political action—that is, agreements portrayed as conduct in the First Amendment's marketplace of ideas—transgress competition policy? Isn't agreement, consensus, in the political sphere sacrosanct?

It was only a matter of time before the Supreme Court would be asked to rule on concerted action seeking political restraints on competition. It had been clear at least since the mid-1930s that states could pass economic regulation without offending the Fourteenth Amendment and that the antitrust laws were no barrier to state regulation. Now the *Noerr Motor Freight* case (1961) required the Court to look behind the state action and into the political process: Did a joint publicity campaign and lobbying effort constitute an illegal agreement in restraint of trade? Did a campaign by a railroad trade association, aimed not at winning over consumers but at urging state legislatures and citizens to reject a bill favoring motor carriers who competed with the railroads for long-haul freight business, violate the antitrust laws? What if the campaign were shown to be "vicious, corrupt and fraudulent"?[47]

Writing for a unanimous Court, Justice Black held the industrywide publicity campaign legal, resting the decision on an "essential dissimilarity" between "persuad[ing] a legislature" to exclude competitors and "help[ing] one another take away the trade freedom of others." The dissimilarity, although somehow "essential," was not entirely clear. First of all, it was likely that the railroads' campaign was intended to accomplish both ends. Certainly publicity campaigns could plausibly be characterized in either political or economic terms. Moreover, both forms of conduct, if successful, would produce identical effects on competition. Finally, the Court was willing to assume that petitioning government often served an "ulterior motive" of financial benefit. In short, Black simply proclaimed a categorical dissimilarity between "petitioning government" and a "common law trade restraint," between politics and economics. The antitrust laws, he observed, were not intended for political conduct, regardless of motive or effect.[48]

Antitrust policy thus projected two sharply different visions of competition—one in economic markets for goods and another in the political marketplace of ideas. At the same time, the theory of monopolistic competition had already transformed commercial rivalry into competition in the marketplace of ideas. Yet, when confronted with agreements between rivals that were characterized as "political," the Court flipped back into something like the classical vision invoked in Justice Holmes's marketplace metaphor for political discourse. In Justice Black's marketplace of ideas, there were no cartels, no profane trusts, no oligarchies; just "the people" petitioning government and seeking consensus. Of course there were cartels and profane trusts. But they were next door—in the economic sphere.

Four years later, Justice Byron White wrote an opinion that confirmed both the antitrust immunity of those seen as petitioning government and the categorical distinction between economic and political collaboration. In *United Mine Workers v. Pennington* (1965), an independent coal operator complained that the UMW and the large coal companies had conspired to raise costs, including wages, to levels that would drive smaller companies out of business. White's opinion divided Pennington's complaint into two categories: Economic collaboration to impose industrywide contracts was illegal per se under the antitrust laws. Political collaboration to influence public officials was, however, legal per se. There was no Rule of Reason, no balancing, just two spheres and two conclusions. White stressed that intent was not relevant in the political sphere. Nor was competitive effect.[49]

What was it that pulled a Court of pragmatic, postrealist judges back into a rhetoric of formalism marked by categorical distinctions between political and economic spheres, direct and indirect effects? From an antitrust perspective, it appears to have been an overreaction to the doubled genealogy of "agreement," an inability to balance the political and economic implications, the sacred and profane legacies, of concerted action. Perhaps it reflected an ethical commitment to a purely political sphere, to an individualist imagery of "one person, one vote"—heedless to both political realities and recent political theory.

Placing these two opinions amid a different group of decisions produces another perspective, but one that nonetheless affirms the state of tension between the twin genealogies of "agreement." The *Noerr* and *Pennington* decisions explicitly refer to the New Deal era cases that made it clear that government regulation did not have to be consistent with the antitrust laws. Accordingly, the federal government could sanction dairy cooperatives and the State of California could regulate rivalry among raisin ranchers, notwithstanding the Sherman Act's prohibition of combinations in restraint of trade. In this line, too, *Noerr* and *Pennington* are seen as cases about a conflict between the antitrust policy against "agreements" and the political virtues of collaborative activity.[50]

Yet, when set into a concurrent line of cases beginning with *Thornhill* (1940)—the decision granting First Amendment immunity to labor picketers in Tuscaloosa County, Alabama—the *Noerr-Pennington* doctrine's turn to formalism can be understood in terms of an ethical commitment and logic unexpressed in Justice White's opinion. Why not look at intent or effect when determining whether conduct should be seen as an exercise of First Amendment rights? Justice Murphy's *Thornhill* opinion viewed as immaterial an intent to persuade customers or suppliers to boycott Thornhill's employer, because such an intent, if taken as evidence of "economic" rather than "political" conduct, would disqualify all picketing from First Amendment protection. Murphy's ingenious strategy characterized the dispute between labor and management in (traditional) political terms, and picketing as a form of political speech, but then proceeded to describe the political sphere with Justice Holmes's marketplace metaphor. Alabama law could not restrain the peaceful, productive competition found in the marketplace of ideas.[51]

In a subsequent labor case, however, decided during the McCarthy era, the Court retreated from Murphy's equation of competing ideas and picketing workers. Applying a Rule of Reason, a balancing jurisprudence to limit First Amendment speech rights, the *Giboney* (1949) decision seems to illuminate an alternative ethical commitment and logic driving the *Noerr-Pennington* doctrine's new formalism. In *Giboney*, Justice Black held "that nothing in the constitutional guaranties of speech or press compels a state to apply or not to apply its antitrade restraint law to groups of workers, businessmen or others." He characterized labor picketing as "more than free speech." It was the use of "economic power" to "bring about coercion." In enforcing its antitrust laws, the State of Missouri was protecting "the interests of the whole public." What were those interests? Borrowing from early First Amendment jurisprudence, Justice Black portrayed the labor picketing as a "clear danger, imminent and immediate," and therefore as a "grave offense against an important public law" whose purpose was "to afford all persons an equal opportunity to buy goods."[52] The Court balanced consumerism with free speech rights, giving more weight to the competition in markets for goods and services than to competition in the marketplace of ideas. In short, Justice Black portrayed the picketing as a "grave offense" against consumer choice, a "clear danger" to the unified body economic.

One year later, another labor case followed *Giboney*'s balancing approach to determining free speech rights in labor disputes. With Justice Black now dissenting, Chief Justice Frederick Vinson wrote an opinion upholding the constitutionality of the Taft-Hartley Act's registration requirement for labor leaders who were members of the Communist Party. In the *Douds* case (1950), the Court found that the clear and present danger to "the free flow of goods" by closet Communists who called "political strikes" (strikes motivated by "political affiliations" rather than by the immediate economic interests of union members) justified the burden upon First Amendment free speech. The Vinson opinion replaced the *Thornhill* decision's categorical protection of speech with a Rule of Reason. "[T]he problem is one of weighing the probable effects of the statute upon the free exercise of the right of speech and assembly," Vinson explained, "against the congressional determination that political strikes are evils of conduct which cause substantial harm to interstate commerce." "Nothing in the Constitution," he concluded, "prevents Congress from acting in time to prevent potential injury to the national economy from becoming a reality." "The Bill of Rights," he proclaimed, is not a "suicide pact."[53]

In a statement that the *Noerr-Pennington* doctrine would repudiate, at least as it applies to the antitrust laws, Vinson insisted: "Those who, so Congress has found, would subvert the public interest cannot escape all regulation because, at the same time, they carry on legitimate political activities." Justice Black was outraged. Although the majority characterized the statutory requirement of registration to be a reasonable regulation based on "political affiliations"—like "business affiliations . . . a rational ground"—Black viewed the statute as an assault on the most basic political freedom: "'Freedom to think is absolute of its own nature; the most tyrannical government is powerless to control the inward workings of the mind.' But people can be, and in less democratic countries have been, made to suffer for their admitted or conjectured thoughts."[54] Both *Douds* and *Giboney* reflected the dangers of submitting First Amendment speech rights to a Rule of Reason. In balancing the impact of an agreement or association on commercial markets with the impact of its regulation on the marketplace of ideas, the post-1937 Court was inclined to defer to legislative judgments.

In contrast to the *Lochner* era's protection of liberty of contract, this Court's turn away from a balancing jurisprudence in *Noerr* and *Pennington* can be understood as a liberal formalism designed to protect "political" or "individual" rights such as petitioning government from *any* infringement by majoritarian action, including the Sherman Act's prohibition of agreements in restraint of trade. Even if the railroad trade association's publicity campaign or labor-management collaboration in the coal industry restrains trade, the mid-1960s Supreme Court declared, joint efforts to petition government would not be restricted. Agreements, when plausibly portrayable as either political or economic, either sacred or profane, would be treated as political and thus as above reproach.[55] The marketplace of ideas, conceptualized in terms of "political" rights, would be understood as a forum for political exchange between individuals to negotiate consensus, a forum free from the economic power of large corporate bureaucracies and industry trade associations, a marketplace whose only perceived threat comes from the heavy hand of majoritarian government seeking to control the hearts and minds of individual citizens. In short, this liberal formalism shared with its conservative predecessor a view of the market uninformed by intervening political and economic theories of oligarchic or monopolistic rivalry. Hence, the unmediated jurisprudence of price-fixing, whether by cartels, lobbying groups, or labor unions: An agreement was either illegal per se (economic and thus profane) or, under the *Noerr-Pennington* doctrine, legal per se (political and thus sacred). A parallel strand of liberal formalism would appear in the Court's merger jurisprudence under the Celler-Kefauver Amendment to Clayton Act § 7, particularly in its exploration of differing approaches to the question of economic power.

Competition Policy, Market Images, and the Problem of Corporate Size

What is a market? There was a time when "market" meant marketplace—a unique place for exchanging goods in relative safety from more violent forms of acquisition, such as plunder and theft. Subsequently, "market" reflected a functional logic: a process of exchange, wherever it took place. Nowadays, "market" is an abstract idea, an institutional complex whose shifting elements depend upon a series of normative judgments. And yet, the very idea of a "market" has been reified—that is, we treat the idea as if it retains a physical or functional existence independent of our policies and institutions. We even call it "the market," as if "it" enjoyed an autonomous existence, perhaps in New York City or Tokyo, or in Adam Smith's eighteenth-century Scotland.

Although "market" as a place or function has no necessary logical relationship with the idea of "competition," the *idea* of a "market" has come to be associated with it. In the 1950s and 1960s, the Supreme Court struggled with the idea of a market, its relationship to competition policies and to the reported trend toward economic concentration. There were variations in the Court's attitude toward the idea of a market, variations that reflected differing views of competition policy.

In antitrust policy, the rhetoric was bipolar, shifting between a narrower competition rhetoric of market power and a broader property rhetoric of economic power. Neither rhetorical extreme seemed satisfactory. Market power, usually inferred from a firm's market share, sometimes appeared to identify dominant firms and other times seemed misleading. Moreover, the very determination of the "market" was a notoriously slippery process. The other rhetorical marker—economic power—was usually associated with corporate size. It often identified dominant firms but also met with the claim that corporate size reflected commercial success and economies of scale. In sum, the idea of market power was utterly incoherent, while the idea of economic power, some claimed, cast too wide a net.

Despite its incoherence, the idea of market power would ultimately provide the touchstone for the Court's antitrust policies. The choice was overdetermined; there were too many good reasons not to think in terms of market power. Here are three of them. First, in its various forms, competition policy had always assumed some idea of a market. With microeconomic theories of all stripes tied to markets—from the classical imperative of individual freedom to pursue any calling, to the multiplication of markets under the theory of monopolistic competition—it made sense to judge commercial activity within the analytical framework of markets. Second, the alternative, the idea that economic power justified antitrust prosecution, was not only alien to the rhetoric of microeconomics but a frontal attack on traditional property rights associated with ownership and control. And, finally, the idea of "punishing" someone for status (large size) rather than behavior (unfair competition of one sort or another) was inimicable to the ideology of individual fault underlying Anglo-American law.

Nevertheless, concerns about corporate size persisted. The Court's efforts to resolve the problem of corporate bigness worked along three lines, each of which shows the tension between the competition rhetoric of market power and the property rhetoric of economic power. The first line, traced through Sherman Act cases, underlined the special solicitude for internal growth expressed in Learned Hand's *ALCOA* opinion (1945) and in the Celler-Kefauver Act's legislative history. The second, seen in a series of vertical restraints cases under the Clayton Act, sought to develop an alternative notion of competitive impact founded in volume of commerce rather than market share—that is, in corporate size. The third and most prominent line supported the Court's merger jurisprudence under the Celler-Kefauver amendment; here, the idea of a "market" was alternatively dilated and constricted, extended and shortened, threatening the continued viability of microeconomic analysis as a framework for antitrust policy. After tracing these three lines, I turn to the Court's 1967 term, whose antitrust jurisprudence retained only the most tenuous rhetorical connection to a microeconomic framework of market analysis.

During that term, the competition policy driving the Court's opinions reflected a property rights rhetoric as well as explicit Jeffersonian concerns about economic power.

For those who believe that competition policy requires attention to market power and its exercise, there is the pragmatic problem of market definition—that is, taking the abstract notion of a "market" and giving it the physical substance it once enjoyed. In its antitrust doctrine, the Court has constructed a market in two dimensions: geographic expanse and product definition. Where is this product bought and sold? And what other products are viewed as close substitutes? These two simple questions, asked in a world of high-speed transportation and increasing product differentiation, have usually elicited controversial answers. On rare occasions, the Court was asked to enjoin the actions of a monopolist in a clearly defined market, such as that of the only newspaper in Lorain, Ohio.[56]

But, most of the time, market definition was indeterminate. It was up for grabs in the sense that there were two or more highly plausible alternative definitions to choose from. The first opinion to consider explicitly alternative market definitions and to give reasons for choosing one over the others was Learned Hand's opinion in *ALCOA* (1945). The Supreme Court followed Hand's example in the *duPont* (1956) decision, also a Sherman Act case, which rejected the Eisenhower Administration's charge that E. I. duPont de Nemours & Company monopolized the production and sale of cellophane packaging material. The decisive issue was the question of monopoly power, which turned on the idea of a market. Was the product cellophane, as the Government argued, or all flexible wrapping materials, as duPont claimed?[57]

DuPont's view prevailed. Six Justices were convinced that duPont's patented cellophane competed in a larger market of flexible packaging materials. Given this view of the market, duPont's 20 percent share was deemed far short of monopoly. Its 75 percent share of a cellophane market would likely have met the Court's standard for monopoly power. The Government argued that other materials were not close substitutes for cellophane because their physical characteristics were different. Justice Stanley F. Reed, writing for the majority, found that the array of other packaging materials was "reasonably interchangeable by consumers for the same purposes." Moreover, Reed introduced the deceptively simple economic concept of "cross-elasticity of demand" to show that there was "great sensitivity" to price changes. This measure of competition between substitutes purported to reflect the rate at which customers abandoned cellophane for other flexible packaging materials when duPont raised its price, or returned when duPont lowered it. In short, the Court applied neoclassical price theory to determine the boundaries between markets: Because customers moved freely between cellophane and other flexible packaging materials, the Court believed, there was competition in what must be "a market." Hence, duPont did not have "the power to control prices or exclude competition."[58]

The Court rejected the Government's argument that cellophane's higher price—two or three times higher than its rivals—was evidence of monopoly power. Although the Court conceded that the higher price reflected product differentiation (customers willing to pay more for cellophane rather than switch to a substitute), Reed insisted that this was not "monopoly power." Chief Justice Earl Warren dissented, arguing that the market definition was wrong. Joined by Justices Douglas and Black, Warren asked how duPont could charge so much more for cellophane if there were close substitutes.[59]

While Justice Reed's majority was willing to rely on the mechanical formulation of cross-elasticity of demand and the neoclassical price theory subtending it, Chief Justice Warren's dissenting faction recognized neoclassical theory's limitations, particularly its failure to take account of the power to control price in the absence of a dominant market share, the power described in the theory of monopolistic competition. Warren, Douglas, and Black were arguing for a market definition coextensive with duPont's successful product differentiation. But the implications were subversive of the very notion of market competition: Each differentiated product, each brand name with customer loyalty, could theoretically define its own market and thus be deemed a monopoly. For this reason, if no other, the theory of monopolistic competition was a dangerous alternative to mainstream price theory.[60] The Court's Sherman Act jurisprudence evaded the danger to its economic grounds by remaining within the neoclassical precincts outlined in Reed's majority opinion.

There was a second thread running through the Court's efforts to resolve the problem of corporate size, a thin thread seen in the narrow confines of Clayton Act § 3, which prohibits agreements to deal exclusively with one trading partner, or to condition the sale of one product on the promise to buy a second one—but only when such agreements "substantially lessen competition." Tugging on that thread was Justice Douglas, who was intent upon formulating an alternative to market power for judging competitive impact. Recall his dissenting opinion in the *Columbia Steel* merger case (1948). Disputing the majority's view that small market shares meant that U.S. Steel's acquisition of Consolidated Steel, an independent steel fabricator, did not offend the Sherman Act, Douglas had observed: "The business of Consolidated amounts to around $22,000,000 annually. The competitive purchases by Consolidated are over $5,000,000 a year. I do not see how it is possible to say that $5,000,000 of commerce is immaterial. . . . [T]he volume of business restrained by this contract is not insignificant or insubstantial." Writing for the majority, Justice Reed had rejected this formulation, much as he would alternatives to a strict neoclassical view in *duPont* (1956), stating that "we do not think the dollar volume is in itself of compelling significance."[61]

The source for Douglas's dissenting formulation was Justice Felix Frankfurter's majority opinion in *International Salt* (1947). The International Salt Company's practice of leasing its patented machines only to those who agreed to buy all salt from International was prohibited, the Court concluded, because it is "unreasonable, per se, to foreclose competitors from any substantial market." Under both the Sherman and Clayton Acts, the effects on competition were substantial when the "volume of business affected by these contracts cannot be said to be insignificant or insubstantial."[62] In short, it was the *amount* of commerce, the *size* of the firm, that counted, not the percentage share of some "market."

One year later, however, Frankfurter joined Justice Reed's majority in the *Columbia Steel* merger case, and Douglas found himself writing a dissenting opinion. The Court continued to flip between the two standards in cases involving the practice of "tying" or conditioning the sale of one good or service to the purchase of a second. The Northern Pacific Railroad, for example, conditioned the sale or lease of land adjacent to its track upon the promise to ship over its lines all goods produced on the land. Justice Black, writing for the Court, explicitly adopted Frankfurter's *International Salt* standard, finding that Northern Pacific's vast land holdings—more than forty million acres granted by Congress—constituted "sufficient *economic* power to impose an appreciable restraint of free competition."[63]

Frankfurter, however, again joined the dissenting opinion, here written by Justice John Harlan, who maintained that the standard should be the "amount of control over the relevant market," including specific findings of "significant percentage control of the relevant market." Black, Douglas, and the others who joined them insisted upon the importance of economic power, regardless of any market power analysis founded in market share.[64]

Three years later, the rhetorical tables turned again in the *Tampa Electric* case (1960). Apparently because the price of coal had dropped dramatically, Tampa sought to escape a long-term requirements contract with the Nashville Coal Company by claiming that the Clayton Act prohibited such exclusive dealing. It was illegal, Tampa claimed, because the $128 million per year contract was "not insignificant or insubstantial," and thus it substantially lessened competition. Justice Clark, writing for the Court, rejected the dollar-volume standard, the corporate-bigness-as-anticompetitive ethic, with the substitution of one crucial word: The test was whether "competition has been foreclosed in a substantial *share* of the line of commerce affected."[65]

Justices Black and Douglas dissented without opinion. What more could they say? After struggling for more than a decade to define competition policy in terms of corporate size, they found themselves severely outnumbered. Henceforth, they seemed to concede, the competition rhetoric of market power would shape antitrust policy. The battle that stood before them in the decade of the 1960s, especially in the highly visible arena of corporate mergers, the remaining struggle, would be fought over opposing microeconomic theories of market power.

The Celler-Kefauver amendment's regulation of corporate mergers provided the third and most prominent battleground for conflicts over competition policy, for rhetorical struggles between those advocating a market-power approach and those calling for antitrust regulation of corporate concentration, that is, regulation of economic power unconstrained by microeconomic analysis of individual markets. For the Court majority, which was committed to a competition policy founded in the microeconomic logic that market share reflects market power, the problem under the Celler-Kefauver amendment was finding some market share short of Sherman Act "monopolization" to give substance to the phrase "substantial lessening of competition." Should the post-merger line be drawn at a 50 percent market share? Thirty percent? Ten? The problem was acute because the amendment's legislative history reflected the desire to halt "trends toward concentration" even before some dangerous level of concentration was reached. Thus, the Court would not only be called upon to formulate some market-share equivalent to a dangerous level, it would also be asked to determine when, over time, cumulative market share increases reflected a trend toward that level.

Even more perplexing, the *Congressional Record* seemed to suggest that the concerns about "economic concentration" bore on the larger sphere of a competitive economy rather than the microeconomic model of a competitive market. Is the larger economic sphere simply the sum of individual markets with competitive structures? Or is economic concentration in the larger sphere a condition inaccessible through the logic of microeconomics? What would the Court, newly committed to the microeconomic logic of markets and market power, do with the egalitarian sentiments, the Jeffersonian rhetoric of "economic concentration" evident in the Celler-Kefauver amendment's legislative debates? In the period from 1957 to 1966, corporate merger policy would prove to be the leading battleground for the struggle between adherents to the microeconomic logic of market power and their opponents, those who believed that economic concentration—corporate bigness—was a policy issue that escaped the narrow confines of microeconomic analysis.

Although Chief Justice Warren's opinion in the *Brown Shoe* case (1962) is generally recognized as the Court's long-delayed acknowledgment of the Celler-Kefauver amendment's concern about the polymorphous consequences of economic concentration through corporate merger, the Eisenhower administration earlier prosecuted an astounding case to undo the duPont family's acquisition of 23 percent of General Motors' common stock, an acquisition that gave them effective control of General Motors. The *duPont (GM)* case (1957) was astounding on three accounts.[66]

First, the Justice Department was seeking an injunction to reverse a stock purchase consummated almost forty years earlier. How could the Court even entertain the thought of an attack on a transaction so old?[67]

Second, this 1919 stock acquisition was prosecuted under the original Clayton Act, whose § 7 language everyone assumed did not apply to vertical integration. DuPont stood accused of taking over its largest customer in order to become its sole supplier of automotive finishes and fabrics. Justices Burton and Frankfurter dissented, insisting there was no precedent for applying the statute to vertical mergers. They argued that the original § 7 applied only to mergers between direct competitors. Writing for the Court,

Justice Brennan turned to statutory language ignored by all those who took the narrow view. The Clayton Act applies to vertical stock acquisitions, Brennan observed, in which the effect may be "to restrain commerce in any section or in any community" or "tend to create a monopoly in any line of commerce" even if, he stressed, there is no lessening of competition.[68] In short, "commerce" is not synonymous with "competition"; it includes relations between customers and suppliers.

Third and most remarkable was the Court's holding that duPont's acquisition did violate the original Clayton Act. General Motors showed that duPont's sales to GM constituted less than 5 percent of all sales of finishes and fabrics, calling it "a negligible percentage of the total market." Dissenting Justices Burton and Frankfurter added that the sales represented an equally small percentage of duPont's business. Justice Brennan's opinion for the Court rejected their market-share logic for determining the competitive impact of the stock acquisition. Instead, Brennan defined a narrow "line of commerce"—automotive finishes and fabrics, observing:

> General Motors is the colossus of the giant automobile industry. . . . In 1955 General Motors ranked first in sales and second in assets among all US industrial corporations and became the first corporation to earn over a billion dollars in annual net income. In 1947 GM's total purchases of all products from du Pont were $26,628,274. . . . Expressed in percentages, du Pont supplied 67% of GM's requirements for finishes in 1946.

Giving great weight to evidence of corporate size and sales volume, Brennan concluded that "du Pont has a substantial share of the relevant market." In short, duPont had captured too much of the business of the largest corporation in perhaps the most concentrated oligopoly in American industry. The vertical merger substantially restrained "commerce" and thus, regardless of its effects on competition in some isolated market, violated the Clayton Act.[69]

The large majority of cases decided under Clayton Act § 7 involved horizontal mergers. Mergers are called horizontal when the corporations seeking to combine sell (or buy) competing products or services in the same geographic area. What begins as a simple statement, however, quickly develops into a complex and mystifying inquiry. With the postwar development of large-scale manufacturing and distribution technologies, the explosion of communications media, and the proliferation of consumer products, there is no obvious answer to the question, "Who competes?" Yet the answer is dispositive of any microeconomic analysis of competition, market definition, and market share: If the merging partners do not encounter one another in the same "market," if they do not compete, then there is no effect on competition, and thus no microeconomic reason to stop the merger. Lingering in the background, moreover, was Justice Brennan's distinction between "commerce" and "competition"—his view in *duPont* (*GM*) that merger jurisprudence should not be circumscribed by the microeconomic logic of market analysis.

In the 1960s, the Court seemed to be searching for a satisfying answer to the question "Who competes?" The investigation explored three issues. First, there was the question of approach: Should the analysis involve a balancing of factors or a bright-line test, a Rule of Reason or a liberal formalism? Second, what do contending models of economic analysis have to say about what it means for two corporations to compete? Finally, should the microeconomic idea of a market give way to a Jeffersonian inquiry into economic concentration, to a metamarket idea of a competitive economy?

In determining "Who competes?" the Court began with a balancing approach that initially took into account a broad array of factors but quickly turned to a bright-line test, a liberal formalism whose jurisprudence had much in common with the *Noerr-Pennington* (1961, 1965) doctrine's categorical distinction between economic and political conduct. Chief Justice Warren's landmark opinion for the Court in *Brown Shoe* (1962) looked to the Celler-Kefauver amendment's legislative history for its Jeffersonian tone and to the *DuPont (GM)* (1957) decision for its economics. From the legislative debates came the "fear of a rising tide of economic concentration in the American economy," the desire to retain " 'local control' over industry," and the commitment to protect small business. In sum, Warren viewed congressional concern about increasing economic concentration to encompass "not just economic but other values."[70]

Although citing for authority Justice Brennan's opinion in *duPont* (*GM*) (1957), in *Brown Shoe* Chief Justice Warren at first seemed to reject the earlier opinion's logic of corporate size, describing market share as "important." Yet, Warren proceeded by characterizing the congressional concern embodied in the phrase "substantial lessening of competition" as permitting mergers only between small companies. But Brown Shoe and its merging partner, Kinney, were "neither small companies nor failing companies." Brown Shoe had assets of $72 million and Kinney had sales of $42 million. As the third largest shoe retailer, moreover, Brown had been "a moving factor" in the industry trend toward increased concentration. Despite a relatively small share of the national market (5 percent), the merger violated the Clayton Act, the Court held, largely because it increased the size of a large national chain and thus the likelihood of other consolidations in a fragmented industry. Along with an extended discourse on submarkets that threatened to explode the very idea of a market, Warren's underlying thematic is clearly Jeffersonian:

> [W]e cannot fail to recognize Congress' desire to promote competition through the protection of viable, small, locally owned businesses. Congress appreciated that occasional higher costs and prices might result from the maintenance of fragmented industries and markets. It resolved these competing considerations in favor of decentralization.[71]

One year later, however, the Court changed its view of the relative importance of market share in assessing the competitive effects of a merger between rivals. Responding to criticism that the *Brown Shoe* opinion offered no guidance to businessmen and their advisors, the *Philadelphia National Bank* (1963) decision dropped the earlier opinion's Jeffersonian tone while reshaping its market analysis into a form described as "fully consonant with economic theory." Citing numerous economic tracts for authority, Justice Brennan without hesitation equated congressional concern about corporate concentration to a microeconomic logic of "the relevant market" and a determination of submarkets and submarket shares. After simply proclaiming an identity between economic concentration and market-share analysis, Brennan took the next step. He devised a bright-line test to aid in "sound business planning." Henceforth, the Court would prohibit mergers resulting in an "undue percentage share" of the market ("at least 30%") and a "significant increase in concentration" ("more than 33%").[72] The discipline of microeconomics provided the logic for a liberal formalism—a conclusive inference of anticompetitive effect taken from the elusive "facts" of market-share percentages.

Certainly, Brennan was aware that there is no necessary relationship, either logical or empirical, between corporate size and the microeconomic logic of market share. Two multi-billion dollar, multinational oil companies could merge and their successor could enjoy far less than 30 percent of an "area of competitive overlap." On the other hand, two relatively small companies could merge and their $20 million successor could hold more than the 30 percent share prohibited under the logic of *Philadelphia National Bank*. Given the congressional concern over economic concentration, "local control" of industry, and protecting small businesses, which merger should pass antitrust scrutiny? The Court's 1964 term produced three merger decisions that sought, by stretching the idea of a "market" to encompass a broader range of rivals and products, to reconcile the congressional concern over economic concentration with the market-share logic of microeconomic analysis. Deploying an expanded economic rhetoric of market analysis, all three decisions prohibited the proposed mergers. Those three decisions would create a new danger, both to mergers involving large corporations and to the status of economic rhetoric.

The threat to mergers involving large corporations was not the peril avoided in *duPont* (*Cellophane*) (1956) and re-presented in *duPont* (*GM*) (1957): the dangerous logic of monopolistic competition theory, a logic that pointed to I. E. duPont as a single-firm market. *DuPont* (*GM*)'s explosive implication was that every firm with customer loyalty has some monopoly power and thus could be seen as violating the antitrust laws. The new threat emerged not from narrowly tailoring market definition to a single firm but instead from expanding the idea of a market beyond competition between practically identical products to include a larger group of substitutes—in short, duPont's winning argument in *duPont* (*Cellophane*) and losing argument in *duPont* (*GM*). Within the contours of the Clayton Act, the implication that firms compete more broadly threatened a strict regulatory regime: The Clayton Act would prohibit more mergers, now seen as combinations between competitors.

Government regulation of mergers would run rampant—unless the Court strictly imposed the *Philadelphia National Bank* (1962) decision's requirement that a merger produce a firm with substantial market share. If small market shares such as those seen in *Brown Shoe* (1962) were enough, then the Jeffersonian rhetoric of a "trend toward concentration" could portray any merger between large firms dealing in similar products as a merger between direct and substantial competitors. Horizontal merger activity, expansively defined, would come to a grinding halt. Mergers in any market showing a trend toward concentration—including, for example, supermarkets in the Los Angeles area—would provoke the strictest scrutiny. Moreover, the very status of microeconomic analysis was endangered because its core concept of a "market," alternately squeezed and expanded, began to resemble less some neutral exercise of social science expertise than the performance of a facile accordionist who can play any tune.

Of the three decisions during the 1964 term, two opinions written by Justice Douglas paid scrupulous attention to the microeconomic rhetoric of market analysis. In the *El Paso Natural Gas* case, the Justice Department was seeking to stop a merger between El Paso, the largest supplier of natural gas to California, and Pacific Northwest, a company that had competed against El Paso and lost. Nonetheless, the Court found that Pacific Northwest had "been a substantial factor in the California market." Even though Pacific Northwest had never sold natural gas in California, "it was so strong and militant that it was viewed with concern, and coveted, by El Paso." It was but a small step for the Court to conclude that "unsuccessful bidders are no less competitors than the successful one."[73]

In *ALCOA* (*Rome Cable*) as well, Justice Douglas presented a detailed market analysis of aluminum and copper conducting cable, both bare and insulated, used to transport electricity above and below ground. Separating the aluminum and copper cable business into separate lines of commerce based upon microeconomic reasoning about price and end-use differences, Douglas found that ALCOA was "the leader in a highly concentrated market," holding a 27.8 percent share in an aluminum cable oligopoly in which the four largest companies together controlled 76 percent. The case's difficulty lay in Rome Cable's small (1.3 percent) share: What difference would Rome's disappearance make? Douglas maintained that Rome Cable was an "important competitive factor" in the market, on account of "its special aptitude and skill in insulation," "the effectiveness of its marketing organization," and "an active and efficient research . . . organization." In short, "Rome seems to us the prototype of the small independent that Congress aimed to preserve by § 7." Douglas framed the Celler-Kefauver amendment with oligopoly theory. "It would seem that the situation in the aluminum industry may be oligopolistic," Douglas observed. "As that condition develops," he reasoned, "the greater is the likelihood that parallel policies of mutual advantage, not competition, will emerge."[74]

The rationales underlying both opinions by Justice Douglas took the form of microeconomic analysis. The first seemed a straightforward application of neoclassical price theory—losers are no less competitors than winners. The second relied on postclassical price theory—the structural logic that oligopoly markets tend to produce tacit cooperation rather than competition. Both opinions stayed within the microeconomic rhetoric of market analysis. In the *Continental Can* decision, however, Justice Byron White's opinion for the Court vacillated between the microeconomic rhetoric of market share analysis and the more expansive discourse of economic concentration and corporate size. Continental Can Company, a metal can manufacturer with $3 billion in annual sales and a 33 percent market share, had acquired Hazel-Atlas, a bottle manufacturer with a 10 percent market share. The Court forged a "combined metal and glass container market" as the "area of effective competition" between Continental and Hazel-Atlas. After the merger, their combined share of this inter-industry market would have been 30 percent—precisely the level defined one year earlier in *Philadelphia National Bank.* Thus far, Justice White traced Justice Brennan's earlier microeconomic analysis.

Lodged in the middle of the opinion, however, was a rhetorical irregularity of alien origin. Although the decision seemed to rest comfortably on the *Philadelphia National Bank*'s liberal formalism of market share, White volunteered that "[w]here a merger is of such size as to be inherently suspect, elaborate proof of market structure, market behavior and probable anticompetitive effects may be dispensed with in view of § 7's design to prevent undue concentration."[75] There it was again: a concern with economic concentration unbounded by market share analysis. Was White saying that the opinion's market share analysis was superfluous—a rhetorical cover for an underlying Jeffersonian normative content? Or, at the very least, a legitimating discourse, a microeconomic rationale, for a congressional concern ultimately unfounded in the idea of a market? What if merger policy were severed from microeconomics? Would the Court be seen as a political institution unconstrained by the logic of economic science? Unconstrained by the neutral principle of competition? Driven by a policy to redistribute property rights in order to level economic power?

Those who continued to rely on Justice Brennan's construction of *Philadelphia National Bank*'s bright-line test—its liberal formalist analysis to assess the competitive effects of horizontal mergers—were shaken three years later by a pair of decisions. Written by Justice Black, the *Pabst Brewing* and *Von's Grocery* opinions (1966) were alarming insofar as they aggressively rejected the microeconomic analysis subtending Justice Brennan's design of clear market-share guidelines that profiled the corporate mergers prohibited under Clayton Act § 7. Although the small market-share percentages found to trigger antitrust interdiction in *Von's Grocery* perhaps provide sufficient evidence to convict the Court of unreconstructed Jeffersonianism, it is the four separate opinions in the unanimous *Pabst Brewing* decision that present with striking clarity the Justices' conflicting views on competition policy and the idea of a "market." The proposed merger between Pabst and Blatz Brewing Companies would have combined "two very large brewers" with combined sales in 1957 accounting for 24 percent of sales in Wisconsin, 11 percent of sales in the three-state area of Wisconsin, Illinois, and Michigan, and 4.5 percent of sales nationally. The District Court dismissed the

Government's case for failure to carry its burden of proof on the issue of geographic market.[76]

Which of the three alternative geographic markets was, according to the *Philadelphia National Bank* decision, an "area of competitive overlap"? Justice Black restated the question, asking, instead, "within the meaning of Section 7," what is "a relevant section of the country"? It is not necessary, stressed Black, "for the Government to show a 'relevant geographic market' in the same way the *corpus delicti* must be proved to establish a crime." Black did not hide his disdain for the microeconomic discourse of market power: "Certainly the failure of the Government to prove by an army of expert witnesses what constitutes a relevant 'economic' or 'geographic' market is not an adequate ground on which to dismiss a § 7 case. . . . Congress did not seem to be troubled by the exact spot where competition might be lessened." For Black and the Court majority, it was enough that the brewing industry was "marked by a steady trend toward economic concentration" and that the merger "brought together two very large brewers competing against each other in forty states." It was corporate size, economic concentration—not market power, not the microeconomic logic of market share—that led Congress to amend the Clayton Act.[77]

While Justice White's one-sentence concurring opinion seems nothing more than a gesture to dissociate himself from the tone of Justice Black's polemic, Justice Harlan's opinion, joined by Justice Stewart, reflects a view of competition policy at odds with the majority opinion in two respects. First, Harlan and Stewart maintained that the statutory question of competitive effect "necessarily involves a study of statistics and other evidence bearing upon market shares, market trends, number of competitors and the like." In short, it is the discourse of microeconomics that provides the necessary logic to "measure" the change in competition. Second, Harlan and Stewart made it plain that their economics was informed by the theories of oligopoly and monopolistic competition. The beer industry's "heavy emphasis on consumer recognition and promotional techniques in the marketing of beer supports the conclusion that there does exist a substantial barrier to a new competitor. . . . [T]his means that those already within such a . . . market can engage in oligopolistic pricing or other practices. . . ."[78]

Justice Abe Fortas was unwilling to join either Justice Black's logic of economic concentration or Justice Harlan's postclassical economics. The Government has a duty, Fortas insisted, to prove "the relevant market." Though the search is "frequently complicated and elaborated beyond reason," it is not "a snipe hunt." "In some situations, arithmetic as to the merging companies' aggregate volume of sales may be impressive. Sometimes, the resulting size of the conjoined companies is great. But unless it can be shown that the effect may be 'substantially to lessen competition' . . . courts are not authorized to condemn the acquisition."[79]

In short, two views of competition policy contended for dominance in merger policy. Justices Black, Douglas, and their cohorts believed that the microeconomic logic of "markets" obscured the real issue of economic power, corporate concentration, and its effects on commerce. Justice White, it seemed, agreed. Justices Harlan, Stewart, and Fortas were certain that market-share analysis was the only viable logic for making sense of Congress's prohibition of mergers that substantially lessen competition. Justice Fortas did not, however, ascribe to the oligopoly theory embraced by Harlan and Stewart.

Mergers are purchase-and-sale transactions. Someone wants to buy and someone wants to sell property, whether physical assets or intangible marks of ownership and control. The question about merger policy is ultimately a simple one: What entitles the government, which presumably reflects a political majority, to deny property owners the most basic of all rights—the right to sell and to buy a business? Since the passage of the Sherman Act, the Justice Department has enforced a congressional expression of the "public interest" entitled "competition policy." While "competition policy" has meant many things, the Supreme Court until the 1950s was consistent in its view that corporate size was not one of them. Indeed, the right to grow and prosper was seen as a fundamental right. After Congress enacted the Celler-Kefauver Act of 1950, however, the Court began pushing the notion of "public interest" beyond competition policy. Just as the New York legislature could set rates for public utilities and just as the Washington legislature could pass a minimum-wage statute for women notwithstanding the effect on the regulated firms' property rights, so could Congress regulate mergers to limit corporate expansion to "internal growth"—the mark of success in "the market." The new merger policy seemed restrained neither by the Sherman Act's traditional competition policy nor by the ancient common-law (and Constitutional) right to sell one's property.

A market-based competition policy, argued Black, Douglas, and White, provided too narrow a view of the pervasive problem of economic concentration. In short, economic concentration can be understood as a competition problem whose solution falls outside the traditional microeconomic analysis of markets. But corporate bigness can also be understood as a property problem whose solution calls for limits on the accumulation of corporate assets. Those who believed that competition policy as seen through the lens of microeconomics was the proper view—particularly Harlan and Fortas—were expressing their disagreement with an assault on economic concentration, on the property right to grow and prosper, an assault launched from somewhere outside the traditional market-logic of competition policy.

The 1967 term produced three anti-trust opinions that immediately provoked controversy, three opinions whose triangulation brings into sharp focus the confrontation between the problem of economic concentration and microeconomic market models of competition policy. The issue of economic concentration, as we have seen, involved social policy questions beyond the scope of any microeconomic theory: Logics of market analysis simply cannot address the larger metamarket problems associated with corporate consolidation, with vast accumulations of wealth and thus economic power. In each of the three cases, the Court was forced to resolve a troubling misfit between competition policy and the problem of economic concentration. It was brought face to face with incongruities among the issue of firm size, the imagery of corporate power, and the idea of market power—for example, a large business's being family owned, a small business's holding great market power, or a large conglomerate corporation's holding none. In sum, the three decisions raised more questions than they answered about the relationship between economic analysis and competition policy. As well, they reintroduced a property rhetoric into antitrust jurisprudence whose implications for competition policy were obscure.

In the *Clorox* case, the Federal Trade Commission sought to enjoin Procter & Gamble from acquiring Clorox, the leading household liquid bleach manufacturer. Writing for a unified Court, Justice Douglas emphasized both Clorox's market power and P&G's size. In a industry whose annual sales were about $80 million, Clorox held almost 50 percent of the national market. With assets of $12 million, Clorox was the only national company in an industry characterized as oligopolistic: The four largest firms accounted for 80 percent of sales, with the remaining 20 percent divided among many small local and regional producers.[80] Clearly, Clorox was the dominant firm.

Although P&G did account for more than 50 percent of packaged detergent sales, Douglas stressed its size: With sales of $1,100 million and assets of $500 million, P&G's $127 million annual advertising budget dwarfed annual sales of the entire bleach industry. Indeed, $67 million in P&G profits almost equaled total bleach industry revenues. P&G was fifteen to twenty times larger than the entire bleach industry. A unanimous Court agreed that the Clayton Act prohibited the acquisition. Justice Douglas wrote an opinion adopting the FTC's policy analysis, which focused on the likely effects of a huge firm's purchase of the dominant firm in an industry of relatively small businesses.[81]

Although the rhetoric was microeconomic, the logic was Jeffersonian—both in the FTC's prosecution and Douglas's opinion for the Court. The FTC asked about the probable market impact of an enormous firm with vast financial resources, with economic power. The Court concurred in the FTC's finding that P&G's economic power would rigidify the current oligopoly structure in the bleach industry by striking fear of massive retaliation into the hearts of its tiny rivals, already led by oligopoly logic to believe that cooperation usually pays. Moreover, the Court agreed that P&G's expertise in developing brand loyalty, its willingness to use advertising as the primary weapon for competitive warfare, along with the monopoly profits from its brand-name products already available as a war chest, would immediately make it an overwhelming force in the liquid bleach industry. Indeed, Clorox was an attractive target because it had already established its brand name, allowing it the monopolistic advantage of charging a higher price for its bleach, a product chemically identical to all other liquid household bleaches. P&G would simply improve upon that success. In short, the FTC maintained that P&G's economic power—its huge size—would aggravate tendencies already seen in the industry, tendencies described in the market-based logics of postclassical microeconomics: the oligopoly logic of cooperation and the monopolistic competitive logic of rivalry through product advertising and promotion.[82]

Only Justice Harlan rejected the Jeffersonian logic impelling the microeconomic rhetorics heard in Douglas's opinion. Although concurring in the result, Harlan insisted upon evidence of "behavior" rather than a "general fear of bigness," reliance on oligopoly theory, or even a pejorative view of advertising. Relying on neoclassical price theory (although there was no explicit acknowledgement of reliance on any particular theory), Harlan called for attention to evidence of market share and, with it, "increase[d] pricing power in the relevant market." Most of all, Harlan stressed that what was important was not a competitor's size but rather the entrepreneurial magic of its management.[83]

Later that term, the Court decided another case that scrambled the categories of economic and market power and thus the rhetorics of property rights and competition. In the *Schwinn* case, the tension between corporate size and market power was evident in Justice Fortas' opinion for the Court. For many years, Arnold, Schwinn & Company had been the largest bicycle manufacturer in America, producing almost one in every four bikes sold. Even though it had lost almost half its market share in the 1950s, Schwinn's unit sales and revenues actually increased. It was not a small or failing company. Yet Fortas also thought it significant that Schwinn was a "family-owned" business, 84 percent of whose sales were through small franchised "bicycle specialty shops." Its competition was described as "giant" bicycle retailers such as Sears and Wards.[84]

The Justice Department sued to enjoin Schwinn's resale price maintenance and other restraints on distribution of its bicycles. The issue before the Court was limited to Schwinn's nonprice restraints on its distributors and retailers—provisions, for example, confining sales to specific territories and classes of customers. Justice Fortas resolved the question of restraining competition in Schwinn bicycles by reviving the distinction between sold and consigned goods, a distinction seemingly rejected three years earlier in *Simpson v. Union Oil* (1964).

At this juncture, it is useful to recall the doctrinal context for this narrow question—the legality of nonprice restraints on sold and consigned goods. Only four years earlier, Justice Douglas, writing for the Court in *White Motors* (1963), had applied a Rule of Reason to a small truck manufacturer's nonprice restraints. Influenced by a Jeffersonian ethic, the Court was willing to consider the possibility that White Motors's restrictions on its dealers would improve competition with the Big Three automotive giants. In the following year, Justice Douglas, again writing for the Court in *Simpson* (1964), had declared that competition policy trumped consignments, at least in an oligopolistic oil industry in which the only price competition likely was at the dealer level. In both decisions, Douglas's opinions were derived from competition policy and informed by a Jeffersonian logic, an egalitarian ethic. In both opinions, property rights were reshuffled to conform with an oligopoly theory of competition.

In the *Schwinn* opinion, however, a seeming ambivalence about the bicycle manufacturer (large, yet family owned) was accompanied by a surprising departure from the microeconomic rhetoric of market share. Justice Fortas, who had insisted so strenuously on microeconomic analysis in *Pabst Brewing* just one year earlier, now reached back into the dark recesses of common-law property rights to distinguish between reasonable and unreasonable restraints. Schwinn's restraints accompanying consignments were reasonable, Fortas declared, because it retained title and thus ownership of consigned bicycles. Implicit was the sense that Schwinn was not, after all, Union Oil Company or Pabst Brewing but a "family-owned" business. There was no coercion lurking about, no massive corporate bureaucracy weighing upon independent entrepreneurs. On the other hand, resale limitations accompanying *sold* bicycles, wrote Fortas, transgressed the "ancient rule against restraints on alienation." Schwinn went too far in "limiting the [small independent] retailer's freedom as to where and to whom it will resell."[85] Here, Schwinn was acting too big for its breeches.

In short, Fortas split the difference as a way of resolving this ambivalence toward Schwinn: Restraints ancillary to consigned bikes were reasonable; those accompanying sold bikes were not. He was intent upon making sense of the scrambled categories of big and small, of coercion and freedom, of faceless and family-owned enterprise. The scrambled category of a large, successful (but) family-owned business even led Fortas to argue that small manufacturers would benefit from more lenient treatment of restraints accompanying consignments. This argument is obviously wrong: Consignments require a manufacturer to have the financial resources to postpone payment until each consigned item is sold. As Justice Stewart correctly observed in his dissenting opinion, not only consignment but franchising more generally seems to promise some degree of entrepreneurial independence to *retailers*.[86]

Finally, Fortas's desire to resolve Schwinn's ambivalent position—a large, successful (but) family-owned business—led him from the microeconomic logic of market share to the classical logic of freedom of contract, informed by a Jeffersonian commitment seen most prominently in Justice Black's antitrust opinions, particularly *Fashion Organizers Guild* (1941) and *Klor's* (1959). In his *Schwinn* opinion, Fortas derived competition policy from freedom of contract, from the recognition of common-law property rights. Market share and the like were wholly irrelevant; their acknowledgment would have identified Schwinn as a powerful presence in the bike market.

Had property rights again become the major premise in competition policy—but now property rights informed by a Jeffersonian ethic, a commitment to rough equality among market rivals? And what of the egalitarian sentiment? Wasn't Schwinn, though a family business, awfully large and strong for a small firm? Amid such questions, the resurgence of property rhetoric seems to have been motivated nonetheless by a desire to get at economic concentration, to overcome the limits of microeconomic analysis of markets. Yet, microeconomic analysis *did* provide a powerful and persuasive framework for competition policy. And market power *was* important, although economic power was, too.

The foregoing questions and the ambivalences they reflect, the scrambled categories of large and small, powerful and weak, bureaucratic corporation and family-owned business, exploded in the *Utah Pie* case (1967). Here are two renditions of the economic circumstances—both entirely accurate. The first, as seen by Justice Byron White for the Court majority, evokes a Jeffersonian ethic, a preference for localism, and a denunciation of corporate concentration:

> The plaintiff, Utah Pie Company, was a family-owned business whose only plant was located in Salt Lake City. The company made and sold frozen dessert pies. Of its eighteen employees, nine were owner-family members. During the five years in question, corporate net profits averaged less than $6,000 a year. Corporate net worth never exceeded $68,802.13. The three defendants charged with trying to drive Utah Pie out of business were large multi-national food conglomerates—ITT-Continental, Pet Foods, and Carnation. Their prices in Salt Lake City were lower than their prices in the rest of the country and sometimes below their costs of production. Moreover, at least one of them sent industrial spies to Utah Pie. The Supreme Court affirmed the lower court's finding that the three national firms violated the antitrust laws. (Utah Pie eventually filed for bankruptcy and went out of business.)[87]

Now compare the economic circumstances, as seen by Justice Potter Stewart, who dissented:

> Three national firms were selling frozen dessert pies in the Salt Lake City area. A local company, Utah Pie, later opened a plant in the area and began to sell frozen dessert pies at lower prices, in order to attract customers, especially supermarket chain stores. In response to these price cuts, each of the national firms lowered prices, though not in any coordinated way. The Salt Lake City market during the five years in question saw intense price competition. Utah Pie, taking advantage of its local plant, was able to undercut the national firms' prices often enough to maintain almost a 50 percent market share. Yet Justice White's majority affirmed the jury's finding that the three national firms violated the antitrust laws. (The lower court's finding that Utah Pie had violated the antitrust laws was not appealed.)

Justice Stewart, joined by Justice Harlan, concluded his dissent in the clear rhetoric of market economics: "I cannot hold that Utah Pie's monopolistic position was protected by the federal antitrust laws from effective price competition."[88]

Justice White's opinion for the Court whipped up a rhetorical omelet of competition policies and property rights even more scrambled than Fortas's *Schwinn* opinion. Amid behavioral references to buccaneering and slashing prices below costs, competitive impact is described in very different terms: depressing market prices, deteriorating price structure, and long-term market price decline. White and those who joined him—Black, Douglas, Clark, Brennan, and Fortas—seemed unaware of the discontinuity between "slashing" conduct and "deteriorating" consequences. How can deep price cuts only depress? Or buccaneering only erode? It appears that the property rhetoric of buccaneering and slashing, the images of piracy and pillage, all of them visions of predatory conduct akin to theft, impelled the Court to find antitrust violations even though the competitive effects appeared moderately (though depressingly) beneficial.

Indeed, isn't pricing decline and lasting impact precisely what we want of competition? On the contrary, the Court majority seemed to compound its antitrust heresy, its rejection of competition policy, with an approving reference to an earlier decision that was "not impressed by the argument that the effect of [lowering price] had been to terminate a [local] monopoly and to create a competitive market." Apparently, White and his majority were interested not in promoting "the game" of competition but in protecting the "advantage of a local plant." White maintained that a local competitor was not "fair game" for the predatory tactics of large national competitors—neither the invasion of privacy by industrial spying nor the ferocious price slashing supported by "treasur[ies] used to finance the warfare drawn from interstate, as well as local, sources." National competition could also be localized predation.[89]

In portraying the national firms' conduct as evidence of predatory intent, of personalized strategies aimed at pirating a small family business, White's opinion projects an image for understanding the Jeffersonian ethic—its egalitarian impulse and its antipathy toward economic concentration. The vision of national competition as localized predation brings to light the doubleness of "private" rights and the "personal" realm, the doubleness of liberty sentiments animating not only the rhetoric of private property rights but also its free competition counterpart. Although individual market transactions are private in a very basic contractual sense, their market-registered sum is public: their cumulative consequences include allocation of resources and distribution of wealth. Utah Pie Company represented for the Court not just a business but a local family enterprise; not just a firm competing in the public arena of competition but also a private domain to be protected from the intrusion of personalized predation.

Both literally and figuratively, Justice White's opinion for the Court is about the price of "homemade apple pie." Doubtless it is chance that explains the opposing parties' pre-trial agreement literally to adopt an "apple pie" standard for their study of the pricing conduct under scrutiny: They stipulated that apple pie prices would represent all fruit pie prices.[90] And perhaps it is equally accidental that Utah Pie Company, family owned and operated, produced them locally: homemade apple pies.

Yet the symbolic import of this image grows from deep sociopolitical roots—the sanctity of a private domain recognized in the political tradition of liberalism as well as the constitutional protection of liberty and property. Indeed, its revered symbol in America has been "homemade apple pie," which can have no substitutes or rivals. Irreplaceable at any price, its inelasticity of demand labels it a (local) monopoly. Moreover, it describes—symbolizes—the personal, the private domain of our lives. This sanctuary must be preserved, protected from the public rigors of business rivalry. Out there, impersonal and fierce competition is proper and effective. Out there, exchange value guides an invisible hand's allocation of market shares—pieces of a public and competitive pie. But in here, it is use value that prevails and fair shares that evidence a visible hand—Mom's division of her homemade apple pie.[91]

Justice White was intent upon raising an antitrust shield between the (price) slashing of three large national firms and the apple pie baking of a family (business). (Market share was simply irrelevant; monopoly was presumed.) The opinion projects a desire to effect an impossible mediation: Utah Pie Company's dual location in both public and private domains. It insists upon a mirrored image of two hands working, each one shielded from the other, neither one entitled to undercut the other, but both obliged to divide the same pie.

The issue of economic concentration, as we have seen, involved social policy questions just beyond the grasp of microeconomic theory: Logics of market analysis simply did not reach the larger metamarket problems associated with corporate consolidation, with vast accumulations of wealth and thus with economic power. As the preceding section describes, the Supreme Court experimented with two approaches to this misfit between theory and practical problem.

First, the Court sought to expand competition theory, to strengthen microeconomic analysis of markets, by incorporating the postclassical theories of oligopoly and monopolistic competition. Rejected by mainstream policy makers and practitioners in the influential *1955 Attorney General's Report*, these theories brought with them dangerous revisions to the traditional view of markets. Oligopoly theory introduced a structural logic as the determining factor in what was, after all, the most common industrial structure in America. The danger was twofold: First, most industries would call for restructuring to allow competition. Second, individual intent would be seen as the product of an external structure rather than the internal engine for free-willed action.

Monopolistic competition theory introduced a view of economic markets that threatened to paint the commercial sphere as a three-ring circus for monopolistic bedlam. With the compelling microeconomic logic that product differentiation grants many firms some customer loyalty, some power over price and thus some monopoly power, monopolistic competition theory suggested that many firms, especially large firms with the financial power to invest heavily in advertising, had put enough distance between themselves and their rivals to define an entire "market" in terms of one differentiated product, one brand name.

The Court's second approach to resolving the misfit between competition theory and the problem of economic concentration took a direct path to the issue of economic power. Turning from competition rhetoric to a property rhetoric, a number of Court opinions took up Congress's explicitly Jeffersonian tone, the polymorphous concerns about corporate bigness expounded in the debates over the Celler-Kefauver amendment of 1950. Recall that the debates and the statute reflected a compromise on corporate bigness based on a tension between competition and property rights. On the one hand, independent entrepreneurs were seen as the active agents, the intellectual engines driving competitive markets, while large corporations were seen as the spreading virus of anti-competitive bureaucracy. On the other hand, some large corporations were, it seemed, the result—the reward—of competitive success. What to do? Congress differentiated internal from external growth, attacking corporate bigness only when it was the result of external growth, of buying up one's rivals rather than overcoming them.

There were two very different dangers couched in the Court's second approach, its turn to the rhetoric of property rights to trump the competition rhetoric of microeconomics. One danger emerged in the *Utah Pie* decision: Did Justice White's opinion reflect an inability to contain or a decision to reject the congressional compromise? Was there emerging from this egalitarian ethic a generalized assault on corporate concentration, an attack on corporate bigness not confined to mergers? The second danger in the Court's turn to the rhetoric of property rights lay in its tenuous link to a Jeffersonian tone, to an egalitarian ethic. If the rhetoric of property rights were to lose its Jeffersonian anchor, as threatened in the *Schwinn* opinion, a libertarian rhetoric of property rights would then produce competition policy unconcerned with the size and economic power of economic actors. In effect, there would be a return to classical property rights, to a *Lochner*ian freedom of contract and, ironically, a total disregard for economic concentration, for the metamarket effects of large corporations.

The twin dangers in property rights rhetoric pointed in opposite directions. Now seemingly unconstrained by the microeconomic logic of market-based competition, would the Court move toward a Jeffersonian vision of commerce free of gross inequalities of economic power or instead toward a retrenchment of property rights—freedom of contract unbound by an egalitarian ethic? In either case, what would be the implications for competition policy, not only for the regulation of commercial markets but also for the intertwined constitutional jurisprudence regulating the marketplace of ideas? The era seemed to end where it began—with congressional, jurisprudential, and social scientific images of marketplace processes to resolve differences, haunted still by the persistence of disparities of power expressed in the Jeffersonian imagery of corporate dominance, the civil liberties discourse of individual freedom, and the civil rights rhetoric of equality.

5

Rhetorics of Free Competition, 1968–1980: Efficiency, Property Rights, and Equality

For many of us, the year 1968 and the quarter century since then may be too close to observe as history. As historical perspective shortens, events loom larger on the horizon. There is the tendency to grant greater importance to more recent events, events that have touched our lives. The 1968 murders of Senator Robert F. Kennedy and the Reverend Martin Luther King Jr. seem to cast longer shadows than does the 1881 assassination of James A. Garfield, the last President of the United States born in a log cabin and a respected politician whose death was deeply mourned at the time. The shorter the temporal distance, the more discernible the past becomes in its particulars, the more complex in its insinuations. The recent past approaches like a crowd of counter-memories pushing against the present—an unsettling re-collection of what the present might have been, for better and for worse.

But 1968 is in fact far away if not long ago. Richard Nixon won the presidency that November and the Watergate scandal was still in the future. Televised across the country, the 1968 Democratic convention in Chicago presented a stark contrast between formalized decorum inside and violent protest in the streets; clearly, Franklin Roosevelt's New Deal coalition had exploded. Almost ten million voters, most of them southern Democrats, attracted by a law-and-order rhetoric and a well-known commitment to segregation, cast their ballots for third-party candidate George Wallace of Alabama. But for the anomalous single-term presidency of Jimmy Carter at the close of the 1970s, Republicans would occupy the White House for the next quarter century. Public perceptions of politics would veer between images of corruption and incompetence. Racial strife, the Vietnam War, generational conflicts, and, later, the articulation of gender and class differences would further rend the veil of consensus. Neither common values nor common interests, neither peaceful process nor open political institutions were in evidence in 1968.

The year 1968 marked a rupture from hopeful images of Eisenhowerian happy days and Kennedyesque Peace Corps volunteers. In this sense, the events of 1968 defined the sixties era—not the commercialized flower-child images attached to the Haight-Ashbury neighborhood in San Francisco and later to the "Woodstock generation," but rather the troubled spirit of a fragmented body politic, with its waves of dissensus, its surges of distrust, its furious political protest. Not only in the United States, where shortly before his death Martin Luther King led a march against the Vietnam War—a cooperative venture between the civil rights and anti-war movements—but also in Paris, Prague, and dozens of other cities, factory workers and clergy, scholars and activists, citizens and newcomers, and, most of all, students, took to the streets. The Prague Spring's street violence was understood as the product of political repression. But what of Chicago? Paris? The engines of democratic politics—consensus and compromise—were stalled, perhaps broken down. There was, in the deepest sense, a legitimacy crisis.

It was the anomalous presidency of "outsider" Jimmy Carter whose rhetoric of effective and responsive government began to recast America's 1960s era of political illegitimacy. Promising to manage the federal government efficiently, just as he had his duties as a Navy nuclear engineer, a peanut farmer, and governor of Georgia, Carter introduced a new rhetoric of expertise, related to but different from Franklin Roosevelt's "Brains Trust." Carter advocated deregulation and expressed confidence in the private sector. He brought with him people such as economist Alfred Kahn, whose job as head of the Civil Aeronautics Board was to deregulate the commercial airline industry—in short, to eliminate his own job. The deregulation rhetoric later adopted by Ronald Reagan, the move to lessen direct government supervision of commercial and banking activities, the elevation of "efficiency" to something akin to a neutral principle of government, the call to rally 'round the flag of managerial expertise and its sanitizing logic of market economics, appeared prominently in the presidential election of 1976 and Jimmy Carter's presidency.

Public policy initiatives and Supreme Court jurisprudence during the Nixon and Carter presidencies reveal some continuities and some changes in underlying political economy. Most striking was the change in attitude toward government regulation. Whereas Nixon began his first term with an executive order creating the Environmental Protection Agency, Carter began with promises to dismantle the Civil Aeronautics Board and to rein in other agencies. During Nixon's first term, Congress created the Occupational Safety and Health Administration (OSHA) and passed the Economic Stabilization Act of 1970, giving the President power to set prices and wages through boards and commissions reminiscent of Franklin Roosevelt's NRA. By the end of Carter's presidency, Congress was poised to dismantle the Federal Trade Commission.

Despite these sharp differences, there was a common thread running through the early Nixon and the Carter administrations. Even after Watergate, there were those in the public sector who retained the belief—or at least the hope—that government could, with honest people in office, be effective in managing the country. After all, hadn't Congress done its job in rooting out those responsible for the Watergate affair? Hadn't Nixon and his advisors resigned, several of them convicted of criminal misconduct? Indeed, Carter was elected on the belief that he was that honest person, and on the promise that he would revoke regulatory shelter of entrenched corporate/political interests. Carter, himself a businessman, claimed that commercial competition, under proper government supervision, would serve both consumer and citizen interests.

Supreme Court jurisprudence would shift with the arrival of Nixon appointees Warren E. Burger, Harry A. Blackmun, Lewis F. Powell, and William H. Rehnquist. In antitrust, concern about corporate concentration dwindled, and by 1974 competition policy had returned to the neoclassical logic of market price analysis. This turn away from Jeffersonian sentiment was accompanied by an expansion of corporate speech, particularly the First Amendment rights of corporations to spend more freely in the "marketplace of ideas" than federal campaign reform legislation would have allowed. At the same time, individual speech rights were curtailed by an expanded notion of private property rights.

Finally, there was a persistent and growing movement already under way when Nixon took office. A group of legal scholars, including Robert Bork and Richard Posner, as well as economists such as George Stigler, were reviving neoclassical economics as an approach to criticize and reformulate public policy. Early influence would be seen in Supreme Court antitrust jurisprudence. Carter's deregulation policies would also take something from their work. The greatest impact, however, would be felt later—in the unbounded legitimation afforded to Reagan administration policies by the neo-Chicago School's rhetorics of efficiency, consumer welfare, and free competition.

By examining antitrust and free speech policies, as well as the influential "New Learning" espoused by adherents to the Chicago School of law and economics, this chapter takes up the shifting discourse of free competition in the years between 1968 and 1980—its changing relationship to property rights, individual liberty, and equality. It concludes with an investigation of the imagery of populism and efficiency that inspired the Carter administration's deregulation policies, an imagery whose underlying impulse was a belief that responsive government could actively serve the public interest, both by regulating in the public interest and by eliminating regulatory capture by private commercial interests. The trick was distinguishing between good regulation and bad. Late in Carter's term, however, both congressional rhetoric and public opinion began to reflect a categorical distrust of activist government. It was Reagan's simple promise of less government that would later captivate the electorate's collective imagination.

The Nixon-Ford Years, 1968–1976: Industrial Concentration, the Marketplace of Ideas, and the Ascendancy of Chicago-School Law and Economics

The Nixon years were a time of turmoil, a time when the public sphere was battered by waves of progress and decay. The year 1973 is emblematic of the era's roiling excess: The Supreme Court's decision in *Roe v. Wade*, which recognized the centrality of a woman's choice to proceed with a pregnancy, as well as the Paris Peace Accords' formally ending the Vietnam War, seemed to herald progress. Yet, decay—both political and economic—was evident in the melodrama of Nixon's Watergate scandal and in the trauma of the OPEC cartel's oil embargo. It should come as no surprise, therefore, that the era's competition policies and rhetorics were volatile: While Congress passed legislation that increased federal regulation of marketplaces with little regard for the microeconomic consequences, both the Nixon administration and the Supreme Court shifted toward rhetorics of microeconomics and ultimately to the deregulatory logic of neoclassical price theory. Moreover, both the Court and an ascending Chicago School battalion of policy analysts began to pay more attention to the property-rights consequences of competition policy—both in commercial markets and in the political marketplace of ideas. Indeed, in some respects, the Chicago School's "New Learning" produced a property-rights rhetoric closer to the classical economic discourse of individual liberty than to modern economics and its concern with actual effects on markets.

Antitrust Policy: Free Competition and Industrial Concentration

Although little noticed, both the Democratic Congress and Nixon's Department of Justice supported competition policy that reflected consumerist distrust of large bureaucratic corporations. Expressing approval of the Antitrust Division's Merger Guidelines issued by Ramsey Clark in the last year of Lyndon Johnson's presidency, Nixon appointee John Mitchell even called for their application to conglomerate mergers. By the end of Nixon's first term, administration attitudes had shifted. During Gerald Ford's stewardship, open debate over deconcentration policies would rage both in Congress and the Supreme Court.

The 1968 Merger Guidelines expressed the Antitrust Division's commitment to corporate deconcentration—that is, to an evaluation of large mergers according to a market-share analysis founded on the tenets of oligopoly theory. Somewhat more lenient than recent Supreme Court merger doctrine, the Guidelines announced the Division's enforcement policy by describing typical situations in which mergers would usually be challenged. For example, in a market described as "highly concentrated," where the four largest firms produce 75 percent of the output, the Division would challenge a merger between two firms, each of whom held only 4 percent market shares, or a merger between two firms whose market shares were 15 percent and 1 percent. While questioning a merger between two 4 percent firms seems to go too far, perhaps so far as to protect the largest firms' industry leadership, the Guidelines were consistent with the congressional intent to stem the tide of industrial concentration as well as recent Court opinions' structural approach to competition.[1]

In nominating Richard McLaren to head the Antitrust Division, Nixon and Mitchell chose someone who not only intended to follow the new Guidelines but believed as well that "the antitrust laws and more particularly section 7 of the Clayton Act are able to reach conglomerate mergers." McLaren agreed with the recommendations of the influential 1968 Neal Report. Commissioned by the Carter administration, the report had called for vigorous government antitrust initiatives to restructure much of American industry. Antitrust Chief McLaren concurred, stating that he wanted "to stop this merger trend that was leading more and more toward economic concentration." The anticoncentration policy subtending the Neal Report, the Merger Guidelines, and recent Supreme Court doctrine provoked a series of cases designed to arrest pending conglomerate mergers.

By 1969, a second commission, appointed by Nixon and headed by Chicago School economist George Stigler, had published its report recommending against a government policy of deconcentration. At the same time, fellow Chicago School adherents Robert Bork, Richard Baxter, and others expressed public criticism of the Neal Report and the Antitrust Division's corporate deconcentration policy. Small wonder that Nixon began to question McLaren's deconcentration program and ultimately withdrew his support. This withdrawal was evidenced not only by McLaren's replacement by a less activist Chief, but also by subsequent discovery of Nixon administration corruption: its subterfuge of agency challenges to ITT's series of pending conglomerate mergers.[2]

Still, the Federal Trade Commission persisted in its deconcentration policies, issuing along the way its "Staff Report, Conglomerate Merger Performance" (1972), which found that sizable mergers were followed by insignificant operational changes directed at improving efficiency. Three years later, a study headed by former FTC economist Frederick Scherer found more generally that large mergers resulted in minimal efficiency benefits. FTC deconcentration policy would continue through the Nixon, Ford, and Carter years. It was Carter appointee Michael Pertschuk who would bring FTC consumerism to a crescendo and, at the same moment, to the brink of annihilation, at the hands of a deregulation-minded Congress in 1980 and later the Reagan administration.[3]

Wielding a rhetoric of private property rights, the Supreme Court had already articulated metamarket concerns about economic power in its 1967 triumvirate of antitrust opinions dealing with corporate size and scope. By the mid-1970s, however, a microeconomic logic of market analysis would emerge triumphant. In *Fortner Enterprises, Inc.* (1969), for example, the Court had an opportunity to find that the huge size and enormous economic power of U.S. Steel called for scrutiny of its practice of tying special credit terms to the sale of its prefabricated houses. But the opinion looked instead for "economic power *in the market*," described as "some power over buyers"—whether because of a patent, copyright, or "their strong preference for the product."[4] This concern for consumers was a rhetorical departure from the Jeffersonian commitment to small producers articulated in opinions such as *Proctor & Gamble* (*Clorox*) and *Utah Pie* during the 1967 term. Certainly, the *Fortner* Court's consumerism, expressed in terms of Chamberlin's theory of monopolistic competition, represented the outermost limit of microeconomic market analysis. After all, the Court did recognize that strong brand loyalty could give rise to an inference of "economic power in the market." But that would be as far as the Court would go. Henceforth, antitrust decisions would shift among alternative theories of competitive *markets*. Never again would the Court step outside the market-based discourse of microeconomics into the property discourse of economic power to judge corporate dominance.

Perhaps the clearest example of the Court's commitment to microeconomics discourse, particularly to oligopoly theory, was Justice Douglas's opinion in *Container Corp.* (1969), a trade association case about the troublesome question of disseminating information to member firms. How does the assemblage and delivery of information about market price, including specific sales to identified customers, affect competition? There was undisputed evidence that the "result of this reciprocal exchange of prices was to stabilize prices." Yet, since entry into the corrugated box business did not require a large initial investment, the number of manufacturers and plants almost doubled during the time under scrutiny. As dissenting Justice Thurgood Marshall pointed out, there was "active price competition." Nonetheless, Douglas expressed the majority's view that "price information exchanged in some markets may have no effect on a truly competitive price. But the corrugated container industry is dominated by relatively few sellers." Where the product is fungible and where there are no close substitutes, oligopoly theory suggests that the "exchange of price data tends toward price uniformity."[5] Despite evidence of competitive behavior, the Court majority reposed in a purely structuralist version of oligopoly theory to condemn the exchange of price information.

By the mid-1970s, however, the Court's strict reliance on market structure—its liberal formalist rendition of oligopoly theory—had softened into the more flexible analysis of market structure, conduct, and performance espoused by Harvard School centrists Joe Bain, Carl Kaysen, and Donald Turner. Even the severe market share logic subtending the Court's horizontal merger doctrine (as well as the Antitrust Division's 1968 Merger Guidelines) was opened to doubt. In the *General Dynamics* decision (1974), for example, the Court approved a merger between two leading coal producers, despite the Government's evidence that the "coal industry was concentrated among a small number of larger producers" and that "the trend had been toward increasing concentration." Justice Potter Stewart wrote that "the District Court was justified in finding that other pertinent factors affecting the coal industry . . . mandated the conclusion that no substantial lessening of competition occurred or was threatened by the acquisition." In his dissenting opinion, Justice Douglas insisted that by not discussing "the effect of the combination on industry concentration," the discrict court departed from the market share logic of precedent such as *Philadelphia National Bank* (1963) and *Brown Shoe* (1962).[6]

Later that term, the Court, following the market-definition logic established in *General Dynamics*, approved a second merger challenged by the

Antitrust Division. Just as Justice Stewart found that the two coal companies, one engaged in strip-mining and the other in deep mining, were not competitors, so did Justice Lewis Powell in *Marine Bancorporation* (1974) write that two regional banks in the State of Washington, one doing business in the eastern metropolitan area of Spokane and the other in western Portland, did not compete. The Government argued that Washington's bank regulation (like all state legislation) had the practical effect of defining the state as "an economically differentiated region." Moreover, Marine was a potential competitor known to all and thus an important competitive factor. Nonetheless, the Court not only defined the merger between two Washington state banks as conglomerate rather than horizontal, but dismissed even the possibility that the doctrine of potential competition, by then well established in assessing a pending conglomerate merger's effects on competition, rendered the merger illegal. Justice Powell turned aside the arguments with a technical definition of "the market" as "the area in which the acquired firm is an actual, direct competitor." Since neither merging partner currently competed in Washington outside its metropolitan area, the Court rejected the Government's claim that the merger would substantially lessen competition, even though there was evidence that such competition had been seriously contemplated. As in *General Dynamics*, there was no competition to lessen.[7]

Dissenting in both cases, Justice Byron White in *Marine Bancorporation* protested that "[f]or the second time this Term, the Court's new anti-trust majority has chipped away at the policies of § 7 of the Clayton Act." Referring to Nixon appointees Burger, Blackmun, Powell, and Rehnquist, White wrote that the new majority "redefines the elements of potential competition," in the process ignoring "a severely concentrated commercial banking market." The newly constricted rhetoric of "market" definition and analysis again prevailed. With "competition" understood as market-specific and "the" market viewed in narrow terms, not only would some horizontal mergers be redefined as conglomerate (thus lessening only potential competition), but conglomerate mergers as a category would be judged according to a withered standard of potential competition. "In the last analysis, one's view of this case, and the rules one devises for assessing whether this merger should be barred turns," Justice White acutely observed, on one's view "of the policy of § 7 of the Clayton Act to bar mergers which may contribute to further concentration in the structure of American industry."[8] The new antitrust majority's concern was not economic concentration, but market power—itself limited by a pinched definition of "the" market.

The Court's twin decisions in 1974 seemed to provoke some in Congress to demand a revived antitrust policy of economic deconcentration. In addition to urging the FTC to pursue deconcentration efforts under the more flexible standard of FTCA § 5, Congress considered numerous amendatory bills. While Senator Philip A. Hart's (D.Mich.) 1976 "no-fault" monopolization bill never reached the Senate floor, he and forty-four of his colleagues did vote in favor of legislation calling for vertical divestiture of the major oil companies. Other similar bills were considered as well. Moreover, the Naderian wave of consumerism, characterized by linked demands for safer products, more competition, industry deconcentration, and closer scrutiny of large corporations, did lead to some congressional antitrust legislation—none of it, however, aimed at reviving deconcentration policy. First, the Consumer Pricing Act of 1975 repealed the Miller-Tydings Resale Price Maintenance Act of 1937. State fair-trade laws (few of which remained) could no longer allow manufacturers to set resale prices. Second, the Hart-Scott-Rodino Act of 1976 not only empowered state attorneys general to sue on behalf of their citizens for antitrust injury but also imposed premerger notification requirements on principals in large corporate mergers and acquisitions.[9] What was perhaps the strongest statement made about competition policy did not, however, appear in an antitrust statute. As we shall see, it was the egalitarian commitment expressed in the 1974 amendments to the Federal Election Campaign Act that sought to regulate the marketplace of ideas by limiting campaign contributions and spending.

The "New Learning": The Phoenix of Neoclassical Economics

Congressional and judicial enthusiasm for industrial deconcentration had ebbed. Certainly, the Supreme Court, with four Nixon appointees, was turning away from the deconcentration logic of opinions such as *Philadelphia National Bank* (1963), *Pabst* (1966), and *Proctor & Gamble* (1967), shifting its jurisprudence to the microeconomic logic of market analysis. After the 1974 merger decisions, simply demonstrating corporate size and oligopolistic market structure would no longer be enough to convince the Court that competition policy should be invoked to stop a merger (and perhaps other conduct under antitrust scrutiny). But vigorous debate over the significance of corporate size and market structure continued, spurred by the politically charged setting for Naderian consumerism, by persistent FTC activity, and by recurring congressional consideration of new antitrust legislation.

At the center of the debate was Edward Chamberlin's oligopoly theory, proselytized by antitrust chief Donald Turner and his thoughtful collaborator, economist Carl Kaysen, and corroborated in studies headed by economists such as Joe Bain, Frederick Scherer, and Walter Adams. The debate attracted two generations of opponents to oligopoly theory. As I discussed in chapter 4, the first generation was led by economist John M. Clark, who argued as early as 1940 that industrial restructuring was an overreaction to economic concentration. Adopted in the *1955 Attorney General's Report on the Antitrust Laws*, Clark's theory of "workable competition" reflected a sanguine attitude toward large-scale enterprise.

A second generation of rivals to the dominant school of oligopoly theorists joined the fray as early as 1963 in a much-discussed exchange appearing in *Fortune* magazine, later expanded and dutifully footnoted in the *Columbia Law Review*. Yale law professors Ward Bowman and Robert Bork insisted that rational antitrust policy required strict adherence to the dictates of efficiency —that is, to determining effects on market price and output. Columbia law professors Harlan Blake and William Jones took a broader view, asserting that economics meant more than any particular efficiency logic, although agreeing nonetheless that economics should provide the ground for competition policy. Drawn by the early writings of Bork and Bowman, inspired by University of Chicago law professor Aaron Director, and guided by the writings of Chicago economics professors George Stigler and Ronald Coase, a new "Chicago School" rendition of neoclassical economics emerged.[10]

Formerly a forceful proponent of economic deconcentration, George Stigler experienced a conversion to neoclassical price theory—that is, to the view that concentrated industries were the result of economies of scale and, moreover, that oligopolists were no less driven by an unrelenting instinct to compete. In time, he came to believe, inefficient firms would crumble of their own weight. Stigler's sympathetic view of large corporate bureaucracies was accompanied by an acceptance of Marver Bernstein and Mancur Olsen's visions of large government agencies as tending to serve the interests of those most affected—typically, regulated firms. In his influential article "The Theory of Regulation" (1971), Stigler explored and sharpened his theory of regulatory capture, a theory in which government agents metaphorically appear as sellers in a market for economic regulation.[11]

Even more influential, both to Chicago Schoolers and to mainstream economists, was Ronald Coase's article titled "The Problem of Social Cost" (1960). The celebrated "Coase Theorem" imagines that "when the pricing system works smoothly" (i.e., when there are no information, bargaining, or enforcement costs), regardless of initial entitlements, the parties always bargain to an agreement that maximizes efficiency. Any shift in entitlements—for example, shifting from a firm's right to pollute a river to a local resident's right to swim in clean water—will only produce a wealth transfer. The parties will always bargain to that magic social good of efficiency—that is, to the same level of pollution. Stigler would add a stunning amendment to the Coase Theorem, asserting that in such "smoothly" working markets, even monopolies "act like competitors."[12] The social policy implications were unmistakable: Simply assure smoothly functioning markets and then step out of the way. Let the parties, pursuing their self-interest, bargain to socially optimal agreements. Adam Smith was born again—this time without the need for a divine invisible hand. Or was it *Lochner*'s constitutionalized freedom of contract—but without need for a constitutional hand?

As it turns out, the strength and appeal of the Coase Theorem lies in its abstraction, its tautological beauty: In idealized markets devoid of transaction costs and related imperfections, Coase reasoned, parties bargain to the most efficient solution. Of course they do. No one in her right mind, under conditions of perfect information and costlessly available substitutes, would agree to anything less. No one would agree to a deal that is worse than the best deal available, which, under ideal conditions, would be *the* best deal available—for both parties. That is, no one *could* be better off making another deal. Like flies at a picnic, however, the annoying omnipresence of transaction costs spoils this perfect allocation of goods and services. In real-world markets, parties will settle for less-than-perfectly acceptable terms, perhaps calling off the picnic or the deal altogether. Economists and policy makers of all stripes would take notice of the Coase Theorem. Those inclined to trust government intervention could justify their policies by pointing to the need to adjust "markets," whether commercial or implied, thrown off kilter by transaction costs. Most markets could be described as off kilter. Such policy makers imagined mid-August picnics in the Florida Everglades. Those inclined to distrust government intervention, many of them Chicago Schoolers or neoclassical price theorists, tended to analyze "markets" in idealized terms devoid of messy complications such as transaction costs and oligopoly market structure. They imagined fly-free picnics—Valentine's Day barbecues along the Arctic Circle.

During the Nixon-Ford years, the most prolific and influential Chicago Schooler was Richard Posner, who, unlike many fellow travelers, did wrestle with some of the difficult questions raised by the neoclassical faith in the natural efficiency of markets free of government supervision. In addition to numerous journal articles, Posner published two celebrated books. The first, *Economic Analysis of Law* (1973), was an effort to describe the actual workings of not only commercial markets but also noncommercial arenas as consistent with an overarching hypothesis that "common-law rules and institutions tend to promote economic efficiency." That is, Posner was arguing that government regulation inconsistent with the common law was inefficient. The second book, *Antitrust Law, An Economic Perspective* (1976), was in large part a gathering of earlier journal articles criticizing oligopoly theory–based antitrust and offering a neoclassical alternative.[13] Before exploring Posner's effort to argue that economic efficiency provides a legitimate liberal premise for all government regulation, I want to examine the pivotal rhetorical strategy he deployed in *Economic Analysis of Law*.

Both in *Economic Analysis of Law* and in his later references to the book, Posner was obsessed with convincing his readers that his project was positive, not normative; scientific, not ideological. He was not arguing, he insisted, that economic efficiency *ought* to be the beacon guiding public policy and legal rule-making. He was, instead, testing a hypothesis, a scientific theory, about the way human institutions *actually* work. Indeed, Posner likened his "scientific study of law" to the study of physics and astronomy. Economic efficiency, like the "big bang" theory, "must be taken seriously . . . because it has scored some successes" and "provides a coherent theoretical framework for" future investigation.[14]

But his claims about the scientific character of this efficiency hypothesis were ill founded. Of the many reasons for their untenability, I offer two: First of all, Posner himself admitted "the paucity of quantitative testing" as well as "the frequency and stubbornness . . . of anomalies." This low threshold for success, together with the strong criticism and empirical falsification of the hypothesis during the last fifteen years, describes an efficiency hypothesis with little to recommend it. Indeed, other Chicago Schoolers, including Robert Bork, have found themselves celebrating the very unverifiability of the hypothesis.[15] Hardly the stuff of science.

Second, Posner's efficiency hypothesis provides an unworkable model for research. One striking example of its inadequacy is the "theory of second best," which is a restatement of the general proposition that no hypothesis about the relationship between two variables can be tested empirically unless all other pertinent variables are controlled. In determining the efficiency of commercial conduct in one market, neoclassical price theorists ignore numerous variables. For example, they make crucially false assumptions about the competitive state of all other markets and the static nature of the economy in general. Thus, the effects of monopoly in related markets or new products or changing consumer tastes simply are ignored. Perhaps Yale law professor Arthur Leff put it best when he criticized Posner's approach: "If a state of affairs is the product of *n* variables, and you have knowledge of or control over less than *n* variables, if you think you know what's going to happen when you vary 'your' variables, you're a booby."[16] In sum, Posner's aspiration for a scientific enterprise founded in his efficiency hypothesis remains unfulfilled and, it seems, unfulfillable.

Moreover, even Posner's working definition of efficiency is fraught with difficulties—shifting meanings and, within his most favored meaning, both internal inconsistency and limited normative appeal. These frailties in the very substance of "efficiency" seem destructive of his anti-trust enterprise, whether scientific or political, whether positive or normative, insofar as Posner insists in his *Antitrust Law* that "since, in an economic analysis, we value competition because it promotes efficiency—*i.e.*, as a means rather than as an end—it would seem that whenever monopoly would increase efficiency it should be tolerated, indeed encouraged."[17] In short, Posner turns on its head the traditional view that competition is important both in and of itself, as a fair, meritocratic process, and in light of a whole ensemble of expected benefits including not only efficiency but also low prices to consumers, product innovation, and a preference for independent entrepreneurs. Posner's normative structure derives solely from efficiency. His enterprise can make sense only to the extent that efficiency does.

What, then, does Richard Posner, perhaps the most thoughtful and candid Chicago Schooler, mean by "efficiency"? First of all, Posner sometimes means "productive efficiency" and at other times "allocative efficiency." Most economists and policy makers think of productive efficiency as an "engineering" concept—that is, in terms of producing the most with the resources available. For Chicago Schoolers, allocative efficiency means getting goods and services to those who value them the most. These distinctly different concepts have no necessary logical relationship. For example, consumers may prefer electrical energy from a less efficient oil-fired generation plant to that produced in the most efficient nuclear reactor. As the example suggests, Posner's shifting between productive and allocative efficiencies creates both analytical and normative ambiguity in his work. Moreover, there are no self-evident meanings in Posner's explicit references to "strict economic-efficiency grounds," "inefficient or anticompetitive in some legitimate economic sense," and "efficiency in the economic sense." Even if we assume that all of these phrases mean "allocative efficiency," they nonetheless remain confusing because mainstream economists mean one thing and Richard Posner (along with other Chicago Schoolers) mean another by the term. Is he attempting to distinguish among two or more ideas of allocative efficiency or does he always mean the same idea?[18] Although this question remains unanswered, what is clear is that Chicago Schoolers and mainstream economists do use the term in radically different ways.

When mainstream economists and Chicago Schoolers refer to allocative efficiency, their intentions differ in two important respects. First of all, mainstream economists generally concern themselves with utility, while Chicago Schoolers focus on wealth. Thus, mainstream economists are committed to assessing policy by looking at effects on subjective utilities—in other words, personal satisfaction. One serious difficulty with assessing personal satisfaction, many economists agree, is that such preferences are not quantifiable for many empirical purposes. The Chicago Schoolers' turn to assessing policy by looking at the effects on wealth solves the problem of measurability: Wealth—the market value of all exchangeables—offers data for making calculations. Posner leaves no doubt that the "only kind of preference that counts in a system of wealth maximization is . . . one that is backed up by money."[19] In short, only money counts.

Second, mainstream economists and Chicago Schoolers apply alternative measures for assessing the relative efficiency of two states, whether the value is wealth, utility, or something else. Formulated by Italian political economist Wilfredo Pareto, the mainstream economic standard holds that moving to a new state of affairs, a new rule or right, is "better" or more "efficient" than the current state of affairs only when at least one person is better off and no one is worse off.[20] This standard would seem to favor the status quo insofar as few changes produce only benefits. Chicago Schoolers have adopted the far less demanding formulation favored by Jeremy Bentham and other Utilitarians: Moving to a new state of affairs is more "efficient" if, on balance, the benefits outweigh the costs. Putting together the concern for wealth and the Benthamite standard of comparison, Chicago Schoolers define allocative efficiency as "wealth maximization." Thus, for example, Posner asserts that monopoly is more "efficient" than competition when the increase in wealth to management, shareholders, and others outweighs the decrease in wealth to consumers, competitors, and others. Benthamite Utilitarians would try to gauge, instead of wealth, the net change in satisfaction, asking: Overall, is society better off? Those mainstream economists following Wilfredo Pareto would ask first if any individual is worse off. Their form of allocative efficiency is termed "Pareto superiority."

With the Chicago Schoolers' turn from utility to wealth, a Benthamite balancing seems possible: Simply measure the net changes in wealth by looking at increases and decreases in relevant market values. Despite the virtue of measurability, wealth maximization as the foundation for a moral code or political economy is undermined by logical infirmities and normative controversy. Posner's writing about wealth maximization evidences both frailties. There are two fault lines slicing through his logic of wealth maximization.

The first fault is produced by Posner's participation in the habitual enterprise of seeking to portray microeconomics (the study of firms and markets) as a scientific endeavor devoid of politics. Following economist Alfred Marshall's call just before the turn of the century for a science of microeconomics, economists (and fellow travelers such as Posner) have envisioned a quarantine of macroeconomics—the politics-infested vocation concerned with taxing and fiscal policy, the stuff of Roosevelt's New Deal and Keynesian fiscal policy. Microeconomists, whether Edward Chamberlin or Ronald Coase, would not concern themselves with government policies intended to distribute wealth by, for example, government borrowing in the 1930s to fund the WPA or taxation in the 1980s and 1990s to fund the savings and loan bailout. Instead, they would study markets in splendid isolation from such political acts. The problem with this bifurcation, well known to Posner and others who live by it, is that allocative efficiency, whether Pareto efficiency or wealth maximization, is logically and empirically dependent upon the distribution of wealth. That is, when wealth distribution changes, Posner recognizes that the pattern of demands can change. If preferences change, then resources must be reallocated. The status quo is by definition no longer efficient. In short, different distributions of wealth produce their own efficient allocations of resources. And because changing competition policy tends to change the distribution of wealth, the wealth effects on efficiency must be accounted for. In his *Antitrust Law*, Posner explicitly calls distributional concerns "political" or "social" objections better left outside an antitrust policy informed by the science of microeconomics, a dubious distinction that is even less persuasive when the value is wealth rather than utility.[21]

The "Law of Demand" rends a second fault line through the logic of wealth maximization. Perhaps the most fundamental tenet of economics, the "Law of Demand" holds that the more of a good—ice cream, for example—people consume, the less each additional scoop will satisfy them and the less they will pay. Posner applies this principle to absolutely everything but money—the very measure of wealth. His economic analysis proceeds as if a dollar has the same value to someone living in the streets of Manhattan as to someone else living in a penthouse sixty floors above the street. What could lead to such an absurd claim? It is the belief that "treating a dollar as worth the same amount to everyone, or, in economics jargon, ignoring distributive considerations" can solve the problem of wealth maximization's dependence upon the "political" issue of wealth. Now, Posner can imagine a sanitized, scientific hypothesis of efficiency, ignoring the "political" question of who wins and who loses. Just as long as a monopolist gains enough wealth to pay the losses of consumers, rivals, and others (although there is no call to do so), the monopoly is "efficient." In addition to the normative controversy raised by this treatment of wealth, its logic flies in the face of the very foundation of economic rationality, the "Law of Demand."[22]

Such illogical and counterfactual treatment of wealth by Posner and fellow Chicago Schoolers seems to remove any possibility of defining their enterprise as scientific. It is neither logically coherent nor open to rigorous empirical testing nor neutral in some political or normative sense. The normative content is as controversial as the logic is porous. In consequence, simply asserting that an antitrust policy is "efficient" is not enough. Some moral or political argument must be made to justify the resulting distribution of wealth, the identity of winners and losers, the severity of gains and losses, and, most of all, the controversial choice of wealth as the value to be maximized, rather than utility, fairness, environmental impact, a preference for independent entrepreneurs, or even a preference for multinational firms. At the very least, Chicago Schoolers should show more candor by consistently calling their normative ground "wealth maximization" rather than "efficiency" or "consumer welfare."

Within the narrower confines of antitrust policy, Richard Posner mounted an assault on oligopoly theory by seeking to insert the logic of competition into oligopoly theory's logic of cooperation. Recall the context: Edward Chamberlin developed a theory of perfect oligopoly and its logic of cooperation, tempered by effects of market imperfections and other economic circumstances. Thus, an oligopolist might compete rather than cooperate under such conditions as, for example, imperfect information. In his influential treatment of oligopoly theory, however, Harvard law professor and Antitrust Division chief Donald Turner simply assumed perfect oligopoly and thus concluded that antitrust prosecution to mandate competitive conduct—economically irrational behavior, under perfect oligopoly conditions—would be both futile and somehow reprehensible. Moreover, he asserted that the only effective approach—industry deconcentration—lay outside the legitimate reach of the antitrust laws.[23]

Whereas Turner imagined oligopolists as imprisoned in a structural logic of cooperation, Posner declared their independence from market structure. He insisted upon a universal logic of rivalry, a fundamental drive to compete unconstrained by industry structure. When oligopolists do not compete, according to Posner, they are engaging in recognizable behavior deemed "tacit collusion." Moreover, such behavior can and should be enjoined under current antitrust laws. Thus, there was no need in the mid-1970s to adopt pending legislation calling for the expensive, time-consuming, and inefficient remedy of industrial deconcentration. To identify and prosecute those who engage in tacit collusion, Posner offered a twelve-step investigation of "conditions favorable to collusion," followed by a listing of twelve "sorts of evidence—evidence of collusive behavior—relevant to such a demonstration." Posner's complex and expensive procedure, his unwieldy set of twenty-four factors for identifying tacit collusion, seems an elaborate overcompensation for Turner's simple and perhaps simplistic approach of looking only at market structure. What was lost between the extremes is Edward Chamberlin's original formulation—which is certainly translatable into manageable antitrust policy through presumptions and burdens of proof.[24] Posner's alternative presents an economic analysis so unmanageable that investigations would be few and far between. The practical consequence would be maintenance of the status quo. But for a few initiatives trickling out of the FTC and perhaps the Antitrust Division, no one (neither state attorneys general nor private plaintiffs) could afford the costs of investigation and prosecution. Taking much from the *1955 Attorney General Report*'s rendition of workable competition theory, Posner's approach, too, sought to discredit both structuralist oligopoly theory and its implication that industry deconcentration affords the only effective remedy.

Of course, Richard Posner was not the only prominent Chicago Schooler striving to replace competition policy with efficiency and to redefine efficiency as wealth maximization. Another prolific and influential policy analyst was Yale law professor Robert Bork, who in the mid-1960s had already claimed that the Sherman Act was intended to serve wealth maximization, which he termed "consumer welfare." This erroneous claim, repeated in his *Antitrust Paradox* (1978), was not seriously challenged until the mid-1980s, when more careful historians returned to the Act's legislative history, finding, for example, that neither economists nor legislators in the Sherman Act era had yet imagined allocative efficiency. Moreover, Bork's treatment of the legislative history ignored the crucial fact that the Sherman Act as passed jettisoned the very language of consumerism upon which his interpretation rested.[25] Nonetheless, Bork's justification for wealth maximization, framed in the historical rhetoric of "original intent," was accepted alongside Posner's policy arguments.

Convinced that a legitimate judiciary requires something akin to Herbert Wechsler's neutral principles, Bork's turn to the Sherman Act's legislative history follows his own general guidelines for deriving a neutral principle. Both his conviction and his guidelines appear in a well-known article entitled "Neutral Principles and Some First Amendment Problems" (1971). In it, Bork characterized constitutional law just as he would antitrust in the *Antitrust Paradox*: The jurisprudence in both areas, he was disturbed to find, reflected a "lack of theory," a scarcity of "principled decisions." Bork's bad-theory criticisms, put side by side, laid the groundwork for his common approach to supplying good theory. Indeed, he asserted in *Neutral Principles* that "the category of constitutional property [or "rights"] might usefully follow the progress of thought about economic property."[26] His approach, along with two inconsistencies in its application to constitutional and antitrust problems at best sheds light on his differing views of the economic and political spheres. At worst, they reflect logical inconsistency.

The possibility that his common approach does reflect a logical inconsistency is perhaps destructive of Bork's enterprise insofar as he presents himself as a devotee of deductive logic. Despite criticisms of deductive logic heard from Socrates and the Skeptics to Holmes and the Legal Realists, Bork seems bent upon defying them all. In what appears as a truculent allusion to Holmes's aphorism that "The life of the law has not been logic: it has been experience," Bork writes that "logic has a life of its own, and devotion to principle requires that we follow where logic leads." Logic must be followed even though, he laments, "I do not suggest that [it] will make anything approaching a mechanical jurisprudence possible." Yet, without properly derived neutral principles, logically applied, how are we "to know that the decisions are correct?"[27] Only a legal formalist could be so sure of a pristine deductive process, so sure of deriving something called the "correct" decision.

For a true believer in the deductive logical maxim that general principles can decide concrete cases, the worst of all possible errors is the tautology—a circular argument whose "conclusion was contained entirely in the major premise." Thus did Bork criticize Judge Skelly Wright's view of "constitutional rights and liberties," characterizing "the Judge's syllogism" as "no more than an assertion of what it purported to prove." Were the constitutional argument a proper syllogism, Bork would have been satisfied—at least with the logic if not with the premises. Yet the very foundation for Bork's antitrust policy is unmistakably tautological. His normative argument for "consumer welfare" as the best policy for antitrust is impeccably circular. It begins with the assumption that consumers maximize their welfare and ends with the conclusion that what is chosen maximizes "consumer welfare." Simply the fact that products are purchased is "proof" of allocative efficiency. Otherwise, consumers would have purchased something else. In short, "consumer welfare" is defined in terms of what consumers purchase, which is then presented as proof of "consumer welfare." All that is necessary is a free market, which, for Bork, means an economic sphere free of antitrust and other government regulation. In an astonishing public admission, he has stated more recently that his "system is entirely circular, which is its strength because circular logic is not rebuttable."[28]

The second inconsistency in Bork's treatment of constitutional and antitrust theory is normative. In "Neutral Principles," he argues against the First Amendment jurisprudence that Justices Holmes and Brandeis first articulated in *Schenck* (1919), against their view that the First Amendment should protect speech unless it presents "a clear and imminent danger of some substantial evil which the state constitutionally may seek to prevent." Bork's argument against waiting until a danger is "clear and present" comes directly out of Justice Edward Sanford's majority opinion in *Whitney* (1927). The state, Bork quotes Sanford approvingly,

> cannot reasonably be required to defer the adoption of measures for its own peace and safety until the revolutionary utterances lead to actual disturbances of the public peace or imminent and immediate danger of its own destruction; but it may, in the exercise of its judgment, *suppress the threatened danger in its incipiency.*

Despite the benefits of narrowly political speech—whether the expressive value to the speaker or the instrumental value to society—and despite the vague and distant danger to "peace and safety," Bork is adamantly *in favor* of state power to *suppress political speech* "in its incipiency." Yet Bork is adamantly *opposed* to state power to *suppress economic power* in its incipiency. In fact, his condemnation of the incipiency doctrine has led him to disapprove of the entire Clayton Act (1914), passed, in the words of the Senate Committee on the Judiciary, "to arrest the creation of trusts, conspiracies, and monopolies *in their incipiency*." The idea that something short of monopolization should provoke antitrust scrutiny, Bork maintains, carries the germ of protectionism into the healthy body of free and naturally efficient markets: "[T]he focal point of the infection is the Clayton Act. . . . That makes [it] the 'Typhoid Mary' of the protectionist disease."[29]

Are these two views of incipiency logically inconsistent? Or do they perhaps reflect a change in attitude after seventeen years of further thought about incipiency? On the assumption that neither faulty logic nor changed outlook explains the discrepancy, we can consider a third alternative—that Bork believes in different standards for identifying danger in the economic and political spheres. He apparently condones price discrimination, tying, mergers, and other behavior prohibited by the Clayton Act, even when the actors are dominant firms whose conduct substantially lessens competition. Such wealth-maximizing conduct is prized despite such anticompetitive effects as higher prices to consumers, higher costs of doing business, destruction of rivals (typically smaller and sometimes more productively efficient), and spillover into the political sphere. At the same time, Bork agrees with Justice Sanford's *Whitney* decision, which holds, in dissenting Justice Holmes's words, that the First Amendment should not protect "the surreptitious publishing of a silly leaflet by an unknown man."[30]

Is it that Bork imagines entirely separate political and economic spheres? Apparently not, insofar as Bork has written that "it is difficult to see how a constitutional court could properly draw the distinction" between danger to "functions essential to effective democracy" and threatened "destruction of property."[31] If economic and political spheres are not separate, then what is wrong with recognizing the "political" content of antitrust or the "economic" content of constitutional jurisprudence? What is wrong, for example, with recognizing in traditional, pluralistic terms the social costs of mergers between multi-billion dollar oil companies—even when they maximize wealth?

Does Bork's neutral principle of wealth maximization simply trump his other values, including regulation of "dangerous" speech? In short, does he mean to say that wealth-maximizing behavior, whether or not speech, merits broader protection than narrowly political speech? Thus, for example, should child pornography constitute protected speech simply because it, like any other market transaction, presumably maximizes wealth? Certainly, difficulties in formulating norms for government regulation of commercial and political competition were not limited to Bork's writing. As we shall see, distinct images of political and economic rivalry guided both Congress and the Supreme Court in their efforts to adjudicate conflicts between private property rights and protected public speech.

The Marketplace of Ideas: Free Competition and Property Rights

During the Nixon-Ford years, Congress considered a series of bills aimed at corporate deconcentration. The bills failed to pass, although their lengthy consideration throughout the mid-1970s invigorated antitrust activism in the enforcement agencies and provoked the reactivist scholarship of Chicago Schoolers. Still, congressional concerns about corporate concentration and its links to political corruption, amplified by the Watergate scandal, did lead to election campaign regulation. The Federal Election Campaign Act (1972) and amendments (1974) were only the most recent in a long line of campaign financing legislation, beginning with the Tillman Act of 1907, which prohibited corporations from making monetary contributions to candidates running for federal office. Indeed, the Supreme Court approved legislation passed shortly before the 1950 Celler-Kefauver amendment to the Clayton Act's merger provision with these words:

> The Sherman Law was a response to the felt threat to economic freedom created by enormous industrial combines. The income tax law of 1894 reflected congressional concern over the growing disparity of income between the many and the few. No less lively, although slower to evoke federal action, was popular feeling that aggregated capital unduly influenced politics, an influence not stopping short of corruption.[32]

Few doubted the overlap between economic power and political influence, the link between dominance in markets for goods and danger of corruption in the marketplace of ideas. Indeed, three decades of "public choice" theorists—Marver Bernstein, Mancur Olsen, and George Stigler—had already fashioned persuasive arguments supporting the view that concentrated economic interests lead to more focused and persistent attempts to influence (to "purchase" the supply of, in Stigler's terms) government legislation and regulation.

Although both Congress and theorists spanning the ideological spectrum recognized the likely dangers of political corruption attending economic power, the Supreme Court was spinning its own web of competition doctrines across economic markets and speech marketplaces, doctrines that reflected other concerns. Those concerns included a view of legislative politics, expressed in American jurisprudence at least as early as Justice Stephen Field's opinions, as dangerously corrupt; an image of citizens as speech consumers, seen in a few opinions during the latter New Deal, particularly the *Thornhill* decision (1940); and a need to reconcile the public exercise of free speech with the rights of private property owners.

First of all, the Court, in a unanimous decision authored by Justice Douglas, described the political arena as already so corrupt that legislative lobbying deserved little judicial scrutiny. In *California Motor Transport* (1972), an antitrust plaintiff sued a trade association for conspiring to exclude it from entering the market. The association, an industry group that pooled economic resources to lobby for favorable legislation and regulation, responded that their efforts to petition the legislature were constitutionally protected from antitrust liability. The excluded rival asserted that their lobbying efforts were built upon fraudulent claims, and thus according the Court's "sham" exception were outside constitutional protection of "political expression." Justice Douglas observed that there are many "forms of illegal and reprehensible practice which may corrupt the administrative or judicial processes and which may result in antitrust violations. Misrepresentations, condoned in the political arena," he determined, "are not immunized when used in the adjudicatory process."[33] In short, the lethal coupling of economic combination and fraudulent techniques was condoned in legislative corridors, at least under the antitrust laws, even though the Court did have doctrinal weapons at hand to deal forcefully with such corruption. The Court would not regulate concerted legislative lobbying because, it seemed to the Justices, the political arena was already depraved.

Outside antitrust doctrine, in a celebrated *per curiam* opinion the Court finally adopted, as Justice Holmes had conceived long before and civil libertarians had demanded ever since, a more expansive view of protected speech—that is, a more limited notion of what speech constitutes a "clear and present danger." For my purposes, however, the *Brandenberg* decision (1969) holds another significance: It reflects, at the very moment of perceived change, a longstanding consensus. The opinion is founded in a long-lived constitutional agreement about the *kinds* of "danger" that disqualify speech from First Amendment protection. The constitutional discourse of "clear and present danger" has been the same—whether expressed in criminal syndicalism, antiwar protest, school desegregation demonstration, or labor picketing cases, and whether judging the danger of one unknown speaker on a soapbox or the danger of mass protest in the streets of Montgomery, Alabama. The concern has been over *forcible* overthrow of the government, over *physical* violence to persons or property. But *economic* corruption of the political process, perhaps because its dangers are more insidious, less visible, gradual rather than clear and present, had never been part of First Amendment doctrine. Not until the 1970s has congressional concern about economic corruption, congressional legislation to limit corporate participation in the political sphere and commercial "speech," come to be seen as raising constitutional questions.[34]

Distinctions between market and marketplace, between commercial conduct and political speech, persisted in First Amendment doctrine long after antitrust policy, inspired by the work of Berle and Means and provoked by the Celler-Kefauver amendment, struggled with both the economic and political implications of corporate concentration. By the mid-1970s, however, the Supreme Court shied away from antitrust concerns about concentration and turned to the narrower microeconomic focus on markets and market power. Although congressional oversight committees did pressure enforcement agencies to pursue corporate deconcentration policies, there was ultimately a slow but deliberate abandonment of such initiatives.

In Court decisions managing the imagined marketplace of ideas, three rhetorical trends emerged, each with interesting implications for the relationship between such marketplaces and economic markets: Citizens were seen as speech consumers in the marketplace of ideas. Speech producers were denied access to an expanded domain of private property, which included shopping malls. Finally, corporate spending in the public marketplace of ideas was equated with individual speech.

The Court applied the rhetoric of consumerism to citizens in *Red Lion Broadcasting Co.* (1969), which upheld the FCC's "fairness doctrine." The FCC rule required broadcasters "to afford reasonable opportunity for the discussion of conflicting views on issues of public importance." Even after this rule was withdrawn, *Red Lion*'s doctrine remained influential in one important respect. Though it justified regulation of broadcasters on the assertion that broadcasting frequencies constitute a scarce resource, the Court explicitly stated that it was restricting broadcasters' First Amendment rights to strengthen those of radio listeners and television viewers. In short, the rights of speech consumers trumped those of speech producers. This Schumpeterian view of democracy as a marketplace inhabited largely by compliant consumers was no aberration. In *Virginia State Board of Pharmacy* (1976), Justice Blackmun could write, over only Justice Rehnquist's dissent, that consumers have standing to assert First Amendment protection of advertisers. "As to the particular consumer's interest in the free flow of commercial information," Blackmun maintained, "that interest may be as keen, if not keener by far, than his interest in the day's most urgent political debate." The Court was willing to protect commercial "speech," the lifeblood of modern economic markets—whether it was old-fashioned price competition or the brand differentiation driving monopolistic competition. In politics as in commerce, the predominant strategy was mass advertising; the weapon, ideas; and the idealized framework, a marketplace. Certainly, society has "a strong interest in the free flow of commercial information." The marketplace of ideas was understood in economic terms, with citizens imagined as consumers to be protected rather than producers to be encouraged.[35]

The Court's vision of consumer protection in the marketplace of ideas was accompanied by two lines of decisions governing the production of speech: the first a series of "shopping mall" cases, and the second *Buckley v. Valeo* (1976)—perhaps a line in and of itself, with seven opinions extending to 295 pages—which was followed two years later by the *Bellotti* decision.[36]

The shopping mall cases presented the Court with conflicts between those seeking to exercise free speech rights and others asserting private property rights to evict them. What made the conflicts so difficult was the functional doubleness of the suburban shopping mall: On the one hand, shopping malls are commercial enterprises built on private property, for profit. On the other, a mall serves as the commons once provided by the "community business block." Traditionally, a speaker was not permitted to place her soapbox in the aisle of a commercial enterprise, but was permitted to perorate on the commons. Justice Thurgood Marshall, over the surprising dissent of First Amendment champion Hugo Black, wrote that "peaceful picketing carried on in a location open generally to the public is, absent other factors involving the purpose or manner of the picketing, protected by the First Amendment." As to the question of whether "businesses situated in the suburbs could largely immunize themselves from . . . criticism by creating a *cordon sanitaire* of parking lots around their stores," Marshall concluded in *Logan Valley Plaza* (1968) that "[o]wnership does not always mean absolute dominion." "The more an owner, for his advantage, opens up his property for use by the public in general," he determined, "the more do his rights become circumscribed by the . . . rights of those who use it."[37] In consequence, the Amalgamated Food Employees Union Local 590 was permitted to picket peacefully in the shopping center.

Four years and four Nixon appointees later, the Court denied constitutional protection to anti-Vietnam War activists who were distributing leaflets in a shopping mall. Writing for a new majority in *Lloyd Corp. v. Tanner* (1972), Justice Lewis Powell's logic is reminiscent of the Four Horsemen opinions before *Nebbia* (1934), particularly Justice Sutherland's narrow view of the "public interest" justifying state power to regulate. Powell declared that property does not "lose its private character merely because the public is generally invited to use it for designated purposes." "The essentially private character of a store and its privately owned abutting property," he concluded, "does not change by virtue of being large or clustered with other stores in a modern shopping center."[38]

In emphasizing the commercial nature of this marketplace, Powell recounted how the property owners' policies were driven by the single-minded purpose "to create 'customer motivation' as well as customer goodwill in the community." Thus, "political use is . . . forbidden, except that presidential candidates of both parties have been allowed to speak in the auditorium." As the mall manager explained, however, "We do that for one reason and that is great public interest. It . . . brings a great many people to the Lloyd Center who may shop before they leave." Justice Powell did not flinch even at banning perhaps the most traditional exercise of speech and press rights: "handbilling, which was considered likely to annoy customers, to create litter. . . ." Five Justices felt certain that mandating a public marketplace of ideas would disturb the fragile ethos of consumerism cultivated in what was once seen as a "community business block."[39] In retrospect, their outlook coincides with the view unveiled in Robert Bork's "Neutral Principles" (1971) article—that wealth-maximizing behavior can merit broader protection than political speech. At the very least, Powell's bare majority did impose a corresponding logic of private property rights to protect commercial conduct from disruption by political activity. The Court concluded that someone's freedom of speech must yield to someone else's liberty to sell and buy.

In *Buckley v. Valeo* (1976), the Court was again asked to determine the proper balance between private property rights and freedom of speech. At issue was the constitutionality of the Federal Election Campaign Acts—legislation aimed at limiting campaign contributions and spending in presidential campaigns. No one doubted the impact of wealth, of campaign spending, especially in a marketplace recently dominated by broadcast media. How would the Court respond to Congress's attempt to reconcile a political arena founded in the ideology of "one person, one vote" with a free market system whose by-product has been inequality of wealth?[40]

The Court equated spending with speech and property with liberty, thereby eviscerating a statute intended to limit the use of wealth to amplify voice in the marketplace of ideas. The opinion transformed the political ethic of "one person, one vote" into a commercial logic of "one dollar, one vote." Yet there was no political logic that *required* the equation of spending and speech. To the contrary, one individual's freedom of speech, enhanced by extreme wealth, tends to diminish and can overwhelm the effect of others' speech. Indeed, whether Rousseau or de Tocqueville, Rawls or Dworkin, advocates of liberal democracy have called for a conception of liberty, of individual freedom, ultimately founded in rough equality. Set in the last two centuries of democratic theory, the Court's equation of free speech and free spending therefore appears normatively suspect—particularly the Court's statement that "the concept that government may restrict the speech [that is, the spending] of some elements of our society in order to enhance the relative voices of others is wholly foreign to the First Amendment."[41] Rather, the view that the First Amendment prohibits Congress from regulating independent campaign spending by third parties, particularly political action committees, is reminiscent of the laissez-faire ideology rejected in *Nebbia* (1934) and repudiated in the "constitutional revolution" of 1937. Even if the Court in *Buckley* was intent upon reshaping the "marketplace of ideas" along the logical lines of commercial markets by attributing speech properties to campaign spending, surely laissez-faire, in 1976, was not the political economy of choice outside a narrow fringe of post-Watergate American society.

Nonetheless, a framework for understanding *Buckley*'s conception of the marketplace of ideas can be found at the intersection of the Court's shopping mall cases and its antitrust jurisprudence. Recall that in *Lloyd Corp.* (1972) the Court had imposed a logic of private property rights permitting shopping mall owners to prohibit the political activity of handbilling in a space seen only four years earlier as a commons. The transformation of public space to private property, the subordination of speech rights to commercial interests, derived from the Court's view that it was merely enforcing ownership rights. It was only recognizing the legitimate exercise of dominion, the right to control access to one's property. In *Buckley*, too, the Court was only protecting the freedom of corporate "persons" to put their money where their mouths are, the liberty to deploy their property in the marketplace of ideas, to seek advantage over and even to control access, just as they do in markets for goods and services. The consequence, of course, is that (borrowing George Stigler's metaphor) someone's freedom of speech yields to someone else's liberty to buy and sell political advantage in the marketplace of ideas.

Moreover, the Court had charted a new course for antitrust doctrine just a few years before *Buckley*. Although the mid-1970s is usually identified with a competition policy of corporate deconcentration founded in structuralist oligopoly theory, the Court by 1974 had already indicated that it understood oligopoly theory in microeconomic terms. That is, it interpreted the oligopoly problem as one of market power, not economic power. Thus, corporate size and industrial concentration were no longer antitrust issues. Indeed, meta-market concerns were simply invisible through the lens of microeconomic analysis. As a result, the Court refused to give credence to antitrust arguments founded in corporate size, just as it refused to allow Congress to regulate the effects of great wealth in political markets.

Finally, there were rhetorical conditions of possibility conducive to the Court's treatment of political speech: What made the treatment possible was the rhetorical shift to property rights in the "populist" antitrust opinions—*Utah Pie, Procter & Gamble* (*Clorox*), and *Schwinn*—during the 1967 term. The Court, in each opinion, subordinated a microeconomic logic of market-based competition to some sort of property right. The danger, I have suggested, was that the Court's property rights rhetoric pointed in two opposed directions—one toward a commitment to an egalitarian ethic and the other, away from it. Which direction was taken? The Court moved away from a Jeffersonian vision of commerce free of gross inequalities of economic power, and turned instead toward classical freedom of contract—a property rhetoric unbound to an egalitarian ethic.[42] The Court's indifference to equality (that is, its formal assumption of equality in all "persons") hurled it away from one notion of "free competition" toward its antinomy, away from a model of competition free of economic power toward a vision of competition free of government intervention. Together with a microeconomic focus on *market* power, the Court could pursue a competition policy that did not offend the property rights rhetorics legitimizing *economic* power.

Within this framework, the *Buckley* decision does not seem to be an isolated return to the laissez-faire ideology of *Lochner*ian constitutionalism. Rather, it appears consistent with the Court's developing competition policy—that is, a growing tendency, approved in the newly influential work of Richard Posner, Robert Bork, and other Chicago Schoolers—to ignore issues of wealth and corporate size, whether in commercial markets or political marketplaces of ideas.

The Carter Years, 1977–1980: Deregulation, Populism, and Efficiency Logics

At first blush, the *Buckley* decision, published in January 1976, seems to sit comfortably alongside the campaign rhetoric of deregulation that would win Jimmy Carter the presidency that November. Moreover, the Carter campaign's promises of honest and efficient management seem to share the Court's rationale for upholding congressional limits on direct contributions to candidates—that is, the rationale of avoiding "the reality and appearance of corruption." However, the Court's First Amendment jurisprudence as well as its antitrust policy actually reflect a relationship between competition policy and private property rights different from Carter's "neopopulist" approach to deregulation, different from the Naderite, interventionist vision of political economy issuing from both populist politics and postclassical economics.

In those years, "efficiency" became the talisman both for Jimmy Carter's deregulation policies and for the burgeoning literature of Chicago School theorists spearheaded by the work of Richard Posner and Robert Bork. What emerged in the period were two contending formulations of efficiency—one a Naderite commitment to consumer empowerment and the other a pledge to wealth maximization, termed "consumer welfare," although wealth more often accrued powerful producers. Perhaps it is an irony of history that the early successes of the Carter Administration, particularly its activist FTC under Michael Pertschuk, produced a populist sense of consumerism whose ideological residue would legitimate the profoundly different policy of "consumer welfare" developed by Chicago School theorists and adopted by the Reagan-Bush Administrations. However, when Carter's activist FTC became the primary target for congressional critics as well as Reaganite deregulators espousing "consumer welfare," irony verged on the burlesque.

The Marketplace of Ideas: Corruption, Commerce, Property Rights

An ethos of deregulation, of "free competition," surrounded the Court's *Buckley* decision. Political spending in a marketplace of ideas, unfettered short of direct purchase of candidates and regulated largely to dispel the appearance of corruption, was now protected as First Amendment speech. Two years later, the Court would extend the same sort of marketplace logic to strike down a Massachusetts statute limiting corporate spending. In *First National Bank of Boston v. Bellotti* (1978), managers of several business and banking corporations wanted to advertise their opposition to a referendum amending the Massachusetts constitution to allow a personal income tax. The statute permitted those running commercial corporations to expend corporate funds to influence public opinion only where the issue was one "materially affecting" corporate business interests. Were the advertiser a natural person, Justice Powell remarked, "no one would suggest that the State could silence their proposed speech."[43]

But the advertisers were not natural persons, according to the Court or, for that matter, according to legal discourse generally. Rather, they were defined by statutes and court doctrines as economic entities whose purpose is to maximize returns to their owners. The legal duties imposed upon their managers derive from the obligation to pursue profits. Corporate managers have a fiduciary duty to ensure that all corporate conduct and corporate speech be commercial. In that fundamental sense, whether conduct or speech, regardless of content, corporate spending must always be a commercial activity. If the statute in *Bellotti* had been seen as state regulation of an individual's commercial speech, would it have been protected under the First Amendment? Later that term, the Court would reaffirm its view that commercial speech occupies a "subordinate position in the scale of First Amendment values"—somewhere, apparently, between politics and obscenity. Thus, rather than the close scrutiny actually given in *Bellotti*, an amorphous, deferential balancing test would have been applied. Notwithstanding Powell's statement to the contrary, the Court could easily have found that the Massachusetts statute's regulation of commercial speech was constitutionally innocuous.[44]

But Justice Powell did not rest his argument on a dangerous analogy between natural and unnatural persons. Nor did he take up the First Amendment interests of consumers as listeners, recently raised in *Virginia Pharmacy* (1976). Rather than look to the nature of the speaker or the listener, Powell looked at the content of the message. Because each advertisement in *Bellotti* endorsed a view about amending the state constitution, it was deemed an "expression that the First Amendment was meant to protect." This "political content" approach, while appealingly neutral in its purport, perpetuated the *Buckley* decision's commercial logic of "one dollar, one vote." Indeed, Powell expressly approved of the earlier opinion's indifference to the dangers of corporate economic power in the marketplace of ideas. Moreover, he insisted that "if the First Amendment protects the right of corporations to petition" government from liability under the antitrust laws, "there can hardly be less reason for allowing corporate views to be presented openly to the people."[45]

In short, "political content" was protected, even when it originated in corporate managers commanded by legal rules to stay within the bounds of commercial conduct. Although within the legal bounds of commercial conduct, corporate speech in pursuit of pecuniary gain was unregulated when imagined within a marketplace of ideas. The difficulty raised is two-sided. From the commercial perspective, corporate speech can be seen as anticompetitive, as seeking to trump commercial market mechanisms by petitioning for political intervention. From the political perspective, corporate speech can be seen as amplified voice in a political sphere whose most effective arenas—large metropolitan newspapers and radio and television broadcast media—often require the purchase of expensive amplification.

In the murky waters between political and commercial domains, competition policies informed by a commitment to equality have yielded to convergent notions of individual liberty and property, notions made all the more troubling by the well-settled "person"hood of corporations. The Court resolved a doubled vision of "free competition" (competition free from political and economic power) into a unitary image of competition free of government intervention by turning toward a conception of "individual" liberty unmitigated by concerns about substantive equality.[46]

The Supreme Court and Antitrust Doctrine: Allocating Private Property Rights in Commercial Markets

Three seemingly unrelated opinions, when juxtaposed, suggest that the Court established a rhetorical pattern to reconcile competition policy and private property rights in commercial markets. In the aggregate, the opinions illuminate a persistent recourse to property rights as the rhetoric for shaping competition policy—property rhetoric stripped of the egalitarian commitment expressed ten years earlier in cases such as *Utah Pie* and *White Motors*.

In *Brunswick Corp. v. Pueblo Bowl-O-Mat* (1977), the Court addressed the question of antitrust injury—a seemingly obscure issue with extremely practical consequences: "Any person who shall be injured in his business or property by reason of anything forbidden in the antitrust laws" has a claim for treble damages and attorney fees.[47] But those who fall outside the zone of protected interests, those whose injuries are attributed to "competition," are awarded no damages. The problem, of course, is that the two categories—"competition" and "anything forbidden in the antitrust laws" are neither self-evident nor mutually exclusive. Both categories (and their relationship) are rhetorical consequences of judicial definition and interpretation.

The Court faced the kind of difficult question often associated with declining sectors of the economy—in this instance, the bowling industry. Brunswick, one of the two largest manufacturers of bowling equipment, acquired 222 failing bowling centers. The obvious problem for Brunswick was disposing of equipment abandoned or given up by defaulting debtors. Brunswick sold some equipment, closed some bowling centers, and itself operated 168 centers that held the promise of cash after expenses. Pueblo Bowl-O-Mat, an independent bowling alley, sued Brunswick, claiming that the acquisitions constituted an illegal merger. But gaining a dominant position in the bowling alley business did not seem to be Brunswick's purpose. Rather, the apparent intent was to reduce the losses resulting from the declining popularity of bowling. Nonetheless, the district court held that Brunswick did violate Clayton Act § 7. Brunswick did not appeal the holding. It did not even assert the strong defense, long recognized by the Court, that its acquisitions were "failing companies" and thus entirely legal. In this procedural setting, Justice Marshall wrote for a unanimous Court that plaintiff Pueblo Bowl-O-Mat suffered no antitrust injury. The Court was convinced that the bowling alley owner was really complaining about competition: "[B]y acquiring the failing centers [Brunswick] preserved competition, thereby depriving [Pueblo] of the benefits of increased concentration."[48]

The incongruity of finding that an illegal merger increased competition is striking. The incongruity derives from the courts' divergent competition policies. On the one hand, the trial and appellate courts upheld jury findings of an injury to competition primarily because Brunswick was a large corporation, because someone with a "deep pocket" entered a market of "pygmies." This view of competition policy was founded in the concerns about corporate concentration expressed in the Celler-Kefauver bill debates, as well as merger opinions through 1967 and the 1968 Merger Guidelines. On the other hand, the Supreme Court, given the opportunity, would have found the merger lawful. The Court would have reversed, I believe, not only because the acquired alleys were "failing companies" but also because the lower courts' concern about corporate size was outside the Supreme Court's microeconomic analysis of markets adopted in merger opinions since 1974. To recover damages, Marshall wrote, Pueblo would be called upon to demonstrate that Brunswick "had abused its deep pocket by engaging in . . . predation."[49]

The requirement of proving "predation" was unprecedented in Clayton Act § 7 cases. Yet it was consistent with the Court's narrowed approach to defining "relevant markets" as well as its indifference to claims of increasing trends toward concentration, both of which were seen in the Court's 1974 term. The Court would not prohibit a merger, it seemed, simply because the result was a dominant firm. Some unacceptable conduct within the microeconomic confines of a market, beyond the merger, was called for. The framers of Clayton Act § 7 and its amendments would have been astounded. The implication was that neither economic power nor market power, neither size nor market share, would give rise to an inference of antitrust injury. Someone's fundamental property right to buy and sell a business was now seen as consistent with competition policy until the power associated with increased size was actually abused. The Court refused to infer competitive injury either from the structuralist logic of oligopoly theory or from metamarket theories about corporate concentration. The assumption, instead, was that firms, big and small, tend to compete in acceptable ways. It is not surprising that federal court dockets have shown few merger cases since 1977, despite a massive merger movement that began only a few years later.

The second example of an opinion applying a property rhetoric to resolve questions of competition policy was *Broadcast Music, Inc. v. CBS, Inc.* (1979). There, the Court applied a property metaphor to absolve the defendants of antitrust's gravest sin—price-fixing among competitors. CBS argued that the bundling of copyrighted musical compositions into indivisible blocks by BMI and ASCAP—the two dominant firms in the business of licensing such music—constituted illegal price fixing. Applying the Rule of Reason to conduct that appeared to be price fixing, Justice Byron White maintained that the blanket licenses were reasonable because they enabled copyright holders to enforce their property rights under the Copyright Act of 1976, property rights otherwise subject to multiple use without consumption and without the owner's knowledge, which left the owner without "any real way to demand reimbursement for the use of his property." Although White did write that BMI's and ASCAP's blanket licenses were "procompetitive" insofar as they created a rationalized market where none existed before, it was a property metaphor that inspired the opinion. White characterized the repertoire of music created by the blanket license as an entirely "different product," and ASCAP and BMI each as "a separate seller offering its blanket license, of which the individual compositions are the raw materials." "Here the whole is truly greater than the sum of its parts."[50] This extended metaphor gave life to an entirely new property right independent of, and in addition to, statutory copyright entitlements. Following the property logic of White's allegory, the licensing arrangement was not even a restraint among competing composers. It couldn't be. The bundled music was new property owned by one new property owner—the licensing agency. Questions of competition and restraint, therefore, did not even arise.

By contrast, for dissenting Justice Stevens, the blanket license created neither a new product nor new owners. Instead, the license was a tying together of old products and an agreement restraining price competition among numerous individual property owners. Deploying a rhetoric sharply different from the majority's property metaphor, Stevens insisted that competition policy required the Court to limit the value of copyrights to that obtainable by individual holders under the property rights—"the statutory monopoly privileges"—granted by the copyright statute. Most of the opinion goes on to portray the licenses' anticompetitive effects—higher prices, additional benefits to already popular composers, and harms to other composers.[51]

Although there was disagreement over the outcome, both majority and dissenting opinions agreed that this price-fixing agreement was not illegal per se. Underlying the consensus was a more basic agreement that the Rule of Reason meant a balancing of commitments to competitive markets and private property rights. For Justice White's majority, ASCAP and BMI had the operative property rights and hence the freedom to alienate a new product. For Justice Stevens, copyright holders are granted a statutory entitlement that must be construed in the larger context of competition policy—that is, construed to exclude the liberty to maximize their return by entering into agreements with other holders. Thus far, both analyses turn on the allocation of property rights. But because both allocations are highly plausible conclusions of property rights logic, the outcome is indeterminable—that is, the property logic of ownership itself cannot mechanically allocate property rights.[52] Some other principle must intervene. For Stevens, it was an image of competitive markets. For White, it was the property metaphor, the image of a "new product."

My third example of the Court's turn to property rhetoric for formulating competition policy is the *GTE Sylvania* opinion (1977). Speaking through Justice Powell, the Court permitted a manufacturer, short of fixing prices, to control the disposition of products held by independent distributors and retailers. Much as *Bellotti* (1978) would adjudicate the interplay of freedom of speech among citizens in the marketplace of ideas, *GTE Sylvania* portrayed competition policy as the consequence of allocating property rights among trading partners in commercial markets. Recall that the *Schwinn* decision (1967) had prohibited a manufacturer from imposing restraints on distributors and retailers who purchase bicycles. Unless the bicycles were consigned, unless Schwinn retained title to the property, restraints were simply prohibited. The rationale derived entirely from common-law notions of title to property: Whoever "owns" the bicycles controls the conditions of their sale. In practical terms, retention of title to property allowed Schwinn to restrain competition among its distributors and dealers. Ten years later, Justice Powell's opinion for the Court in *GTE Sylvania* changed all of that. It allowed the manufacturer to impose (reasonable) restraints on all distributors and dealers, regardless of who held title to the goods. Powell began by describing Justice Fortas's consignment logic in *Schwinn* as a "perversion of antitrust analysis," as providing "no analytical support" for distinguishing between consignments and sales.[53] Of course, Powell's description is erroneous. First, consignment logic provides "no analytical support" only if analysis is limited to competition rhetoric. Second, property rhetorics have always had a hand in producing antitrust doctrine—as they would later in Powell's opinion.

Reasoning as though competition policy had always provided the only legitimate ground for antitrust doctrine, Powell proceeded to narrow the idea of competition, simply asserting that "interbrand competition . . . is the primary concern of antitrust law." Thus, Sylvania could reasonably restrain its dealers from competing among themselves in order to coordinate competition against Sony, RCA, and other brand-name producers. But, as Justice White observed in his concurring opinion, intrabrand competition (here, rivalry among Sylvania dealers) had always been an important antitrust concern—whether because a source of price competition or an arena for the "independent businessman's interest in controlling the terms on which he trades his own goods."[54]

The disagreement between Powell and White about the value of intrabrand competition derives from differing views of a fundamental property right: Who has the right to control the sale of a product—the producer or the retailer who now owns it? White contended that Sylvania dealers should be allowed to compete against one another in the sale of their "own goods." Powell maintained that Sylvania must have the right to restrain its dealers from competing against one another, to allow Sylvania and other manufacturers to manage "the efficient marketing of *their* products."[55] Only after Powell's majority imagined Sylvania televisions sitting in dealer warehouses, bought and paid for but still somehow Sylvania's property—only after competition is understood as purely interbrand, as rivalry between the Sylvanias and Sonys of the world—does the Court's underlying concern, its curious fixation on "free riders," make sense.

What are "free riders"? In Justice Powell's eyes, they are dealers who do not promote GTE Sylvania products, dealers who do not offer the service or repair facilities necessary to help GTE Sylvania "compete more effectively against other manufacturers."[56] "Free riders" are despicable price cutters who live off the marketing efforts of their fellow dealers. They misappropriate the value of such efforts, receiving the benefits without paying the costs.

Of course, free riders need not be imagined as thieves in the night. By the traditional lights of competition policy, they are heroes. For they engage in price competition. Even in Justice Powell's eyes, when Sylvania dealers compete against Sony dealers on price, they become heroes again. The ambivalent attitude toward price cutters, the idea of free riding, and the very bifurcation of competition based on "brand" all derive from a complex property logic. The logic begins with the manufacturer's right to control goods, to manage their movements in the stream of commerce long after ownership has ended. It ends with protection of the promoting dealer's "goodwill" from theft by "free riders." To connect these property rights, the Court extended managerial capitalism—the control without ownership closely observed by Berle and Means—beyond corporate assets to goods already sold to independent entrepreneurs. What requires this extension, the Court suggests, is the need for product promotion and other activities associated with what is, after all, monopolistic competition—the product differentiation, the market fragmentation through advertising and promotion, and the pursuit of brand loyalty leading to higher costs and higher prices first described by economist Edward Chamberlin. In short, the Court's "free rider" logic subordinates price competition to the purchase of brand loyalty.

Still, GTE Sylvania, although not quite a failing company, was a "faltering firm." Would this property logic of extended control, this long-armed restraint of independent retailers, be limited to struggling manufacturers such as GTE Sylvania and White Motor? Or would the notion of a "faltering firm" itself be extended to all businesses, seen as struggling in a "world market" of dangerous competitors? Such questions would raise controversy well into the 1980s.

The Chicago School's Vision of Virtue and Commerce

Insofar as all manufacturers, even monopolists, face the risk of faltering, Chicago Schoolers have argued since the early 1960s that all restraints by manufacturers on their dealers should always be permitted. Following economist Lester Telser's account of how manufacturers and consumers together benefit from restraints on their distributors and dealers, Richard Posner, Robert Bork, and fellow travelers mounted a "free rider" defense of complete manufacturer sovereignty over "their" goods from production to consumption. The defense is founded on the claim that such restraints are always motivated by the desire to lower transaction costs. Thus, vertical restraints are always benign.[57]

These arguments and others posed by Chicago Schoolers ultimately derive from the normative claim that wealth maximization ought to provide the only goal for competition policy. During the Carter years, Robert Bork and Richard Posner sought to go beyond the unpersuasive position that wealth maximization is a principle whose neutrality, and thus whose primacy, is self-evident. Both scholars endeavored to make moral arguments of sorts to justify wealth maximization as the fundamental value underlying their view of the good society. Although taking different paths, both ultimately found justification in one particular image of individual liberty—freedom of contract.

In his *Antitrust Paradox* (1978)—probably still the most influential book about antitrust policy—Bork made three kinds of arguments to claim that wealth maximization ("consumer welfare") ought to be the unrivaled social good guiding antitrust policy. I have already mentioned his appeal to Sherman Act legislative history—an analysis whose deep flaws numerous careful scholars have already exposed. In the second argument, Bork claimed that only the logic of efficiency can provide an administrable standard for antitrust policy. I will not repeat here the numerous criticisms of that claim, including my earlier explications of efficiency's internal incoherence and its dependence upon the excluded macroeconomic variable of wealth distribution. I want to examine Bork's third kind of argument—the normative claim, the moral argument, that wealth maximization is the only justifiable goal for antitrust.

For Bork, "productive efficiency" is a crucial component of wealth maximization: When he uses the word "efficiency" alone, Bork informs us, "productive efficiency is meant." However, he rejects as "unsatisfactory" the mainstream view of productive efficiency as a "mechanical or engineering operation." After two pages of argumentation, he concludes that "the relative efficiency of firms is . . . measured by their relative success in the market."[58] How does Bork arrive at a social Darwinist vision of productive efficiency as commercial success?

Bork begins his radical revision of "productive efficiency" by calling upon the work of Chicago economist Frank H. Knight, who defined the idea as the "effective coordination of the various means of production in each industry as will produce the greatest result." For Bork, who views this idea through the normative lens of unfettered competition, "effective use" appears as "any activity by a business firm that creates wealth." Thus, Knight's "effective coordination" becomes Bork's "free market system." Yet, depending upon one's view of proper "competition policy," "effective coordination" can mean anything from monopoly to government-protected cartel to atomistic competition. Moreover, Knight's "greatest result" becomes Bork's "wealth." Again, depending upon the normative content of "result," industries can be coordinated to maximize output, price, employment, local control, and so on. All of these alternative meanings for "result" were taken seriously in 1933, when Knight published his book on industrial organization.[59]

Indeed, Frank Knight was part of an earlier generation of Chicago School economists who saw their discipline quite differently than their modern-day successors. His equally distinguished colleague, Henry C. Simons, was persuaded by the structural logic running through Edward Chamberlin's oligopoly theory to publish a book whose subject was the restructuring of concentrated industries into small independent businesses. Knight himself expressed disdain for the spurious rigor of strict price theory: "[A] fetish of "scientific method" in the study of society is . . . romantic folly . . . current among the educated. . . . [A] natural or positive science of human conduct . . . is not what we need; indeed, the idea is an absurdity."[60] Bork begins his revision of price theory as a natural science (though in the nineteenth century mode of Herbert Spencer's *Social Statics*) on the shoulders of Chicago School economists who understood themselves as engaged in the policy science of political economy. After the stock market crash of 1929 and amid the Great Depression, Frank Knight and his colleagues rejected the ideology of unfettered competition.

Only in a Spencerian world in which the fittest survive, in which those who survive must be the fittest, can Bork conclude that "[s]ince a free market system assumes that consumers define their own welfare, it follows that productive efficiency consists in offering anything . . . that consumers are willing to pay for." We must, of course, take all of this—including the assertions that we are essentially consumers and entirely free—on faith alone. Bork's logic is circular and thus closed to the empirical investigation that makes social sciences scientific. "[A]ntitrust must avoid any standards that require direct measurement and quantification of either restriction of output or efficiency," he warns, because "[s]uch tasks are impossible."[61] Bork's idea of productive efficiency as the commercial facsimile of natural selection, were it followed rigorously, would lead to an antitrust policy of competition free of all government supervision. Its logical conclusion would demand tolerance even of the price-fixing cartels and monopolies-by-merger that Bork identifies as the only legitimate targets for antitrust policy. In short, there would be no antitrust enforcement.

The social Darwinist vision animating Robert Bork's *Antitrust Paradox* (1978) and its rendition of "consumer welfare" had already inspired an earlier generation of economic and social policy makers. Ultimately, decisions such as *Lochner* (1905) had portrayed commercial markets as a natural preserve to be ruled by individual desires, as a private sphere to be governed by freedom of contract. The "Coase Theorem" (1960) later seemed to validate such sentiments, purporting to demonstrate that parties bargain to an efficient solution in the absence of transaction costs. It was time for someone to take up the banner of contractarianism, to forge a formal connection between wealth maximization and liberty of contract. Seeking to hinge all legal regulation on the "hypothesis of economic efficiency," Richard Posner would make the explicit argument that wealth maximization can be derived from freedom of contract. In a series of articles appearing during the second half of Jimmy Carter's term, Posner sought to demonstrate that wealth maximization consummates the Western tradition of individual liberty, that it fulfills the emancipatory ethic established in philosopher Immanuel Kant's formulation of "personal autonomy."[62]

In brief, Posner claimed that wealth maximization can be understood as a liberal value because it is the product of market transactions between willing buyers and sellers. An individual willingly enters into a market transaction (or other transaction that Posner characterizes as market-like) only when she believes that she will be better off than she is before the transaction. If the transaction results in a loss, then we can assume that she *ex ante* consented to the loss. Posner claims that all consensual market transactions are therefore conduct serving the Kantian notion of personal autonomy and, presumably, the liberal value of individual liberty. Market transactions, because they instantiate the ideal of personal autonomy, should be the rule. Thus Posner concludes that wealth maximization can serve as a proxy for personal autonomy.

Moreover, the goal of wealth maximization emerges as a neutral principle, even though some individuals lose wealth. It is neutral because the freedom of contract required for wealth maximization is, at the same time, a mechanism that allows *every* participant to exercise personal autonomy. In short, wealth maximization serves an underlying commitment to liberty—in particular, freedom of contract. Hence, competition free of government meddling not only maximizes wealth but safeguards individual liberty.[63] This formulation of wealth maximization intimates that *Lochner* (1905) was correctly decided and that antitrust, if not eliminated entirely, should be confined to *Stan-*

dard Oil's (1911) Rule of Reason—its common-law notion of restraints of trade. Indeed, an even larger claim followed—the efficiency of "the common law," that is, the assertion that common-law rules allow parties to bargain to the most efficient solutions. In this view, the only legitimate role for government is to intervene when markets dysfunction, by lowering transaction costs and generally employing economic logic to guide dysfunctional markets in mimicking efficient ones.

Certainly there are deep difficulties connected with asserting that the common law maximizes wealth, beginning with normative concerns about the treatment of those without dollars to express their preferences and ending with technical questions about the underlying process of common-law adjudication. Within the descriptive claim lies a prescriptive one that the common law is preferable to legislation precisely because it maximizes wealth. Even if the descriptive claim were true, why should maximizing wealth be more important than some other public policy? Furthermore, there are questions about the character of the claim: Does it refer to any set of common-law rules? Or only to those common-law rules that purport to minimize transaction costs? (Per se rules in antitrust, for example?) Or a particular set of common-law rules associated with some historical moment? (1805? 1905? 1985?) I want to put aside these difficulties for now[64] in order to assume Posner's view of efficiency and to pursue his explicit corollary regarding relations among competition, efficiency, and populism. The corollary—that efficiency and populism are contradictory policies—is an important rhetorical formation in the Chicago School literature. Indeed, it is the very contradiction described in Posner's *Antitrust Law* (1976) and elaborated in Bork's *Antitrust Paradox* (1979).

Posner's discussion of monopoly provides a clear example of "populism" in Chicago School terms. In sharp contrast to the "liberty" rhetoric underlying wealth maximization, Posner presents "populism" as founded in a primary commitment to equality. For Posner, Bork, and their cohorts, it is an asserted conflict between commitments to liberty and equality that underlies the paradox imagined between wealth maximization and "populism," between "economic" and "sociopolitical" concerns.

Posner deposits objections to monopoly into two categories—economic and sociopolitical. His example of a sociopolitical objection to monopoly is the "policy of restricting the freedom of action of large business firms to promote small business." According to this view, the populist commitment to equalizing rivalry, to promoting effective competition, is built upon the practice of restricting large business firms' freedom of contract. While many controversial claims underlie this characterization of "populism," for the sake of efficiency, I will address only the most obvious one:[65] the explicit claim that "populism's" commitment to equality is founded in the restraint of large firms' liberty. This claim makes sense only if Posner assumes first that free competition must serve liberty and, second, that anything beyond a formal notion of equal opportunity is antithetical to liberty. But neither assumption stands up to scrutiny.

To begin, it is not clear that free competition must serve large firms' liberty. For example, enjoining a merger or a cartel can be seen as serving free competition by restricting the liberty of large business organizations. Moreover, even if one believes that free competition must always serve *some* commitment to liberty, liberty and equality need not be seen as antithetical. Indeed, it is a commonplace that liberty and equality are always interdependent, that each requires the other as a condition for its livelihood. For example, the greater a dominant firm's power, the more it diminishes the liberty of rivals, customers, and suppliers. Diminishing that firm's market power might increase total liberty. One might even find that it maximizes liberty, although it would leave the dominant firm with less of it. In short, "populism's" substantive commitment to rough equality does not preclude a commitment to liberty. Posner's (and Bork's) assumption notwithstanding, "populism" can be entirely compatible with free competition, liberty, and equality.

The true paradox lies in the fact that both wealth maximization and "populism" can be (in)compatible with free competition. The claimed conflict between wealth maximization and "populism" reflects an underlying tension between commitments to liberty of contract and substantive equality. It is the tension captured in the conundrum of "free competition": Chicago Schoolers' wealth maximization rests on a preference for liberty of contract and the associated ideology of competition free of government power. "Populism" rests on the resolve to eliminate gross inequalities and on the associated ideology of competition free of private economic power. Posner's (and Bork's) price theory proceeds from a commitment to individual liberty, liberty which is presented as antithetical to substantive equality. In sharp contrast, "populism" treats a strong commitment to equality as part and parcel of a dedication to individual liberty.[66]

Finally, both wealth maximization and "populism" include a politics of wealth distribution: Both a regime of liberty of contract and a regime committed to recognizing the impact of economic power in bargain transactions produce predictable patterns of wealth distribution. The difference lies in the patterns produced, in who wins and who loses. As Ronald Coase correctly concluded in his "Theory of Social Cost" (1960), any shift in entitlements effects a distribution of wealth. In sum, both efficiency and populism involve normative choices and, in consequence, are inescapably political.

Deregulation of Commercial Markets: Populism and Efficiency

Jimmy Carter took office with the promise that deregulation would break up the cozy relationship between regulatory agency and regulated firm. No longer would airlines, for example, be protected from competition. Informed by Senator Edward Kennedy's (D.Mass.) subcommittee hearings and the subsequent Kennedy Report (authored largely by current Justice Stephen Breyer), Congress would pass the Airline Cargo Deregulation Act of 1977 and the Airline Deregulation Act of 1978.[67] The anticipated payoff was better value for consumer dollars because more airlines would compete for their patronage. Under the guidance of economist Alfred Kahn, the Civil Aeronautics Board would be disbanded, ending big business "protectionism" and introducing rivalry. Almost everyone believed that the new competition would spur efficiency, more and better service, and lower prices.

There was, however, a fundamental disagreement among economists about how this new competition would emerge. Both rationales, in fact, appeared in Kahn's writings and testimony.[68] The two opposed views did assume the same point of departure—that economies of scale were not important and thus were not barriers to new competition. From that assumption (now seen as erroneous), two opposing inferences were made. Traditional economists reasoned that deregulation would allow easy entry and exit, and thus more competition would take hold. The implication was that the antitrust laws were still needed, for example, in making sure that mergers would not gobble up competitors, especially since mergers could not be justified by economies of scale. Chicago School economists inferred something radically different. Because economies of scale are not important, they reasoned, even monopolies will price at cost because of the unrelenting threat of potential competition in an industry where entry and exit are cheap. This theory of "contestable markets," as it came to be known, had no use for antitrust.

In the larger context of Carter administration attitudes toward antitrust enforcement, however, there was a noticeable tilt toward active antitrust enforcement. First of all, John Shenefield, who headed the Antitrust Division, favored a strong government hand. Indeed, Carter's Commission for Review of Antitrust Laws and Procedures (1979), chaired by Shenefield, even supported a pending Senate bill calling for no-fault monopolization—that is, a purely structuralist approach to market power rejected by the Supreme Court a few years earlier. Moreover, the Federal Trade Commission, under the leadership of Commissioner Michael Pertschuk, would investigate advertising and other trade practices in an enforcement program informed by Chamberlin's theory of monopolistic competition and inspired by a Naderite zeal for exposing Vance Packard's "hidden persuaders." Whether seeking to regulate the practices of the "funeral trade" or to break up the breakfast cereal oligopoly, the FTC's active regulation of "unfair or deceptive acts or practices" and "unfair methods of competition" under FTC Act § 5 reflected a "populism" or "consumerism" sensitive to unequal bargaining power, concerned about mass advertising in the broadcast media, and intent upon improving consumer access to market information. In sum, both Shenefield's Antitrust Division and Pertschuk's FTC distrusted unregulated freedom of contract.[69]

There was no conflict perceived between populism and competition, nor between populism and efficiency. Perhaps English philosopher Isaiah Berlin captured best the misgivings about modern commercial markets informing the Carter administration's mix of consumerism and populism: "If I find that I am able to do little or nothing of what I wish, I need only contract or extinguish my wishes, and I am made free. If the tyrant (or 'hidden persuader'") manages to condition his subjects (or customers) into losing their original wishes and embrace ('internalize') the form of life he has invented for them, he will, on this definition, have succeeded in liberating them."[70] Liberty of contract without economic parity was regarded as a pernicious mirage. In the same vein, mass advertising and its power to beguile, especially children, became the focus for FTC activity. But FTC policy makers along with their Antitrust Division counterparts were out of step with the times—as the Reagan landslide victory would soon show. But even earlier—in the decade before the 1980 presidential election—Supreme Court doctrine and influential scholarly work had already turned away from the egalitarian concerns reflected in the Carter administration's theoretical commitments to oligopoly and monopolistic competition, its blend of deregulation and managed competition, its ideological mix of populism and efficiency.

6

Rhetorics of Free Competition, 1980–1992: Free Market Imagery, Corporate Control, and the Problem of Equality

By 1980, the Supreme Court had turned away from the Warren era's ethic of substantive equality. Yet, no clear position on equality had replaced that ethic. Perhaps the most striking example of the resulting quandary was the Court's *Bakke* (1978) decision.[1] On the one hand, the University of California's affirmative action program to set aside a number of positions for minority candidates in the medical school's entering class was outlawed as racial discrimination. On the other, it was permissible for admissions committees to take race and other characteristics into account. Similar quandaries about equality also emerged in the Court's First Amendment speech jurisprudence, producing sharp-angled changes in the treatment of corporate and commercial speech.

In the Reagan administration, however, there was no equivocation. The social policy theorists who had been spinning out the implications of wealth maximization and its ethic of "one dollar, one vote" were now advising the Reagan administration, making policy for federal agencies, and sitting as federal judges. The wealth-maximization form of efficiency provided the normative ground for a political economy favoring freedom of contract—economic markets free of government action to determine fairness or to adjust for historically unequal bargaining power. This shift to economic laissez-faire coincided with the increased efficiency of those in the business community to assert their interests. There was a more visible Business Roundtable (founded in 1972), a revitalized American Chamber of Commerce, as well as the usual trade and professional groups, and, most of all, in the wake of the *Buckley* (1976) and *Bellotti* (1978) decisions, literally thousands of political action committees representing corporate and other commercial interests (as well as religious and other ideological groups). Consumer, environmental, and labor groups were no longer the best-organized lobbyists.

The social and cultural context had also changed. Lyndon Johnson's Vietnam War and Richard Nixon's Watergate scandal heightened our traditional distrust of the state, embittering citizens and turning them against the federal government that had rescued them from the Great Depression. Now, that bitterness was accompanied by the belief that government was just incompetent. The Carter administration could not deliver on its promises. Economic problems associated with the high rate of inflation, high interest rates, and high oil prices were attributed to the Carter people's inability to manage. In contrast, corporations were represented as economically rational, potentially efficient captives of regulation, yearning to be free. The Iranian hostage crisis seemed to symbolize all of this—all that was wrong and how it could be made right. Depicted as the gang who couldn't shoot straight, the Carter administration seemed to be doing everything wrong—whether directing the U.S. Army or regulating the U.S. economy. By promising to right these wrongs, Ronald Reagan was not only elected president but also portrayed as the good guy, wearing the white hat, astride the white horse. He was the western hero who could turn national tragedy into a cowboy romance.

The Reagan administration's policies were wrapped in a rhetoric of "traditional values," later taken up by the Bush administration as "family values." Those values were offered as the solution to the America's woes. They embraced not only a promise to unshackle corporate America from government restraints, but also recommitments to a strong military, individual initiative, and traditional social roles, including family, gender, sexual preference, and race relations. It was a promise, most of all, to return to a robust economy founded in a regime of corporate control, subject only to the discipline of "the free market." Public policy would no longer interfere with the efficient management of private property. At the same time, social roles and moral questions were brought out of the closet, out of the private sphere. Now they were seen as the social infrastructure, the foundation necessary for the resurgence of a "strong America." This "return" to "traditional values," with its imagery of "the free market" and its commitment to an economy subject only to "corporate control," was accompanied by a complex ideological inversion of public and private spheres—that is, a flip-flop in attitude about the proper subjects for public policy.

"Traditional values" meant that the government should not seek to distribute power by, for example, enforcing anti-race or anti-sex discrimination policies. Rather, they should "allow" the play of "the free market"—whether in employment, gender, or race relations. This domestic "freedom of contract" regime, portrayed as necessary to unleash the economic power of American business, was accompanied by a massive military buildup, whose geopolitical consequences were largely symbolic. "Wars" with Grenada and Iraq produced more smoke than fire. Reagan proposed the "Star Wars" fantasy of a heavenly shield against the "evil empire" of the Soviet Union. There were, nevertheless, consequences. Increased defense spending turned more industrial resources toward military production and helped create massive budget deficits. Moreover, these initiatives set a tone that reinforced traditional social roles, including gender roles. Recall the public image of Jimmy and Rosalyn Carter: a weak man and strong woman; a President seeking international cooperation, both military and economic, and held hostage by Iran's Ayatollah Khomeini. Compare Ronald and Nancy Reagan: a strong man, tall in the saddle, with a doting wife; a President spurring international competition, both geopolitical and economic, and willing to deploy American military power without remorse.

By the end of the 1980s, George Bush's inability to measure up to Reagan's manliness in a fragmented post–Soviet Union world allowed Southerner Bill Clinton, a consensus-seeking "policy wonk" in the image of Jimmy Carter (strong wife and all), to win the presidency. Clinton's rhetorical imagery articulated a desire for cooperation rather than competition, for domestic consensus within a society fragmented by identity politics and economic decline, as well as for international agreements in a world economy characterized by ruinous competition.

Even before Ronald Reagan's campaign for the presidency in 1980, the public rhetoric of deregulation had begun to shift. Unlike the interventionist moral discourse of "traditional values," the accompanying economic rhetoric of efficiency meant getting government off the backs of business. The Reagan revolution was not so much a turn toward economic deregulation; Carter had already moved the country in that direction. Rather, it was the shift from a consumerist to a corporatist vision of deregulation.

There were large differences between the Carter and the Reagan rhetorics of efficiency and goals for deregulation. Perhaps most significant was the imagined relationship between government regulators and regulated corporations. For Carter, the logic of deregulation was regulatory capture—the corruption of the political process symbolized by the illegal corporate support of the Watergate episode—as well as the corporate irresponsibility publicized by Ralph Nader and his consumerist movement. The postregulatory environment would reflect free competition—that is, competition free of excessive corporate power, supervised according to prevailing policies of environmental, antitrust, and health and safety regulation. For Reagan, the logic of deregulation was the unburdening of corporate America, the loosening of government constraints on a natural corporate inclination to compete through more efficient processes and innovative products. The postregulatory environment was imagined as a different sort of free competition—competition free of government supervision.

Unlike the complex cross-currents swirling through the Nixon and Carter presidencies, the Reagan administrations were, if nothing else, clear as to ideology. The 1980s' translucence derives from a unifying image and a dominant agenda. The decade's unifying image was "the free market"—a postmodernist Leviathan, an idealized, efficient, all-encompassing sovereign compelling rivalrous individuals, side by side yet in splendid isolation, each one making rational choice after rational choice to maximize wealth. All the world was a market, filled with consumers and producers yearning to be free of government regulation.

The dominant agenda was corporate control, seen most clearly in three related domains. First, in labor relations, Reagan sent a message early in his presidency with the swift firing of the nation's striking air traffic controllers, a message that the country was better off supporting management. Congress expressed its own antilabor sentiments with the passage of legislation denying food stamps to striking workers. The Supreme Court approved the legislation and held, in another case, that the bankruptcy laws permitted employers to rescind or change collective bargaining agreements without the approval of the bankruptcy court or the National Labor Relations Board. In this instance, however, Congress did pass legislation overruling the Court. Further eviscerating the mediation process embodied in the NLRB's statutory mandate, the Court also held that the National Labor Relations Act does not preempt state common-law causes of action by strike replacement workers. First and foremost, corporate control meant the subjugation of labor unions.[2]

Second, the agenda of corporate control embodied an image of commercial markets as stacked in three levels. On the ground floor was the commercial marketplace for goods and services, freed of burdensome regulation, including antitrust enforcement. Thus, corporate managers could exercise commercial judgment to increase efficiencies and to maximize profits, unimpeded by political constraints. Presumably, these managers were disciplined not only by the unrelenting competition they faced, but also by market demands originating at the next higher level. That is, superordinate financial markets would register poor management performance: Stock prices would decline, bond ratings would drop, and hence the cost of new capital would rise. But there was also a third level of commercial market—for "efficient management" or "corporate control"—to which financial markets responded. When current stock prices or corporate bond ratings reflected inefficient management, the highest order of market would discipline those currently in control. The underperforming corporation would be acquired by someone who would install new managers to instill the ethic of efficiency, to raise profits. Financial markets would register the improved performance with higher stock prices and better bond ratings.

In the merger-and-takeover wave of the 1980s, trafficking in corporate entities was assessed with little attention to antitrust effects in markets for goods and services. The activities of corporate raiders, the benefits to shareholders of the targeted firm, the transaction costs of fees paid to middlemen, the risks of high interest rate junk bond liabilities, the effects on employees and employee pension plans—all of these financial consequences—were justified by reference to a market for corporate control. Responding to Berle and Means's critical portrayal of the modern bureaucratic corporation's management as unconstrained by corporate owners (shareholders), the 1980s version of "free competition" produced a laissez-faire solution to the problem of management discretion. Trafficking in corporations, it was asserted, was motivated by the belief that current management was inefficient. An emancipated market for corporate control allowed more efficient managers to take over slumbering corporations, to make them "lean and mean" and to revive American competitiveness in world markets for goods and services.

Finally, the agenda of corporate control created policy controversy in a third domain—the marketplace of ideas. It was there that both legislative initiatives and Court doctrine grappled with the question of equality. Should political and commercial speech be treated identically? Should discrimination be made between individuals and corporations? Or between profit and nonprofit corporations? In general terms, what should be done, if anything, about the distorting effects of wealth in the marketplace of ideas? The underlying concern was corporate control of the marketplace of ideas. Whether handbilling in shopping malls or in utility bills mailed to customers, whether Federal Election Commission rules or state utility commission regulations, should advertising expenditures and practices be limited? Or should the commercial practices of monopolistic competition, of product advertising and brand identification, be permitted in the marketplace of ideas when the ideas are political and the products are candidates for political office?

Together, the dominant image of "the free market" and the dominant agenda of "corporate control" marked the 1980s. They depended upon and, to some extent, influenced a series of ideological inversions. In an ironic way, political discourse appropriated the feminist maxim that what is personal is political, what is private is public. The watershed year was 1988, when Democratic presidential hopeful Gary Hart invited journalistic scrutiny of his private life. Hart would withdraw from the primary campaign under pressure produced by disclosures of the kinds of marital infidelities traditionally ignored by the press corps. Tabloid journals now served as the model for political journalism in America—the obsessive reportage of lifestyles of the rich and famous. The irony in this revision was its perfect subversion of feminist concerns. Feminists were arguing that traditional gender roles were social constructs and thus, at least in part, the product of public policies enacted to sustain them. One implication was that the private sphere should not be viewed as somehow outside the domain of public policy that supported its practices and relations. In sharp contrast, the journalistic turn to private voyeurism tended to eclipse the very debate over public policy issues demanded by feminists (and by others whose subordinate positions were presumed to be natural or otherwise outside the proper boundaries of the public sphere).

This inversion of the traditional views of public policy and individual privacy came to define political discourse beyond the conduct of political campaigns. Indeed, some of the major public policy issues of the decade reflected this inversion. Encouraged by the Reaganite rhetoric of "traditional values," religious fundamentalists organized political action committees, mass media networks, and political campaigns to press moral positions in the political sphere—positions on school prayer, public displays of religious observances, gender roles, sexual practices, and, most divisively, abortion. Whether the half-million pro-choice advocates who marched in Washington or those who picketed Planned Parenthood offices, whether the Reagan administration's "litmus test" for appointing federal judges or the Supreme Court's struggle with *Roe v. Wade*, private issues and moral questions were contested in the public marketplace of ideas.

Less visibly, ideological inversions produced stunning reversals in competition policies applied to commercial markets. For example, economic actors were now using antitrust laws to restrain local political institutions. Moreover, in corporate law, Berle and Means's concern about corporate management beyond the control of ownership was turned on its head. A new rhetoric of marketplace rivalry—called "contestability theory"—emerged, based on a presumption that all markets were always subject to new entrants. The implication was that government regulation was unnecessary and perhaps pernicious. This counterfactual hypothesis, coupled with the new faith in "markets for efficient management," revised the traditional view of managers as unbridled corporate sovereigns.

Instead, a top corporate executive was now portrayed as simply one contractual relationship among many that defined a corporation at any given moment. A chief executive officer, like any supplier or customer, was nothing more than one filament in a nexus of contracts. The real problem, therefore, was making sure that managers could not insulate themselves from the discipline imposed by the "market for efficient management." How was that to be accomplished? By allowing unfettered corporate mergers, acquisitions, and takeovers. No longer were corporations to be treated as entities separate from the markets they inhabited. Rather, they were understood as temporary bundles of contracts floating atop a sea of available alternative contracts. Markets and corporations were made of the same basic materials. And they needed the same primordial environment to allow survival of the fittest: freedom of contract. Government regulation would only skew the incentives away from the efficiency-seeking, profit-maximizing predisposition of naturally functioning free markets.

The unifying image of "the free market" and a dominant agenda of "corporate control" redefined competition policies in the 1980s. Traditional public regulation of economic activities was now seen as more properly a matter for private decision. Intensely private questions became the stuff of political debate and mass media attention. I begin my examination of the translucent 1980s with the earliest example of ideological inversion—the Federal Trade Commission's turn away from traditional economic regulation. Next, I investigate the decline of antitrust as the site for commercial competition policy. Not only did the Supreme Court allow private actors to restrain political entities under the antitrust laws but the Reagan administration declined to contest mergers between powerful multinational corporations. During those years, conservative academics and Reagan administration policy makers developed and implemented the new economics of pluperfect competition—that is, a radically simplified model of "contestable markets," under which *all* markets were seen as self-policing. I then explore parallel developments in corporate law to understand the changes in free competition rhetoric that allowed the merger and takeover explosion, and that made the corporate raider the cultural icon of the decade. I conclude with the Supreme Court's struggle to come to grips with the ethic of equality in the most troubling of markets, one teeming with individuals and corporations, with citizens and consumers, with economic and political images—the marketplace of ideas.

The Federal Trade Commission: From "Social" to "Economic" Regulation

The earliest example of ideological inversion was the change in attitude toward the Federal Trade Commission. In 1975, Democratic leaders in Congress warned President Gerald Ford against excessive regulatory reform, writing that "[r]egulation is as American as hot dogs, baseball, apple pie and Chevrolet." Congress, after delay attributable to growing ambivalence toward the FTC, finally heeded two well-publicized reports issued in 1969, one by a Ralph Nader study group and the other by the American Bar Association, portraying the FTC as moribund and ineffectual. Congress passed the Magnuson-Moss Warranty and FTC Improvements Act of 1975, which expanded the FTC's enforcement powers and confirmed its authority to issue industry-wide regulations.[3]

It was only a few years later that the *Washington Post*, a citadel of liberal politics, would ridicule the FTC's proposals to regulate children's advertising in an editorial titled "The National Nanny": "[T]he proposal, in reality, is designed to protect children from the weaknesses of their parents—and the parents from the wailing insistence of their children. That, traditionally, is one of the roles of a governess—if you can afford one. It is not a proper role of government." Ridicule was soon accompanied by expression of outrage. Congressman William Frenzel (R.Minn.) proclaimed on the House floor that the FTC "is a king-sized cancer on our economy." "It has undoubtedly added more unnecessary costs on American consumers who it is charged with protecting," he charged, "than any other half dozen agencies combined." In 1980, Congress passed another FTC Improvements Act, this one imposing numerous restrictions on specific proceedings to consider industry trade rules—most conspicuously the children's advertising project. Moreover, Congress included a provision for legislative veto of FTC rules, the veto later overturned by the Supreme Court as transgressing the constitutional mandate for separation of powers.[4] But the new tone was set.

When the Reagan administration took office in 1981, the FTC was already seen as misguided and overzealous. Now the Executive joined Congress and the business sector in viewing the FTC as the most egregious example of government meddling in the economy. Indeed, Reagan named James Miller III, who helped shape the campaign's deregulation rhetoric, as FTC chairman. Miller declared that FTC's "social" regulation, its excessive activism, would yield to "economic" analysis: "The role of the Commission in the area of consumer protection should be to replicate, to the degree feasible, the workings of an efficient marketplace. Whatever the merits of various 'social goals,' we believe that Congress is the appropriate forum for addressing these issues." Congress, Miller knew, would be reticent, reflecting the antipathy of the new electoral majority who had just elected a conservative Republican president. Compare the view of Carter appointee Michael Pertschuk: "The marketplace creates incentives which produce innovation and efficiency and productivity, but those incentives are so strong that they often lead to pressures to undermine the standards of a civilized society, to lie, to coerce, to cheat, to overreach. . . ." Miller's reorientation of the FTC would serve the ideological function of symbolizing the Reagan revolution—the withdrawal of government from the commercial marketplace and the return of unfettered private enterprise, with its natural instincts for efficiency and innovation.[5]

The Naderite alliance between government regulators and consumers withered. In its place, there emerged a neoconservative corporatism that held that consumers (as well as citizens and workers) are really better off deferring to the business sector. The new alliance was reflected in the anti-FTC offensive, in Antitrust Chief William Baxter's categorical insistence that consumers benefit when manufacturers are allowed to fix retail prices, in corporate raiders' claims that not only shareholders but American competitiveness profit when takeovers are freed from government oversight and, finally, in Reagan's message, dispatched in the swift firing of the nation's striking air traffic controllers, that the country is better off with strong management control over workers, despite serious health and safety concerns expressed by overworked controllers, the frightening risks created by their novice replacements, and the consequent dangers to airline passengers.

Antitrust Law: From Regulation of Commercial Competition to Restraint of Political Power

A confluence of ideology and material circumstances signaled antitrust's decline in the 1980s. The idea of an autonomous world "market" was combined with the experience of American industrial collapse to produce the sense that unfettered domestic competition and more corporate consolidation were the answers. No longer would competition policy revolve around government supervision of domestic commercial markets—whether antitrust or other economic regulation. The new focus was international competitiveness—a neomercantilism—beginning with Reagan's view that military power was the prerequisite and shifting after the demise of statist communism in Eastern and Central Europe to Clinton's "common market" view that government-spurred innovation—a USA, Inc.—in a Western Hemispheric free-trade zone was the answer. Much like the early New Deal years, Reagan's corporatist regime and Clinton's vision of democratic corporatism (or, in the international context, corporate democracy), left little room for domestic antitrust.

Although it is too early to tell whether domestic antitrust's decline is permanent or cyclical, there has clearly been a shift toward guarding against unfair competition in international trade. That shift has been accompanied by an exclusive (and narrow) focus on conduct in what remains of domestic antitrust. There is little concern about market power and none about corporate size. That does not, of course, mean that domestic competition policy, particularly concern about economic power, has disappeared. To a significant degree, its production sites have moved across antitrust's borders to other legal domains—to the realms of corporate and securities law and corporate speech—that I take up later in the chapter.

As for the commercial competition policy that remained, the Reagan-Bush years produced an antitrust inversion. Consistent with the conservative Republicans' deregulatory ideology of freeing commercial enterprise from government constraints, antitrust doctrine emerged as a weapon for privately owned businesses to attack the power of political subdivisions. Supreme Court doctrine projected two images of city and local governments. They were portrayed either as commercial actors or as renegade fiefdoms whose anticipated abuses of political power were to be governed by commercial competition policy. Meanwhile, the Reagan and Bush administrations implemented antitrust policies that promoted the consolidation of economic power. Although the Supreme Court issued a number of important decisions consistent with those policies, they were largely continuations of trends begun in the Carter years—especially trends narrowing the liability of manufacturers for imposing restraints on distribution of their products, the culpability of large firms for price discrimination and, generally, the cognizable scope of "antitrust injury."[6] More important in those years were the cases that never reached the Supreme Court, the disputes settled by the FTC and Justice Department, and, finally, the enforcement policies that left undisturbed transactions that would have provoked scrutiny in prior years—particularly large corporate mergers.

Antitrust and Political Power

Although commercial actors are constitutionally protected from antitrust scrutiny when they petition government entities, government entities themselves are sometimes subject to antitrust attack. The seeming contradiction arises when the government entity is not strictly a sovereign state, but rather one of its subdivisions, such as a state agency, a city council, or a municipal power company. Thus, for example, trade association activities to blockade state licensing of new competitors has been constitutionally protected while a city's efforts to promote competitive bidding for cable franchising has been held subject to antitrust liability. The Sherman Act's framers would have been astounded. An antitrust statute passed to enhance government authority to control the abuse of economic power was now being used by private economic actors to control government authority. As we shall see, Congress did respond, however equivocally, to this inversion of competition policy by passing legislation to shield cities and localities from damages, but not injunctions, in such lawsuits.

Since the later New Deal case of *Parker v. Brown* (1943), the Supreme Court has recognized that the Sherman Act does not preempt economic regulation by states.[7] Moreover, private actors compelled by state regulation to act in ways that restrain competition are immune from antitrust liability. Finally, political subdivisions have been treated much like private economic actors in business to make a profit. The treatment is surprising, given the nonprofit, social welfare aims of political subdivisions. The *Parker* doctrine has been applied in two kinds of cases involving political subdivisions. In one, the Supreme Court has explicitly treated nonprofit, municipally owned utilities and hospitals as private economic actors. In the other, the Court has often seen political subdivisions as renegade sovereigns, as local pockets of resistance against a federal policy of free trade. Although the treatment of political actors has varied in recent years, the important point remains: Their antitrust status has been no better than that of private economic actors claiming "state action" immunity under the *Parker* doctrine.

In the *City of Lafayette* case (1978), Louisiana Power & Light Company, an investor-owned, for-profit corporation, sued the city for "various antitrust offenses" in the conduct of its own electric power company, which was a not-for-profit corporation. Justice Brennan, writing for a plurality of four, brushed off the city's argument that political purposes should always merit antitrust immunity:

> [The City's] argument that their goal is not private profit but public service is only partly correct. Every business enterprise, public or private, operates its business in furtherance of its own goals. . . . the economic choices made by public corporations in the conduct of their business affairs, designed as they are to assure maximum benefits for the community constituency, are not inherently more likely to comport with the broader interests of national economic well-being than are those of private corporations acting in furtherance of the interests of the organization and its shareholders.

The Court plurality determined that the interests of communities in, for example, maintaining local control over the provision of necessary services such as electricity, are not to be privileged over shareholder interests in maximizing return on investment. They are not to be given special treatment unless there is a statewide policy "requiring the anticompetitive restraint," a policy "affirmatively expressed," "compelled," and "actively supervised by the State." The plurality opinion expressed concern that the locality-owned electrical utilities, unregulated by a state, in concert with other municipally owned utilities such as water and natural gas providers, "would necessarily have an impact on the regulated public utility whose service was displaced." In his concurring opinion, Chief Justice Burger carried that logic a step further, posing a formal distinction between a "proprietary enterprise" and traditional "governmental" conduct. "This," he concluded, "is an ordinary dispute among competitors in the same market."[8]

Four Justices dissented from the view that the antitrust laws apply to local government. Dissenting Justice Potter Stewart observed that, in passing the Sherman Act, "Congress was concerned with attacking concentrations of private economic power unresponsive to public needs." The Court plurality, according to the dissenting faction, "blurs, if indeed it does not erase, [the] logical distinction between private and governmental action." It is "senseless," they insisted, "to require a showing of state compulsion when the State itself acts through one of its governmental subdivisions."[9]

For a narrow majority of the Court, the political accountability of the city of Lafayette to its citizens and the Louisiana legislature was not enough to distinguish it from "private corporations" acting for the benefit of their shareholders and managers. Rather, five Justices imagined some sort of preexisting "market" whose commercial nature turns all participants, short of entire states, into "economic" actors—that is, subject to the antitrust laws. The same vision of an autonomous "market," somehow independent of the legal rules (contract, property, tort, antitrust, and so on) that define market relations, led a divided Court to apply the Robinson-Patman Act to the State of Alabama. In *Jefferson County Pharmaceutical Association* (1983), Justice Powell held that wholesaling of prescription drugs at a lower price to state and local government hospitals for resale in competition with disfavored private pharmacies is subject to prosecution for price discrimination. Again, the Court imagined "*the* private retail *market*" that "a State has chosen to compete in." The University of Alabama's hospital, in dispensing prescriptions to patients, including students and indigents, was envisioned as an outsider who entered a preexisting arena, who intruded upon a purely economic domain. The outsider, Powell reasoned, must be made to abide by that domain's code of ethics. He concluded that Congress intended for all entities, public and private, save the federal government, to abide by that code.[10]

Justice Stevens, dissenting from the Court's vision, saw no universal market. Moreover, he insisted that had Congress placed federal and state agencies on equal footing. Both were seen as political actors. Neither was understood as competing—fighting for customers and profits—with private hospitals. Echoing the views expressed in Stewart's dissenting opinion in *City of Lafayette*, Stevens found no entitlement granted to profit-seeking businesses to impose an economic logic upon the conduct of political actors, no right to compete as if all rivals are firms composed of private property, constrained to seek profits. But the majorities in these two cases created such an entitlement; they simply could not tolerate commercial markets populated, at least in part, by organizations composed of public property and constrained only by political process.[11] For these bare majorities, competition policy required an imaginative commitment to private property rights.

Situated between these two portrayals of political subdivisions as economic actors was the *City of Boulder* case (1982), in which the Court treated a small city as a renegade sovereign, as seeking to undermine the "free trade" policy enshrined in the antitrust laws. Boulder's sole cable T.V. provider claimed a conspiracy between the city and a potential competitor to restrain trade. The claim arose out of a City Council ordinance prohibiting the cable provider from expanding into other areas of the city for three months. The moratorium would allow the Council to draft a model cable T.V. ordinance and to invite other cable providers to enter the market. In short, Boulder was seeking to introduce competitive bidding into a monopolized market.[12]

Boulder is a "home rule" municipality under the Colorado constitution, entitling it to exercise "the full right of self-government in both local and municipal matters." Indeed, in such matters, the "City Charter and ordinances supersede the laws of Colorado." Despite this constitutional grant of full state authority to Boulder, the Court refused to extend Colorado's governmental immunity to Boulder, Justice Brennan writing that the Constitution recognizes only a "'dual system of government,' which has no place for sovereign cities." This distrust of localism, this fear of "parochialism," led the Court to the proposition that "civil and criminal sanctions upon 'persons,' of course, apply to municipalities as well as to other *corporate* entities."[13] Boulder was subject to the antitrust laws because, according to the Court's logic, its attempt to introduce competitive bidding did not reflect a "clearly articulated state policy" to displace competition with regulation. Nor did Colorado "compel" Boulder to regulate.

Justice Rehnquist, joined by Burger and O'Connor, wrote a stinging dissent. First, because the case involved two sovereigns (the federal government and, by the home-rule provision in the Colorado constitution, Boulder), Rehnquist insisted that the issue was not exemption from liability under the antitrust laws but rather preemption under the Supremacy Clause. Under no circumstances should Boulder be subject to damages. Instead, the Court should seek to reconcile the federal and local policies (here, both favoring competition), at worst finding the local ordinance preempted. The majority was simply wrong in treating "a political subdivision of a State as an entity indistinguishable from any privately owned business." The result, warned Rehnquist, would be a "*Lochner*-like" substantive due process analysis of every local ordinance, asking whether the enactment comports with the antitrust laws' competition policy. Along with the well-known renunciation of substantive due process jurisprudence, a universal standard—now competition rather than freedom of contract—was inconsistent with the recognized obligations and authority of localities. "Competition," Rehnquist observed, "simply does not and cannot further the interests that lie behind most social welfare legislation."[14]

The case provoked a strange juridical alignment: Court liberals, led by Justice Brennan, were insisting on doctrine whose effect was corporate dominance over majoritarian sentiments—both state and local. Justice Rehnquist characterized their position as "*Lochner*-like"—anathema to liberals both on and off the Court. The alignment is evidence of the unstable ideological valences of competition rhetoric. Here, for example, the question of local politics also resonated with recent experience in school desegregation and First Amendment speech cases, along with the commitments to liberty and equality they provoked. Justice Brennan in particular could feel strongly about the importance of a federalized framework, given the recent constitutional history of local majoritarianism. Yet pulling in the same direction was the Reagan era's dominant agenda of corporate control and its commitment to freedom of contract.

Local and state government officials across the country were outraged by the decision. Nonetheless, Reagan's FTC extended its own program of unfettering competition from government supervision. In 1984, the FTC sued the cities of New Orleans and Minneapolis, charging that their regulation of local taxi companies violated the FTC Act. That year, Congress finally passed the Local Government Antitrust Act, acceding to pressure by local officials and to criticisms echoing concerns expressed in recent Supreme Court dissenting opinions. In large part overruling *City of Boulder*, the Act shields localities from antitrust damages, although not from injunction.[15]

The *Hallie* case (1985) seems to mark a retreat in the scope of antitrust limitations on political actors. Four unincorporated Wisconsin townships claimed that the adjacent city of Eau Claire ran afoul of the Sherman Act by monopolizing "the provision of sewage treatment services." Unlike the *City of Boulder*'s cable regulation, Eau Claire's entry into sewage treatment followed the clear path opened by state legislation. An elaborate Wisconsin statute authorized localities to do precisely what Eau Claire did—demand annexation to the city as the condition for providing the service. The town of Hallie, seeking to retain its residents (although not its sewage), claimed that the "state action" doctrine did not protect from antitrust scrutiny Eau Claire's "tying" of sewage treatment and annexation, because the Wisconsin statute did not "compel" such conduct. Under the *City of Lafayette* (1978) standard, argued Hallie, "authorization" by state law was not enough to invoke a "state action" exemption. Writing for a unanimous Court, Justice Powell read the 1978 opinion as standing for the proposition that "it is sufficient that the statutes authorize the City to provide sewage services and also to determine the areas to be served." Thus, something more than Boulder's "home rule" charter was still necessary—an "affirmatively expressed . . . state policy."[16] But something less than compulsion was now sufficient to exempt municipal regulation from the commercial ethic of competition policy.

Lest Justice Powell's opinion be misunderstood as adopting a more lenient standard for municipalities than private businesses, one need only turn to the very next decision appearing in the U.S. Reports: Powell's opinion in *Southern Motor Carriers Rate Conference v. U.S.* (1985), holding that a "rate bureau"—a legislatively authorized cartel of trucking companies—qualified for the "state action" exemption. In short, political subdivisions dispensing social welfare services and privately owned businesses seeking profits would continue to receive equal treatment under the antitrust laws.[17]

In one fundamental respect, however, the Court has discriminated between political subdivisions and privately owned businesses. With an unincorporated locality, state agency, or incorporated city, the antitrust question has been sovereign control: Is the sewage disposal agency authorized? Is the electrical utility subject to state control? Is the city following a clearly articulated state policy? The Court as a matter of common practice pierces the political veil of state sovereignty over its subdivisions. The implicit assumption is that without explicit state direction, localities are out of control, and act upon parochial interests. Somehow local political processes cannot be trusted even though, presumably, virtually all state legislatures can trump local policies—just as virtually all corporate boards of directors or CEOs can control division managers. Yet, unlike corporate subdivisions, political subdivisions are regulated by the commercial tenets of antitrust doctrine.

With a parent corporation and wholly owned subsidiaries, effective control is presumed. Their joint action is assumed to be the "conduct of a single firm." Their "officers are not separate actors." Nor are there "two separate corporate consciousnesses." For antitrust purposes, a parent and its subsidiaries are like a "team of horses" with a "single driver." Following a traditional, managerialist view of the bureaucratic corporation as a coherent, hierarchical entity, the Court, at least since the *Copperweld* decision (1984), has been respectful of the corporate veil. In this view, antitrust tenets of competition policy do not apply to intracorporate relations. Rather, the logic of private property rights and its bargain theory of contracts depicts a pyramidal structure of corporate control.[18]

This line of cases raises two interesting questions, neither explicitly addressed by the Court: If political subsidiaries of states were viewed as pyramidal power structures, would their intramural activities—whether individual or concerted—escape the commercial ethic of competition? Or does the absence of an invested property logic in political subdivisions, the presence of a social welfare rationale, simply mark them as dangerous intruders in a "free market" driven by free contracting?[19]

Antitrust and Economic Power

Of the 10,000 merger notifications filed during the 1980s, Justice's Antitrust Division challenged only 28. Whether multi-billion-dollar mergers, such as General Electric's acquisition of RCA or U.S. Steel's purchase of Marathon Oil, or "joint ventures" between American auto oligopolists and major foreign rivals, such as that between GM/Toyota or Ford/Mazda, Antitrust Chief William Baxter applauded corporate consolidation: "There is nothing written in the sky that says that the world would not be a perfectly satisfactory place if there were only 100 companies." Thus, he announced that, in his Antitrust Division, "an industry trend toward concentration is not a factor that will be considered." Attorney General Edwin Meese later declared that corporate consolidation would "make the United States more competitive." The late Malcolm Baldridge, Secretary of Commerce, warned: "The world economy has changed, trade patterns have changed, but the antitrust laws have not. . . . [T]hey place additional and unnecessary burdens on the ability of U.S. firms to compete. Repeal of Clayton 7 will increase the efficiency of U.S. firms and strengthen their competitiveness in world markets."[20] Behind such simplistic views of the benefits of corporate size lay a more complex economic argument for permissiveness in merger policy, an argument founded in dazzling new conceptions of competition. However, before examining that argument, we must examine the Reagan-Bush policies that encouraged the merger maelstrom of the 1980s. Those policies were codified in new Merger Guidelines (1982) issued by the Justice Department and emulated by the FTC. My examination begins with an example—the FTC's approval of the Texaco/Getty and Chevron/Gulf oil industry mergers in 1984.

It concludes with a close look at the Merger Guidelines—their policy and their enforcement.

On January 6, 1984, Texaco informed the FTC of its contemplated merger with Getty. Texaco had revenues of $48 billion and assets of $27 billion; Getty's revenues were $12.3 billion and its assets $10 billion. Their combined net income for 1982 was just short of $2 billion. On February 2, the FTC conditionally approved the merger. As part of the final consent order allowing the merger, Texaco and Getty agreed to divestiture of assets in twenty-nine states and the District of Columbia. After the $10 billion dollar tender offer, Texaco was the second largest petroleum company in the United States. But that was July. By the end of October, Texaco would fall to the third position. Superseding Texaco would be an even larger Chevron Corporation. Combined with Gulf Oil, the new Chevron Corporation had revenues of $62 billion, assets of $43 billion, and refinery capacity of more than 2.2 million barrels per day. After Exxon, Chevron was not only the second largest domestic oil company but also the second largest industrial corporation in the United States.[21]

How was it that Reagan's FTC approved these mergers? All four firms were "fully integrated petroleum compan[ies], engaged in the exploration for and production of crude oil and natural gas, refining, the transportation of crude oil, natural gas and refined products, and the distribution and marketing of refined products and natural gas."[22] All four were multi-billion dollar, multinational corporations. Weren't the antitrust laws written to block the buildup of massive economic power by combination—especially when the two companies are rivals in the same industry? The FTC's logic of consent was sublime: In both reviews, the FTC defined the geographic market as worldwide, with particular "lines of commerce" such as refining or transportation, partitioned into "relevant geographic markets." Each line of commerce was inspected for competition between the merging parties. Where the FTC found competing assets—Chevron and Gulf refineries in Port Arthur, Texas, for example—one had to be sold. After negotiating divestiture of offending assets, two horizontal mergers—the Clayton Act's vision of mating Tyrannosaurus Rex—emerged from the FTC's magical chrysalis as harmless butterflies. Chevron and Texaco were seen as unthreatening firms disciplined by a worldwide market full of oil companies. At the same time, they were firms whose corporate predecessors, after divestitures, were no longer rivals. In short, these oil industry mergers were transformed, for domestic purposes, into conglomerate mergers.

Commissioner Michael Pertschuk dissented, asking: "What are the social benefits of this merger?" The FTC had concluded that "this acquisition does not present . . . efficiencies, . . . notwithstanding [Chevron's] statements that it does." Pertschuk thus observed that "the Commission is accepting substantial risks in relying on a complex, uncertain remedy in a case where a merger clearly appears to be unlawful, and offers few, if any, benefits other than to the private parties." But William Baxter, speaking for the Reagan administration, had already told Congress that "vertical and conglomerate mergers have ceased to be a major enforcement focus." Attorney General William French Smith opined that "[b]igness doesn't necessarily mean badness." Douglas H. Ginsburg, a later Antitrust Chief (and failed Supreme Court nominee), stated that he "never saw a conglomerate merger [he] disliked that much." Indeed, both the Justice Department and FTC adopted a common set of Merger Guidelines,[23] which institutionalized the view that "competition" means only horizontal rivalry. This pair of multi-billion dollar mergers between multinational oil companies, imagined as conglomerates in a world market, could not by (re)definition "substantially lessen competition."

It is an irony of antitrust history that these and other mergers in the oil industry have reunited large pieces of John D. Rockefeller's Standard Oil Trust—the Progressive Era's symbol for corporate buccaneering that inspired passage of the Sherman Act in 1890 and its Clayton Act amendments. Under the 1982 Merger Guidelines (as well as Supreme Court doctrine since the mid-1970s), antitrust orthodoxy was able to justify this vulgar irony of history with the divine reason of microeconomics. Indeed, it was the heavenly logic of neoclassical price theory that informed the 1982 Guidelines' radical departure from their 1968 predecessor.

At first blush, the economic theory underlying the 1968 and 1982 policies appears to be the same. Whether the earlier "Four-Firm Concentration Ratio" or the more recent "Herfendahl-Hirschman Index" (HHI), both techniques are intended to describe the degree of concentration in an industry. Both derive from oligopoly theory's structuralist logic of cooperation. In light of such structural concerns, there has been persistent criticism of agency underenforcement during the 1980s—at both the FTC and Justice Department.[24] A closer look at the policies articulated in the 1982 Guidelines suggests, however, that the extremely low level of enforcement is entirely consistent with their triangular framework for evaluating mergers. The framework includes a price-theory basis for determining the "relevant market," a model of all markets as "contestable" regardless of structure, and a financial theory of competition. In sum, the three pieces fit together as a nonstructuralist justification for a permissive attitude toward mergers. The attitude, of course, is that mergers do not produce anticompetitive effects.

According to the HHI, to calculate "market" concentration, the "relevant market" must be identified. The 1982 Guidelines' approach to defining a relevant market begins with the merging firms' combined output at current market prices, and then asks: How many customers will be lost or how many new firms will respond to a "small but significant and nontransitory increase in price"? The Guidelines explain this abstruse language as the measure for gauging response to a hypothetical "five percent price increase lasting one year." Those customers who would leave or those new firms who would enter in that year are included in "the relevant market."[25] Seemingly neutral, the procedure incorporates a fundamental bias in favor of businesses that already have market power. That is, the "5 percent" technique for determining "the relevant market" makes it just as easy for large firms in an already concentrated market to merge as for small firms in a competitively structured one.

Such consequences, of course, defeat the very purpose for measuring industry concentration.

Here is how the bias works: When one of the merging firms is currently exercising market power by charging higher prices, many past customers will already have defected to close substitutes. With the price already high, an increase of 5 percent would send current customers to products they earlier rejected at a competitive price as distant substitutes. The Guidelines, by beginning at the current (higher) price, thus draw *distant* substitutes inside the bounds of the "relevant market." A larger "relevant market" results, yielding a lower market share and thus undervaluing the firm's market power. Responding to such criticism, Antitrust Chief William Baxter has written that in his opinion the purpose of Clayton Act § 7 is to stop mergers that "lessen competition" below the current level, not to reduce the amount of market power already being exercised. Apparently, a larger firm with more market power is seen as making little difference in a market already dominated by powerful firms.[26]

The rationale for tolerating mergers between already powerful firms is couched in a codicil to the HHI market-share standard for judging a merger's effects on competition: "If entry into a market is so easy that existing competitors could not succeed in raising price for any significant period of time, the Department is unlikely to challenge mergers in that market."[27] When read by Antitrust Chief William Baxter and other disciples of "contestability theory," this statement takes on a meaning not apparent to the uninitiated reader. These disciples claim that industries as a rule have no real barriers to entry and exit—that is, no technological or financial obstacles that cannot be overcome. The implication is that large firms with market power, even monopolies, are always threatened by swarms of potential competitors circling overhead, burrowing below, and attacking from all sides. According to this view, mergers never lessen competition. I will have more to say about contestability theory in the following section.

The third element in the triangular framework for understanding the extremely low level of enforcement under the 1982 Guidelines is expressed in their opening section, titled "Purpose and Underlying Policy Assumptions": "Although they sometimes harm competition, mergers generally play an important role in a free enterprise economy. They can penalize ineffective management and facilitate the efficient flow of investment capital and the redeployment of existing productive assets."[28] The policy expressed clearly deemphasizes a corporate merger's effects on competition in product and service markets. Neither does the section reflect the preference for internal growth, the compromise on corporate bigness, expressed in the 1950 Celler-Kefauver amendment to the Clayton Act. Stressed instead are the virtues of mergers for efficiency in financial markets and for rivalry in markets for efficient management. Corporations are understood according to recent financial theories of the firm, theories which portray corporate managers and potential managers as competing for shareholder loyalty and thus for the power to control corporate assets.

Antitrust's traditional concern with product markets has been replaced by the finance theory that legitimized Wall Street's takeover frenzy of the 1980s. Together with "contestability theory," this new vision of corporate governance has employed the principles of wealth maximization to empty antitrust of its normative content. This foundation for competition policy, a facsimile of *Lochner*'s constitutional freedom of contract, signifies a deferential attitude toward private enterprise. Productive rivalry is seen in the takeover wars between corporate management and raiders, between once and future sovereigns. Competition policy is understood as facilitating corporate takeovers to allow more efficient managers to control productive assets.

Thus have theoretical debates about competition policy shifted in the 1980s. In what remains of economic debate over antitrust policy, traditional economists research the claimed efficiency effects of mergers and question the tenets of "contestability theory." That dispute became more important during the Bush administration, which increased the level of antitrust enforcement. Moreover, state antitrust enforcers were not persuaded by the theory. If anything, they were convinced that increased state activity was necessary to make up for the federal agencies' neglect.[29] At the same time, traditional corporate law theorists, as well as policy makers in the states, were engaging in a passionate war of words and policy initiatives with those who espouse the financial theory of the firm. Before examining corporate law as the new site for struggles over competition policy, a brief look at "contestability theory" is in order.

The Theory of PluPerfect Competition: Contestable Markets

Contestability theory was stated with crystalline clarity early in Ronald Reagan's first term:

> A contestable market is one in which the positions of incumbents are easily contested by entrants. [It is a market] in which entry is completely free, from which exit is costless, in which entrants and incumbents compete on completely symmetric terms, and entry is not impeded by fear of retaliatory price alterations.

Like a perfectly competitive market, a contestable one appears in theory only. Despite the theory's severe differences from real-world markets, neoclassical price theorists, including both Carter and Reagan-Bush policy makers, formulated competition policies in light of this abstract, counterfactual model. For Chicago Schoolers and Reagan-Bush policy makers who inflated contestability theory into a full-blown ideology of unfettered competition, the beauty was that a more expansive theory would dispense with the need for actual competitors.[30]

Instead of actual competitors, there need only be potential ones. And they are everywhere—in the abstract. Thus, theorists could claim, even monopolies are disciplined by potential competitors.[31] Although they sound similar, contestability theory is nothing like the potential competition policies used in the 1960s to evaluate conglomerate mergers. Then, specific firms were identified as potential competitors and on that account prohibited from entering certain markets through merger. Their economic value lay in the perception of their potential entry. Now, potential competition in the abstract is assumed to exist without regard to particular potential competitors, who, in consequence, are free to enter any market through merger.

Visions of contestable markets depend upon conditions too extreme to describe actual markets. For example, the potential competitor must be poised to enter instantaneously, at a scale large enough to capture the market. By the same token, the entrant must be able to exit immediately, without any loss of investment. To make contestability claims about the real world, deregulation-minded theorists had to show that the ideal conditions were met—more or less. Rightly believing that locating actual markets with no barriers to entry would provide strong corroboration for their theory of contestable markets, Chicago Schoolers have devoted endless attention to the topic. Their general approach, however, has not been the traditional social-scientific, empirical investigation of real markets. Instead, they have sought, by abstract argument, to constrict the traditional definition of entry barriers.[32]

Although the traditional view of barriers to entry derives from the work of Harvard economist Joe Bain, the Chicago School relies on George Stigler's work. Bain and others who follow Chamberlin's oligopoly theory see concentrated industries and the higher prices they produce as the result of barriers to entry. What would prevent new entrants? The advantages of incumbents, which allow them to maintain prices above competitive levels. Such advantages may include economies of scale, product differentiation, vertical integration, patents, and other conditions deterring new entrants. All of these conditions are seen as barriers to entry. George Stigler, however, has taken a narrower view of what constitutes a true barrier to entry. Stigler has written that a barrier to entry is "a cost of producing . . . which must be borne by firms which seek to enter an industry but is not borne by firms already in the industry."[33] In this view, there are very few "true" barriers to entry. New entrants need only match the investment of incumbents in scale, technology, or advertising to compete effectively.

Stigler's narrower view has been influential: Courts and commentators are now more circumspect in analyzing entry barriers. For example, product differentiation through advertising is no longer seen as barring entry, but only as delaying it. Stigler's view, nonetheless, does raise some serious policy concerns. Perhaps most troubling is the distinction made between a barrier and a delay. As many of Stigler's disciples have made plain, the notion of delaying new rivals does not distinguish between short time periods of weeks or months and delays as long as decades. For instance, the formation of U.S. Steel some seventy-five years ago allowed a dominant firm to avoid robust competition for about fifty years, until foreign imports (though subject to import tariffs) began to offer cheap steel produced in some instances by more efficient technology and in others by lower priced labor.[34] Stigler's static view ignores the economically significant factor of time.

Furthermore, there have been fundamental criticisms that, if taken to their logical conclusion, refute Stigler's view in its entirety. Perhaps the most devastating criticism has come from economist Oliver Williamson, who argues persuasively that new entrants can face a barrier to entry in the form of higher costs of capital. In short, when new ventures present greater risks than established firms, financial markets will take the greater risk into account by charging more for venture capital. The risks are even greater when the new entrant is not an already large diversified firm or when the existing firm has a reputation for strategic pricing behavior. Williamson's criticism is devastating because it theoretically assumes what the Chicago School does: perfectly efficient markets, including capital markets. Even in theory, new ventures are now seen as facing barriers to entry. Moreover, if the counterfactual assumption of efficient capital markets is loosened, other barriers to entry arise.

Williamson's criticism, together with the severe conditions required for claims that markets have no true barriers to entry and thus that they are surrounded by potential competitors poised to "hit and run," seem to corroborate the obvious: Real-world markets do present barriers to entry. Contestability theory, the ground for much of the Chicago School's claims about competition policy (and for the Merger Guidelines since 1982), simply does not have descriptive value. In consequence, it has little to say about the workings of actual markets. The theory does, however, provide an attractive prescription—a vision of efficiency-seeking commercial actors in markets unfettered by government regulation. In consequence, both federal agency enforcement and court doctrine in the 1980s were strongly influenced by contestability theory—at least its core concept of (no) barriers to entry.

Corporations and Securities Law: The New Site for Commercial Competition Policy

Although these dazzling visions of free competition, unencumbered by the experience of actual markets, entered Reagan administration antitrust policy without public fanfare, they were nonetheless the subject of continuing debate and controversy during the takeover movement of the 1980s. Most debate was aired not in the traditional language of antitrust but in a new language of corporate theory. Alongside antitrust's decline, corporate theory emerged as the new site for struggle over competition policy and its relationship to private property rights.

As far back as the mid-nineteenth century, long before the appearance of Berle and Means's landmark study of corporations and private property rights, corporate law was the site for mediating between, on the one hand, individualism and its associated visions of the corporation as a "person" or an entity and, on the other hand, the material reality of corporations as associations of people joined as groups, as aggregations for commercial purposes.[35] For most of this century, policy makers have imagined the corporation as having a separate existence, at least in the sense that corporations are distinct "persons" or "firms" or "groups" functioning in commercial markets. Antitrust and corporate law, in a rough division of labor, have reflected the division between corporations and the markets they inhabit. As a general matter, antitrust has regulated intercorporate behavior, while corporate law has provided the rules for intracorporate activities. Antitrust has been understood in terms of competition policy, while corporate law has dealt with private property relations.[36]

But, since 1980, corporate theory has expanded into areas traditionally occupied by a more robust antitrust law, thereby providing new images of both inter- and intra-corporate relations. The process can be understood as a shift in levels—from the traditional understanding of corporations as inhabiting product and geographic markets to a new understanding of corporations as residing in financial markets. Following this "financial" theory of the firm, competition rhetoric entered corporate law with a vengeance. New notions of corporate competition have produced new metaphors, changing ways of thinking about relations between managers and shareholders and about boundaries between firms and markets. Like all economic metaphors, they can be understood as the product of recent experience and enduring habits of thought. In particular, they reflect the application of competition policy and private property logics to explain and, in some respects, to legitimate the tidal wave of corporate takeovers that engulfed the business sector.

Much as "contestability theory" informed antitrust's decline in the 1980s, so have price-theoretical visions of efficient capital markets and unfettered competition for corporate control inspired recent reconceptualizations of traditional corporate governance. Yet a spirited debate among those holding differing views persists. Indeed, there has been a divergence in views between federal and state policy makers, paralleling the divergence in antitrust enforcement. Many state policy makers have doubted the new theories—whether contestability in antitrust or finance theory in corporate governance.

Intercorporate Contestability: The Market for Corporate Control

The metaphor of a "market for corporate control" first appeared as an attempt to explain the logic of conglomerate mergers in the 1960s. In response to the prevailing view derived from antitrust policies against deconcentration, a new portrait of corporate managers was drawn: Relatively unconcerned with rivalry in markets for goods and services, corporate decision makers were really stock portfolio managers who were seeking to lower risk to stockholders by accumulating a diverse mixture of stock ownership in wholly owned subsidiaries. This financial theory of corporate management assumed a property-rights logic of maximizing shareholder return. The underlying rationale depended upon the belief that financial markets were "efficient" in processing information. Individuals, regardless of their own insights, could do no better than "the efficient market," because pricing patterns appeared as a "random walk." This random walk accurately reflected the correct valuation of all market information. Hence, second-guessing "the efficient market" was just that—guessing—and thus a losing strategy. Even extrapolating market trends was futile, given the market's appearance of randomness. In consequence, the best one could hope for was to approximate "the market" by investing in a diversified portfolio and holding onto it. Conglomerates were no more than diversified portfolios, producing two distinct benefits. Not only would returns on investment approximate the market, but financial markets would recognize the wisdom of management's strategy by charging less for the money conglomerates would need: Interest rates would be lower and stock prices for new issues would be higher.[37]

One implication of this reconceptualization was that conglomerates reflect positive financial innovation rather than anticompetitive danger. Antitrust policy makers would soon lose interest in conglomerate mergers. Thereafter, concerns about corporate concentration in general fell by the wayside. By the takeover movement in the 1980s, oligopoly theory's structuralist concerns about market power had given way to a revival of price theory, bolstered by the view that commercial markets, regardless of concentration levels, were contestable. Federal antitrust enforcement agencies were inclined to see takeovers as benign—whether U.S. Steel's acquisition of Marathon Oil or mergers between two oil companies such as Texaco and Getty.

Price theorists were appropriating the financial theory of the firm to revise the image of a market for corporate control comporting with their belief in contestable markets: Corporate raiders were "financial entrepreneurs," seeking to wrest control of large corporations from slumbering management by purchasing stock on the open market. They claimed they could manage corporate assets more efficiently than current managers. Typically, some combination of the target corporation's cash, assets sold off for cash, and high-interest "junk" bonds ultimately financed most hostile takeovers. Stock prices soared on rumors of impending takeovers. Current stockholders gained by selling or exchanging at the inflated price—at the "market" price, which by definition "correctly" anticipated new and efficient management.[38]

Now, it was argued, corporate managers no longer enjoyed sovereign control. They were disciplined, constrained to deploy strategies approved by those in capital markets. If a manager's investment strategies were unacceptable, financial entrepreneurs would take over the corporation and hire better managers. It was J. P. Morgan's successors who sat in the seats of power, overseeing pale impressions of John D. Rockefeller and Henry Ford. Captains of industry had devolved into mere employees serving at the will of investment bankers and advisors. At the same time, the new Morgans were portrayed not as autocrats but as representatives elected by stockholders who voted with their shares. Although price theorists characterized the rivalry in market terms and thus as a form of economic competition, the rhetoric suggested a sort of economic democracy, usually with two management teams (like two political parties) suing for the trust of stockholder and investment banker constituencies. Occasionally, third-party candidates would appear on the investment horizon, sometimes beckoned as "white knights." The icon for the decade was H. Ross Perot, the 1980s billionaire who mounted a third-party campaign in the 1992 presidential election—H. Ross Perot, that postmodernist, high-tech cross of Harry Truman and Daddy Warbucks, that emblem of ambivalence toward large corporate enterprise, that embodiment of the dilemma of free competition.

Everyone agreed that corporate takeovers produced side-effects reaching far beyond shareholders and senior managers. There were employee layoffs and plant closings, draining the pecuniary lifeblood out of localities and regions. "Junk bond" financing imposed daunting debt loads, taking funds away from research and development and other productive activities, and sometimes throwing the newly acquired corporations into bankruptcy. At the same time, whether successful or not, corporate raiders usually walked off with hundreds of millions of dollars. Investment bankers, accountants, lawyers, public relations firms, and others in the typical dealmaker's entourage received enormous fees, matched by the "golden parachutes" given to deposed managers. Even unsuccessful assaults produced similar effects. In short, these takeover battles were not simple two-party sales contracts without significant transaction costs or third-party effects.

The intense debate centered on third-party effects, whose significance could not be denied—either practically or theoretically. As for the practical consequences, price theorists and their apprentices pointed to the tremendous wealth produced. For example, law professor David Ruder, later chairman of the Securities and Exchange Commission, testified before Congress that the benefits to stockholders outweighed job losses and other disruptions to local communities. Moreover, even billion-dollar fees to promoters and their helpers were a small percentage of the wealth produced for stockholders. This wealth-maximizing view of efficiency was expressed in price-theoretical scholarship as well.[39]

Responses were widespread, variously taking the forms of empirical studies, ethical criticism, and antitakeover legislation in the several states. Some responses pointed to the opportunity costs of expending funds on takeovers rather than on new plants, exploration, or research and development. Others simply refused to balance job losses and community disruptions on a scale calibrated only in dollars gained and lost. Still others pointed to the typically disappointing performance of postacquisition firms as well as the minor changes in management that often ensued. A number of states enacted antitakeover statutes. Some states (North Carolina, for example) have explicitly recognized a wide range of third-party effects as the predicate for regulating corporate takeovers. Others—Wisconsin, for example—have defined more broadly "the best interests of the corporation" to include not only shareholders but also "employees, suppliers, and customers of the corporation, and communities. . . ." Even in the bastion of corporate influence, the Delaware supreme court defined "the corporate enterprise" to include nonstockholder interests.[40] Among Reaganite policy makers and their intellectual antecedents, however, competition policy at the federal level entailed the lowering of barriers in the "market for corporate control," the unleashing of financial entrepreneurs to seek out and destroy corporate inefficiency.

Intracorporate Contestability: Nexus of Contracts Theory

There emerged a new view of the corporation itself, a view that duplicated the deregulatory implications of modeling corporate activity within a "market for corporate control." Since the early 1980s, Chicago Schoolers have developed an alternative to the traditional managerialist view of the corporation, the view that managers hold a special place in the corporation not only because of their entrepreneurial expertise but also because they are bound by legal duty and corporate theory to act as agents for corporate ownership, for shareholders. The new theory presents the corporation in radically different terms—as a bundle of contracts essentially indistinguishable from other market transactions.[41] Inspired by Ronald Coase's "Nature of the Firm" (1937), derived from neoclassical price theory, and shaped by finance theory, this "nexus of contracts" metaphor for corporations explodes the boundary between firm and market.

In some respects, the view is an old one: Corporations are seen as aggregates rather than entities. What's new is that the logic ultimately points to a molecular disaggregation, a nuclear fission of identifiable interests. Managers, like other employees, become nothing more than an input factor. Shareholders are similarly abstracted as providers of capital. Yet the contractarian view is at least as old as Chief Justice John Marshall's opinion in *The Trustees of Dartmouth College* (1819), which characterized the corporate charter as a contractual association of individuals.[42]

Recall that Ronald Coase analyzed the firm as a bundle of contracts managed by a cost-minimizing entrepreneur whose logic was binary: His choices were either to internalize a function (thereby increasing the size of the firm) or to externalize it by purchasing the input on the open market. The implication was that corporate management exercised a special entrepreneurial skill whose efficiency-seeking calculus would only be restrained by government regulators. Management decisions were better left to those who must answer to the logic of private property rights.

Nexus of contract theory erased the line between firm and market assumed both by Coase and by traditional corporate theorists. When viewed as simply one strand in a "nexus of contracts," corporate managers suddenly looked like help hired to maximize return on investment. Moreover, firms were no longer imagined as participants in particular commercial markets for goods and services. Rather, they were re-presented as floating bundles of contractual relations seeking opportunities for more profit. Pointing to a "corporation" in a market was seeing a momentary eddy in the stream of commerce.

The U.S. Steel Company's life cycle can stand as an historical exemplar. Formed in 1901 by J. Pierpont Morgan to dominate the steel industry, U.S. Steel was the corporate consolidation of 170 steel companies. Later, to maintain its power in the steel industry, U.S. Steel purchased both suppliers and customers—not only railroads, iron mines, and coal companies, but also steel fabricators. Whether lobbying Congress for import tariffs or seeking to keep new technology from its domestic rivals, U.S. Steel's corporate self-image was that of a steel company, the biggest steel company. Ultimately, its strategies, devoid of investment in new technology, became clear. By the 1980s, U.S. Steel no longer saw itself as a steel company, having shut down numerous plants and fired thousands of employees. Between 1982 and 1986, it acquired three oil companies, the largest a $6 billion purchase of Marathon Oil.[43] Indeed, in 1982, U.S Steel had already changed its name to USX—a proper name for a firm understood as a nexus of contracts, a firm prepared to answer to "the efficient capital market," the abstracted successor to J. P. Morgan.

In drawing an idealized, ahistorical portrait of contractual exchange, the "nexus of contracts" view of corporations reflects its *Lochner*ian heritage as well as its price theoretical legacy. It is idealized in the sense that the neoclassical view presents exchange as occurring between two roughly equal parties, each with other attractive opportunities. That is, markets are presumed to be perfectly contestable. The extent of unequal bargaining power and the impact of corporate hierarchies are both ignored. The view is ahistorical in two respects. First, the exchanges are viewed outside of time, as if intracorporate transactions are isolated events devoid of reliance on prior dealings, empty of past relations. But relations among corporate constituencies are actually less like ordering from a mail-order catalogue or buying gasoline along an interstate highway during a cross-country trip than like dealing with one's plumber, ex-spouse, or astrologer. Second, the view is ahistorical insofar as it depends upon an extremely narrow view of the common law of contracts, which is, after all, the ground that remains after the edifice of "regulation" is razed. Within the confines of a "bargain" theory of contracts, the common law has been both more capacious and less coherent than the neoclassical view allows.

Even within the category of "bargain contracts," numerous unexamined possibilities emerge. If a corporation is understood as a bundle of bargain contracts, why not, for example, give voice to any party to any contract negotiated with corporate management? Why privilege the input factor called "stockholders," rather than management, or employees, or local taxpayers who typically subsidize corporations? Why not, moreover, evaluate the adequacy of consideration—the relative value of the promises exchanged? What of the expectations developed during a series of employment contracts? Although taking such questions seriously conflicts with an abstracted, ahistorical view of contract, they permeate the traditional common law's "bargain" theory of contract.[44]

Like any general theory, "nexus of contracts" is open not only to internal stress analysis but also to external critique. Most obviously, in addition to the "bargain" theory, traditional contract doctrine has included other theories, which often conflict with it.[45] Indeed, they have been applied in just those situations in which there is no bargain, in which a judicially expressed sense of fairness has called for protecting an injured party's interests. Thus, for example, promises have been enforced even without a contractual exchange, simply to protect reasonable reliance on promises. Moreover, the ancient common-law writ of *quantum meruit*, later known in equity as restitution, and more recently called a "contract implied in law," allows recovery in the absence of a promise, in the name of justice. Neither of these traditional theories of contract requires a bargain. Both seek to account for a world more complex than the abstract, ahistorical view supporting the "nexus of contracts" metaphor for contracts.

Common-law doctrines of contractual exchange have painted a more subtle picture of commercial transactions and, even more broadly, of cultural exchange. Each doctrine, after all, is an application of selected social norms to concrete cases. The view of corporations and markets as a series of isolated bargains presents only one aspect of the common law's multifaceted figure of commercial and cultural exchange. A nexus of contracts theory of intracorporate rivalry threatens to dissolve the very notion of a corporation—for good or for ill—just as the theory of contestable markets threatens to disintegrate the very idea of a market. The consequence, ultimately, would be a Hobbesian vision of individuals whose connections to others, and thus to collectivities, are adversarial, episodic, and economically self-interested. Traditional notions of community and commitment would fall out of the rhetoric and the imaginative structure.

The Marketplace of Ideas: Property Rights and the Problem of Equality

The new corporate law portrayed commercial exchange as fundamentally financial in nature: What we do or buy or sell ultimately owes its value to the well-informed decisions made every day in financial markets. The market for corporate control reflects commercial virtue of the highest order—competition motivated by the desire to squeeze the last penny of efficiency out of productive enterprise. Markets for goods and services, as a matter of economic logic, fall into line. At every level, commercial markets and thus the corporate bundles of contracts within them are contestable, so long as they are free of the corrupting influence of politics.

With its ideological inversion of the Carter years' concern about the corrupting influence of commerce, this Reagan-era credo of virtuous commerce met its match in the marketplace of ideas. Legislation, both congressional and state, sought to limit the advantages of wealth in political transactions. It is no surprise, in our "information age," that these opposing attitudes toward commerce, these conflicting visions of virtue and corruption, were adjudicated in the Supreme Court, whose First Amendment speech jurisprudence is, after all, the last word in the marketplace of ideas.

According to promoters of the new corporate law, commercial competition is a perpetual motion machine that runs on its own inexhaustible supply of energy—information. Whether stock prices, quarterly earnings, industry trends, inflation indices, or world currency exchange rates, self-correcting markets both produce and consume information and depend upon its interpretation and manipulation. Overlapping these commercial markets is a grid of informational channels, some networked and others not, comprising today's "marketplace of ideas." But this uneven grid, convoluted and turned back on itself, here spiraling into the horizon and there stopping without warning, this postmodernist institution of intersecting planes, of overlapping logics, is a cultural space, not just the economic or political marketplace Holmes imagined. Here are crossings of literary and scientific discourse, product advertising and public referenda, stock prices and debate over reproductive choice, union handbilling and corporate bond offerings, the Christian Broadcasting Network and *Hustler* magazine.[46]

In our "information age," where competition means mass product advertising, televised political debates, endlessly repackaged talk-show telecasts of the tediously perverse, and computerized access to stock markets, as well as handbilling, union picketing, and precinct organization, what sense can be made of legal doctrine founded in Holmes' *Lochner*ian metaphor—the "marketplace of ideas"?[47] At a time when great wealth produces the media exposure needed to reach the masses (two recent examples being Budweiser beer and Ross Perot), should competition in this metaphorical marketplace be regulated to limit individual and corporate property rights to purchase the means to amplify voice? Or to ensure access? Should commercial practices of product advertising and brand identification, practices seeking corporate control in the marketplace of ideas, be subject to majoritarian restraint when the ideas are political and the products are legislation or legislators?

Although federal deregulation of commercial behavior—whether antitrust or environmental law—reflected the corporatist ideology that carried Republicans Reagan and Bush into the White House, the Supreme Court's speech jurisprudence was less sure, more troubled by the implications of substantive inequality in the marketplace of ideas. The rhetoric of "corruption" used to express these concerns had two sources. First of all, there were the majoritarian sentiments persistently seen in the various restraints contested before the Court. Whether federal regulation of political action committees or state supervision of public utilities, barriers were raised to staunch what was seen as the polluting flow of wealth into the political common. Second, the 1980s discourse of First Amendment speech consisted of the classical rhetoric of individual rights—in this instance, freedom of speech. Arguments about contestable marketplaces of ideas were nowhere to be found. Neither did speech jurisprudence or scholarship portray corporations, whether profit or nonprofit, as efficient bundles of bargain contracts. In this marketplace, free exchange meant something different. It meant, in the best of all possible worlds, exchange free of charge, access to anyone who wished to participate in the give and take of ideas and arguments. At the very least, it meant a commitment to individual freedom of speech.

In the 1980s jurisprudence of First Amendment speech, the classical liberal rhetoric of individual rights ran head on into Jeffersonian concerns about commercial corruption. As a consequence, the decade's unifying image of a "free market" and the dominant agenda of "corporate control" assumed sharply different forms when market exchange involved ideas rather than corporate securities. The mechanism of "corporate control," which was imagined as the market-based *solution* to commercial problems of inefficiency, was associated with the political *corruption* that required legislatures to limit corporate spending in the marketplace of ideas. It was the Jeffersonian or Brandeisian rhetoric of menacing corporate power that expressed concerns about the corrosive effects of wealth, of unequal voice, in the marketplace of ideas, especially when the ideas were political. The 1980s response to Jeffersonian fears of corruption took the rhetorical form associated with Justice Sutherland and the Four Horsemen—their freedom of contract jurisprudence, with its commitment to formal equality—that today appears as a *Lochner*ian freedom of speech.[48]

Recent speech doctrine has raised again the dilemma of free competition by posing the question, "From what tyranny do we want to free competition?" For some on the Court, tyranny in the marketplace of ideas meant the exercise of private economic power by corporations and associations to dominate exchanges involving speech. For others on the Court, tyranny meant the exercise of political power by government to regulate speech. In the marketplace of ideas, an intractable problem of inequality produced Court factions with conflicting attitudes toward the corrosive effects of wealth. In consequence, shifting factional allegiances produced wavering speech doctrine.

Disputes underlying the Court's speech cases raised two fundamental questions about equal access, both involving the rights of private property holders. One group of disputes took the form of a conflict between property rights and individual liberty—here, freedom of speech: Under what circumstances can someone exclude public discourse from privately owned property—whether a shopping mall or a utility company's billing envelope? The second cluster of disputes displayed a tension between property rights and equality—here, unequal access to the marketplace of ideas: To what extent can political institutions limit the advantages of private property in public discourse—particularly by regulating the recent phenomenon of political action committees?

In the first collection of speech cases, the Court understood itself as trying to accommodate private property rights and public concerns about speech acts, concerns that arose within three different regulatory frameworks. Writing for a unanimous Court in *Pruneyard Shopping Center v. Robins* (1980), Justice Rehnquist affirmed that the California constitution, as interpreted by the California's highest court, could extend speech rights and constrict private property rights without offending the First and Fourteenth Amendments of the federal Constitution. In short, the public right to speak and petition trumped the mall owners' speech and property rights. Although the Court recognized that the right to exclude others is "an essential stick in the bundle of property rights," it is "the several states [that are] . . . possessed of residual authority . . . to define 'property' in the first instance." Although this formulation seems radically state's rights-ist, it is far less deferential to majoritarian sentiments than it first appears. Rehnquist states elsewhere that the state, "in the exercise of its police power, may adopt reasonable restrictions on private property so long as the restrictions do not amount to a taking without just compensation or contravene any other federal constitutional provision."[49] This formulation puts state constitutional provisions into the balancing jurisprudence applied to any regulatory initiative over the last century—state police power weighed against private property rights. In consequence, the state can extend access to shopping malls in the public interest—here, the interest in free speech—to the same extent that it can regulate other economic enterprises, such as electric utility companies or bakeries. The public interests in free speech and petitioning government were neither more nor less important in the Court's constitutional scheme for protecting private property rights.

Despite earlier cases, particularly the *Lloyd* decision (1972) allowing shopping mall owners to exclude handbilling, the Court's traditional approach invited the several states to shift the balance between individual liberty of speech and private property rights. Or so it appeared at the time. Six years later, however, now-Chief Justice Rehnquist found himself dissenting in another case involving the State of California's regulation of access to a site situated both in the private domain of property and the public marketplace of ideas. In *Pacific Gas & Electric* (1986), Justice Lewis Powell, writing for a shifting majority, concluded that the Public Utility Commission could not compel the regulated monopoly to include with its billing statement materials written by a consumer-advocacy group. The regulation was outlawed despite legislation that defined the extra envelope space as public space belonging to customers—an ingenious application of Rehnquist's rationale in *Pruneyard*. In short, the State could not appropriate the extra envelope space to serve as a "commons" for public discourse.[50]

The Court's prohibition against compelling access to the extra envelope space did not turn explicitly on the public or private nature of the space. Indeed, the distinction was characterized as entirely irrelevant. Rather, compelling access was seen as transgressing First Amendment concerns about the perceived impact on the corporation's speech rights: If Pacific Gas & Electric were compelled to allow access, the Court maintained, it would be obliged to respond to speech inconsistent with corporate positions on matters of public concern. The speech right to remain silent would be violated. But despite the Court's assertion that the opinion's logic is independent of the public or private nature of the speech space, it actually depends upon the assumption that the space at issue is to be treated as private property. If the extra envelope space were imagined as a commons, then no one would be compelled to respond because no one is personally identified with a commons. If a compulsion to respond were generally associated with public spaces, then no speech would be permitted on any commons. To the contrary, only when the space is *private* property does the possibility arise that the property owner's mere permission to speak reflects more than disinterested silence. Only an invitation to speak on *private* property can insinuate the property owner's acceptance or agreement with the speech.[51]

As we have seen in the first pair of regulatory frameworks, the Court balanced speech and private property rights, rights derived from both federal and state sources. In *Pruneyard* (1980), the Court imagined state speech rights as trumping state property rights. In *Pacific Gas & Electric* (1986), however, the Court's logic depended upon the view that constitutionally protected common-law property rights (in conflict with explicit state legislation) trumped federal speech rights, as they have since *Lloyd* (1972). Such questions about excluding public discourse from private property also arose within a third regulatory framework—under the National Labor Relations Act. Two recent labor decisions reflect changes consistent not only with the Court's guardianship of private property rights but also with the decade's agenda of promoting corporate control.

Both cases involved handbilling by union members outside shopping malls. Both involved claims of unfair labor practices under the NLRA. In *DeBartolo Corp.* (1988), the Court affirmed the Labor Board's finding that distributing leaflets in the parking lot outside the mall was not an unfair labor practice. Writing for a unanimous Court, Justice White addressed a First Amendment concern beyond the statute. When the union engages in handbilling rather than picketing, when the purpose is persuasion rather than intimidation, White declared, then the question is one of speech rather than conduct. Whatever the outcome under the NLRA, White seemed to be saying, handbilling is a First Amendment right that is more important than the private property right to exclude speakers from the parking lot of a shopping mall.[52]

Four years and four Reagan–Bush appointees later, Justice Clarence Thomas would write for a divided Court in *Lechmere, Inc.* (1992) that union "organizers cannot claim even a limited right of access to a nonconsenting employer's property" unless employees were "otherwise inaccessible." The opinion was startling as much in its silence as in its tone. First of all, the tone: In reversing the Circuit Court as well as a Reaganized NLRB, Thomas declared that not only barring union organizers from distributing handbills but also attempting to remove them from "public property" was a fair labor practice. The possibility of *employer*-provoked violence, certainly a statutory and public concern, was ignored. Now, the silence: The First Amendment rights rhetoric adopted in Justice White's *DeBartolo Corp.* opinion for a unanimous Court was nowhere to be found. For Thomas and for dissenting Justice White as well, the case involved a balancing of private property rights and a statutory entitlement to fair labor practices.[53] Much like the labor opinions written before the New Deal, this one did not even consider First Amendment speech to be an issue.

The recent Court's primary concern for the welfare of private property right-holders is consistent with the Reagan era's ideological commitment to corporate control—here, vis-à-vis labor. Workers were ultimately removed from both the public and private spheres. They had no private rights insofar as they were excluded from the kind of interest-organizing strategies that managers and shareholders undertook as parties to a corporate nexus of contracts, even though their contractual relationships were often of longer duration than that of their managers. They were denied First Amendment protection in their most useful public forum as well—the shopping malls and parking lots adjacent to their employers. *Lechmere, Inc.*, moreover, is part of a general expansion of property rights at the expense of individual freedom of speech protected under the First Amendment. This movement can also be seen in the realm of intellectual property rights, in copyright law particularly, where it has been described as "an ever-increasing array of new or reconstructed property theories . . . cannibalizing speech values at the margin."[54]

Questions of property rights, First Amendment speech, and access also arose in a second cluster of cases, primarily involving the regulation of political action committees (PACs)—regulation both state and federal. Political action committees are private, not-for-profit organizations whose agenda is ideological and whose sources for funds are contributions by individuals, for-profit organizations (including corporations), and other not-for-profit organizations (including other PACs). Here the disputes were not over access to arguably private space or information. Rather, they erupted over unequal access to the public "marketplace of ideas," unequal access resulting from disproportionate financial resources to amplify voice, to buy space from media corporations who do not own but who do control most of the marketplace.

The Court's rhetorical strategy for dealing with the problem of inequality derived from the premise that commercial and political transactions must be treated differently, although they are found in the same metaphorical marketplace of ideas. In commercial transactions outside the marketplace of ideas, inequality was ignored: Whether corporate mergers or labor handbilling at shopping malls, property rights were not limited by concerns about economic power.[55] The consequence, of course, was a marketplace of ideas that reflected those inequalities. What to do? The Court would draw finer and finer lines between commercial and political precincts, lines heeding the ideological demand to protect political virtue from the threat of commercial corruption.

In *Central Hudson Gas & Electric* (1980), the Court reaffirmed its recent extension of First Amendment protection to commercial advertising, over an extended dissent by Justice Rehnquist. Although the remaining Justices concurred in the judgment that the Public Service Commission of New York could not restrain the regulated monopoly from all promotional advertising, only a bare majority joined Justice Powell's opinion. A solitary Rehnquist offered several reasons for insisting that the PSC could impose the ban. Of those reasons, the most subversive was the argument that commercial speech and commercial conduct were indistinguishable. That is, the agency's prohibition was "akin to an economic regulation to which virtually complete deference should be accorded." The PSC argued that its ban on promotional advertising was part of a larger energy conservation effort. Certainly, Rehnquist maintained, "if the Public Service Commission had chosen to raise the price . . . or to restrict its production," the decisions would be upheld. Banning promotional advertising is "virtually indistinguishable." In short, Rehnquist recognized the functional economic identity of advertising and other commercial conduct—understood by its practitioners long before Edward Chamberlin formalized the understanding in *The Theory of Monopolistic Competition* (1932).[56]

No fellow Justice, however, was willing to acknowledge Rehnquist's point. The danger lurking in the Court's constitutionalization of commercial speech, given the economic reality that advertising is the predominant form of commercial competition, was a collapse of the traditional distinction between trade and ideas and, ultimately, between economic and political endeavor. Even short of that collapse, the implications were troubling. As a practical matter, the remaining distinction between commercial and political speech would wither away. In consequence, First Amendment protection of commercial advertising as freedom of speech would "resurrect the discredited [liberty of contract] doctrine of cases such as *Lochner*" and thus the chief form of commercial competition would be free from state regulation. Rehnquist found that prospect unacceptable because he found "no reason for believing that the marketplace of ideas is free from market imperfections any more than there is to believe that the invisible hand will always lead to optimum economic decisions in the commercial market."[57]

In *Pacific Gas & Electric* (1986), as we have already seen, the Court overturned another Public Service Commission regulation requiring a regulated public utility monopoly to include materials written by a consumer group in its monthly billing statement, accompanied, presumably, by its own promotional advertising. A decade later, in *City of Cincinnati* (1992), the Court would strike down, under the First Amendment, a city ordinance prohibiting racks holding commercial handbills on public property but not those containing newspapers.[58] Thus, elevating sales advertising to the status of commercial speech, following the logically prior differentiation between commercial speech and conduct, was threatening the kind of corporatist, *Lochner*ian regime of unfettered commerce envisioned in Rehnquist's *Central Hudson* dissent.

In the neighboring precinct of political speech, it was already clear that corporations enjoyed First Amendment protection. The Court, again in 1980, affirmed the corporate speech jurisprudence of *Buckley* (1976) and *Bellotti* (1978): The New York Public Service Commission could not ban Con Edison's political advertising, even more surely than it could not prohibit Central Hudson's promotional advertising.[59] So it was that commercial enterprise, with its genius for corrupting political discourse, was incorporated into the marketplace of ideas.

This genius did not, however, go entirely unrecognized. Campaign finance reform legislation, both congressional and state, provoked the Court again and again to draw lines zoning the realm of political speech, lines intended to segregate commercial influence from political enterprise. In *Federal Election Commission v. Massachusetts Citizens for Life (MCFL)* (1986), Justice Brennan wrote for a divided Court that the government could regulate disbursements of commercial corporations but not those of nonprofit ideological entities. The distinction was based upon the observation that "[t]he resources in the treasury of a business corporation . . . are not an indication of popular support for the corporation's political ideas." Thus, the use of such funds constitutes an "unfair deployment of wealth for political purposes," which threatens "the integrity of the marketplace of political ideas."[60]

In *Austin v. Michigan Chamber of Commerce* (1990), Justice Thurgood Marshall interposed two more boundaries between corrupting commercial endeavor and corruptible political speech. First, even though the Chamber of Commerce was a nonprofit organization, it was still commercial and thus subject to regulation regarding its political expenditures, Marshall concluded, because most of its funds were contributed by commercial corporations. *MCFL* was cited for "the legitimacy of Congress' concern that organizations that mass great wealth in the economic marketplace not gain unfair advantage in the political marketplace." The Chamber of Commerce was treated as an agent for commercial influence. In addition to the new category of not-for-profit commercial enterprise, Marshall observed that media corporations and the ideas they produced, although for-profit, were distinguishable from General Motors and the goods it produced.[61] In short, the *New York Times* or the National Broadcasting Company were mirror-image reversals of the Chamber of Commerce: Although for-profit, they were political enterprises and thus worthy of impenetrable First Amendment armor.

Amid these high-minded republicanist concerns expressed about corruption and the line-drawing they prompted, what the *Austin* Court approved was merely the segregation of corporate contributions into separate accounts —a faint-hearted response to the commercial threat of political corruption. There was no ban on corporate political spending. Indeed, such legislation would violate the Court's marketplace logic for the First Amendment. Severely limited by the Court's view of spending as speech, by its equation of financial contribution with political commitment, legislation largely took the trivial form of accounting principles for segregating corporate contributions to PACs. The disparity between a republicanist rhetoric of corrupting corporate wealth and the accounting practice of separating corporate contributions was symptomatic of an underlying ideological constraint limiting regulation of the political marketplace, limiting political oversight of the uses of "immense aggregations of wealth," whether corporate or individual in form. The underlying constraint was reflected in two litigated questions regarding equality in the political marketplace of ideas.

First of all, should individuals and corporations enjoy equal First Amendment protection in their political speech (expenditures)? The Court was unsure, and thus doctrine exhibited violent swings. In a series of four cases, the Court flipped back and forth, beginning with the *Bellotti* (1978) opinion's statement that First Amendment speech rights extended equally to corporations and individuals. In *FEC v. National Right to Work Committee* (1982), however, the Court explicitly permitted Congress to "treat[ ] unions, corporations, and similar organizations differently from individuals"—here, a not-for-profit ideological corporation—"to ensure that substantial aggregations of wealth amassed by the special advantages which go with the corporate form of organization should not be converted into political 'war chests'" But, four years later, in *Pacific Gas & Electric*, the Court reverted to its *Bellotti* rhetoric of equal rights for corporations. Then, in *Austin* (1990), the Court approved Michigan's regulatory scheme, Justice Marshall pointing to "the corrosive and distorting effects of immense aggregations of wealth that are accumulated with the help of the corporate form."[62]

But, in *Austin*, dissenting Justices Antonin Scalia and Anthony M. Kennedy let the ideological cat out of the bag. What, they asked, does a distinction between corporations and individuals have to do with concerns about the corrupting influence of wealth in the political marketplace of ideas? Regulating a struggling corporation but not a wealthy individual makes no sense. Doesn't the logic of corruption, they insisted, require legislation restricting the campaign expenditures of individuals as well as corporations?[63] Their questions were striking, for two reasons: First, because they made perfectly good sense about the corrupting influence of wealth, and second, because their underlying assumption, founded in well-settled Court doctrine, was the unconstitutionality of limiting anyone's expenditures in the marketplace of political ideas (that is, expenditures short of direct contributions to particular candidates).

Indeed, an unbroken line of opinions beginning at least as early as *Buckley* (1976) had already resolved the second question regarding equality by condemning legislative limits on expenditures: "The concept that government may restrict the speech of some elements of our society in order to enhance the relative voice of others is wholly foreign to the First Amendment." Spending limits to equalize speech were held unconstitutional, as were other measures seeking to equalize voice. Even in *Austin* (1990), which recognized the systemic threat of corruption carried by wealth into the political marketplace of ideas (and thus the cost of unequal voice), Justice Marshall was careful to point out that the Michigan statute did not seek "to equalize the relative influence of speakers on elections." Dissenting Justice Scalia agreed on the unconstitutionality of equalizing voice, adding, however, language from *Buckley* that the First Amendment "was designed . . . to assure *unfettered* interchange of ideas" among all persons, whether natural or corporate.[64]

Thus, despite their disagreement, Marshall and Scalia did concur on *Buckley*'s unquestioned baseline: In the political marketplace of ideas, Congress cannot limit political expenditures, except direct contributions to particular candidates, where the appearance of corruption is inescapable. Even though everyone conceded the systemic threat of "great wealth . . . in the political marketplace," no one would approve majoritarian regulation of expenditures to equalize access, or at least to limit unequal voice, in the political marketplace.

On one side of the divide stood the Court majority, with its commitment to "one person, one vote," translated into a marketplace ethic of "one dollar, one idea." Their concerns about wealth were expressed in the republicanist rhetoric of anticommercialism. As a result, the "corporate form" with its corrupting "war chest" became the imaginative location, the linguistic placeholder for concerns about wealth. But *individual* war chests were different.

They were repositories for private property rights whose exercise in the political marketplace of ideas enabled the expression of one person, and thus represented the most sacred of First Amendment rights. The only limit on individual expression (spending) was the danger of corruption associated with direct contributions to particular political candidates (even though the distinction between direct contribution and other expenditures was inconsistent with the recognition that wealth has systemic effects).

On the other side of the divide stood dissenting Justices Scalia and Kennedy, with the same commitment to "one person, one vote," translated into the same marketplace ethic of "one dollar, one idea." They did not, however, share the majority's republicanist concerns about commercial corruption of politics. If anything, they were more concerned about the threat of political majoritarianism. Whereas the Court majority understood free competition to mean political exchange free of commercial corruption, Scalia understood it to mean interchange of ideas unfettered by government restriction. He could criticize the majority's position as inconsistent not only with the First Amendment's libertarian logic of free speech but also with their own commitment to equality. Their conception of free competition, founded in the republicanist distrust of commercial endeavor, was an easy target in an era when individual wealth and corporate power are no longer tied so closely as they were in the Gilded Age. It was an easy target because individual wealth is a concern at once expressed in a somewhat dated rhetoric of republicanism and trapped in the popular metaphor of marketplace liberalism.

What are the alternatives? For those who agree with Justice Scalia, it is a return to the individual liberty celebrated in the marketplace liberal vision of unfettered competition. For those who agree with the Michigan legislature and the Congress that sought to regulate political campaign finance practices, it is a republicanist course of limiting the impact of commercial wealth on politics. More than twenty years ago, Justice Marshall wrote for a unanimous Court that "[t]here is an 'equality of status in the field of ideas,' and government must afford all points of view an opportunity to be heard."[65] In sum, what free competition means is an historical question captured in the rhetorical residues of republicanism and liberalism, which articulate two different visions of society—about the way it works and the way it should.

These visions represent two complex sets of assumptions and beliefs about political economy—that is, about relations between public interests and private property rights, about the value of individual liberty and the costs of inequality, and about economic enterprise in a democratic society. Competition policy in America houses our collective recollections of these political economic visions and accommodates the tensions between them by providing a rhetorical framework for expressing alternative strategies to reconcile material conditions and utopian aspirations, and for adjudicating fundamental disagreements over those strategies.

Concluding Thoughts: On the Limits of Competition Policy

As we have seen, the confines of competition policy during the last century have been capacious. Yet, there have been well-defined limits. Competition policy and its limits have been articulated in twin rhetorics of free competition, in two clusters of images and arguments expressing ethical commitments to liberty and equality. One rhetoric has reflected a primary commitment to individual liberty, to competition free of government power, in appeals to freedom of contract, wealth maximization, private property rights, or freedom of speech. The other rhetoric has reflected a primary commitment to rough equality, to competition free of excessive economic power, in appeals to fair competition, consumerism, majoritarianism, or Jeffersonian entrepreneurialism. Sometimes, one rhetoric has sought to appropriate the other's appeals—for example, to consumerism or freedom of speech. At other times, both rhetorics have incorporated parallel appeals—for example, to fair profits, efficiency, or cooperative enterprise. Although the appeals have shifted from time to time, what has remained constant is each competition rhetoric's primary ethical commitment—one to individual liberty and the other to rough equality.

Since the Sherman Act debates began in 1888, what sorts of relations between liberty and equality have emerged out of the twin rhetorics of free competition? Before the New Deal, a primary commitment to individual liberty was expressed, for the most part, in the traditional discourse of common-law private property rights, constitutional liberty, and classical economics. Since the later New Deal, the dominant metaphor for liberty has been economic. That is, calls for individual liberty have appealed to the economic imagery of free markets. Those expressing a primary commitment to rough equality have appealed first to a Jeffersonian vision of perfect competition, then to unsettling images of industrial concentration, and always to a sense of economic fairness as the consequence of limits imposed by political majorities on the practices of powerful commercial enterprises.

During the last century, these twin rhetorics of free competition have collided, intersected, and bypassed one another, in the historical process inspiring or justifying multiple competition policies. Despite such historical complexity, however, these rhetorical confrontations have produced only three distinct logics to serve as the connective tissue between politics and economics, between public and private spheres. Perhaps most familiar is the classical logic of two distinct spheres whose cherished separation was to be guarded as the basis of a free society. This logic has been carried forward in modern economics' separation of efficiency questions from those of wealth distribution. Given our sensibilities, the logic seems untenable for two reasons. First, the last century of America's history chronicles the indisputable experience of overlapping political and economic—public and private—domains. Second, the theory itself is unappealing insofar as we value the distinction between political and economic domains, in part because we believe that individual (private) success in the economic domain serves public interests and in part because we expect each domain to curb the excesses of the other. In short, we demand a certain amount of overlap.

The second historical logic that has appeared collapses the two spheres into one. That is, one loses its distinctiveness and simply disappears into the other. The economic sphere disappeared into its political counterpart, for example, in the arguments justifying the Hoover era's treatment of labor unions and in the *ALA Schechter Poultry* (1935) opinion's attitude toward the New Deal's National Industrial Recovery Act. In the last two decades, the political sphere has come to be identified as an economic domain—most zealously so under the influence of Chicago School economist George Stigler's market metaphor for government regulation and the Public Choice school that has reified Stigler's metaphor. Thus, the logic of unification produces one domain—whether political or economic—rather than the first logic's bipolar opposition. But the purity produced by the logic of unification comes at a high price: Lost in the collapse is one sphere's ethical principles and social goals. For example, equality may give way to liberty, as happened in the *Lochner* era, or equitable concerns may yield to wealth maximization, as called for by Posner, Bork, and other Chicago School acolytes; more concretely, consumers may pay higher prices as a result of information exchange managed by an industry trade association, or political handbilling may be prohibited from shopping malls because it interferes with the commercial ethos. In both theoretical and practical terms, competition policy comes to reflect only one rhetoric, one vision of society, untempered by its historical counterweight, because the unifying logic of collapsing domains either ignores ethical and teleological differences between economic and political realms or understands them as closed to negotiation.

There is a third logic of political economy that has emerged from free competition rhetoric, a logic that recognizes the value of distinct domains yet allows for some negotiation. The last century has produced numerous instances of a negotiated relationship between public and private, between political and economic spheres. For example, Justice Brandeis's opinion in *International News Service* (1918) defined property rights as a balancing of public and private interests. Some fifty years later, Congress sought to balance private property rights and political speech rights in campaign finance reform legislation. Although such balancing reflects a worthwhile logic of negotiation, it is limited insofar as the interests balanced are understood as incommensurable. That is, public and private domains, political and economic spheres, are treated as independently defined and formed.

Another more appealing notion of negotiation proceeds from the view that public and private domains, political and economic spheres, are more than menacing neighbors: They can be seen as two interdependent and mutually defining discourses, two clusters of images and commitments that both produce and limit one another. Indeed, the historical relationship between political and economic spheres has sometimes reflected such dialogical interaction. For example, treating liberty and equality as intertwined, Chief Justice Hughes, writing for the Court in *West Coast Hotel* (1937), folded the notion of substantive equality into liberty of contract jurisprudence and, in the process, altered the relationship between private commercial transactions and the public interest. In the early 1980s, the California legislature passed a statute consistent with a dialogical understanding of the public and private domains: The law sought to expand the room for public debate by defining extra space in a regulated utility's billing envelopes ("extra" meaning unused for commercial purposes) as a public forum for free speech. But the Supreme Court held the statute unconstitutional. As I discuss in chapter 6, Justice Powell's opinion was the incoherent product of a frozen property logic unable to comprehend the California legislature's negotiation of new borders between public and private domains.

Although the logic of negotiation, especially in its dialogical form, is inherently unstable, inherently the product of *ad hoc* settlements, its very instability represents its strength. Such treatment of economic and political affairs can open the rhetorical space necessary for competition policy to promote public deliberation, to sustain participatory government, while inspiring individual aspirations and economic enterprise. For competition policy to remain a durable good, it must reflect a dialogical sense of political economy. It is in that sense of interdependence between liberty and equality, between individual and collectivity, and, finally, between "the market" and "the state," that we find the continuing possibility of democratic politics and economic opportunity.

Notes

Introduction

1. Although the subjects of domestic competition policy and international trade policy have intertwined histories, rhetorics, and laws—from the Sherman Act debates, through the Webb-Pomerane Act of 1918, to the current view of commercial competition policy as primarily an international issue—this book examines only domestic competition policy, which is itself a project whose containment within a manuscript of manageable length has been challenge enough. Thus, I leave to another day questions of international trade policy.

I also want to say a word about endnote style conventions. As part of my effort to shorten the manuscript, I seldom use more than one note per paragraph. Thus, each note often includes more than one citation reference. Where a note includes multiple page references to one source, the order conforms with the order of citation in the main text. Where a note includes multiple sources, those separated by semicolons refer to the same textual subject matter. Those separated by periods refer to different subjects, all ordered to conform with their appearances in the main text. Where there is some ambiguity, I have included parenthetical cues.

2. This minimalist rendering is an accurate abstract of the majority and dissenting opinions published in the well-known *Northern Securities* case, 193 U.S. 197 (1904), which undid J. P. Morgan's armistice—a merger between warring railroad barons James Jerome Hill and Edward Henry Harriman.

3. Charles River Bridge v. Warren Bridge, 36 U.S. (11 Pet.) 420 (1837). Supreme Court historian Charles Warren has called the decision "one of the two great antitrust cases of the country's early national history." Henry F. Graff, *The Charles River Bridge Case, in* QUARRELS THAT HAVE SHAPED THE CONSTITUTION 84 (John A. Garraty ed. [1962] 1987). For a discussion, see MORTON J. HORWITZ, THE TRANSFORMATION OF AMERICAN LAW 137–39 (1977). Regarding Andrew Jackson's campaign against and veto of the bill to recharter the Bank of the United States, see generally BRAY HAMMOND, BANKS AND POLITICS IN AMERICA FROM THE REVOLUTION TO THE CIVIL WAR (1957); HARRY L. WATSON, LIBERTY AND POWER: THE POLITICS OF JACKSONIAN AMERICA (1990).

4. As a general matter, in any historical period, junctures of material circumstances and reigning ideologies, crossings of economic currents and political countercurrents, produced solutions to local problems whose rhetorical residues are still with us. Whether classical or civic republicanism, libertarianism or New Deal liberalism, these rhetorical residues provide familiar imaginative structures for trying to

make sense of new circumstances. Their historical roots define both their value and their limits. For example, classical republicanism emerged in a time of city-states, a time when "marketplace" meant physical locations for peaceful exchange, often seen as gift-giving. Classical liberalism arose as an emancipatory rhetoric in a time when monarchy embodied a unified power over both political and economic transactions. The limits reached in political ideology to some degree reflect radically changed historical conditions. Thus, for example, classical liberalism's exclusive concern with individual rights against the sovereign is inadequate to the task of evaluating commercial regulation when the sovereign is a majoritarian institution and the "individual" is a multinational corporation. The consequence is a contradiction of sorts: Unfettered commercial enterprise can produce the kind of oppression that inspired classical liberals' demands for individual rights. Yet it is the very limits encountered and contradictions produced within political ideologies, together with the frictions created by their intersections, that open up the rhetorical spaces needed for new formulations, new approaches to current problems.

5. I take up JOSEPH A. SCHUMPETER, CAPITALISM, SOCIALISM AND DEMOCRACY (1942) as well. My reading of Berle and Means diverges from the mainstream view, which holds that they were motivated by the belief that shareholder democracy would solve the problem of unfettered corporate management. I dispute that reading, and demonstrate that their solution was consistent with the early New Deal's vision of public regulation of the economic domain.

I say absolutely nothing about the Keynesian revolution, which can be understood, according to John Kennneth Galbraith and others, as a paradigm shift away from the view that economics cannot justify government "intervention" into markets to stimulate demand. With the death of (Jean-Baptiste) Say's Law, however, Franklin Roosevelt's economic policies became the stuff of macroeconomics—now an intellectually reputable pursuit. But government attempts to increase demand, particularly the New Deal's public funding of what we would today call "infrastructure," later produced its own neoclassical reflex—Milton Friedman's theories about monetary policy. See generally, JOHN KENNETH GALBRAITH, ECONOMICS IN PERSPECTIVE: A CRITICAL HISTORY (1987).

6. Justice William O. Douglas wrote that "[m]isrepresentations [are] condoned in the political arena." California Motor Trans. Co. v. Trucking Unlimited, 404 U.S. 508, 513 (1972).

7. As French theorist Michel Foucault has written, this approach "allows us to establish a historical knowledge of struggles." FOUCAULT, *Two Lectures, in* POWER/KNOWLEDGE 83 (1980) (discussing his use and abuse of Nietzsche's "genealogical" approach). In short, my methodology can be understood as a use and abuse of Foucault. *See generally* FRIEDRICH NIETZSCHE, THE USE AND ABUSE OF HISTORY (A. Collins trans. 2d ed. 1957); FOUCAULT, *Nietzsche, Genealogy, and History, in* LANGUAGE, COUNTER-MEMORY, PRACTICE: SELECTED ESSAYS 139–64 (D. Bouchard ed. 1977). *See also* KENNETH BURKE, ATTITUDES TOWARD HISTORY ([1937] 1984). For recent writings about rhetorical history, *see, e.g.,* Dominick LaCapra, *Canons and Their Discontents* 13 INTELL. HIST. NEWSL. 3, 12 (1991) ("dialogic readings"); JOYCE APPLEBY, LIBERALISM AND REPUBLICANISM IN THE HISTORICAL IMAGINATION, particularly at 30, 126–27, 289 (1992); Robert W. Gordon, *Critical Legal Histories,* 36 STAN. L. REV. 57 (1984); Dorothy Ross, *The Liberal Tradition Revisited and the Republican Tradition Addressed, in* NEW DIRECTIONS IN AMERICAN INTELLECTUAL HISTORY 116 (John Higham & Paul K. Conkin eds. 1979); David A. Hollinger, *Historians and the Discourse of Intellectuals, id.* at 42. My early inclination was to characterize the relationship between competition and property rights within

the narrower deconstructionist confines of logical contradiction rather than the broader rhetorical notions of tension and mediation. Cf. Rudolph J. R. Peritz, *The Predicament of Antitrust Jurisprudence: Price Discrimination and the Monopolization of Antitrust Argument*, 1984 DUKE L.J. 1205, 1278–81.

Chapter 1

1. Chapter 647, 26 Stat. 209 (1890) (codified as amended at 15 U.S.C. §§ 1–7 (1988)). Regarding the debates, see HANS THORELLI, THE FEDERAL ANTITRUST POLICY: ORIGINATION OF AN AMERICAN TRADITION (1955); William L. Letwin, *Congress and the Sherman Antitrust Law: 1887–1890*, 23 U. CHI. L. REV. 221 (1956); Richard Hofstadter, *What Happened to the Antitrust Movement? in* THE PARANOID STYLE IN AMERICAN POLITICS AND OTHER ESSAYS 188 (1965); Rudolph J. Peritz, *The "Rule of Reason" in Antitrust Law: Property Logic in Restraint of Competition*, 40 HASTINGS L.J. 285 (1989); David Millon, *The Sherman Act and the Balance Of Power*, 61 S. CAL. L. REV. 1219 (1988); Robert H. Lande, *Wealth Transfers as the Original and Primary Concern of Antitrust: The Efficiency Interpretation Challenged*, 34 HASTINGS L.J. 65 (1982); John Flynn, *Rethinking Sherman Act Section I Analysis: Three Proposals for Reducing the Chaos*, 49 ANTITRUST L.J. 1593 (1980); Eleanor Fox, *The Modernization of Antitrust: A New Equilibrium*, 66 CORNELL L. REV. 1140 (1981). I have found most useful for understanding the debates' historical context the following: EDWARD A. PURCELL, JR., LITIGATION AND INEQUALITY: FEDERAL DIVERSITY JURISDICTION IN INDUSTRIAL AMERICA, 1870–1958 (1992); PURCELL, THE CRISIS OF DEMOCRATIC THEORY: SCIENTIFIC NATURALISM AND THE PROBLEM OF VALUE (1973); DOROTHY ROSS, THE ORIGINS OF AMERICAN SOCIAL SCIENCE (1991); JOYCE APPLEBY, LIBERALISM AND REPUBLICANISM IN THE HISTORICAL IMAGINATION (1992); J.G.A. POCOCK, THE MACHIAVELLIAN MOMENT: FLORENTINE POLITICAL THOUGHT AND THE ATLANTIC REPUBLICAN TRADITION (1975); PETER NOVICK, THAT NOBLE DREAM: THE "OBJECTIVITY QUESTION" AND THE AMERICAN HISTORICAL PROFESSION (1988); HAYDEN WHITE, METAHISTORY: THE HISTORICAL IMAGINATION IN NINETEENTH-CENTURY EUROPE (1973); G. EDWARD WHITE, JUSTICE OLIVER WENDELL HOLMES: LAW AND THE INNER SELF (1993); WHITE, TORT LAW IN AMERICA: AN INTELLECTUAL HISTORY (1980); DAVID MONTGOMERY, CITIZEN WORKER: THE EXPERIENCE OF WORKERS IN THE UNITED STATES WITH DEMOCRACY & THE FREE MARKET DURING THE NINETEENTH CENTURY (1994); MONTGOMERY, BEYOND EQUALITY: LABOR AND RADICAL REPUBLICANS, 1862–1872 (1967); CHRISTOPHER L. TOMLINS, THE STATE AND THE UNIONS: LABOR RELATIONS, LAW, AND THE ORGANIZED LABOR MOVEMENT IN AMERICA, 1880–1960 (1985); WILLIAM E. FORBATH, LAW AND THE SHAPING OF THE AMERICAN LABOR MOVEMENT (1991); MORTON KELLER, REGULATING A NEW ECONOMY: PUBLIC POLICY AND ECONOMIC CHANGE IN AMERICA, 1900–1933 (1990); LAWRENCE M. FRIEDMAN, A HISTORY OF AMERICAN LAW (1973); ALFRED D. CHANDLER, JR., THE VISIBLE HAND: THE MANAGERIAL REVOLUTION IN AMERICAN BUSINESS (1977); GABRIEL KOLKO, THE TRIUMPH OF CONSERVATISM: A REINTERPRETATION OF AMERICAN HISTORY, 1900–1916 (1963); MARTIN J. SKLAR, THE CORPORATE RECONSTRUCTION OF AMERICAN CAPITALISM, 1890–1916: THE MARKET, THE LAW, AND POLITICS (1988); ARNOLD M. PAUL, CONSERVATIVE CRISIS AND THE RULE OF LAW: ATTITUDES OF BENCH AND BAR, 1887–1895 (1960); MORTON J. HORWITZ, THE TRANSFORMATION OF AMERICAN LAW, 1870–1960 (1992); HORWITZ, THE TRANSFORMATION OF AMERICAN LAW, 1780–1860 (1977); HOWARD GILLMAN, THE CONSTITUTION BESIEGED: THE RISE AND DEMISE OF LOCHNER ERA POLICE POWERS JURISPRUDENCE (1993); ROBERT WIEBE, THE SEARCH FOR ORDER, 1877–1920 (1967); ROBERT STEINFELD, THE INVENTION OF FREE LABOR: THE EMPLOYMENT RELATION IN ENGLISH AND AMERICAN LAW AND CULTURE, 1350–1870 (1992); WILLIAM E. NELSON, THE ROOTS OF AMERI-

CAN BUREAUCRACY (1982); ERIC FONER, FREE SOIL, FREE LABOR, FREE MEN: THE IDEOLOGY OF THE REPUBLICAN PARTY BEFORE THE CIVIL WAR (1980); KAREN ORREN, BELATED FEUDALISM: LABOR, THE LAW, AND LIBERAL DEVELOPMENT IN THE UNITED STATES (1991); J. WILLARD HURST, LAW AND SOCIAL ORDER IN THE UNITED STATES (1977); RICHARD HOFSTADTER, SOCIAL DARWINISM IN AMERICAN THOUGHT (1944); Cass, R. Sunstein, *Beyond the Republican Revival,* 97 YALE L.J. 1539 (1980); Sunstein, *Lochner's Legacy,* 1987 COLUM. L. REV. 873; James May, *Antitrust Practice and Procedure in the Formative Era: The Constitutional and Conceptual Reach of State Antitrust Law,* 1880–1918, U. PA. L. REV. 495 (1987); May, *Antitrust in the Formative Era: Political and Economic Theory in Constitutional and Antitrust Analysis,* 50 OHIO ST. L.J. 257 (1989); Duncan Kennedy, *Towards an Historical Understanding of Legal Consciousness: The Case of Classical Legal Thought, 1850–1940,* 3 RES. LAW & SOC. 3 (1980); Kennedy, *The Role of Economic Thought,* 34 AM. U. L. REV. 944 (1985); Michael L. Benedict, *Laissez-Faire and Liberty: A Re-Evaluation of the Meaning and Origins of Laissez-Faire Constitutionalism,* 3 LAW & HIST. REV. 293 (1985); Charles W. McCurdy, *Justice Field and the Jurisprudence of Government Relations: Some Parameters of Laissez-Faire Constitutionalism, 1863–1897,* 61 J. AM. HIST. 970 (1975); Stephen A. Siegel, *Understanding the Lochner Era: Lessons from the Controversy over Railroad and Utility Rate Regulation,* 70 VA. L. REV. 187 (1984); David M. Rabban, *The First Amendment in Its Forgotten Years,* 90 YALE L.J. 514 (1981); William E. Nelson, *The Impact of the Antislavery Movement upon Styles of Reasoning in Nineteenth-Century America,* 87 HARV. L. REV. 513 (1974); Harry N. Scheiber, *Property Law, Expropriation, and Resource Allocation by Government: The United States, 1789–1910,* 33 J. ECON. HIST. 232 (1973); Scheiber, *The Road to* Munn*: Eminent Domain and the Concept of Public Purpose in the State Courts, in* LAW IN AMERICAN HISTORY (Donald Fleming & Bernard Bailyn eds. 1971).

2. Samuel C.T. Dodd, Rockefeller's attorney, has been credited with devising the commercial trust and with convincing the New Jersey legislature to amend its incorporation statute to permit it. MATTHEW JOSEPHSON, THE ROBBER BARONS 277–78 (1934), citing Dodd, "Combinations, Their Uses and Abuses, with a History of the Standard Oil Trust" (1888) (presented to the New York legislature); Dodd, *The Present Legal Status of Trusts,* 7 HARV. L. REV. 157 (1893).

3. Justice Field, however, strenuously dissented in Munn v. Illinois, 94 U.S. 113 (1877), the only non-railroad *Granger* case, arguing that the public interest should not extend beyond industries benefiting from public grants. Thus, Field would allow regulation of railroads but not of the grain elevators at issue in *Munn.* A few years later, the Court would exert power to review state regulation of railroads. *See* Chicago, Milwaukee & St. Paul Ry. v. Minnesota, 134 U.S. 418 (1890) (holding that the Constitution called for judicial review of the "reasonableness" of rates).

4. Those limited circumstances were reflected in overlapping common-law and constitutional doctrines. The common-law doctrines were special treatment of common carriers and the narrow category of unreasonable restraints of trade. The constitutional law doctrine was the state's police power to protect public health and morals, even if the protection injured private property rights.

5. I discuss the "Rule of Reason's" multiple jurisprudences in chap. 2. For an illuminating description of the federal common law in the *Swift v. Tyson* era, *see* PURCELL (1992), *supra* note 1, at 59–86.

6. I discuss Lochner v. New York, 198 U.S. 45 (1905) in the text accompanying notes 93–100, *infra.* For views that the Court saw democracy as a "corrupt cover for 'rent-seeking' or special-interest legislation, and feared that private interests—including rich corporate private interests—would seek wealth for themselves through the legislative process at the expense of the general welfare," *see* Robert W. Gordon, *The*

Elusive Transformation, 6 YALE J.L. & HUMAN. 137, 150 (1994); Benedict, McCurdy, Siegel, GILLMAN, all *supra* note 1.

7. *See* Peritz, *supra* note 1.

8. H.R. MISC. DOC. NO. 124, 50th Cong., 1st Sess., 19 CONG. REC. 719 (1888) (in substitution of H.R. REP. NO. 67, introduced by Representative William Mason (R.Ill.)). The resolution directed the House Judiciary Committee to investigate certain charges about trusts' high prices to consumers. 1 EARL KINTNER, THE LEGISLATIVE HISTORY OF THE FEDERAL ANTITRUST LAWS AND RELATED STATUTES 53 (1978). REPORT OF THE HOUSE COMMITTEE ON MANUFACTURES, H.R. REP. NO. 3112, 50th Cong., 1st Sess. (July 30, 1888); S. 3440 and S. 3445, 50th Cong., 1st Sess., 19 CONG. REC. 7512 (1888); S. 3445, 50th CONG. REC. 1120 (1889) (as amended).

9. HORWITZ (1992), *supra* note 1, at 83.

10. S. 1, 51st Cong., 1st Sess., 21 CONG. REC. 2901 (1890); 21 CONG. REC. 3152–53 (1890). After several days of deliberation on the Conference Reports the bill was passed. *See* Peritz, *supra* note 1, at 303 n.88.

11. *Mr. Sherman Gives Up Hope*, N.Y. TIMES, Apr. 8, 1890, at 4 (quoting comments appearing in the *St. Louis Globe-Democrat*), *reprinted in* 1 KINTNER, *supra* note 8, at 24 n.1, 153.

12. 21 CONG. REC. 2457 (1890) (industrial liberty); 21 CONG. REC. 2729–30 (1890) (statement of Sen. Orville Platt (R.Conn.) regarding fair price).

13. 21 CONG. REC. 2457 (1890) (statement of Sen. Sherman (D.Ohio)).

14. 20 CONG. REC. 2458 (1890) (remarks of Sen. Sherman, quoting from Craft v. McConoughy, 79 Ill. 346, 350 (1875)); *see also* 20 CONG. REC. 1458 (1889) (statement of Sen. Jones (D. Nev.)) (these combinations could "plunder the public"); 21 CONG. REC. 2561 (1890) (statement of Sen. Teller (R. Col.)); 20 CONG. REC. 1457 (1889) (statement of Sen. Teller); 20 CONG. REC. 1457 (1889) (statement of Sen. Teller); 21 CONG. REC. 2561 (1890) (statement of Rep. Mason).

15. 21 CONG. REC. 2460 (1890) (remarks of Sen. Sherman).

16. 21 CONG. REC. 2729 (1890) (statement of Sen. Platt); *id.* at 5956 (statement of Sen. Stewart).

17. *Id.*; Richard Ely, *Report on the Organization of the American Economic Association*, 1 PUB. AM. ECON. ASS'N 6–7 (Edmund James and Simon Nelson Patten), 27 (Edwin Seligman) (1886).

18. For example, Senator George (D.Ga.) stated: "These trusts and combinations are great wrongs to the people. . . . They increase beyond reason the cost of the necessaries of life and they decrease the cost of the raw material, the farm products of the country. They regulate prices at their will." 21 CONG. REC. 1768 (1890).

19. *See, e.g.*, McCurdy, *supra* note 1, for a useful study of Justice Stephen Field's libertarian formulation of the relationship between the individual and the state.

20. 21 CONG. REC. 2720–21 (1890) (statement of Sen. Platt).

21. *Id.* at 5957 (statement of Rep. Stewart); *see also id.* at 5954 (statement of Rep. Morse (D. Mass.)) (asserting that combination is a legitimate means for assuring a fair return on property). For an exchange between Stewart and Congressman Richard P. Bland (D.Mo.), *see* 21 CONG. REC. 5951, 5953, 5957 (1890). The Cullom Committee's influential Report to Congress characterized its focus as "the railroad problem." For a partial reproduction of the congressional debates over the Interstate Commerce Act, see I THE ECONOMIC REGULATION OF BUSINESS AND INDUSTRY: A LEGISLATIVE HISTORY OF U.S. REGULATORY AGENCIES 255–309 (Bernard Schwartz ed. 1973).

22. *Munn*, 94 U.S. 113, 134 (1877). *See, e.g.*, SOLON J. BUCK, THE GRANGER MOVEMENT: A STUDY OF AGRICULTURAL ORGANIZATION AND ITS POLITICAL, ECONOMIC, AND SOCIAL

RAMIFICATIONS, 1870–1880 123, 159, 166, 179, 194 (1913). The "Granger" cases, all but *Munn* involving railroad regulation, appear in volume 94 of the United States Reports.

23. Stone v. Wisconsin, 94 U.S. 181, 184 (1877) (one of the *Granger* cases). The Court imposed the same common-law standard of "reasonableness" on corporate power. *Railroad Commission Cases*, 116 U.S. 307, 347, 352 (1886) (holding that the state's regulatory power is subject to the "taking" standard of the "due process clause"). The Court declared that the common law was implicitly incorporated in the defendants' corporate charters, so that "[t]he right to fix reasonable charges has been granted, but the [state] power of declaring what shall be deemed reasonable has not been surrendered." *Id.* at 325. *See also* Georgia R.R. & Banking Co. v. Smith, 128 U.S. 174, 179 (1888) (declaring that "carriage is not required . . . upon conditions amounting to the taking of property for public use without just compensation"). Regarding state regulation of rates and the issue of just compensation, *see* Chicago, Minn. & St. P. Co. v. Minnesota, 134 U.S. 418 (1890) (adopting Justice Field's view of property as exchange value); Budd v. New York, 143 U.S. 517, 549 (1892) (Justice Brewer dissenting) ("men are endowed by their creator . . ." with property rights); Bluefield Water Works & Improvement Co. v. Public Serv. Comm'n, 262 U.S. 679, 692–93 (1923) (finding that there is no constitutional right to profits such as are realized or anticipated in highly profitable enterprises); Missouri *ex rel* Southwestern Bell Tel. Co. v. Public Serv. Comm'n, 262 U.S. 276, 291 (1923) (Brandeis J., concurring) (describing methodology for determining a fair return on investment); Smyth v. Ames, 169 U.S. 466, 546 (1898) (stating that a company is entitled to no more than a fair return upon that which it employs for the public convenience).

24. 21 CONG. REC. 3145, 3146, 3152 (1890) (statements of Sen. Hoar); *id.* at 3148, 3152 (statements of Sen. Edmunds). The example given of unfair means is merger—"the unfair buying up of all other persons engaged in the same business." *Id.*

25. Craft v. McConoughy, 79 Ill. 346 (1875) (price-fixing cartel) and Chicago Gas-Light & Coke Co. v. People's Gas-Light & Coke Co., 121 Ill. 530, 13 N.E. 169 (1887) (territorial allocation agreement); People v. Chicago Trust Co., 130 Ill. 268, 22 N.E. 789 (1887) (charter revocation); People v. North River Sugar Ref. Co., 22 Abb. N. Cas. 164 (N.Y. Sup. Ct. 1889) (same); Richardson v. Buhl & Alger, 77 Mich. 632, 43 N.W. 1102, 1110 (1889) (Sherwood, C.J.). For insightful treatments of state common laws as reflections of political and economic values of the times, see sources cited *supra* note 1, particularly May, Letwin, THORELLI.

26. Chief Justice Melville W. Fuller wrote that "while it is justly argued that those rules which say that a given contract is against public policy, should not be arbitrarily extended so as to interfere with freedom of contract, yet, in the instance of business of such character [here, illuminating gas] that it presumably cannot be restrained to any extent whatever without prejudice to the public interest, courts decline to enforce or sustain contracts imposing such restraint." Gibbs v. Consolidated Gas Co., 130 U.S. 396, 408–09 (1889).

27. Mogul Steamship Co. v. McGregor, Gow & Co., 23 Q.B.D. 598, 612, 614–19 (1889), *aff'd*, 1892 A.C. 25.

28. *See* sources cited *supra* note 1, particularly PURCELL (1973), POCOCK, ROSS, APPLEBY, HOFSTADTER (1944), May (1987). According to Purcell, Stewart's view of combination and competition as two great forces was reflected as well in debates about the meaning of evolution—that is, did a species "compete" with itself or only with other species?

29. *See* FRANCIS WAYLAND, THE ELEMENTS OF POLITICAL ECONOMY 4 (1937); HENRY WOOD, THE POLITICAL ECONOMY OF NATURAL LAW 16, 17 (1894); HARRY STEELE COMMAGER,

THE AMERICAN MIND: AN INTERPRETATION OF AMERICAN THOUGHT AND CHARACTER SINCE THE 1880'S (1950).

30. If there were capital expended, then the price would naturally reflect both kinds of input units. *See, e.g.*, JOHN BATES CLARK, ESSENTIALS OF ECONOMIC THEORY 14–17 (1907); WAYLAND, *supra* note 29, at 4–5. As Arthur T. Hadley observed in his well-known study of the railroad industry, "We accept almost without reserve the theory of Ricardo, that under open competition in a free market, the value of different goods will tend to be proportional to their cost of production." HADLEY, RAILROAD TRANSPORTATION—ITS HISTORY AND LAWS 69 (1885). *See also* CLARK at 77; HORWITZ (1977), *supra* note 1, 109–39, 160–88, 253–66; Kennedy (1985), *supra* note 1 (describing the relationship between classical economic and legal thought).

31. *Munn*, 94 U.S. at 113, 126. *See* Williams v. Standard Oil Co., 278 U.S. 235, 240 (1929) (finding that the petroleum industry is not clothed in the public interest).

32. 21 CONG. REC. 4102 (1890) (Rep. Fithian); *id.* at 3151–52 (Sen. Edmunds); *id.* at 3152 (Sen. Hoar).

33. Scholarly responses included the work of neoclassicists like John Bates Clark, who argued that "To regulate combinations is possible and, in some directions desirable; to permanently suppress them is impossible; to temporarily repress them is either to force them into illegal forms, or to restore the internecine war from which a natural evolution has delivered us." CLARK, *supra* note 30, at 61; *see* Northern Sec. Co. v. United States, 193 U.S. 197, 400–10 (1904) (Holmes, J. dissenting) (expressing similar fears).

34. DAVID AMES WELLS, RECENT ECONOMIC CHANGES AND THEIR EFFECT ON THE PRODUCTION AND DISTRIBUTION OF WEALTH AND WELL-BEING OF SOCIETY 74 (1889); Henry Carter Adams, *Publicity and Corporate Abuses, in* 1 PUBLICATIONS OF THE MICH. POL. SCI. ASS'N 109, 116 (1894) (*reprinted in* THORELLI, *supra* note 1, at 108–52). Letwin, *supra* note 1, at 222–40.

35. Roscoe Pound, *The Theory of Judicial Decision*, 36 HARV. L. REV. 641, 653 (1923). Regarding claims of economies of scale, *see, e.g.*, DAVID AMES WELLS, *supra* note 34, at 73–75 (1896); Andrew Carnegie, *Popular Illusions About Trusts, in* THE GOSPEL OF WEALTH, AND OTHER TIMELY ESSAYS 81–82 (2d. ed. 1933); *cf.* John Bates Clark, *The Limits of Competition*, 2 POL. SCI. Q. 46 (1887) (all social classes benefit from increased efficiency achieved through industrialization).

36. 2 JAMES BRYCE, THE AMERICAN COMMONWEALTH 407–08 (1889).

37. 22 AM. L. REV. 926 (1888).

38. Sherman Antitrust Act § 7, Ch. 647, 26 Stat. 209 (July 2, 1890); Sherman Anti-Trust Bill, S. 3445, 50th Cong., 1st Sess. (August 14, 1888). For discussions of common-law treatment of monopolies and contracts in restraint of trade, see Letwin, *supra* note 1, at 241–45; THORELLI, *supra* note 1, at 45–48.

39. *Id.* §§ 1–3, 6. The allusion to smuggling is not surprising, given the intense debates over tariffs that overlapped the Sherman Act deliberations. The confiscation provision remains as "§ 6. Forfeiture of property in transit."

40. Northern Pac. R.R. v. United States, 356 U.S. 1, 4 (1958); Standard Oil Co. v. United States, 221 U.S. 1, 58 (1911); United States v. Aluminum Co. of Am., 148 F.2d 416 (2d Cir. 1945) (L. Hand, J.). This common-law view has led most mainstream antitrust commentators and critics to accord the "legislative history . . . relatively little weight." PHILIP AREEDA & DONALD TURNER, ANTITRUST LAW: AN ANALYSIS OF ANTITRUST PRINCIPLES AND THEIR APPLICATION 14–15 (3d ed. 1981); PHILIP AREEDA, ANTITRUST ANALYSIS: PROBLEMS, TEXTS, AND CASES 314 (3d ed. 1981); 15 U.S.C. § 1 (1988) (emphasis added). J. Auerbach, *President Roosevelt and the Trusts*, 175 N. AM. REV. 877, 891 (1902) (de-

scribing the legislation as "crudely drawn, imperfectly considered, hastily enacted . . ."); United States v. Trans-Missouri Freight Ass'n, 166 U.S. 290, 351–56 (1897) (White, J., dissenting); LAWRENCE SULLIVAN, HANDBOOK OF THE LAW OF ANTITRUST 181 (1977) (rule of reason allows inquiry only into whether an arrangement significantly decreases competition). The modern Chicago School reflects a schizoid attitude toward legislative history. On the one hand, Robert Bork has a great investment in arguing that wealth maximization motivated the Fifty-first Congress because his view of legitimate lawmaking depends upon a kind of originalism. On the other hand, the Chicago School holds to the view that historical study is superfluous because "the market's" current expression of value impounds and thus already reflects history. I discuss these matters in chap. 6. Regarding the new wave of antitrust scholars who recover antitrust history, see *Symposium: Observing the Sherman Act Centennial: The Past and Future of Antitrust as Public Interest Law*, 35 N.Y.L. SCH. L. REV. 767 *et seq.* (1990).

41. Northern Sec. Co. v. United States, 193 U.S. 197, 403 (1904).

42. Holmes decried this federal common law for commerce as a "transcendental body of law outside any state but obligatory within it." Black and White Taxicab and Transfer Co. v. Brown and Yellow Taxicab and Transfer Co., 276 U.S. 518, 523 (1928). Historian Edward A. Purcell, Jr. has written of a parallel shift in the Court's treatment of corporate diversity jurisdiction, as well as changed attitudes, of both sitting Justices and elite lawyers, toward the Court's institutional self-image. PURCELL (1992), *supra* note 1, at 286–91.

43. *See, e.g.*, SKLAR, *supra* note 1, at 118.

44. Swift v. Tyson, 41 U.S. (19 Pet.) 1 (1842); Chicago, Minn. & St. P. Ry. v. Minnesota, 134 U.S. 418 (1890) (Blatchford, J.); Western Union Tel. Co. v. Call Publishing Co., 181 U.S. 92 (1901) (Brewer, J.).

45. 52 F. 104 (C.C.S.D Ohio 1892).

46. United States v. Trans-Missouri Freight Ass'n, 166 U.S. 290, 327–28 (1897).

47. 58 F. 58, 73 (8th Cir. 1893), *rev'd*, 166 U.S. 290 (1897); *see also* Chicago Bd. of Trade v. United States, 246 U.S. 231, 238 (1918) (true test of legality is whether restraint merely regulates rather than suppresses competition); 53 F. 440, 451 (C.C.D. Kan. 1892), *aff'd*, 58 F. 58 (8th Cir. 1893), *rev'd*, 166 U.S. 290 (1897); *cf. In re* Greene, 52 F. 104, 112–13 (C.C.S.D. Ohio 1892) (holding that, constitutionally, the federal government cannot regulate the property of a corporation created by a state). 53 F. at 453.

48. 166 U.S. at 330; Albro Martin, *Railroads and Receivership: An Essay on Institutional Change*, 34 J. ECON. HIST. 685, 705 (1974).

49. *Trans-Missouri*, *supra* n.46, 166 U.S. at 333.

50. *Id.* at 355, 346. A unanimous Court, however, agreed with Peckham's rendition of individual liberty in that term's Allgeyer v. Louisiana, 165 U.S. 578 (1897) ("liberty of contract and freedom of trade"—the individual liberty announced in the Declaration of Independence and embodied in the Fourteenth Amendment's protection of "life, liberty, and property").

51. The seven years since the Sherman Act debates provoked only heightened fears about the breakdown of peace and prosperity. The country was still in the deep economic depression following the financial panic of 1893. A few months before the panic, the Homestead strike against Andrew Carnegie's steel-making empire provoked rampant violence—eighteen people shot to death and many more injured, including strikers, police, and even innocent bystanders. In 1894, the infamous Pullman strike was enjoined under color of the Sherman Act. One year later, however, a unanimous Supreme Court held that the Sherman Act did not reach the Sugar Trust

because it was involved in manufacture, not commerce. United States v. E.C. Knight, 156 U.S. 1 (1895). Combinations of capital and those of labor seemed to call for two different sets of rules. Both sorts of combinations, however, contributed to a sense of instability and powerlessness among small business owners, farmers, laborers, and others outside the small circles of economic and political power.

52. *Trans-Missouri,* 166 U.S. at 322–23, 323–24, 337. *See generally* Elizabeth Mensch, *The Colonial Origins of Liberal Property Rights,* 31 BUFF. L. REV. 635, 733–55 (1982); Gregory S. Alexander, *Time and Property in the American Republican Legal Culture,* 66 N.Y.U. L. REV. 273, 287–89, 325 (1991).

53. It was here, at the threat of political corruption, that the two factions converged. The libertarian concern about corruption, however, focused directly upon the political sphere. Nonetheless, for all the ways in which the Literalist and Rule of Reasonist factions disagreed, their solutions were founded in commitments to individual liberty. For the Literalists, industrial liberty required affirmative congressional policy to salvage some modicum of entrepreneurial equality. For the Rule of Reasonists, the common law, founded in traditional notions of liberty of contract, made sense to the extent that it allowed individuals to protect their property from the ravages of ruinous competition.

54. *Trans-Missouri,* 166 U.S. at 355–56.

55. *In re* Debs, 64 F. 745–55 (C.C.N.D. Ill. 1894), *aff'd as to decree,* 158 U.S. 564 (1895). *See* Peritz (1989), *supra* note 1, at n.161–66.

56. Loewe v. Lawlor, 208 U.S. 274 (1908) (*Danbury Hatters* case).

57. That view was, of course, based on the belief that labor markets were free, i.e., that mobility was great, that employers competed perfectly for labor, and that employers were themselves individuals, rather than groups such as corporations. For helpful discussions of the period between the Civil War and the New Deal, see William Forbath's pair of articles: *The Shaping of the American Labor Movement,* 102 HARV. L. REV. 1109 (1989); *The Ambiguities of Free Labor: Labor and the Law in the Gilded Age,* 1985 WIS. L. REV. 767 (1985). For a discussion of the manufacturers' and unions' lobbying efforts during the Clayton Act drafting process and legislative debates, see Daniel Ernst, *The Labor Exemption, 1908–1914,* 74 IOWA L. REV. 1151 (1989).

58. Certainly, by the turn of the century, Marshall's *Principles,* as well as the work of American economist John Bates Clark, had significant influence among political economists. ALFRED MARSHALL, PRINCIPLES OF ECONOMICS (1890); JOHN BATES CLARK, ESSENTIALS OF ECONOMIC THEORY (1907); JOHN KENNETH GALBRAITH, ECONOMICS IN PERSPECTIVE: A CRITICAL HISTORY 89–126 (1987); ROSS, *supra* note 1. Nonetheless, alongside the economics profession's growing interest in the workings of the market model, the Court was strengthening its commitment to a political economy founded in individual liberty. Although these concurrent movements might seem in conflict, they were, instead, complementary insofar as both were unconcerned with economic inequalities between buyers and sellers, short of perfect monopoly.

59. FRANCIS A. WALKER, POLITICAL ECONOMY 262 (3d ed. 1888); Dr. Miles Medical Co. v. John D. Park & Sons, 220 U.S. 373 (1910); Vegelahn v. Guntner, 167 Mass. 510 (1895). Employers, however, whether the local bakery or Andrew Carnegie's massive steel company, were imagined as "individuals." I discuss the pre–New Deal rhetorics of individualism and collectivity in chap. 2.

60. *See, e.g.,* Hopkins v. Oxley Stave Co., 83 F. 912, 919 (8th Cir. 1897); Kennedy (1980), *supra* note 1. *See* Justice Field's dissenting opinions in *The Slaughterhouse Cases,* 83 U.S. (16 Wall) 36, 88 (1873) and Munn v. Illinois, 99 U.S. 113, 143 (1877), as well as his majority opinion in Chicago, Minn. & St. Paul Ry. v. Minnesota, 134 U.S. 418 (1890).

61. *See, e.g.,* Justice Peckham's opinion in *Trans-Missouri,* 166 U.S. at 323 (describing "opportunities for labor in other departments than those to which they have been accustomed" for employees thrown out of work by new technology).

62. For a discussion of how the emerging entity theory of the corporation made the argument plausible, in formal terms, see Morton J. Horwitz, Santa Clara *Revisited: The Development of Corporate Theory,* 88 W. VA. L. REV. 173 (1985), expanded in HORWITZ (1992), *supra* note 1, 65 *et seq.*

63. Joint Traffic Ass'n v. United States, 171 U.S. 505, 575–76 (1898). Counsel for the railroad cartel rehearsed Justice White's dissenting opinion from *Trans-Missouri*: "A just freedom of contract . . . is one of the most important rights . . . of 'liberty,' for all human industry depends upon such freedom for its fair reward. The use of property is an essential part of it." Responding to this claim of a common-law right to a fair return founded in freedom of contract, Peckham wrote that despite "general liberty of contract . . . there are many kinds of contracts which . . . may yet be prohibited." *Id.* at 533. Accordingly, the issue of an unconstitutional taking of private property "for public use without just compensation . . . is, we think, plainly irrelevant" because Congress has the power to regulate private contracts that restrain interstate commerce. *Id.* at 571.

Regarding the common-law view of speech, *see, e.g.,* Robertson v. Baldwin, 165 U.S. 275, 281 (1897), decided in the same year as *Trans-Missouri. Cf.* Rabban, *supra* note 1. The English common law was, however, the product of persistent clashes in the seventeenth century between government and diverse groups of dissenters, some more successful than others. Moreover, it was Parliament's ordinance for licensing the press, enacted June 14, 1643, that elicited a well-known printer's celebrated defense of free speech: "Areopagetica; a Speech of Mr. John Milton For the Liberty of Unlicenc'd Printing, To the Parlament of England," *reproduced in* JOHN MILTON, COMPLETE POEMS AND MAJOR PROSE 717–49 (Merritt Y. Hughes ed. 1957).

64. *Trans-Missouri,* 166 U.S. at 329, 313, 342; *Joint Traffic,* 171 U.S. at 560, 565, 577.

65. 175 U.S. 211, 213, 244 (1899), *aff'g* 85 F. 271 (6th Cir. 1898).

66. 85 F. 271, 281 (1899) (Taft, J.).

67. *Id.* at 284.

68. 175 U.S. at 238, 230 (citing *Debs,* 158 U.S. at 564), 229.

69. Swift & Co. v. United States, 196 U.S. 375 (1905); *see generally* Barry Cushman, *A Stream of Legal Consciousness: The Current of Commerce Doctrine from* Swift *to* Jones & Laughlin, 61 FORDHAM L. REV. 105 (1992).

70. Still, the *Northern Securities* Court's decomposition into four opinions did not disrupt the earlier understanding that price-fixing cartels always violated the Sherman Act. That understanding had just been corroborated. Montague & Co. v. Lowry, 193 U.S. 38, 44–8 (1904). Rather, the four opinions reflect dissensus over the relationship between cartels and mergers—both of them combinations in restraint of trade.

71. The conception of a "trust" was itself complex. Not only did the corporate trust derive from the fiduciary relations developed in the well-settled relationship among trustee, trust corpus (assets), and beneficiaries, but there was a well-known doctrine of public trust as well. *See, e.g.,* Justice Field's opinion for a divided Court in Illinois Cent. Ry. v. Illinois, 146 U.S. 387, 451 (1892). Field believed that the Court was the proper trustee for supervising the conduct of the public's corruptible representatives—the legislature. This view is different in some significant respects from the later "liberty of contract" jurisprudence, the libertarian individualism driving the

Lochner (1905) Court, particularly in the relationship between legislature and individual. The later view became more oppositional than representational.

72. Plessy v. Ferguson, 163 U.S. 537, 545, 550 (1896). For a similar observation made regarding the civil rights removal statute, *see* PURCELL (1992), *supra* note 1, at 142–47.

73. *Northern Sec.*, 193 U.S. at 320.

74. *Id.* at 320–21, 357–58.

75. *Id.* at 337.

76. *Id.* at 328–29, 331 (citing Hopkins v. United States, 171 U.S. 578 (1898); United States v. Joint Traffic Ass'n, 171 U.S. 505 (1898)) (emphasis in original), 337, 338.

77. 193 U.S. at 332, 342.

78. *Id.* at 397, 368. *See, e.g., id.* at 275, 287, 293.

79. *Id.* at 411, 405.

80. *Id.* at 410, 407, 411. For a thoughtful historical study of social science discourse in late nineteenth century America, see ROSS, *supra* note 1.

81. 193 U.S. at 407, 403.

82. *Id.* at 361. Brewer's shift was plainly consistent with his dissenting opinion in a rate regulation case many years earlier. Arguing against New York State's power to regulate rates, he wrote that "men are endowed by their creator" with the right of property. Budd v. New York, 143 U.S. 517, 549 (1892).

83. *Joint Traffic Ass'n*, 171 U.S. at 571 (1898) (Peckham describing his holding in Allgeyer v. Louisiana, 165 U.S. 578 (1897)).

84. *Northern Sec.*, 193 U.S. at 293, 275, 295.

85. *Id.* at 327, 377.

86. Lochner v. New York, 198 U.S. 45 (1905).

87. 198 U.S. at 53–54; *id.* at 56 (Peckham), 66 (Harlan), 76 (Holmes). But is this the "general proposition" that Holmes criticizes? Such a reading is possible, given his subsequent view that the police power is defined in terms of majoritarian sentiments. *See* Noble State Bank v. Haskell, 219 U.S. 105, 110–12 (1911) ("the police power extends to all the great public needs."). But Holmes did express, in general terms, his belief that there were limits on majoritarianism, in both his *Northern Securities* and *Lochner* dissenting opinions, limits founded in "fundamental principles as they have been understood by the traditions of our people and our law." *Lochner*, 193 U.S. at 76. For a succinct account of legal formalist thinking, see MAX WEBER, *The Categories of Legal Thought, in* ECONOMY AND SOCIETY 657–58 ([1922] 1968).

88. *Lochner*, 198 U.S. at 57, 59.

89. *Id.* at 58, 59, 64.

90. *Id.* at 68, 72.

91. *Id.* at 72.

92. *Id.* at 73. Judicial distrust of the legislature, as expressed in Peckham's opinion for the Court, had been seen as early as Justice Field's dissenting opinion in *The Slaughterhouse Cases* (1873) and in his *Illinois Cent. Ry.* (1892) opinion for the Court.

93. *Lochner*, 198 U.S. at 75–76; Harlan agreed, citing economist William Stanley Jevons for the proposition that "the relation of the State to labor is one of the most debatable and difficult questions of social science." *Id.* at 68, 72. As historian G. Edward White has pointed out, Holmes wrote to Fredrick Pollock about a year later: "My intellectual furniture consists of an assortment of general propositions that grow fewer and more general as I grow older. I always say that the chief end of man is to frame them and no general proposition is worth a damn." Holmes to Pollock, Sep-

tember 24, 1904, I *Holmes-Pollock Letters* 118, *appearing in* WHITE (1993), *supra* note 1, at 556 n.141.

94. *Lochner,* 198 U.S. at 76; *Northern Sec.,* 193 U.S. at 407, 411.

95. The Court's 1904 and 1905 dockets produced open conflict beyond *Northern Securities* and *Lochner.* As historian Edward A. Purcell, Jr. has written, the relationship between corporations and employees split the Court in Northern Pac. Ry. Co. v. Dixon, 194 U.S. 338 (1904). Justice Brewer's opinion for the narrowest of majorities held that the fellow servant rule shielded the railroad from liability for an employee's injury, even though the fellow employee whose negligence caused the injury was many miles away, entirely unknown to the injured employee. Justice White wrote for the dissenting quartet that the result of the majority's attenuated logic was that "recovery cannot be had in any event." 194 U.S. at 352. In Purcell's view, White was insinuating that the majority was acting on the basis of class bias. For a brilliant synthesis of the federal common law in those years, set within the framework of *Lochner* and *Ex Parte* Young, 209 U.S. 123 (1908), see PURCELL (1992), *supra* note 1, 59–86.

96. 1908 was an interesting year for Court opinions. In addition to the four I discuss briefly, there were several other decisions of note. Perhaps the most notable is *Ex Parte* Young, 209 U.S. 123, which narrowed the Eleventh Amendment limit on federal court jurisdiction to hear individual citizens' suits against states. As Edward A. Purcell, Jr. has written, "Together, the two decisions gave the federal courts constitutional authority . . . to serve as the frontline protectors of liberty and property against state interference." PURCELL (1992), *supra* note 1, at 283.

97. Adair v. United States, 208 U.S. 161, 173 (1908) This individualist rhetoric, a surprising turn for Harlan, was criticized by dissenting Justice Joseph McKenna as "deduced" from "abstract propositions." Holmes dissented as well, concluding with the remark that unions, like combinations of capital, have their supporters and thus that even requiring unions could constitute legitimate congressional policy. *Id.* at 191–92. *Danbury Hatters* case, Loewe v. Lawlor, 208 U.S. at 274, 297, 303–04 (1908). Chief Justice Fuller's opinion is filled with references to physical injury—threats, coercion, intimidation, force, destruction, paralysis—rather than economic harm. I discuss in chap. 2 the Court's political and conflictual imagery in labor association cases—a sharp contrast to its economic and competition rhetoric in trade association cases.

98. Muller v. Oregon, 208 U.S. 412, 416, 419 n.1 (abstract of Brandeis brief), 421 (1908); *see* Nancy Woloch, *Feminist Movement, in* THE READER'S COMPANION TO AMERICAN HISTORY 391–97 (Eric Foner & John A. Garraty eds. 1991) and sources cited therein. *Muller*'s view can be seen as a restatement of beliefs long espoused by the Court. In Bradwell v. Illinois, 83 U.S. (16 Wall.) 130 (1873), the Court held, with only Justice Salmon P. Chase dissenting, that the Illinois Supreme Court's denial, solely because she was female, of Myra Bradwell's application for a license to practice law, did not offend the Constitution. Justice Joseph E. Bradley wrote in a concurring opinion, joined by Stephen J. Field and Noah H. Swayne, that the "natural and proper timidity and delicacy which belongs to the female sex evidently unfits it for many of the occupations of civil life. . . . This is the law of the Creator." 83 U.S. at 144–45.

99. Berea College v. Kentucky, 211 U.S. 45, 48, 50, 53–54 (1908). Justice Harlan dissented, arguing consistently with *Santa Clara* that individual liberty of contract should not be obstructed by the corporate form. *Id.* at 58. *See* Santa Clara v. Southern Pac. R.R., 118 U.S. 394 (1886). The mainstream view of *Santa Clara* is slightly different—that the Court treated the corporate entity as itself an entity, a person, for constitutional purposes. That view has been challenged and, I believe, displaced by the

better interpretation described above, developed and forcefully argued by historian Morton Horwitz. For his most recent discussion of the case and its context, see HORWITZ (1992), *supra* note 1, at 65–108.

100. Standard Oil v. United States, 221 U.S. 1 (1911); United States v. American Tobacco Co., 221 U.S. 106 (1911); *Northern Securities*, 193 U.S. at 370.

101. *American Tobacco*, 221 U.S. at 180. For claims that policy conflict only arose at the time of the Clayton Act, *see* FREDERICK ROWE, PRICE DISCRIMINATION UNDER THE ROBINSON-PATMAN ACT xi (1962) ("paradox of antitrust at war with itself"); Robert Bork, *The Place of Antitrust Among National Goals, in* BASIC ANTITRUST QUESTIONS IN THE MIDDLE SIXTIES: FIFTH CONFERENCE ON THE IMPACT OF ANTITRUST ON ECONOMIC GROWTH 12 (Nat'l Indus. Conf. Bd. 1966); for a critique, see Peritz, *The Predicament of Antitrust Jurisprudence*, 1984 DUKE L.J. at 1231–61.

102. Henry George in PROGRESS AND POVERTY ([1879] 1938) grappled with what Dorothy Ross has called "the republican trajectory of progress and progressive decay." Ross, *The Liberal Tradition Revisited and the Republican Tradition Addressed, in* NEW DIRECTIONS IN AMERICAN INTELLECTUAL HISTORY 123 (John Higham & Paul K. Conkin, eds. 1979). George wrote: "I do not believe that inequality is the necessary result of social growth, but that it is the constant tendency of social growth if unaccompanied by changes in social adjustments which, in the new conditions that growth produces, will secure equality." PROGRESS AND POVERTY, *excerpted in* Ross at 124. *Northern Sec.*, 193 U.S at 370 (White, J., dissenting).

103. It was this restriction on freedom of contract that caused "injury to the public." *Standard Oil*, 221 U.S. at 54. *Id.* at 54, 62. For an earlier reference to "the liberty of a trader to engage in business," see Chief Justice Fuller's opinion for a unanimous Court in the *Danbury Hatters* case, 208 U.S. at 293.

104. 221 U.S at 181. In general, however, sovereign involvement was unreasonable since the "centrifugal and centripetal forces resulting from the right to freely contract was the means by which monopoly would be inevitably prevented if no extraneous or sovereign power imposed it and no right to make unlawful contracts having a monopolistic tendency were permitted." *Standard Oil*, 221 U.S. at 62.

105. The date was January 5, 1911. Counsel also appeared briefly ten days later, on the last day of reargument of the *Standard Oil* case. Dr. Miles Medical Co. v. John D. Park & Sons Co., 220 U.S. 373 (1910); *see also* Bobbs-Merrill Co. v. Straus, 210 U.S. 339 (1908) (resale price maintenance for patented articles not enforceable).

106. *Dr. Miles Medical Co.*, 220 U.S. at 385, 390–91, 376, 396 (quoting petitioner's charge), 389. It appears that everyone agreed that a property claim of title retention overrides the Literalist principle, developed in earlier horizontal cartel cases, that competition is the only legitimate arbiter of price. But unlike the broad discretion granted under the "Rule of Reason," *Dr. Miles* required a narrowly circumscribed property interest to entitle a manufacturer to set retail prices.

107. But a problem would always arise in determining what constitutes property ownership. For now, the Court was willing to rest on the common-law doctrine of title, turning for authority to Lord Coke's traditional views on common-law property rights, including the sacred right of alienation, the right to receive property unencumbered by onerous conditions on resale or other transfer. *See* Peritz, *A Genealogy of Vertical Restraints Doctrine*, 40 HASTINGS L. J. 511, 520–23 (1989).

108. *Dr. Miles Medical Co.*, 220 U.S. at 406.

109. See HORWITZ (1992), *supra* note 1, at 65–108. Hale v. Henkel, 201 U.S. 43 (1905) (Fourth Amendment, but not Fifth, applies to corporations).

110. THORSTEIN VEBLEN, ABSENTEE OWNERSHIP AND BUSINESS ENTERPRISE IN RECENT

TIMES 105 (1923). Veblen describes captains of business as entrepreneurs, as the head of a "pecuniary institution." In contrast, the earlier captains of industry were primarily interested in making goods rather than money. *Id.* at 85. This distinction constituted the ground for Veblen's replacement of Marx's working class with engineers to lead the revolution. *See* VEBLEN, THE ENGINEERS AND THE PRICE SYSTEM (1921), particularly chaps. 5 & 6 (describing the logic of technicians and the revolution); THE INSTINCT OF WORKMANSHIP AND THE STATE OF THE INDUSTRIAL ARTS (1914), particularly chaps. 1 & 2. Veblen's earlier THE THEORY OF BUSINESS ENTERPRISE (1904) laid the foundation for his later work. His discussion of "the metaphysics of natural liberty," the "principle of natural (pecuniary) liberty" remains illuminating. *Id.* at 268–301. Herbert Hoover, in contrast, believed that the entrepreneurial spirit, under proper circumstances, produced industrial statesmanship that would be the engine for an evolution in capitalism. I discuss the 1920s in chap. 2. Still the most readable account of the era associated with captains of industry is MATTHEW JOSEPHSON, THE ROBBER BARONS: THE GREAT AMERICAN CAPITALISTS 1861–1901 (1934).

111. George F. Canfield, *Is a Large Corporation an Illegal Combination or Monopoly under the Sherman Anti-Trust Act?* 1909 COLUM. L. REV. 95, 101. SKLAR, *supra* note 1, at 15–16 & n.12. LOUIS GALAMBOS, THE PUBLIC IMAGE OF BIG BUSINESS IN AMERICA, 1880–1940 (1975); ALFRED D. CHANDLER, SCALE AND SCOPE 48 (1990). As late as 1937, Yale law professor Thurman Arnold, in his well-known THE FOLKLORE OF CAPITALISM, could write about the fears provoked by the United Auto Workers' innovative strike strategy: "So firmly fixed in the popular imagination was the belief that General Motors was a big man who 'owned' the plant that the public became alarmed over possible dangers to their own homes because of . . . the sit-down strike." ARNOLD, FOLKLORE at 191. For some reproductions of the era's cartoonry, see THORELLI, *supra* note 1.

112. Coppage v. Kansas, 236 U.S. 1, 17 (1915).

113. Elihu Root, *Some Duties of American Lawyers to American Law, in* ROOT, ADDRESSES ON GOVERNMENT AND CITIZENSHIP 425 (Robert Bacon & James B. Scott eds. 1916). David J. Brewer, *Protection to Private Property from Public Attack,* 55 NEW ENGLANDER AND YALE REV. 97, 107–08 (1891); Brewer, *The Nation's Safeguard,* PROCEEDINGS OF THE NEW YORK STATE BAR ASSOCIATION 39 (1893), *excerpted in* PURCELL (1992), *supra* note 1, at 80. *Budd,* 143 U.S. at 549 (Brewer, J. dissenting).

114. This is James Madison's federalism. For a recent interpretation, see JENNIFER NEDELSKY, PRIVATE PROPERTY AND THE LIMITS OF AMERICAN CONSTITUTIONALISM (1991).

Chapter 2

1. Standard Oil v. United States, 221 U.S. 1 (1911); Lochner v. New York, 198 U.S. 45 (1905); Georgia R.R. & Banking Co. v. Smith, 128 U.S. 174 (1888). The Maginot Line was an intricate and massive system of fortifications built along France's eastern border in the 1930s to prevent a German invasion. Nonetheless, the Germans easily invaded France in 1940 simply by taking a course just north of the Maginot Line near the Ardennes. *See, e.g.,* VIVIAN ROWE, THE GREAT WALL OF FRANCE (1959).

2. For a study of the Bureau of Corporations, see SKLAR, *supra* chap.1, note 1.

3. Peckham wrote the phrase "small dealers and worthy men" in his opinion for a divided Court in United States v. Trans-Missouri Freight Ass'n, 166 U.S. 299, 323 (1897).

4. By "trust," I mean the general category of large commercial or manufacturing organizations that raised public concern in those years, not only the legal entity

formed by strict compliance with the formal procedures required to create a trust in the narrow sense. United States v. United Shoe Mach. Co., 247 U.S. 32 (1918); United States v. U.S. Steel Corp., 251 U.S. 417, 440 (1920).

5. 51 CONG. REC. 14218–21 (1914) (statement of Sen. Thompson). Justice Harlan, as well as some legal commentators and social critics, portrayed the move to a Rule of Reason as a radical shift from the preceding jurisprudence. *Standard Oil*, 221 U.S. at 100–03 (Harlan, J., dissenting in part). ALBERT H. WALKER, THE UNREASONABLE OBITER DICTA OF CHIEF JUSTICE WHITE IN THE *Standard Oil* CASE 1–13 (1911). Walker also wrote the first account of the Sherman Act legislative debates and early case law. WALKER, HISTORY OF THE SHERMAN LAW OF THE UNITED STATES (1910).

6. 51 CONG. REC. 9,267, 14,211–12, 14,520, 15,864, 15,866 (1914). *See also* E. JONES, THE TRUST PROBLEM IN THE UNITED STATES 46–87 (1923). *But see* John S. McGee, *Predatory Price Cutting: The Standard Oil (N.J.) Case*, 1 J.L. & ECON. 137, 143 (1958) (arguing that the trial records contain no evidence of predatory pricing activities). 51 CONG REC. 14520.

7. *See* SKLAR, *supra* chap. 1, note 1.

8. A number of state statutes were enacted before 1911. The figure of twenty statutes is the arithmetic mean of the two different figures that appear in the debates. *See* 51 CONG. REC. 15857 (1914) (Senate: 19 states); 51 CONG. REC. 9157 (1914) (House: 21 states). THE LEGISLATIVE HISTORY OF THE ANTITRUST LAWS AND RELATED STATUTES 2509 (Earl W. Kintner ed. 1978) [KINTNER]. *Hearings Before the Committee on Interstate Commerce of the Senate pursuant to S. Res. 98*, 62d Cong., 1911, Part XVI, at 1156, reproduced in ALEXANDER M. BICKEL, THE UNPUBLISHED OPINIONS OF MR. JUSTICE BRANDEIS 119 (1957). *Hearings on H.R. 11380, Before House Committee on the Judiciary*, 62d Cong., 2d sess., at 104–05, 129–30 (1912); S. 3276, 62d Cong., 1st Sess. (Aug. 19, 1911) (*Standard Oil* was decided on May 15). H.R. 15926, 62 Cong., 2d Sess. (1911). KINTNER at 1385.

9. Clayton Act, ch. 323, 38 Stat. 730 (1914) (current version at 15 U.S.C. § 18 (1982)). Federal Trade Commission Act of 1914, ch. 311, 38 Stat. 717 (current version at 15 U.S.C. § 41 (1982)).

10. One example of Holmes's leading a conservative majority is Penn Coal Co. v. Mahon, 260 U.S. 393 (1922) (holding state regulation an unconstitutional taking of property).

11. United States v. U.S. Steel Corp., 251 U.S. 417, 442, 444 (1920) (4–3 decision). Justices Brandeis and McReynolds took no part in the decision. Dissenting Justices Day and Clarke agreed with Pitney that sheer size, attained by merger, did not violate the Sherman Act. There was, however, a massive record of industry-wide conspiracies to fix prices and to charge a standard freight rate, regardless of the origin and destination of any given steel shipment. It was these "Gary dinners," convened in Gary, Indiana, that the dissenting faction believed violated the Sherman Act. "To permit this," wrote Day, "would be to practically annul the Sherman Law by judicial decree." *Id.* at 461.

12. *Id.* at 450.

13. 253 U.S. 421, 422–29 (1920) (Brandeis & Clarke, JJ., dissenting).

14. *Id.* at 427. This limited view of the FTC's power held sway until the New Deal years. For an expansive view of Commission jurisdiction, see FTC v. Sperry & Hutchinson Co., 405 U.S. 233, 244 (1972).

15. PAUL L. MURPHY, THE CONSTITUTION IN CRISIS TIMES, 1918–1969 42–43 (1972). *See* John E. Edgerton, *Annual Address of the President, in* PROCEEDINGS, NAT'L ASS'N OF MANUFACTURERS 114–15 (1924) and HERBERT HOOVER, THE NEW DAY: CAMPAIGN SPEECHES OF HERBERT HOOVER, 1928 16, 162–63 (1928), *referenced in* MURPHY, at p.67 n.80. *See gen-*

erally FRIEDRICH VON HAYEK, THE ROAD TO SERFDOM (1944); George Stigler, *Wealth, and Possibly Liberty*, 7 J. LEGAL STUD. 213 (1978). *Gilbert*, 254 U.S. 325, 343 (1920). The Court held that the First Amendment does not prohibit a state from criminalizing the counseling of young men against the draft. Chief Justice White joined Brandeis's dissent.

16. Munn v. Illinois, 94 U.S. 113, 143 (1876). *The Railroad Commission Cases*, 116 U.S. 307 (1886) (holding that the state's regulatory power is subject to the "taking" standard of the "due process clause").

17. *See* John Nockelby, *Tortious Interference with Contractual Relations in the Nineteenth Century: The Transformation of Property, Contract and Tort*, 93 HARV. L. REV. 1510 (1980); Kenneth Vandevelde, *The New Property of the Nineteenth Century: The Development of the Modern Concept of Property*, 29 BUFFALO L. REV. 325 (1980); HORWITZ (1992), *supra* chap. 1, note 1, at 145–68 (summary and sources for writings on the dephysicalization of property).

18. International News Serv. v. Associated Press, 248 U.S. 215 (1918).

19. *Id.* at 231, 235, 236.

20. *Id.* at 236, 238, *aff'g*, 245 F. 244 (2d Cir. 1917), *modifying*, 240 F. 983 (S.D.N.Y. 1917).

21. 248 U.S. at 247 (Holmes, J., dissenting). *Cf.* FTC v. Beechnut Packing Co., 257 U.S. 441, 456 (1922) (Holmes, J., dissenting) (arguing that property ownership allows discretion over terms of resale and thus trumps both "competition" and "unfair" under FTC Act § 5).

22. *International News Serv.*, 248 U.S. at 249–52, 263 (Brandeis, J., dissenting). Brandeis wrote that if the framework was the common-law of trade secrets, then INS's lawful acquisition would resolve the dispute in its favor and not as the majority held. INS was "merely using [AP's] product without making compensation." Finally, if the public interest in copyright provided the analogy, the issue was even more troubling: Granting special property rights to AP would conflict with copyright protection policy and doctrine by permitting "curtailment of free use of knowledge and ideas." *Id.* at 260, 263.

23. A corresponding conflict between differing views of private property and public interest persisted in antitrust cases in which competition was identified as the public interest.

24. The rate cases raise some interesting questions that suggest the severe limitations imposed upon the states. In those cases, regulated corporations, typically utilities, were complaining that regulated prices did not permit a "fair return" to investors. The regulated utility and the regulating state often disagreed on how to value the utility's property. *See, e.g., Bluefield Water Works*, 262 U.S. 679 (1923) (Brandeis, J., concurring without opinion); *Missouri* ex rel *Southwestern Bell*, 262 U.S. 275, 291 (Brandeis, J., concurring); *Georgia Ry. & Power*, 262 U.S. 625 (Brandeis, J., for the Court).

25. 291 U.S. 502 (1934). Tyson Bros.-United Theatre Ticket Offices, Inc. v. Banton, 273 U.S. 418 (1927) (theatre ticket agents); Ribnik v. McBride, 277 U.S. 350 (1928) (employment agents); Williams v. Standard Oil of La., 278 U.S. 235 (1929) (gasoline).

26. *Tyson Bros.*, 273 U.S. at 427 (quoting Packard v. Banton, 264 U.S. 140, 143 (1924)); *Id.* at 428 (McReynolds, J., dissenting) (declaring that "the right of the owner to fix a price at which property shall be sold is an inherent attribute of property itself"). In Nebbia v. New York, 291 U.S. 502, 532 (1934), Justice Roberts wrote for the Court that price setting is not "sacrosanct." In his dissenting opinion, Justice McReynolds wrote that the New York statute's regulation of milk prices was a

"temerarious interference with the rights of property and contract . . . and with the natural law of supply and demand." *Id.* at 558.

27. *Tyson Bros.*, 273 U.S. at 430. Sutherland's view of the public interest was much more limited than Justice Field's formulation some fifty years earlier. The earlier view was not confined to a closed common-law category, but included any undertaking that involved a public grant. *See, e.g.*, Field's dissenting opinion in Munn v. Illinois, 94 U.S. 114, 136 (1876).

28. *Tyson Bros.*, 273 U.S. at 446. (Holmes, J., dissenting). Holmes had already characterized the police power in broad terms accepted by an earlier Court majority. *See* Noble State Bank v. Haskell, 219 U.S. 105, 110–12 (1911) ("the police power extends to all the great public needs . . ."). Justices Harlan Fiske Stone and Edward T. Sanford wrote separate dissenting opinions. Brandeis and Holmes also signed on to Stone's opinion.

29. In sharp contrast, the Supreme Court rarely overturned state antitrust statutes, just as it did not find the Sherman Act unconstitutional. *See* May (1986), *supra* chap.1, note 1.

30. United States v. Trenton Potteries Co., 273 U.S. 392 (1927). *Tyson Bros.*, 273 U.S. at 451. (Stone, J., dissenting). Sutherland's opinion is consistent with the classical economic model of competition derived from maximizing individual freedom of contract, while Stone's approach seems to derive from the neoclassical market model of competition.

31. *Williams*, 278 U.S. at 240.

32. *See* chap. 1; Roscoe Pound, *Liberty of Contract*, 18 YALE L. J. 454 (1909); Felix Cohen, *Transcendental Nonsense and the Functional Approach*, 35 COLUM L. REV. 809 (1935); THURMAN ARNOLD, THE FOLKLORE OF CAPITALISM 207–29 ([1937] 1962).

33. For a careful historical treatment of the associationalist movement in the United States, see Ellis Hawley, *Three Facets of Hooverian Associationalism: Lumber, Aviation, and Movies, 1921–1930*, in REGULATION IN PERSPECTIVE 95–123 (Thomas K. McCraw ed. 1981); for a study of the Commerce Department directly after the war, see Robert F. Himmelberg, *Business, Antitrust Policy and the Industrial Board of the Department of Commerce, 1919*, 42 BUS. HIST. REV. 1 (1968).

34. My analysis of trade associations is indebted to GEORGE STOCKING & MYRON WATKINS, MONOPOLY AND FREE ENTERPRISE (1951). *Id.* at 231–35, 238 (Stevenson). Clair Wilcox, *Competition and Monopoly in American Industry*, TNEC MONOGRAPH NO. 21 at 238–49 (1940).

35. Hawley, *Three Facets, supra* note 33, at 95 (Hoover). JOHN M. CLARK, STUDIES IN THE ECONOMICS OF OVERHEAD COSTS 432–35 (1923). American Column & Lumber Co. v. United States, 257 U.S. 377, 412 (Holmes, J., dissenting). *Id.* at 417 (Brandeis, J., dissenting).

36. THE INDEPENDENT, June 22, 1918, 482–83, *reprinted in* DONALD R. BRAND, CORPORATISM AND THE RULE OF LAW: A STUDY OF THE NATIONAL RECOVERY ADMINISTRATION 50 (1988) (Dewey). ARTHUR JEROME EDDY, THE NEW COMPETITION (1914); *see also* MILTON N. NELSON, OPEN PRICE ASSOCIATIONS (1922).

37. STOCKING & WATKINS, *supra* note 34, at 37 n.48. Hawley, *Three Facets, supra* note 33, at 98–9.

38. For an account of the artisan strain of antiindustrialism, antimodernism, and its cooption into the market logic of industrialism, see T.J. JACKSON LEARS, NO PLACE OF GRACE 59–96 (1981); see also G. EDWARD WHITE, THE EASTERN ESTABLISHMENT AND THE WESTERN EXPERIENCE 5–6, 172–177 (1968) ("contradictory attitudes toward industrial-

ism" later seen in Teddy Roosevelt's conservationism, antimonopoly sentiments, and faith in the "yeoman farmer").

39. Board of Trade of Chicago v. United States, 246 U.S. 231, 237, 238 (1918).

40. *Id.* at 238, 240. For a discussion of the four categories of competitive effects that the Court would evaluate over the next fifty years—unfair methods of competition, wealth transfers, efficiencies of different varieties, and economic power—see Peritz, *A Counter-History of Antitrust Law*, 1990 DUKE L.J. 263, 280–85.

41. Straus v. American Publisher's Ass'n, 231 U.S. 222 (1913). In all, there were ten trade association cases between 1913 and 1933.

42. *Chicago Board*, 246 U.S. at 244. American Column and Lumber Co. v. United States, 257 U.S. 377, 412–13 (1921) (Holmes, J., dissenting).

43. EDDY, *supra* note 36, at 1.

44. *American Column & Lumber Co.*, 257 U.S. at 385–86, 378, 383. Examples of explicit price-fixing include Straus v. American Publishers Ass'n, 231 U.S. 222 (1913); Ramsay v. Associated Bill Posters of Am., 260 U.S. 501 (1923).

45. *American Column & Lumber Co.*, 257 U.S. at 387–89.

46. *Id.* at 391–412, 394, 402, 403, 408, 405.

47. *Id.* at 393, 399, 410, 411–12. *See* THORSTEIN VEBLEN, ABSENTEE OWNERSHIP 128 (1923) (characterizing combinations as founded in view that the true domain of competition lay between absent owners and consumers).

48. *American Column & Lumber Co.*, 257 U.S. at 412–14 (Holmes, J., dissenting).

49. *Id.* at 414–15, 418 (Brandeis & McKenna, JJ., dissenting).

50. *Id.* at 417, 418.

51. 262 U.S. 371, 379, 386, 386, 389 (1923).

52. Even in *Chicago Board*, Brandeis abided the coercion in all contracts exposed in stunning manner by Robert Hale, *Coercion and Distribution in a Supposedly Non-Coercive State*, 38 POL. SCI. Q. 470 (1923).

53. Robert Hale, *Bargaining, Duress, and Economic Liberty*, 1943 COL. L. REV. 603; *see also* Hale, *Coercion and Distribution*, *supra* note 52.

54. For the information in this section, I am particularly indebted to the work of Ellis Hawley, *Three Facets*; Hawley, *Herbert Hoover, the Commerce Secretariat, and the Vision of an 'Associative State,' 1921–1928*, J. AM. HIST. 116–40 (1974); Hawley, *Herbert Hoover and the Sherman Act, 1921–1933: An Early Phase of a Continuing Issue*, 74 IOWA L. REV. 1067–1104 (1989). *See also* ROBERT F. HIMMELBERG, THE ORIGINS OF THE NATIONAL INDUSTRIAL RECOVERY ADMINISTRATION: BUSINESS, GOVERNMENT, AND THE TRADE ASSOCIATION ISSUE, 1921–1933 (1976); PAUL L. MURPHY, THE CONSTITUTION IN CRISIS TIMES 68–96 (1972); STOCKING & WATKINS, *supra* note 34, at 38, 405.

55. Hawley (1989), *supra* note 54, at 1073–85.

56. Maple Flooring Mfrs. Ass'n v. United States, 268 U.S. 563, 582–83, 566–67, 577 (1925).

57. *Id.* at 567–68.

58. *Id.* at 579.

59. For discussion of the price-fixing cases, see Peritz, *A Counter-History of Antitrust Law*, 1990 DUKE L.J. at 279–99.

60. Vegelahn v. Guntner, 44 N.E. 1077, 1081 (1896) (Holmes, J., dissenting).

61. TOMLINS, *supra* chap. 1 note 1, at 32–95; William Forbath, *The Shaping of the American Labor Movement*, 102 HARV. L. REV. 1109, 1112 n.12 (1989) (citing Samuel Gompers's view, as early as 1901, that the best thing for labor was that the state leave labor alone).

62. PURCELL (1973), *supra* chap. 1. note 1, at 117–27.

63. William H. Taft, *The Right of Private Property*, 3 MICH. L.J. 215, 231 (1894). *See generally* FELIX FRANKFURTER & NATHAN GREENE, THE LABOR INJUNCTION (1930); CLYDE SUMMERS, HARRY WELLINGTON & ALAN HYDE, CASES AND MATERIALS ON LABOR LAW 186–89 (2d ed. 1982); Alpheus Mason, *The Labor Decisions of Chief Justice Taft*, 78 U. PA. L. REV. 585 (1930); Edgar A. Jones, Jr., *Picketing and Coercion, A Jurisprudence of Epithets*, 39 VA. L. REV. 1023 (1953); Haggai Hurvitz, *American Labor Law and the Doctrine of Entrepreneurial Property Rights: Boycotts, Courts, and the Juridical Reorientation of 1886–1895*, 8 INDUS. REL. L.J. 307 (1986); Dianne Avery, *Images of Violence in Labor Jurisprudence: The Regulation of Picketing and Boycotts, 1894–1921*, 37 BUFF. L. REV. 1 (1988).

64. Some labor historians have argued that unions gave up their political agenda in the face of the dominant legal regime's relentless opposition, especially the federal courts, an agenda that reappeared in aspects of the New Deal. *See, e.g.*, Forbath, *supra* note 61, at 1112. However, recent work by Katherine van Wezel Stone, as yet unpublished, suggests that the political agenda changed—from seeking rights to seeking immunities.

65. Loewe v. Lawlor, 208 U.S. 274, 304–05 (1908).

66. Roscoe Pound, *Liberty of Contract*, 18 YALE L.J. 454 (1909); *see* Peritz, *The "Rule of Reason" in Antitrust Law: Property Logic in Restraint of Competition*, 40 HASTINGS L.J. 285, n.16, 51, 255–61 (1989). For a thoughtful treatment of the republicanist ideology that permeated labor associations before the turn of the century and the anti-individualist epithets it provoked from opponents and commentators, see TOMLINS, *supra* chap. 1 note 1, at 63–95.

67. Francis B. Sayre, *Criminal Conspiracy*, 35 HARV. L. REV. 420 (1921). For a description and insightful analysis of the question of union incorporation, particularly a public debate between Samuel Gompers and Louis Brandeis in 1902, see TOMLINS, *supra* chap. 1 note 1, at 86–91.

68. National Ass'n of Window Glass Mfrs. v. United States, 263 U.S. 403, 411 (1923).

69. *Id.* at 412–13.

70. Bedford Cut Stone Co. v. Journeyman Stone Cutters' Ass'n of Am., 274 U.S. 37, 48, 52–54, 60 (1927); *id.* at 65 (Brandeis, J. dissenting, joined by Holmes, J.). In addition to citing early labor injunction cases, Sutherland referred to Eastern States Lumber Ass'n v. United States, 234 U.S. 600 (1914), an early trade association case decided according to classical cartel doctrine. 274 U.S. at 54. Sutherland made no mention of the more recent *Maple Flooring* decision and its approval of trade associations.

71. *Bedford Cut Stone Co.*, 274 U.S. at 65. FORBATH, *supra* chap. 1 note 1, 193–98 (Appendix A).

72. FREDERICK H. COOKE, THE LAW OF COMBINATIONS, MONOPOLIES, AND LABOR UNIONS 33 (2d ed. 1909). *See generally* HERBERT HOVENKAMP, ENTERPRISE AND AMERICAN LAW 207–240 (1991) and sources cited therein. I ARTHUR JEROME EDDY, A TREATISE ON THE LAW OF COMBINATIONS 412 (1901). Hopkins v. Oxley Stove Co., 83 F. 912, 919 (8th Cir. 1897). *See also* CHRISTOPHER G. TIEDEMAN, A TREATISE ON STATE AND FEDERAL CONTROL OF PERSONS AND PROPERTY IN THE UNITED STATES 452–53 (1900) ("fettering of the individual, glaringly at variance with that freedom in the pursuit of happiness . . . guaranteed to all").

73. *See generally* C. Bertrand Tompson, *Relations of Scientific Management to Labor*, 30 Q. J. ECON. 311 (1915); Tompson, *The Literature of Scientific Management*, 31 Q. J. ECON. 506 (1914); James Laurence Laughlin, *The Unions v. Higher Wages*, 14 J. POL. ECON. 129 (1906); R. F. Hoxie, *Why Organized Labor Opposes Scientific Management*, 31 Q. J.

ECON. 62 (1916). Among the writings of John Bates Clark, see *The Possibility of a Scientific Law of Wages*, 4 PUBLICATIONS, AM. ECON. ASSN. 37 (1889); *Distribution as Determined by a Law of Rent*, 5 Q. J. ECON. 289 (1891); THE DISTRIBUTION OF WEALTH (1899). For claims of organized labor's increased efficiency, *see* John R. Commons, *Labor's Attitude toward Industrial Efficiency*, 1 AM. ECON. REV. 563 (1911). *See also* Frederick W. Taylor's writings, especially SHOP MANAGEMENT (1911) and THE PRINCIPLES OF SCIENTIFIC MANAGEMENT (1911). The tenets of "Taylorism," of assembly-line production associated with the early success of Henry Ford, were quickly understood as antithetical to the labor movement in two ways. First, the specialization of assembly-line workers de-skilled them, taking away their "property" of specialized knowledge and thereby their bargaining power. In the process, trade unions also lost bargaining power. Second, "Taylorism" produced a gap, a hierarchy, between workers, now unskilled, and management, now knowledgeable. In this context, scientific management must be understood in terms far broader than Hoover's conferences to increase productive efficiency, standardize industry practices, and decrease waste. Just as important was the long-term effect of disempowering workers.

74. For an extended analysis of *Dr. Miles*, *see* Peritz, *A Genealogy of Vertical Restraints Doctrine*, 40 HASTINGS L. J. 511, 516–27 (1989). Holmes wrote of employer-employee competition in Vegelahn v. Guntner, 167 Mass. 92, 107, 44 N.E. 897, 904 (1896); *see also* Holmes, *Privilege, Malice, and Intent*, 8 HARV. L. REV. 1 (1894).

75. JOHN KENNETH GALBRAITH, ECONOMICS IN PERSPECTIVE: A CRITICAL HISTORY 5, 108–12, 266 (1987); THOMAS KUHN, THE STRUCTURE OF SCIENTIFIC REVOLUTION (2d ed. 1970).

76. It was Arthur C. Pigou, successor to Alfred Marshall at Cambridge, who attacked the marginalists' anomalous position that the marginal utility of money, unlike everything else, did not decline with increasing amount. That is, Pigou held that a pound sterling or dollar is worth more to the poor than to the rich. Thus, there is an allocative efficiency logic in redistributing wealth. PIGOU, THE ECONOMICS OF WELFARE (1920). Mainstream economists continue to deny the Pigovian formulation or, in the alternative, to treat it as unworkable.

Productive efficiency—the operational engineering notion of getting the most from the least—has no necessary relationship with allocative efficiency, except in the platonic world of perfect competition. *See, e.g.*, Lewis Kornhauser, *A Guide to the Perplexed Claims of Efficiency in the Law*, 8 HOFSTRA L. REV. 591, 596 (1980).

77. William H. Taft, *The Right of Private Property*, 3 MICH. L.J. at 219, 231 (1894); letter from William Howard Taft to Helen Herron Taft (July 1894), *quoted in* JUDITH ICKE ANDERSON, WILLIAM HOWARD TAFT: AN INTIMATE HISTORY 63 (1981); ARNOLD PAUL, CONSERVATIVE CRISIS AND THE RULE OF LAW: ATTITUDES OF BAR AND BENCH, 1887–1895 153 (1960); for a more recent treatment, *see* Avery, *supra* note 63.

78. Atchison Topeka & Santa Fe Ry. v. Gee, 139 F. 582, 584 (C.C.S.D. Iowa 1905); United States v. Debs, 64 F. 724, 759–60 (1894); Farmers' Loan & Trust v. Northern Pac. Ry., 60 F. 803, 821 (C.C.E.D. Wisc. 1894); *In re* Phelan, 62 F. 803, 815 (C.C.S.D. Ohio 1894) (Taft, J.).

79. Duplex Printing v. Deering, 254 U.S. 443 (1921); Truax v. Corrigan, 257 U.S. 312 (1921) (any business activity is an extension of property rights). ALEXANDER BICKEL, THE UNPUBLISHED OPINIONS OF MR. JUSTICE BRANDEIS 78–84 (1957). Foreshadowed three years earlier in Justice Pitney's *International News Service* (1918) opinion, which defined a property interest as any "pecuniary right," the *Duplex* opinion's formulation was expanded even more in American Steel Foundaries v. Tri-City Cent. Trades Council, 257 U.S. 184, 204 (1921), which propounded a "property right of access of the employer." *See* Hurvitz, *supra* note 63, at 342–44. Pitney's capacious view of in-

timidation as including "persuasion" was not inconsistent with the narrow, common-law view of speech rights expressed in the Court's adoption of the "clear and present danger" doctrine. I discuss *Schenck* (1919) and its progeny later in this chapter. The "persuasion" question was, however, more complicated. A few months after *Duplex*, Chief Justice Taft wrote in *American Steel Foundaries*, 257 U.S. at 208–11, that the Clayton Act protected persuasive activities by employees and, moreover, that common-law doctrine protected such activities by others with a future interest in working for the particular employer being picketed. *See* Avery, *supra* note 63, at 85.

80. *Truax*, 257 U.S. at 368. For an explication and elaboration of the notion of property as sovereignty, see the work of legal realists Robert L. Hale and Morris Cohen, particularly Hale, *Rate Making and the Revision of the Property Concept*, 1922 COLUM. L. REV. 209, 214 and *Coercion and Distribution in a Supposedly Non-Coercive State*, 38 POL. SCI. REV. 470 (1923), and Cohen, *Property and Sovereignty*, 13 CORNELL L.Q. 8 (1927).

81. For a study of the legislative history behind the "ambivalent" language of the labor exemption, see Daniel R. Ernst, *The Labor Exemption*, 1908–1914, 74 IOWA L. REV. 1151 (1989). The Clayton Act provision, currently codified at 15 U.S.C. § 17 (1992), ultimately took the form: "The labor of a human being is not a commodity or an article of commerce." That formulation had particular rhetorical resonances, particularly in the key of property rights. In short, its non-commodity-ness implied that property rights arguments were unavailable for claims of labor's right to organize. At the same time, business enterprise was commodified—that is, identified as property by way of injury to profits. Within this rhetorical structure, property rights arguments were available only to owners.

82. United States v. Wheeler, 254 U.S. 281 (1920); MURPHY, *supra* note 54, at 31, 36. Regarding the railroad shopman's strike, see ZECHARIAH CHAFEE, JR., THE INQUIRING MIND 198 ff. (1928). *See generally* SAMUEL P. ORTH, THE ARMIES OF LABOR (1919); ROBERT H. WIEBE, THE SEARCH FOR ORDER, 1877–1920 (1967); Mark Kelman, *American Labor Law and Legal Formalism: How "Legal Logic" Shaped and Vitiated the Rights of American Workers*, 58 ST. JOHN'S L. REV. 1 (1983); Tomlins, *supra* chap. 1, note 1; B. W. Poulson, *Criminal Conspiracy, Injunctions, and Damage Suits in Labor Law*, 7 J. LEG. HIST. 212 (1986).

83. A narrow pathway into the cultural imagination, perhaps only that of the cultural elite, opens in the entry for "cooperation" found in the ENCYCLOPAEDIA BRITANNICA 745 (11th ed. New Volumes 1922). "Cooperation," defined as "economic organization," gives as examples consumers, industrial producers, credit and banking, and agriculture. Missing is any reference to labor unions as a form of economic organization.

84. Justice McReynolds, writing for the Court in Meyers v. Nebraska, 262 U.S. 390 (1923), held the foreign-language-teaching statutes unconstitutional, despite an expansive reading of the liberty interests protected under the Fourteenth Amendment. The historical information in this paragraph is gleaned from THE READER'S COMPANION TO AMERICAN HISTORY (Eric Foner & John A. Garrity eds. 1991); THE TIMETABLES OF HISTORY: A HORIZONTAL LINKAGE OF PEOPLE AND EVENTS (Bernard Grun ed. 1979); ENCYCLOPAEDIA OF THE SOCIAL SCIENCES (Edwin R.A. Seligman ed. 1937).

85. Debs v. United States, 249 U.S. 211 (1919). *See generally* NICK SALVATORE, EUGENE V. DEBS: CITIZEN AND SOCIALIST (1982).

86. Schenck v. United States, 249 U.S. 47 (1919); Froework v. United States, 249 U.S. 204 (1919); Debs. v. United States, 249 U.S. 211 (1919); Abrams v. United States, 250 U.S. 616 (1919).

87. *Schenck*, 249 U.S. at 47 (Holmes, J., writing for a unanimous Court) ("clear

and present danger"); *Abrams*, 250 U.S. at 630 (1919) (Holmes, J., dissenting) ("free trade in ideas"). For an illuminating discussion, see WHITE (1993), *supra* chap. 1, note 1, at 412–54.

88. For historical and cultural studies of advertising, see, for example, STEWART EWEN, CAPTAINS OF CONSCIOUSNESS (1976); ROLAND MARCHAND, ADVERTISING THE AMERICAN DREAM: MAKING WAY FOR MODERNITY, 1920–1940 (1985); DANIEL POPE, THE MAKING OF MODERN ADVERTISING (1983); SUSAN STRASSER, SATISFACTION GUARANTEED: THE MAKING OF THE AMERICAN MASS MARKET (1989); STEWART EWEN & ELIZABETH EWEN, CHANNELS OF DESIRE, MASS IMAGES AND THE SHAPING OF AMERICAN CONSCIOUSNESS (1982); RICHARD S. TEDLOW, NEW AND IMPROVED: THE STORY OF MASS MARKETING IN AMERICA (1990).

89. *Gompers*, 221 U.S. 418, 420 n.1, 436–39 (1911); WHITE (1993), *supra* chap. 1, n.1, at 350–51, 413–14; Rabban, *supra* chap. 1, n.1, at 531–3. The English common law treated speech, as Holmes described it in private correspondence in 1919, as another "act you don't like" and thus, Holmes wrote, "free speech stands no differently than freedom from vaccination." Holmes's letter excerpts are quoted and discussed in WHITE, *id.* at 425–26.

90. The earliest attempt to organize labor associations at the national level seems to have been the National Labor Union conference held in Baltimore in 1866. DAVID MONTGOMERY, BEYOND EQUALITY: LABOR AND THE RADICAL REPUBLICANS, 1862–1872 176–96 (1967). Of those attending the 1866 meeting, the National Typographical Union, founded in 1850, has the earliest date of origin, according to Montgomery's Appendix B, at 458, although it is not clear that the organization used the same name since its inception. For a collection and synthesis of studies investigating the links between labor unions and free speech during this period and into the New Deal, see Note, *A New Deal for Free Speech: Free Speech and the Labor Movement of the 1930s*, 80 VA. L. REV. 291, 300–04 (1994) (by student author Geoffrey D. Berman). *See generally* PAUL L. MURPHY, WORLD WAR I AND THE ORIGIN OF CIVIL LIBERTIES IN THE UNITED STATES (1979).

91. Gitlow v. New York, 268 U.S. 652, 657–59 (1925).

92. American School of Magnetic Healing v. McAnnulty, 187 U.S. 94, 98, 104 (1902).

93. Meyer v. Nebraska, 262 U.S. 390 (1923) (Holmes & Sutherland, JJ., dissenting); for discussion of pre-1918 speech cases, see Rabban, *supra*, chap. 1, note 1. *Gitlow*, 268 U.S. at 672 (Holmes & Brandeis, JJ., dissenting).

94. *See generally* POPE, *supra* note 88; Leverett S. Lyon, *Advertising*, I ENCYCLOPAEDIA OF THE SOCIAL SCIENCES 469 (1930); TEDLOW, *supra* note 88; for an exploration of World War I and its impact, see DAVID M. KENNEDY, OVER HERE: THE FIRST WORLD WAR AND AMERICAN SOCIETY (1980). MURPHY, *supra* note 15, at 1–8; JAMES R. MOCK & CEDRIC LARSON, WORDS THAT WON THE WAR: THE STORY OF THE COMMITTEE ON PUBLIC INFORMATION (1939). In 1917, Wilson also issued a proclamation forbidding any alien from Germany or its allies from publishing criticism of the United States government. One year later, alien registration and arrests began. PAUL MURPHY, WORLD WAR I AND THE ORIGIN OF CIVIL LIBERTIES IN THE UNITED STATES 74 (1979).

95. The information for this description came from the "advertisement" entry in I NEW VOLUMES 11–12 (1922) to ENCYCLOPAEDIA BRITANNICA (11th ed. 1910).

96. These statements are compiled and reproduced in MARCHAND, *supra* note 88, at 5–6.

97. I ENCYCLOPAEDIA BRITANNICA 235–42 (11th ed. 1910).

98. I NEW VOLUMES 11–12 (1922) to ENCYCLOPAEDIA BRITANNICA (11th ed. 1910).

99. MARCHAND, *supra* note 88, at xx–xxii); POPE, *supra* note 88, at 6–16; EWEN, *supra* note 88, at 64–65 ("great Americanizer"), 68 ("answer to Bolshevism").

100. EDWARD L. BERNAYS, PROPAGANDA 31 (1928) and BERNAYS, CRYSTALLIZING PUBLIC OPINION 47–48 (1923); EDWARD A. FILENE, SUCCESSFUL LIVING IN THE MACHINE AGE 147 (1931); EWEN, *supra* note 88, at 88–91 (quotations and Parker Pen Company advertisement).

101. Stromberg v. California, 283 U.S. 359 (1931) (free speech) (McReynolds & Butler, JJ., dissenting); Near v. Minnesota, 283 U.S. 697 (1931) (freedom of the press) (Butler, Van Devanter, McReynolds & Sutherland, JJ., dissenting).

102. Although both Harold Hotelling and Joan Robinson published research that overlapped Chamberlin's work in some significant respects, Chamberlin's is not only more influential in the United States but also more accessible. Thus, I focus on his work. Harold Hotelling, *Stability in Competition*, 39 ECON. J. 41 (1920); JOAN ROBINSON, THE ECONOMICS OF IMPERFECT COMPETITION 88–90, 179 (1933) (defining "imperfect competition" in terms of imperfectly elastic demand; setting out a rigorous definition of marginal revenue); *see also* Piero Sraffa, *The Laws of Returns Under Competitive Conditions*, 26 ECON. J. 535–50 (1926) ("Monopoly, not competition, is the normal market situation."), cited in both CHAMBERLIN and ROBINSON. Perhaps most influential of all was the withering attack on the sufficiency of any political economy limited to microeconomics, limited to the self-regulating price mechanism of markets, in JOHN MAYNARD KEYNES, THE GENERAL THEORY OF EMPLOYMENT INTEREST AND MONEY (1936).

103. EDWARD H. CHAMBERLIN, THE THEORY OF MONOPOLISTIC COMPETITION 4, 8, 9 (1933).

104. *Id.* at 46, 48.

105. *Id.* at 56, 57.

106. *Id.* at 71. I take up Chamberlin's usage of the term "advertising" to mean the larger category of expenditures intended to "alter the shape or the position of the demand curve for a product." *Id.* at 117. There is a fourth strategy available—that of an oligopolist. *Id.* at 100–04.

107. *Id.* at 273–74. As we approach the twenty-first century, this transformation seems to raise difficult constitutional questions about the extent to which First Amendment speech jurisprudence should shield commercial actors' exercise of economic power for purely economic purposes, much like the questions raised by the *Lochner*ian freedom of contract jurisprudence that protected commercial actors from government regulation in the first third of the twentieth century.

108. JOSEPH A. SCHUMPETER, CAPITALISM, SOCIALISM AND DEMOCRACY 83 (1942) [emphasis added]. For his earlier and more circumspect description of economic development as "revolutionary" or discontinuous change by entrepreneurs, see SCHUMPETER, THE THEORY OF ECONOMIC DEVELOPMENT (first German language edition 1911) (R. Opie trans. 1934), particularly his discussion of the "fundamental phenomenon of economic development" at 57–94.

109. SCHUMPETER (1942), *supra* note 108, at 106.

110. BERLE & MEANS, THE MODERN CORPORATION AND PRIVATE PROPERTY 356 (1932). *See also* THORSTEIN VEBLEN, THE ENGINEERS AND THE PRICE SYSTEM chaps. 5 & 6 (1921) (*On the relationship between technicians and the revolution*).

111. The orthodox view of Berle and Means places them in a debate with E. Merrick Dodd about the corporation's proper constituency. In this view, Berle and Means are associated with the argument that shareholders are the sole constituency that management should serve, while Dodd is associated with the argument that a broader constituency is appropriate. The orthodox view is based on an exchange of articles between Berle and Dodd. Adolf Berle, *Corporate Powers as Powers in Trust*, 44 HARV. L. REV. 1049 (1931); E. Merrick Dodd, *For Whom Are Corporate Managers Trust-*

ees?, 45 HARV. L. REV. 1145 (1932); Berle, *For Whom Corporate Managers Are Trustees: A Note*, 45 HARV. L. REV. 1365 (1932) [hereinafter *A Note*]; Dodd, *Is Effective Enforcement of the Fiduciary Duties of Corporate Managers Practicable?*, 2 U. CHI. L. REV. 194 (1935). But Berle's views must be distinguished from those appearing in the *Modern Corporation* book. In sharp contrast to the position taken in the Berle and Means book, Berle wrote that "economic civil war" would be the practical consequence of rivalry among corporate stakeholders. *A Note*, 45 HARV. L. REV. at 1369. The *Modern Corporation* book, noted at 45 HARV. L. REV. at nn.4 and 9, not only expressed agreement with Dodd in theory, but offered a practical framework of government supervision. Indeed, Berle would change his opinion more than once. Twenty years later, he portrayed corporate management as disciplined by the methods and values constituting professional expertise. *See* ADOLF BERLE, THE TWENTIETH CENTURY CAPITALIST REVOLUTION 63–64 (1954); BERLE, POWER WITHOUT PROPERTY 108–09 (1959); *see generally* JORDAN A. SCHWARZ, LIBERAL: ADOLF A. BERLE AND THE VISION OF AN AMERICAN ERA (1987). For an earlier exposition of the progressive socio-economic possibilities attendant to business managers' development of a professional attitude, see LOUIS BRANDEIS, BUSINESS—A PROFESSION (1925)

Chapter 3

1. ARTHUR SCHLESINGER, THE AGE OF ROOSEVELT: THE POLITICS OF UPHEAVAL 279 (1960).

2. National Industrial Recovery Act of 1933 [NIRA], 73d Cong., Sess. 1, Ch. 90, Pub. Law No. 67, June 16, 1933, 15 U.S.C. §§ 701–12. *See generally* ROBERT F. HIMMELBERG, *supra* chap. 2 note 54. Perhaps the most influential treatment of competition policy during the New Deal is ELLIS W. HAWLEY, THE NEW DEAL AND THE PROBLEM OF MONOPOLY (1966). Hawley's political history pays no attention, however, to the rhetorics at play and in consequence deals only in passing with the imaginative framework for the interest group politics he chronicles so well. For a recent and compelling analysis of fiscal policies during the New Deal, see ALAN BRINKLEY, THE END OF REFORM: NEW DEAL LIBERALISM IN RECESSION AND WAR (1995).

3. The term "liberal" can be confusing here. I have used the term to reflect an ideology which animated the "conservative" Supreme Court under Chief Justices White and Taft between 1910 and 1930, a Court committed to liberty of contract as the major premise for both constitutional and antitrust policy. New Deal liberals viewed the classical rendition as conservative because they were portrayed as conserving the status quo. In seeking to minimize the confusion, I call the New Dealers, as well as the more progressive faction on the Court (composed of some progressives, some New Deal liberals, and others) "new liberals" or "New Deal liberals." I call the more conservative faction "classical liberals" or "conservatives."

The orthodox view of the New Deal held by historians, although acknowledging diverse and conflicting strands of political economy, has two foci, each presented as a binary opposition. First, much has been made of the conflict between the conservative Supreme Court majority and the political mandate for a liberal New Deal. For a recent discussion of the influence of legal doctrine on the "constitutional revolution" of 1937, particularly Justice Robert's "switch in time," *see* Barry Cushman, *Rethinking the New Deal Court*, 80 VA. L. REV. 201 (1994) and Edward A. Purcell, Jr., *Rethinking Constitutional Change*, 80 VA. L. REV. 277 (1994) (commenting on the Cushman article). Second, close attention has been paid to substantial policy shifts: from early suspension of the antitrust laws under the statist National Industrial Recovery Act of 1933, to a reinvigorated commitment to "free competition," culminating in 1938 with Arnold's antitrust crusade. Indeed, following historian Arthur M. Schlesinger, Jr., many see the Roosevelt administration's shift to free enterprise beginning as early as the congressional session following the midterm elections of 1934. SCHLESINGER, THE AGE OF ROOSEVELT: THE POLITICS OF UPHEAVAL 272–394 (1960). Yet, mainstream historians seem to share Richard Hofstadter's view that the New Deal never really followed any single, coherent vision, but rather reflected both conflict and compromise. For Hofstadter, the conflict, while exhibiting numerous strains, was driven most forcefully by a long-lived tension between an ideology of individualism and the material benefits of large-scale organization. The compromise involved a "chaos of experimentation," a "masterly shifting equipoise of interests" in securing the new fiscal role of government. Nonetheless, like their progressive forebears, the New Deal liberals were committed to some positive government role in the nation's economic life. RICHARD HOFSTADTER, THE AGE OF REFORM: FROM BRYAN TO FDR 5, 217–22, 272–317 (1955). *See also* PAUL MURPHY, THE CONSTITUTION IN CRISIS TIMES 128–69 (1972); ELLIS W. HAWLEY, THE NEW DEAL AND THE PROBLEM OF MONOPOLY 4, 472 ([1966] 1969).

4. *ALA Schechter Poultry v. United States*, 295 U.S. 495 (1935).

5. *Hearings before the Committee on Ways and Means*, H.R. 73d Cong, 1st Sess.; on H.R. 5664, A Bill to Encourage National Industrial Recovery, to Foster Fair Competition, and to Provide for the Construction of Certain Useful Public Works, and for Other Purposes (May 18, 19, 20, 1933), NATIONAL INDUSTRIAL RECOVERY HEARINGS AND REPORTS (Library of Department of Commerce 1933) [HEARINGS AND REPORTS]. Wagner Statement, *id.*, May 18, 1933, at 91. Harriman Statement, *id.*, May 19, 1933, at 132.

6. NIRA § 1; HEARINGS AND REPORTS at 96.

7. HEARINGS AND REPORTS at 134.

8. *Id.* at 78–79. DONALD BRAND, CORPORATISM AND THE RULE OF LAW 88 (1988).

9. HAWLEY, *supra* note 3, at 29.

10. Statement of Donald R. Richberg, HEARINGS AND REPORTS, May 18, 1933, at 75–85.

11. 73d Cong., 1st Sess., Ch. 90, Pub. Law No. 67, June 16, 1933; 15 U.S.C. §§ 701–12, NIRA § 7(a). PETER H. IRONS, THE NEW DEAL LAWYERS 205 (1982) (Sen. Wagner).

12. *Id.* at 96 (Sen. Wagner). HEARINGS AND REPORTS at 66–71 (May 18, 1933) (Richberg).

13. HEARINGS AND REPORTS at 406 (Senate Hearings May 22, 26, 29, 31, June 1, 1933).

14. Senator Arthur Capper (R.Kan.) and Representative Dennis W. Marland (D.Okla.) sponsored the original oil regulation provision. HEARINGS AND REPORTS at 35–273.

15. HEARINGS AND STATEMENTS (Sen. Comm. on Finance) at 273–74 (Emery). *Id.* (House Ways and Means Comm.) at 138 (Treadway and Harrison), 108 (Crowther).

16. HEARINGS AND REPORTS at 100–01 (House hearings). CONG. REC., 73d Cong., 1st Sess., 1933, 77:5165, quoted in DONALD R. BRAND, CORPORATISM AND THE LAW 87 (1988).

17. HEARINGS AND REPORTS at 73 (Jenkins in House hearings), 394 (Lamont in Senate hearings), 388–89 (Hook in Senate hearings).

18. HEARINGS AND REPORTS at 404–06 (Senate hearings). Lewis could have added that steel industry members typically associated twice: once to form a corporation or firm, and a second time to form a trade association. The Norris-LaGuardia Act of 1932, passed overwhelmingly in the last year of Hoover's presidency, had already granted workers the rights to organize and strike. Known as the anti-injunction stat-

ute, it was endorsed by progressives and conservatives alike. The Supreme Court declined to review lower court decisions enforcing the statute until 1938, when it upheld the statute. *See* MURPHY, *supra* note 3, at 117–18.

19. HEARINGS AND REPORTS at 15 (Gore in Senate Hearings), 160 (same), 209 (Titus).

20. ARTHUR SCHLESINGER, THE COMING OF THE NEW DEAL 88 (1958).

21. HAWLEY, *supra* note 3, at 56–58.

22. SCHLESINGER, *supra* note 3, at 447. HOFSTADTER, *supra* note 3, at 306–16. Hawley, *supra* note 3, at 57–67. IRONS, *supra* note 11, at 31–37. STOCKING & WATKINS, MONOPOLY AND FREE ENTERPRISE 43–44 (1951); BRAND, *supra* note 16, at 11–18, 81–83 (1988). ALA Schechter Poultry Corp. v. United States, 295 U.S. 495 (1935).

23. STOCKING & WATKINS, *supra* note 22, at 44; HOFSTADTER, *supra* note 3, at 272–317; HAWLEY, *supra* note 3, at 66; IRONS, *supra* note 11, at 29–31, 39–40. The nineteen cases mentioned in the text all involved questions of constitutional law. IRONS, *supra* note 11, at 55.

24. HAWLEY, *supra* note 3, at 83–98; IRONS, *supra* note 11, at 38–40.

25. HEARINGS AND REPORTS at 26 (Senate). HAWLEY, *supra* note 3, at 21–26; IRONS, *supra* note 11, at 203–25; BRAND, *supra* note 16, at 229–60.

26. HAWLEY, *supra* note 3, at 62–67; IRONS, *supra* note 11, at 30–32, 203–06.

27. HAWLEY, *supra* note 3, at 22, 61–67; IRONS, *supra* note 11, at 30–33, 203–15; BRAND, *supra* note 16, at 232–69.

28. National Labor Relations Act, ch. 372, § 1, 49 Stat. 449 (1935), codified at 29 U.S.C. § 151 (1992). The NLRA did recognize the disparate treatment of labor and capital collectives and its impact on bargaining power in labor relations: "The inequality of bargaining power between employees who do not possess full freedom of association or actual liberty of contract, and employers who are organized in the corporate or other forms of ownership association substantially burdens and affects the flow of commerce, and tends to aggravate recurrent business depressions, by depressing wage rates and the purchasing power of wage earners in industry and by preventing the stabilization of competitive wage rates and working conditions within and between industries." *See generally* Katherine Stone, *The Post-War Paradigm in American Labor Law*, 90 YALE L.J. 1509 (1981) (industrial pluralism as basis for labor relations theory and practice); Karl Klare, *Labor Law as Ideology: Toward a New Historiography of Collective Bargaining Law*, 4 IND. REL. L.J. 450 (1981) (historical materialism as a viable approach).

29. HAWLEY, *supra* 3, at 51–65, 78–94; IRONS, *supra* note 11, at 31–33; BRAND, *supra* note 16, at 99–120; STOCKING & WATKINS, *supra* note 22, at 43–45, 232–37.

30. 295 U.S. 495, 535, 527, 537, 535 (1934). In Panama Refining Co. v. Ryan, 293 U.S. 388 (1935), the Court held NIRA § 9(c) an unconstitutional delegation of congressional power to state regulatory commissions. For a thoughtful analysis of delegation doctrine, based on Public Choice theory, see DAVID SCHOENBROD, POWER WITHOUT RESPONSIBILITY: HOW CONGRESS ABUSES THE PEOPLE THROUGH DELEGATION (1993).

31. Sugar Inst. v. United States, 297 U.S. 553 (1936). Nebbia v. New York, 291 U.S. 502 (1934). Although the minority faction was composed of progressives and "new liberals," I use "progressive" as a short-hand rendition. While that can be misleading insofar as it suggests that the minority faction was always "led" by post-progressive sentiments, it does make sense in dealing with questions of political economy to the extent that the minority faction shared the sometimes conflicting views that the judicial role called for deference to the legislature and that social welfare called for a balancing of public policy with individual interests, including but not limited to private property rights. For illuminating analyses of both the progressive/

liberal distinction and the jurisprudential persona of the sitting Justices, see G. EDWARD WHITE, THE AMERICAN JUDICIAL TRADITION 150–77 (Holmes and Brandeis), 178–99 (Sutherland, Butler, McReynolds, and Van Devanter), 200–29 (Hughes and Stone) (1988). For a helpful discussion of the progressive/liberal traditions in politics, see HOFSTADTER, *supra* note 3, at 18, 302–28; SCHLESINGER, *supra* note 3, at 385–94.

32. O'Gorman & Young v. Hartford Fire Ins. Co., 282 U.S. 251 (1931). Justice Roberts was the junior member of the Court. Chief Justice Hughes, however, was neither new nor junior. Not only was he the Chief Justice but he had served as an Associate Justice between 1910 and 1916.

33. New State Ice Co. v. Liebmann, 285 U.S. 262, 277, 302, 204 (1932).

34. Home Building & Loan Co. v. Blaisdell, 290 U.S. 398 (1934). *See* WHITE, *supra* note 31, at 192–212 (1988) (Roberts, J.).

35. *Nebbia*, 291 U.S. at 506, 507.

36. *Id.* at 518, 529–30.

37. *Id.* at 523–30. Roberts wrote that price-setting is not "sacrosanct"—that is, state price-fixing does not call for stricter scrutiny than other economic regulation. *Id.* at 532.

38. *Id.* at 523, 524.

39. *Id.* at 524, 537, 538. Roberts does assert a distinction between property rights and freedom of contract: Property rights involve use of one's property while contract rights need not. Apparently, Roberts overlooked or misunderstood the implications of Justice Pitney's opinion in *International News Service* (1918), defining any right that has some market value as a property right. That collapse of property into contract rights was given its modern structure by Wesley Hohfeld in *Some Fundamental Legal Conceptions as Applied in Judicial Reasoning*, 23 YALE L.J. 16 (1913).

40. *Morehead*, 298 U.S. 587 (1936). Adkins v. Children's Hosp., 261 U.S. 525 (1923) (Taft, Sanford, Holmes, JJ., dissenting; Brandeis, J., not voting).

41. *Morehead*, 298 U.S. at 610, 617.

42. 290 U.S. 399, 441, 448–51, 488 (Sutherland, J., dissenting). Sutherland concluded with as good a description of legal formalism as can be found: Provisions of the Constitution are "pliable in the sense that . . . they have the capacity of bringing within their grasp every new condition which falls within their meaning. . . . But their meaning is changeless; it is only their application which is extensible." Compare Max Weber's short description of legal formalism in WEBER, *supra* chap. 1, note 87.

43. *Id.* at 429 (emphasis added), 428 (citing Ogden v. Sanders, 12 Wheat. 212, 286, 6 L. Ed. 606 (1827)).

44. *Adkins*, 261 U.S. at 569–70 (Holmes, J., dissenting). *Tipaldo*, 298 U.S. at 626. (Hughes, J., dissenting).

45. 298 U.S. at 629. One year later, Hughes's view would attract Roberts and reappear as the majority opinion in West Coast Hotel v. Parrish, 361 U.S. 841 (1937), one of the decisions producing the "constitutional revolution" of 1937.

46. Appalachian Coals, Inc. v. United States, 288 U.S. 344, 359–61, 382 (1933).

47. Sugar Inst., Inc. v. United States, 297 U.S. 553 (1936), *aff'ing* 15 F. Supp. 817.

48. *Appalachian Coals*, 288 U.S. at 373; *Sugar Inst.*, 297 U.S. at 598.

49 . *Sugar Inst.*, 297 U.S. at 598.

50. *Id.* at 599.

51. *Id.* at 599–601.

52. *ALA Schechter Poultry*, 295 U.S. 495, 538.

53. *Id.* at 529.

54. *Id.* at 533.

55. *Id.* at 531, 533.

56. *Id.* at 532–34.

57. *Id.* at 539. The ICC was also called an "expert body," implying that agency discretion was limited not only by judicial review but also by the expertise of those making the decisions. The opposition between expertise and politics has been a legitimating discourse for agency discretion since the New Deal. Richard Stewart, *The Reformation of American Administrative Law*, 88 HARV. L. REV. 1667 (1975); Gerald E. Frug, *The Ideology of Bureaucracy in American Law*, 97 HARV. L. REV. 1276 (1984).

58. The requirement of judicial review was already seen not only in *Gratz* but also in Ohio Valley Co. v. Ben Avon Borough, 253 U.S. 287 (1920), which held unconstitutional a Pennsylvania statute authorizing a state commission to set utility rates without judicial review.

59. 295 U.S. at 537 (delegation to trade associations unconstitutional).

60. SCHLESINGER, *supra* note 3, at 447–48.

61. Wagner Act, 49 Stat. 449 (1935); 29 U.S.C. §§ 151–68 (1988). As Katherine Stone has written, the Wagner Act served the vision of "the workplace as private democracy." Stone, *supra* note 28, at 1525; *see also* Stone, *The Legacy of Industrial Pluralism: The Tension Between Individual Employment Rights and the New Deal Collective Bargaining System*, 59 U. CHI. L. REV. 575 (1992); Karl Klare, *Judicial Deradicalization of the Wagner Act and the Origins of Modern Legal Consciousness, 1937–1941*, 62 MINN. L. REV. 265, 284–93 (1978).

62. The Public Utility Holding Company Act of 1935, Pub. L. No. 101–550, codified in 15 U.S.C. §§ 79z–5n (1988).

63. REPORT OF THE HOUSE COMMITTEE ON INTERSTATE AND FOREIGN COMMERCE (accompanying S.5), H.R. REP. NO. 2755, 74th Cong., 2d. Sess. (May 22, 1936). This notion of "consumer welfare" is in sharp contrast to its revisionist use by recent Chicago Schoolers. *See* Peritz, *Counter-History*, 1990 DUKE L.J. at 311. There was, of course, a close connection between the competition-based "consumer welfare" policies of the later New Deal and the Roosevelt administration's desire to increase consumption. Though massive government borrowing began in 1933, true "Keynesian" deficit spending did not commence until 1939—after an alarming recession in the winter 1937–1938. For an interesting and thoughtful discussion of the consumption side of consumer wellbeing, see BRINKLEY, *supra* note 2, at 65–85. In short, it is important to remember that consumer wellbeing had both its macro- and microeconomic sides.

64. Gardiner C. Means, *Industrial Prices and their Relative Inflexibility*, S. DOC. NO. 13, 74th Cong., 1st Sess. (January 17, 1935) (by letter of transmittal dated January 15, 1935, from H.A. Wallace, Secretary of Agriculture, to Col. Edwin A. Halsey, Secretary of the Senate) [Means Report].

65. Means Report at 1–2.

66. Means Report at 2–9.

67. Mans Report at 9–13.

68. Means Report at 13–18, 28–30 (Appendix F). These prescriptions track those offered in ADOLF BERLE & GARDINER MEANS, THE MODERN CORPORATION AND PRIVATE PROPERTY (1932).

69. Means Report at 14.

70. See sources cited *supra* note 57.

71. 49 Stat. 803, 821, 15 U.S.C. § 79k(b)(2). This section owes a great deal to the research reflected in STOCKING & WATKINS, *supra* note 22, at 40–81, 431–37; HAWLEY, *supra* note 3, at 325–43. The approach taken and the conclusions drawn, however, tend to differ from the earlier scholarly work.

72. Frequent newspapers accounts and Senator Hugo Black's committee investigating political lobbying publicized the financial power and abusive tactics of the utility lobby in its efforts to defeat the PUHC Act. Those controlling public utility holding companies were seen as engaged in "spoliation, mismanagement, and faithless stewardship." Pepper v. Litton, 308 U.S. 295, 308 (1939) (Douglas, J.). Such conduct provoked three overlapping regulatory regimes. First, there were the state public utility commissions, overmatched and overwhelmed by the massive resources and financial complexities of multitiered, multinational holding companies. As governor of New York, Franklin Roosevelt had sought to regulate utility holding companies. HAWLEY, *supra* note 3, at 324–43. Second, stock manipulation and other financial abuses were seen as securities industry problems. Indeed, the PUHCA is codified amid the Securities Act of 1933, 15 U.S.C. §§ 77a–77aa, and the Investment Company Act of 1940. 15 U.S.C. §§ 80a-1 to 80a-52. And it is the Securities and Exchange Commission, not the Department of Justice or FTC, that oversees utility holding companies, even beyond matters of corporate finance. 15 U.S.C. § 79. Third, the "Power Trust" raised antitrust anxieties and, under PUHCA § 11, faced the ultimate antitrust remedy—the controversial "death sentence" of corporate dissolution. The very phrase—"Power Trust"—declared the distrust of corporate bigness that motivated John Sherman, Woodrow Wilson, Louis Brandeis, and their disciples.

73. Electric Bond & Share Co. v. S.E.C., 303 U.S. 419 (1938).

74. American Power & Light Co. v. SEC, 329 U.S. 90, 98, 99 (1946). With citations to antitrust decisions ordering corporate dissolution—both *Northern Securities* (1904) and *Standard Oil* (1911)—Murphy turned aside the defendants' claims that corporate dissolution was an unconstitutional taking of property. *Id.* at 100 n.7.

75. The Robinson-Patman Act of 1936, ch. 592, 49 Stat. 1526 (June 19, 1936). For a rhetorical analysis of law and economics approaches to price discrimination, see Peritz, *The Predicament of Antitrust Jurisprudence*, 1984 DUKE L.J. 1205.

76. Clayton Antitrust Act of 1914, ch. 323, § 2, 38 Stat. 730 (original version).

77. Robinson-Patman Act § 2(f). *Hearings on H.R.4995, H.R.5062, H.R.8442 Before the House Committee on the Judiciary* (Bills to Amend the Clayton Act), 74th Cong., 1st Sess., July 19, 1935, at 200–02, 260–61.

78. Clayton Antitrust Act § 2. According to both the House and Senate Committee Reports, the new language was necessary because "[t]he existing law has in practice been too restrictive in requiring a showing of general injury to competitive conditions in the line of commerce concerned, whereas the more immediately important concern is in injury to the competitor victimized by the discrimination. Only through such injury in fact can the larger, general injury result." Report of the House Committee on the Judiciary (on H.R. 8442), H.R. REP. NO. 2287, Pt.1, 74th Cong., 2d. Sess. (March 31, 1936). For almost identical language, see Report of the Senate Committee on the Judiciary (on S. 3154), S. REP. NO. 1502, 74th Cong., 2d Sess., February 3 (legislative day, January 16), 1936. Although orthodox antitrust scholars understand this provision as extending a cause of action to injured buyers, both the House and Senate reports characterize the new language as aimed at adding a new injury standard for the benefit of injured small businesses.

79. Goodyear Tire & Rubber Co. v. FTC, 22 FTC 232 (1936), *order set aside*, 92 F.2d 677 (6th Cir 1937), *rev'd and remanded*, 304 U.S. 257 (1938), *on remand*, 101 F.2d 620 (6th Cir. 1939), *cert. denied*, 308 U.S. 557 (1939). Rep. Patman went so far as to enter the FTC Cease and Desist Order into the record. House Debate, 74th Cong., 2d sess., March 5, 1936, 80 CONG. REC. 3382–85.

80. Report of the House Committee on the Judiciary, H.R. REP. NO. 2287, Pt.1,

74th Cong., 2d Sess. (March 31, 1936). Report of the House Committee on the Judiciary (Minority Views), H.R. REP. NO. 2287, Pt.2, 74th Cong., 2d Sess. (March 31, 1936). Here is the example Celler gives in his "Minority Views" of the House Committee Report: A manufacturer typically has "large plant capacity"—"probably . . . excess plant capacity" with a "slack season in his line during which he would ordinarily lay off many men." "He would be set up to make and market a run of production resulting from the usual flow of small-lot orders." Some time later, a large buyer would propose that the manufacturer make up an order to the buyer's specification, according to the manufacturer's optimum production schedule. Under these circumstances, Celler insisted, neither sales, warehousing, nor research costs should be part of the selling price.

What are the tacit assumptions underlying Celler's persuasive example? For example, what of the assumption that a large buyer simply steps onto the scene, while smaller buyers do not? What if, instead, we imagine small buyers seeking to buy from excess capacity? Cellers assumed that the manufacturer has an ongoing relationship with small buyers, while the large buyer shops around. Don't small buyers shop around? Even if they don't, then should we, in any event, allow the large buyer to skim the cream off the top, while the small buyers pay the upkeep for manufacturers who are thus in positions to compete for large buyers' business? Moreover, how does the large buyer already know about the manufacturer's facilities? Certainly from salesmen or other advertising. Moreover, was it the manufacturer's research department that helped to develop those facilities now sought by the large buyer? The actual outcome of Celler's admonition is that long-term customers, both large and small, subsidize their short-term rivals. That outcome raises questions entirely different from the asserted conflict between large and small firms.

81. This debate can be understood as a disagreement over pricing at cost—marginal, average variable, or average total. The neoclassical economist proceeds on the assumption that price competition means pricing at marginal cost (the increase in total cost associated with the last unit sold). Aside from the notorious difficulties of determining marginal cost and the commercial realities of determining price by other means, there is a vast literature on this debate as it applies to price discrimination under the Robinson-Patman Act and its analogue—predatory pricing—under Sherman Act § 2. For the origin of the orthodox position, see Philip Areeda & Donald Turner, *Predatory Pricing and Related Practices Under Section 2 of the Sherman Act*, 88 HARV. L. REV. 697 (1975).

82. Minority View at 1–2, 26–27.

83. 80 CONG. REC. 7324 (May 14, 1936).

84. Act of Aug. 17, 1937, ch. 690, tit. VIII, 50 Stat. 693, *amending* Sherman Act § 1 (15 U.S.C. § 1), *repealed by* the Consumer Goods Pricing Act of 1975, Pub. L. No. 94–145, § 2, 89 Stat. 801.

85. Senate Debate, 75th Cong., 1st Sess., July 23, 1937, 81 CONG. REC. 7495. The Supreme Court recognized the importance of allowing small manufacturers more competitive leeway in White Motor Co. v. United States, 372 U.S. 253 (1963) (Douglas, J.). *See* Peritz, *A Genealogy of Vertical Price Restraints*, 40 HASTINGS L.J. 511, 554–62 (1989). The Supreme Court established the constitutionality of state fair-trade laws, and did so by putting all manufacturers on an equal footing, in Old Dearborn Distrib. Co. v. Seagram-Distillers Corp., 299 U.S. 183 (1936).

Regarding loss leaders, *see, e.g.*, Additional Views Submitted by Mr. Celler, in Report of the House Committee on the Judiciary (with Additional Views), H.R. REP. NO. 382, 75th Cong., 1st Sess. (March 11, 1937); Dr. Miles Medical Co. v. John D. Park

& Sons, 220 U.S. 373, 375, 394 (1911). "Loss-leader pricing" refers to the strategy of selling a product at a loss in order to entice customers into the store, hopefully to buy other products at higher prices. The idea is to make up the loss and gain a handsome profit from the bundle of goods purchased.

86. H.R. REP. NO. 382, *supra* note 85. Moreover, Franklin Roosevelt opposed the bill because his advisors counseled that it "will seriously raise the cost of many articles to the consuming public." Because, however, the bill was attached as a rider to an important funding bill, Roosevelt signed it, hoping that its effects "will not be as serious as it is feared." Statement by President Franklin D. Roosevelt upon Signing H.R.7472, August 18, 1937, *reproduced in* 1 THE LEGISLATIVE HISTORY OF THE ANTITRUST LAWS AND RELATED STATUTES 538 (Earl W. Kintner ed. 1978) [KINTNER]. For detailed histories of both the Robinson-Patman and Miller-Tydings Acts by two historians, see JOSEPH C. PALAMOUNTAIN, JR., THE POLITICS OF DISTRIBUTION (1955); HAWLEY, *supra* note 3, at 247–70. Hawley ascribes to Edward Levi's view that "small merchants" were successful in "disguising" the two statutes as antitrust legislation. HAWLEY, *supra* note 3, at 266; Edward Levi, *The Robinson-Patman Act—Is It in the Public Interest?*, ABA SEC. ANTITRUST L. 60 (1952); *see* Peritz, *Predicament of Antitrust Jurisprudence*, 1984 DUKE L.J. at 1231–34. Hawley describes the two statutes as second-best solutions sought by the same "political agitators" who failed to convince Congress to pass anti-chain store tax legislation. "The two laws were not very effective for the purposes intended." The Robinson-Patman Act in particular failed its sponsors because the FTC and the courts "stress[ed] an interpretation under which the act might really be used to strengthen competition rather than protect small competitors. In practice, too, the act had something of a boomerang effect." In short, Hawley presumes that congressional sponsors were "really" intent upon protecting small inefficient merchants from large efficient firms. HAWLEY at 261–67. This view depends upon controversial assumptions: for example, a purity of motive, a total disconnection between congressional rhetoric and the "real" and pure motive, a dichotomy between smallness and efficiency, an identity between size and efficiency, a view of actual market competition as purely meritocratic (efficiency-based), a view of legislative politics as purely factionalized (protectionist).

87. Remarks of Rep. John E. Miller, 81 CONG. REC. A873–74, 75th Cong., 1st Sess., April 19, 1937.

88. Report of the House Committee on the Judiciary (with Additional Views), H.R. REP. NO. 382, 75th Cong., 1st Sess. (March 11, 1937) (Additional Views Submitted by Mr. Celler).

89. Remarks of Representative John E. Miller, 81 CONG. REC. A874–75; H.R. Rep. No. 2287, 74th Cong., 2d Sess. (March 31, 1936); S. REP. NO. 1502, 74th Cong., 2d Sess. (Feb. 3, 1936); Senate Debate, 75th Cong., 1st Sess. (July 23, 1937), 81 CONG. REC. 7495–96 (Senator Tydings), 7497 (Senator Warren R. Austin (R., Vt.)).

90. Wheeler-Lea Act of 1938 of March 21, 1938, ch.49, 52 Stat. 111.

91. FTC v. Raladam, 283 U.S. 643 (1931) (requiring evidence of injury to competition). Annual Report of the Federal Trade Commission 14 (1935), *reproduced in* 6 KINTNER, *supra* note 86, at 4837. Report of the House Committee on Interstate and Foreign Commerce (with Additional Views), H.R. REP. NO. 1613, 75th Cong., 1st Sess. (August 19, 1937) (FTC recommending amendment to FTC Act § 5(a)).

92. H. R. REP. NO. 1613, 75th Cong., 1st Sess. (August 19, 1937). The Wheeler-Lea Act also made FTC cease and desist orders final after 60 days, eliminating the original requirement for Court of Appeals approval under § 5(b).

93. "I do not think there is one case in a thousand in which the Commission

cannot go ahead and make a showing of some competition." *Hearings on S. 3744 Before the Senate Committee on Interstate Commerce*, 74th Cong., 2d Sess. (1936) (FTC Commissioner Davis), *reproduced in* 6 KINTNER, *supra* note 86, at 4808 n.9.13). FTC v. Winsted Hosiery Co., 258 U.S. 483 (1922) (holding false and misleading advertising to be an unfair method of competition).

94. THURMAN ARNOLD, THE FOLKLORE OF CAPITALISM 207–29 ([1937] 1962). ARNOLD, THE BOTTLENECKS OF BUSINESS 263 (1940). *Cf.* HOFSTADTER, *supra* note 3, at 312–16; HAWLEY, *supra* note 3, at 420–56.

95. HAWLEY, *supra* note 3, at 436 n.12.

96. *Relative Efficiency of Large, Medium-Sized, and Small Business*, MONOGRAPH NO. 13, THE TEMPORARY NATIONAL ECONOMIC COMMITTEE (1941) [TNEC EFFICIENCY STUDY]. For a political history of TNEC's creation, see HAWLEY, *supra* note 3, at 410–19.

97. TNEC EFFICIENCY STUDY at 12–14.

98. *Id.*

99. *Id.*

100. When America entered World War II, the Antitrust Division's prosecution of domestic corporations slackened in deference to the Roosevelt administration's efforts to mobilize industry for the war effort. The Division turned its attention to international cartels and their American members, especially those cartels seen as benefiting German companies.

101. The exigencies of World War II would, however, bring back the kind of corporatist cooperation between government and business that arose during World War I, cooperation that brought to a halt Woodrow Wilson's similarly adversarial "New Freedom" platform.

102. For contemporary criticism of the Court's use of delegation doctrine, see Louis L. Jaffe, *Law Making by Private Groups*, 51 HARV. L. REV. 201 (1937).

103. I will not travel this well-trodden path. For recent renditions of the 1937 revolution, see MURPHY, *supra* note 3, at 128–70; ALFRED H. KELLY, ET AL., THE AMERICAN CONSTITUTION 467–508 (7th ed. 1991); IRONS, *supra* note 11, at 272–90; CHARLES A. & MARY R. BEARD, THE BASIC HISTORY OF THE UNITED STATES 420–30 ([1944] 1960); Barry Cushman, *Rethinking the New Deal Court*, 80 VA. L. REV. 201 (1994). Justice Van Devanter retired in 1937.

104. Olsen v. Nebraska, 313 U.S. 236 (1941).

105. Truax v. Corrigan, 257 U.S. 312, 354–55, 367–68 (1921) (Brandeis, J., dissenting). In *Privilege, Malice, and Intent*, 8 HARV. L. REV. 1 (1894), Holmes portrayed competition as a defense to claims of injury to property. For discussions of the article, see G. EDWARD WHITE, JUSTICE OLIVER WENDELL HOLMES: LAW AND THE INNER SELF 215–18, 289–90 (1993); HORWITZ, *supra* chap. 1, note 1, at 129–31. For an impassioned dissent arguing that a state can regulate corporations without regard to contract and property rights because incorporation is not a vested right but rather a privilege conferred by the state, see Justice Brandeis's opinion in Liggett v. Lee, 288 U.S. 517, 541–80 (1933) (dissenting in part) (asserting that the Florida anti-chain store tax was entirely constitutional). For an echo and an amplification of this position, see Justice Hugo Black's opinion in Connecticut Gen'l Life Ins. Co. v. Johnson, 303 U.S. 77 (1938) (arguing that a corporation should not be treated as a "person" under the Constitution).

106. West Coast Hotel v. Parrish, 300 U.S. 379 (1937).

107. *Id.* at 406 (Sutherland, J., dissenting).

108. *Id.* at 391, 391–92 (citing Chicago, Burlington & Quincy R.R. Co. v. McGuire, 219 U.S. 549, 565 (1911)), 399, 393, 395.

109. *Jones & Laughlin Steel*, 301 U.S. 1 (1937).

110. Thornhill v. Alabama, 310 U.S. 88, 97, 105 (1940) (citing both *Schenck*, 249 U.S. at 52 (Holmes, J.) and *Abrams*, 250 U.S. at 630 (Holmes, J., dissenting), though Holmes had nothing to say about a marketplace of ideas in *Schenck*. Justice Murphy also relies upon Justice Brandeis's opinion in Senn v. Tile Layers Union, 301 U.S. 468, 478 (1937), which recognizes a right to disseminate facts of a labor dispute. 310 U.S. at 103.

111. *Thornhill*, 310 U.S. at 102, 104.

112. *Id.* at 103, 104.

113. *Id.* at 104.

114. *Id.* at 105.

115. James Harrington called for redistribution of property, whereas John Locke, of course, did not. JAMES HARRINGTON, THE COMMONWEALTH OF OCEANA (1656); JOHN LOCKE, SECOND TREATISE OF GOVERNMENT § 124 (1690).

116. *Thornhill*, 310 U.S. at 92.

117. Indeed, the *Thornhill* opinion made reference to the two decisions that introduced the new constitutional jurisprudence of "preferred freedoms" residing in the Bill of Rights, or at the very least, the constitutional calculus that political rights and questioned state action which limited them were to be balanced. Palko v. Connecticut, 302 U.S. 319 (1937) (Cardozo, J.); United States v. Carolene Products, 304 U.S. 144 (1938) (Stone, J.). But two years after *Thornhill*, when confronted with an explicit claim of protection for commercial speech, Justice Roberts for a unanimous Court would write a four-page opinion holding that commercial speech did not merit First Amendment protection. Valentine v. Chrestensen, 316 U.S. 52 (1942).

118. Apex Hosiery v. Leader, 310 U.S. 469 (1940).

119. *Id.* at 481–82.

120. *Id.* at 493, 493 (emphasis added), 500–01, 514 (Hughes, C.J., dissenting.).

121. *Sugar Inst.*, 297 U.S. at 601.

122. *Id.* at 598. 15 F.Supp. 817, 906 (S.D.N.Y. 1934).

123. *FOGA*, 312 U.S. 457, 462, 466 (1941).

124. *Id.* at 457 (citing *Addyston Pipe*, 175 U.S. at 242).

125. Interstate Circuit v. United States, 306 U.S. 308 (1939), is a good example of the Court's typical success at reconciling consumer and producer interests by folding two (and sometimes three) visions of competition policy into one opinion. *Cement Institute*, 333 U.S. 683, 713–15 (1948).

126. United States v. Socony-Vacuum Oil Co., 310 U.S. 150, 168, 214, 218, 223, 225 n.59, 221, 214 (1940).

127. 312 U.S. at 467 (quoting *Trans-Missouri Freight*, 166 U.S. at 323).

128. United States v. Aluminum Co. of Am., 148 F.2d 416 (2d Cir. 1945). A Second Circuit panel of three judges heard this appeal after four members of the Supreme Court recused themselves; the matter was referred to the circuit court under the 1944 amendment to 15 U.S.C. § 29. An Act to Amend the Expediting Act, ch. 239, 58 Stat. 272 (1944), *repealed by* Judicial Code and Judiciary Act, ch. 646, 62 Stat. 869, 989 (1948). In its following term, a unanimous Supreme Court in American Tobacco v. United States, 328 U.S. 781, 811 (1946), explicitly approved the *ALCOA* decision, citing extensive passages from Judge Learned Hand's opinion.

129. *FOGA*, 312 U.S. at 458–59, 467–68.

130. *Associated Press*, 326 U.S. 1 (1945), *aff'ing* 52 F.Supp. 362, 372 (S.D.N.Y. 1945).

131. 326 U.S. at 19, 20.

132. American Tobacco Co. v. United States, 328 U.S. 781, 786, 790–94, 809–11 (1946).

133. Rostow, *The New Sherman Act: A Positive Instrument of Progress*, 14 U. CHI. L. REV. 567, 567, 569, 574, 577–83, 589 (1947).

134. United States v. Columbia Steel Co., 334 U.S. 495 (1948) (5–4 decision). Because U.S. Steel purchased assets rather than stock, the suit was brought under the Sherman Act rather than the pre-1950 Clayton Act, which applied only to stock transactions. *ALCOA*, 148 F.2d at 429.

135. *Columbia Steel*, 334 U.S. 495, 534–36 (1948) (Douglas, J., dissenting).

136. For a thought-provoking description and analysis of the Bretton Woods Conference and its aftermath, see ROBERT KUTTNER, THE END OF LAISSEZ-FAIRE 25–54 (1991).

137. 334 U.S. 1 (1948). For discussions, *see, e.g.*, Donald Cahen, *The Impact of Shelley v. Kraemer on the State Action Concept*, 44 CAL. L. REV. 718 (1956); Louis Henkin, *Shelley v. Kraemer: Notes for a Revised Opinion*, 110 U. PA. L. REV. 473 (1962); II ALFRED KELLY, ET AL., *supra* note 103, at 583, 593; HORWITZ, *supra* chap. 1 note 1, at 207.

138. 304 U.S. 64, 78–79 (1938) (citing Holmes's dissent in Black & White Taxicab Co. v. Brown & Yellow Taxicab Co., 276 U.S. 518, 532–36 (1928)). For a brief but useful discussion, see PURCELL (1992), *supra* chap. 1 note 1, at 224–30.

Chapter 4

1. Gray v. Sanders, 372 U.S. 368, 381 (1963) (Douglas, J.); Brown Shoe Co. v. United States, 370 U.S. 294, 316 (1962) (Warren, C.J.). For a recent treatment of the fifties through the lens of gender relations, see BARBARA EHRENREICH, HEARTS OF MEN: AMERICAN DREAMS AND THE FLIGHT FROM COMMITTMENT (1984). See generally DAVID HALBERSTAM, THE FIFTIES (1993).

2. PURCELL (1973), *supra* chap.1 note 1, at 235–66.

3. There was also an outpouring of literature about the corporation as a social institution and about the social conformity that the institution seemed to demand. Most prominent were the writings of C. Wright Mills, David Reisman, and Sloan Wilson. MILLS, WHITE COLLAR (1951) and THE POWER ELITE (1956); REISMAN, THE LONELY CROWD: A STUDY OF THE CHANGING AMERICAN CHARACTER (1950); WILSON, THE MAN IN THE GRAY FLANNEL SUIT (1955).

4. GEORGE W. STOCKING & MYRON W. WATKINS, MONOPOLY AND FREE ENTERPRISE 87–89 (1951); ROBERT TRIFFIN, MONOPOLISTIC COMPETITION AND GENERAL EQUILIBRIUM THEORY 17 (1949).

5. JOE BAIN, BARRIERS TO NEW COMPETITION 110–12 (1954). Walter Adams & Joel Dirlam, *Big Steel, Invention and Innovation*, 80 Q.J. ECON. 167 (1966). *Accord*, Ward Bowman, *Towards Less Monopoly*, 101 U. PA. L. REV. 577 (1953); MARK J. GREEN, THE CLOSED ENTERPRISE SYSTEM 23 (1972). CORWIN EDWARDS, BIG BUSINESS AND THE POLICY OF COMPETITION 1–6, 131–32 (1956); *accord*, Louis Schwartz, *Institutional Size and Individual Liberty: Authoritarian Aspects of Bigness*, 55 NW. U. L. REV. 4 (1960). *But see* ADOLF BERLE, THE TWENTIETH CENTURY CAPITALIST REVOLUTION (1954) (arguing that large modern corporations, finding themselves in the public eye, develop a sense of social responsibility).

6. George Stigler, *The Case Against Big Business*, FORTUNE, May 1952, at 267; *cf.* GEORGE STIGLER, FIVE LECTURES ON ECONOMIC PROBLEMS 46 (1949) ("the industrial distribution and their strength and patterns of behavior are obviously also important variables"). Donald Turner, *The Definition of Agreement under the Sherman Act: Conscious Parallelism and Refusals to Deal*, 75 HARV. L. REV. 655 (1962).

7. Carl Kaysen & Donald F. Turner, Antitrust Policy: An Economic and Legal Analysis (1959).

8. *Id.* at 11–14. The debate over static efficiency analysis and dynamic change—both their limits and their relationship—has not been resolved.

9. Joe Bain, Barriers to New Competition 142 (1956). Stocking & Watkins, *supra* note 4, at 320–21. Donald Turner, *Conglomerate Mergers and Section 7 of the Clayton Act*, 78 Harv. L. Rev. 1313, 1332 (1965).

10. The Court has shared those concerns from time to time. For an early expression *see Procter & Gamble (Clorox)*, 386 U.S. 568 (1967), which is discussed later in this chapter. There was also the long-lived and ultimately abandoned investigation into the breakfast cereal industry. In Re: Kellogg, 99 FTC 8 (1982). For a more recent though implicit indication, *see* Eastman Kodak Co. v. Image Technical Servs., Inc., 112 S.Ct. 2072 (1991) (holding that Kodak's differentiated product—its replacement parts—can constituted a separate product market). For an interesting discussion of advertising as an antitrust issue, see Elizabeth Mensch & Alan Freeman, *Efficiency and Image: Advertising as an Antitrust Issue*, 1990 Duke L.J. 321.

11. For a critical discussion of the *AG Report's* self-presentation as neutral, its view of "workable competition" as a neutral principle, a "rule of thumb," and its attempt to represent the old "Rule of Reason" in the newer language of workable competition, *see* Peritz, *Predicament of Antitrust Jurisprudence*, 1984 Duke L.J. at 1223–31. For conference papers, largely composed by Committee members, which applaud the *AG Report, see* Conference of the Antitrust Laws and the Attorney General's Committee Report (James A. Rahl & Earle Warren Zaidins eds. 1955). Edward S. Mason, *Symposium*, 39 Am. Econ. Rev. 713 (1949); J.M. Clark, *Toward a Concept of Workable Competition*, 30 Am. Econ. Rev. 241–56 (1940).

12. *See* Stocking & Watkins, *supra* note 4, at 97–102.

13. Joseph A. Schumpeter, Capitalism, Socialism and Democracy 269–84 (1942) (see esp. chap. 22, *Another Theory of Democracy*).

14. *Id.*

15. Robert A. Dahl, A Preface to Democratic Theory 138 (1956); *see also* David Truman, The Governmental Process (1951). Richard B. Stewart, *The Reformation of American Administrative Law*, 88 Harv. L. R. 1667, 1711–15 (1975); Purcell (1973), *supra* chap. 1 note 1, at 260–61; Horwitz (1992), *supra* chap. 1 note 1, at 253–57. In sociology, it was Talcott Parsons. Historian Edward A. Purcell, Jr. has termed the marketplace pluralist view the "relativist theory of democracy." Purcell (1973) at 260–63.

16. Robert A. Dahl, Who Governs? Democracy and Power in an American City 91 (1961); Purcell (1973), *supra* chap. 1 note 1, at 260–61. United States v. Carolene Prods. Co., 304 U.S. 144, 152 n.4 (1938).

17. In re Gault, 387 U.S. 1, 21 (1967) (Fortas, J.). The immanent normativity of process was confronted in the case law following *Erie* (1938), when the Court attempted to distinguish between substance (state law) and procedure (federal law) by treating as substantive those rules that were deemed "outcome-determinative." Guaranty Trust Co. v. York, 326 U.S. 99, 109 (1945) (Frankfurter, J.) and Byrd v. Blue Ridge Rural Elec. Coop, Inc., 356 U.S. 525 (1958) (Brandeis, J.). More recently, social theorists have sought to deal with this problem. Two well-known attempts are John Rawls, A Theory of Justice (1971) ("original position") and Jürgen Habermas, Communication and the Evolution of Society (Thomas McCarthy trans. 1979) ("ideal speech situation").

18. A.V. Dicey, Introduction to the Study of the Law of the Constitution (1885); Marver Bernstein, Regulating Business by Independent Commission (1955); Mancur

OLSEN, THE LOGIC OF COLLECTIVE ACTION (1965); George Stigler, *The Theory of Regulation*, 2 BELL J. ECON. 3 (1971); *Cf.* DONALD R. BRAND, CORPORATISM AND THE RULE OF LAW 1–11 (1988).

19. Edward S. Mason, *Introduction*, THE CORPORATION IN MODERN SOCIETY 1–3 (Mason ed. 1959). Eugene V. Rostow, *To Whom and for What Ends is Corporate Management Responsible? in id.* at 63, 70–71. Carl Kaysen, *The Corporation: How Much Power? What Scope?* in *id.* at 85–105. W. Lloyd Warner, *The Corporation Man in id.* at 106–21. Earl Latham, *The Body Politic of the Corporation in id.* at 218–36. Latham points out that the Hobbesian perspective had been taken up by others before him, including Yale Law School economist Walton Hamilton, sociologist C. Wright Mills, and, of course, Adolf Berle. *Id.* at 219.

20. Sociologist Talcott Parson's organic view of society as a self-regulating system seeking to attain consensual goals is, at the very least, consistent with the ideological thrust of competition rhetoric that participants engage in something entirely different from the dangerous political processes of conflict and struggle. An integrative function, something like a neoclassical invisible hand, keeps society on this efficient course toward group-wide satisfaction. TALCOTT PARSONS, ESSAYS IN SOCIOLOGICAL THEORY (1954). *See* PURCELL (1973), *supra* chap. 1 note 1, at 261–62.

21. Brown v. Board of Educ., 347 U.S. 483 (1954); Herbert Wechsler, *Toward Neutral Principles of Constitutional Law*, 73 HARV. L. REV. 1 (1959).

22. Wechsler rejected equality because, quoting the Court in *Plessy* (1896), "'enforced separation stamps the colored race with a badge of inferiority' . . . solely because its members choose 'to put that construction upon it.'" Wechsler's astonishing conclusion is that "a denial of equality" is not a neutral principle because it cannot be applied equally to whites, who do not feel the sting of segregation. The conclusion is astonishing not only because of its implications for race relations but also because of its failure to understand the very logic of such discrimination: It occurs only when there is a power inequality, only when the more powerful party does not feel the sting of discrimination, feeling instead some benefit from the unequal treatment. Wechsler then considered whether the "freedom to associate" is a neutral principle. He observed that the principle applied both to those who prefer integration and to those who impose segregation, but concluded that the principle of liberty is not neutral because the Court would be forced to decide whether to deny or to impose association. Wechsler's view would dismantle most constitutional jurisprudence—whether *Locher*ian liberty of contract (one party was injured and the other benefited) or its equality-based successors. 73 HARV. L. REV. 1, 33–34.

23. Katzenbach v. McClung, 379 U.S. 294 (1964) (Ollie's Barbecue).

24. HENRY HART & ALBERT SACHS, THE LEGAL PROCESS (1958); *see generally* G. Edward White, *The Evolution of Reasoned Elaboration*, 59 VA. L. REV. 279 (1973); Richard Parker, *The Past of Constitutional Theory and its Future*, 42 OHIO ST. L.J. 223 (1981); Gary Peller, *Neutral Principles in the 1950's*, 21 U. MICH. J.L. REF. 561 (1988); HORWITZ (1992), *supra* chap. 1 note 1, at 253–55.

25. Charles A. Reich, *The New Property*, 73 YALE L.J. 733 (1964).

26. *Id.* at 733, 765–67, 771–78, 786–87. For a criticism of Reich's approach as limited by an ideology of individualism and thus ineffective in the kinds of "public interest" controversies that do not fit into the traditional model of bipolar disputes, see Stewart, *supra* note 15, at 1721–22.

27. PURCELL (1973), *supra* chap. 1 note 1, at 235–66.

28. 95 CONG. REC. 11485 (August 5, 1949) (Statement of Rep. Celler). 96 CONG. REC. 16450 (Dec. 12, 1950) (Sen. Kefauver). Report of the Federal Trade Commission:

The Merger Movement: A Summary Report 7 (1948); Report of the House Committee on the Judiciary, H.R. Rep. No. 1191, 81st Cong., 1st Sess. (Aug. 4, 1949) (accompanying H.R. 2734).

29. Temporary National Economic Committee Final Report, S. Doc. No. 35, 77th Cong., 1st. Sess. 5 (March 3, 1941). FTC Report, *supra* note 28, at 68–69; 96 Cong. Rec. 11, 486 (1950) (remarks of Rep. Celler).

30. FTC v. Western Meat Co., Thatcher Mfg. Co. v. FTC, Swift & Co. v. FTC, 272 U.S. 554 (1926). 95 Cong. Rec. 11489 (Aug 15, 1949) (Reps. Ellsworth and Celler). *Id.* at 11491 (Rep. Jennings).

31. *Id.* at 11492.

32. Chief Justice Warren noted in Brown Shoe Co. v. United States, 370 U.S. 294, 322 n.37 (1962), that some supporters of the Celler-Kefauver amendment expressed concern that passage of the bill "would amount to locking the barn door after most of the horses have been stolen, but urged approval of the measure to prevent the theft of those still in the barn." *Id.* (citing 95 Cong. Rec. 11489, 11494, 11498 (remarks of Reps. Keating, Yates, Patman) and 96 Cong. Rec. 16444 (remarks of Sens. O'Mahoney, Murray)).

33. *FTC Report, supra* note 28, at 23. 95 Cong. Rec. 11493, 81st Cong., 1st Sess. (Aug. 15, 1949).

34. Chicago School Price Theory is discussed *infra* chaps. 5 and 6. This conservative program rests on an "efficiency" logic largely derived from the free competition rhetoric of private property rights.

35. Theatre Enters. v. Paramount Film Distrib. Corp., 346 U.S. 537, 540–41 (1954).

36. Turner, *supra* note 6, at 658, 663–69.

37. *Id.* at 671–73. Turner's extreme view of a deterministic oligopoly logic ultimately allowed the domestication of the radical potential in Chamberlain's original formulation.

38. Kieffer-Stewart Co. v. Jos. E. Seagram & Sons, 340 U.S. 211, 215 (1951), overturned in Copperweld Corp. v. Independence Tube Corp., 469 U.S. 927 (1984) (over a strenuous dissent by Stevens, Brennan, and Marshall, arguing that the original Sherman Act's primary concern was with trusts, or what today are called holding companies). Although intracorporate conspiracy makes no sense when viewed within the legal logic of corporations as entities or Coase's theory of the firm as an economic unit, corporation law has long included a deviant doctrine of apparent authority. The doctrine is deviant in the sense that it protects reasonable reliance by a customer, supplier, employee, or other third party on appearances, even in the absence of actual authority. By the 1950s, courts were taking an expansive view of the apparent authority doctrine, as they were the contract doctrine of promissory estoppel, which protects reasonable reliance on a promise despite the absence of a bargain contract. *See, e.g.,* Lee v. Jenkins Bros., 268 F.2d 357 (2d Cir. 1959), *cert. denied,* 361 U.S. 931 (1959). Promissory estoppel was enshrined in § 90 of both the Restatement and Restatement (Second) of Contracts. For a historical treatment of promissory estoppel, see Jay Feinman, *Promissory Estoppel and Judicial Method,* 97 Harv. L. Rev. 678 (1984).

39. Klor's Inc. v. Broadway-Hale Stores, Inc., 359 U.S. 207, 208, 213 (1959).

40. *Parrish* (1937) and *Tipaldo* (1936) are discussed *supra* chap.3.

41. For example, in United States v. Parke-Davis & Co., 362 U.S. 269 (1960), the Justice Department presented evidence that Parke-Davis had employed an elaborate enforcement scheme, including threats of termination to some retailers who cut prices. The Court held that, while the *Colgate* (1919) doctrine permitted "mere announcement of his policy and the simple refusal to deal," Parke-Davis's use of "other means

which effect adherence to his resale prices" was going too far. It crossed the line between liberty of contract and coercion, between reasonable and unreasonable restraints. This coercive course of conduct violated the Sherman Act, even though "there results the same economic effect" on both sides of the line. The Court's concern was not competitive effect but coercion—the exercise of grossly disproportionate economic power. *Id.* at 44, 45. United States v. Colgate & Co., 250 U.S. 300 (1919); for discussion of the *Chicago Board* (1918), coercion, and the *Colgate* doctrine, see *supra* chap. 2. For more on *Colgate,* see Peritz, *Genealogy,* 40 HASTINGS L.J. 511, 527–31 (1989). The Supreme Court recognized the coercive, government-enforced essence of private contracts in Shelley v. Kraemer, 334 U.S. 1 (1948), the civil rights case in which the Court found court enforcement of a racially restrictive covenant to be unconstitutional state action.

42. Simpson v. Union Oil Co., 377 U.S. 13, 20–21, 18 (1964). There was an implied question of which property rights were at risk: Were all consignments subject to the federal antitrust laws? Douglas said as much. What of other property rights? Certainly, Douglas could not subordinate all property rights to competition policy. For a discussion of this question, see Peritz, *Genealogy,* 40 HASTINGS L.J. at 531–44.

43. *Simpson,* 377 U.S. at 21, 22 n.9.

44. White Motor Co. v. United States, 372 U.S. 253, 256–76 (1963). For an amplified discussion of *White Motor,* see Peritz, *Genealogy,* 40 HASTINGS L.J. at 554–62.

45. *White Motor,* 372 U.S. at 261 (illegal per se), 278 (Clark, J., dissenting).

46. The per se illegality of express price-fixing and boycott agreements was stable during the period specified. At other times, such agreements have been treated differently. For an overview, see Peritz, *Counter-History,* 1990 DUKE L.J. 263.

47. Eastern R.R. Presidents Conf. v. Noerr Motor Freight, Inc., 365 U.S. 127, 129 (1961). United Mine Workers of Am. v. Pennington, 381 U.S. 657 (1965). The "state action" immunity from antitrust liability was formalized in Parker v. Brown, 317 U.S. 341 (1943). *See also* United States v. Rock-Royal Cooperative, 307 U.S. 533 (1939) (price-fixing under the Agricultural Marketing Act of 1937 not an unconstitutional "taking" of private property).

48. *Noerr Motor Freight,* 365 U.S. at 136, 138–39, 145. Justice Black's portrayal of the economic effects of political action as "incidental" is a categorical conclusion, not a description, given the neglected "ulterior motive" of financial benefit. Numerous difficulties result from the assertion that political and economic conduct can be essentialized and thus neatly cordoned off from one another. I suggest only two. First of all, it seems that the Court was much too willing to view an advertising campaign, built upon the misrepresentation of paid performers as disinterested third parties, arguably directed at consumers, as a political campaign directed at citizens and legislatures. Second, Black's opinion paints the political process as a marketplace of ideas free of powerful groups. Much as neoclassical economists were blind to gradations of power between pure competition and pure monopoly, Black wrote of "the people" as a unified body of individuals: Government acts "on behalf of the people." The right to petition government protects "the ability of the people to make their wishes known." Without this protection, "the people cannot freely inform the government." *Id.* at 137. The impression conveyed had little to do either with the reality of a powerful railroad association's advertising campaign or with the recent attempts of theorists to reconcile traditional democratic theory with the presence of oligarchic elites. See, *e.g.,* Samuel P. Huntington, *The Marasmus of the ICC: The Commission, The Railroads, and the Public Interest,* 61 YALE L.J. 467 (1952). *Hearings: Trucking Mergers and Concen-*

tration, Senate Small Business Committee, 85th Cong., 1st Sess. 211–384 (July 1, 2, 11, 12, 1957) (report of Walter Adams and James B. Hendry).

49. United Mine Workers of Am. v. Pennington, 381 U.S. 657, 672 (1965).

50. *See supra* note 47.

51. Thornhill v. Alabama, 310 U.S. 88 (1940). The Court would soon decide that "commercial speech" deserved less constitutional protection than "political speech." Valentine v. Chrestensen, 316 U.S. 52 (1942).

52. Giboney v. Empire State Storage, 336 U.S. 490, 501, 503, 503 n.6, 504 (1949).

53. American Communications Ass'n v. Douds, 339 U.S. 382, 387, 390, 392, 394, 400, 406, 409 (1950). The Court cited its "commercial speech" opinion, *Valentine, supra* note 51, for the general authority of Congress to regulate the conduct of individuals, though "at the same time, they carry on legitimate political activities."

54. *Douds*, 339 U.S. at 412, 446.

55. The same structural logic is seen Time Inc. v. Hill, 15 N.Y.2d 986, 207 N.E.2d 604, *rev'd and remanded*, 385 U.S. 374 (1967). The New York Court was willing to make a distinction between "trade purposes" and "news," between markets for the sale of newspapers and magazines, and the marketplace of ideas. Placing the *Life* magazine story in the first category, seeing it as something like commercial speech, the New York Court imposed a more stringent standard. The U.S. Supreme Court refused to uphold the more stringent standard because it characterized the distinction between commercial markets and the marketplace of ideas as "too close to call."

56. Lorain Journal Co. v. United Sates, 342 U.S. 143 (1951).

57. United States v. E. I. duPont de Nemours & Co. 351 U.S. 377 (1956).

58. *Id.* at 379, 391, 394–95, 399–400.

59. *Id.* at 380, 392–93. While Burton clearly signaled a refusal to define Sherman Act monopoly power in terms of Edward Chamberlin's theory of monopolistic competition, and a determination to stay within the confines of neoclassical price theory, Burton later in the opinion remarked, surprisingly, that it was product "quality and salesmanship," not price, that determined customer choice between cellophane and its substitutes. What is this but a step into the rejected theory of monopolistic competition? *Id.* at 402. *Id.* at 414–18, 426 (Warren, C.J., dissenting).

60. At the same time, the Court's refusal to go beyond the traditional notion of market definition and market power reflected an appreciation of the commercial success resulting in internal growth. A subsequent case brought under Sherman Act § 2, United States v. Grinnell Corp., 384 U.S. 563 (1966), appears to have adopted the theory of monopolistic competition to define the "market." At least according to dissenting Justice Abe Fortas, the majority's determinations of "geographical and product markets . . . have been tailored precisely to fit the defendants' business." *Id.* at 587. In other words, Fortas complained that substitutes should have been included to define a broader market. The majority, led by Justice Douglas, found that the defendant's "insurance accredited central station protection services" was so differentiated from substitutes that it defined its own market.

61. United States v. Columbia Steel Co., 334 U.S. 495, 537, 527 (1948). This purchase of corporate assets was bought under the Sherman Act case because the pre-1950 Clayton Act governed only stock transactions.

62. International Salt Co. v. United States, 332 U.S. 392, 396 (1947).

63. Northern Pac. R.R. Co. v. United States, 356 U.S. 1, 9–11 (1957) (emphasis added).

64. *Id.* at 13, 19.

65. Tampa Elec. Co. v. Nashville Coal Co., 365 U.S. 320, 325, 327 (1961).

66. United States v. E. I. duPont de Nemours & Co., 353 U.S. 586 (1957).

67. *Id.* Brennan later wrote: "The statutory policy of fostering free competition is obviously furthered when no supplier has an advantage over his competitors from an acquisition of his customer's stock likely to have the effects condemned by the statute." *Id.* at 607, 619–26 (Burton and Frankfurter, JJ., dissenting) (arguing that transaction too old to be of concern).

68. *Id.* at 590–93.

69. *Id.* at 594–96, 608. *DuPont* (*GM*) did not resolve the controversial question of defining markets and determining competitive effects: Was it conduct or industry structure or corporate bigness that offended the Clayton Act? Six years later, the Federal Trade Commission issued a cease-and-desist order to dissolve another merger more than a decade after its completion. FTC v. Consolidated Foods Corp., 380 U.S. 592 (1965). The FTC's rationale was conduct-based. Justice Douglas's opinion for the Court was strongly influenced by the industry's oligopoly structure. Justices Harlan and Stewart concurred in the result, but disapproved of Douglas's oligopoly rationale. *Id.* at 598–99, 600–01, 603–05.

70. Brown Shoe Co. v. United States, 370 U.S. 294, 311–16 (1962). The merger had both vertical and horizontal aspects: Each firm both manufactured and retailed shoes. Moreover, the case involved questions of both product and geographic market definitions.

71. *Id.* at 302, 325, 328, 331–32, 343–44. Justice Harlan would have applied the volume of commerce rationale recently rejected in *Tampa Electric* (1961); *id.* at 371–74. *Id.* at 344.

72. United States v. Philadelphia Nat'l Bank, 374 U.S. 321, 362–64 (1963). Justice Brennan observed that the Clayton Act prohibited mergers which substantially lessened competition in *any* line of commerce, in *any* section of the country. He took this to mean that anticompetitive consequences in any market could not be weighed against claims that the merger was beneficial in some other respect or in other markets. Thus, PNB's argument that its merger with Girard Bank would make it a stronger rival to the New York City banks in the market for large corporate lending fell on deaf ears. *Id.* at 370–71.

73. United States v. El Paso Natural Gas Co., 376 U.S. 651, 658, 661 (1964).

74. United States v. Aluminum Co. of Am., 377 U.S. 271, 277–78, 280–81 (1964).

75. United States v. Continental Can Co., 378 U.S. 441, 447, 457–58, 461 (1964).

76. United States v. Von's Grocery, 374 U.S. 270, 271–73, 281, 288 (1966); United States v. Pabst Brewing Co., 384 U.S. 546 (1966).

77. *Pabst Brewing Co.*, 384 U.S. at 548–51; Justice Douglas concurred, including in an appendix a recent article by humorist Art Buchwald, whose point was that microeconomic market analysis was just a way of obscuring the continuing social issue of economic concentration. *Id.* at 553–55.

78. *Id.* at 555, 559–61.

79. *Id.* at 562.

80. FTC v. Procter & Gamble Co., 386 U.S. 568, 571 (1967).

81. *Id.* at 571–72.

82. The FTC's theories, adopted in Douglas's opinion, also included the theory of potential competition. The FTC argued that Procter & Gamble's size, its range of household cleansing products, and its desire to include a bleach product, made it the most likely firm to enter the bleach industry on its own. This theory, consistent with the preference for internal growth over external, holds that the perception of a

potential competitor waiting in the wings makes a market more competitive, so long as the perception holds. *Id.* at 575, 578. In the 1980s, the theory would be abstracted into a theory of "contestable markets," in which anti-interventionist policy makers would argue that there were always potential competitors waiting in the wings, even in monopolistic markets. Thus, government intervention to maintain or reinstitute competition was never necessary. The theory of contestable markets is discussed *infra* chap. 6.

83. *Id.* at 590–603 (Harlan, J., concurring).

84. United States v. Arnold, Schwinn & Co., 388 U.S. 365, 368–69, 376 (1967). The District Court expressed no ambivalence, characterizing Schwinn as a "pygmy against a Cyclops . . . a microscopic Lilliputian." 237 F.Supp. 323, 334 (N.D. Ill. 1965).

85. *Schwinn*, 388 U.S. at 378–80.

86. *Id.* at 380 (Fortas), 386–87 (Stewart).

87. Utah Pie Co. v. Continental Baking Co., 386 U.S. 685 (1967).

88. *Id.* at 706.

89. *Id.* at 690, 702 ("ground rules for the game"), 703 n.14 ("Fair game for discriminatory price cutting" and citing *Mead*, 348 U.S. at 119 ("treasur[ies] use to finance . . .")).

90. *Id.* at 690 n.6.

91. Of the many powerful feminist analyses of the public/private dichotomy and the ideology of the market, I have been influenced most by the work of Frances Olsen. See particularly Olsen, *The Family and the Market: A Study of Ideology and Legal Reform*, 96 HARV. L. REV. 1497 (1983); *The Myth of State Intervention in the Family*, 18 U. MICH. J.L. REF. 835 (1985).

Chapter 5

1. Department of Justice, *Merger Guidelines* (1968).

2. NEIL FLIGSTEIN, THE TRANSFORMATION OF CORPORATE CONTROL 203–12 (1990); William Kovacic, *Failed Expectations: The Troubled Past and Uncertain Future of the Sherman Act as a Tool for Deconcentration*, 74 IOWA L. REV. 1105, 1136–39 (1989); RICHARD DUBOFF, ACCUMULATION AND POWER: AN ECONOMIC HISTORY 107–11 (1989). The ITT affair, including Attorney General Kliendienst's misdemeanor conviction for misleading the Judiciary Committee about the secret settlement negotiations, inspired Congress to pass legislation requiring the publication of consent decrees, court findings, and other relevant documents sixty days prior to the effective date of the judgment. The Antitrust Procedures and Penalties Act of 1974, Pub. L. No. 93–528, 88 Stat. 1796 (codified as amended at 15 U.S.C. § 16 (1988)).

3. Federal Trade Comm'n Staff Report, *Conglomerate Merger Performance: An Empirical Analysis of Nine Corporations* (1972). FREDERICK SCHERER, ET AL., THE ECONOMICS OF MULTI-PLANT OPERATION—AN INTERNATIONAL COMPARISONS STUDY (1975).

4. The *Clorox*, *Schwinn*, and *Utah Pie* decisions (1967) are discussed *supra* chap. 4. Fortner Enters., Inc. v. U.S. Steel, 394 U.S. 495, 503–04 (1969) (emphasis added).

5. United States v. Container Corp., 393 U.S. 333, 336, 344, 337 (1969).

6. United States v. General Dynamics Corp., 415 U.S. 486, 494, 498, 522 (1974) (Douglas, J., dissenting).

7. United States v. Marine Bancorp., Inc., 418 U.S. 602, 619, 622–23 (1974).

8. *Id.* at 642, 653.

9. 121 CONG.REC. 32, 289–96 (1975) (concerning vote S. 2387, 94th Cong., 1st Sess.

(1975), entitled Petroleum Industry Act of 1976); *Cf. Hearings on S.2387 and Related Bills Before the Subcommittee on Antitrust and Monopoly of the Senate Committee on the Judiciary*, 94th Cong., 1st Sess. (1975); Monopolization Reform Act of 1976, S. 3429, 94th Cong., 2d Sess. § 3, 122 CONG. REC. 13,872 (1976). *See, e.g.*, Industrial Reorganization Act (proposing to restructure seven concentrated industries), discussed in *Hearings on S. 117 Before the Subcommittee on Antitrust and Monopoly of the Senate Committee on the Judiciary*, 93d Cong., 1st Sess. 3 (1973). *See generally* Note, *A Legislative Approach to Market Concentration: The Industrial Reorganization Act*, 24 SYRACUSE L. REV. 1100 (1973); Note, *The Industrial Reorganization Act: An Antitrust Proposal to Restructure the American Economy*, 73 COLUM. L. REV. 635 (1973); Kovacic, *supra* note 2, at 74. Miller-Tydings Resale Price Maintenance Act of 1937, Ch. 690, 50 Stat. 693 (1937), *amended by* McGuire Resale Price Amendment of 1952, ch. 745, 66 Stat. 631 (1952), *repealed by* Consumer Pricing Act of 1975, 89 Stat. 801 (1975); Hart-Scott-Rodino Antitrust Improvements Act of 1976, Pub. L. No. 94–435 (1976) (codified at 15 U.S.C. § 7A (1988)). The Supreme Court soon limited the scope of the 1976 Act in Illinois Brick Co. v. Illinois, 431 U.S. 720 (1977) (limiting damage remedy to direct purchasers). Ralph Nader's influence began with his UNSAFE AT ANY SPEED: THE DESIGNED-IN DANGERS OF THE AMERICAN AUTOMOBILE (1965) and continued with, for example, MARK GREEN, ET AL., TAMING THE GIANT CORPORATION (1976).

10. Robert Bork & Ward Bowman, *The Crisis in Antitrust*, FORTUNE, Dec. 1963, at 138. Harlan Blake & William Jones, *The Goals of Antitrust: A Dialogue on Policy*, 65 COLUM. L. REV. 363 (1965). By "oligopoly theorists," I refer to the larger group of economists who took industry structure seriously. One of the Chicago Schoolers' most successful efforts at legitimating their approach resulted from their participation in a conference at Columbia Law School, precipitated by Senator Hart's proposed legislation calling for widespread deconcentration of American industry. A group of essays and edited conference transcripts, collected in INDUSTRIAL CONCENTRATION: THE NEW LEARNING (Harvey J. Goldschmid, H. Michael Mann, & J. Fred Weston eds. 1974), counterposed oligopoly theorists and Chicago School price theorists in a series of debates over questions regarding the theoretical presuppositions and empirical grounding of the dominant oligopoly theory of industrial concentration. Ward S. Bowman, Jr., *Tying Arrangements and the Leverage Problem*, 67 YALE L.J. 19 (1957); Robert Bork, *Legislative Intent and the Policy of the Sherman Act*, 6 J.L. & ECON. 7 (1966); GEORGE J. STIGLER, *A Theory of Oligopoly* and *Barriers to Entry, Economics of Scale, and Firm Size*, *in* THE ORGANIZATION OF INDUSTRY 39, 67 (1968); Robert Bork's writings in antitrust, published as law review articles in the 1950s and 1960s, would reappear in his landmark book THE ANTITRUST PARADOX (1978).

11. George J. Stigler, *The Theory of Regulation*, 2 BELL J. ECON. 3 (1971).

12. Ronald H. Coase, *The Theory of Social Cost*, 3 J.L. & ECON. 1, 2 (1960). George J. Stigler, Jr., *The Law and Economics of Public Policy: A Plea to the Scholars*, 1 J. LEG. STUD. 12 (1972). This argument is a precursor to the "contestability theory" that legitimized much of the deregulation championed by Alfred Kahn during the Carter administration and carried forward in the laissez-faire ideology of the Reagan administrations.

13. RICHARD POSNER, ECONOMIC ANALYSIS OF LAW (1973); POSNER, ANTITRUST LAW, AN ECONOMIC PERSPECTIVE (1976).

14. Richard Posner, *Some Uses and Abuses of Economics in Law*, 46 U. CHI. L. REV. 281, 295 (1979) (quoting STEVEN WEINBERG, THE FIRST THREE MINUTES: A MODERN VIEW OF THE ORIGIN OF THE UNIVERSE 119 (1977).

15. *Id. See* ROBERT BORK, THE ANTITRUST PARADOX 116–33 (1978) (method of anti-

trust analysis); Bork, *Judicial Precedent and the New Economics, in Changing Antitrust Standards,* CONF. BD. RESEARCH BULL. NO. 144, 10 (1983); *see also* Mario Rizzo, *The Mirage of Efficiency,* 8 HOFSTRA L. REV. 641 (1980). *See* Peritz, *Counter-History,* 1990 DUKE L.J. at 300–11; for a collection of criticisms and alternative policy formulations, including reviews of empirical research, see *Symposium, The Past and Future of Antitrust as Public Interest Law,* 35 N.Y.L. SCH. L. REV. 767 et seq. (1990). For studies finding significant statistical correlations between firm size and profitability, see David J. Ravenscraft, *Structure-Profit Relationships at the Line of Business and Industry Level,* 65 REV. ECON. & STAT. 22 (1985); Mark Glick & Hans Ehrbar, *Long-Run Equilibrium in the Empirical Study of Monopoly and Equilibriium,* 28 ECON. INQ. 151–62 (1990).

16. Arthur Leff, *Economic Analysis of Law: Some Realism about Nominalism,* 60 VA. L. REV. 451, 476 (1974) (reviewing RICHARD POSNER, ECONOMIC ANALYSIS OF LAW (1973)).

17. POSNER (1976), *supra* note 13, at 22.

18. *See, e.g.,* R. LIPSEY & P. STEINER, ECONOMICS 172–73 (3d ed. 1972). Only under conditions of perfect competition do productive and allocative efficiency coincide. *See, e.g.,* Lewis Kornhauser, *A Guide to the Perplexed Claims of Efficiency in the Law,* 8 HOFSTRA L. REV. 591 (1980). For a critique of Posner's use of productive efficiency, see Peritz, *Predicament of Antitrust Jurisprudence,* 1984 DUKE L.J. at 1283–4. *See, e.g.,* POSNER (1976), *supra* note 13, at 4, 11–15; RICHARD POSNER, THE ROBINSON-PATMAN ACT 7–10, 27 (1976); for a critical analysis, see Peritz, *Predicament of Antitrust Jurisprudence,* 1984 DUKE L.J. at 1284–95; *see also* Frank I. Michelman, *A Comment on Some Uses and Abuses of Economics in Law,* 46 U. CHI. L. REV. 307, 308–09 (1979).

19. *See, e.g.,* PAUL A. SAMUELSON, ECONOMICS 609–11, 617–18 (1967); Peritz, *Predicament of Antitrust Jurisprudence,* 1984 DUKE L.J. at 1285. RICHARD POSNER & FRANK EASTERBROOK, ANTITRUST 9–10 (1980); Posner, *supra* note 14, at 291. *See generally* Jules Coleman, *Efficiency, Utility, and Wealth Maximization,* 8 HOFSTRA L. REV. 509 (1980). Many values can be maximized or otherwise privileged—freedom of association, affirmative action, and workplace democracy are just three examples. For yet another value, see Peritz, *Competition Policy: its History and its Promise for Localism in a Global Economy, in* COMMUNITY EMPOWERMENT AND ECONOMIC DEVELOPMENT (Toni Taibi ed.) (forthcoming, U. Ill. Press) (formulating efficiency norm to maximize local economic development). Richard Posner, *Utilitarianism, Economics, and Legal Theory,* 8 J. LEGAL STUD. 103, 119 (1979); *but see* Mark Kelman, *Choice and Utility,* 1979 WIS. L. REV. 769, 778–82 (arguing that whether a transaction is beneficial cannot be measured solely by choice of consumer at time of transaction). SAMUELSON, *supra,* at 419 (suggesting that most present-day researchers do measure utility—behavioristically, and in "greater than" or "less than" terms rather than in cardinal numbers); G.C. ARCHIBALD & R. LIPSEY, AN INTRODUCTION TO MATHEMATICAL ECONOMICS 284–88 (1976) (explaining that utility need only be represented as ordinal to derive demand curves).

20. WILFREDO PARETO, COURS D'ÉCONOMIE POLITIQUE (1897) (first Eng. trans. 1936). *See* Peritz, *Predicament of Antitrust Jurisprudence,* 1984 DUKE L.J. at 1249, 1279–95.

21. POSNER (1976), *supra* note 13, at 4–5; POSNER & EASTERBROOK *supra* note 19, at 10; *see* Peritz, *Predicament of Antitrust Jurisprudence,* 1984 DUKE L.J. at 1285–95; Guido Calabresi & Douglas Melamed, *Property Rules, Liability Rules, and Inalienability,* 85 HARV. L. REV. 1089, 1096 (1972); *see generally* Coleman, *supra* note 19. Of course, Chicago economist Milton Friedman has applied the price-theoretical logic of supply and demand to macro-economic questions of monetary policy.

22. POSNER & EASTERBROOK, *supra* note 19, at 9–10. The marginal utility of money was recognized long ago in ARTHUR C. PIGOU, THE ECONOMICS OF WELFARE (1920); *see* JOHN KENNETH GALBRAITH, ECONOMICS IN PERSPECTIVE 212–13 (1987); Peritz, *Predicament*

of Antitrust Jurisprudence, 1984 DUKE L.J. at 1289–90. For a powerful critique of the view that human beings are motivated only by self-interest, see Amartya Sen, *Rational Fools: A Critique of the Behavioral Foundations of Economic Theory*, 6 PHIL. & PUB. AFF. 317 (1977).

23. POSNER (1976), *supra* note 13, at 39–78.

24. *Id.* at 55–71. The list seems to be a reworking of the 1955 ATTORNEY GENERAL REPORT's approach, informed by GEORGE J. STIGLER, *A Theory of Oligopoly, in* THE ORGANIZATION OF INDUSTRY 39 (1968). In a concentrated industry, for example, there could be a presumption of tacit collusion, with a burden of proof imposed upon industry members over a certain size to show cause why the industry should not be deconcentrated. Without here parsing through the specifics, rebuttal evidence could include a manageable number of factors derived from Chamberlain's analysis of imperfect oligopoly, Posner's twenty-four point plan, and more recent work by others. The important differences are two. First, concentrated firms would have the burden of proof. Second, the number and shape of rebuttal factors would be manageable.

25. Robert Bork, *Legislative Intent and the Policy of the Sherman Act*, 9 J. L. & ECON 7 (1966); *The Rule of Reason and the Per Se Concept* (pts. I & II), 74 YALE L.J. 775 (1965), 75 YALE L.J. 373 (1966). By "consumer welfare," Bork means wealth maximization, which includes "producer welfare" as well. For a contrast between this notion of "consumer welfare" and the values subtending Ralph Nader's consumer movement, see Peritz, *Counter-History*, 1990 DUKE L.J. at 311–2. For an excellent analysis and useful bibliography of historical scholarship regarding the Sherman Act's legislative history, see James May, *Historical Analysis in Antitrust Law*, 35 N.Y.L. SCH. L. REV. 857 (1990).

26. Robert H. Bork, *Neutral Principles and Some First Amendment Problems*, 47 IND. L.J. 1, 1–5, 18 (1971). BORK, ANTITRUST PARADOX 382–401 (1978); for criticisms, see Peritz, *Predicament of Antitrust Jurisprudence*, 1984 DUKE L.J. at 1246–62; Peritz, *Counter-History*, 1990 DUKE L.J. at 301–12.

27. Bork (1971), *supra* note 26, at 5, 8, 18. Bork seems to have some difficulty in deciding exactly what he means by logical derivation, which usually refers to a deductive process. Induction is the "weaker" logic of extracting general principles from concrete cases—usually called empiricism. What then does he mean when he writes that rights must be "derived logically by finding and extrapolating a more general principle"? *Id.* at 8. General principles are starting points in deduction and interpretive conclusions in induction. Holmes's aphorism, as stated, comes from THE COMMON LAW 1 (1881)

28. Bork, *supra* note 26, at 5–6. For the parallel view of the proper judicial role in antitrust cases, see Bork, *The Role of Courts in Applying Economics*, 54 ANTITRUST L.J. 21, 24 (1985). Bork, *Judicial Precedent and the New Economics, in Changing Antitrust Standards*, CONF. BD. RESEARCH BULL. NO. 144, 10 (1988).

29. Gitlow v. New York, 268 U.S. 652, 669 (1925) (emphasis added); Schenck v. United States, 249 U.S. 47, (1919) (Holmes, J., dissenting) ("clear and present danger"); Whitney v. California, 274 U.S. 357, 375 (1927) (Brandeis, J., concurring) ("clear and imminent danger"); Bork (1971), *supra* note 26, at 32–33. S. REP. NO. 698, 63d Cong., 2d Sess. 1 (July 22, 1914). Bork, *The Place of Antitrust Among National Goals, in* BASIC ANTITRUST QUESTIONS IN THE MIDDLE SIXTIES, FIFTH CONFERENCE ON THE IMPACT OF ANTITRUST ON ECONOMIC GROWTH 18 (Nat'l Indus. Conf. Bd. 1966). For an extended analysis, see Peritz, *Predicament of Antitrust Jurisprudence*, 1984 DUKE L.J. at 1258–62.

30. Abrams v. United States, 250 U.S. 616, (1919) (Holmes, J., dissenting). The Court, of course, characterized Abrams's handiwork as a clear and present danger.

Most observers today would agree with Holmes and Brandeis, who saw the speech as anything but dangerous. For Bork, it seems, the question of danger is immaterial. Justice Sanford's formulation in *Whitney* (1927) certainly adopts that view.

31. Bork (1988), *supra* note 28, at 34.

32. United States v. United Auto Workers, 352 U.S. 567, 570 (1957). Tillman Act of 1907, Ch. 420, 34 Stat. 864, 865; Federal Election Campaign Act of 1971, Pub. L. No. 92–225, 86 Stat. 3 (1972); The Federal Election Campaign Act Amendments of 1974, Pub. L. No. 93–443, 88 Stat. 1263 (1974) (codified as amended at 2 U.S.C. §§ 431–55 (1988)).

33. California Motor Trans. Co. v. Trucking Unlimited, 404 U.S. 508, 513 (1972).

34. Even when the Court did consider the danger of economic inequality in the marketplace of ideas, it was the "imminent danger" test formulated by Justice Holmes in *Schenck* (1919) to reflect concerns about physical violence, forcible overthrow. *Bellotti*, 435 U.S. at 792.

35. *Red Lion*, 395 U.S. 367 (1969). Congress subsequently enacted the doctrine into law and later repealed it. Legislation imposing upon newspapers an obligation to allow a right to reply, however, was deemed unconstitutional. Miami Herald Publishing Co. v. Tornillo, 418 U.S. 241 (1974). For a thoughtful discussion of First Amendment ideology, see David Cole, *Agon at Agora: Creative Misreadings in the First Amendment Tradition*, 95 YALE L.J. 857 (1986) (applying the theoretical approach of Yale literary critic Harold Bloom); *First Amendment Antitrust: The End of Laissez-Faire in Campaign Finance*, 9 YALE L. & POL'Y REV. 236 (1991). In his more recent piece, Cole's otherwise insightful analysis is blemished by a seeming unfamiliarity with the shift in antitrust ideology in the mid-1970s, a shift from his view to a benign neglect of corporate size and economic concentration, to, by the 1908s, the very laissez-faire ideology he rejects.

Virginia State Bd. of Pharmacy v. Virginia Citizens Consumer Council, Inc., 425 U.S. 748, 763 (1976). The opinion followed Justice Blackmun's opinion in Bigelow v. Virginia, 421 U.S. 809 (1975) (two years after his opinion in Roe v. Wade), in which he wrote for a strong majority that a Virginia newspaper's advertisement about abortions available in New York merited First Amendment protection because it "contained factual matter of clear public interest." The extension of speech protection from information about abortion to sale prices of house brand aspirin is not, however, self-evident. One interesting ambivalence raised by this development can be seen in the Court's declaration, in Gertz v. Robert Welch, Inc, 418 U.S. 323, 339 (1974), that "[u]nder the First Amendment there is no such thing as a false idea." Aside from the untenable distinction Justice Powell posited between false ideas and "false statements of fact" (which do not merit constitutional protection), the Court could not maintain this no-false-idea doctrine and sustain FTC regulation under the FTC Act § 5 of false or misleading advertising. The Court would even uphold a Texas statute barring optometrists from practicing under trade names. Friedman v. Rodgers, 440 U.S. 1 (1979). Some distinctions between citizens and consumers, between political and economic speech, were still necessary, it seemed.

36. Buckley v. Valeo, 424 U.S. 1 (1976); First Nat'l Bank of Boston v. Bellotti, 435 U.S. 765 (1978).

37. Amalgamated Food Employees Union Local 590 v. Logan Valley Plaza. Inc., 391 U.S. 308, 313, 324 (1968). Perhaps First Amendment-absolutist Black's dissent in this speech case was not so surprising, given his earlier opinion in *Giboney* (1949) depicting labor picketing as always involving more than speech. The best-known "public function" or "company town" case is Marsh v. Alabama, 326 U.S. 501 (1946).

38. Lloyd Corp. v. Tanner, 407 U.S. 551, 569 (1972). Echoing Justice Sutherland's decision in Williams v. Standard Oil, 278 U.S. 235 (1929), Justice Powell wrote: "We hold that there has been no such dedication of Lloyd's privately owned and operated shopping center to public use." 407 U.S. at 570.

39. *Lloyd Corp.*, 407 U.S. at 569, 554–55. Moreover, striking employees would no longer be permitted to picket their employer's place of business, if in a shopping center. Hudgens v. NLRB, 424 U.S. 507, 520–21 (1976). Recall that Chief Justice Vinson wrote that "[n]othing in the Constitution prevents Congress from acting in time to prevent potential injury to the national economy from becoming a reality." *Douds*, 339 U.S. at 406, 409. Not only did the Court expand the scope of employers' property rights, but it defined employees' rights narrowly. In Bishop v. Wood, 426 U.S. 341 (1976), for example, Justice John Paul Stevens refused to acknowledge a permanent employee's entitlement to due process upon discharge. The decision was particularly surprising because the employee was a city police officer and thus, there was no constitutional question of state action—the issue analogous to "public function" in the shopping center cases. Justice Brennan wrote in his dissenting opinion that the dismissal was unconsititutional because "'liberty' or 'property' [is] guaranteed against state deprivation without due process of law." *Id.* at 351.

40. Buckley v. Valeo, 424 U.S. 1 (1976). For useful analyses of Buckley and its progeny, see Harold Leventhal, *Courts and Political Thickets*, 77 COLUM. L. REV. 345 (1977); J. Skelly Wright, *Money and the Pollution of Politics: Is the First Amendment an Obstacle to Political Equality?*, 82 COLUM. L. REV. 609 (1982); William Patton & Randall Bartlett, *Corporate "Persons" and Freedom of Speech: The Political Impact of Legal Mythology*, 1981 WIS. L. REV. 494; David Cole, *supra* note 35; CHARLES LINDBLOM, POLITICS AND MARKETS (1977); C. EDWIN BAKER, HUMAN LIBERTY AND FREEDOM OF SPEECH (1989).

41. *Buckley*, 424 U.S. at 48–49.

42. Of course, it is possible to describe the dynamic in terms of an egalitarian ethic similar to the one which informed the *Lochner* Court—a formal sense of equality. But, as Roscoe Pound wrote at the time, "Why do so many [courts] force upon legislation an academic theory of equality in the face of practical conditions of inequality? Why do we find a great and learned court in 1908 taking the long step into the past of dealing with the relation between employer and employee in railway transportation, as if the parties were individuals—as if they were farmers haggling over the sale of a horse?" Roscoe Pound, *Liberty of Contract*, 18 YALE L.J. 454 (1909).

43. First Nat'l Bank of Boston v. Bellotti, 435 U.S. 765, 777 (1978), *rev'g* First Nat'l Bank of Boston v. Attorney General, 371 Mass. 773, 359 N.E.2d 1262 (1977).

44. Ohralik v. Ohio State Bar Ass'n, 436 U.S. 447, 456 (1978). *See, e.g.*, Central Hudson Gas & Elec. Corp v. Public Service Comm'n, 447 U.S. 557 (1980).

45. *Bellotti*, 435 U.S. at 765, 775, 784 n.20, 792 n.31. There is, of course, the difficulty of distinguishing between commerce and politics, whether content- or intent-based. *See, e.g., Chrestensen*, 122 F.2d at 516 (2d Cir. 1941) (Clark, J.) ("if intent and purpose must be measured, how can we say that plaintiff's motives are only or primarily financial? Is he just engaged in an advertising plot, or does he really believe in his wrongs?").

46. For an argument that the solution calls for a redistribution of wealth, see Lucas A. Powe, Jr., *Mass Speech and the Newer First Amendment*, 1982 SUP. CT. REV. 243. Numerous philosophers and social theorists have argued that equality is the foundation for liberty. See, e.g., JOHN RAWLS, A THEORY OF JUSTICE (1971) ("original position"); Ronald Dworkin, *Philosophy and Politics: Dialogue with Ronald Dworkin, in* MEN OF IDEAS (Bryan Mages ed. 1976); Dworkin, *What is Equality? Part 2: Equality of Re-*

sources, 10 PHIL. & PUBL. AFF. 283 (1981); H.L.A. HART, THE CONCEPT OF LAW 195 (1961); JÜRGEN HABERMAS, COMMUNICATION AND THE EVOLUTION OF SOCIETY 1–69 (Thomas McCarthy trans. 1979) ("ideal speech situation")

47. Brunswick Corp. v. Pueblo Bowl-O-Mat, 429 U.S. 477, 485 (1977); Clayton Act, Ch. 323, § 4, 38 Stat. 730 (current version at 15 U.S.C. § 15 (1988)).

48. *Brunswick Corp.*, 429 U.S. at 488; United States v. Philadelphia Nat'l Bank, 375 U.S. 321, 372 n.46 (1963) (failing company defense, recognized in both Senate and House reports); Citizens Publishing Co. v. United States, 394 U.S. 131 (1969) (same).

49. 429 U.S. at 490; Marshall's call for proof of predation seems to invoke the Sherman Act standard for attempts to monopolize—some proof of egregious conduct as the evidentiary basis for finding predatory purpose.

50. Broadcast Music, Inc. v. Columbia Broadcasting Sys., 441 U.S. 1, 19–20, 21–22 (1979) (portraying ASCAP and BMI as agencies to "integrate sales, monitoring, and enforcement against unauthorized copyright use"). Copyright holders retained the right to license their works independently. For a more detailed analysis, see Peritz, *Counter-History*, 1990 DUKE L.J. at 291–94.

51. *Broadcast Music*, 441 U.S. at 28, 37.

52. Although the property rights here derived from the Copyright Act, the pull of property rights more generally would lead to an unstable doctrine of price fixing, with the Court veering between the pure competition logic of per se illegality and the "Rule of Reason" weighing of property and competition concerns. Regarding the problem of indeterminability of property rights in the context of vertical restraints doctrine, see Peritz, *Genealogy*, 40 HASTINGS L.J. at 525–27.

53. Continental T.V., Inc. v GTE Sylvania, Inc., 433 U.S. 36, 53–54 (1977). In my discussion of this case, all references to "restraints" mean non-price restraints.

54. *Id.* at 52 n.19, 67–9.

55. *Id.* at 55.

56. *Id.*

57. Lester Telser, *Why Should Manufacturers Want Fair Trade?*, 3 J.L. & ECON. 86 (1960); Richard Posner, *The Next Step in the Antitrust Treatment of Restricted Distribution: Per Se Legality*, 48 U. CHI. L. REV 6, 8 (1981). For insightful criticisms of this view, see William S. Comanor, *Vertical Price-Fixing, Vertical Market Restrictions and the New Antitrust Policy*, 95 HARV. L. REV. 983 (1985); Frederick Scherer, *The Economics of Vertical Restraints*, 52 ANTITRUST L.J. 687 (1983).

58 ROBERT BORK, THE ANTITRUST PARADOX 90–91, 104–06 (1978). For a fuller treatment, see Peritz, *Predicament of Antitrust Jurisprudence*, 1984 DUKE L.J. at 1246–61.

59. BORK, *supra* note 58, at 90–91. FRANK H. KNIGHT, THE ECONOMIC ORGANIZATION 9 (1933) (defining economic policy in terms of allocating and coordinating functions).

60. FRANK H. KNIGHT, *The Role of Principles in Economics and Politics*, *in* his ON THE HISTORY AND METHOD OF ECONOMICS 250, 260–61 (1956); HENRY C. SIMONS, A POSITIVE PROGRAM FOR LAISSEZ-FAIRE (1934). Regarding economic rationality as a logic of "satisficing" rather than maximizing, see HERBERT SIMON, MODELS OF BOUNDED RATIONALITY (1982) (two volumes, including essays dating back to 1937).

61. BORK, *supra* note 58, at 117. Yet Bork seeks to exclude, parenthetically, from his definition of productive efficiency, "goods and services . . . that society outlaws for other reasons—addictive drugs or prostitution, for example, is obvious." The exclusion must, of course, be parenthetical (cordoned off) because it conflicts with the norms of efficiency, conflicts with the assumption of a "free market." Once Bork concedes that a "free market" can include social norms other than efficiency, he must make normative arguments about each and every one. For example, why exclude

cigarettes or prostitution if consumers want it? Or why exclude special solicitude toward local producers if consumers want such government policy? The progression, of course, is endless. Moreover, each example reflects a conflict between individual desires and majoritarian sentiments. Small wonder that Bork wants to contain within parentheses any "exception" to unrestrained consumer choice—that is, any activity that "society outlaws for other reasons."

62. Richard Posner, *Utilitarianism, Economics, and Legal Theory*, 8 J. LEG. STUD. 103 (1979); *The Ethical and Political Basis of the Efficiency Norm in Common Law Adjudication*, 8 HOFSTRA L. REV. 487 (1980); *Change in the Common Law: Legal and Economic Perspectives*, 9 J. LEG. STUD. 189 (1980). *See* Peritz, *Counter-History*, 1990 DUKE L.J. at 305 n.165. Of course, both generations impose limits on freedom of contract. For the *Lochner* generation, it was the legitimate police power to regulate matters of health, safety, and public morals. For Bork, it is "outlaw[ed]" contracts. In both, liberty of contract would yield, at some point, to other social values. Once that is admitted, however, the determination of precisely which social values trump the social value of liberty of contract becomes itself a matter of social value judgments. Thus, as soon as freedom of contract was seen as limited by other social values, both Justice Sutherland's Four Horsemen and Robert Bork faced the same slippery slope, the same nondeductive logic of balancing social values: If some contracts are unenforceable because they violate the law (that is, the social values expressed in legislative enactment or in constitutional provision), liberty of contract is no longer sacrosanct.

63. Posner's formulation can be understood as an attempt to recoup the loss suffered in the move from the traditional Pareto Optimality standard to the Kaldor-Hicks version of allocative efficiency, which is something approaching a Utilitarian balancing. That is, the appeal of the Paretan determination is its dependence on the fact that no one can be worse off—pretty close to a neutral standard. Kalder-Hicks, however, allows for losers so long as there is a net gain. With the turn to "personal autonomy," Posner can claim that even losers are better off. It is the process that is good, even when the result is not. Even losers are winners, just for the taste of it, just for the freedom of exercising one's commercial preferences. Wealth maximization would seem to offend both Utilitarian and Libertarian ethics. Utilitarians would not recognize wealth as an adequate representation of utility. Libertarians (following Kant) would view the wealth maximization form of cost-benefit analysis as anunsatisfactory proxy for personal autonomy because its methodology shares Utilitarianism's unsatisfactory view of individuals as means, not ends. Posner's analysis can be seen as a deeply flawed attempt to synthesize Utilitarian and Libertarian ethics. For more on this, see Peritz, *Counter-History*, 1990 DUKE L.J. at 305 n.164.

64. Many of them have been amply discussed. *See, e.g.*, Duncan Kennedy & Frank Michelman, *Are Property and Contract Efficient?*, 8 HOFSTRA L.REV. 711 (1980), published shortly after Posner's piece.

65. POSNER (1976), *supra* note 13, at 19. Recent studies of the relationship between firm size and productive efficiency, understood in traditional non-Borkian terms, find little support for economies of scale as applied to very large firms. For sources, see Peritz, *Counter-History*, 1990 DUKE L.J. at 283–84 n.79. Thus, notwithstanding Ronald Coase's "Theory of the Firm" (1937), neither the size nor the success of large businesses can be attributed categorically to productive efficiency. One plausible alternative theory is that such success is based instead on the "background" rules—the contract, tort, and property law that Posner, Bork, and their cohorts call "the common law." In other words, what we call liberty of contract might favor large firms so much that small and medium-sized firms' efficiency advantages are lost. If large firms

were permitted to enter into contracts "freely," then, for example, a large multinational firm could sell below cost to drive a more efficient local firm out of business and finance its losses from monopoly profits in uncontested locations or from brand-identified products. Indeed, if permitted, they could perhaps convince banks to loan money for the purpose of driving small rivals out of business. A (populist) policy of "protecting" local firms from such practices would be consistent with competition on the merits. Here, populism, (traditional) productive efficiency, and competition are entirely compatible. Nonetheless, following Posner's "economic logic" of wealth maximization, restricting the liberty of large firms would be anticompetitive and inefficient.

66. For a closely reasoned argument demonstrating that neither private property nor freedom of contract regimes are necessarily more efficient than state-of-nature or forced-sharing-for-need regimes, see Kennedy & Michelman, *supra* note 64, at 712. Of course some notions of equality may be compatible with a primary commitment to liberty of contract—formal equality as seen in *Lochner* (1905) or nondiscrimination as seen in *Bakke* (1978) are two examples. The point remains, however, that Chicago School price theory and its norm of wealth maximization reflect a primary commitment to liberty of contract that is antithetical to substantive equality.

67. Civil Aeronautics Board Practice and Procedures, Senate Subcomm. on Administrative Practice of the Judiciary Comm., 96th Cong., 1st Sess. (1976) (Kennedy Report); Airline Deregulation Act of 1977, Pub. L. No. 95–163, 91 Stat. 1281 (Nov. 9, 1977); Airline Deregulation Act of 1978, Pub. L. No. 95–504, 92 Stat. 1705 Oct. 24, 1978) (codified as amended at 49 U.S.C. § 1301 et seq.). *See generally* Peter C. Carstensen, *Evaluating "Deregulation" of Commercial Air Travel: False Dichotomization, Untenable Theories, and Unimplemented Premises*, 46 WASH. & LEE L. REV. 109 (1989); PAUL S. DEMPSEY, FLYING BLIND, THE FAILURE OF AIRLINE DEREGULATION (1990); STEVEN BREYER, REGULATION AND REFORM 197–222 (1982); MARTHA DERTHICK & PAUL J. QUIRK, THE POLITICS OF DEREGULATION 17–27, 99–100, 124–25, 152–55 (1985).

68. Compare *Hearings on H.R. 11145 Before the Aviation Subcommittee of the House Public Works and Transportation Committee*, 95th Cong., 2d. Sess. 178 (March 6, 1978) (statement of Alfred E. Kahn) with *id.* at 178–79, 1137. Kahn later revised his views of contestability theory. *Airline Deregulation, Hearing Before the Subcomm. on Antitrust of the Senate Judiciary Comm.*, 100th Cong., 1st Sess. 64 (1987). DEMPSEY, *supra* note 67, led me to these sources. Kahn would also point to the Reagan administration's lax merger policies as a crucial reason for the failure of airline deregulation—both from the consumer's and the carrier's perspectives. Alfred Kahn, *Airline Deregulation—A Mixed Bag, But a Clear Success Nevertheless*, 16 TRANSP. L.J. 229, 251 (1988).

69. *See, e.g., Hearings (Mergers & Economic Concentration) on S.600 Before the Subcommittee on Antitrust, Monopoly & Business Rights of the Senate Committee on the Judiciary*, 96th Cong., 1st Sess. 61–70 (March 8, 1979) (Statement of John H. Shenefield, Assistant Attorney General, Antitrust Division) (1979); *see also id.* at 38–41 (Statement of Ralph Nader and Mark Green); *cf. id.*, vol. II at 9–17 (Statement of Richard Posner). I REPORT TO THE PRESIDENT AND THE ATTORNEY GENERAL OF THE NATIONAL COMMISSION FOR THE REVIEW OF ANTITRUST LAWS AND PROCEDURES vi–ix (1979). MARC A. EISNER, ANTITRUST AND THE TRIUMPH OF ECONOMICS 5, 146–49 (1991) (arguing generally that in antitrust, "expertise provides a fundamental role in the definition and implementation of policy" and specifically that Shenefield's commitment to deconcentration did not filter down into a Justice Department whose economists and lawyers were already committed to price theory). FTC Act, 15 U.S.C. § 45 (a)(1). See Kovacic, *supra* note 2, at 1138; MICHAEL PERTSCHUK, REVOLT AGAINST REGULATION 78–79, 100–05 (1982).

70. ISAIAH BERLIN, *Two Concepts of Liberty*, *in* FOUR ESSAYS ON LIBERTY 139–40 (1969). Here, "contract" reflects a doubleness—not only to constrict or diminish but to agree or bargain.

Chapter 6

1. Regents of the Univ. of Cal. v. Bakke, 438 U.S. 265 (1978). Justice Powell was disturbed by the "illogical end of insulating each category of applicants with certain desired qualifications from *competition* with all other applicants." *Id.* at 315 (emphasis added). See also *id.* at 305, 319 n.53 (twice) for additional references to affirmative action as a subversion of an admission process otherwise assumed to be a purely meritocratic competiton.

2. *See, e.g.*, Howell Raines, *Tower Power: Controllers Discover the Ceiling after Reagan Hits It*, N.Y. TIMES, Aug. 9, 1981, at D1; Lyng v. International Union UAW, 485 U.S. 360 (1988) (upholding statute denying food stamps to strikers); NLRB v. Bildisco & Bildisco, 465 U.S. 518 (1984) (permitting revocation of collective bargaining agreement upon filing of bankruptcy), legislatively overruled by 29 U.S.C. § 151 et seq. Belknap, Inc. v. Duwayne E. Hale, 463 U.S. 491 (1983) (holding that the NLRA does not preempt state common law). See also SAMUEL BOWLES, ET AL., BEYOND THE WASTE LAND: A DEMOCRATIC ALTERNATIVE TO ECONOMIC DECLINE (1983).

3. Congressional Democratic Policy Statement on Regulatory Reform, paper presented to the White House (June 25, 1975), *excerpted in* MICHAEL PERTSCHUK, REVOLT AGAINST REGULATION 20 (1982). For a careful study of the FTC, see RICHARD A. HARRIS & SIDNEY M. MILKIS, THE POLITICS OF REGULATORY CHANGE 140–224 (1989). EDWARD F. COX, ET AL., THE NADER REPORT ON THE FEDERAL TRADE COMMISSION (1969); AMERICAN BAR ASSOCIATION, REPORT OF THE COMMISSION TO STUDY THE FEDERAL TRADE COMMISSION (1969).

4. *The National Nanny*, WASH. POST, Mar.1, 1978, at A22. 125 CONG. REC. 10, 757–58 (Nov. 14, 1979) (statement of Rep. Frenzel). The FTC Improvements Act of 1980, Pub. L. No. 96–252, 94 Stat. 374; INS v. Chadha, 462 U.S. 919 (1983); Consumers Union v. FTC, 691 F.2d 575 (D.C. Cir. 1982), *aff'd*, 463 U.S. 1216 (1983).

5. *Transition Report, Conclusions and Recommendations*, G1 (1980), *excerpted in* HARRIS & MILKIS, *supra* note 3, at 188 (Miller's statement). *FTC Reauthorization: Hearings Before the Subcomm. on Commerce, Trans. and Tourism, Comm. on Energy and Commerce*, 97th Cong., 2d Sess. 174 (Apr. 1, 20, 1982) (Pertschuk statement). Miller's appointment was seen as making the FTC the "textbook case" of deregulation. NAT'L J., Dec. 5, 1981, at 249, *noted in* HARRIS & MILKIS at 141.

6. *See, e.g.*, Cargill, Inc v. Monfort of Colo., Inc., 479 U.S. 104 (1986) (antitrust injury); Monsanto v. Spray-Rite, 465 U.S. 752 (1984) and BEC v. Sharp Elecs., 485 U.S. 717 (1988) (resale price maintenance); J. Truett Payne v. Chrysler Motors Corp., 451 U.S. 557 (1981) (price discrimination). The Court has also expanded the circumstances under which a defendant can prevail on a motion for summary judgment, therby avoiding a full trial. Matsushita Elec. Indus. Co. v. Zenith Radio Corp., 475 U.S. 574 (1986). The Reagan administration's Justice Department submitted an *amicus curiae* brief in *Monsanto*, urging the Court to overturn its treatment of resale price maintenance as illegal per se. The Court declined the invitation. For Chicago School scholarship making the argument, *see, e.g.*, Richard Posner, *The Next Step in Antitrust Treatment of Restricted Distribution: Per Se Legality*, 48 U. CHI. L. REV. 6, 8 (1981); William Baxter, *Resale Price Maintenance as a Reasonable Restraint of Trade*, 14 ANTITRUST L. &

ECON. REV. 13, 26 (1982); Frank Easterbrook, *Vertical Arrangements and the Rule of Reason*, 53 ANTITRUST L.J. 135 (1984). *Cf.* Robert Pitofsky, *In Defense of Discounters: The No-Frill Case for a Per Se Rule Against Vertical Price Fixing*, 71 GEO. L.J. 1487 (1983); Frederic Scherer, *The Economics of Vertical Restraints*, 52 ANTITRUST L.J. 687 (1983); William Comanor, *Vertical Price-Fixing, Vertical Market Restrictions, and the New Antitrust Policy*, 98 HARV. L. REV. 983 (1985); Peritz, *A Genealogy of Vertical Restraints Doctrine*, 40 HASTINGS L.J. 511 (1989).

My use of the word "trends" is not meant to suggest coherence or continuity. A number of cases seem to point in other directions. *See, e.g.*, Aspen Skiing Co. v. Aspen Highlands Skiing Corp., 472 U.S. 585 (1985) (monopolization); Eastman Kodak Co. v. Image Technical Services, Inc., 112 S. Ct. 2072 (1992) (market definition under Sherman Act); *compare* Arizona v. Maricopa County Medical Soc'y, 457 U.S. 332 (1982) *with* Atlantic Richfield Co. v. USA Petroleum Co., 495 U.S. 328 (1990) (horizontal v. vertical maximum price-fixing).

7. Parker v. Brown, 317 U.S. 341 (1943).

8. City of Lafayette v. Louisiana Power & Light Co., 435 U.S. 389, 403, 404, 410 ("expressed," "compelled," "supervised"), 422–24 (Burger, J. concurring) (1978).

9. *Id.* at 428, 431, 432 (Stewart, J., dissenting).

10. Jefferson County Pharmaceutical Ass'n v. Abbott Labs., 460 U.S. 150, 154 (1983) (emphasis added).

11. Justice Stevens also joined Justice O'Connor's strange dissenting opinion, as did two fellow Justices. The peculiar basis for O'Connor's opinion favoring an exemption to the State of Alabama was reliance upon long-standing business practices. Given this reliance, the Court should not "fill gaps" in the statute and upset "structured . . . marketing relationships." 460 U.S. at 180, 188 (O'Connor, J., dissenting).

12. Community Communications Co. v. City of Boulder, 455 U.S. 40 (1982). This image of the renegade sovereign seems out of place, at least to the extent that the Court has recognized that Congress passed the Sherman Act and later legislation with private economic power in mind. The rhetoric of free trade among the states sounds very much like opinions in "dormant Commerce Clause" cases, including recent opinions treating states, when "market participants," differently. *See, e.g.*, Brown-Foreman Distillers Corp v. New York State Liquor Auth., 476 U.S. 573 (1986); Bendix Autolite Corp. v. Midwesco Enters., Inc., 486 U.S. 888 (1988).

13 455 U.S. at 43, 44, 49, 56 (emphasis added). In a footnote, the Court also cited *City of Lafayette* for the proposition that it "may be that certain activities which might appear anticompetitive when engaged in by private parties, take on a different complexion when adopted by a local government." *Id.* at n.20, *citing City of Lafayette*, 435 U.S. at 417 n.48. That possibility remains unexplored.

14. 455 U.S. at 66, 60 (Rehnquist, J. dissenting).

15. The Local Government Antitrust Act, 15 U.S.C. §§ 35, 36 (1984). For a brief discussion of the FTC prosecutions and sources, see HARRIS AND MILKIS, *supra* note 3, at 208–09.

16. Hallie v. City of Eau Claire, 471 U.S. 34, 36, 42, 39 (1985).

17. Southern Motor Carriers Rate Conf. v. United States, 471 U.S. 48 (1985). The Court seemed to be embarking on an ad hoc approach to qualification of private parties for the "state action" exemption. Here, the Court found that the joint rates submitted were not required. Individual motor carriers could file lower rates, if they desired. The Court's view that lower rates were a strong likelihood offers perhaps the clearest example of the Court's rejection of oligopoly theory and its presumption

that firms in such circumstances would appreciate the logic of cooperative action and would, accordingly, hold the line on higher prices.

In a series of cases beginning at least as early as California Retail Liquor Dealers Ass'n v. Midcal Aluminum, Inc., 445 U.S. 97 (1980), the Court also applied a preemption analysis to determine whether a state statute or a local ordinance, "on its face," conflicted with the Sherman Act. This Supremacy Clause analysis led the Court, in a case decided contemporaneously with *City of Boulder*, to determine that the Sherman Act did not preempt a California statute allowing distillers to designate authorized importers. Rice v. Norman Williams Co., 458 U.S. 654 (1982). In Fisher v. City of Berkeley, 475 U.S. 260 (1986), the Court made it clear that the preemption doctrine applied as well to municipalities. The Court determined, even before reaching the "state action" question, that the Sherman Act had not preempted the city's rent control ordinance. Justice Marshall determined that since the ordinance "on its face" did not conflict "irreconcilably" with the Act, the antitrust laws simply did not apply and thus, the Supremacy Clause was not offended. What is odd about the opinion is that its "preemption" analysis consisted of a substantive evaluation of the ordinance. Echoing the *Colgate* (1919) doctrine that unilateral action by a commercial actor is not a violation of Sherman Act § 1, Marshall found that the City of Berkeley, as well, had acted unilaterally. Applying a substantive analysis borrowed from evaluation of commercial actors, the Court found that the political corporation of Berkeley could control rents without fear of preemption by the antitrust laws. In the context of Rehnquist's criticism and the concerns of those seeking to maximize local autonomy, the preemption opinions seem to retrace the substantive due process steps threatened in *City of Boulder*, though perhaps at a slight remove from the close scrutiny of all local regulation.

18. Copperweld Corp. v. Independence Tube Corp., 469 U.S. 927 (1984). In terms of corporate theory, the decision is consistent with Ronald Coase's theory of the firm as a network of contracts surrounding an efficiency-seeking entrepreneur, so long as the entrepreneur sits at the top of a rigorously controlled hierarchy of contracting parties and so long as the entrepreneur's interests coincide with those of the shareholders.

19. Of course, I do not mean to say that competition rhetoric does not inform regulation of corporations. For an interesting analysis of commercial markets without "private" property rights, see John E. Roemer, *The Morality and Efficiency of Market Socialism*, 102 ETHICS 448 (1992).

20. The FTC and Justice Department had antitrust agendas that went beyond cutting staff and decreasing activity. For the most part, the two agencies focused on price-fixing. *See, e.g.,* Walter Adams & James Brock, *Reaganomics and the Transmogrification of Merger Policy*, 33 ANTITRUST BULL. 309, 314 (1988) (reviewing budget and staff cuts, observing that by 1988, Justice Department Antitrust Division was little more than half of 1981 staff); MARC ALLEN EISNER, ANTITRUST AND THE TRIUMPH OF ECONOMICS 195 (1991) (price-fixing agenda). *Big Shift in Antitrust Policy*, DUN'S REV., Aug. 1981, at 38; William Baxter, *Responding to the Reaction: The Draftsman's View*, 71 CAL. L. REV. 618, 630 (1983). Malcolm Baldridge, *The Administration's Legislative Proposal and its Ramifications*, 55 ANTITRUST L.J. 29, 34 (1986).

21. In the Matter of Texaco, Inc., and Getty Oil Company, 104 FTC 241 (July 10, 1984) (Consent Order); In the Matter of Chevron Corporation and Gulf Corporation, 104 FTC 597 (Oct. 24, 1984) (Consent Order).

22. *Id.* (Chevron).

23. Consent Order, 104 F.T.C at 261–63 (Pertschuk dissenting). *Oversight of Gov-*

ernment Merger Enforcement Policy: Hearings Before the Senate Comm. on the Judiciary, 97th Cong., 1st Sess. 51 (1982) (Baxter testimony); Taylor & Crock, *Reagan Team Believes Antitrust Legislation Hurts Big Business,* WALL ST. J., July 8, 1981, at 1 (Smith statement); *Interview with Douglas H. Ginsburg,* 55 ANTITRUST L.J. 255, 262 (1986) (Ginsburg statement). U.S. Department of Justice, Merger Guidelines, 47 Fed. Reg. 28,493 (1982) [*Merger Guidelines*].

24. *See, e.g.,* William Kovacic, *Failed Expectations,* 74 IOWA L. REV. 1105, 1145 & n.250 (*citing* Leddy, *Recent Merger Cases Reflect Revolution in Antitrust Policy,* LEGAL TIMES, Nov. 3, 1986, at 17, col.1 (showing that Antitrust Division practices reflected lower merger enforcement thresholds than those set out in the HHI)). For a blow-by-blow description of enforcement under the Guidelines, see Walter Adams & James Brock, *Reaganomics and the Transmogrification of Merger Policy,* 33 ANTITRUST BULL. 309 (1988).

25. *Merger Guidelines,* Section 2.11. The more recent Guidelines include some changes, some deletions, and some additions. Nonetheless, the underlying triangulation of justifications for a permissive attitude toward mergers remains.

26. William Baxter, *Responding to the Reaction: The Draftsman's View,* 71 CAL. L. REV. 618, 623–24 at n.35 (1983). It should be noted that the theory underlying the Merger Guidelines' 5 percent solution is elasticity of demand—much as Justice Reed applied in *duPont* (*Cellophane*) (1956).

27. *Merger Guidelines,* Section 3.3. There is a second available rationale for Baxter's response. The first is a rejection of the weak, "tacit collusion" version of oligopoly theory espoused, for example, by Richard Posner in his ANTITRUST LAW (1976). Recall Posner's argument that oligopoly structure, while not imposing a logic of cooperation, does make tacit collusion easier to monitor and thus increases the difficulty of secretly lowering prices. Apparently, Baxter believes that the costs of preventing the merger (including potential efficiency losses) are greater than the costs of postmerger collusion. Or perhaps he simply rejects the view that increased concentration raises the probability of higher prices through tacit collusion. Moreover, Baxter mentioned a third rationale—the possibility of achieving efficiencies—that has no logical relationship to this criticism. Rather it goes to Baxter's general sentiments in favor of large businesses.

28. *Merger Guidelines,* Section 1.

29. Robert H. Lande, *When Should States Challenge Mergers: A Proposed Federal/State Balance,* 35 N.Y.L. SCH. L. REV. 1047, 1066 (1990). While industrial organization economists have continued their work—not only their criticisms of neoclassical price theory, but also their research and theorizing about the significance of industry structure and other factors—there has emerged a new wave of antitrust legal scholars whose historical studies and policy analyses have raised fundamental questions about current views of competition policy. For a collection of such work, along with other thoughtful approaches to issues of competition policy, see *Symposium,* 35 N.Y.L. SCH. L. REV. 767 *et seq.* (1990).

30. WILLIAM J. BAUMOL, ET AL., CONTESTABLE MARKETS AND THE THEORY OF INDUSTRIAL STRUCTURE 349 (1982). In theory, three conditions must be met: (1) no barriers to entry; (2) no advantage to any buyer or seller; (3) no predatory pricing. Economist William G. Shepherd has written devastating criticisms of the theory—both its empirical implausibility and its theoretical inconsistencies. Shepherd, *Economic Analysis to Guide Antitrust Enforcement: Prospects for Section 2,* 35 N.Y.L. SCH. L. REV. 917 (1990); *Three "Efficiency School" Hypotheses About Market Power,* 33 ANTITRUST BULL. 395 (1988). Two of the original theorists have taken issue with the Reagan administration's laissez-

faire interpretation: "Contestability theory does not, and was not intended to, lend support to those who believe (or seem to believe) that the unrestrained market automatically solves all economic problems and that virtually all regulation and antitrust activity constitutes a pointless and costly source of economic efficiency." William J. Baumol & Robert D. Willig, *Contestability: Developments Since the Book*, in STRATEGIC BEHAVIOUR AND INDUSTRIAL COMPETITION 9 (Derek J. Morris, et al. eds. 1986).

31. *See, e.g.*, William J. Baumol, *Contestable Markets: An Uprising in the Theory of Industry Structure*, 71 AM. ECON. REV. 1–15 (1982); Eugene F. Fama & Arthur B. Laffer, *The Number of Firms and Competition*, 62 AM. ECON. REV. 670 (1972); William J. Baumol, et al., *Weak Invisible Hand Theorems on the Sustainability of Multiproduct Natural Monopoly*, 67 AM. ECON. REV. 350 (1977); J.C. Panzar & Robert D. Willig, *Free Entry and the Sustainability of Natural Monopoly*, 8 Bell J. Econ. 1 (1977); BAUMOL, ET AL., CONTESTABLE MARKETS, *supra* note 30, at 222.

32. For a critical appraisal, see Shepherd, *supra* note 30. There is, however, a body of literature seeking to show that predatory pricing (and thus, retaliation) is not an effective method of monopolizing. The abstract analysis derives from economist John S. McGee's claims about the Standard Oil Company prior to 1911, in *Predatory Price Cutting: The Standard Oil (NJ) Case*, 1 J.L. & ECON. 137 (1958). Most of the derivative literature is collected in B.S. Yamey, *Predatory Price Cutting: Notes and Comments*, 15 J.L. & ECON. 129 (1972). For a strong criticism and a persuasive argument that predatory pricing can be an effective method of monopolizing, see RICHARD POSNER, ANTITRUST LAW 184–95 (1976).

In perhaps the best explication of barriers to entry, Chicago School economist Harold Demsetz insightfully wrote that "defining ownership is precisely that of creating properly scaled legal barriers to entry." Whether the grant of a taxi medallion or trademark, whether privileging dispersed ownership or economies of scale, the "entire problem of desirable and undesirable `frictions' in economic systems" involves, in my terms, a balancing of private property rights and public interests in competition (and other types of government regulation). As Demsetz put it: "Even the operation of an unregulated market system presupposes the general recognition of property rights, *but the problem of defining ownership is precisely that of creating properly scaled legal barriers to entry*. Harold Demsetz, *Barriers to Entry*, 72 AM. ECON. REV. 47, 52, 56, 49 (1982) (emphasis in the original).

33. GEORGE J. STIGLER, *Barriers to Entry, Economies of Scale, and Firm Size, in* THE ORGANIZATION OF INDUSTRY 67 (1968). JOE S. BAIN, BARRIERS TO NEW COMPETITION: THEIR CHARACTER AND CONSEQUENCES IN AMERICAN MANUFACTURING INDUSTRIES 3 (1956); BAIN, *Chamberlain's Impact on Microeconomic Theory, in* ESSAYS ON PRICE THEORY AND INDUSTRIAL ORGANIZATION (1972). In Bain's view, advertising costs raise the highest barrier, for two reasons. First, large firms can achieve economies of scale in differentiating their products. Second, advertising presents the greatest risk and thus, the greatest deterrent to new entrants because, unlike failed investment in tangible assets, failed investment in advertising leaves nothing to be sold. *See, e.g.*, Richard Schmalensee, *Ease of Entry: Has the Concept Been Applied Too Readily?*, 56 ANTITRUST L.J. 41 (1987); for a debate between Yale Brozen (Chicago Schooler) and H. Michael Mann (Bainian) over advertising, see *Advertising as an Impediment to Competition, in* INDUSTRIAL CONCENTRATION: THE NEW LEARNING 114–60 (1974). The issue was central to the Supreme Court's holding in *Procter & Gamble (Clorox)*, 386 U.S. 568 (1967). *See generally* Elizabeth Mensch & Alan Freeman, *Efficiency and Image: Advertising as an Antitrust Issue*, 1990 DUKE L.J. 321. Finally, if the Bainian view of advertising holds, it has something important to say about campaign financing, particularly within the "public choice"

view of contributors as purchasers or investors in a market for political goods: The growing emphasis on political advertising in the broadcast media, and the large investment needed to compete, create a barrier to entry that can justify government intervention.

34. For a spirited description of U.S. Steel's corporate life cycle, see WALTER ADAMS & JAMES BROCK, DANGEROUS PURSUITS 90–96 (1989).

35. Oliver Williamson, *Dominant Firms and the Monopoly Problem: Market Failure Considerations*, 85 HARV. L. REV. 1512 (1972); Book Review, 83 YALE L.J. 647 (1974). On strategic pricing behavior (and the special case of predatory pricing), see RICHARD POSNER, ANTITRUST LAW 184–96 (1976). For a criticism of Williamson, see *id.* at 93–94. It should be noted that Posner's criticism proceeds from two fundamental errors. First, his argument ignores Williamson's basic assumption about real markets—that imperfections tend to increase costs of entry. Posner's response ignores the pervasive presence of market failure. Second, Posner claims that diversified firms can raise money cheaply. But the counterexample assumes that financial markets cannot assess the risk of the particular venture or that a diversified firm would be willing to subsidize a risky venture at a cost greater than attributed by financial markets. This argument not only is inconsistent with arguments about the illogic of a large firm's subsidizing predatory pricing, but suggests as well that either the diversified firm or the financial markets have made a miscalculation. Even if all of that is wrong, Posner's solution of markets filled only with large diversified firms is unattractive on several accounts. *See* Peritz, *Predicament of Antitrust Jurisprudence*, 1984 DUKE L.J. at 1271–79.

36. *See, e.g.*, Morton J. Horwitz, Santa Clara *Revisited: The Development of Corporate Theory*, 88 W. VA. L. REV. 173 (1985); William Bratton, *The New Economic Theory of the Firm: Critical Perspectives from History*, 41 STAN. L. REV. 1471 (1989); Bratton, *The "Nexus of Contracts" Corporation: A Critical Appraisal*, 74 CORNELL L. REV. 407 (1989); Bratton, *Corporate Debt Relationships: Legal Theory in a Time of Restructuring*, 1989 DUKE L.J. 92; David Millon, *Theories of the Corporation*, 1990 DUKE L.J. 201; Gerald E. Frug, *The Ideology of Bureaucracy in American Law*, 97 HARV. L. REV. 1276 (1984); Ian R. MacNeil, *Economic Analysis of Contractual Relations, Its Shortfalls and the Need for a "Rich Classificatory Apparatus,"* 75 NW. U. L. REV. 1018 (1981); JAMES WILLARD HURST, THE LEGITIMACY OF THE BUSINESS CORPORATION IN THE LAW OF THE UNITED STATES 1780–1970 (1970).

37. Henry G. Manne, *Mergers and the Market for Corporate Control*, 73 J. POL. ECON. 113 (1965). For a detailed discussion, see Bratton, 41 STAN. L. REV. at 1517–20. *Cf. Conglomerate Mergers and Acquisitions: Opinion & Analysis*, 44 ST. JOHN'S L. REV. 1–1163 (1970). Franco Modigliani & Gerald A. Pogue, *An Introduction to Risks and Return: Concepts and Evidence*, 30 FIN. ANAL. J. 68 (1964); Eugene F. Fama, *Random Walks in Stock Market Prices*, 21 FIN. ANAL. J. 55 (1965); RICHARD A. BREALEY, AN INTRODUCTION TO RISK AND RETURN FROM COMMON STOCKS (1969); Oliver Williamson, *Organization Form, Residual Claimants and Corporate Control*, 26 J.L. & ECON. 351 (1983). Empirical claims were also disputed. *Compare* Paul A. Malatesta, *The Wealth Effects of Merger Activity and the Objective Functions of Merging Firms*, 11 J. FIN. ECON. 155 (1983 *with* Michael C. Jensen & Richard S. Ruback, *The Market for Corporate Control: The Scientific Evidence*, 11 J. FIN. ECON. 5 (1983).

38. *See, e.g.*, Lucian A. Bebchuck, *The Case for Facilitating Competing Tender Offers*, 95 HARV. L. REV. 1028 (1982); Frank H. Easterbrook & Daniel R. Fischel, *The Proper Role of a Target's Management in Responding to a Tender Offer*, 94 HARV. L. REV. 1161 (1981). The market price was the correct price by definition. There is, according to

the financial theory of the firm, no intrinsic value in stocks or other assets—only market or exchange value. Some of the takeovers were "leveraged buyouts"—that is, acquisitions by current managers or small groups of investors, who essentially turned publicly held into privately held corporations. These and other restructurings were common in the mid-1980s. Bratton, 41 STAN. L. REV. at 1520–21.

39. Nathaniel Nash, *A Hands-Off Takeover Stance*, NY TIMES, July 23, 1987, at D1, *cited in* Bratton, 41 STAN. L. REV. at n.236. *See* Jonathan Macey, *State-Anti-Takeover Legislation and the National Economy*, 1988 WIS. L. REV. 467; Macey, *Externalities, Firm-Specific Capital Investments, and the Legal Treatment of Fundamental Corporate Changes*, 1989 DUKE L.J. 173; Frank Easterbrook & David Fischel, *Voting in Corporate Law*, 26 J.L. & ECON. 395 (1983). Echoing Robert Bork's criticism of an antitrust with multiple normative grounds, some protested that multiple considerations would produce doctrinal incoherence. Gilson & Kraakman, *Delaware's Intermediate Standard for Defensive Tactics: Is There Substance to Proportionality Review?*, 44 BUS. LAW. 247, n.65 (1989).

40. For a thoughtful discussion of the managerial myopia resulting from the agency-cost analysis of price theorists, see Aleta G. Estreicher, *Beyond Agency Costs: Managing the Corporation for the Long Term*, 45 RUTGERS L. REV. 513 (1993). Compare the critique in Robert W. Hamilton, *Private Sale of Control Transactions: Where We Stand Today*, 36 CASE W. RES. L. REV. 248, 256–59 (1985) (observing that buyer may be purchasing the possibility of increasing agency costs). For studies of links between increased corporate debt loads and decreased research and development, see, e.g., Estreicher, *supra*, at 516 and sources cited at n.6; Adams & Brock, 33 ANTITRUST BULL. at 341–42 and sources cited therein. For arguments that non-shareholder constituencies should be taken into account, see Clyde Summers, *Codetermination in the United States: A Projection of Problems and Potentials*, 4 COMP. CORP. L. & SEC. REG. 155, 170 (1982); John C. Coffee Jr., *Shareholders v. Managers: The Strain in the Corporate Web*, 85 MICH. L. REV. 1, 81–86 (1986); MASAHIKO AOKI, THE COOPERATIVE GAME THEORY OF THE FIRM 56–57 (1984); Joseph Singer, *The Reliance Interest in Property*, 40 STAN. L. REV. 611 (1988); *cf.* Carol M. Rose, *Women and Property: Gaining and Losing Ground*, 78 VA. L. REV. 421 (1992). For references to studies indicating poor performance after mergers, see Peritz, *Counter-History*, 1990 DUKE L.J. at n.79; Estreicher, *supra*, at nn.20 and 106; Adams and Brock, 33 ANTITRUST BULL. at nn.113–26 (including a study by Murray Weidenbaum, former Chief of Reagan's Council of Economic Advisors, that the "evidence suggests that *shareholders* generally benefit from takeovers does not hold up to serious analysis." M. Weidenbaum & S. Vogt, *The Pot versus the Kettle*, CHALLENGE, Sept/Oct 1987, at 57 (emphasis added)).

North Carolina Shareholder Protection Act, 1987 N.C. Sess. Laws 124; Act of June 9, 1987, Ch. 13, 1987 Wis. Laws 45; *see generally*, Lyman Johnson & David Millon, *Missing the Point About State Takeover Statutes*, 87 MICH. L. REV. 846 (1989). Unocal v. Mesa Petroleum Co., 493 A.2d 946, 955–56 (Del. 1985); *see also* Paramount Communications v. Time, Inc., [1989 Transfer Binder] FED. SEC. L. REP. (CCH) ¶ 94, 514 (Del.Ch. 1989), *aff'd*, 565 A.2d 280 (Del. 1989). *See generally*, Millon, 1990 DUKE L.J. at 232–36, 251–61.

41. Armen A. Alchian & Harold Demsetz, *Production, Information Costs, and Economic Organization*, 62 AM. ECON. REV. 777 (1972); Michael C. Jensen & William H. Meckling, *Theory of the Firm: Managerial Behavior, Agency Costs and Ownership Structure*, 3 J. FIN. ECON. 305 (1976). By the 1980s, the neoclassical price theoretical view filled law journals. See, e.g., Frank H. Easterbrook and Daniel R. Fischer, *Corporate Control Transactions*, 91 YALE L.J. 698 (1982); Steven N.S. Cheung, *The Contractual Nature of the Firm*, 26 J.L. & ECON. (1983); Robert Hessen, *A New Concept of Corporations: A*

Contractual and Private Property Model, 30 HASTINGS L.J. 1327 (1979); Jonathan Macey, *From Fairness to Contract: The New Direction of Rules Against Insider Trading,* 13 HOFSTRA L. REV. 9 (1984). For critical evaluations, see Richard Buxbaum, *Corporate Legitimacy, Economic Theory, and Legal Doctrine,* 45 OHIO ST. L.J. 515 (1984); Deborah DeMott, *Beyond Metaphor: An Analysis of Fiduciary Obligation,* 1988 DUKE L.J. 879; Bratton, 41 STAN. L. REV. 1471 (1989); Bratton, 74 CORNELL L. REV. 407 (1989); Millon, 1990 DUKE L.J. 201.

42. Trustees of Dartmouth College v. Woodward, 17 U.S. (4 Wheat.) 518, 636 (1819).

43. For a short history of the steel industry, see WALTER ADAMS & JAMES BROCK, DANGEROUS PURSUITS 12–15, 57–58, 65–66, 90–96, 128–89 (1989); see Walter Adams & Hans Mueller, *The Steel Industry, in* THE STRUCTURE OF AMERICAN INDUSTRY 80 (W. Adams ed., 7th ed. 1986).

44. See, e.g., Michael C. Jensen, *Organization Theory and Methodology,* 58 ACCT. REV. 319, 327 (1983); Ian MacNeil, *Economic Analysis of Contractual Relations: Its Shortfalls and the Need for a "Rich Classificatory Apparatus,"* 75 NW. U. L. REV. 1018 (1981); Bratton, 41 STAN. L. REV. at 1478–80. There is a long-lived and rich literature on the traditional bargain principle and more recent alternative foundations for contractual liability. A good start would include GRANT GILMORE, THE AGES OF AMERICAN LAW (1977); GILMORE, THE DEATH OF CONTRACT (1974); PATRICK S. ATIYAH, THE RISE AND FALL OF FREEDOM OF CONTRACT (1979). See also Jay Feinman, *Promissory Estoppel and Judicial Method,* 97 HARV. L. REV. 678 (1984); Melvin A. Eisenberg, *The Bargain Principle and its Limits,* 95 HARV. L. REV. 741, 798–99 (1982) (noting that the bargain principle's fairness and efficiency arises only in perfectly competitive markets).

45. As Holmes observed about the current theory's ancestors, general principles do not decide concrete cases. This internal critique of legal formalism applies not only to the "nexus" theory of corporations but to the Chicago School's larger enterprise of formalizing legal analysis. It was French philosopher Jacques Derrida and the deconstructionist movement in the 1970s who added the jiu-jitsu motion—the turning of a formal argument's strength against itself. Taken up by literary critics and later passed on to critical legal scholars, deconstruction is an ethical criticism with independent roots in American legal realism. That judo flip, that inversion, is the deconstructive moment. For early rehearsals, see Jacques Derrida, *Structure, Sign and Play in the Discourse of the Human Sciences, in* THE STRUCTURALIST CONTROVERSY 247 (Richard Macksey & Eugeno Donato eds. 1970); JACQUES DERRIDA, OF GRAMMATOLOGY (G. C. Spivak ed. 1976). More recently, the term "deconstruction" has come to mean any analysis that is critical. An earlier ethics of textual criticism appeared in the work of some legal realists. Two of the legal realist works that brilliantly anticipated the methodology were Robert Hale, *Coercion and Distribution in a Supposedly Non-Coercive State,* 38 POL. SCI. Q. 470 (1923) and Felix Cohen, *Transcendental Nonsense and the Functional Approach,* 35 COLUM. L. REV. 809 (1935). See also COHEN THE ETHICAL BASIS OF LEGAL CRITICISM (1959).

46. The analysis that follows does not address questions involving freedom of the press, questions of church and state, and pornography. While I believe that those questions—particularly regarding freedom of the press—can be understood, in some useful sense, within the framework I suggest, other important issues come into play—gender relations, for example—that would call for a more wide-ranging discussion than this chapter, as I have developed it, can support.

47. The metaphor, first expressed in Holmes's *Abrams* (1919) dissent, is *Lochner*ian in two senses. First, Holmes seemed to choose the image of an unfettered marketplace because it was consistent with the Court majority's political economy,

its ideology of state-market relations. It is *Lochner*ian in the second sense that current First Amendment jurisprudence treats the marketplace of ideas much like Justice Peckham treated labor relations in *Lochner*—as largely protected from state regulation by a constitutional freedom.

48. The Jeffersonian rhetoric also invokes the 1937 "constitutional revolution's" egalitarian rhetoric framing Chief Justice Hughes' new liberty of contract rationales for his dissent in *Tipaldo* (1936) and then for his majority opinion in *Parrish* (1937), which portrayed state economic regulation as legitimate. These opinions are discussed *supra* chap. 3. See also CASS R. SUNSTEIN, DEMOCRACY AND THE PROBLEM OF FREE SPEECH (1993). Sunstein calls for a "New Deal" for First Amendment speech. As an initial matter, there is some question about the likelihood of success of a call for any sort of program described in the rhetoric of the New Deal. The impulse to describe all property rights, and thus all commercial activity, in fundamentally positivist terms is, as Sunstein points out, an old one, going back in modern times to the work of legal realists Robert Hale and Morris Cohen. In short, Sunstein's approach to the problem of free speech derives from a belief that there are no natural rights, at least no natural property rights, that political conduct is fundamentally different from economic in both intent and result, and that commerce is inferior to politics as a social enterprise. Although this logic, unconditioned by intermediate normative judgments, could lead to majoritarian tyranny over individual commercial enterprise, Sunstein does not let it get out of hand. As he understands all too well, the historical linkages between individual liberty and property rights retain some utility, if not the superordinate value attributed by his colleague Richard Epstein. RICHARD EPSTEIN, TAKINGS: PRIVATE PROPERTY AND THE POWER OF EMINENT DOMAIN (1985).

49. Pruneyard Shopping Ctr. v. Robins, 447 U.S. 74, 82, 84, 81 (1980); for the Supreme Court of California, Justice Newman wrote that "to protect free speech and petitioning is a goal that surely matches the protecting of health and safety, the environment, aesthetics, property values and other societal goals that have been held to justify reasonable restrictions on private property rights." Robins v. Pruneyard Shopping Ctr., 23 Cal.3d 899, 908; 592 Pac.2d 341, 346; 153 Cal. Rptr. 854, 859 (1979).

50. Pacific Gas & Elec. v. Public Utility Comm'n, 475 U.S. 1, 9 (1986).

51. *Id.* at 9 (Powell, J.). Dissenting Justice Rehnquist insisted that, like the Pruneyard Mall, the extra envelope space was a public forum. Thus, he concluded, there was no interference with the monopoly's speech rights. *Id.* at 24–26. Dissenting Justice Stevens pointed out that the lower standard for commercial speech was easily met. Pacific Gas & Electric's rights could not provide the basis for denying voice, granted by the state, to those expressing views about ratemaking decisions, just as their rights did not allow them to exclude customers from public hearings. *Id.* at 36.

52. DeBartolo Corp. v. Florida Gulf Coast Bldg. & Constr. Trades Council, 485 U.S. 568, 571, 576 (1988). For another example of the long-held view that private property is threatened by violence whenever labor picketing (rather than, for example, handbilling) occurs, see Sears, Roebuck & Co. v. San Diego Dist. Council of Carpenters, 436 U.S. 180, 208 (Blackmun, J., concurring), 213 (Powell, J., concurring) (1978).

53. Lechmere, Inc. v. NLRB, 112 S.Ct. 841, 843, 846 (1992) (White, Blackmun, Stewart, JJ., dissenting). The three other Reagan–Bush appointees—Antonin Scalia, Anthony M. Kennedy, David H. Souter—joined Thomas. The dissenters agreed insofar as they neither expressed concern about First Amendment speech nor cited *DeBartolo* as precedent. Justice White wrote that the NLRA grants the Labor Board wide discretion, "leaving open the question of how § 7 and private property rights

were to be accommodated." Thus, White insisted, "a court should not substitute its own judgment for a reasonable construction by the Board." *Id.* at 853.

54. Diane Leenheer Zimmerman, *Information as Speech, Information as Goods: Some Thoughts on Marketplaces and the Bill of Rights*, 33 WM. & MARY L. REV. 665, 667 (1992). But the issues are slightly more complex than Zimmerman suggests. Thus, for example, while the Court in Time, Inc. v. Hill, 385 U.S. 374, 380–83 (1967), did allow a suit over a popular play's use of Hill's ordeal as a hostage, there was no question that a for-profit corporation—Time, Inc.—could report on the play. Nor was there any question that Larry Flynt's *Hustler* magazine could publish a vulgar parody involving Jerry Falwell's mother without liability to him. Hustler Magazine v. Jerry Falwell, 485 U.S. 46 (1988). Here, exercise of protected First Amendment rights produced for *Hustler* and Time copyrightable property with market value. Thus, for example, Falwell could not deface copies of *Hustler* or even photocopy the parody without Flynt's approval. For a theory that legal doctrine and public policy regarding information are ultimately founded in property rights derived from the "attributes of romantic authorship," see James Boyle, *A Theory of Law and Information: Copyright, Spleens, Blackmail, and Insider Trading*, 80 CAL. L. REV. 1413 (1992). For an argument that society's interest in limiting patent rights to the social value of the invention requires courts to exercise their equity powers to impose compulsory licensing, see Martin J. Adelman, *Property Rights Theory and Patent-Antitrust: The Role of Compulsory Licensing*, 52 N.Y.U. L. REV. 977 (1977).

The ascendant view of corporations as bundles of contracts, the view that legitimized open securities markets to allow takeovers by more efficient managers, implies something new about labor relations. It suggests that contracts with workers are just as much a part of the economic firm as contracts with managers (who themselves are seen as workers). Thus, there would be no question of private property open to managers but closed to other workers, and no privileged status given to management's view of unionization. Moreovoer, unions would be given the same opportunity as corporate raiders to "take over" the firm's labor and other factors of production.

55. Cargill v. Monfort, 479 U.S. 104 (1986) (finding no antitrust injury resulting from merger of industry's dominant firms); *Lechmere, Inc.*, 112 S. Ct. 841 (1992) (overruling NLRB finding that employer's bar of union organizers from distributing handbills in parking lot at shopping center was an unfair labor practice).

56. Central Hudson Gas & Elec. Corp. v. Public Serv. Comm'n of N.Y., 447 U.S. 557, 584, 591 (1980) (Rehnquist, J., dissenting).

57. *Id.* at 592.

58. City of Cincinnati v. Discovery Network, Inc., 113 S.Ct. 1505 (1993). The city was concerned that the advertising literature would ultimately land on the streets and sidewalks, given the public's low regard for its value. Compare the Court's approval of banning political speech in shopping malls on account of concern about litter. *Lloyd*, 407 U.S. 551 (1972).

59. Consolidated Edison Co. v. Public Serv. Comm. of N.Y., 447 U.S. 530 (1980).

60. Federal Election Comm. v. Mass. Citizens for Life, 479 U.S. 238, 279, 257 (1986).

61. Austin v. Michigan Chamber of Commerce, 494 U.S. 652, 660–61, 666 (1990). This treatment of corporate activity was radically different from earlier doctrine, particularly the *Noerr-Pennington* doctrine, which grants First Amendment immunity from antitrust liability to associations petitioning government.

62. Federal Election Comm'n v. Nat'l Right to Work Comm'n, 459 U.S. 197, 207, 210–11 (1982). *Austin*, 494 U.S. at 660.

63. *Austin*, 494 U.S. at 679 (Scalia, J., dissenting), 695 (Kennedy, J., dissenting).

64. *Buckley*, 424 U.S. at 48–49 ("wholly foreign"), citing, among other decisions, Eastern R. Conf. v. Noerr Motors, 365 U.S. 127 (1961), which grants antitrust immunity to trade restraints when they take the form of petitioning government. The Court would later take an expansive view of that immunity when the conduct occurs in the legislative branch, precisely because "illegal and reprehensible conduct . . . [are] condoned in the political arena." California Motor Transp. Co. v. Trucking Unlimited, 404 U.S. 508, 513 (1972). Federal Election Comm'n v. Nat'l Conservative Pol. Action Comm., 470 U.S. 480 (1985); Clark v. Community for Creative Non-Violence, 468 U.S. 288 (1984) (holding that there is no constitutional duty to equalize opportunities for speech); *MCFL*, 479 U.S. at 251–52 (same). Justice Rehnquist, in his *Pacific Gas & Electric* dissent, interpreted the constitutional limitation more narrowly, writing that a "State can use its own funds to subsidize, but not to interfere with another's speech." 475 U.S. at 24 (1986). *Austin*, 494 U.S. at 660 (Marshall), 685 (Scalia, citing *Buckley*, 424 U.S. at 48–49) (emphasis added).

65. Police Dep't of Chicago v. Mosley, 408 U.S. 92, 95–96 (1972) (Marshall, J., writing for a unanimous Court); *see, e.g.*, Lucas A. Powe, Jr., *Mass Speech and the Newer First Amendment*, 1982 SUP. CT. REV. 243, 282–83 (arguing that concerns about the corrupting effects of wealth are best addressed by redistributing wealth); *see also* Kenneth L. Karst, *Equality as a Central Principle in the First Amendment*, 43 U. CHI. L. REV. 20 (1975).

Index

Abstract individual self-assertion and economic inequality 23
Adair v. U.S. (1908) 49
Adams, Henry Carter 23, 79
Addyston Pipe & Steel Co., United States v. (1899) 36, 81, 172
Adkins v. Children's Hospital (1923) 134–35
Administered prices 145. *See also* Oligopoly theory
Administrative Procedure Act of 1946 189
Advertising 105–06, 263
Agreement, economic and political views of 199–209
Airline Cargo Deregulation Act of 1977 262
Airline Deregulation Act of 1978 262
ALA Schechter Poultry Corp. v. United States (1935) 6, 111, 130–31, 136, 172
ALCOA (1945) 174. *See also Aluminum Co. of America, United States v.* (1945)
Allgeyer v. Louisiana (1897) 43
Aluminum Co. of America, United States v. (1945) 174–75, 177, 199, 210–11
Aluminum Co. of America, United States v. (Rome Cable) (1964) 218
Amalgamated Food Employees Union Local 590 v. Logan Valley Plaza (1968) 249
American Association of Foreign Language Newspapers 105
American Chamber of Commerce 265
American Column & Lumber Co. v. U.S. (1921) 82, 87, 102, 171
American Communications Ass'n v. Douds (1950) 208–09
American Economic Association 16
American Federation of Full Fashioned Hosiery Workers 167
American Federation of Labor, First Amendment protection denied to 101
American Linseed Co., United States v. (1923) 84, 86
American Power & Light Co. v. SEC (1946) 148
American School of Magnetic Healing v. McAnnulty (1902) 102
American Tobacco Co., United States v. (1911) 50–51, 60, 75, 79–80
American Tobacco Co., United States v. (1946) 175–77
Antitrust, formative period
  cartel and trust doctrines, logics driving 56
  cartel doctrine, accommodation between Supreme Court factions 36
  federal common law regime 29
  Literalists and Rule of Reasonists 29, 34
    alternative view through lens of rhetorical analysis 27
    orthodox view 26
  Supreme Court cycles 28–38, 39–58
  unanimity in labor cases 37
Apex Hosiery v. Leader (1940) 164, 167–68
Appalachian Coals, Inc. v. U.S. (1933) 136, 173
Armstrong Bureau of Related Industries 85
Arnold, Schwinn & Co., United States v. (1967) 223–24, 228, 256
Arnold, Thurman
  adversarial antitrust policy, force driving 114, 159, 179
  anti-corporatist approach to competition policy 111
  The Bottlenecks of Business (1940) 158
  consumer welfare, interest in while Antitrust Division Chief 157
  The Folklore of Capitalism (1937) 158
Associated Press v. U.S. (1945) 174–75
Associations
  commercial, and labor 33, 34
  economic 91–94
  labor 94–95, 96–100
  labor and trade, perceived and treated differently 97
  persons, as opposed to 55
  political economy of 5, 63
  trade, labor, political compared 63
Austin v. Michigan Chamber of Commerce (1990) 297–98

Bacon, Henry 13
Bain, Joe
  Barriers to New Competition (1956) 183
  broad view of barriers to entry 283
  product differentiation as a barrier to entry 185
Balancing jurisprudence and political economy 302–03
Baldridge, Malcolm 278
Barriers to entry 283–84, 358n32
Baxter, William 272, 278–80
Bedford Cut Stone Co. v. Journeyman Stone Cutters' Ass'n (1972) 93
Bellotti decision (1978). *See First Nat'l Bank of Boston v. Bellotti*
Bentham, Jeremy 240
Berea College v. Kentucky (1908) 49

Berle, Adolf 129, 145, 187, 190, 204
The Modern Corporation and Private Property (1933) 6, 107, 110, 327–28n111
Berlin, Isaiah 263
Bernays, Edward 106
Bernstein, Marver 187, 189, 237
Black, Hugo
antitrust rhetoric of 173, 204
opinion in *Giboney* (1949) 207–08
opinions in antitrust cases
Associated Press (1945) 174
Fashion Organizer's Guild (1941) 171–73
Klor's, Inc. (1959) 202–03
Pabst (1966) 219–20
and 30-hour work week bill 127
Blake, Harlan 237
Borah, William E. 123
Bork, Robert
antitrust debate with Blake and Jones 236
Antitrust Paradox (1978) 258, 260–61
deductive logic, views of 243–44
free competition and First Amendment speech, views of 243
"Neutral Principles and Some First Amendment Problems" (1971) 243–45, 249
Sherman Act legislative history, view of 243
Bowen, Lord 21
Bowman, Ward 236
Bradwell v. Illinois (1873) 316n98
Brand, Donald R., *Corporatism and the Rule of Law* (1988) 115
Brandeis, Louis
Bedford Cut Stone Co. (1927) dissent 93
Chicago Board (1918) opinion 78–80, 85, 89, 161
Erie Railroad (1938) opinion 180
FTC power argued for in *Gratz* (1920) dissent 67
Gilbert (1920) dissent 69
labor injunctions, argued for in *Truax* (1921) dissent 98
liberty and property, views of 162
Muller v. Oregon (1908) brief 49, 135
private profit as good public policy, argued for in *American Col. & Lumber* (1921) dissent 77
property as balancing public and private interests, in *International News Service* (1918) dissent 71
relationship between competition policy and property rights, views of 166
testimony in congressional hearings 64–65
trade associations, view of 83, 84
Brandenberg v. Ohio (1969) 247
Brennan, William J. 214–15
Bretton Woods Accords 178
Brewer, David J.
defection to Rule of Reason faction in *Northern Securities* (1904) 39, 43
majoritarianism, view of 57
Muller (1908) opinion 36, 49, 135
Breyer, Steven 262
Broadcast Music, Inc. v. CBS, Inc. (1979) 255–56
Brown Shoe Co. v. U.S. (1962) 214–16
Brown v. Board of Education (1954) 61, 182, 192, 199
Brown, Henry Billings 38
Brunswick Corp. v. Pueblo Bowl-O-Mat (1974) 254
Bryce, James 24
Buckley v. Valeo (1976) 248–52, 265, 296, 298
Budd v. New York (1892) 58
Bureau of Corporations 60, 64
Bush, George 267
Business Roundtable 265
Butler, Pierce 130, 132, 134
California Motor Transport Co. v. Trucking Unlimited (1972) 246
Captains of industry 62
Cardozo, Benjamin N. 130
Carnegie, Andrew 23, 55
Carolene Products Co., United States v. (1938) 188
Carroll, John A. 197
Carter, Jimmy 7, 8, 229–31, 262, 266–67
Celler, Emmanuel
economic concentration, concerns about 196
Miller-Tydings Act, opposition to 154–55
Robinson-Patman Act, opposition to 151–52
Celler-Kefauver Act of 1950 195–99
Cement Institute, FTC v. (1948) 172
Central Committee for Lumber Standards 87
Central Hudson Gas & Elec. Corp. v. Public Serv. Comm'n of N.Y (1980) 295–96
Chamberlin, Edward H. 170–71, 236, 241–42, 258–59, 283, 296
innovation, views on 109
monopolistic competition theory 185
perfect oligopoly 184
product differentiation, expansive view of 108
theories, influence of 145, 157, 183
The Theory of Monopolistic Competition (1932) 6, 107
Charles River Bridge v. Warren Bridge (1837) 5
Chevron and Gulf oil companies, 1984 merger of 279
Chicago Board of Trade v. U.S. (1918) 203
fair competition, rhetoric of, compared to *ALA Schechter Poultry* (1935) 136
modern Rule of Reason, compared to common-law version 78–80
trade association cases 1913–1925, as precedent for 81
Chicago School 258–62. *See also* Bork, Robert; Posner, Richard
Cincinnati, City of v. Discovery Network, Inc. (1992) 296
Citizens
liberty of, and trusts 14
market participants, seen as 169
as speech consumers 187, 248
utopian vision of 6, 113, 118, 122–23, 130, 142
City of Lafayette v. Louisiana Power & Light Co. (1978) 274
Civic virtue 7, 10, 51
Civil Aeronautics Board 230, 263
Civil Rights Act of 1948 181
Civil Rights Act of 1964 192–93
Clark, John B. 95
Clark, John M. 90, 236
labor organizations, view of 119
trade associations, approval of 77
workable competition, theory of 185–86
Clark, Ramsey 232
Clark, Tom 201
Clarke, John H. 82
Classical economics 169–172, 302
Classical political economy 10, 48
Classical view of competition
cartel doctrine, informing 113, 144, 172–73, 202–03
freedom of contract, relationship to 33
liberty and equality, informing relationship between 24
monopoly, informing view of 22, 23
Clayton Act of 1914
Bork's view of 245
labor exemption 98, 325n81

rhetoric of competition, significance of 63
Rule of Reason, passed in reaction to 61, 64–65
Clear and present danger test. *See* First Amendment speech
Cleveland, Grover 13
Clinton, Bill 267
Coase, Ronald 241
"The Nature of the Firm" (1937) 110, 288
"The Problem of Social Cost" (1960) 237, 262
Coase Theorem. *See* Coase, Ronald, "The Problem of Social Cost" (1960)
Coercion
freedom of contract, relationship to 138
all contractual relationships, part of 85
trade association cases, views of reflected in 84–85, 171–72
Columbia Steel, United States v. (1948) 176, 201
Combination, early views of 16, 22, 24
Commerce Department 75
Commission for Review of Antitrust Laws and Procedures 263
Committee on Public Information, Division of Advertising 104
Common law, views of
ancillary restraints in corporate merger case 39, 44
cartel doctrine 36–37, 171
competition 44
conspiracy doctrine 175, 202
restraint of trade doctrine, late nineteenth century 19
Sherman Act language 11
speech rights 35, 88, 147–50
Commonwealth, views of 11, 19
Community Communications Co. v. City of Boulder (1982) 275–76
Competition 16, 22, 65, 97, 344n82. *See also* Chamberlin, Edward H.; Competition policy; Free competition; Monopolistic competition; Oligopoly Theory
Competition policy
antitrust injury doctrine in corporate merger cases 254
consumers, serving interests of, in later New Deal 157–58
efficiency, derived from 239
"family-owned" business 226
hands, invisible and visible, formulated by 227
imagined in terms of economic agreements and political agreements 199–209
in the information age 291
limits 301–03
copyright 253, 255–56
property rights 3, 223–24
local monopoly, confronted by 226
market-based logic, produced by 221
municipally owned utilities, applied to 274–78
oligopoly theory 234
positive law, enacted as 8
property rights, allocating 253–58
shifting locus, from markets for goods to marketplace of ideas 281–82
shifting models of 169–71
Concentration, industrial 219. *See also* Corporate size
Conflict between labor and management 97
Congressional legislation, in later New Deal 147–157
Consignment of goods in antitrust vertical restraints doctrine 223, 256
Conspiracy, intracorporate, and doctrine of apparent authority 341
Constitutional revolution of 1937 162
Consumer
and First Amendment speech 293, 296
in jettisoned Sherman bill of 1888 and associated debates 13
in later New Deal 172
and unified body economic 6, 142
under Wagner Act 143, 168
Consumer Pricing Act of 1975 236
Consumer welfare
New Deal period, as understood in 156–57
redefined by Chicago Schoolers to mean wealth maximization 238–43, 345n25
Wheeler-Lea Act of 1938 144
Container Corp., United States v. (1969) 234
Contestability theory 270, 282–84, 290
Continental Can Co., United States v. (1964) 219
Continental T.V. Inc. v. GTE Sylvania (1977) 256
Cooke, Frederick 94
Coolidge, Calvin 86
Cooperative competition 62, 75–76. *See also* Associations; Eddy, Arthur Jerome; Hoover, Herbert; Open competition
Coppage v. Kansas (1915) 57
Copperweld Corp. v. Independence Tube Corp. (1984) 278
Copyright Act of 1976 255
Copyright and competition policy 253, 255–56
Corcoran, Tommy 111
Corporate and political subdivisions, antitrust treatment of 277–78
Corporate control 265, 267–70, 285–87
Corporate merger policy. *See also* Merger Guidelines
in formative period of antitrust, 1904–1911 38–58
in liberal formalist period, 1950–1974 214–22
in period of return to market power analysis, 1974–1980 234–36
in Reagan administrations 278–282
Corporate personality 50, 54–56, 74–75, 92
Corporate size 210. *See also* Economic concentration
antitrust doctrine, effects on
"family owned" business 223
Rule of Reason before New Deal 61, 68
jurisprudence in 1960s 219
and First Amendment speech doctrine 251
compared to market share 225–27
profitability, correlation with 347n15
Corporate speech as necessarily commercial 252–53
Corporate theory during the 1980s 284–90
Corporation
as bureaucracy 110
and corruption 297–99
economic and political rhetorics of 190–91
and First Amendment speech rights 296–99
as "person" under Fifth and Fourteenth Amendments 50, 55, 188, 336n105
in sociological literature of 1950s 338n3
Corruption and commerce 252, 291–96, 314n71
Crowther, Frank 122

Dahl, Robert A. 187–189
Danbury Hatters case (*Loewe v. Lawlor* (1908)) 33, 37, 49, 92
Darrow, Clarence 126
DeBartolo Corp. v. Florida Gulf Coast Bldg. & Constr. Trades Council (1988) 294
Debs, Eugene V. 32, 60, 99
Debs, In re (1895) 32, 33, 36
Deconstruction 361n45
Delegation doctrine 130
Department of Agriculture 82
Deregulation 8
commercial markets 251–52, 261–64, 267–72

differences between Carter and Reagan administrations 267
marketplace of ideas 291, 296–99
political economies of 7, 267
Desegregation 192–93
Dewey, John 77
Dialogical sense of political economy 303
Dicey, A. V. 189
Director, Aaron 237
Douglas, William O.
antitrust opinions compared to those of Black 173, 204
Columbia Steel (1948) (dissent) 203–05, 212–13
duPont (Clorox) (1967) 220–22
economic due process jurisprudence, view of 161
Simpson (1964) 203–05
Socony-Vacuum Oil Co. (1940) 173
White Motors (1963) 204–05, 223
Dr. Miles Medical Co. v. John D. Park & Sons (1910) 53–55, 69, 81, 96, 153, 205
Duke, James B. 52, 62
Duplex Printing v. Deering (1921) 98
DuPont (E.I.) de Nemours & Co., United States v. (Cellophane) (1956) 211–12
DuPont (E.I.) de Nemours & Co., United States v. (GM) (1957) 214–15

E.C. Knight Co., United States v. (1895) 37–38
Economic concentration. *See also* Corporate size; Economic power
in Celler-Kefauver Act 199
congressional concerns about 196
and market power 214–17, 219
Supreme Court approaches to problem of 210–28
Economic due process doctrines
and antitrust policy 58, 66–69, 79
and associations 60
and class, gender, and race 48
and common-law judiciary 57, 180
and competition policy 73–75
and corporate mergers 45
and deductive style of argument 10, 72, 80
and equality 57, 135–36, 161
and First Amendment speech 296
and gender 49, 162
and liberty 10, 72–7
and race 38, 49
and types of cases heard by Supreme Court 72
Economic power. *See also* Corporate size; Economic concentration
market power, compared to 210–28
threatening political liberty 24
threatening political corruption 11, 39, 246
Economic Stabilization Act of 1970 230
Economic theories
of competition's imperfections 183–87
in Supreme Court competition policy in 1960s 218
Eddy, Arthur Jerome 90, 102, 116, 137
describing workers' labor as their capital 94
The New Competition (1914) 78, 116
Edmunds, George F. 13, 20, 23
Edwards, Corwin, *Big Business and the Policy of Competition* (1956) 183
Efficiency. *See also* Competition policy; Consumer welfare
civic virtue, surrogate for 6
and common law 261
and deregulation 231
and economies of production 259
and Jeffersonian entrepreneurialism 333n80
and liberty 65, 352n63, 260
and marginal utility of money 324n76, 347n22
and populism 261–62, 263–64
shifting meanings of 238–42
theory of "second best" 239
and wealth 96, 240
Eisenhower, Dwight 182, 192
El Paso Natural Gas, United States v. (1964) 218
Electric Bond & Share Co. v. SEC (1938) 148
Ellsworth, Harris 197
Emery, James A. 122
Entitlements and property rights 194
Environmental Protection Agency 230
Equality. *See also* Chicago School; Classical view of competition; Corporate size; Economic due process doctrines
economic due process as normative commitment to formal view of 11, 57
efficiency compromise under the Robinson-Patman Act of 1936 153
First Amendment speech 298–99
freedom of contract 21, 163
Jeffersonian rhetoric in Sherman Act debates 15
and labor unions, treatment of 11
liberty 3, 261
"fictitious equality," producing 163
free competition rhetorics of 301
and marketplace of ideas 299
and private sphere 180
Erie Railroad v. Tompkins (1938) 180
Espionage Act of 1918 99–100

Fair competition 112. *See also* National Industrial Recovery Act; National Recovery Administration; Trade associations; Unfair competition
antitrust
and Rule of Reason 51
in Sherman Act debates 13, 16, 19
commercial rhetorics of 136–39
early New Deal rhetoric of 118–19
labor relations 119
link between competition and price regulation 75
NIRA and *ALA Schechter Poultry* (1935) opinion 139–42
political rhetorics of 130–36
in trade association cases 88
Fair profit 13, 17–19, 69
Fashion Organizer's Guild of America v. FTC (1941) 171
Federal Election Campaign Act (1972, 1974) 236, 246
Federal Election Commission 269
Federal Election Committee v. Massachusetts Citizens for Life (1986) 296–97
Federal Election Committee v. National Right to Work Committee (1982) 297
Federal Trade Commission
advertising, regulation of 263
as "National Nanny" (1978) 271
NIRA, authorized under 116
and Reagan administrations 70–72, 271–72
staff reports 147, 233
Federal Trade Commission Act of 1914 61, 63–65
Fictitious prices 21–22
Field, Stephen J. 19, 39, 51, 69
Fifth Amendment rhetoric, and Sherman Act 39, 41, 44. *See also* Fourteenth Amendment
Fiftieth Congress 9, 12, 13
Fifty-first Congress 21
Filene, Edward 106
Financial theory of corporation 281, 285–86
First Amendment speech
annoying customers, balanced against 249
antitrust and 206

"clear and present danger" test
adopted 100
limited 106
Bork's view of 244
danger to commerce as sufficient 207–09
non-economic nature of danger 247
commercial and political speech 296
commercial corruption, threatened by 291, 296–99
commercial markets, protected in 247–51
commercial shopping malls, not protected in 248–51
common law of. *See* Common law
consumers as protected class 165, 293
corporate size in Supreme Court doctrine 250–51
corporate speech, as necessarily commercial 252
corporation's right to 296–99
economic due process and 296
equality and 298–99
free competition images for 164, 291–99
free trade in ideas metaphor 100
jurisprudence of 101–04
labor picketing and 101, 164–65, 294–95
political action committees and 295–99
postclassical economics and 295–96
property rights and 164, 246, 248–51, 291–99
public commons and 293
silence and 293
speaker, identity of, or content of message as basis 253
spending as 250, 298–99
Stigler's model of markets for regulation 250
World War I and 104–06
First Nat'l Bank of Boston v. Bellotti (1978) 248, 252–53, 256, 265, 296–98
Fithian, George W. 22
Ford, Gerald 7, 232
Ford, Henry 128
Fortas, Abe 189
Fortner Enterprises, Inc. v. U.S. Steel (1969) 233
Foucault, Michel 306n7
Four Horsemen. *See* Butler, Pierce; McReynolds, James C.; Sutherland, George; Van Devanter, Willis
Fourteenth Amendment. *See also* Economic due process doctrines
and corporations as persons 55
and First Amendment speech 35, 103
and industrial liberty 43
and price-fixing, public 18, 22, 72–75, 131–36
Sherman antitrust bill and 18
Free competition rhetorics
competition policies, relationships to 3
contestability theory and 270
corporate takeovers, justifying 270
efficiency and populism, underlying 261–64
First Amendment speech and 291–99
freedom of contract and 3, 12, 31
freedom of press and 174
liberty and equality, relationships to 3, 261–62
market for efficient management, portrayed in 270
New Deal calls to 112
property rights and 3, 246–51
Reagan administrations, imagery of 265–70
Sherman anti-trust bill, expressed in 11
three logics of political economy, underlying 301–03
two sets of commitments, expressed in 3, 301–03
Free labor 34, 101
Free market 8
"Free rider" doctrine 205, 257–58
"Free trade in ideas" 63, 100, 101–04
Freedom of contract 52, 361. *See also* Economic due process doctrines; Liberty; Price fixing
cartels and 36
coercion and 138
corporate mergers and 41–43
government coercion required for 85
other social values impinging upon 32, 42, 351n61–62
state regulation and 133–36
Freedom of the press, and free competition rhetorics 174
Frenzel, William 271
FTC v. See name of other party
Fuller, Melville W. 49, 92

Gadd, F. R. 83
Gary, Elbert 75
General Dynamics Corp., United States v. (1974) 234
Giboney v. Empire State Storage (1949) 207–08
Gilbert v. Minnesota (1920) 69
Ginsburg, Douglas H. 280
Gitlow v. New York (1925) 102
Goldberg, Arthur 193
Gompers v. Buck's Stove & Range Co. (1911) 101
Gompers, Samuel 106
Goodyear Tire & Rubber Co. v. FTC (1936) 150–51
Gore, Thomas P. 124
Government legitimacy crisis 6, 229–30, 251–52
Granger cases (1876), and property rights 10, 18, 69
Gratz, FTC v. (1920) 67
Greene, In re (1892) 29–31
GTE Sylvania (1977). *See Continental T.V. Inc. v.*

Hale, Robert 85
Hallie v. City of Eau Claire (1985) 277
Hand, Augustus 174
Hand, Learned 174–75, 177
Harding, Warren G. 86, 91
Harlan, John M. (the elder) 39–41, 45–48, 49
Harlan, John M. (the younger) 213, 220, 223, 225
Harriman, Edward Henry 39, 55
Harriman, Henry I. 116–17, 122
Harrington, James 166
Harrison, Benjamin 13
Hart, Henry, *The Legal Process* (1958) 191, 193–94
Hart, Philip A. 235
Hart-Scott-Rodino Act of 1976 236
Hawley, Ellis 78, 86, 125, 129
Haymarket Affair 9
Hill, James J. 39
Hill, Joseph L. 117
Historical contingency 4
Hoar, George F. 20
Holmes, Oliver Wendell, Jr., 66–67, 110, 164, 180, 244, 247
antitrust Rule of Reason 27, 50
and associations
labor 93
labor and capital 89, 93
social and economic 45, 47–48
trade 83–84, 137–38
competition policy 4, 27, 43, 50, 84, 96
consumer prices 77
economics
classical 34, 53, 61
neoclassical 77, 96
First Amendment speech 100, 103
general principles 41–43, 45, 47–48, 93, 315n87
interstate commerce power of Congress 37
majoritarianism and its limits 41–43, 45, 47–48, 73–74
price fixing 37, 53, 77, 83

property rights 53, 71
women's suffrage and equality 135
Home Building & Loan Ass'n v. Blaisdell (1934) 132, 134–35, 162
Hook, Charles R. 123
Hoover, Herbert 59
American Column & Lumber (1921), reaction to 87
industrial self-governance, belief in 86
laissez-faire ideology, transgression of 112
and large government bureaucracy 91
libertarian rendition of collectivist mentalité 111
political economy, view of 69
and Reconstruction Finance Corporation 106
scientific management, belief in 77
trade associationalism, champion of 62, 75
Horwitz, Morton 188
House committees
Committee on the Judiciary 65
Committee on Manufactures 13
Special Comm. on Investigation of the Amer. Retail Federation 150
Un-American Activities Committee 181
Ways and Means Committee 116
Hughes, Charles Evans
miners in Bisbee deportation, representing before Supreme Court 98
opinions
ALA Schechter Poultry (1935) and fair competition rhetorics 139–41
Dr. Miles (1910) 53–54
Blaisdell (1934) and freedom of contract doctrine 134–36
Morehead (1936) (dissenting) 134
Sugar Institute (1936) 138
West Coast Hotel (1937) 163
and Roberts, Owen J. 131–36
shaky ground for opinion in *ALA Schechter Poultry* (1935) 130

Illinois Central Railway v. Illinois (1892) 39
Industrial concentration 232. *See also* Corporate size; Economic concentration
Industrial liberty
classical liberal view of 86
Information Age and competition policy 291
Jeffersonian entrepreneurial view of 15, 31. *See also* Small dealers and worthy men
in Sherman Act debates 13, 16–17
Information
in commercial markets and marketplace of ideas 290–91
exchange 82, 83–85
as public good and private property 175
Innovation 109
International News Service v. Associated Press (1918) 63, 69–72
and *Chicago Board* (1918) 80
and *Associated Press* (1945) 175
International Salt Co. v. U.S. (1947) 212
Interstate Commerce Act of 1887 9, 10
fair profit, rhetoric of 18
NIRA hearings, referenced in 117
railroad price-fixing cartels 30

Jackson, Andrew 5
Jackson, Howell E. 29, 31, 42
Jefferson County Pharmaceutical Ass'n v. Abbott Labs. (1983) 275
Jefferson, Thomas 135, 166
Jeffersonian entrepreneurialism 11. *See also* Black, Hugo; Brandeis, Louis; Douglas, William O., Peckham, Rufus; Small dealers and worthy men
antitrust Rule of Reason, relationship to 61
corporate size, concerns about 223
efficiency, relationship to 333n80
industrial liberty, relationship to 28
labor cases under the Sherman Act, relationship to 33
Literalist jurisprudence in antitrust's formative period, relationship to 31
microeconomic analysis of market share, relationship to 225–27
Sherman Act debates, as heard in 15
Jenkins, Thomas A. 123
Jenks, Jeremiah W. 55
Jennings, John E., Jr. 197
Johnson, General Hugh 125, 126, 129
Johnson, Lyndon 232
Johnson, William, cited by Charles Evans Hughes in *Blaisdell* (1934) 135
Johnson-Reed Act of 1924 99
Joint Traffic Ass'n v. United States (1898) 35, 81
Jones & Laughlin Steel, NLRB v. (1937) 164
Jones, John P. 15
Jones, William 237

Kahn, Alfred 8, 230, 263
Kaysen, Carl 234, 236
Antitrust Policy: An Economic and Legal Analysis (1959) 184
"The Corporation in Modern Society" (1959) 190
Kefauver, Estes 196. *See also* Celler-Kefauver Act of 1950
Kennedy, Edward 262
Keynes, John Maynard 178, 306n5, 327n102
Kieffer-Stewart Co. v. Jos. E. Seagram & Sons (1951) 202
King, Martin Luther 229
Klor's Inc. v. Broadway-Hale Stores, Inc. (1959) 202, 224
Knight, Frank H. 259
Knutson, Harold 120
Ku Klux Klan 59

La Follette, Robert 65, 98
Labor, views of 91–100, 119–20, 207–08, 249, 294–95, 325n81
Labor boycotts 33, 89, 97, 144, 160–68. *See also* Associations
Labor unions and trade associationalism 62–63. *See also* Associations
Laissez-faire constitutionalism. *See* Economic due process doctrines
Lamar, Lucius Quintas Cincinnatus 101
Lamont, R. P. 123
Latham, Earl, "The Body Politic of the Corporation" (1959) 191
Laughlin, Lawrence 55
Lechmere, Inc. v. NLRB (1992) 294–295
Leff, Arthur 239
Legal process 191, 193–94, 339n17
Lewis, John L. 120, 123
Liberalism, political 62
Liberty. *See also* Freedom of contract
efficiency, relationship to 65, 352n63
equality, relationship to 3
in First Amendment speech policy 250
in free competition rhetorics 301
in liberty of contract jurisprudence of New Deal Court 163
in marketplace of ideas 299
property, relationship to 69. *See also* Property
two facets of 43, 44, 52
two views of before 1911 51

tyranny, result of 3, 263
views of compared 113
Lloyd Corp. v. Tanner (1972) 249–50, 293, 294
Local Government Antitrust Act of 1984 277
Lochner v. New York (1905) 5, 45–48, 57, 62, 103
Locke, John 81, 166
Logan Valley Plaza (1968). *See Amalgamated Food Employees v.* 249

Magnuson-Moss Warranty and FTC Improvements Act of 1975 271
Majoritarianism 46, 72–75. *See also* Price fixing
Maple Flooring Mfrs. Ass'n v. U.S. (1925) 87, 91, 102, 136
Marginal utility of money 324
Marginalist revolution 94–96
Marine Bancorporation, United States v. (1974) 235
Market, conceptions of 209–11
Market for efficient management. *See* Corporate control
Market of public opinion 165
Market power
compared to economic power 210–28
versus economic concentration 214, 217, 219–28
Market share in corporate merger doctrine 212–21, 232–36. *See also* Corporate merger policy; Merger Guidelines; Neoclassical economics
Market size 212. *See also* Corporate size
in corporate merger doctrine 212–15
in Clayton Act §3 doctrine 212–13, 220–21
Marketplace of ideas, relationships to
commercial markets 247–51
competition policy 291–99
corruption 252–53, 297–99
deregulation 291
free competition rhetoric and property rights 246–51
Lochner (1904) era jurisprudence 361n47
property rights 247–51, 291–99
recognition of workers' right to picket 144, 164
wealth, corporate and individual 298–99
Marketplace pluralism 188
Marshall, Alfred, *Principles of Economics* (1890) 33, 79, 94
Marshall, John 133, 288
Mason, Edward S. 184, 190
Mason, William 15
Master and servant 46, 50–55
McCarthy, Joe 181–82
McLaren, Richard 232–32
McReynolds, James C. 67–68, 84–85, 103, 136, 141, 168
Means, Gardiner C.
The Modern Corporation and Private Property (1932) 6, 107, 110
report (1935) 144, 145–47
Meese, Edwin 278
Merger Guidelines (1968) 232
Merger Guidelines (1982) 280–82
Meyer v. Nebraska (1923) 103
Mill, John Stuart 77
Miller, John E. 150, 154–55
Miller-Tydings Resale Price Maintenance Act of 1937 153–54, 236
Mitchell, John 232
Moley, Raymond, *After Seven Years* (1939) 115
Monopolistic competition 107, 185, 205. *See also* Chamberlain, Edward H.; Postclassical economics
Monopolization, "no fault" bill in 1976 235
Montague & Co. (1904) 41
Morehead v. New York ex rel Tipaldo (1936) 132, 134–35
Morgan, J. P. 39, 56, 286, 288–89
Muller v. Oregon (1908) 49
Municipally owned utilities, and competition policy 274–278
Munn v. Illinois (1876) 18, 22
Murphy, Francis 148, 164–66, 172, 207
Murphy, Paul L. 69

Nader, Ralph 235–36, 252, 263, 267, 271–72
National American Woman Suffrage Association 49
National Ass'n of Window Glass Mfrs. v. U.S. (1923) 92
National Association of Manufacturers 69
National Committee on Wood Utilization 87
National Consumers League 49
National Industrial Recovery Act (1933) 169
Berle and Means, concerns held in common with 110
congressional hearings 115–24
dystopian experience 124–30
fair competition, new rhetoric of 120, 124
political economy of 113
political norm of equal representation 114
statist impulse, seen as 111–12
utopian vision of an organic body politic 122
Wagner Act of 1935, compared to 128
National Power Policy Committee, report (1935) 147
National Recovery Administration 6
industry codes 125, 126, 128–30
labor unions 127–28
in NIRA hearings 116
political arena for negotiation in positive-sum game 113
reasons for failure 129
Nebbia v. New York (1934) 132–34
ALA Schechter Poultry (1935), compared 131
price-fixing, public 72
property and state regulation, conflict between 162
Thornhill (1940), compared 166
Neoclassical economics
in *American Col. & Lumber Co.* (1921) 82
ascendancy of 62
classical and postclassical compared to 169–71
in *Columbia Steel* (1948) opinion 177
maximizing returns assumed in 110
and metamarket concerns 211–12, 222
politics and 241–42
postclassical compared to 108
price theory and the "New Learning" emerging from 236–245
science, aspiration toward, and 241–42
Neutral principles 191–93, 243, 249
New Deal 5, 112, 114. *See also ALA Schechter Poultry* (1935); Arnold, Thurman; Consumer welfare; Fair competition; National Industrial Recovery Act; National Recovery Agency; *Thornhill* (1940)
Supreme Court decisions
antitrust 168–78
First Amendment speech 164–66
government regulation of price 160–64
labor 160–68
views of historians 328–29n3
New State Ice Co. v. Liebmann (1932) 132
Nexus of contracts theory 288–90
NIRA. *See* National Industrial Recovery Act
Nixon, Richard 7, 8, 229–33
NLRB v. See name of other party
Noerr Motor Freight, Eastern R.R. Presidents Conf. v. (1961) 206–07, 209, 216
Northern Securities v. United States (1904) 27, 39–45, 47–51, 64, 84
cartel and merger doctrines compared 38

corporations and individuals distinguished 55
harbinger of *Standard Oil* (1911) 28
Sherman Act as affront to property rights 57
N. Pacific R. R. Co. v. U. S. (1957) 213, 343n63
NRA. *See* National Recovery Agency

O'Gorman & Young v. Hartford Fire Ins. Co. (1931) 131–32
Occupational Safety and Health Administration 230
Oligopoly theory. *See also* Chamberlin, Edward H.; Economic concentration; Market share; Postclassical economics
Chamberlin's early theories of 107–08
common-law cartel doctrine, relationship to 201–03
common-law conspiracy doctrine, relationship to 175–76
competition and cooperation, views of 242
early opposition to 236–38
liberal formalist rendition, in Supreme Court doctrine 217, 234
structure of discourse during 1950s and 1960s 184–85
Olney, Richard 36
Olsen, Mancur 194, 246
administrative agencies, critique of 187, 189–90
Logic of Collective Action (1965) 189, 237
Open competition 66. *See also* Associations; Cooperative competition; Fair competition
Organic body politic 142
Orwell, George 106

Pabst Brewing Co., United States v. (1966) 219, 224
Pacific Gas & Electric v. Public Utility Comm'n (1986) 293–294, 296, 298
Pareto, Wilfredo 240
Parker v. Brown (1943) 273
Parsons, Talcott 340n20
Peckham, Rufus
and Rule of Reason faction 39, 43
economic due process adherent, in *Lochner* (1905) opinion 45–46
cartel and labor cases, views in 33
Literalist opinions
Addyston Pipe (1898) 36–37
Joint Traffic (1898) 35
shifting rationales 35–37
Trans-Missouri (1897) 30
Pennsylvania Public Service Commission Act 66
Perot, H. Ross 286–87, 291
Pertschuk, Michael 233, 252, 263, 271, 279
Petitioning government, as defense to price-fixing charges 206–07, 246
Philadelphia National Bank, United States v. (1963) 217, 219–20, 234, 236
Pinkertons 97
Pitney, Mahlon
in *Coppage* (1915), protecting property rights 57
in *Duplex Printing* (1921), seeing in labor strikes threat of class warfare 98
in *International News Service* (1918), creating "quasi-property" rights 69–73
Platt, Orville 16, 18
Plessy v. Ferguson (1896) 38, 45, 50
Pluralism, and disparities of power 6
Pluralistic society 182
Political action committees 295, 296–99
Political corruption, and economic power 11, 39, 246. *See also* Corruption; First Amendment speech; Marketplace of ideas
Political economy in America 301–03
Political ideology, and historical context 305–06n4
Political theory of oligarchic competition 187–91

Populism 7, 261
Posner, Richard
Antitrust Law, An Economic Perspective (1976) 238, 242–43
Economic Analysis of Law (1973) 238–41
monopoly, view of 261
ealth maximization, view of 258, 260–61
Postclassical economics 171, 177. *See also* Chamberlin, Edward H.; Monopolistic competition; Oligopoly
classical and neoclassical, compared 169
First Amendment speech, crossing of 295–96
two new models 107
Pound, Roscoe 23, 92
Power Trust 147, 333n72
Price fixing 29–30
cartels 36–37
oligopoly theory and 175
private 73
property rights and 255–56
public 72. *See also* Economic due process doctrines; Price regulation
public and private, compared 74–75
Price regulation 74. *See also* Economic due process doctrines
Private interests 71
Proctor & Gamble Co., FTC v. (Clorox) (1967) 222–23, 233
Producers, discussed in Sherman Act debates 14
Property rights
barriers to entry, as 358n32
competition policy and 3, 70, 223–24
control of products granted to manufacturers in Supreme Court doctrine 257
and corruption in marketplace of ideas 297–99
defenses limited in antitrust cases 174–75
differing views of 71
equality and 228
in free competition rhetorics 3, 221–28
in First Amendment speech doctrine 251
entitlements rejoin, with liberty 194–95
First Amendment speech and 164, 291–99
industrial and individual, and equality 194
labor exemption in Clayton Act 325n81
liberty and, in the marketplace of ideas 292–99
pecuniary rights, as any 63, 69–72
rhetorics appearing in early antitrust opinions 42
state regulation and 133–36
Pruneyard Shopping Center v. Robins (1980) 292–94
Public choice theory 187–89, 302
Public interest 9, 10, 73
Public Utilities Holding Company Act of 1935 143, 147
Purcell, Edward A., Jr. 90

Railroads, regulation of 9
Reagan, Ronald 8, 267
Reasonable prices, as logic for price-fixing 30
Red Lion Broadcasting Co. v. FCC (1969) 248
Regents of the Univ. of California v. Bakke (1978) 265
Regulation 13, 133–36
Rehnquist, William 248, 276, 292–96
Reich, Charles A., "The New Property" (1964) 194–95
Report of the Attorney Gen.'s Natl. Comm. to Study Antitrust Laws (1955) 186–87, 201, 227, 236, 243
Resale price maintenance 53–56, 153, 255–56
Restatement Second of Contracts 135
Restraints on distribution, effects of consignment 53, 153, 203–05, 223
Ricardoan labor theory of value 22

Richberg, Donald
industrial statesmanship, belief in 126
labor organizations, view of 119
labor under NIRA, view of 120
NRA, view of 125
small enterprise, view of 117
Riner, John A. 29, 30
Roberts, Owen J. 131–36
Robinson-Patman Act of 1936 148–50, 151–53
Rockefeller, John D. 9, 10
corporate personality, and 55
personification of corporate bureaucracy 50
principal with corporate agents 62
Roe v. Wade (1972) 61, 232, 269
Roosevelt, Franklin D. 6, 111–12, 123–24, 196, 229
Bretton Woods Accords 178
National Recovery Administration and trade associationalism of Hoover, Herbert 78
negotiated NIRA auto industry code 128
and NIRA's passage 115
Roosevelt, Theodore 39, 60
Root, Elihu 57
Rostow, Eugene V. 176–78, 190, 201
Ruder, David 287
Ruinous Competition 13, 16, 40
Rule of Reason, antitrust
common-law version 50–52
in era of cooperative competition 1911–1933 59
modern version 79
public reactions and legislative initiatives provoked by 53–66
two forms
common-law and modern 78–80
Standard Oil (1911) and *Chicago Board* (1918), compared 167
application to trade and labor associations 89, 94–96

Sachs, Albert, *The Legal Process* (1958) 191, 193–4
Sadowski, George G. 152
Sanford, Edward T. 103
Santa Clara v. Southern Pacific Railroad (1886) 50, 55
Schenck v. U.S. 244
Scherer, Frederick 233
Schumpeter, Joseph A.
Capitalism, Socialism and Democracy (1942) 109
competition by innovation 109
theories of imperfect competition 183, 185–86
theory of democracy 187–88, 193
Schwinn (1967). *See Arnold, Schwinn & Co.*
Second National Bank 5
Securities and Exchange Commission, and "Power Trust" 147
Sedition Act of 1918 99, 104
Senate committees
Finance, Senator Sherman's anti-trust bill 13
Interstate Commerce, 1914 antitrust legislation 65
Judiciary 13, 20, 245
Shelley v. Kraemer (1948) 179
Shenefield, John 263
Sherman Act debates
common-law language, significance of change to 19–20
competition and property rhetorics heard in 14–20
echoed in NIRA hearings 117
free competition rhetoric 14, 30
overview of 12
property rhetoric of fair price 18–19
short-horn cattle monopoly discussed in 20, 22, 25
two factions and two rhetorics in 12
uncommon-law remedies 25–26
Sherman Act doctrine
Fifth Amendment and 29, 39, 41, 44, 51
First Amendment and 174–75
free trade in ideas and 102
labor picketing and consumer welfare 168
"*Lochner*-like" economic due process jurisprudence of application to municipalities 276
sit-down strikes 167
weapon to block local government 273–78
Sherman bill, Judiciary Committee's substitute for 12, 13
Sherwood, Thomas R. 21
Shopping malls and First Amendment speech 248–51
Simons, Henry C. 259
Simpson v. Union Oil Corp. (1964) 203, 205, 223
Sloan, Alfred 126
Small dealers and worthy men 40. *See also* Jeffersonian entrepreneurialism
centralization under Hoover and 77
industrial liberty 28
phrase used in *Fashion Organizer's Guild* (1941) 173
phrase used in Trans-Missouri (1897) 31
Sherman Act debates, evoked in 14–15
Smith, Adam, and "Coase Theorem" 237
Smith, William French 280
Socony-Vacuum Oil Co., United States v. (1940) 173–74
Southern Motor Carriers Rate Conference v. U.S. (1985) 277
Spencer, Herbert 66, 259
Standard Oil Co. v. United States (1911) 26, 80–81, 103, 167, 203
common-law Rule of Reason 52, 79
dissolution, effects of 64
Northern Securities (1904), foreshadowed by 28
opinion of White, Edward D., analyzed 50–52
public currency 61
State action exemption to antitrust liability 273–78
State regulation of corporate takeovers 287
Stevenson consulting firm
Stevenson, Charles R. 76, 107
trade association movement and 81
Stewart, John W. 16–19, 22
Stigler, George 7
and industry structure, importance of 183, 237
narrow view of barriers to entry 283–84
and Olsen's similar theory of regulatory capture 187
"The Theory of Regulation" (1971) 187, 189
Stocking, George W. 183, 185, 186
Stone, Harlan Fiske
Fourteenth Amendment and antitrust jurisprudences compared 73
labor sit-down strikes and consumer welfare in *Apex Hosiery* (1940) opinion 167
Sherman Act and consumer welfare 168
trade associations, views of 87–88
Straus v. American Publisher's Ass'n (1913) 81
Sugar Institute v. U.S. (1936) 131, 137, 171
Sutherland, George 81, 134, 249, 292
Four Horsemen's view of constitutionally protected property rights 73–75, 134–35
New State Ice (1932), opinion in 132
West Coast Hotel (1937), dissenting opinion in 163–64
Swift & Co. v. United States (1905) 37
Swift v. Tyson (1842) 29
Swope, Gerard 125–26

Taft, William Howard 60, 66, 68, 162
in *Addyston Pipe* (1898) 36

anti-labor decisions 91, 98
anti-labor sentiments 97
General Electric (1927), opinion in 153–54
Taft-Hartley Act of 1947 178
Tampa Electric Co. v. Nashville Coal Co. (1960) 213
Tarbell, Ida 77
Tariff Commission 122
Teagle, Walter 126
Teegarden, H. B. 148–150
Teller, Henry M. 15
Telser, Lester 258
Temporary National Economic Committee Report No. 13 (1941) 157–59, 196
Texaco and Getty oil companies, 1984 merger of 279
The Civil Rights Cases (1883) 192
Theatre Enterprises v. Paramount Film Distributors Corp. (1954) 201
Thompson, William 64
Thornhill v. Alabama (1940) 164–67, 207–08
Tillman Act of 1907 246
Tipaldo. See Morehead (1936)
Titus, Louis 124
TNEC. *See* Temporary National Economic Committee
Trade association
distinguished from cartel and trust 75
ethic of "Equitable Sharing of Business" 77
fair competition rhetoric compared to *ALA Schechter Poultry* (1935) 137
industry wide esprit de corps aimed at buyer as common rival 83
labor union and, different images of 62–63
rise of 76–78
Trade association cases 80–89
Traditional values and Reagan administration rhetoric of free markets 266–67
Trans-Missouri Freight Ass'n, United States v. (1897) 29–32, 35, 41–42, 51, 81, 173
Treadway, Allen T. 122–23
Trenton Potteries, United States v. (1927) 73–74
Truax v. Corrigan (1921) 98, 162, 166
Trustees of Dartmouth College v. Woodward (1819) 288
Trusts 9, 39
Turner, Donald
antitrust relevancy of advertising efficiency, view of 185
Antitrust Policy: An Economic and Legal Analysis (1959) 184
moderate approach to mergers 199
pure structuralist rendition of oligopoly theory 183, 202
Tydings, Millard E. 154
Tyson Bros.-United Theatre Ticket Offices, Inc. v. Banton (1927) 73, 74

U.S. Steel Corp., United States v. (1920) 61, 67, 79, 288
Unfair competition 69, 70. *See also* Fair competition; Federal Trade Commission
Unified body economic, image of 157
United Auto Workers, United States v. (1957) 246
United Mine Workers v. Pennington (1965) 206–07
United Shoe, United States v. (1918) 61
United States Strike Commission 97
United States v. See name of other party
Utah Pie Co. v. Continental Baking Co. (1967) 225–27, 233
Utterback, Hubert 151

Van DeVanter, Willis 161
Veblen, Thorstein 55, 110, 317n110
Vegelahn v. Gunter (1896) (dissenting opinion of Holmes) 93
Victory Loan campaign 104
Vinson, Fred M. 179, 208
Virginia State Bd. of Pharmacy v. Virginia Citizens Consumer Coun. (1976) 248
Von's Grocery, United States v. (1966) 219

Wagner Act of 1935 143
Wagner, Robert F. 115, 117, 119, 123
Waite, Morrison R. 19
Walker, Francis, *Political Economy* (1888) 34
Wallace, Henry 145
War Industries Board (World War I) 75
Warner, W. Lloyd, "The Corporation Man" (1959) 190
Warren, Earl 212, 214, 216
Watkins, Myron W. *See* Stocking, George W.
Wealth, effects in marketplace of ideas 298–99
Wealth maximization 240, 258
Wechsler, Herbert, "Toward Neutral Principles of Constitutional Law" (1959) 191
Wells, David Ames 23
Wells, H. G. 106
West Coast Hotel v. Parrish (1937) 163, 166, 180, 201, 203, 302
Wheeler-Lea Act of 1938 156, 168
White Motor Co. v. U.S. (1963) 204–05, 223, 254
White, Byron 206–07, 294
and market share versus market size debate 219–21, 235
property rights and competition, views of 225–28, 255–57
Utah Pie Co. (1967), opinion in 225–28
White, Edward Douglass
in Bisbee deportation case 98
cartel and labor opinions, compared 33
property rights and competition policy in *Northern Securities* (1904) (dissenting) 42
Rule of Reason opinions in *Standard Oil* (1911) and *American Tobacco* (1911) 50–51
"reasonable" interpretation of Sherman Act called for in *Trans-Missouri* (1897) (dissenting) 27, 30
Whitney v. California (1927) 244–45
Wilhelm, Kaiser 90
Williams v. Standard Oil (1929) 74
Williamson, Oliver 284
Wilson, Woodrow 66, 76
Committee on Public Information 104
"New Freedom" approach to monopoly 60
War Industries Board 75, 78
trade associations, impact of World War mobilization on 90
Women's Trade Union League 49
Wood Waste Committee 87
Workable competition 77, 185–87. *See also* Clark, John M.; Report of Attorney General's National Commission to Study Antitrust Laws (1955)
World War I 59, 104–06
Wright, Skelly 244

Yates, Sidney R. 198